Client/Server Programming with RPC and DCE

Written by David Gunter

with

Steven Burnett
Gregory L. Field
Lola Gunter
Thomas Klejna
Shankar Lakshman
Alexia Prendergast
Mark C. Reynolds
Marcia E. Roland

que®

Client/Server Programming with RPC and DCE

Copyright© 1995 by Que® Corporation.

Library of Congress Catalog No.: 95-71419

ISBN: 0-7897-0182-0

97 96 95   6 5 4 3 2 1

Interpretation of the printing code: the rightmost double-digit number is the year of the book's printing; the rightmost single-digit number, the number of the book's printing. For example, a printing code of 95-1 shows that the first printing of the book occurred in 1995.

Screen reproductions in this book were created using Collage Plus from Inner Media, Inc., Hollis, NH.

Dedication

To Lola, with love.

Credits

President and Publisher
Roland Elgey

Associate Publisher
Joseph B. Wikert

Editorial Services Director
Elizabeth Keaffaber

Managing Editor
Sandy Doell

Director of Marketing
Lynn E. Zingraf

Senior Series Editor
Chris Nelson

Title Manager
Bryan Gambrel

Acquisitions Editors
Lori Jordan
Fred Slone

Product Director
Forrest Houlette

Production Editor
Maureen A. Schneeberger

Editors
Kelli Brooks
Thomas Cirtin
Susan Shaw Dunn
Patrick Kanouse
Gill Kent
Nanci Sears Perry
Midge Stoker

**Assistant Product Marketing
Manager**
Kim Margolius

Technical Editor
James McGovern

Acquisitions Coordinator
Angela Kozlowski

Operations Coordinator
Patty Brooks

Editorial Assistant
Michelle Newcomb

Book Designer
Ruth Harvey

Cover Designer
Dan Armstrong

Production Team
Steve Adams
Claudia Bell
Brian Buschkill
Heather Butler
Jason Carr
Anne Dickerson
Bryan Flores
DiMonique Ford
Trey Frank
Jason Hand
John Hulse
Damon Jordan
Daryl Kessler
Bob LaRoche
Stephanie Layton
Michelle Lee
Kaylene Riemen
Bobbi Satterfield
Scott Tullis
Kelly Warner

Indexer
Carol Sheehan

Composed in *Stone Serif* and *MCPdigital* by Que Corporation.

About the Authors

David Gunter is a consultant and computer author based in Cary, NC. His areas of interest include UNIX systems management, and network and systems programming. David holds a Masters degree in computer science from the University of Tennessee. During his free time, David enjoys traveling, reading, and spending as much time as possible with his wonderful wife.

Steven Burnett is a technical writer, editor, and teacher of artificial linguistics, with a Master of Science in technical communication from North Carolina State University. He's also dealt with Internet issues for several years.

Gregory L. Field is a software development specialist with Radio Computing Services, where he works doing multiplatform GUI development using object-oriented methodologies. He is a graduate of the University of North Carolina-Asheville, where he received a B.S. in computer science.

Lola Gunter is a technical consultant in Raleigh, NC. She has worked in multimedia software development, as a computer consultant, and as a manager of technical documentation. She has a Bachelor's degree in computer science from the University of North Carolina-Asheville. Other than multimedia and the Internet, her interests include working with stained glass, roughhousing with her German Shepherd, and traveling.

Tom Klejna is a Sr. Distributed Computing Consultant for OSF Professional Services and has over fourteen years of industry experience. He is responsible for managing and delivering consulting to OSF customers on OSF's Distributed Computing Environment (DCE) as well as standards-based client/server architecture. His consulting assignments included enterprise architecture for the integration of large mainframe systems, minicomputers, UNIX workstations, and PCs using LAN and WAN topologies. Tom has a B.S. in computer information science from Bentley College in Waltman, MA.

Shankar Lakshman works as a software engineer for Wandel & Goltermann Technologies, Inc., located in Research Triangle Park, N.C. Shankar has worked on both the embedded systems and user interface aspects for 100 Base-T Ethernet (Fast Ethernet) and High Speed Serial Interface (HSSI). During his spare time, Shankar enjoys writing, reading, gardening, playing with his son, and listening to music. He has recently finished his new house in Cary, N.C.

Alexia Prendergast works for an applications development company as a publication specialist. She writes manuals and other technical documentation, and edits a quarterly technical journal. Previously, she worked as a senior technical writer, editor, and instructor for an engineering and construction company in the metals industry. She received her degree in professional writing from Carnegie Mellon University.

Mark C. Reynolds has been involved in network programming in a UNIX environment since the original release with 4.1 BSD. He is the creator of several large-scale RPC applications. He has also edited and translated a number of works of mathematics, including Stanislaus Ulam's posthumous collection of essays, "Science, Computers and People: From the Tree of Mathematics." He is currently a consultant to Adaptive Optics Associates, Inc., where he works on device drivers, image processing, and computer special effects. When he is not programming, he can be found groping his way up the cliffs of New Hampshire and upstate New York.

Marcia E. Roland is the Middleware Product Manager for Seer Technologies, Inc. During Ms. Roland's 12 years in the computer industry, she has focused on many emerging technologies, from expert systems and artificial intelligence to middleware technology and operating systems. Marcia began her career with Digital Equipment Corporation.

Acknowledgments

I'd like to thank everyone at Que who worked to make this book a reality. Lori Jordan approached me with this book idea back in March, and both she and Fred Slone have worked very hard to guide this project to completion. The entire Que editorial and production staffs did their usual excellent job with this project.

I am grateful to all the writers who worked on this book, for without them this book would not exist. Special thanks goes to Marcia Roland for being such a wealth of DCE information!

We'd Like to Hear from You!

As part of our continuing effort to produce books of the highest possible quality, Que would like to hear your comments. To stay competitive, we *really* want you, as a computer book reader and user, to let us know what you like or dislike most about this book or other Que products.

You can mail comments, ideas, or suggestions for improving future editions to the address below, or send us a fax at (317) 581-4663. For the online in-clined, Macmillan Computer Publishing has a forum on CompuServe (type **GO QUEBOOKS** at any prompt) through which our staff and authors are available for questions and comments. The address of our Internet site is **http://www.mcp.com** (World Wide Web).

In addition to exploring our forum, please feel free to contact me personally to discuss your opinions of this book: I'm **75230,1556** on CompuServe, and I'm **bgambrel@que.mcp.com** on the Internet.

Thanks in advance—your comments will help us to continue publishing the best books available on computer topics in today's market.

Bryan Gambrel
Product Development Specialist
Que Corporation
201 W. 103rd Street
Indianapolis, Indiana 46290
USA

Contents at a Glance

Introduction

Introduction to RPC

Introduction to DCE

Windows Development

OS/2 Development

Multiplatforms

Contents

3 Communications Protocols   75

4 Client/Server Development Overview   121

5 Responsibilities of a Client   151

9 External Data Representation   225

10 Language Specification   259

IV Windows Client/Server Development 445

17 Introduction to OLE   447

18 Client/Server Development with OLE   459

19 Using Open Database Connectivity (ODBC)   489

V OS/2 Client/Server Development   519

20 Introduction to OS/2 Client/Server Development 521

24 A Survey of Commercial Client/Server Products   677

25 Messaging and Middleware   695

Introduction

As computer systems drop in cost and increase in power, they are becoming more and more common in everyday life. With the development of high-speed networks, it is easier for computers to communicate and interoperate. As a result, much of today's software is based on the client/server computing model.

Learning to develop client/server applications is a non-trivial process. Just as there are many different types of computers, there are also many different types of networks and client/server communication methods. Some of these methods adapt well to several different platforms, while others tend to be "vendor specific" and are not easily implemented in a multiplatform environment. The goal of this book is to provide an introduction to some of the different client/server methodologies, and help you evaluate them to determine which will best fit your needs.

Who Should Use This Book?

As you might guess, client/server programming is a complex topic. To really master the subject, you need to have a good understanding of the different client/server methods that are available, how network communications work, what operating systems support what methods, and how the whole thing interacts. In this book, we mainly discuss RPCs and DCE, with some exploration of the client/server features of different operating systems.

This book is primarily aimed at the software engineer or systems designer who is wanting to learn the fundamentals of client/server development.

How This Book Is Organized

In order to cover the diverse issues related to client/server development, this book is divided into six sections.

Part I, "Introduction to Client/Server Programming," provides a preface to the client/server paradigm and looks at the networking aspects in detail. It gives an introduction to the various communications protocols and the different types of client/server communications that can be used. Chapters 4, 5, and 6 provide a thorough introduction to client/server development and discuss the characteristics and responsibilities of a good client and a good server.

Part II, "Introduction to RPC," covers the remote procedure call (RPC) interprocess communication mechanism in detail. Chapter 7 gives an introduction to RPCs. In Chapters 8, 9, and 10, you learn some of the details of the RPC environment such as authentication and the external data representation (XDR) mechanism. Chapters 11 and 12 show how to develop RPC applications.

In Part III, "Introduction to DCE," you learn about the Distributed Computing Environment (DCE). Chapter 13 provides an introduction to DCE. Chapter 14 discusses the various security protocols that DCE provides. Chapters 15 and 16 show how to develop applications using DCE.

Part IV, "Windows Client/Server Development," examines the client/server mechanisms that are available under Microsoft Windows. This section introduces the various client/server methodologies, and provides a detailed introduction to OLE and Open Database Connectivity (ODBC).

Part V, "OS/2 Client/Server Development," introduces the client/server environment that is available under OS/2. It gives an introduction to client/server development under OS/2 and looks at the named pipes communication mechanism.

Finally, Part VI, "Multiplatform Client/Server Development," looks at the details involved in developing client/server applications in a multiplatform environment. Chapter 23 discusses the important issues to consider when developing a multiplatform application. Chapter 24 gives you a look at some of the commercially available client/server development tools and applications. Chapter 25 introduces the multiplatform concepts of messaging and middleware.

There is no way that one book can provide you with all the information that is available about client/server programming. In this book, we have tried to bring together the important concepts of client/server development, introduce the major components and platforms, and show how to bring these components together to develop robust multiplatform applications.

How to Use This Book

You may prefer to read this book from cover to cover. The information tends to progress from simple to complex as you move through the chapters. However, because the information is separated into six parts, each with its own particular emphasis, you can choose to read only those areas that appeal to your immediate needs. But don't let your immediate needs deter you from eventually giving attention to each chapter as you have time. You'll find a wealth of information in them all!

Conventions Used in This Book

This book uses several special conventions that you should be aware of. These conventions are listed here for your reference.

Because client/server development, by its nature, requires multiple platforms, you should be aware that many operating systems, such as UNIX, are case-sensitive. That means that when this book instructs you to type something at a command or shell prompt, you must type exactly what appears in the book exactly as it is capitalized.

Several type and font conventions are used in this book to help make reading it easier:

- *Italic type* is used to emphasize the author's points or to introduce new terms.

- Screen messages, code listings, command samples, and code the user needs to enter appear in `monospace typeface`.

- If you are instructed to type something, what you are to type appears in **`bold in the special typeface`**.

Keys are sometimes pressed in combination; when this is the case, the keys are represented in this way: Ctrl+H. In this example, you must press and hold the Ctrl key, press the letter "H," and then release both keys.

When discussing the syntax of a particular command, this book uses some special formatting to distinguish between the required portions and the variable portions. Consider the following example:

```
lp filename
```

In this syntax, the `filename` portion of the command is variable; that is, it changes depending on what file you want the `lp` command to work with. The `lp` is required; it is the actual command name. Variable information is presented in *italics*; information that must be typed exactly as it appears is presented in `non-italic` type.

In some cases, command information may be optional; that is, it is not required for the command to work. Square brackets (`[ ]`) surround those parts of the command syntax that are optional. In the following example, notice that the `device1` parameter is variable and optional (it is in italics as well as surrounded by square brackets); however, to use the optional `abc` parameter, you must type it exactly as it appears (it is not in italics; it is a *literal* option):

```
command filename [device1] [abc]
```

Tip

Tips present short advice on a quick or often over-looked procedure. These include shortcuts that will save you time.

Note

Notes present interesting or useful information that isn't necessarily essential to the discussion. A note provides additional information that may help you avoid problems, or offers advice that relates to the topic.

Caution

Cautions serve to warn you about potential problems that a procedure may cause, unexpected results, and mistakes to avoid.

Sidebars

Longer discussions not integral to the flow of the chapter are set aside as sidebars. Look for these sidebars to find out even more information.

Troubleshooting

Troubleshooting sections anticipate common problems in the form of a question.

The response provides you with practical suggestions for solving these problems.

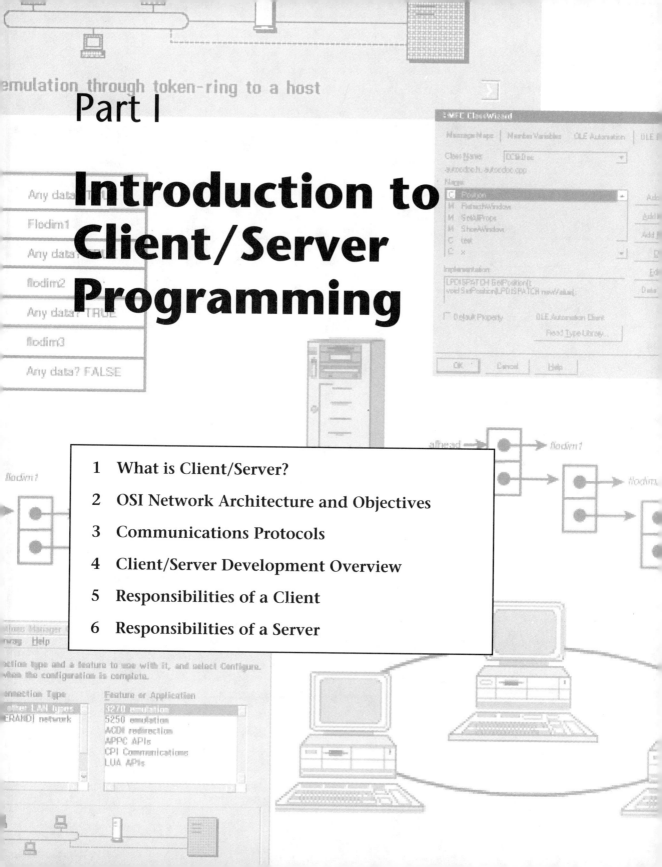

Part I

Introduction to Client/Server Programming

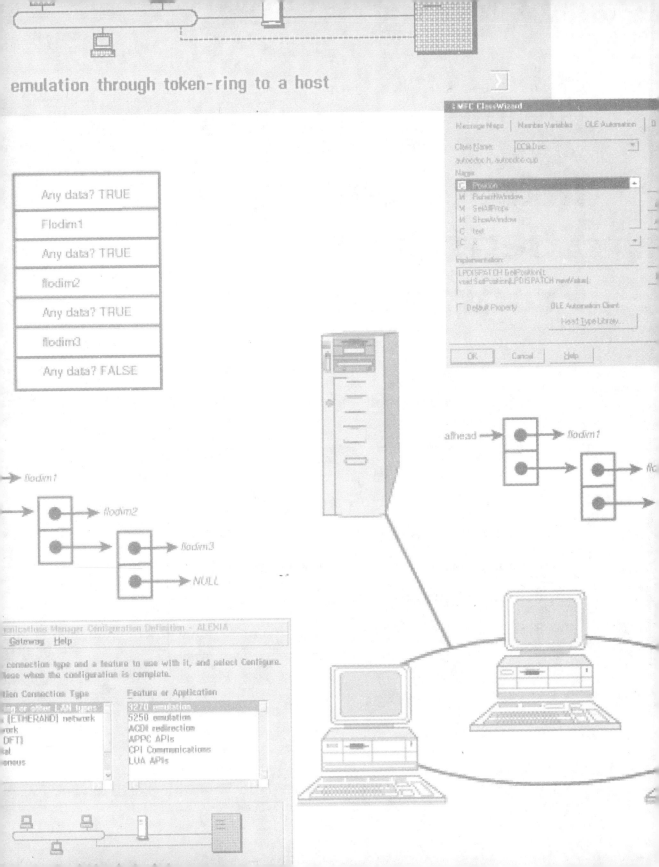

emulation through token-ring to a host

Chapter 1

What is Client/Server?

Everywhere you turn, people are talking about client/server, but what exactly is it? In the most general sense, *client/server* refers to a basic change in computing style—the shift from machine-centered systems to user-centered systems.

More specifically, a client/server system is one in which a network ties various computing resources together so clients (the front end) can request services from a server (the back end) that can supply information or additional computer power as needed.

Why is client/server such a hot topic? It is mainly because some of the expected goals of client/server computing include the following:

- Use computing power more effectively and efficiently by conserving resources

- Decrease maintenance costs by creating client/server systems that require less maintenance and cost less to upgrade than mainframes

- Increase productivity by providing users with transparent access to needed data through standard, easy-to-use interfaces

- Increase flexibility, interoperability, and portability by using standards to create open systems—systems that support multiple environments

As you can see from these goals, organizations that move forward to client/server technology greatly increase their competitive edge.

In this chapter, you learn the following:

- How client/server technology evolved

- What makes up the client/server model

- What standards govern the client/server model

- How client/server application development is different than traditional application development

- What your end user can look forward to in your client/server program

How Did Client/Server Technology Develop?

Tip

A client/server architecture refers to a computing system made up of multiple clients and one or more (usually more) servers. Users can work with multiple client/server applications at the same time.

Computer technology has been steadily evolving, with each successive architecture taking advantage of the latest technology in order to exploit the computer to its fullest. Computers today are smaller, faster, and cheaper than ever before. As a result, the trend is to distribute the processing of information and the information itself among a number of these new computers.

The term *architecture* is usually used to describe database management systems, operating systems, and other highly complex software/hardware mechanisms. *Architectures* describe how hardware devices and software packages fit together to form an easily-used and easily-modified whole.

The Dark Ages of Computing

Classical computing consists of a mainframe host with one or more non-programmable terminals (NPT), as figure 1.1 shows. Applications are centrally controlled and reside on the host. All data management, application logic, and presentation formatting takes place on the host. Users interact with the central system through NPTs that only display data. This is the most common architecture today.

A well-managed system using a classical architecture offers these capabilities:

- A high level of reliability

- Central control and management of information

- Strong data management and storage capabilities

However, classical applications limit flexibility for the end user. The user interface is not graphical, which makes the system harder to use and means that the user must learn how to use the host's command language. Also, the application is dependent on one platform, which means if anything happens to the host, the user is unable to use the system until the system is up and running again.

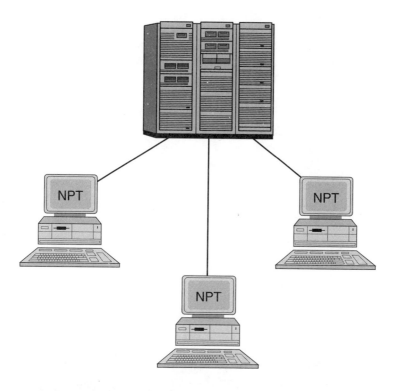

Fig. 1.1
The NPT accesses the host and emulates the screens locally.

> **Note**
>
> Client/server systems assume you have some type of network with a communication architecture that conforms to one of the available standards and assures the reliable transfer of data.

The Wave of the Future

With client/server computing, a client application runs on a *programmable workstation*. A programmable workstation can be a PC, a UNIX workstation, or a Mac, for example. The client application relies on the services provided by a server—whether it is a host or LAN-based server—and the two communicate through protocols, such as the Internet protocols (TCP/IP) or Novell's IPX/SPX. Figure 1.2 shows a client/server architecture made up of three clients and one server.

A client/server environment has many advantages over classical architectures. User-interface management and other processing is off-loaded from the host, while the server still provides centralized control of corporate resources. Further, because the client communicates with the server via a defined interface,

Tip
Computing systems that have been in use for many years use older technology and application development methods. These systems are called *legacy systems*. The term *legacy* refers to the fact that these older systems must continue to operate and be integrated into the newer systems. Classical computing certainly falls in this category. Note that with the rapid development of client/server technology, legacy client/server systems already exist!

the client need never know where the server resides or how it is implemented. The workstation runs the application and displays the information to the user. Only when accessing data does the client establish communication with the server. The work load lessens dramatically on the host as the power of the workstation is exploited.

Fig. 1.2
Generally, client/ server architectures connect individual servers with multiple clients.

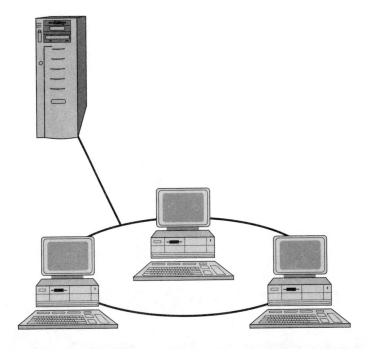

> **Note**
>
> The most common client/server systems have a client run applications and a server store data. However, note that applications can also be stored and run from a server.

Remote data management architectures require more information than classical architectures. With classical systems, security takes place on the host by user ID—for example, when user USERID logs on. The question of who the user is becomes critical in client/server systems because security can take place on the workstation or on the host. Security can be controlled in several dimensions. Two ways security can be determined is by user ID (for example, user ID USERID can access system) or by user group (for example, only if USERID belongs to user group DEVELOPMENT, can USERID access system). You can even define access to a particular component on a particular workstation, although this may not be the most efficient way to apply security measures.

How Did We Get Here From There?

Organizations deal with more data than ever before, which must be managed and shared. The increase in data, coupled with organizations' efforts to cut costs, increase productivity, and improve customer service (both by better use of data and faster response times to customers) all have contributed to the push for a client/server architecture.

In addition to changing business needs, the development of client/server technology has been driven by the following:

- Hardware advancements

- Software advancements

- Network advancements

Hardware Advancements

Desktop capabilities have increased dramatically while prices have dropped. The original IBM PC/XT, which operated at a speed of 4.77 MHz and had 64K of memory, has been replaced by machines that are 20 times faster and have 1,000 times more memory—for about the same price as the XT. Another type of processor, the Reduced Instruction Set Computing (RISC; pronounced *risk*) processor, is taking over an increasing amount of the market because it offers even faster processing speeds.

In addition to offering more computing power for your money, PCs and workstations also offer far more flexibility in building and upgrading networks. Instead of limiting an organization to particular machines, a network can connect almost any PC, workstation, minicomputer, or other server—all while still presenting a uniform interface to the user.

In contrast, mainframe technology has not developed nearly as quickly, nor has this technology managed to outpace costs. A mainframe costs about 150 times more to operate than a PC, and certainly does not offer 150 times more processing power. These changes have prompted a change in focus from mainframe to the desktop computer.

Software Advancements

Advances in the software used in client/server environments greatly increase the ease and efficiency with which the user can access information. Early systems could not request specific information; users had to download an entire data set from the host and process the information locally. Meanwhile, other users would be "locked out," or denied access, from that data set. However, now clients can formulate requests for specific records. The use of the

Structured Query Language (SQL) lets users request specific data without learning to use the server operating system or the server *Database Management System* (DBMS). Database management systems are not only able to access data residing in a relational database structure, but can access legacy data residing on different machines (data from the dark ages of computing)!

What makes this data easily accessible to the user is the development of standard, easy-to-use graphical user interfaces. The *graphical user interface* (GUI, pronounced *goo-ey*) is the means by which the end user communicates with the presentation and business logic of the application.

As opposed to the non-programmable terminals in classical systems which just emulated mainframe screens, the workstation becomes responsible for presenting the information and uses more sophisticated graphical displays, including more complicated graphics and even animation. The GUI concept is based on the understanding that people respond better to pictures rather than words alone. The industry has shown that the most popular computer systems use graphical user interfaces.

> **Note**
>
> GUIs are made up of combo boxes, radio buttons, list boxes, push buttons, and other graphically-oriented input objects, in addition to traditional editable fields.

Graphical windows also allow many different events to be captured within the application. Multiple windows, and even multiple instances of the same window, are now all possible on the same screen within the same application. Using windows this way never applied to programming 3270 interfaces.

Multi-threaded processing is also one of the most important software developments in computing. *Threads* are capabilities of the operating system that let applications run multiple instructions concurrently. The original operating systems were single-threaded, which meant that they could only execute one instruction at a time. However, client/server systems can process multiple threads at a time, which means that client/servers are able to make more efficient use of the system's hardware and software.

Network Advancements
Of course, without the *local area network* (*LAN*), client/server technology would not exist. Support for platforms is only complete if the communications to and from those platforms are supported as well. Networks provide

the communications support needed to connect multiple machines and even multiple platforms.

A *network* is a system that transfers data and messages between processes. A network architecture has rules, or *protocols*, that define how transfers occur within that architecture. Different hardware and software can communicate as long as they use the same protocols and data formats.

Advances in networking technology let workstations connect to multiple data sources, creating a user-centered environment where the user has transparent access to whatever data is needed regardless of where that data is located. Transparent access means that the user can access data on remote machines without ever having to interact directly with those machines or even being aware that other machines are involved in the process. You might be hooked up to networks across town, across the country, or across the world.

Probably the most important development in networking technology has been the development of standards. Initially, LAN components did not adhere to any standards, which made interoperability very difficult, if not impossible. The development of standards by the Institute of Electrical and Electronic Engineers (IEEE) has created network components that are almost generic, and therefore easily integrated into a system.

What is the Client/Server Model?

In the client/server model, a client issues a request and the server returns a response or takes a series of actions. The server can act on the request immediately or add the request to a queue. Acting on a request immediately might mean the server calculates a number and returns it right away to the client. Adding the request to a queue might mean the request has to "wait in line" to be served. A good example of this is when you print a document to a network printer. The server puts your request in a queue along with print requests from other clients. It then processes the request according to priority, which, in this case, is determined by the order in which the server received the request.

The Basic Client/Server Model

The client process first sends a message to "wake up" the server. Once the client and server have established communication, the client can submit the request (see fig. 1.3).

Fig. 1.3
The client sends a
request to the
server. The server
returns the
requested data or
services.

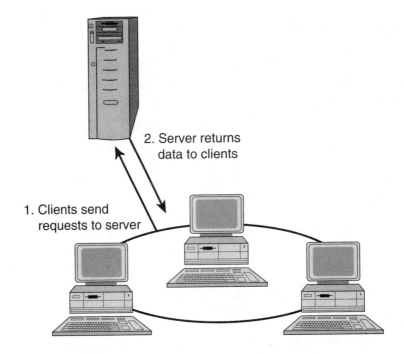

2. Server returns
   data to clients

1. Clients send
   requests to server

The Client

The client is the requester of services. Even though the graphic used for this concept shows a workstation, a client is no more than a process. Services requested by a client may exist on the same workstations or on remote workstations and hosts connected via a network. The client always initiates the communication.

> **Note**
>
> The client is the most important part of the client/server system. The client should be the only part of the system that the user is aware of, and the network and server should exist to answer the client's needs.

▶ See "What
   Exactly is a
   Client?,"
   p. 151

The components of the client are fairly simple. A client machine must be able to do the following:

- Run the presentation software (the GUIs).

- Generate the data request and send it to the server.

- Store the received data.

Those requirements determine how much memory is needed, what processing speeds would improve response time, and how much storage is required. Remember that to the user, the client *is* the system. The interactions with the server are transparent. Keeping that in mind, it is important that the interface be error free, flexible, and easy-to-use.

The Server

Servers respond to requests made by clients. Just as clients are processes, so are servers. Servers are the process that responds to client requests by performing the desired actions. A client can act as a server if it is receiving and processing requests as well as sending them (for example, a workstation also used as a printer server for others). Servers do not initiate communication—they listen for client requests.

Let's return to our simple example of a network printer server. The client asks the server to print a document on a specific printer, the server adds the print job to the queue then notifies the client when the document has been successfully printed. The client process may physically reside on the same workstation as the server process. In this example, a print command could be issued on the network server workstation, making use of the print server process on that workstation.

The components of the server are fairly simple. A server machine must be able to do the following:

- Store, retrieve, and protect data.

- Review data requests from clients.

- Generate and send data requests to other servers.

- Handle data management tasks such as locking, backing up, or recording audit trails.

- Manipulate data.

A server's tasks typically fall into one of six areas: managing files, managing applications, managing and storing data, passing on client requests and server responses, managing databases, and helping with network communication. The type of server used depends on the task requested. There are six types of servers which are as follows:

- File servers

- Application servers

Tip

The power of the server can range from the equivalent of the client to mainframes. This flexibility is what makes client/server systems so scalable.

▶ See "The
Server,"
p. 125

- Data servers

- Compute server

- Database servers

- Communications servers

Networks

Networks are the cloudiest component of the client/server equation—and that means that client/server computing is doing its job. People generally don't know much about how networks really work with client/server systems because client/server systems are designed to make the network transparent to the user. In addition to being transparent to users, networks must be reliable. Without the network, the client/server system does not exist. Therefore, the network must be able to maintain connections, detect errors, and recover immediately from failures.

▶ See "Networks
in General,"
p. 28

Networks have operating system software and management software to control the server's communication services and to protect client and server programs from having direct contact with each other. The management software focuses on providing reliable service, minimizing traffic across the network, and minimizing downtime.

Beyond the Basic Client/Server Model

If the client/server architecture is so basic, why do you hear so many different terms, such as *distributed systems* and *peer-to-peer computing*? These terms are just different ways of referring to client/server computing—although, there can be some small differences in construction and application.

> **Note**
>
> Distributed computing generally means the same thing as client/server computing. Distributed processing takes the client/server model a step further, because with a distributed architecture, both process and data can be distributed among clients and servers.

In a fully distributed environment, there are many applications across many platforms communicating with one another as figure 1.4 shows. In the classical environment discussed earlier, each application runs independently on its own platform and is unaware of other applications. In a distributed environment, many applications may share both data and processing. Further, a single application may be spread across multiple platforms, without any concern for exactly where an application resides.

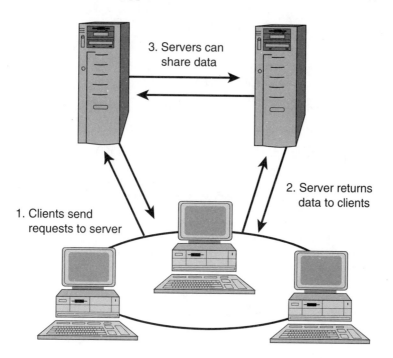

3. Servers can share data

2. Server returns data to clients

1. Clients send requests to server

I

Introduction

Fig. 1.4
In addition to servicing client requests, servers in distributed systems can make requests of other servers, and in effect become clients themselves.

Distributed logic systems are the first of the more advanced technologies. Parts of the application are stored on the host as well as the workstation. Distributed database systems keep all the application logic on the workstation but divide the database between the host and the workstation.

> **Note**
>
> Distributed logic is an *application* that is divided between the client and server. For example, some of your processing logic may reside on the client, and that logic may send requests to logic on the server. Distributed logic is different than distributed data, which is a *database* that stores some data on the client and some on the server.

Distributed processing can save on resources by off-loading data from the mainframe and distributing it among different servers, and by off-loading processes and distributing them as well. However, even though distributed processing can save on resources by off-loading data and logic, it also means that maintenance becomes more complicated. More servers must be maintained, there is no centralized data integrity verification, and the maintenance to back up data on each server is greater than for one central backup.

The Ideal Client/Server System

Theoretically, any user at a client workstation can get information services from any type or size of server machine that is hooked up to the network. The ideal client/server environment has the following features:

- Machine-independent data representation tools to let different machines exchange data.

- A protocol to specify low-level client and server responsibilities during a remote procedure call.

- A protocol compiler that packages client requests and server responses.

- Methods to provide security during remote access.

- Services that let applications find conventional network objects and bind to particular network services.

- A network time service for host synchronization to establish a single absolute network time.

- A system that distributes information rather than having to store multiple copies of the same information.

What Governs the Client/Server Model?

To be able to use a variety of hardware and software products from different vendors, the hardware and software must work together, or *interoperate*, correctly. Standards let applications understand multiple languages and protocols, and provide a way to unify resources. The Open Systems Interconnection reference model, communication protocols, and communication paradigms are the three most common areas in which standards help hardware and software work together successfully.

Open Systems

Open systems follow standards that allow different machines and platforms to communicate with each other as if they were the same. The standards define the format in which data is exchanged, how remote systems are accessed, and how systems are invoked. The seven-layer Open Systems

Interconnection (OSI) reference model created by the International Standards Organization (ISO) offers a standard for developing applications and a way to compare different networking architectures (see fig. 1.5).

OSI Model

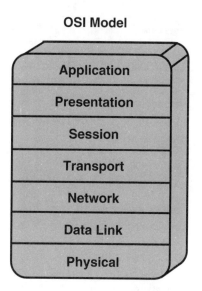

I

Introduction

Fig. 1.5
The Open Systems Interconnect model standardizes the network architecture.

The OSI model defines an overall architecture for the complex software and hardware that make up networks. The architecture describes how machines can communicate with each other in a standardized and highly flexible way by defining layers of software that should be implemented in each communicating machine. The OSI model does not define the software itself or even detailed standards for that software; it simply defines the broad categories of functions that each layer should perform. Table 1.1 describes the function of each layer of the OSI model.

Table 1.1   The Seven-Layer OSI Model

Layer Number	Layer	Function
7	Application	Supports applications
6	Presentation	Codes and formats translation
5	Session	Manages dialogue between client and server
4	Transport	Controls quality of packet transmission

(continues)

Table 1.1 Continued		
Layer Number	**Layer**	**Function**
3	Network	Routes data through the network
2	Data Link	Creates frames
1	Physical	Transmits signals

The seven layers of the model act as both clients and servers; each layer requests services or data from the layer above it, and satisfies requests from the layer below it. The layers are explained as follows:

■ Layer 1, the physical layer, deals with the actual hardware (cables, hubs) required to create a connection between two devices.

■ Layer 2, the data link layer, moves the transmitted signal from the hardware to the software. In other words, a network adapter card helps move the signal from the wire to the computer memory for further processing.

■ Layer 3, the network layer, determines the actual physical routing of information from node to node.

■ Layer 4, the transport layer, uses protocols to package, address, and route information among local network nodes.

■ Layer 5, the session layer, lets two processes establish and control a *communication session*, which is simply a group of transactions.

■ Layer 6, the presentation layer, provides the interface between the application and the services it requires.

▶ See "The OSI Model in General," p. 44

■ Layer 7, the application layer, is the part of the application the user interacts with directly.

Communication Protocols

Both the client and server must follow a specific set of rules when converting and transmitting requests and data over a network. The rules that they follow are called *protocols*.

There are three major categories of protocols: asynchronous, binary-synchronous, and bit-oriented. The asynchronous and binary-synchronous protocols are both character-oriented, which means that the protocol uses a particular code set for transmission, with some of the characters in the code set reserved for control functions. A bit-oriented protocol means that the protocol is independent of any particular code set, and no character codes are reserved for control functions.

All communication protocols perform the following functions:

- **Synchronizing**: establishes and maintains a connection between the client and server, so the client and server are not disconnected while transmitting instructions or data.

- **Framing**: marks the beginning and end of each transmission frame, so the receiver (whether client or server) knows where the transmission begins and ends.

- **Controlling**: performs some set of control functions—such as terminating and releasing the session, or expediting data transfer—depending on the type of communication.

- **Error detecting**: detects errors and implements error recovery. For example, the network may detect a break in the connection between client and server. The system may send a message to the users asking them if they want to reestablish the connection—or the system may just go ahead and reestablish the connection automatically.

Some communication protocols also perform these functions:

- **Addressing**: manipulates network addresses, for example, preparing the client request to be sent to the appropriate server.

- **Retransmitting**: resends frames when errors are detected, which would happen if data were corrupted during transmission.

- **Pacing**: controls the rate at which data is transmitted to make sure the client is not sending data faster than the server can receive it, or vice versa.

- **Inquiring**: inquires about the status of other clients or servers— for example, to see whether or not a server is available to receive a request.

Communication Paradigms

There are several major communication paradigms available to clients and servers. Communication paradigms define the methods by which clients and servers communicate.

Remote Procedure Calls

Tip

RPCs are supported by runtime libraries. When an application makes a request of a remote server, the runtime library finds the server and passes the request on. As far as the user can tell, the RPC functions just like a local

Clients use remote procedure calls (RPCs) to make requests of remote services. Clients send the remote service some input parameters and, in return, receive output parameters which are the results of the request. An RPC is the method by which one process invokes another process which resides on a remote system.

During a remote procedure call, the client sends a request out over the network. The server is constantly listening for requests. When it receives a request, the server executes the requested procedure and assembles a reply. The reply is then returned over the network to the client. RPCs are the backbone of the client/server architecture.

Messages

When using *messaging*, a process sends a message to another process across the network in a form from which the receiving partner recognizes specifying the destination by name. For example, if Process A on the client sends a message to Process B on the server, Process A's address is included in the message so that Process B knows where the message came from.

> **Note**
>
> *Messaging* is one of the three basic programming practices used in object-oriented programming. The other two practices are inheritance and encapsulation.

Subscriptions

When using subscriptions, clients "subscribe" to a particular service. The service sends messages to the client until the client cancels the "subscription." This is different from messaging, because it is at a higher level and implies a broadcasting capability by the provider. Messaging requires one process to send a message to another. However, if a client subscribes to a print service, that client can receive printer status messages that are broadcast to all clients that subscribe to that same service.

What Does the Client/Server Model Mean to Application Development?

The client/server architecture lets you exploit the particular capabilities of clients, servers, and networks when you develop your application. To take advantage of those capabilities, you must change the way you think. Remember that the most common function of a client/server application is to give the user access to data—efficiently and easily. You need to integrate GUIs, distributed applications, relational databases, and networks. Tools that help you design client/server applications assume that you are familiar with GUIs, desktop computing, and SQL databases. Data is no longer stored and controlled by central mainframes. Instead, data is spread throughout organizations on servers.

Since client/server computing is so different from classical models, it amplifies all the shortcomings of traditional development methodologies for developing systems. The maintenance information that controls this system is exponentially larger than the previous architectures. Security is regulated at several different levels including workstation, data, and time. The location of process and data across the system is dynamic. Clients and servers become defined by the software not the hardware. RPCs, which allow a client to request a service from a server, are central to client/server computing.

Developing Applications

Developing client/server applications is quite a bit different than traditional programming. To develop an RPC application, you follow these generic steps:

1. Specify the protocol for client/server communication.

2. Develop the client and server programs.

3. Compile the programs.

4. Link the stubs and libraries.

5. Test the applications by launching the server on a remote machine and running client locally.

Because of the complexity of the client/server architecture, client/server application development requires more detailed planning—specifically, how to partition the application among client and server, and how to distribute the data between client and server. Applications that use RPCs are intrinsically distributed because the RPCs are essentially client and remote server processes. The applications themselves are usually divided into two parts—the client portion and the server portion. Clients make the call, and servers service the call. RPCs make requests to a server process on another machine look just like requests to a server process on the same machine.

When a client makes a request, processing passes from the client to a client stub which packages the function parameters. The package is transmitted to the server stub, which unpacks it. Once unpacked, the client request parameters invoke a remote procedure. The result is then repackaged and returned to client (see fig. 1.6).

Fig. 1.6
RPCs help make the calls to remote servers transparent to the user.

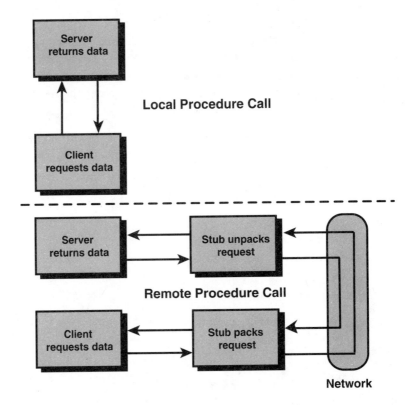

▶ See "RPCs, Distributed Computing, and the Client/ Server Model," p. 196

Partitioning Applications

Figure 1.7 shows some examples of how applications are partitioned across the client/server architecture.

The user interface resides on the client; no longer does the host have to generate the user display. You can also partition the application layer to partially reside on the client. Tasks which typically work well on the client are formatting queries to the server, generating reports, and error checking. Application logic on the client is called the *front end*.

The server, on the other hand, is primarily responsible for retrieving, manipulating, and securing data. Of course, that also depends on how the data is distributed. Application logic on the server is called the *back end*.

Distributing Data

After you decide how to partition your application between the client and the server, you need to decide how to distribute the data. One of the main reasons you want to distribute your data is to minimize its movement and therefore cut down on network traffic. You have four main data distribution options which are as follows:

- Have multiple identical copies.

- Divide data among several locations.

- Derive data from other locations.

- Partially replicate data in high-speed access areas.

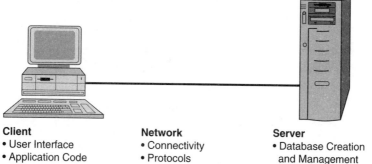

Fig. 1.7
Tasks are divided among the client, the network, and the server.

Client
- User Interface
- Application Code
- SQL Generation
- Application Control and Switching

Network
- Connectivity
- Protocols
- Network Topology
- Communications Software

Server
- Database Creation and Management
- Transaction Management
- SQL Execution
- Stored Procedures and Triggers
- Recovery and Backup

▶ See "What Is a Client/Server Application," p. 121

The concept which plays a large part in determining how to distribute data is *nodal residency*. What nodal residency means, is that data is stored closest to the users who need it. So if a reference file that is not going to be changed often is used by multiple users, it may make sense to have multiple copies of that file stored on the clients. If some data is used by all clients and other data is specific to particular clients, it may be more practical to store the commonly-used data on the server, and the client-specific data on the client. If some data that changes often can be calculated quickly from existing data on the server, you may not want to waste the time or space storing it. Or, if clients regularly use the same parts of files, you might want to copy the parts your users need each time they request the information. Once you have planned carefully how to split the tasks and data between the client and server, you can write your programs.

What Do Client/Server Applications Mean to Your End Users?

Client/server applications move the focus of computing from being machine-centered to user-centered. Here is what your end users can look forward to:

- Enhanced data sharing—Data collected as part of normal business operations that used to be stored on the host is now available to all authorized users.

- Integrated services—All information is available on the desktop so users don't have to interact directly with the server.

- Resource sharing among diverse platforms—Users have the opportunity to really achieve open system computing because platforms don't matter anymore.

- Data interchange and interoperability—Users can exchange data between platforms using a standard Distributed Relational Database Architecture (DRDA) that lets multiple vendors access Data Base Management Systems (DBMSes).

- Masked physical data access—Users can access data from anywhere in the network.

- Easier Maintenance—When standards are used, applications and data are easier to maintain because similar principles apply to all applications, code standards, structure standards, and naming standards.

From Here...

For more information on the topics in this chapter, please refer to the following chapters:

- Chapter 4, "Client/Server Development Overview," discusses how to develop a client/server application and how developing client/server applications differs from developing classical applications.

- Chapter 5, "Responsibilities of a Client," explains what makes up a client, what the role of the client is in the client/server process, and what responsibilities the client has.

- Chapter 6, "Responsibilities of a Server," discusses what makes up a server, what the role of the server is in the client/server process, and what responsibilities the server has.

Chapter 2

OSI Network Architecture and Objectives

In this chapter, you will gain a brief overview of the OSI structure, an introduction to various communication hardware, and so on. Communication hardware has made tremendous progress in the last decade: switching technology while making great strides in providing faster and reliable means of communication has changed the very approach to it. With the advent of new technology, users are finding that more and more data can be squeezed on to the network, thus opening new areas of sharing information.

Protocols, software, and other related communication areas have also made great strides. Several new protocols have been introduced into the market, quite a few of them proprietary in nature. Software, while taking over some of the work that hardware was doing, still relies on extremely fast chips to handle the guts of communications at current high speeds.

While communications is playing an important role in people's lives, it is also equally important to know that there is a lot going on behind the scenes. This chapter hopes to provide the reader with a better understanding of the technology out there and how to become a part of it.

Some of the concepts that are discussed in this chapter are the following:

- OSI layers
- Bridges, routers, and switches

Networks in General

Networking in general is the art of distributing information, of any kind, to a group. The key to this age of computers is to collect this information as accurately as possible and to distribute it as fast as possible. As information becomes widely available and required by researchers around the world, networking becomes even more of an urgent necessity. The concept of storing information or processing it all at a centralized location is fast becoming obsolete and prohibitively expensive.

Networks, or to be more specific, computer networks, are quickly becoming the technology of the future, allowing machines at great distances from each other to communicate and exchange information. This connection or communication can take place over different media, some examples being copper wire, fiber, microwaves, and satellites. Some of the obvious uses of sharing information and having it available at the action of a command or the touch of a button are providing immense cost savings, resource-sharing, and reliable alternate sources of information distribution.

Generally, networks provide flexibility, offer a great number of applications, and improve overall performance. Some of the applications supported provide accessibility to remote programs and databases (airplane reservations, electronic banking, commerce, and so on), electronic mail (both video and text), and data communications.

Physical Elements

Several objects or elements go into forming a computer network. Some are relatively inexpensive, while others cost so much that many individual users or groups of users may have to share the overall cost. Maintenance and upgrading of these physical elements are another issue, and add to the complexity of the task. Compatibility between different vendors, different networks, different protocols, and so on is another problem. These physical elements have to satisfy the following four important characteristics in general:

- Electrical

- Mechanical

- Functional

- Procedural

There are several elements that go into forming a network. They can be broadly grouped under the headings of hardware and software.

While
hardware involves elements such as routers, switches, bridges, and so on,
software involves protocols, frames, packets, and more. All these will be discussed in the following pages.

Hardware

In any situation, before installing a computer network, one has to pay a lot
of attention to hardware, in particular, cost and the user's needs and future
expansion. While cost is definitely a significant factor, it should not act as a
deterrent because the payoffs of a satisfactorily working network are immense. The other factors also need to be considered because updating networks on a frequent basis causes expenses to be high and may also cause a
decrease in productivity. Under the category of hardware, we can further
subdivide the network into the following areas:

- Network interface cards
- Servers
- Switches
- Routers
- Bridges
- Communication media

Network Interface Cards (NIC). In a *local area network* (*LAN*) environment
consisting of several personal computers (PCs), the computers all need to be
connected to one another in order to share information, printers, files, and so
on. Each PC has a LAN card, known as the *network interface card* (*NIC*),
through which it communicates to a common file storage place called the *file
server* or *LAN server*, or to printers. From the NIC a user on a PC can also communicate outside the LAN using special devices. Some of these devices, as
indicated previously, are switches, routers, bridges, and others. Each of these
topics will be discussed in greater detail in the following sections.

Servers. *Servers* are devices that several NICs are connected to as nodes. Servers act as a central storage media and local information distribution center.
Usually applications that can be shared by several users are found on servers.
They serve as the last common point of a network address before an end
node is reached. Likewise, they are the first common point before any data
has to be sent to either another node or to the outside.

Switches. There are several varieties of switching technologies involved in the information-sharing process. Some of them are the following:

■ *Private Automatic Branch Exchange (PABX).* This contains stepper switches and crossbars. Crossbars are devices that connect different switches. For example, when a telephone number is dialed using a rotary dial, each number in the telephone number represents a stepper switch. The exchange gets to the next number in the sequence via these crossbars, thus finally identifying the destination number that the source number needs to be connected.

■ *Electronic Private Automatic Branch Exchange (EPABX).* In this technology, the mechanical switches are replaced with electronic switching matrices. These, in turn, can use either analog or digital switching techniques. They are also known as *solid-state PBX.*

■ *Computerized Branch Exchange (CBX).* Allows a microprocessor to be used to control the operation of the switch. Analog signals are converted to digital signals before being transmitted, and digital switching is employed to transfer the bits of data.

■ *Time Division Multiplexing (TDM).* In this technique, after an analog signal is converted into digital form, it is then switched through a TDM mechanism and vice versa (the digital signal was converted back to an anolog signal at the destination side).

■ *Circuit, Message, Packet Switching.* When enormous amounts of data are involved, switching systems are employed to allow a set of communications equipment to be used and shared between a group of users. Data-switching systems fall into three categories: Circuit, Message, or Packet.

Circuit switching is the oldest among the three systems and shares a lot of technology with the telephone system. It consists of two parts: a switch matrix that carries the data to be switched, and a switch controller that runs the operation.

Message switching offers some improvements over circuit switching. It relieves the problems of circuit setup time and single circuit connection. Data is grouped into blocks or messages, and the switching system decides how best it can move the data as quickly as possible towards its destination. The process of sending a message involves three steps: submission, transmission, and delivery.

Packet switching makes use of the qualities of both circuit and message switching, while also offering data error control and flow control. Messages are formed into packets according to the specifications of the packet-switching system. Each packet has three parts: *header, body*, and *trailer*. The header contains information such as destination address, flow control information, and type of service. The body contains the actual data. The trailer contains error detection information. In most computer communications, packet switching is adopted as standard.

Presently, several hardware manufacturers of switches, such as Fore, Nortel, and AT&T, offer a variety of data switches that offer not only very high throughput rates, but also with very low latency.

Routers. Logical division of networks running appropriate software is usually accomplished by a device known as a router. Routers interconnect multiple networks, primarily those running at the same high-level protocols (TCP/IP, XNS, IPX and others). They make forwarding decisions at the network layer of the OSI (*Open Systems Interconnection*) model. Routers are provided with more software intelligence than simple bridges (see the next section, "Bridges"), and hence are well-suited for complex environments or large inter-networks. Particularly, they support active, redundant paths (loops) and allow logical separation of network segments.

Routers work with network numbers that are embedded into the data portion of the packet (unlike bridges, which operate at the data-link layer and only on the MAC (*Media Access Control*) addresses in the packet) and determine the forwarding of each packet based on the network number. These network numbers are similar to geographic area code numbers in the telephone system. For local calls, one simply dials the seven-digit number. The switching offices of the telephone system will automatically route the call locally to its destination.

Packets that are bound for non-local networks (i.e., network stations that are usually geographically separated) are sent to a router by the software that resides in the network layer of the OSI model. Depending on the type of network operating software (TCP/IP, XNS, IPX or others), there are many different ways of traversing the routers.

When the network-layer software receives data from its upper-layer software, it looks at the network address (not the physical address) of the destination packet and compares it to its local network address. If the network number is different, then the software will know that the packet is bound for a remote network. It then attempts to find a router that can process this packet via the shortest route. Routers are the only device that may forward a packet to a remote device on an internet.

> **Note**
>
> The section in this chapter, "The OSI Model in General," is suggested for reading if reader is a bit rusty about OSI and its layers.

Network numbers are assigned to workstations in various ways. An end station may hold a table of network numbers and their associated routers in its network-layer software. These entries contain the router's physical address, which network numbers the router is associated with, and the distance to the final destination. If the network number is not in the table, or the end station does not support holding a table, the station will request the routers on the network to send it information about a particular destination.

On obtaining this information, the station will address its packet to be handled by a router or a series of routers, thus enabling the packet to reach its final destination. It will submit a packet to the network with the destination MAC address set, not to its final destination, but to a particular router. Embedded somewhere in the network-layer header of the packet is the final destination network and host number. Thus, each router in the path to the destination will know where to forward the packet: it reads the network header information in the packet to determine the final destination.

Each router that receives the packet reads the fields of the packet that contain the routing information, particularly the destination network number. If the destination network number is directly attached to the router, the router simply forwards the packet, physically addressed to the final destination. Each router also holds a list of other routers that it knows about in a routing table. The table has the address of the router next in line to the final destination network, if the destination network is not directly attached to that router. The router will then physically address the packet directly to that next router. When the next router receives that packet, it will invoke the same algorithm as the previous router to get the packet to its final destination.

When the packet finally reaches the router with the destination network, it will physically address the packet to the final destination. The physical source address of the packet will be that of the router, so that the destination will know how to address any response packets. Any return packets from the destination network station will be addressed directly to that router, and the response packet will be forwarded in the same manner to the originator of the packet.

Some routers allow for different-sized packets on the network. If one segment of the network allows for only 1,518 bytes (the maximum Ethernet (IEEE 802.3) packet size) and the other segment allows for 4472 (Token Ring (IEEE 802.5) maximum per 4 Mbps (Mega bits per second), most 16-Mbps networks will use the 4 Mbps packet size of 4472. Routers fragment the original packet and then reassemble it at the destination network. They also allow for multiple paths to the same destination station. One network station could use one path to reach a destination and another network station might use an entirely different path but still reach the same destination. Routers do not forward broadcast packets, which are sent to everybody on the network; this eliminates problems referred to as *broadcast storms* (a lot of packets at any given time).

Bridges. Internet-working devices that link LANs at the OSI data link layer, or, more specifically, the MAC layer are known as *bridges*. They can function without the knowledge of the higher-level protocols and applications that are being transported through them. The fundamental operations of a MAC layer bridge are the following:

- *Relaying.* A MAC layer bridge relays individual user data frames between the LAN systems connected to its ports. Frames are a data structure, usually consisting of a header, payload, and a checksum. The order or sequence of frames received on one port and transmitted on another are maintained. The bridge relay function includes the following:

    Frame reception

    Frame discarding

    Frame forwarding

    Recalculation of the *Frame Check Sequence (FCS)*

    Frame transmission

> **Note**
>
> Frame Check Sequence is defined as an error-checking number that indicates if all the bits in the frame have been received correctly.

■ *Filtering.* A MAC layer bridge *filters* frames in order to prevent the duplication of frames. Bridge filtering functions include the following:

Permanent configuration of reserved addresses

Explicit configuration of static filtering information

Automatic learning of dynamic filtering information (through frame examination)

Aging out of filtering information that has been automatically learned

■ *Configuration management* includes the following functions:

Identifies all bridges that make up an inter-network, and locations of end stations attached to the LAN segment.

Remotely resets or reinitializes bridge operation.

Controls the priority with which a bridge port transmits frames.

Forces a specific configuration of the spanning tree.

Controls the propagation of frames with specific MAC addresses to certain ports of the bridge.

Bridge Architecture. Each bridge port is capable of receiving and transmitting frames to and from the LAN to which it is attached. Each bridge port has three entities:

■ The *MAC Service* entity handles all MAC layer functions. Here, individual MAC addresses or group addresses associated with a bridge port are examined.

■ The *MAC Relay* entity handles relaying of frames between bridge ports, filtering frames and learning filtering information.

■ The *Bridge Protocol* entity is used for the spanning tree algorithm and protocol, which is responsible for configuration of bridge topology in a network. Bridge Protocol entities between bridges communicate with one another via the *Bridge Protocol Data Unit (BPDU).*

> **Note**
>
> *Spanning Tree Algorithm* (*STA*) is a protocol that allows the physical loop to exist, but not a logical loop. It is an IEEE-approved protocol that enables bridges to interconnect more than one of the same cable feeds or to provide for a redundancy in the network.

Bridge Operation. The following describes the operation for the MAC layer bridge:

- The *Forwarding Process* forwards received frames that are to be relayed to other bridge ports, and filters frames based on information contained in the *Filtering Database*.

- The *Learning Process* or *Listening Process* is where each bridge port observes the source address of each frame received and updates the filtering database with an address entry based on which port it came from.

- The *Filtering Process* discards frames that are part of the filtering database.

Port State information specifies whether a bridge port is in Learning Mode, Filtering Mode, or Forwarding Mode.

Bridging Applications. There are many different reasons for using bridges as an internetworking device within local and enterprise-wide networks. These may be the result of physical limitations and/or network enhancement reasons. Common bridge application reasons include the following:

- Node population exceeds maximum specifications.

- Need to connect two or more remote sites.

- Network management improvements are needed.

- Enterprise-wide internetworking is required.

- Need to isolate building floor or departmental LANs from common backbone systems.

For remote access or WAN connectivity to existing LAN systems, a remote internetworking link is required. This link is comprised of a pair of bridges that function as if they were locally attached to one another. A remote bridge link provides a transparent and seamless connection between LANs. Remote bridges work just like transparent bridges.

> **Note**
>
> In a LAN-WAN-LAN connection mechanism, two bridges are required; one from LAN-WAN and the other from WAN-LAN.

For many organizations, implementation of a network backbone throughout entire buildings, such as campuses, allows for data connectivity throughout the information systems environment. Isolation of localized network traffic is an important step that is critical to supporting future growth and maintaining optimal performance. When bridges segment departmental LANs, network traffic typically remains local to the department.

Backbone networks are best used to transport interdepartmental traffic or to provide connectivity to shared resources and other host systems. Departmental LANs can interconnect to the backbone via a bridge. Many networks include bridges housed in the *Intermediate Distribution Frame (IDF)* or wiring closet for interconnectivity to the backbone systems.

> **Note**
>
> IDF can be thought of as a series of bridges that are connected to each other via a backbone of wiring, thus allowing several LANs to talk to each other without a WAN.

Types of Bridges. There are several types of bridges available on the market. Depending upon the requirements of any network, the appropriate type of bridge must be selected. Some of the important types of bridges are discussed in this section.

- *Transparent*. Transparent bridging has the following characteristics:

    It is used for local LAN-to-LAN connections.

    It does not logically separate networks.

    It does not interconnect different data link architectures.

It utilizes the MAC layer learning process, forwarding process, and filtering process.

It does not alter the frame.

In most cases, it does not depend on protocols.

It is susceptible to multicasts and broadcast frames causing a lot of unnecessary network traffic.

> **Note**
>
> *Multicast frames* are those that are addressed to a group of nodes.

- *Transparent Spanning Tree.* As networks grow and become more complex, the possibility of creating multiple paths or loops between LANs increases. Loops can cause havoc to a network based solely on transparent bridging. Duplication of packets and broadcast storms will degrade network performance. To combat the active loop problem, a bridging algorithm known as the *Spanning Tree Algorithm* (*STA*) is needed. The STA provides the following functionality:

    It configures a predictable active topology of bridged LANs into a single Spanning Tree so that there is, at most, one logical path between any two LAN segments, thus eliminating any network loops.

    It provides a fault-tolerant path by introducing automatic reconfiguration of the Spanning Tree topology in the event of bridge failure or a breakdown in the data path.

    It consumes a minimal amount of bandwidth to establish and maintain a Spanning Tree bridge path.

    It operates in a manner transparent to the end nodes.

- *Translational.* A translational bridge is a special form of a transparent bridge that provides a network connection between LANs that have different physical and data link architectures (for instance, Token Ring to Ethernet). Translational bridges have the following characteristics:

    They are used for local LAN-to-LAN connections.

    They do not logically separate networks.

They translate from one physical data link layer type to another.

They are protocol-independent, but data-link-dependent.

They are susceptible to multicast and broadcast traffic.

Bandwidth may be wasted.

- *Source-Route.* The term source-routing was coined by IBM to ascribe a method of bridging frames across Token Ring networks. Source-routing requires that the message source supply the information needed to deliver a message to its intended recipient; therefore the message source is responsible for determining the address of the message destination. Source-routing information consists of a list of ring and bridge numbers, which determines the route to the message destination. Because the message is required to specify the route to the destination, a route discovery process is required.

- *Encapsulating.* An encapsulating bridge provides LAN connection services by totally encapsulating the original frame within a new envelope associated with one type of LAN. An encapsulating bridge is generally associated with backbone topologies such as IEEE 802.3 (Ethernet) and IEEE 802.5 (Token Ring) connections to FDDI (Fiber Data Distribution Interface).

> **Note**
>
> IEEE 802.3 is a physical layer standard that specifies a LAN using the CSMA/CD access method, operating at 10/100 Mbps; IEEE 802.5 is a physical layer standard that specifies a ring topology LAN with a token-passing access method, operating at 4/16 Mbps.

Encapsulating bridges have the following characteristics:

They are used for remote or local LAN-to-LAN connections.

They connect LANs of the same or different physical media.

They encapsulate the data link layer of one LAN into the data link layer of another.

They do not alter the frame from the source node to destination node in any way.

They are vendor-proprietary.

They add overhead to the frame transmission.

They are susceptible to multicast and broadcast traffic.

They do not logically separate networks.

Processing performed by an encapsulating bridge is dependent upon the data link layer architectures. No stripping of protocol headers is performed. The integrity of the original IEEE 802.3, IEEE 802.5 or FDDI frame is maintained with an encapsulating bridge.

■ *Source-Route Transparent.* One major drawback that traditional IBM Token Ring environments have is their reliance on source-route bridges. In typical network environments, support for both transparent and source-routed packets is required. This lack of integration between transparent and source-route bridging forced IBM to develop and implement the *Source-Route Transparent (SRT)* bridge specification. An SRT bridge is a combination transparent and source-routing bridge that provides a network connection between LANs that have both non-source-routed and source-routed data link architectures. With an SRT bridge, network systems can interconnect and run different types of protocols simultaneously, including non-source-routed and IEEE 802.5 source-routed packets. The following summarizes the characteristics of source-route transparent bridges:

They are used for local or remote LAN-to-LAN connections.

They do not logically separate networks.

They support both transparent and source-route bridging.

They use the standard source-route algorithm.

They are susceptible to multicast and broadcast traffic.

Bridging or Routing Issues. The network manager's dilemma is to choose between a bridge or a router. The following issues should be considered before making the decision.

■ *Cost*: As in any investment decision, budget dictates the type of equipment to be purchased. In this respect, bridges are less expensive than routers and a more efficient usage of the available bandwidth is made by routers.

- *Expertise*: To reduce downtime or cost, it is in everybody's interest that the equipment is installed and working as soon as possible. In this regard, No up-front configuration, except in the case of filter setup, is required for bridges. They also build and learn address tables on the fly. Routers, on the other hand, require knowledge of the protocols that are to be implemented and of frame formats.

- *Reliability of Transmission*: Reliable transmission is one of the primary requirements of any network. With this in mind, Message delivery is not guaranteed with bridges, because they operate at the data link or MAC layer. Routers, however, facilitate network layer protocols, so guaranteeing delivery.

- *Error Detection*: In addition to reliable transmission, it is also required that data be error-free. In this respect, Data link layer Frame Check Sequence (FCS) error checking is performed by bridges. Routers perform both data link FCS and network layer (protocol-specific) error checking.

- *Security*: Security of networks is one of the primary issues to be concerned with. While firewalls can be built to prevent illegal entry, both bridges and routers provide some sort of security. Bridges provide MAC layer and protocol filtering functionality. Intelligent bridges are also capable of filtering a variety of traffic according to source and destination addresses. Routers provide MAC layer, protocol, and network layer filtering functionality. Some routers also provide optional sliding-window filters that can be defined by the user.

Wiring and Communications Media

Various methods of communication media are available today for carrying data across networks. In past years, these communication methods have been heavily oriented towards wire conductors. Communication paths can be grouped into four categories: open wire, twisted pair cable, coaxial cable, and the latest fiber-optic cable.

Wire will continue to be utilized around the world for some more time because of its extensive usage. Most of this wire is copper because of its resistance to corrosion; copper is also a good conductor of electrical signals.

Twisted pair cable came into being in order to provide better electric current flow. It is composed of copper conductors insulated by either plastic or paper and twisted into pairs. These pairs are further twisted into units which, in turn, are twisted into the finished cable. The cable is covered by lead or plastic.

This arrangement worked well with transmission frequencies of up to one megahertz (Mhz).

Above these frequencies, for long-distance simultaneous transmission of multiple conversations, interference in the form of cross talk causes problems. Therefore, coaxial cables were developed. These allowed higher frequencies to be used, thereby providing greater bandwidth and more information-carrying capabilities. Developments in the field of laser technology have helped in construction of thin fiber that can carry information at frequencies in the visible light spectrum. This allows over 1.3-gigabit-per-second information transmission for over 20 miles. Constant improvements in fiber technology keep taking place, which, in turn, lead to better and longer transmission of data without the need to regenerate the signal.

Satellite Communications

With the launch of satellites in low geosynchronous orbit, radio signals are being used for communication purposes. These use the very high frequency (VHF), ultra high frequency (UHF), and microwave bands. Signals are sent to these satellites and bounced off to various distant places.

Software

Various topics dealing with the hardware and its related issues have been discussed, but simply having the hardware does not solve the problem of data transmission and receiving. Different vendors following various specifications provide a sea of products that, in a lot of cases, prove to be incompatible with each other. In order to resolve this problem, software in the form of protocol is laid on top of the hardware. This solves the issue of handshaking between communication equipment and the problem of ensuring that a proper data path is established. In the following pages, various methods of communication using these protocols will be discussed.

> **Note**
>
> *Protocol* can be defined as the rules and conventions that need to be followed when two machines are conversing with each other. *Handshake* is the actual method of starting a conversation (REQ/ACK/NAK) between two machines.

Topologies

Networks are based on topologies. Topologies are architectural drawings that represent the cable layout and methodologies used for a LAN or WAN.

Topologies can be hardware-dependent, i.e., when a particular LAN is chosen, a specific topology must be followed when implementing the LAN. Some LANs have the capability of representing many types of topologies.

Bus Topology

The *bus topology* is sometimes known as the linear-bus topology (see fig. 2.1). It is a simple design that uses a single length of cable (also known as the *medium*) with network stations attached to this cable. All stations share this single cable, and transmissions from the station can be received from any station attached to the cable (a *broadcast medium*). There are end points to the cable segment, commonly known as *terminating points*.

Fig. 2.1
Stations connected in a bus network.

Bus Topology

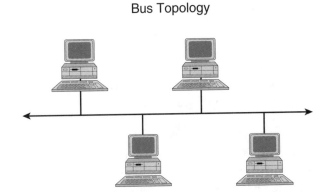

Given the simplicity of this topology, the cost of implementing it is usually low, but the management costs are high. No single station on the LAN can be individually administered easily, as compared to a star topology. There are no management designs (no controller) in stations that are attached to a single cable. The single cable can lead to a major problem: it contains a single point of failure. If the cable breaks, then no station will have the ability to transmit. The LAN that best represents this topology is the Ethernet access method.

Star Topology

The *star topology* is probably the oldest topology used for communications (see fig. 2.2). It was first introduced with analog and digital switching devices known as Private Branch Exchanges (PBX). In the star topology all stations are attached to one common point. This common point is usually a wiring hub with all stations attached via cables that extend from it. Since the stations are on a point-to-point link with the central wiring hub, the cost and the amount of cable may increase as stations are added. Considering the type of cable used, however, the overall cost is about equal to that of other topologies.

Star Topology

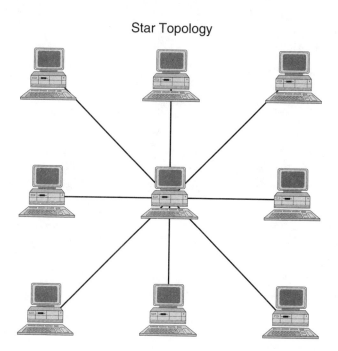

Fig. 2.2
Stations connected to a central hub in a star pattern.

There are two primary advantages to this topology. First, there is no single point of potential cable failure that would affect the whole network. If one of the cables should develop a problem, only the station directly using that cable would be affected. The example of the telephone can be used here. If the wire that connected your telephone were broken, only your telephone would be disabled. All other phones would remain operational. Similarly, all other network stations would remain operational. Second, the star topology allows for better network management.

The disadvantage of this topology is the centralized hub. If the hub fails, all connections to it are disabled. Most centralized hubs have passive backplanes and dual power supplies to enable 100% uptime.

With the advent of a new wiring system for Ethernet networks, known as *Unshielded Twisted Pair* (*UTP*), the star topology, which replaces the bus topology as the most common topology used for Ethernet networks.

Ring Topology

In the ring topology, all stations attached to the ring are considered repeaters on the LAN that is enclosed in a loop. A diagram of the ring configuration is shown in figure 2.3. There are no endpoints to this cable topology as in the star topology. The repeater, for our purposes, is the controller board in the station that is attached to the LAN.

Fig. 2.3
Stations arranged in a Ring formation.

Ring Topology

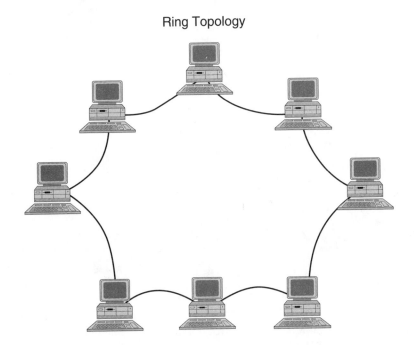

Each station will receive a transmission on one end of the repeater and repeat the transmission, binary bit by binary bit, with no buffering, on the other end of the repeater. Data is transmitted in one direction only, and received by the next repeater in the loop.

The most common cable design for this topology is the star-wired ring. The LAN that implements it is the Token Ring. A combination of the star topology and the ring topology is used for the physical cabling system of token ring. The token ring topology is commonly known as the star-wired ring.

The OSI Model in General

OSI stands for *Open Systems Interconnection*, an international standard issued by ISO, the International Organization of Standards, an organization founded in the 1940s to promote standards in a variety of technical (and non-technical) fields. The organization is composed of the national standards organizations of the member countries, such as the American National Standards Institute (ANSI). ISO proposed and accepted a model for network communications which became the OSI layered model.

There are seven layers of the OSI model; these layers form a stack. Each layer provides a level of abstraction for the layer above. Machines communicate across layers, that is, layer *n* on machine *A* communicates with layer *n* on machine *B*. The devices can also be different processes on the same machine. This ability is what provides the basis for the client server model.

The conversation is carried across the lower layers transparently to the upper layer. Each layer thus provides certain services to the higher layers, while hiding the implementation of the service from the higher layer.

Each layer in the stack passes both data and control information to its corresponding layer on the other machine, or corresponding process.

The seven layers of the OSI model are shown in Table 2.1.

Table 2.1 The Seven Layers of the OSI Model

Layer Number	Name
1	Physical
2	Data Link
3	Network
4	Transport
5	Session
6	Presentation
7	Application

Some of the functions and services offered by each layer are summarized in Table 2.2. Detailed discussion of each layer is provided in the following pages.

Introduction

Table 2.2 The OSI Layers

Layer	Description
Physical	Concerns the transmission of unstructured bit stream over physical medium; deals with the mechanical, electrical, functional, and procedural characteristics to access the physical medium.
Data link	Provides for the reliable transfer of information across the physical link; sends blocks of data (frames) with the necessary synchronization, error control, and flow control.
Network	Provides upper layers with independence from the data transmission and switching technologies used to connect systems; responsible for establishing, maintaining, and terminating connections.
Transport	Provides reliable, transparent transfer of data between end points; provides end-to-end error recovery and flow control.
Session	Provides the control structure for communication between applications; establishes, manages, and terminates connections (sessions) between cooperating applications.
Presentation	Provides independence to the application processes from differences in data representation (syntax).
Application	Provides access to the OSI environment for users; also provides distributed information services.

The Physical Layer

The physical layer forms the lowest layer in the OSI stack. All the other layers are on top of this layer. The physical layer specification defines signal voltages, encoding schemes, and the physical connections for sending bits across a physical media. It specifies the methods used to transmit and receive data on a network. This layer is comprised of the wiring, the devices that are used to connect a station's network interface card (NIC) to the wiring, the signal involved in transmitting and receiving data, and the ability to detect and if possible correct errors on the network media. Services and functions provided by the physical layer have been summarized in Table 2.3.

Table 2.3 Services and Functions of the Physical Layer

Services	Description
Physical connections	Connection of systems via transmission medium.
Physical SDUs (Service Data Units)	Consists of a single bit

Services	Description
Physical connection end points	Identifies a unique physical point of attachment to a transmission medium.
Data circuit identification	Identifier of physical communication paths for reference by higher layers.
Sequencing	Bits are delivered in the order in which they are submitted.
Fault condition notification	Data-link entities are notified of fault conditions.
Quality-of-service parameters	Characterization of quality of transmission path.

Functions	Description
Physical connection activation and deactivation	Control of the physical link.
Physical SDU transmission	Synchronous or asynchronous transmission of bits.
Physical layer management	Management activities related to physical layer.

The Data-Link Layer

This layer lies on top of the physical layer. This is the first layer where bits are collected and data is handled as packets. Synchronization of transmission of data and handling of frame-level error check and recovery are performed at this layer. While the physical layer receives and transmits a stream of bits without any regard to beginning or end, the data-link layer performs the job of providing some format to the data. It does frame formatting and CRC (Cyclic Redundancy Check, which checks for errors in the whole frame) at this layer. In situations such as lost frames, duplicate frames, and so on, the data-link layer decides whether to request the lost frames or discard the duplicate frames before passing them on to the next layer—the network layer. The data-link layer also performs the function of controlling the flow of data by providing the necessary buffer space, thus ensuring a smooth transfer of data. Some examples of typical protocols available at this layer are *High-level Data Link Control* (*HDLC*) and *Synchronous Data Link Control* (*SDLC*). Services and functions provided by the data-link layer have been summarized in Table 2.4.

Table 2.4 Services and Functions of the Data-Link Layer

Services	Description
Data-link connection	Connection of network entities
Data-link SDUs	Exchange of SDUs
Data-link connection endpoint identifiers	Identifies connection at SAP
Sequencing	Ordered delivery
Error notification	Notification of unrecoverable error
Flow control	Controls SDU rate
Quality-of-service parameters	Optionally selectable

Functions	Description
Data-link SDU mapping	One-to-one, SDU to PDU (Protocol data unit)
Data-link connection splitting	One data-link connection onto several physical connections
Delimiting and synchronization	Framing of bits
Sequence control	Ordered delivery
Error detection	Transmission, format, and operational errors
Error recovery	Retransmission of PDUs
Flow control	Between data link entities
Identification and parameter exchange	Controls information between entities
Control of data-circuit interconnection	Provides for network layer control
Data link layer management	Management activities related to data link layer

The Network Layer

The network layer performs the function of determining how packets or frames get forwarded or routed between stations. There are several ways that these routes are determined. They can be based on tables that are "plugged into" the network and usually remain the same. They can also be provided at the beginning of each communication session. Another method is to have the route determined on a packet-by-packet basis. Another function performed by the network layer is to make sure that congestion does not take place and to prevent bottlenecks. Devices such as bridges, gateways, and routers provide the necessary means for the network layer to ensure that a packet of information arrives at the correct device on the correct subLAN.

The network layer also has built-in accounting functions to keep track of things such as the number of packets that have been sent to each station. In this way, billing information can be provided to the service providers. It also resolves various problems of interconnecting different networks that might otherwise be incompatible, thus ensuring that the correct data reaches its destination. Special protocols and addressing methodologies help the network layer in this endeavor.

This is also the first layer where some filtering is performed to separate packets that are supposed to go to a particular network, thereby reducing cost and network traffic. Devices that handle these protocols, known as routers, are used for this purpose. Based on certain information embedded in the packet itself, this layer will allow data to be transferred in a sequential manner between stations in the most economic path, both physically and logically. Some protocols that operate at this level are Internet Protocol (IP) of TCP/IP and Novell Netware's Inter-network Packet Exchange (IPX). Services and functions provided by the network layer have been summarized in Table 2.5.

Table 2.5   Services and Functions of the Network Layer

Services	Description
Network addresses	Identifies transport entities uniquely.
Network connections	Identifies connection of transport entities.
Network connection endpoint identifiers	Identifies connection at SAP (*Service access points*).
Network SDU transfer	Exchange of SDUs.
Quality-of-service parameters	Optionally selectable.
Error notification	Unrecoverable errors are reported.
Sequencing	Ordered delivery.
Flow control	Control of SDU rate.

(continues)

Table 2.5   Continued

Services	Description
Reset	NSDUs (Network SDUs) in transit are discarded and the logical connection is reinitialized.
Release	Network connection is released and the transport entity at the other end is notified.

Functions	Description
Routing and relaying	Intermediate open systems may provide relaying; a route through these is determined.
Network connections	Using data-link connection or tandem subnetwork connections.
Network connection multiplexing	Multiple network connections are mapped onto a data-link connection or subnetwork connection.
Segmenting and blocking	NSDUs may be segmented or blocked to facilitate transfer.
Error detection	Uses data-link error notification and additional mechanisms.
Error recovery	Recovery from detected errors.
Sequencing	Ordered delivery.
Flow control	Between network entities.
Reset	Supports the reset service.
Service selection	Ensures that the service is the same at each end of a network connection that spans several dissimilar networks.
Network layer management	Management activities related to the network layer.

The Transport Layer

The primary function of the transport layer is to provide end-to-end (origination station to destination station) data transmission. It makes sure that data is transferred in a reliable manner with a guarantee that it will be delivered in the same order that it was sent in a timely fashion. The transport layer accepts data from the session layer above, repackages it in smaller packets if necessary, passes it to the network layer below, and ensures that data arrives correctly at the destination. It provides a distinct network connection for each transport connection needed by the session layer. The transport layer will create multiple network connections if necessary, thereby dividing the data among the connections to improve throughput. On the other hand, several transport connections may be multiplexed on the same network connections to achieve reductions in cost.

The type of service needed by the session layer and ultimately by the users of the network is also determined by the transport layer. A common type of transport connection is an error-free point-to-point channel that delivers packets in the order they were sent. In addition to providing a transport connection, and multiplexing several packets onto one channel, the transport layer also takes care of deleting connections across the network. One example of a protocol that operates at this level is Transmission Control Packet (TCP) of TCP/IP. Services provided by the transport layer are as follows:

- Transport connection establishment

- Data transfer

- Transport connection release

Functions provided by the transport layer are as follows:

- Mapping transport addresses onto network addresses

- Multiplexing transport connections onto network connections

- Establishment and release of transport connections

- End-to-end sequence control on individual connections

- End-to-end error detection and any necessary monitoring of the quality of service

- End-to-end error recovery

- End-to-end segmenting, blocking, and concatenation

- End-to-end flow control on individual connections

- Supervisory functions

- Expedited TSDU transfer

The Session Layer

As the name indicates, the session layer allows users on different machines to establish a session between them. It provides the means of organizing and synchronizing the dialog between the two machines, thereby managing the data exchange between them. The session layer offers three methods of interaction between users. They are simultaneous two-way traffic (full duplex), alternate two-way traffic, and one-way traffic. In two-way simultaneous, both parties involved can transmit and receive at the same time. In the two-way alternate, there is more of an inquiry/response relationship. As the name indicates, one-way only allows data to flow one way.

Another service offered by the session layer is known as *token management*. In some protocols, if both sides attempt to perform the same operation, it can cause severe problems (a lot of data can get affected). To prevent such occurrences and manage these activities, the session layer provides tokens that can be exchanged. The side holding the token can perform the critical operation. The session layer also offers another service that allows the ability to *establish synchronization points* within a dialog and, in the event of errors or accidental session termination, to resume the dialog from the last synchronization point. Services and functions provided by the session layer have been summarized in Table 2.6.

Table 2.6 Services and Functions of the Session Layer

Services	Description
Session connection establishment	Connects presentation entities.
Session connection release	Releases in an orderly way without loss of data.
Normal data exchange	Exchanges SDUs.
Quarantine service	Allows presentation entity to request quarantining of one or more SDUs.
Expedited data exchange	Expedites handling of SDUs.
Interaction management	Two-way simultaneous, two-way alternate, or one-way interaction.
Session connection synchronization	Allows presentation entities to define synchronization points and resynchronize to those points.
Exception reporting	Notifies presentation entity.

Functions	Description
Session connection to transport connection mapping	One-to-one mapping.
Session connection flow control	No *peer flow control* (flow control done by transport protocol); backpressure on transport connection.
Expedited data transfer	Supports expedited data service, which frees data from token and flow control constraints.
Session connection recovery	Reestablishes transport connection after failure.
Session connection release	Supports release service.
Session layer management	Management activities related to the session layer.

The Presentation Layer

This layer provides a common means of representation that can be used in communications between end users. It performs certain functions that are needed often enough that an overall solution can be thought of, rather than each user resolving the problem independently. In particular, unlike all the lower layers, which are just interested in moving bits reliably from here to there, the presentation layer is concerned with the syntax and semantics of the information transmitted. As we cross the boundary from the session layer to the presentation layer, there is a significant change in the way that data is viewed. For the session layer and below, the user data parameter of a service primitive (features) is specified as the binary value of a sequence of octets.

The application layer, however, is concerned with the user's view of data. In general, that view is one of a structured set of information, such as text in a document, a personal file, an integrated database, or a visual display of videotex information. The user is concerned only with the meaning of the data values in use, that is, the semantics of the data. The presentation layer must provide a representation of this data that is or can be converted into binary values; that is, it must be concerned with the syntax of the data. Consider that there are three syntactic versions of the information to be exchanged between application entities:

- The syntax used by the originating application entity.

- The syntax used by the receiving application entity.

- The syntax used between presentation entities.

The last is referred to as the transfer syntax. The presentation layer is responsible for translating the representation of the information between the transfer syntax and each of the other two syntaxs as required.

The approach taken by ISO to provide the linkage between semantics and syntax is as follows.

At the application layer, information is represented in an abstract syntax that deals with data types and data values. The abstract syntax formally specifies data independently from any specific representation. The presentation layer communicates with the application layer in terms of this abstract syntax. The presentation layer translates between the abstract syntax of the application layer and a transfer syntax that describes the data values in a binary form suitable for interaction with the session service. The transfer syntax is the representation of the data to be exchanged between presentation identities. The translation from the abstract syntax to the transfer syntax is accomplished by means of encoding rules that specify the representation of each data value of each data type.

The ISO standards make no assumptions about the way in which abstract or transfer syntaxs are specified. The presentation service is general-purpose and is intended to support all application protocols and any appropriate syntax's.

The presentation layer is also concerned with other aspects of information representation. For example, data compression can be used here to reduce the number of bits that have to be transmitted, and cryptography is frequently required for privacy and authentication. Services of the presentation layer are as follows:

- Transformation of syntax

- Selection of syntax

The functions of the presentation layer are as follows:

- Session establishment request

- Data transfer

- Negotiation and renegotiation of syntax

- Transformation of syntax, including data transformation, formatting and special-purpose transformations

- Session termination request

The Application Layer

The application layer is at the boundary between the open systems environment and the application processes that use that environment to exchange data. To support the wide variety of possible applications, the protocols and services potentially available in the application layer are many and varied. They include facilities of general utility to many applications and facilities specific to distinct classes of applications.

Application processes in different open systems that wish to exchange information do so by accessing the application layer. The application layer contains application entities that employ application protocols and presentation services to exchange information. It is these application entities that provide the means for application processes to access the OSI environment. We can think of the application entities as providing useful services that are relevant to one or more application processes.

The OSI document suggests a grouping of functions that clarifies the task of the application layer and also serves as a guide to standardization efforts. The grouping consists of three types of elements:

- *User element:* that part of an application process specifically concerned with accessing OSI services

- *Common application service elements*: provides capabilities that are generally useful to a variety of applications

- *Specific application service elements*: provides capabilities required to satisfy the particular needs of specific applications.

The common and specific application service elements do not form sublayers of the application layer, as was found in the network layer. The common application service elements exist as peers with specific application service elements, and provide a set of functions that would have to be present in each specific application service element if they were not provided separately.

Each application process is represented to its peer and exchanges data with that peer by means of an application entity. An application entity consists of one user element and a set of application service elements needed to support the particular application. Thus, application service elements are combined in different ways to support different applications. In the application, the user must implement a user element that knows how to access the services of those service elements required for the exchange. Services of the application layer are the following:

■ Information transfer

■ Identification of intended communication partners

■ Determination of the current availability of the intended communication partners

■ Establishment of authority to communicate

■ Agreement of privacy mechanisms

■ Authentication of intended communication partners

■ Determination of cost allocation methodology

■ Determination of the adequacy of resources

■ Determination of the acceptable quality of service

■ Synchronization of cooperating applications

■ Selection of the dialogue discipline, including initiation and release procedures

■ Agreement on responsibility for error recovery

■ Agreement on the procedures for control of data integrity

■ Identification of constraints on data syntax

Miscellaneous Layers

The discussion of the network layers in the previous pages of this chapter have been mainly focused on the OSI model. In this section, the *Medium Access Control (MAC)* sublayer is dealt with in some detail. It is especially important in Local Area Networks (LANs), which all use multi-access channel as the basis of their communications. *Wide Area Networks (WANs)*, however, use point-to-point as their basis, the only exception being satellite networks.

The IEEE (Institute of Electrical and Electronic Engineers) has developed several standards for LANs. These are collectively known as IEEE 802, and include CSMA/CD, token bus, and Token Ring. The various standards differ at the physical layer and MAC sublayer, but are compatible at the data-link layer. MAC provides the logical connection for the electrical signals onto the physical medium. The 802.2 standard describes the upper part of the data-link layer, which uses the *Logical Link Control (LLC)* protocol.

Figure 2.4 illustrates the viewpoints of both OSI and IEEE 802.

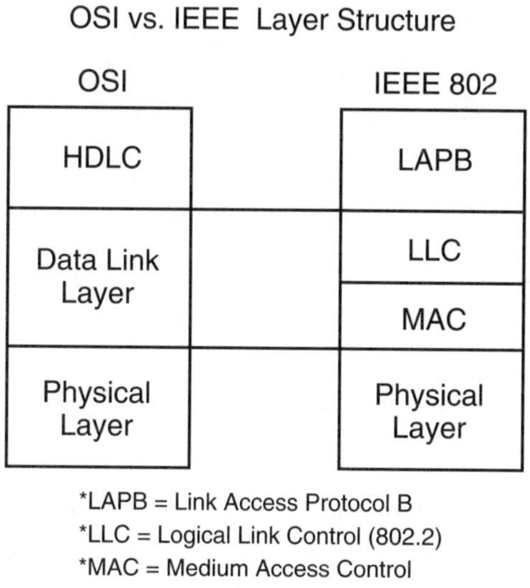

OSI vs. IEEE Layer Structure

OSI	IEEE 802
HDLC	LAPB
Data Link Layer	LLC
	MAC
Physical Layer	Physical Layer

*LAPB = Link Access Protocol B
*LLC = Logical Link Control (802.2)
*MAC = Medium Access Control

Fig. 2.4
OSI versus IEEE layer structure.

The OSI Protocol

The OSI protocol encompasses all seven layers of the OSI model. These, in turn, encompass several different protocols. The OSI protocol structure is rather complex in its architecture. Hence a small set of functions that form the core or basis of all protocols will be discussed briefly. While all these functions may not be present at the same layer or level in all the protocols, they can generally be found somewhere in the different layers. The protocol functions can be grouped in the following sections:

- Segmentation and Reassembly

- Connection Control

- Flow Control

- Ordered Delivery

- Error Control

- Multiplexing

- Encapsulation

Segmentation and Reassembly

A protocol is concerned with exchanging streams of data between two entities. Usually the transfer can be characterized as consisting of a sequence of blocks of data of some bounded size. At the application level, we refer to a logical transfer of a *message*. Whether the application entity sends data as messages or in a continuous stream, lower-level protocols may need to break up the data into blocks of some smaller bounded size. This process is called *segmentation*. For convenience, we shall refer to a block of data exchanged between two entities via a protocol as a PDU (Protocol Data Unit).

There are a number of motivations for segmentation, depending on the context. These are among the typical reasons for segmentation:

- The communications network may accept blocks of data only up to a certain size. *Advanced Research Projects Agency Network* (*ARPANET*), for example, accepts messages up to 8,063 bytes in length.

- Error control may be more efficient with a smaller PDU size. If an error is detected, only a small amount of data may need to be retransmitted.

- More equitable access to shared transmission facilities, with shorter delay, can be provided. For example, without a maximum block size, one station could monopolize a shared medium.

- A smaller PDU size may mean that receiving entities can allocate smaller buffers.

- An entity may require that data transfer comes to some sort of closure from time to time, for checkpoint and restart/recovery operations.

There are several disadvantages to segmentation that argue for making blocks as large as possible:

- Each PDU contains a fixed minimum of control information. Hence the smaller the block, the greater the percentage of overhead.

- PDU approval may generate an interrupt that must be serviced. Smaller blocks result in more interrupts.

- More time is spent in processing smaller and more numerous PDUs.

- All of these factors must be taken into account by the protocol designer in determining minimum and maximum PDU size.

■ The counterpart of segmentation is reassembly. Eventually, the seg-
mented data must be reassembled into messages appropriate to the
application level. If PDUs arrive out of order, this task is complicated.

Connection Control

An entity may transmit data to another entity in an unplanned fashion and
without prior coordination. This is known as *connectionless data transfer*. Although this mode can be useful, it is less common than connection-oriented
transfer.

Connection-oriented data transfer is often required if stations anticipate a
lengthy exchange of data and/or if certain details of their protocol must be
worked out dynamically. A logical association, or connection, is established
between the entities. Three phases occur:

■ Connection establishment

■ Data transfer

■ Connection termination

With more sophisticated protocols, there may also be connection interrupt
and recovery phases to cope with errors and other sorts of interruptions.

During the connection-establishment phase, two entities agree to exchange
data. Typically, one station will issue a connection request (in connectionless
fashion) to the other. A central authority (router/server) may or may not be
involved. In simpler protocols, the receiving entity either accepts or rejects
the request and, in the former case, away they go. In more complex propos-
als, this phase includes a negotiation concerning the syntax, semantics, and
timing of the protocol. Both entities must, of course, be using the same protocol. But the protocol may allow certain optional features, and these must be
agreed upon by means of negotiation. For example, the protocol may specify
a size of up to 8,000 bytes; one station may wish to restrict this to 1,000
bytes.

After connection establishment, the data transfer phase is entered. During
this phase both data and control information (about flow control and error
control, for instance) are exchanged. Finally, one side or the other wishes to
terminate the connection by sending a termination request. Alternatively, a
central authority might forcibly terminate a connection.

The key characteristic of connection-oriented data transfer is that sequencing is used. Each side sequentially numbers the PDUs that it sends to the other side. Because each side remembers that it is engaged in a logical connection, it can keep track of both outgoing numbers, which it generates, and incoming numbers, which are generated by the other side. Indeed, one can essentially define a connection-oriented data transfer as one in which both sides number PDUs and keep track of both incoming and outgoing numbering. Sequencing supports three main functions:

- Flow control

- Ordered delivery

- Error control

These three functions will be discussed in greater detail in the following sections.

Flow Control

Flow control is a technique for assuring that a transmitting entity does not overwhelm a receiving entity with data. The receiving entity typically allocates a data buffer with some maximum length. When data are received, the receiver must do a certain amount of processing (that is, examine the header and strip it from the PDU) before passing the data to a higher-layer user. In the absence of flow control, the receiver's buffer may fill up and overflow while it is processing old data.

In a connection-oriented protocol, the sequence numbers can be used to provide a flow control mechanism. At any given time, the sender is allowed to send PDUs whose numbers are in a contiguous range. Once those PDUs are sent, the entity can send no more until it receives permission from the other entity. For example, the transport protocol in host *A* has permission to send PDU numbers 1 through 7. After it sends these, it waits. At some time, the transport protocol in host *A* receives a message from the transport protocol in host *B*, indicating that it is now prepared to receive numbers 8 through 15.

Flow control is a good example of a protocol function that must be implemented in several layers of an architecture.

Ordered Delivery

When two entities are in different hosts connected by a network, there is a risk that PDUs will not arrive in the order in which they were sent, because they may traverse different paths through the network. In connection-oriented protocols, it is generally required that PDU order be maintained.

For example, if a file is transferred between two systems, we would like to be assured that the records of the received file are in the same order as those of the transmitted file, and not shuffled. If each PDU is given a unique number, and numbers are assigned sequentially, then it is a logically simple task for the receiving entity to reorder received PDUs on the basis of sequence number.

Error Control

Error control is a technique that allows a protocol to recover from lost or damaged PDUs. As with flow control, it is based on the use of sequence numbers. Three mechanisms come into play:

- Positive acknowledgment

- Retransmit after time-out

- Error detection

In a connection-oriented protocol, each PDU is numbered sequentially. For error control, it is the responsibility of the receiving protocol entity to acknowledge each PDU that it receives; this is done by sending back the sequence number of the received PDU to the other side. If a PDU is lost in transit, then the intended receiver will obviously not acknowledge it. The sending entity will note the time that it sends each PDU. If a PDU remains unacknowledged after a certain amount of time, the sender assumes that the PDU did not get through, and retransmits that PDU.

There is another possibility: the PDU gets through but the bits have been altered by errors in transit. To account for this contingency, an error detection technique is needed. The sending entity performs a calculation on the bits of the PDU, and adds the result to the PDU. The receiver performs the same calculation, and compares the calculated result to the result stored in the incoming PDU. If there is a discrepancy, the receiver assumes that an error has occurred, and discards the PDU. As before, the sender fails to receive an acknowledgment and retransmits the PDU. There are several check sum calculations that can be adopted. Some of the more common ones are:

- Cyclic redundancy check—16 bit (CRC-CCITT)

- Cyclic redundancy check—32 bit

Multiplexing

Multiplexing is a function that may be exercised when more than one layer of a communications architecture employs a connection-oriented protocol. The network access protocol may be connection-oriented, allowing a host to set up one or more logical connections to other hosts on the network. In packet-switched networks, these network logical connections are referred to as virtual circuits. The transport protocol will set up a logical transport connection for each pair of SAPs that wish to exchange data. For each transport connection, a separate network connection could be set up. This is a one-to-one relationship, but need not be so.

Multiplexing can be used in one or two directions. Upward multiplexing occurs when multiple higher-level connections are multiplexed on, or share, a single lower-level connection. This may be done to make efficient use of the lower-level service. For example, public packet-switched networks generally charge for each network logical connection that is set up. Thus, if several transport connections are needed between a pair of hosts, these could all be multiplexed on a single network connection. Downward multiplexing, or splitting, means that a single higher-level connection is built on top of multiple lower-level connections. This technique may be used to improve reliability, performance, or efficiency.

Encapsulation

Each block of data contains not only the actual data or payload but also some sort of control information. In fact, some PDUs consist solely of control information and no data. The control information generally falls into three categories:

- *Address*: The address of the sender and/or receiver may be indicated.

- *Error Detection Code*: Some sort of code is often included for error detection.

- *Protocol control*: Additional information is included to implement the protocol functions.

The addition of control information to data is referred to as *encapsulation*. Data are accepted or generated by an entity, and encapsulated into a PDU containing that data plus control information.

Routing

Routing is the actual process of selecting the correct interface and is the next destination for a packet being forwarded. A route can be said to be the path that network traffic follows from its source point to its destination point. The routing architecture of the OSI can be divided into three major components.

Routing Domain (RD)

Routing Domain can be explained as the method or schematic by which a group of intermediate systems (IS) will operate a specific routing protocol such that it is the same for each intermediate system in the overall network. These domains can be depicted in two forms: *hierarchical* or *flat*. As indicated by the name, hierarchical domain has more than one level. For example, IS-IS has two levels known as level 1 and level 2. Flat domains contain one level only.

There is another domain called the administrative domain. In this type of domain, each one contains a group of ISes that a single organization owns and that are administered as a single entity. In a number of instances, both the routing and administrative domains are viewed as a single entity, and are commonly referred to as the domain.

Intermediate System (IS)

The intermediate system referred to in the routing domain described in the previous section is usually a router. As indicated before, a router is an intelligent piece of equipment that forwards data through the most economical and logical path to reach its final destination. It also sends data packets directly to another router in the path towards the data's final destination, or a node, if the destination happens to be that node.

The difference between intermediate systems and end systems (to be discussed below) is that the intermediate systems must contain the intelligence to decipher and route packets in the correct path. Another requirement is that they must contain information about the networks on which they reside. This information consists of the different paths, both logical and economical, that make up the entire network to which they are connected.

End Systems (ES)

This is the last of the three components that make up a routing architecture. An end system is considered to be some sort of device or node that is at the end of the chain in the network. In most cases, it is either a personal computer, a host system, or a minicomputer. An end system usually needs to know only the destination and the associated intermediate system to which it can transmit a message in order to have it forwarded to its ultimate destination.

The routing algorithm that is used with the OSI is called a *Link State Algorithm* (*LSA*). It is vastly different from the more common routing algorithm that is found in most protocols today. This is known as the *Distance Vector Algorithm* (*DVA*), and it is found in protocols such as TCP/IP, XNS, AppleTalk, IPX, and others. Link state algorithm offers several benefits when compared to the distance vector algorithm. It offers faster convergence time (reducing the amount of time that loops may form) and lower bandwidth consumption (only bad links are reported, instead of the whole routing table). This algorithm truly represents a hierarchical architecture consisting of two or more layers.

As indicated before, link state algorithm overcomes the convergence and scalability problems experienced by distance vector algorithm. When a router is disabled or a new router is added on to the network, one router having the responsibility of being the "trusted router" detects a change and informs all the other routers of the change. In a link state algorithm network, only one router is given this responsibility. On the other hand, in the distance vector algorithm internets, all the routers have this responsibility, and therefore will eventually update each other of any changes.

With the link state algorithm, routers are divided into levels 1 and 2. While level 1 routers provide routing within an area, level 2 forms the backbone of the network, providing routing between the areas. In this way, information about changes that affect only one section of a non-backbone area is limited to that area only and to the level 2 router connected to the level 1 routers in the area. This provides for faster convergence, because only the routers that need to know about the change are updated. This also provides for fewer lost sessions and better response times. Since internets designed with link state algorithms converge faster, bandwidth is better utilized on the whole network.

Addressing

One of the most complex addressing schemes is the OSI addressing scheme. This addressing scheme was designed for virtually every different type of data communications environment possible. The primary unit of the OSI address is known as the *Network Access Point (NSAP)*. In the addressing scheme, instead of simply identifying a host with a number, the addresses can vary in length and contain many parts.

The OSI addressing scheme consists of four parts:

- *Initial Domain Part* (*IDP*)—This contains the Authority Format Identifier (AFI) and the Initial Domain Identifier (IDI).

- *Authority Format Identifier (AFI)*—This contains a two-digit value be-tween 0 and 99. This number indicates two things: first, it is used to describe the IDI format and the syntax of the Domain-Specific Part (DSP); second, it is used to identify the authority responsible for allocating the values of the Initial Domain Identifier.

- *Initial Domain Identifier (IDI)*—This describes the addressing domain.

- *Domain-Specific Part (DSP)*—This contains the address determined by the network authority (through ISO). It may contain addresses of end-user systems on an individual network. The DSP identifies the NSAP to the final subnetwork point of attachment (SNPA). In other words, this is the final point at which the network forwards the data to the destina-tion network for delivery to the network node.

Transport Layer

The transport service specification of the OSI is called the Connection-Oriented Transport Specification. As described in the previous pages of this chapter, the primary purpose of the transport layer is to provide end-system-to-end-system communication in a reliable fashion. Protocol used to accom-plish this enables sequential transfer of data between two stations. In other words, data packets should be received in the same order that they were sent. If not, an error message should be generated and necessary corrections made. In this regard, there are five classes of transport layers:

Class 0—Simple Class

This is the simplest form of transport protocol; it makes an assumption that reliable services are embedded in the network layer. It is mainly used for messaging systems, and requires the connection-oriented network service (CONS).

Class 1—Basic Error Recovery Class

Class 1 is similar to class 0, but adds sequencing. It was developed by the CCITT for use with X.25 protocols for providing access to packet-switched data networks. Class 1 also requires CONS.

Class 2—Multiplexing Class

Class 2 is an advanced version of class 0. It provides multiple transport connections to be created using a single network connection. This class also requires connection-oriented network service.

Class 3—Error Recovery and Multiplexing Class

As the name indicates, class 3 is a combination of both class 1 and class 2 and, like these classes, requires CONS service.

Class 4—Error Detection and Recovery

This class is by far the most widely used and implemented. It provides the common transport mechanisms that enable reliable data to be transferred between two stations, and it can operate over the CONS service. While it is the only class that does not require CONS service, it can operate over the Connectionless Network Service.

A session is established when a connection is made at one end of the link and the other end accepts the connection. This connection is usually made when the transport layer receives a request from the session layer. The transport layer then transmits a session request to the intended destination. During this time, parameters are negotiated between the two stations, including the type of transport class that will be supported, and any alternative classes. A "connection confirmed" message is transmitted by the destination on acceptance of the connection packet.

Once a connection is setup, data can flow across the session. In order to provide for flow control on the path circuit, the OSI transport protocol uses a system called credits. The credits determine the number of messages that the destination station can receive. On the same token, a source station can only transmit data packets as determined by the amount of credits. Class 4 has two types of flow control fields. They are known as the *normal* and the *extended* flow control fields. The normal flow control field has 7-bit sequence numbers and 4-bit credit fields. Extended flow control has 31-bit sequence and 16-bit credit fields. One example of the requirement of the extended flow control field is that in high speed networks (for example, FDDI) the possibility exists of a sequence number wrapping to the starting sequence number before a previous sequence number has left the network. The problem with this scenario is that two different packets of data with the same sequence number can be present on the network at any given instant.

Class 4 type transport layer in the OSI model has another unique feature built into it, known as the congestion-avoidance algorithm. This allows a network station to indicate in a transmitted packet that it was experiencing network congestion. The network layer informs the transport layer of congestion possibilities, and the transport layer in turn adjusts its flow control window to proportionately reduce the number of packets on the network. Once the congestion is reduced, the flow control window increases, and so does the number of packets on the network. This also allows for retransmission of packets if any get lost in the network. One other aspect of the transport layer not present in other network protocols is that it allows fragmentation of session layer data into multiple packets if it receives a packet that is larger than it can transmit. It is up to the destination station's transport layer to reassemble the packets.

As far as terminating a session is concerned, the station or user that decides a connection is no longer needed will disconnect the session. It transmits a disconnect request to the other side of the connection; upon receiving the request, the remote side transmits a packet confirming the disconnection.

Session

As indicated previously, the session control layer is the layer in the OSI model that resides between the transport layer and the application layer. Its responsibility is in organizing communication between two applications, and also in managing the communications. The session control layer provides several services beyond that of the connection control facilities in the transport layer. It provides services such as allowing a temporary entity of one system to be connected and to get access to the services of another system without the account control information. This can be viewed as providing access from a guest account. The session control layer also has the responsibility of determining whether the requested application exists, and if the application does not respond to the connection request, issuing an error message back to the requesting node. Buffering for the data sent to and from the application is done using the session control layer. In this regard, three types of data support are provided:

- *Message interface*—This can send and receive messages of any desired size.

- *Segment interface*—This method can send and receive messages of predetermined size only. This usually corresponds to the allowable transport data unit size.

- *Stream interface*—In this type, data is seen as a stream of bytes with an "end of message" marker inserted.

Some of the other responsibilities of the session control layer include monitoring of the connection. The session control layer also monitors the transport connection and, if necessary, forces a disconnect if it discovers that the transport layer has detected a probable network disconnect or when the transport layer does not receive any response to a connection attempt.

Introduction

Application

The application layer in the OSI model has been described in detail under the seven layers in the earlier part of this chapter. Here, some of the issues and services provided by the application will be discussed. Some of the issues include file transfer, remote file access, electronic mail, and virtual terminals. It should be clarified that these application service providers do not form sublayers of the application layer as found in the network layer.

Three of the most common applications in any computer network are file transfer, printing, and remote file access. OSI has standardized the protocol that is to be followed in these applications. Application programs can access, print, and transfer remote files without having the necessity of knowing details of the process involved. Most applications have certain things in common, such as how to manage connections and how to coordinate activities among three or more parties. OSI provides these as standard application building blocks that go a long way in helping any new application with these functions. They are the following:

- Association Control Service Element (ACSE)

- Commitment, Concurrency, and Recovery (CCR)

Association Control Service Element (ACSE)

Association Control Service Element (ACSE) is specifically architectured for managing connections, which are known in the application layer as associations. ACSE has primitives that are shown in Table 2.7.

Table 2.7   OSI ACSE Primitives

OSI ACSE Primitive	Description
A-ASSOCIATE	Establishes an association
A-RELEASE	Releases an association
A-ABORT	User-initiated abort
A-P-ABORT	Provider-initiated abort

Each ACSE primitive maps one-to-one with the corresponding presentation layer service primitive.

Commitment, Concurrency, and Recovery (CCR)

This is a service element in which multiparty interactions are coordinated in a foolproof way, even when repeated system crashes take place. Almost all applications that have to operate reliably, use CCR. CCR resolves many problems where it is imperative that all parties involved in a transaction successfully complete their assigned tasks.

CCR provides a function called atomic action. An atomic action is a collection of messages and operations that either succeeds or can be rolled back to the original state, as if no actions at all had occurred. CCR also provides primitives, which are listed in Table 2.8.

Table 2.8 OSI CCR Primitives		
OSI CCR Primitive	**From**	**Description**
C-BEGIN	Master	Begins an atomic action.
C-PREPARE	Master	Ends phase 1; prepares to commit.
C-READY	Slave	Indicates a slave is able to do its work.
C-REFUSE	Slave	Indicates a slave is not able to do its work.
C-COMMIT	Master	Commits the action.
C-ROLLBACK	Master	Aborts the action.
C-RESTART	Either	Announces that a crash has occurred.

OSI has produced models and standards for file transfer, electronic mail, virtual terminals, directory service, and other applications.

The OSI FTAM model is based on the idea of a virtual filestore that is mapped to a real filestore by software. The virtual filestore definition by itself is highly complex, with lots of fancy attachments. It is highly connection-oriented, with a series of nested regimes. Each regime, in turn, has a series of operations that are permitted during the regime. Some of the more frequently used FTAM service primitives are shown in Table 2.9.

Introduction

Table 2.9   FTAM Service Primitives

FTAM Service Primitive	Description
F-INITIALIZE	Establishes a connection with the filestore
F-TERMINATE	Releases a connection with the filestore
F-U-ABORT	Indicates a user-initiated abort
F-P-ABORT	Indicates a provider-initiated abort
F-SELECT	Selects a file for manipulation or transfer
F-DESELECT	Terminates a selection
F-CREATE	Creates a file
F-DELETE	Destroys a file
F-RECOVER	Re-creates open regime after a failure
F-CANCEL	Abruptly terminates data transfer regime
F-CHECK	Sets a checkpoint
F-RESTART	Returns to a previous checkpoint

Electronic Mail

The OSI electronic mail system, MOTIS, is based on X.400 series of recommendations. It uses a system of Originator/Recipient names for its addressing. One advantage of this system is that the directory service can be consulted for *Presentation Service Access Point* (*PSAP*) addresses, routes, and any other technical information users may not remember. For sending mail, the user constructs the message using a user agent, which, in turn, passes the message to the message transfer agent. On acceptance of the message by the message transfer agent, this agent looks up the address of the next transfer agent, and hands the whole thing over to the next agent using RTS (Reliable Transfer Service). This is designed to prevent lost mail, even during repeated system crashes. After each message is sent, it is confirmed before another is sent. The reliable transfer service primitives are as indicated in Table 2.10.

Table 2.10 RT Service Primitives	
RT Service Primitive	**Description**
RT-OPEN	Establishes an association
RT-CLOSE	Releases an association
RT-U-ABORT	Indicates a user-initiated abort
RT-P-ABORT	Indicates a provider-initiated abort
RT-TRANSFER	Transfers one message
RT-TURN-LEASE	Please give me the "token"
RT-TURN-GIVE	Here is the "token"

Virtual Terminals

Terminals, in general, fall into three categories. They are scroll mode, page mode, and form mode. Scroll mode terminals do not have any processing capability, and hence cannot communicate with the network using any standard protocol. Page mode terminals have the capability of displaying up to a page of data (25 lines of 80 characters each); they cannot communicate with the network either. The last type is the form mode. It has built-in processing power, and hence is relatively powerful. This type is used often in applications such as banking and airline reservations.

The OSI VTS (Virtual Terminal Service) is very similar to the form mode virtual terminal. It can perform all the operations listed in Table 2.11.

Table 2.11 VTS Service Primitives	
VTS Service Primitive	**Description**
VT-ASSOCIATE	Establishes a connection.
VT-RELEASE	Releases a connection.
VT-U-ABORT	Indicates a user-initiated abort.
VT-DATA	Indicates data operation.
VT-DELIVER	Flushes out all buffered data.

(continues)

Table 2.11 Continued	
VTS Service Primitive	**Description**
VT-ACK-RECEIPT	Acknowledges VT-DELIVER.
VT-GIVE-TOKEN	Passes the token in synchronous mode.
VT-REQUEST-TOKEN	Requests the token in synchronous mode.
VT-SWITCH-PROFILE	Negotiates the use of a standard profile.

Directory Service

The OSI directory service allows users to look up names based on attributes. It consists of a hierarchy that incorporates the various private directories as well as conventions followed by different countries. Each entry in the directory consists of a set of attributes and an access control list. The access control list specifies read and write capabilities. Each attribute incorporates four properties: a type, an interpretation, a qualifier, and a value. One attribute in each directory is mandatory, and known as the key. The directory system provides for features such as building mailing lists, the ability to provide aliases, and other features.

Job Transfer and Management

Frequently, in large organizations, individuals with personal computers need to execute or run part of their work on bigger machines, such as mainframes, with the results being sent back to their individual machines. Sometimes such work entitles the usage of departmental computers such as minicomputers for some necessary data or files. In order to perform this kind of remote job, OSI provides another application, known as Job Transfer and Management (JTM). JTM arranges for the work and its associated files to be transferred to the location of the execution machine and after the work is completed to have the results transferred to the designated place.

OSI uses the term document instead of files as a general purpose information carrier. It performs the work primarily by interacting with four kinds of agencies:

- *Initiation agency*—The person or process who needs the work to be done.
- *Source agency*—The file system that provides the required files.
- *Sink agencies*—The file system that allows files to be kept for storage.
- *Execution agencies*—The execution machines that perform the task at hand.

From Here...

Computer communication has come a long way in a very short span of time. With advances in technology, coupled with rapid decrease in cost of hardware, upgrading of network equipment is being done more often than ever. Newer concepts and faster communication methods have also helped in providing global access for data and information.

For more information on the topics discussed in this chapter, refer to the following:

- Chapter 3, "Communications Protocols," gives you more information on both LANs and WANs and other key communication protocols such as NetBios, TCP/IP, SNA.

- Chapter 4, "Client/Server Development Overview," acquaints you with the client/server model and discusses the various protocols that are available in the market.

Chapter 3

Communications Protocols

The previous chapter discussed the OSI model, its seven layers, and the various details associated with it. This chapter presents a detailed discussion of communications protocols with respect to the OSI model. Both LAN and WAN communications protocols will be covered, especially the more common ones. Some of the most current technologies such as Ethernet, FDDI, and ATM and several key communications protocols such as NetBios, TCP/IP, and SNA will also be discussed.

Communications protocols can be defined as the method or form of communication between two users across the network. There are several protocols, some very simple and others very complex. Communications protocols can be divided into three broad categories:

- *Proprietary* protocols were developed by companies solely for their own purposes.

- *Public* protocols were developed according to some standards that may be subject to periodic changes or modifications.

- *Hybrid* protocols combine proprietary and public protocols with specific features.

Protocol Functions

Protocols are designed and developed with a set of features and functions in mind. Some of these are as follows:

- Station addressing

- Error checking and correcting

- Segmenting and sequencing

- Establishing quality of service and flow control

- Application identifying and checkpointing

- Multiplexing, peer-to-peer, and client server

Connectivity

Connectivity is broadly defined as the ability to link with networks outside a Local Area Network (LAN). A network operating system can provide connectivity facilities such as these:

- Allowing a personal computer not attached to a LAN to access the LAN over communication facilities such as telephone lines, via remote access. Operating systems such as Windows NT provide additional facilities such as Remote Access Service (RAS) entries. These entries provide auxiliary support to users to remote access LANs.

- Providing a focal point or a shared communication facility that allows stations on a LAN to access a computer that is not part of the network. This connectivity feature is also known as *communication server*.

- Providing the ability to interconnect two or more LANs that may or may not be of the same type. This connectivity between networks can also be provided via a Wide Area Network (WAN).

Different forms of connectivity and their functions are often provided in the Network, Transport, and Session layers of the OSI model. Connectivity involves a couple of specific issues:

- Network names are a service provided by the Network, Transport, and Session layers of the OSI model so that network users and application programs can interface to the network using those names rather than network addresses. Those layers also provide facilities that translate the network names to addresses. This is accomplished either by each station having its list of names and their addresses or by a central facility maintaining a table of network names associated with different stations and their corresponding addresses.

- Routing and addressing were discussed extensively in the previous chapter. Additional information about addressing is provided in the following pages.

Two types of operation are defined as part of the specification for the interface between the Network layer and the Logical Link Control sublayer:

- Connectionless service

- Connection-oriented service

Connectionless Service

Connectionless service eliminates the need to establish a logical connection between the transmitting and receiving stations; each data unit that is sent is processed independently. There is no sequence checking to ensure that all data units are received in the same order in which they were sent. In addition, the receiving station does not send any sort of acknowledgment that it has received the data units. As a corollary, there is no flow control or error recovery.

Connection-Oriented Service

Connection-oriented service requires that a logical connection be established between the transmitting and receiving stations before it can begin. This is usually referred to as a *virtual circuit* through the network. Sequence checking is performed to ensure that data units are received and processed in the same order in which they were transmitted. Flow control and error recovery are also provided as part of the service, including retransmission of data units not correctly received. Table 3.1 summarizes the differences between the two services.

Table 3.1 Comparison of Connection-Oriented Service and Connectionless Service

Function	Connection-Oriented Service	Connectionless Service
Setup overhead	Yes	No
Sequencing	Yes	No
Error control	Error detection and correction	Per packet

(continues)

Table 3.1 Continued		
Function	**Connection-Oriented Service**	**Connectionless Service**
Delivery	Guaranteed	Best effort
Addressing	Per connection	Per packet
Usage	Mainframe environment	LAN environment

Note

As in any case, there are exceptions to this, one of the most common examples being IP (Internet Protocol). IP can be either connection or connectionless and environment independent.

Addressing

Addresses in data networks are similar to postal addresses. As a means of identification, they provide information about the physical or logical placement of an entity. Typically, to communicate on a data network, users need three forms of addresses:

- *Physical address*—Used by the Physical layer to examine the destination address, the physical address identifies a computer or a workstation on a network.

- *Data-link address*—The IEEE 802.5 standards make use of another address called the LAA (Locally Assigned Address). Its purpose is to identify the type of link protocol that is being used above the Media Access Control layer. It is possible to use a single address at both the Physical and the Data Link layers, a practice used in some WANs. LANs tend to use separate physical and data-link addresses.

- *Network address*—A network address identifies the network; it is a higher-level address than a physical or data-link address. It is also not concerned with lower-level addresses.

The use of these addresses not only provides for clean interfaces, but it also gives network administrators flexibility in configuration of network resources. However, just having these addresses is not sufficient to get a data packet to its final destination. In addition, upper-layer protocols require some sort of protocol ID to distinguish between applications. The Internet standards use names and addresses as indicated in Table 3.2.

Table 3.2   Internet Standards Names and Addresses

Layer	Name/Address Used at This Layer
User Application	End user ID
Internet Application	Port number
Transport	Protocol name
Network	IP address
Logical Link Control	LSAP number
Media Access Control	MAC address
Physical	None

Synchronization

Synchronization, a service provided by the Session layer of the OSI model, is used to move session entities back to a known state in the event of an error or disagreement. This is required because the Transport layer below is only designed to remove communication errors. The Session layer sets up synchronization points that allow it to reset to the last known synchronization point and establish resynchronization. With this ability, session users can insert these points in the message stream.

There are two different kinds of synchronization—major and minor. The units delimited by major synchronization points are usually significant pieces of work logically and are known as *dialog units*. These points play a significant role because it is possible to go back only as far as the most recent major synchronization point. They are also explicitly confirmed or acknowledged. Minor synchronization points allow the user to go back any number of points to resynchronize. Again, the limiting factor is the last major synchronization point. However, minor synchronization points are not confirmed. Setting a synchronization point, be it major or minor, requires the possession of relevant tokens. When resynchronization occurs, all the tokens are restored to the positions they had at the instant the synchronization point was set.

Flow Control

Frequently, circumstances arise in networks in which the load on the network is far greater than can be handled even with optimal routing. Bottlenecks tend to arise if no precautions are taken to restrict the entry of traffic into the network. Excess traffic can cause packet delays, possibly violating maximum delay specifications. These problems require some measure of flow control on the traffic in the network. Flow control is required at various layers in the OSI stack. There are several approaches to flow control:

■ *Packet discarding*. In many cases, packets need to be discarded if a particular node has no available buffer space. In addition, packets can be discarded even though buffer space is still available, if the packets belong to sessions that have used up their share of resources and are likely to cause congestion.

■ *Call blocking*. In this approach, a session is blocked from getting onto the network if the network cannot provide the minimum guaranteed data rate that the session requires.

■ *Packet scheduling*. In this approach, a node can exercise flow control by expediting or delaying the transmission of packets of different sessions.

Error Detection and Correction

Errors on the line can be caused by various reasons:

■ *Noise*—Caused by unwanted signal combining with and thereby distorting the data signal intended for reception; this includes thermal noise, impulse noise, intermodulation noise, and crosstalk.

■ *Attenuation*—The data signal strength decreases with distance over any transmission medium. Sometimes attenuation can be high enough for the receiver to have difficulty obtaining the data from the received signal.

■ *Attenuation distortion*—Attenuation is an increasing function of frequency. Hence, frequency components of a signal are differentially affected, which introduces distortion into the signal.

■ *Collisions*—Collisions can take place in a bus or tree topology; if two stations transmit at the same time, the signals overlap and neither signal can be successfully received.

■ *Delay distortion*—The velocity of propagation of a signal through a guided medium varies with frequency; the velocity tends to be highest near the center frequency of the signal and fall off toward the two edges of the signal's bandwidth.

Errors tend to come in bursts on the line rather than individually most of the time. In order for errors to be detectable, some degree of redundancy must be built into the messages being transmitted. One of the most common methods used in detecting errors is the 32-bit *cyclic redundancy check* (CRC). CRC uses a polynomial code in which on a p-bit frame or packet, the transmitter generates an n-bit sequence known as the frame check sequence (FCS), such that the resulting frame consists of $p+n$ bits. This is divisible exactly by some predetermined number. The receiver then divides the incoming frame by the same number and, if there is no remainder, it is assumed that there was no error in the frame.

When errors have been detected, some action needs to be taken to correct the problem. Enough redundancy is usually present in the transmitted information so that the receiver can deduce what the transmitted character must have been. In other cases, the transmitter may be required to retransmit the erroneous data.

Network Protocols in General

Network protocols perform multiple levels of functions that include the interaction among several levels of logical and physical functions. They are also usually described with the Open System Interconnect (OSI) architecture in mind. There are several OSI protocols that are available to the user at all layers. These protocols perform specific functions at the different layers before passing data on to the next layer. Network protocols can also be broadly classified under the following two categories:

- Local Area Network (LAN) protocols

- Wide Area Network (WAN) protocols

LAN Basics

In the technology of today, nothing has spread as rapidly and made information as easily available as the personal computer. As use of personal computers has grown, so has the need for these computers to interact with one another and with centralized data computers. Networking technology has developed Local Area Networks (LANs) as a means of meeting the requirements of short-distance communication between intelligent devices. The IEEE defines a LAN as follows:

> A datacomm system that allows a number of otherwise independent devices to communicate directly with each other, within a moderately sized geographic area over a physical communications channel of moderate data rates.

A LAN can be used for a variety of purposes. Some of the most common LAN functions are allowing shared access to data, accessing files between computers, sharing printers, and providing electronic mail facilities. An important use of high-speed LANs is cooperative processing, in which an application can run partly from a personal computer and partly from a mainframe computer. Because a LAN provides so many uses, the benefits of installing a LAN usually far outweigh the capital expenditure of investing in cables, network interface cards, operating system, software, and personnel to establish and maintain the LAN.

WAN Basics

Networks that tie together users who are widely separated geographically are known as Wide Area Networks (WAN). Bridges can be used to connect LANs that are widely separated; this collection of LANs and bridges has a connection to a WAN. Frames for remote LANs travel over the WAN. In order to connect two different WANs, WANs (with the exception of satellite networks) use point-to-point links.

Because the reliability in a WAN is low, error handling is introduced in each layer. Important issues include WAN bit errors, router and WAN congestion, and dropped packets. One technique being explored for handling errors is compression. Compression can help curb the demand for costly WAN bandwidth. It can also help free enough bandwidth on mainframe nets to allow LAN traffic to be added without extra circuits. At present, a number of routers compress data over frame relay and other WAN services, such as these.

Some of the commonly available WAN services are these:

■ *56-Kbps*—This is a low-bandwidth, leased line, point-to-point service. A user installs a Channel Service Unit/Data Service Unit (CSU/DSU) at either end of the link, and the carrier establishes the connection between the sites.

■ *Switched 56*—Charges for a switched 56 line are usually less than for a dedicated 56-Kbps line.

■ *ISDN*—Integrated Services Digital Network (ISDN) is a switched service that includes three possible types of service:

B is a channel service that runs at 64 Kbps and is used for voice, circuit-switched data such as dialing remote computers, or packet-switched data such as linking to an X.25 network.

D is a channel service that runs at 16 Kbps and is typically used for sideband signaling information but can be used for low-bandwidth packet-switched data connections.

H is a channel service that runs from 384 Kbps to just under 2 Mbps and is intended for high-bandwidth multimedia or file transfer applications.

- *X.25*—This is relatively slow and is thus less than ideal for any but low-speed LAN interconnection. In this, each packet of data has all the necessary source and destination addressing, by which the switches within a value-added network (VAN) can choose alternate routes to get the data to its destination. Typically, a maximum bandwidth connection to a VAN is 64 Kbps.

- *Frame relay*—Frame relay is often characterized as fast X.25. It does not have the overhead of X.25; it omits packet sequencing and error checking. Frame relay is designed to accommodate the occasional bursts of traffic that LANs typically generate, thereby letting users transmit at fairly high rates.

- *T1*—Bell System introduced the T1 carrier, which can handle 24 voice channels multiplexed together at a rate of 1.544 Mbps. Sometimes referred to as *DS1 channel*, T1 service has been a high-bandwidth communications service of choice for users supporting their own data and voice networks.

- *Fractional T1*—This is obtained by breaking a T1 line into 24 segments of 56 Kbps each. Customers can then choose a number of segments for a specific point-to-point connection. While setup costs are similar to T1, monthly service charges are less expensive, since customers only pay for needed bandwidth.

- *SMDS*—Switched Multimegabit Data Service (SMDS) offers high-bandwidth, packet-switched circuits. It supports bandwidths up to 45 Mbps. This requires high-performance communications equipment such as high-end DSU/CSUs and routers.

Specific Network Protocols

In this section, specific protocols will be discussed. Some protocols are becoming very popular and will remain so for the next few years. Several protocol vendors are offering these services, driving the costs slowly but surely down. Some of the protocols discussed here are:

- Ethernet

- Token Ring

- Fiber Distributed Data Interface (FDDI)

- Frame Relay

- Asynchronous Transfer Mode (ATM)

- High Level Data Link Control (HDLC)

- Point-to-Point Protocol (PPP)

- Switched Multimegabit Data Service (SMDS)

- SMDS Interface Protocol (SIP)

- Synchronous Optical Network (SONET)

- Xerox Network System (XNS)

- DECNet

Ethernet

Ethernet was developed in the early 1970s for LAN systems. Ethernet is a multi-access, packet-switched network that uses a passive broadcast medium, with no central control. Data units transmitted over the network reach every station. Each station is responsible for recognizing the address in a data unit and for accepting data units addressed to it from the transmission medium.

Note

Messages are formed into packets according to the specifications of the packet-switching system. Each packet has three parts—header, body, and trailer. It also provides data error control and flow control.

Ethernet Frame Format

The data encapsulation/decapsulation primary functions performed by the Data Link layer are producing a correctly formatted frame for transmission across the network and then processing a received frame to be sure it has arrived correctly before passing it on to the Client layer. Ethernet frame format is as follows:

- *Preamble*—The preamble is used to provide synchronization and to mark the start of a frame. The same bit pattern is used for the Ethernet preamble field as in the IEEE 802.3 preamble and start frame delimiter fields.

- *Destination Address*

- *Source Address*—Address fields include both source and destination address fields. While Ethernet specifies the use of 48-bit addresses, IEEE 802.3 allows either 16-bit or 48-bit addresses.

- *Type Field*—Ethernet does not support the use of length field and padding. Instead these two bytes contain a type field that is meaningful to the higher network layers. However, this field is defined as part of Ethernet specification.

- *Data Field*—This is payload data in multiples of eight bits. Ethernet defines a minimum frame size of 72 bytes and a maximum of 1,526 bytes including the preamble. A minimum size is required to reduce collision handling problems.

- *Frame Check Sequence*—This is provided in an Ethernet frame as a way of providing error checking. A cyclic redundancy check (CRC) value is calculated from the other fields in the frame. This value is calculated again when the frame is received and is compared with the value in the frame. An error has occurred if the two do not match.

The IEEE 802.3 frame format is as follows:

- Preamble

- Starting Delimiter

- DA

- SA

- Length

- Data Field

- Pad Bytes

- Frame Check Sequence

Ethernet Transmission Specifications

The most common Ethernet implementation uses baseband transmission over coaxial cable at a data rate of 10 Mbps. With newer schemes and faster hardware, Ethernet is currently in the process of being implemented at 100 Mbps. While this technology is available at routers and beyond servers, it will probably be available very soon at each and every desktop computer. Presently, there are two different approaches in the 100 Mbps Ethernet strategy:

■ *100 Mbps Base-T Ethernet*—This is being sponsored by a collection of vendors who perceive that the existing 10 Base-T can be easily upgraded to the 100 Mbps. Several of these vendors have already announced products that can handle both 10 Mbps and 100 Mbps at the same time on the same network interface card (NIC). The advantage of this technology is that the Ethernet specification being used is exactly the same as that of the 10 Base-T specification. This technology in general has gained greater acceptance even among users who see the tenfold gain in speed with very little cost in upgrades.

■ *100 Mbps VG AnyLan*—This was primarily designed and developed by Hewlett-Packard and is gaining a lot of support. It provides speeds of 100 Mbps with expectations of reaching 400 Mbps to 1 Gbps. While 100 Mbps Base-T can only handle Ethernet frames, VG AnyLan can handle both Ethernet and Token Ring frames. In addition, VG AnyLan can also handle voice and video data. Because it has a different specification from the widely installed Ethernet user base, acceptance among vendors and customers has been a little slow. However, they are beginning to realize that it is a better technology and are planning accordingly.

Ethernet has been around for years and will continue to do so with advances in technology. It provides data encapsulation/decapsulation, link management, data encoding/decoding, and other useful functions.

> **Note**
>
> The highest layer of the local area network communications architecture is the IEEE 802.2—Logical Link Contrl (LLC). All of the medium access control (MAC) standards and FDDI sit below LLC. Its main purpose is to provide a method of data exchange between LLC users across a MAC-controlled link.

Token Ring

IEEE 802.5 Token Ring guarantees sequential access, where access to the network is granted via a token frame that is passed from station to station. Token Ring transmission can be at either 4 Mbps or 16 Mbps and can be supported on both shielded twisted-pair (STP) and unshielded twisted-pair (UTP) transmission media. Token Ring is probably the oldest ring-control technique, originally proposed in 1969. It is based on the use of a particular bit pattern, called a *token*, that circulates around the ring when all stations are idle.

Token Ring is based on a physical star, logical ring topology. Logically, a Token Ring network works sequentially, similar to a ring. Physically, the workstation cabling is installed in a star-wired manner from a centrally located wiring closet. One station (the first station on the ring) assumes the responsibility of the Active Monitor. The Active Monitor is responsible for the following:

- Ensuring that a token is not lost
- Purging ring when garbled frames appear
- Making sure frames don't circulate endlessly
- Taking action when ring breaks

If a station detects no Active Monitor, it can issue a Claim Token frame. If a station receives its own Claim Token, it becomes the Active Monitor.

The IEEE 802.5 standard encompasses both the Media Access Control and the Physical layers. It can be viewed as having four parts:

- MAC service specification
- MAC protocol
- Physical layer entity specification
- Station attachment specification

The MAC protocol is the heart of the IEEE 802.5 standard, which is often referred to simply as the Token Ring standard. The specification defines the frame structure and the interactions that take place between MAC entities.

The overall MAC frame format consists of the following fields:

- *Starting Delimiter* (SD)—Indicates the start of token or frame.

- *Access Control* (AC)—Contains the priority and reservation bits, which are used in the priority mechanism, and the monitor bit, used in the ring maintenance mechanism.

- *Frame Control* (FC)—Indicates whether this frame contains LLC data or is a MAC control frame.

- *Destination Address* (DA)—Specifies the station(s) for which the frame is intended.

- *Source Address* (SA)—Specifies the station that sent the frame. The SA size must equal the DA size.

- *Information*—Contains LLC data or information related to a control operation of the MAC protocol.

- *Frame Check Sequence* (FCS)—A 32-bit cyclic redundancy check, based on FC, DA, SA, and Information fields.

- *Ending Delimiter* (ED)—Contains nondata symbols to indicate the end of the frame.

- *Frame Status* (FS)—Contains the A (address recognized) and C (frame copied) bits. Because the A and C bits are outside the scope of the FCS, they are duplicated to provide a redundancy check to detect erroneous settings.

> **Note**
>
> Occasionally, the token either gets lost or the timer runs out and a new token is created. This way, the old token could still be hanging around. Thus, it is possible to have multiple tokens on some networks.

Fiber Distributed Data Interface (FDDI)

Fiber Distributed Data Interface (FDDI) is a 100 Mbps, high-speed internetworking backbone option serial LAN originally created to support high-speed and bandwidth-intensive applications. FDDI can be used as either a departmental LAN transport system or as a high-speed, fiberoptic backbone network. It seems to be finding its place within many organizations as a building and campus backbone transport system; however, it is only capable of transporting IEEE 802.3 and IEEE 802.5 network protocols. Other technologies such as SONET, BISDN, and ATM have emerged as potential backbones for WANs. FDDI specification includes a Physical Medium Dependent (PMD) specification, Physical Sublayer (PHY) specification, and the Station Management (MST) specification.

The FDDI includes the following characteristics:

- Uses a 100 Mbps token-passing LAN using fiberoptic cable as the transmission media.

- Incorporates a token-passing media access control method.

- Implements a dual, counter-rotating ring for redundancy.

- Allows a maximum of 500 physical connections.

- Provides for 2 Km maximum length between stations and 200 Km total maximum length.

- Allows for an 11 decibels (dB) maximum link loss budget.

FDDI's link and station failure mechanisms provide an extra level of redundancy and fault tolerance. When a failure occurs, the ring reconfigures by wrapping the primary ring to the secondary ring, thus isolating the failed station from the ring. The FDDI frame structure is similar to the IEEE 802.5 Token Ring frame structure; however, it uses a different encoding scheme and symbol format. FDDI utilizes 4B/5B encoding [4-bit patterns (16 combinations) with 5-bit patterns (32 combinations)].

The FDDI frame structure is composed of the following:

- Start Delimiter is a 1-byte field.

- Frame Control is a 1-byte field that identifies the type of packet.

- Destination Address is a 2- or 6-byte field that identifies the frame recipient.

- Source Address is a 2- or 6-byte field that identifies the originator of the frame.

- Information Field is a variable-length information field carrying data.

- Frame Check Sequence (FCS) Field is a 32-bit error-checking frame based on a CRC.

Frame Relay

Frame Relay is a streamlined Data Link Layer protocol, which is often compared with X.25. It provides a simple connection-oriented frame transport service. Frame Relay is an ISDN packet-mode bearer service that transfers frames of information from the network side of one user-network interface (UNI) to the network side of another UNI. Some of the applications that Frame Relay offers are block-interactive data applications, such as high-resolution graphics or CAD/CAM; file transfers for large amounts of data; multiplexing low bit-rate applications onto one high-speed channel; and character-interactive traffic, such as text editing, which requires short frames, low delays, and low throughput.

Frame Relay architecture consists of a limited Data Link layer and no Network layer. Frame Relay service architecture is defined as two planes: the C-plane performs control functions, and the U-plane interacts with the user functions.

Frame Relay protocol, as the name implies, relays frame information across the LAN, MAN (Metropolitan Area Network), or WAN, as well as the internetworking devices that connect those elements. This protocol is designed to transfer frames of information with the least possible overhead.

Frame Relay format consists of five fields: beginning and ending Flags, an Address field, an Information field, and an FCS. It also includes some control functions in the Address field. Frame Relay networks have two ways of notifying the networks of and/or controlling congestion: *explicit congestion notification* and *implicit congestion notification*. Frame Relay networks use protocols built on the Data Link layer of the OSI reference model. They provide mechanisms to manage permanent virtual circuits, establish switched virtual circuits, and encapsulate higher-layer protocols. Multiprotocol support is also provided by encapsulating higher-layer protocols such as LAN traffic inside a Frame Relay frame. Fragmentation, which is one aspect of multiprotocol encapsulation, divides a long Network packet into multiple Frame Relay frames and then reassembles the packet at the receiving end of the connection.

> **Note**
>
> Sometimes, traffic arriving at a resource exceeds the network's capacity. This causes congestion. In order to alleviate the problem, Frame Relay has the Backward Explicit Congestion Notification (BECN) and the Forward Explicit Congestion Notification (FECN) bits. These bits are set appropriately by a congested network to notify the user that congestion avoidance procedures should be initiated where applicable for traffic.

Asynchronous Transfer Mode (ATM)

One of the hottest technologies talked about today is Asynchronous Transfer Mode (ATM). It is a broadband ISDN technology that has been touted as the next revolution in LAN and WAN communication. It is a type of cell-switching protocol that was originally conceived in 1988 by CCITT as B-ISDN. ATM provides connection-oriented service with minimal switching overhead to support speeds of more than 100 Megabits/sec. There are two types of ATM connections: *Permanent Virtual Circuit* (*PVCs*) and *Switched Virtual Circuits* (*SVCs*). ATM switching is based on Virtual Paths (VPs), which group Virtual Channels (VCs) and switch them as a unit. ATM switching nodes can switch VPIs, VCIs, or both.

ATM uses digital carrier systems and digital encoding to provide error-free performance. It can support file transfer, interactive data, voice, and video. ATM uses fixed-size cells, providing it Time Transparency. ATM cell stream starts with the signals from individual users or sources. Signals may include constant bit-rate service (such as a DS1 line), variable bit-rate service (such as compressed video), or burst rate service (such as LAN traffic). It then segments the signals into 48-octet payloads and prefaces them with a 5-octet header that contains addressing information. This resulting 53-octet packet is known as a *cell*. Table 3.3 summarizes ATM services.

Note

Real-time synchronous traffic can be provided on packet switching networks due to random delay jitter caused by variable length packets and store and forward delay. ATM eliminates this problem by its fixed size cells, and this provides time transparency.

Table 3.3 ATM Services Summary

ATM Service	Accuracy	Delay	Throughput
File transfer with a large degree of idle time	Cell loss results in retransmission and thus a lower throughput. Low cell loss is acceptable.	Tolerant to variation and end-to-end delay.	Sustained burst

(continues)

Table 3.3 Continued			
ATM Service	**Accuracy**	**Delay**	**Throughput**
Interactive data	No cell loss is tolerable unless link service	Delay sensitive end-to-end delay < 100 µsec. Provides error correction in which case cell loss results in delayed response.	Low transfer rate, no high bursts. High transaction rate.
Video broadcast idle	No cell loss is tolerable	Very sensitive to both variation and end-to-end delay.	Sustained transfer rate, no bursts
Voice predictable	High cell loss is tolerable relative to human speech, up to 1%.	Sensitive to both variation and end-to-end delay. Echo canceling required for delay > 250 µsec round trip.	Short burst, pattern of idle.

ATM Layers and Sublayers

ATM comprises several layers and sublayers. The layers include Physical (PHY), ATM, ATM Adaptation Layer (AAL), and higher. The Physical layer sends and receives bits on the transmission medium. It also sends and receives cells to and from the next highest layer, the ATM layer. The ATM layer then switches these cells to the appropriate circuit to connect with an end system and its specific application. The payload within the cell is generated at, or destined for, the AAL, a layer that interfaces the higher layer functions and processes with the ATM layer. The Physical layer has two sublayers: Physical Medium (PM) and Transmission Convergence (TC). They perform bit-level transmission, frame generation, cell delineation, Header Error Correction generation, and so on. The ATM layer performs four operations: multiplexing, VPI/VCI translation, header generation, and flow control.

The AAL maps the higher layers onto ATM layer. It consists of two sublayers: the Segmentation and Reassembly (SAR) sublayer and the Convergence sublayer (CS) The SAR performs a very important function. It segments the variable-length higher-layer information to be transmitted into fixed-length ATM payloads and reassembles the received payloads into the higher-layer information. The CS performs functions required by the AAL type in use and therefore is service-independent.

ATM Interfaces

The ATM forum has defined a number of options for the Physical layer interface at either public or private UNI. The Synchronous Optical Network (SONET) STS-3c interface that operates at 155.52 Mbps uses multimode or single-mode fiber. An interface for private UNIs operates at 15.520 Mbps with an 8B/10B data-encoding scheme over multimedia fiber, or shielded twisted-pair cables.

Another private UNI operating at 100 Mbps over multimode fiber often called a Transparent Asynchronous Transmitter/Receiver Interface (TAXI) was developed by Advanced Micro Devils, Inc. TAXI uses 4B/5B encoding based on the encoding scheme used with FDDI. The DS3 interfaces operate at 44.736 over coaxial cables. The specifications also mention two new interfaces: E3, operating at 34.368 Mbps, and E4, operating at 139.264 Mbps.

ATM DXI Protocol

The DXI Physical layer uses V.35, EIA 530, RS 449, or EIA 612/613 High Speed Serial Interface (HSSI) interfaces. The DXI Data Link layer protocol is derived from the HDLC protocol. Information from the DTE is encapsulated within the DXI frame and sent to the DCE. The DCE converts the frame to the appropriate ATM protocol suite.

Internetworking ATM

ATM is an emerging technology, which makes internetworkability a particular issue. Some of the problems facing internetworking are various technical, administrative, and tariffing problems. For example, Frame Relay is an established broadband networking protocol, and many organizations would like to see their investment in Frame Relay hardware continue to reap benefits while migrating to ATM. While agreements between the Frame Relay Forum and the ATM Forum have clarified most of the issues concerning Frame Relay over ATM, other difficulties, especially in interoperability, remain. These issues are important enough to cause problems in switches/hubs that are implementing Frame Relay/ATM. Some of the interoperability issues are:

- Conversion between Frame Relay and ATM protocols

- Mapping between Frame Relay and ATM virtual circuits

- Alignment of Frame Relay and ATM traffic-management parameters, such as the conversions of the frame relay CIR into a meaningful parameter for ATM traffic

- Mapping of the local management information (the LMI used at the FRUNI and the ILMI used at the ATM UNI)

Internetworking with SMDS is another important area. A few different methods have been proposed for ATM/SMDS internetworking:

■ An end user can connect to an ATM network using a UNI to access an SMDS service offering. This means that an end user can use the ATM UNI to access SMDS in the same way that other users would use the SNI or DXI/SNI to access SMDS.

■ An SMDS Interface Protocol (SIP) L3-PDU can be encapsulated inside another protocol, the Inter Carrier Interface Protocol Connectionless Service (ICIP_CLS). The AAL 3/4 then transports the ICIP_CLS_PDU.

High Level Data Link Control (HDLC)

HDLC is a bit-oriented line protocol that has achieved wide use throughout the world. The HDLC protocol has been used as a basis for the development of a number of other widely used link layer protocols.

Major HDLC Implementations

Some of the major implementations of HDLC are:

■ Link Access Procedure Balanced (LAPB) protocol is a link layer protocol used on X.25 interfaces. It operates within an X.25 three-layer stack of protocols at the Data Link layer and is used to ensure that the X.25 packet is delivered safely between the user device and the packet network.

■ Link Access Procedure for the D channel (LAPD) is employed on ISDN interfaces. Its purpose is to deliver ISDN messages (and perhaps, user data) safely between user devices and the ISDN node.

■ Logical Link Control (LLC) protocol is employed on IEEE 802 and ISO 8802 local area networks (LANs). It is configured in a variety of ways to provide different types of HDLC services. It rests atop any 802 or 8802 LAN.

■ Link Access Procedure for Modems (LAPM) protocol is relatively new and gives modems a powerful HDLC capability. It operates within V.42 modems and, as one might expect, it is responsible for the safe delivery of traffic across communications links between two modems.

■ Point-to-Point Protocol (PPP) also is a derivation of HDLC. It is employed on a number of Internet point-to-point links. Its primary purpose is to encapsulate network PDUs (Protocol Data Units) and to identify the different types of network protocols that may be carried in the I field of the PPP frame.

■ Multilayer protocol stack. It is responsible for the safe delivery of traffic.

HDLC Characteristics

HDLC provides a number of options to satisfy a wide variety of user requirements. It supports both half-duplex and full-duplex transmission, point-to-point and multipoint configuration, and switched or nonswitched channels. HDLC uses the term *frame* to indicate the independent entity of data (protocol data unit) transmitted across the link from one station to another. The frame consists of four or five fields; Table 3.4 indicates the field sizes relevant to HDLC's frame format, and figure 3.1 shows the frame format.

Table 3.4 HDLC Frame Format

Field Name	Field Size
Flag field (F)	8 bits
Address field (A)	8, or multiples of 8, bits
Control field (C)	8, or multiples of 8, bits
Information field (I)	variable length; optional
Frame check sequence field (FCS)	16 or 32 bits

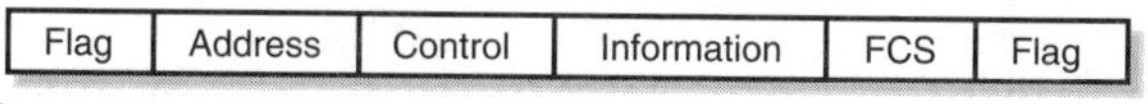

Flag	Address	Control	Information	FCS	Flag

Fig. 3.1
Frame format of HDLC protocol.

All frames must start and end with the flag sequence fields (F). The stations attached to the data link are required continuously to monitor the link for the flag sequence. Once the receiving station detects a nonflag sequence, it is aware that it has encountered the beginning of the frame, an abort condition, or an idle channel condition. Upon encountering the next flag sequence, the station recognizes that it has found the full frame. HDLC is a code-transparent protocol. It does not rely on a specific code (ASCII/IA5, EBCDIC, and others) for the interpretation of line control.

The address field (A) identifies the primary or secondary station involved in the frame transmission or reception. A unique address is associated with each station. The control field (C) contains the commands, responses, and sequence numbers used to maintain the data flow accountability of the link between the primary stations. The format and the contents of the control field vary, depending on the use of the HDLC frame. The information field (I) contains the actual user data. The information field resides only in the frame under the Information frame format. It usually is not found in the Supervisory or Unnumbered frame, although one option of HDLC allows the I field to be used with an Unnumbered frame. The frame check sequence field (FCS) is used to check for transmission errors between the two data-link stations. The FCS field is created by a cyclic redundancy check.

Using the concepts of encapsulation and decapsulation, the fields of the HDLC frame are constructed at the transmit side and used at the receive side to invoke the desired operations. The order of the operations is important. HDLC serves as a foundation for many widely used data-link protocols. Its features of asynchronous balanced mode and normal response mode provide a flexible means of configuring point-to-point, peer-to-peer operations, or multipoint master/slave operations. The HDLC family has spread into the inventory of practically every vendor offering a data-link control product.

Point-to-Point Protocol (PPP)

Point-to-Point Protocol (PPP) provides a standard method for transmitting IP datagrams over serial Point-to-Point links, allowing for the multivendor serial links of TCP/IP LAN systems. PPP uses HDLC as the basis for data encapsulation. The links must be full duplex and can be either dedicated or circuit switched. PPP is comprised of three main components:

- A method for encapsulating IP dataframes over serial links

- A Link Control Protocol (LCP) for establishing, configuring, and testing the data-link connection

- A family of Network Control Protocols (NCPs) for establishing and configuring different network layer protocols

The PPP frame format is as follows:

- The Flag field is a 1-byte field that indicates the beginning and end of a frame.

- The Address field is a 1-byte field that contains the binary sequence 11111111, FF hex, representing the All Stations Address.

- The Control field is a 1-byte field that contains the binary sequence 00000011 or 03 hex.

- The Protocol field is a 2-byte field that identifies the protocol encapsulated in the Information field.

- The Information field is a 0- to 1500-byte field that contains the datagram for the protocol specified in the Protocol field.

- The Frame Check Sequence (FCS) field is 2-byte frame check sequence calculated over all bits of the Address, Control, Protocol, and Information fields.

Switched Multimegabit Data Service (SMDS)

Switched multimegabit data service (SMDS) is virtually the same as Frame Relay except it is fully connectionless and operates at high speeds (1.544 Mbps to 45 Mbps). It is a public switching service based on Cell Relay techniques. SMDS was introduced as an on-demand type service that can support the bursty traffic demands of LAN traffic through WANs. Today SMDS is restricted to intra-LATA (Local Access and Transport Area) connectivity within Regional Bell Operating Companies (RBOCs) domains; however, it is anticipated that SMDS services will expand beyond the LATA. Some of the more familiar SMDS features include the following:

- Connectionless

- Based on 802.6 standard or ATT ISDN ATM standard

- Error detection but no error correction

- Multiplexing to destinations

- 56K to 600 Mbps per second

- Capability of carrying voice

Some of the characteristics of SMDS are as follows:

- Uses addressing schemes similar to the direct-dial telephone

- Includes a group addressing capability to support multicast or broadcast transmissions

- End nodes capable of designating multiple addresses (up to 16) to a single Subscriber Network Interface (SNI)

- Allows access classes to be created to support different traffic characteristics

SMDS Interface Protocol (SIP)

SMDS Interface Protocol (SIP) specifies how the end user gains access to the
SMDS network across the IEEE 802.6 compliant Subscriber Network Interface
(SNI). SIP includes addressing, framing, and physical transport functions. SIP
is a connectionless, three-layer protocol that covers the first two layers of the
OSI model: layer 1 provides the physical layer functions, layer 2 provides
framing and error-detection functions, and layer 3 associates the appropriate
SMDS addressing information with the SMDS PDU passed from the end user.

Synchronous Optical Network (SONET)

Many applications requiring high bit rates for the transfer of voice, video,
and data information are turning to the Broadband ISDN (B-ISDN) protocols
(known commonly as Asynchronous Transfer Mode or ATM) to provide the
packet structure for the information. In addition, the Synchronous Optical
Network (SONET) format and framing structure is being utilized to provide
the Physical layer for transporting the packetized information to its destination. When the ATM cells are transported in a SONET frame structure, it is
called a SONET ATM network.

SONET is a standardized, hierarchical transport scheme originally developed
for public carrier use, designed to carry traffic payloads of almost any size
over fiberoptic networks. The SONET format carries a rich amount (by tele-
communications standards) of overhead used for network management, status monitoring, and fault isolation in the complex public network spanning
thousands of route miles and crossing several different carrier jurisdictions.

SONET's basic building block is a 125-μsec frame that comes in two sizes,
STS-1 and STS-3. The bit rate for STS-1 is 51.84 Mbps and that of STS-3c is
155.52 Mbps. One of the advantages of the SONET format is that the overhead and payload fields are completely separate. The byte-oriented payload
field can be used for virtually any type of digital traffic.

The most obvious advantage to using SONET is enhanced compatibility
between LANs and WANs. Using a combination of ATM and SONET,
tomorrow's workstations will produce messages with both Layers 1 and 2
already network-compatible. Because the message arriving at the LAN/WAN
interface is already in the proper rate and format for forwarding, much less
processing is required, and message handling is much faster. Using SONET as
a LAN protocol ensures that the rates match across the interface, eliminating
the need for rate conversion or buffering. Indeed, it will be possible to attach
data sources directly to the network, if required.

SONET's high efficiency will also be critical in twisted-pair applications. The ATM Forum is vigorously pursuing a standard for ATM LAN service over twisted-pair copper cable, preferably unshielded. SONET sits at the bottom of the OSI layered model as the Physical layer to support ATM LAN services. Above SONET sits the ATM layer and the ATM adaptation layer which actually creates the ATM cells from user data.

Xerox Network System (XNS)

Xerox Network System (XNS) was the first protocol commercially implemented over Ethernet. The protocol is fairly straightforward; its architecture includes certain individual protocols:

- *The Internet Datagram Protocol* (IDP)—This network-level protocol provides the routing functions needed to route data in an internet. This protocol provides network-level addressing, routing, datagram packet formatting, and so on.

- *Routing Information Protocol* (RIP)—RIP will be discussed.

- *Error Protocol*—This protocol allows one network station to notify another network station that an error has occurred in a received packet.

- *Echo Protocol*—This protocol allows for testing of a network path or for recording round-trip delay times.

- *Sequence Packet Protocol* (SPP)—A transport-level protocol, this protocol allows for a reliable data exchange between two stations.

- *Packet Exchange Protocol* (PEP)—PEP is a request-and-response protocol used in transaction-oriented applications.

- *Courier*—This is a session-level protocol that provides remote procedural call services.

- *Clearinghouse*—Clearinghouse provides for the naming services to exist as XNS.

- *File Service*—A file transfer service.

- *Printing Service*—This is a remote printing service.

- *Time of Day*—This provides date and time service.

The most popular implementation of the XNS protocol is Novell NetWare's IPX. IPX imitates this protocol only up to the network layer, IDP (which includes the RIP function). Novell implements SPP in a protocol known as Sequence Packet Exchange (SPX), but this is used primarily for peer-to-peer services such as RCONSOLE, SNA gateways, and so on. After the Transport layer, Novell implements proprietary protocol stack.

XNS can run over any data-link protocol, including Token Ring and Ethernet. XNS sequencing occurs on a packet basis. Every packet transmitted will have at most one sequence number. This is in contrast to protocols such as TCP/IP, where every byte of the data is assigned a sequence number. This is known as a *byte-oriented protocol*.

DECNet

Much of the Digital Network Architecture (DNA), Digital Equipment Corporation's proprietary network architecture, is identical with that of the ISO standard protocols, because in many cases ISO protocols are derived from DNA protocols. DNA is strictly layered and follows very closely the layering in the OSI reference model. One departure from standard OSI layering is that DNA offers two options above the Transport Layer. Figure 3.2 shows that one option is DNA Session and DNA Application layers; the other option is OSI Session, Presentation, and Application layers.

Fig. 3.2
DNA's Session and Application layers and OSI's upper layers.

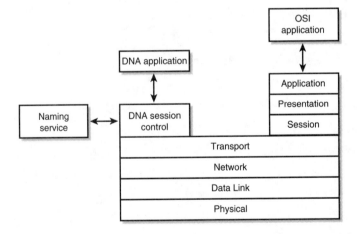

For DNA, the LAN Data Link header consists of Dest, Source, Length, DSAP, SSAP, Ctl, user data, Pad, and CRC. Many functions are available in DECnet:

■ With file access and transfer, files can be accessed remotely in the same manner as if they are stored locally, even across heterogeneous file systems. Files can be created, deleted, modified, and renamed remotely.

■ Remote terminals allow users to type at their local system, as if they were typing at the remote system.

- Users can send and receive messages with electronic mail, which supports the X.400 suite of protocols and a highly reliable store-and-forward system of mail delivery.

- With DECnet's SNA Gateway application, DNA provides application protocols for communicating with systems conforming to IBM's SNA protocols.

- DNA's Time Service is an architecture for providing and maintaining correct time in a distributed system.

IEEE 802.2 Logical Link Control

The Logical Link Control (LLC) sublayer constitutes the top portion of the OSI Model Data Link layer and is common to the various Medium Access Control (MAC) methods (Token Ring, CSMA/CD). The relationship between the LLC sublayer and the Network layer can be categorized by two forms of services: unacknowledged connectionless mode and connection mode.

LLC PDU Structure

The LLC Protocol Data Unit (LLC PDU) consists of a sequence of three octets delivered as a unit to or from the MAC sublayer and contains the following:

- Destination Service Access Point (DSAP) address, which is eight bits

- Source Service Access Point (SSAP), which is eight bits

- Control field, which is eight or 16 bits

- Information field (optional) where D is an integer greater than zero, which is D × eight bits

LLC Types of Operation

The LLC defines three types of operation for data communications between SAPs as follows:

- Type 1—Connectionless

- Type 2—Connection-oriented

- Type 3—Acknowledged connectionless. This service does not require an established data link connection between the origin and destination nodes; however, acknowledgments are required from the destination node. Error recovery is included in this type of operation.

Introduction

LLC is a data-link protocol. It controls the link between two stations. It has nothing to do with the upper-layer protocols that may run on top of it. The data-link layer is divided into two entities—the MAC layer and the LLC layer. The MAC portion of the data-link layer is protocol specific. LLC is placed between the MAC layer specification of the data-link layer and a network-layer implementation. LLC2 (connection-oriented) is used to link a LAN to a WAN and between network stations and SNA hosts.

Systems Network Architecture (SNA)

SNA is a network architecture intended to allow IBM customers to construct their own private networks. Prior to SNA, IBM had multiple communication products, with several data-link protocols. SNA was designed and developed to eliminate this chaos and to provide a coherent framework for loosely coupled distributed processing. SNA architecture is more complicated in places due to the constraints at the time of development. It also performs a number of functions not found in other networks, which, although valuable for certain applications, tend to add to the overall complexity of the architecture.

An SNA network consists of nodes, of which there are four types:

- Type 1 nodes are terminals.

- Type 2 nodes are controllers, machines that supervise the behavior of terminals and other peripherals.

- Type 4 nodes are front-end processors, devices whose function is to relieve the main CPU of the work and interrupt handling associated with data communication.

- Type 5 nodes are the main hosts themselves, although with the advent of low-cost microprocessors, some controllers have acquired some host-like properties.

Surprisingly, there are no type 3 nodes.

Each node contains one or more Network Addressable Units (NAUs). An NAU is a piece of software that allows a process to use the network. To use the network, a process must connect itself to an NAU, at which time it can be addressed and can address other NAUs. The NAUs are the entry points into the network for user processes.

There are three kinds of NAUs:

- A logical unit (LU) is the usual variety to which user processes can be attached.

- A physical (PU) unit is a special, administrative NAU associated with each node. The PU is used by the network to bring the node on-line, take it off-line, test it, and perform similar network management functions. A PU provides a way for the network to address a physical device, without references to which processes are using it.

- The Systems Services Control Point (SSCP) is an NAU of which there is normally one per type 5 node and none in the other nodes. The SSCP has complete knowledge of, and control over, all the front-ends, controllers, and terminals attached to the host. The collection of hardware and software managed by an SSCP is called a domain.

Figure 3.3 provides a representation of the SNA architecture.

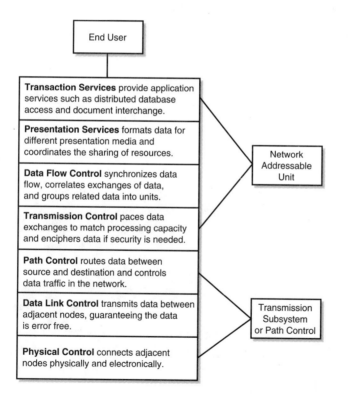

Fig. 3.3
Architecture of SNA protocol.

AppleTalk

In the early 1980s, Apple Computer released the Macintosh computer architecture that included an internal networking scheme based on LocalTalk. Apple's network architecture was called AppleTalk. AppleTalk is a pure, client/server networking system that relies on nodes sharing network resources (servers, printers, files, and so on) together. Interactions between nodes and servers appear transparent to end users as the AppleTalk protocol engages in network interaction and broadcasting functions to communicate between end nodes and resources. Components of an AppleTalk network are Macintosh workstations, cable, routers (ports), servers and printers, and AppleTalk Zones.

The AppleTalk protocol suite consists of many different protocols that perform functions similar to the TCP/IP protocol suite:

- Datagram Delivery Protocol (DDP) is responsible for end-to-end delivery of AppleTalk packets between nodes on an internetwork.

- Router Table Maintenance Protocol (RTMP) is used by AppleTalk routers to exchange and update routing information. RTMP calculates the shortest path to each destination.

- AppleTalk Echo Protocol (AEP) tests the transmission path between two nodes. Troubleshooters use the AEP to determine whether a particular node exists on the internetwork and to measure the round-trip transmission delay between source and destination nodes (i.e., PING in TCP/IP).

- AppleTalk Transaction Protocol (ATP) provides a reliable transport mechanism for Session layer protocols. ATP performs tasks called transactions, between one socket in the requesting node and another in the responding node.

- Name Binding Zone (NBP) is a mechanism that translates between the entity names that users specify for network resources and those specified by the network itself (e.g., Domain Name Server and others).

- AppleTalk Data Stream Protocol (ADSP) communicates directly with the Network layer DDP. ADSP assures that the data stream between two AppleTalk sockets is delivered full-duplex, in sequence, and without duplication.

- Zone Information Protocol (ZIP) translates between network numbers and zone numbers within the internetwork. A *zone* is a logical grouping of nodes that organize a large internetwork. ZIP provides the following three functions:

- Provides a mapping service within routers via ZIT (Zone Information Table).

- Distributes mapping information to other nodes via ZIS (Zone Information Sockets).

- Informs the node of the valid cable range number for a network.

■ AppleTalk Session Protocol (ASP) adds Session layer services to the AppleTalk Transaction Protocol (ATP) in the Transport layer. This service establishes and disconnects the logical connection or session between two nodes.

■ Printer Access Protocol (PAP) is a connection-oriented protocol for communications between workstations and printer servers.

AppleTalk is a routable protocol. AppleTalk routing uses the routing table maintenance protocol (RTMP), which is an RIP-based, distance vector routing algorithm that uses hop count as its metric. It can be encapsulated in all of the major data-link formats for LANs and WANs such as these:

■ LocalTalk—a 230 Kbps baseband LAN system based on daisy-chained, twisted-pair.

■ EtherTalk—a 10 Mbps baseband LAN system based on IEEE 802.3, SNAP header format.

■ TokenTalk—a 4/16 Mbps Token Ring LAN system based on IEEE 802.5, SNAP header format.

■ FDDI Talk—a 100 Mbps Token Ring LAN system based on ANSI X3T9.5, SNAP header format.

AppleTalk is a very chatty protocol. When the AppleTalk chooser menu is opened at a Macintosh workstation, periodic broadcasts are sent out to query for AppleTalk services available on the network. Given the connectionless, broadcasting behavior of AppleTalk, a method for containing or limiting broadcasts was needed, which is the reason the concept of zoning was introduced. AppleTalk broadcasts are contained within a local zone called an *AppleTalk Zone*. Zones are like subnets within an AppleTalk Domain. Routers keep track of zones via the ZIP protocol. Routers keep track of neighbor zones via the ZIP and NBP protocols.

Advanced Program-to-Program Communication (APPC)

Advanced Program-to-Program Communication (APPC) provides application developers on mainframes, minicomputers, and personal computers with a standard protocol that can be used in transferring messages between intelligent machines. Acceptance of the APPC protocols as an international standard makes it more likely that the machines of different vendors will be able to communicate in a compatible manner.

SNA-APPC differs from VTAM SNA in the following ways:

■ No VTAM is required to set up sessions.

■ LU 6.2 allows distributed processing.

■ PU 2.1 provides a dynamic LAN to WAN environment.

■ 3270 display compatibility exists.

■ Distributed application processing is available.

NetBios

NetBios is an upper-layer LAN protocol, which means that it supports Session, Transport, and Function layers. It supports full-duplex Session level transmission service, a choice of both reliable transport service and datagram service (no acknowledgments).

NetBios Functions

NetBios offers a variety of functions. Some of NetBios functions are these:

■ *Name service*—Multiple logical names can be used in a single station. Source and destination names are passed over the LAN to bring up a session between two users. Addressing is not used to route in NetBios.

■ *Session service*—The session built between two users supports full-duplex transmission, flow control using a windowing technique, as well as sequence numbering and acknowledgment services.

■ *Datagram service*—Information is sent and received without first establishing a session. No session is built and no sequence numbering or acknowledgment routines are used.

■ *Routing*—Token Ring source routing is the primary technique for routing packets. Because NetBios does not support a routable header (no addresses), NetBios packets are transmitted over bridged rather than router networks.

NetBios Routing

NetBios uses source routing. The sending station is responsible for providing routing information for messages that cross multiple network segments. The sending station acquires routing information by means of the MSG.FIND.NAME command, which is used to determine the location or locations of a particular name. Responses to this command provide station addresses, and, if necessary, routing information for reaching stations that have this name defined. A message control block (MCB) is used as a protocol header to implement the protocols. NetBios message format is as shown in figure 3.4.

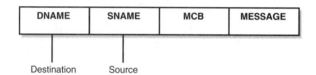

| DNAME | SNAME | MCB | MESSAGE |

Destination   Source

Fig. 3.4
Message format of NetBios.

Names are up to 16 characters and can be added or deleted in the local name table found in each station. Once the names are passed and a session is established, a session number is selected. From then on, packets require only an MCB with the session number. However, NetBios limits up to 255 sessions per net on most Operating Systems. This is usually not a problem for medium to average companies. Larger companies, where more than 255 sessions may be required, have a problem. This has been resolved by Windows NT, which has adapted NetBios to get around this limitation.

Transmission Control Packet/ Internet Protocol (TCP/IP)

Transmission Control Packet/Internet Protocol (TCP/IP) is a family of protocols used extensively in computer communications; it forms the basis in accessing the Internet. TCP and IP are both separate protocols. The TCP/IP protocol family includes protocols such as these:

- Internet Protocol (IP)

- Address Resolution Protocol (ARP)

- Internet Control Message Protocol (ICMP)

- User Datagram Protocol (UDP)

- Transport Control Protocol (TCP)

- Routing Information Protocol (RIP)

Introduction

- Simple Mail Transfer Protocol (SMTP)

- Telnet

- Domain Name System (DNS)

- Network Information Services (NIS)

- BOOTstrap Protocol(BOOTP)

TCP/IP addresses have two components: a network component and a host component. Addresses used in TCP/IP are four-byte (32-bit) quantities called simply IP addresses. They can be assigned in a number of ways. Network layer contains the Internet Protocol (IP) and the Internet Control Message Protocol (ICMP). The Protocol layer contains TCP and the User Datagram Protocol. IP is an example of a connectionless service. Because datagrams could be lost between two end user stations, a higher-level Transport layer protocol such as TCP is essential to recover from these problems. IP does not provide error recovery, flow-control mechanisms, and so on. It supports fragmentation operations.

IP Datagram

The fields in the IP datagram are as follows:

- The version field identifies the version of IP in use.

- The header length field contains 4 bits set to a value to indicate the length of the datagram header.

- The Type of Service (TOS) field can be used to identify several Quality of Service (QOS) functions provided for in Internet.

- The total length field specifies the total length of the IP datagram. It is measured in octets and includes the length of the header and the data. IP subtracts the header length field from the total length to compute the size of the data field.

The IP protocol uses three fields in the header to control datagram fragmentation and reassembly. These fields are the identifier, flags, and fragmentation offset. The *time-to-live* (TTL) parameter is used to measure the time a datagram has been in the Internet. The protocol field is used to identify the next level protocol above the IP that receives the datagram at the final destination. The header checksum is used to detect a distortion that may have occurred in the header. IP carries two addresses: source and destination in the datagram.

These remain the same value throughout the life of the datagram. The padding field may be used to make certain that the datagram header field aligns on exact 32-bit boundary.

IP Source Routing

A mechanism known as *source routing* is used by IP as part of its routing algorithm. This allows an upper-layer protocol to determine how the IP gateways route the datagrams. When IP receives a datagram, it looks at the addresses in the source routing field to determine the next intermediate hop. IP provides two options in routing datagrams to their final destinations:

- *Loose source routing* gives the IP modules the option of using intermediate hops to reach the addresses obtained in the source list as long as the datagram traverses the nodes listed.

- *Strict source routing* requires that the datagram travel only through the networks whose addresses are indicated in the source list.

IP also provides the options of route recording, timestamping, fragmentation, and reassembly. When it receives a datagram that is too big, it divides it into two or more pieces making sure that alignment is done on 8-octet boundaries. To each of these fragmented pieces, a header is attached containing information, addressing, and so on. The fragmented pieces also have information attached to them indicating the position of the fragment within the original datagram. Likewise, at the destination point, IP reassembles the fragments into the original datagram.

IP is a widely used gateway protocol. It has been implemented on both LANs and WANs. IP remains transparent to the underlying network and thus can be placed on a variety of networks. It is designed to discard datagrams that are outdated or those that have exceeded the number of permissible transit hops in an Internet.

Transmission Control Packet (TCP)

In many situations, applications require the assurance that all datagrams have been delivered successfully to the destination. In addition, the transmitting user may want to know if the data was delivered to the receiving user. In this aspect, Transmission Control Packet (TCP) has the necessary mechanisms to provide these important services. TCP resides in the Transport layer of the OSI model. TCP is designed to reside in the host machine or in a machine that does the end-to-end integrity of the transfer of data. Some of the major features provided by TCP are these:

- Reliable data transfer and connection-oriented data management

- Push functions and stream-oriented data transfer

- Resequencing, flow control, and multiplexing

- Full-duplex transmission, precedence, and security

Because TCP is a connection-oriented protocol, it maintains status and state information about each user data stream flowing into and out of the TCP module. TCP provides reliable transfer of data; it uses sequence numbers and positive/negative acknowledgments. This is known as a *virtual circuit*. It has a unique way of knowing the amount of traffic on each virtual circuit. Because it is hard to estimate the amount of time for time-outs and retransmissions, TCP does not use a fixed retransmission timer but an adaptive retransmission timer. Some other considerations in using TCP are these:

- TCP stream data are acknowledged by the receiver on a byte basis.

- If necessary it will retransmit lost or erroneous data.

- A push function is available to force the TCP to send data immediately, thereby ensuring that traffic is delivered and avoided deadlock at the other end.

TCP also has the potential to provide a wealth of information to a network manager. Some of the frequently used applications/protocols in TCP/IP are File Transfer Protocol (FTP), Telnet, and Simple Mail Transfer Protocol (SMTP). TCP provides acknowledgment and sequence numbers in the packet format that are unique. In addition, before any TCP/IP application is started, a three-way protocol handshake needs to be completed. It consists of the following:

User 1	SYN	User 2
User 2	SYN	User 1
User 1	ACK	User 2

Internet protocols have been designed and developed to facilitate the sharing of resources across different networks. This has gained tremendous popularity among users in the past couple of years and promises to continue, with the growing number of applications and services that vendors have been providing on the Internet. With its ease of use, availability across different operating systems and ever-increasing protocol suite, it will make accessing the Internet easier than ever before.

Internet Control Message Protocol (ICMP)

ICMP is a maintenance protocol that handles error messages to be sent when datagrams are discarded or when systems experience congestion. Because IP is a connectionless, unreliable delivery service, allowing routers and hosts on an Internet to operate independently, there are certain instances when errors will occur on the Internet. These are some of the possible errors: a packet is not routed to the destination network, the router is too congested to handle any more packets, or a host cannot be found on the Internet. There is no provision in IP to generate error messages or control messages. ICMP is the protocol that handles these instances for IP.

ICMP datagrams are routable because they use IP to deliver their messages. Because TCP protocol is not used, these messages themselves have the capability of being lost or generating an error. However, no mechanisms exist to detect lost or erroneous ICMP messages themselves, because IP is incapable of detecting whether datagrams were delivered to the proper destination. Figure 3.5 shows how an ICMP message is encapsulated in an IP packet.

Introduction

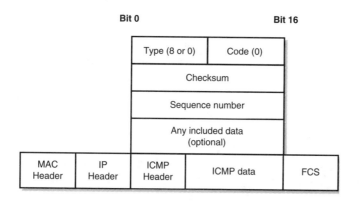

Fig. 3.5
ICMP message encapsulated in an IP packet.

One of the most common uses of this protocol is the PING program. PING (packet internet grouper) is an ICMP message that tries to locate other stations on the Internet to see whether they are active or to see whether a path is up. It can also be used to test intermediate networks along the way to the destination. Another use is to find the address mask of the local network. ICMP running in a router can respond to a host's request to find the subnet address mask for its network. A host, upon start-up, can request of a router the subnet mask assigned to the network.

There are many other uses of the ICMP protocol. When a router receives a datagram, it may determine a better router that can provide a shorter route to the destination network. This is an ICMP redirect, and this informs the sender of a better route. A user's workstation can request a time stamp from a router asking it to repeat the time when it received a packet. This is used for measuring delay to a destination.

File Transfer Protocol (FTP)

One of the more popular and frequently used TCP/IP applications is the file transfer application. File Transfer Protocol (FTP) is a connection-oriented file transfer application and is typically used for large file transfers or client-server file transfers. FTP utilizes the TCP Transport Layer protocol which includes acknowledgments, sequence numbering, and window sizing for dynamic flow control.

FTP is rather unusual in that it maintains two logical connections between the machines. One connection is used for the login between machines and uses the Telnet protocol. The other connection is used for data transfer. This logical connection, called the *data transfer process* (DTP), performs data management during the file transfer. After the DTP has performed its functions and the user's request has been satisfied, the PI is used to close the connection.

FTP also permits transfers between devices other than the original server and client. This operation is typically known as *third-party transfer*. A client opens a connection to two remote machines that both play the role as servers. The purpose of such a connection is to request that the client be given permission to transfer files between the two servers' file systems. If the requests are approved, one server forms a TCP connection with the other server and transfers data across the sending FTP module, the TCP modules, and into the receiving FTP module.

FTP uses a number of commands for preliminary identification, password authentication, and ongoing file transfer operations. Table 3.5 lists the acronyms for some of these commands and a brief description of their functions.

Table 3.5   FTP Commands and Associated Functions

Commands	Function
USER	Identifies the user; required by the server
PASS	User password; preceded by USER
ACCT	User account ID

Commands	Function
CWD	Change working directory
QUIT	Terminate connection
STOR	Accept data and store it
DELE	Delete specified file at the server site
RMD	Remove directory
PWD	Return (print) name of current working directory
HELP	Retrieve helpful information from the server

Trivial File Transfer Program (TFTP)

TFTP can be said to be an alternative to FTP. It is a simplex file transfer program primarily used to bootstrap diskless network workstations. However, unlike FTP, it does not provide a reliable service and hence uses the transport services of UDP instead of TCP. In addition, the size of a datagram is restricted to 512 bytes, and every datagram must be acknowledged.

Network News Transfer Protocol (NNTP)

Although the flooding algorithm is used on most lines, within the backbone, a protocol called NNTP is commonly used. The reason for the distinction is that most sites only have a single news fee, so there is little danger of receiving a message twice from independent sites. Backbone sites connect to multiple sites, so a more sophisticated protocol is needed to avoid wasting bandwidth. NNTP provides about half a dozen commands that allow messages to be selectively downloaded. The NEWSGROUPS command allows one machine to ask another if it knows about any newsgroups created after a given date and time (specified as a parameter). In this way, the existence of new groups can be propagated.

Similarly, the NEWNEWS command allows one machine to ask for a list of news messages received after a given date and time, usually the date and time of the last contact. Once the receiver has this list, it can request the messages it is missing within the ARTICLE command. The LIST and GROUP commands can be used to ask for numbers of the first and last messages held for all newsgroups or one specific newsgroup, respectively. New messages can be posted to the network with the POST command.

Routing Information Protocol (RIP)

Routing Information Protocol (RIP) is a distance vector algorithm. These algorithms keep track of their route between source and destination address in terms of *hop count* (the number of routers a packet must cross). The above algorithm imposes a maximum of 15 hops for any route. One inherent negative with this is that the route path selection is actually based on hop count and does not take into account network congestion or traffic, line speed, or line error information. One of the biggest problems with RIP on a WAN is that it constantly sends out its entire routing table on each router to update other internetwork routers of path availability.

RIP can be classified under Interior Routing Protocols (IRP) and is designed to operate within a single domain or Autonomous System (AS). Routers in this system share information via the same IRP. IRP determines the optimal route to each subnet dynamically. RIP is a UDP-based protocol most widely used in IP-based networks. The RIP hop count is measured relative to the sender's routing table. RIP is not well suited for long-haul, WAN Internets because of its broadcasting nature and hop count threshold.

The following characterizes the RIP protocol:

- It relies on network broadcasts to indicate current connectivity information to neighbors.

- Broadcast messages carry hop information as its metric (relative to the senders routing table).

- Routers transmit router updates every 30 seconds.

- If a route deletion occurs, a garbage collection timer is started (120 seconds) before the route is eliminated and a route change flag is set.

The RIP frame format is as follows (see fig. 3.6):

- Every RIP datagram contains a command and a version number. Command types include a Request for a router to send its routing table and a Response message sent in response to a request or poll or an update message.

- Routers send requests and wait for responses. In the event of a time-out (180 seconds without a response as the metric reaches 16 hops), the route is no longer valid, and neighbors can be notified that the route has been dropped.

- The Address Family Identifier field equals 2 for IP routing.

- The IP Address field contains the traditional IP address format.

- The Metric field must contain an integer value between 1 and 15 (inclusive), specifying the current metric for the destination, or the value 16, which indicates that the destination is not reachable.

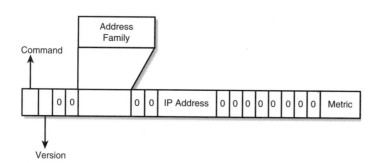

Fig. 3.6
RIP frame format.

Simple Mail Transfer Protocol (SMTP)

The Simple Mail Transfer Protocol (SMTP) standard is one of the most widely used upper-layer protocols in the IP stack. As its name implies, it is a protocol that defines how to transmit messages (mail) between two users. SMTP uses the concept of spooling. The idea of spooling is to allow mail to be sent from a local application to the SMTP application, which stores the mail in some device or memory. Typically, once the mail has arrived at the spool, it has been queued. A server checks to see if any messages are available and then attempts to deliver them. If the user is not available for delivery, the server may try later. Eventually, if the mail cannot be delivered, it will be discarded or perhaps returned to the sender. This is known as an *end-to-end delivery system*, because the server is attempting to contact the destination to deliver, and it will keep the mail in the spool for a period of time until it has been delivered.

The address has the general format of `localpart@domain-name`. By this, the Domain name format can be recognized. From here the user would enter a data message and send this message off to the network to be handled by the mail server. Figure 3.7 shows the SMTP model.

Fig. 3.7
SMTP model.

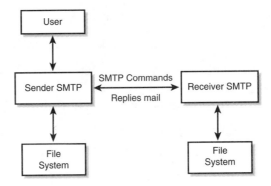

There are two entities to this system: the Sender SMTP and the Receiver SMTP. The Sender SMTP will establish communications with a Receiver SMTP. The sender will send the command MAIL, and the receiver should return an acknowledgment. The last step would be to transmit the data, a line at a time, and end it with a special control sequence. The server should terminate the process with a QUIT command.

Simple Network Management Protocol (SNMP)

The Simple Network Management Protocol (SNMP) evolved from the early developments of network management for the Internet's TCP/IP-based and Ethernet-based networks. SNMP requires only datagram transportation to function. Some of the goals of the SNMP architecture include the following:

■ Keep it simple, stupid (KISS)—minimize the number and complexity of the agent's management functions.

■ Make SNMP monitoring and control extensible—allow for unanticipated changes of network operation, monitoring, or control functions.

■ Make SNMP architecture independent—create structure independent of any particular vendor or host architectures.

With SNMP, a network manager can query any network device or node for network management information such as performance, status, and network errors or send control information to network devices. SNMP accomplishes this dialogue with network devices and nodes by defining managers and agents.

SNMP architecture is comprised of three architectural components:

■ *Managers*—A *manager* is a software program that runs in a network management station. The manager can issue requests, queries, and commands.

■ *Agents*—An *agent* is a software program that runs within a managed device or node. An agent is a data repository for network management information.

■ *Management Information Bases (MIB)*—A MIB is a database element of managed objects.

In addition, to support a heterogeneous environment of vendor equipment, SNMP includes software called proxy agents that allows monitoring and control for network devices that are not addressable using SNMP. The following are the advantages of the SNMP network management scheme:

■ It is easy to implement.

■ It has been used and tested on the Internet for several years.

■ SNMP products are a proven network management scheme.

■ SNMP products are commercially available now.

■ SNMP products are not cost prohibitive.

■ A large population of vendor manufacturers already support SNMP network management functionality.

The following are some of the disadvantages of SNMP:

■ *Minimal security features*—SNMP protocol does not include confirmation that an SNMP datagram received by an agent actually originated from an actual manager. There are merely specific read-only/read-write specifications for MIS variables.

■ *Lack of international acceptance*—SNMP is primarily a U.S.-based network management standard. Although it is rapidly becoming a *de facto* network management standard, SNMP is currently challenged by the OSI implementation of the Common Management Information Protocol (CMIP).

■ *Trap command*—The Trap command, which is used for timing and polling, does not have well-defined specifications for information transfer.

The SNMP Manager is a device typically used for global, enterprise-wide network management systems. Agents can reside on multivendor hardware platform as long as they comply with the standard SNMP MIB definitions. SNMP is a network management tool that can help the network manager with network management responsibilities. The protocol acts as an interpreter through which the network manager can ask devices simple questions. The standard MIBs represent a core set of standard network management questions. SNMP does not manage the network by itself.

Domain Name System (DNS)

Like many addressing schemes (such as the ISO and CCITT standards), the Domain Name System (DNS) uses a hierarchical scheme for establishing names. One attractive aspect of hierarchical naming is that it allows naming administrators to manage their own names at the lowest level of the hierarchy. This approach permits a high-level authority to assign to a lower level (an agent) in a *hierarchical name space* the responsibility for administering a subdomain name space. Even though authority for naming passes from a higher level, the designated agents are permitted to cross the hierarchy to send information to each other regarding names. Therefore, partitioning can be done in any manner deemed appropriate by an upper-level hierarchy, and the name space division can be made small enough to make the whole operation manageable.

Domains and Subdomains

Each domain is identified by an unambiguous *domain name*. Because of the hierarchical nature of the DNS, a domain may be a subdomain of another domain. Subdomains are achieved by the naming structure, which allows encapsulation of naming relationships. The DNS provides two ways of viewing a name. One is called an *absolute name*, which consists of the complete name in the DNS. In contrast, a *relative name* consists of only a part of the name within a complete entry in the DNS.

In order to map user-friendly names to IP addresses, an Internet user must work with the concepts of domain name resolution. Here, the user need only provide a set of arguments to a local agent called a *name resolver*, which is responsible for retrieving information based on a domain name or sending the request to a *name server*. The name servers may store some of the same information that is stored at the name resolvers for purposes of efficiency and backup. Regardless of how the information is stored at the name server, the name resolver must know the name of at least one name server in order to begin the query. The query is passed to the name server from the resolver. The server, in turn, must then provide a response or make a referral to yet another name server.

Resource Records (RR)

Each node contains information about its resources (if no resources are available, the node would have an empty resource). The resource information associated with a node and name is called a *resource record* (*RR*). A resource record is contained in a database and is used to define domain zones. The RRs are also used to map between domain names and network objects. The structure of the DNS permits a relatively simple and easy addition of entries into the RR database.

These messages are transferred between name servers to update the RRs. Consequently, some of the fields in the message are similar to the format of the RR. DNS provides the first international standard for name server protocols. It allows Internet users to map names to addresses and addresses to names. It also supports mailbox operations and the storing of host profiles about operating systems, hardware, and applications architectures. Recent additions provide address and naming services for X.25 and ISDN systems.

User Datagram Protocol (UDP)

The reader may recall that the connectionless protocol provides no reliability or flow control mechanisms. It also has no error recovery procedures. The UDP is classified as a connectionless protocol. It is sometimes used in place of TCP in situations where the full services of TCP are not needed. For example, the Trivial File Transfer Protocol (TFTP) and the Remote Procedure Call (RPC) use UDP.

UDP serves as a single application interface to the IP. It serves principally as a multiplexer/de-multiplexer for the receiving and sending of IP traffic. UDP makes use of the port concept to direct the datagrams to the proper upper layer applications. The UDP datagram contains a destination port number and a source port number. The destination number is used by the UDP module to deliver the traffic to the proper recipient. The format of the UDP message is as follows (see fig. 3.8):

- *Source port*—This value identifies the port of the sending application process. The field is optional with a value of zero if not used.

- *Destination port*—This value identifies the receiving process on the destination host machine.

- *Length*—This value indicates the length of the user datagram including the header and the data, with a minimum of eight octets.

■ *Checksum*—This value is the 16-bit one's complement of the one's complement sum of the pseudo-IP header, the UDP header, and the data. It also performs a checksum on any padding.

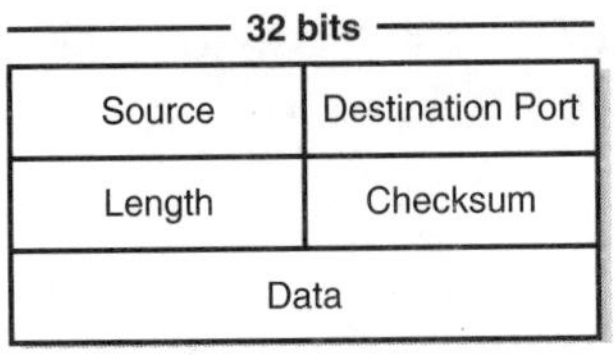

Fig. 3.8
UDP message
format.

```
————— 32 bits —————
┌─────────────┬──────────────────┐
│   Source    │ Destination Port │
├─────────────┼──────────────────┤
│   Length    │     Checksum     │
├─────────────┴──────────────────┤
│             Data                │
└─────────────────────────────────┘
```

UDP is a minimal level of service used in many transaction-based application systems. However, it is quite useful if the full services of TCP are not needed.

From Here...

Communication protocols have come a long way in making networking friendlier and an important part of our day-to-day life. Information gathering, processing, distributing, and storing are proving to be daunting, full-fledged tasks. However, with the advent of faster and better technology, this is becoming easier and less cumbersome. Newer and improved protocols are being designed and developed to help data, voice, and video become accessible on a global scale. The benefits and rewards to be gained by this are tremendous.

With more and more companies becoming network-oriented, protocols are proving to be of great help to get them on the information superhighway. Protocols are also making the work of a network manager less cumbersome by providing various services that help in improving and maintaining the network. With World Wide Web sites springing up everywhere, Internet access is becoming very important. In addition, Internet users are requesting faster information download to save time and money. Thus, there is a tremendous need for the development of new protocols and improvement of existing ones.

For more information on the topics discussed in this chapter, refer to the following:

■ Chapter 4, "Client/Server Development Overview," acquaints you with the client/server model and discusses the various protocols that are available in the market.

■ Chapter 23, "Multiplatform Applications," gives an expanded view of using different platforms to create a client/server system.

Chapter 4

Client/Server Development Overview

Developing client/server applications follows the same basic process as developing classical applications, but the emphasis differs to reflect the differences between the client/server application and the classical application. Client/server applications present specific challenges that must be addressed.

In this chapter, you learn the following:

- What is a client/server application?

- What challenges do you face?

- What is the software development life cycle?

- How do you develop an application for one platform?

- How do you develop an application for multiple platforms?

What Is a Client/Server Application?

Since there is no single definition of a client/server application that everyone agrees with, we can offer a very general definition along with some characteristics of client/server applications.

The general definition of a client/server application is an application in which logic and data are partitioned between a client (the requester of services) and the server (the provider of services) (see fig. 4.1).

Fig. 4.1
The client sends requests to the server, and the server provides services in response.

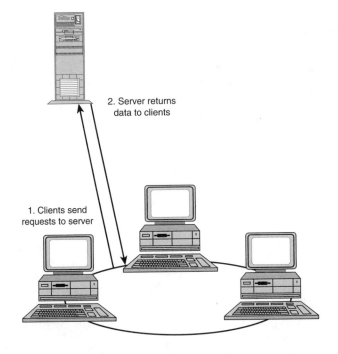

2. Server returns data to clients

1. Clients send requests to server

Tip
Initially, client/ server applications required that all the application logic remained on the client and the data on the server. Now, however, client/server applications can have both distributed logic and distributed data.

Some general characteristics of client/server applications include the following:

- The client and server are processes that usually run on separate machines connected by a network.

> **Note**
>
> Technically, any process that makes requests is a client, and any process that responds to those requests is a server. Therefore, you have client and server processes on the same machine. You can also have a process which is both a client and a server process. An example of such a process would be one that makes a request *of* another process in response to a request *from* another process.

- The client/server application divides function between the client and server based on the idea of a requester of services and a provider of services. However, the division in function is not evident to the end user.

- A server can provide services to many clients at one time. In some cases, clients can make requests to multiple servers.

- Servers wait passively for client requests.

- Multiple client and server platforms can work together.

- Clients and servers communicate through the passing of messages through a network.

- Once the client requests a service, it is up to the server to figure out how to get the job done.

- Upgrading a server does not affect the client as long as the message interface does not change.

- Client/server applications let you add or remove clients from the network without affecting the application.

- The server code and data are centrally maintained, which lets you control data integrity more carefully. The clients, on the other hand, are decentralized.

- The client or server can each be upgraded without affecting the other platform.

- The client has a user-friendly graphical user interface (GUI).

> **Note**
>
> A GUI is an important, though not required, part of a client/server application. However, note that very few clients do not support presentation logic.

- Most client/server applications use a structured query language (SQL) to request and receive data.

- The server provides some measure of security to prevent unauthorized access and to protect the data.

The Client

Many users are only aware of the client portion of the application, which does the following:

- Provides the user interface, accepting user input and displaying output

- Sends requests for information to the server, using remote procedure calls

■ Accepts data returned from the server

■ May perform some actions on the returned data, such as calculating totals or editing fields

Tip
You know your client/server application is a success if your end users are unaware of the processing going on behind the scenes on the server.

For example, if you work for a hotel and you are using a reservation application, one of the application's functions is to let you check reservations for customers. The client displays a screen, asking you to provide the customer's name and confirmation number. The client accepts the input, and sends a request to the server asking for the dates and other details of the customer's reservation. After the server returns the information, the client then accepts the data and displays it to you. At this point, the customer might ask you to change the reservation dates.

The user interface—most often a GUI—is what you see and use to complete your tasks on the client (see fig. 4.2).

Fig. 4.2
The GUI is what you see and use to complete your tasks.

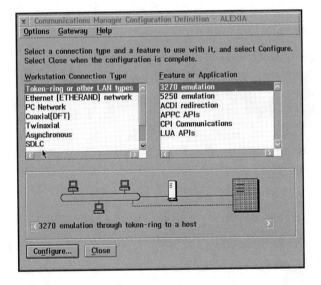

Standard GUIs let novice and experienced users learn applications more easily, move between applications without needing to learn different interfaces, and increase their productivity and efficiency. The most common GUI elements include the following:

■ *Windows* that appear on your screen are used to present information. Windows can overlap, appear next to each other, or pop up in the center of the screen.

- *Menus* give you a list of choices to select. Once you make a choice, the client may present you with a dialog box.

- *Icons* are small pictures that represent a file or application. By selecting an icon, you can open the file or application.

- A *pointer*, usually an arrow controlled by a mouse, lets you make selections on the screen.

- *Scroll bars* let you show more information in the window by moving the information up, down, to the left, or to the right.

- *Buttons* let you select certain actions, like confirming a request, or one option out of a list.

Once the client has submitted a request, the server takes over.

▶ See "User Interface," p. 158

The Server

The server portion of the application provides services to one or more clients. You do not interact directly with the server—the client is your go-between. The server portion of the application takes on the following responsibilities:

- Stores data submitted by the client

- Manipulates data in response to client requests

- Retrieves data in response to client requests

- Protects data from unauthorized access and change, and from failures in the system

Let's return to our example (in which you work for a hotel and you are using a reservation application). When the client sends a request to the server asking for the dates and other details of the customer's reservation, the server validates the client's request. Then the server searches the database for the requested data based on the customer's name or confirmation number. When the server finds the information, it passes it back to the client. If the customer asks you to change the reservation dates, the client passes the changed information back to the server so the server can change the dates in the database.

As you can see, the database is central to the server. The following several characteristics developed by Chris J. Date, an expert in relational databases (which happen to be client/server in nature), should give you a good working definition of distributed databases:

- The database sites are independent of each other. They have their own *database management systems* (*DBMSes*), and those DBMSes control security, data integrity, and recovery for that site. One central site may provide coordination among all the sites.

- No activity should shut down the server, including backing up or recovering the database.

- The data should be transparent to the user. In other words, the data might be split up and located among several different servers, but the data should look to the user as if it were local. Also, *replicated data* (multiple copies of data held at different sites) must be synchronized so that if one site is updated, all of the other sites holding that same data get updated as well. If the remaining updates do not occur for some reason, then the system needs to roll back the original update.

- The database should be independent of hardware, operating systems, and network topologies or protocols.

Some servers manipulate data through stored procedures and triggers. A stored procedure is compiled code that resides on the server and uses structured query language (SQL) to access the database. Since the code is compiled already on the server and does not have to be transmitted over the network, the code executes faster and reduces network traffic—both important performance issues. Triggers are a type of stored procedure that execute automatically in response to predefined events instead of in response to a particular client request. In addition to SQL, there are also other methods of manipulation where logic is declarative.

The type of server used depends on the task requested. There are several types of servers, which are as follows:

- **File servers** manage applications and data files so they can all be shared by a workgroup. File servers pass a large amount of data over the network, and only one person can use the data at a time.

- **Application servers** are host replacements, and make applications available to multiple users.

- **Data servers** are used only for data storage and management, and are used in conjunction with compute servers. These servers search and validate data, but generally don't transmit large amounts of data over the network.

- **Compute servers** pass client requests for data to data servers, and then forward the results of the requests back to the client.

- **Database servers** accept requests for data, retrieve the data from one or more databases, and send the data back to the client. As you'll notice, the function of the database server is the same as the joint function of the data server and compute server.

- **Communications servers** translate network protocols and connect multiple LANs, computers, and platforms.

The network connects clients and servers; networks provide transparent access to servers.

The Network

The *local area network* (*LAN*) passes requests from clients to servers, and returns the results. Since this communications technology is what allows you to hook together different machines running on different platforms, you must understand how it works in conjunction with the client and server.

The LAN connects your clients and servers. Typically, a LAN has different types of servers to provide different types of services. For example, a LAN will have a file server to store user data files and a print server to manage users' printing needs. Basic communication on the LAN is handled by the *network operating system* (*NOS*). LANs may be connected to form *wide area networks* (*WANs*), which are similar to LANs—just larger (see fig. 4.3).

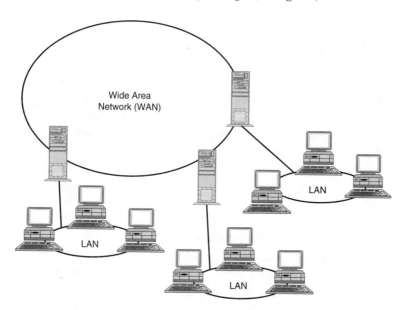

Fig. 4.3
Because LANs and WANs have different capacities, you may experience some degradation in throughput.

You need to determine where your users are located (clients), what resources you have (servers), and how those resources are connected (LAN and WAN), to be able to design your client/server application.

What Challenges Do You Face?

Client/server applications, in their various forms, offer many advantages. However, while these applications are easier to use and offer more flexibility and interoperability, they are also harder to design, implement, and maintain. With proper analysis and design, you can overcome the difficulties described below.

What Happens if Something Breaks?

The client/server architecture itself can cause problems, because there are far more possibilities for failure—and each mode of failure can produce different results. For example, if your client/server architecture consists of one client, one server, and the network connecting them, you have three potential sites for failure: the client, the server, or the network. If you take a more complicated example where your architecture consists of four clients, two servers, and the network, you can see that your potential sites for failure increase. And remember, failures can be full, where, for example, a client is down; or failures can be partial, where, for example, one of a server's two disk drives fails. When designing client/server applications, you must consider the kinds of errors that may happen and include ways for the system to handle those errors.

Anticipating Potential States

If a client/server configuration can have that many modes of failure, just imagine how many potential states that configuration can have. Each client and server can have multiple states. In the previous paragraph, we discussed computers in terms of being up (running) or down (in a state of failure), but a computer can actually be in any one of a variety of states: reading data, processing data, waiting for data, writing data, and so on. Since this is the case, just trying to anticipate failure is not enough—rather you must try to consider how clients and servers in various states in a client/server architecture will affect each other.

Running Multiple Processes

Similarly, client/server applications can run multiple processes at one time, while classical applications run one process at a time. This type of simultaneous processing is difficult to understand since it is so different from the way we, as humans, operate. When we process information or carry out procedures, we generally think about one thing at a time. For example, you are reading the newspaper while the television is on. You hear something that catches your interest. You stop reading and watch the TV. When a commercial comes on, you return to reading the newspaper. It is difficult to imagine devoting your full attention to multiple pieces of unrelated information at once—yet that is what you must do when designing client/server applications.

The mechanism that shows how client/server applications can run multiple processes at one time is the flowchart. In classical applications, the flowchart shows one process leading to another (see fig. 4.4).

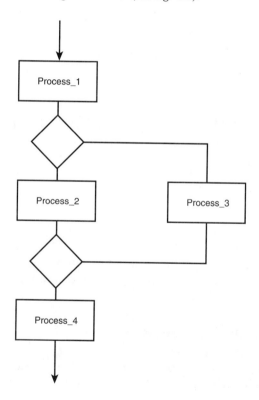

Fig. 4.4
Traditional flow-charts show a linear progression through the processes that make up the application.

However, in the client/server application, the flow is not so clearly defined, nor does one process necessarily lead to another. Isolated pieces of code can execute in a variety of sequences (see fig. 4.5).

Fig. 4.5
In a client/server application, the process flow is not linear.

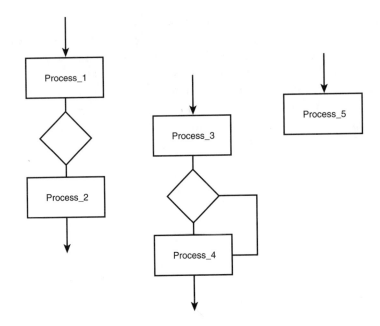

Synchronizing Time-Dependent Processes

Because client/server applications can execute on different machines simultaneously and those machines can have different states, the next logical assumption is that timing events can become complicated. Some processes are time-dependent, but how do you determine time when you are dealing with multiple machines and network paths? The odds are that the system clocks in each client and server are not set to the same exact time, and there is no way to predict exactly how long a process will take to complete or how long it will take for the network to return the results of the process. It is important to realize before you design your application that synchronization may play an important role.

Securing Client/Server Applications

One of the most common topics in the client/server area right now is the challenge of securing client/server applications. How do you secure an application that runs on multiple machines, multiple platforms, and over a network? The same flexibility and accessibility that make client/server systems so desirable are what make client/server systems difficult to secure. Unauthorized users can break into a system by intercepting a password, using administration tools, or by tapping into network phone lines. Be sure to provide ways to secure your application on the client, server, and network levels.

Planning for Performance

Once you develop your whiz-bang client/server application, how do you make sure it operates quickly and reliably enough to be useful?

Many times performance issues are key requirements in the eyes of customers, and many will not buy applications that cannot meet minimal performance benchmarks. Performance is normally difficult to estimate and plan for, and performance on client/server systems is even more so—especially since client/server systems are relatively new and each application has so many external dependencies that vary depending on what configuration the application is used on. Some specific performance issues to consider include the following:

- What is the capacity of each of the network components?

- How efficient are the network protocols?

- What are the processor speeds of the clients and servers?

- What is the memory capacity of the clients and servers?

- What operating systems are being used?

- What client/server configuration is being used?

- How many other applications are being used?

Of course, this list is not complete, but it gives you an idea of some of the factors that can affect system performance.

Standardizing Your Application

In a more general sense, there is a lack of standardization and consistency in the area of client/server technology. Client/server technology can be divided into client technology, server technology, and network technology. Each of these areas can be divided further still into their own various individual technologies. In marrying these areas, you can run into different standards, varying definitions, and certain incompatibilities. These differences make it crucial for you to be very clear when you design, construct, test, and implement your application. If you do not define clearly what your intentions and assumptions are at the outset, you may run into failure during testing or implementation—when working around the problem will be costly.

Tip
You can use development methodology to track where you are in the development process just as you use a clock to see what time it is.

Don't Give Up

I don't want you to read the descriptions of these problems and think that maybe developing a client/server application isn't worth it. I just want to make you aware of some of the challenges to client/server programming, and that you can combat these potential problems through careful planning and the use of a client/server methodology for development.

What is the Software Development Life Cycle?

The *software development life cycle* (*SDLC*) for client/server applications is a development methodology that points out what needs to be done and in what order. The SDLC is made up of six stages: analysis, design, construction, testing, implementation, and maintenance (see fig. 4.6).

Fig. 4.6
The SDLC points out what needs to be done and in what order.

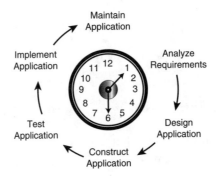

Traditional methodologies fall short when you try to apply them to client/server development because of several reasons:

- They show a linear flow of activities, when in reality the activities may occur in multiple iterations.

- They describe, in general terms, how to develop an application, but not exactly what needs to be done.

- They do not distinguish between the scopes of different sized projects.

The SDLC for client/server applications, however, recognizes the need for multiple iterations; discusses the development process not only in terms of stages, but also in terms of inputs and outputs; and allows for the fact that larger applications require more time and effort in particular stages than smaller applications. Developing applications in rapid iterative cycles results in higher quality systems that you can develop in shorter periods of time. See Table 4.1 for the inputs and outputs of each stage.

Table 4.1   Inputs and Outputs of the SDLC

Stage	Inputs	Outputs
Analysis	User interviews and surveys, Joint Application Development (JAD) sessions, Reviews of existing applications	User requirements—defined, categorized, and without conflicts
Design	User requirements	Defined interfaces and processes
Construction	Defined interfaces and processes	Compiled code
Testing	Compiled code	Tested application, ready for execution
Implementation	Tested application	Application, running satisfactorily
Maintenance	Reports of problems Requests for changes	Improved application, running satisfactorily

Analysis

The analysis phase of the software development life cycle studies the situation and produces user requirements. The purpose of this phase is for you to clearly understand why you are developing the new application. It is especially important for users to be involved early in the analysis and design stage, because that is the only way you can make the client/server application be the best—and the most user-friendly, which is one (if not the main) goal of client/server technology.

Design

The design phase of the software development life cycle translates the "what"—the user requirements—into the "how"—a high level design of the application, including designs for screens and decision processes. You may also design a prototype that you can demonstrate for the users to get their input.

Standards are significant when designing client/server applications because they aim for normalization, which lets you design portable, interoperable systems. The International Standards Organization (ISO) developed the Open Systems Interconnection (OSI) model to address these issues.

Construction

Tip
Networks, database query languages, graphical user interfaces, and operating systems have clearly defined standards. However, development and data standards are still being developed.

If you have thoroughly analyzed and designed the application, you should now only have to translate the design into code and compile the code. This process sounds simple, and it should be with the methodology guiding you. With good project management and team leadership, the construction phase can be the most painless stage of the development process.

Testing

Once you have compiled your code, you can test it. There are several levels of testing. First, you test each compiled module by itself. Then you test the modules that have to work with each other. Finally, you test all the modules together.

Implementation

Implementation involves many concurrent tasks, the most immediate being getting the application running. However, just saying "getting the application running" is deceptively simple. What is actually involved is loading the programs onto the clients and servers; loading the data; converting that data, if necessary; establishing management, recovery, and reorganization procedures; completing the documentation; and training the users.

Maintenance

The maintenance stage is really an abbreviated version of the software development life cycle as a whole, with fewer reviews and less testing because of the frequency and urgency of the requests. Maintenance also involves less planning since you can't anticipate what the next change will be.

How Do You Develop an Application for One Platform?

When you develop an application for one platform, you go through each of the six stages of the SDLC: analysis, design, construction, testing, implementation, and maintenance. Each stage is important—no stage can be skipped or skimmed. Each stage serves as a foundation for the next one, and if you skip one, you will have to go back later and revisit it in retrospect—which will cost you time and money.

Analysis

When defining the requirements, be sure to work directly with users. Don't make assumptions when it comes to what users want—you might be surprised! By defining and refining the requirements with the users, you are given a clear picture of what the end product should be. Without that clear picture, you risk wasting time programming "in circles" and developing an ill-defined client/server application. You should not be deciding what you are programming once development begins. This is a colossal waste of time and effort.

In addition to interviewing the users directly, have a brainstorming session with the other people involved in the project. These brainstorming sessions are called *Joint Application Design* (*JAD*) sessions and create an atmosphere for spontaneity and creativity, which stimulate the flow of ideas. Another useful place to find information is to examine related existing applications. If related systems have already been built, there will be some similarities—and you may find strengths you want to emulate or weaknesses you want to avoid.

Tip
Application development tools can be used to analyze user requirements and prototype applications quickly.

Along with structured data gathering processes like JAD sessions and user interviews, have a file to collect all bits of potentially useful data that might not fit in a particular place in your plan right now. Once you have a general feel for the requirements, the next step is to translate those requirements into tasks and categorize the tasks into related modules. Questions to ask yourself are:

- What do my users need to do?

- What do my users want to do?

- What similar applications exist?

Before you exit the analysis stage of the SDLC, make sure you are confident that you do the following:

- Define the requirements as much as possible

- Categorize the requirements

- Make sure that the requirements do not conflict with each other

Design

The detailed design phase focuses on determining how data will be stored, distributed, accessed, and structured. The outputs at this point are the technologies that you will use, and the presentation logic, application logic, and DBMSes you will use.

Technology

The first step in the design process is determining exactly what technology is needed to meet the requirements defined in the analysis stage. Beyond this point, the design process depends on what technology is going to be used—specifically, the hardware platform, the operating system on each machine, the database management system (DBMS), the network software and operating system, and the language to be used for development. In addition to determining the technology used, you need to define how data is going to be handled; in other words, what the attributes of the data are and how the type of data is identified.

Presentation Logic

When designing GUIs, make sure that they are as intuitive as possible, follow standards, and make the GUIs consistent across the application. Remember that GUIs for client/server applications differ from GUIs used in PC applications in that the client/server GUIs do quite a bit of the data housekeeping tasks, like checking and verifying data.

Several standards for GUI applications exist, including standards created by IBM, Microsoft, and Apple. These standards describe how to present information to the user using a standard format for icons, windows, menus, and so on.

The following are important notes about GUIs:

- GUIs make systems easier to use and allow multitasking and data interchange among applications.

- GUIs can be time-consuming to build—using GUI-building tools speeds up the process.

- Lack of consistency in the user interface can frustrate end users. Follow standards.

- Tools are available to create generic interfaces that are portable to a variety of platforms.

- End users can have different GUIs operating on their workstations at the same time.

In addition to developing layouts for screens, windows, reports, and forms, you must specify how the application and data are going to be distributed, and how and where they will tie together.

Application Distribution

When you distribute the application, you have to determine how to divide the logic and where to store it. Most client/server applications put the presentation logic on the client, the data on the server, and the application logic is split between the two. Some procedures that are used often on the server, like common queries, can be stored on the server to save processing time and resources. They execute quickly because they are stored compiled code. Stored procedures can be nested, and can make remote calls to stored procedures on other servers. Stored procedures can also be maintained more quickly and easily.

The important thing to remember when you are deciding how to distribute the application functions is that you must try to determine the effects of where you place the functions before the application is constructed and implemented (see Table 4.2).

Table 4.2 Distribute Applications Depending On User Needs

Client/Server Architecture	Mainframe	Server	Client
Classical	Presentation Application Database Management		
Intelligent Presentation	Application Database Management		Presentation
Distributed Data Access	Database Management	Database Management	Presentation Application
Distributed Application Logic	Application Database Management		Presentation Application
Distributed Data Access and Application Logic	Application Database Management	Database Management	Presentation Application
Distributed Database	Database Management	Database Management	Presentation Application
			Database Management

▶ See "What Responsibilities Does the Client Have?" p. 160

You can readjust the application distribution once you have implemented your application, but you cannot completely redesign the application. If you load too much on the client, you end up with a *fat client*; if you load too much on the server, you end up with a *fat server*. By *fat*, I mean a client or server that has a disproportionate amount of logic for the tasks it has to do. By planning ahead, you can determine what division will give you the most balanced, efficient application.

▶ See "Understanding Server Distribution" p. 187

When you decide what functions are going to be stored where, you also need to define what the inputs and outputs are, and what data the function requires to complete its task. Also, you need to understand what functions are dependent on other functions. For example, if two steps need to finish before the third can start, and the first two steps are independent of each other, those two steps can execute at the same time on the same or different platforms—but the third step must wait for the completion of both of the first two steps. When you design your application, you must be able to control concurrent and sequential processes.

Functions should be designed independent of the GUI and data source. That way, if you change the GUI or data sources, the program itself won't need to be changed. Also, GUI- and data-independence lets you move the application among platforms easily.

Data Distribution

When you distribute data, you have to decide how to divide it. Do you duplicate the data in more than one place? Do you split the data? If you duplicate the data, you must make sure that you can update all copies of the data at the same time when the user makes a change. If you split the data, you must make sure that you can pull together the appropriate parts of the data when required.

Databases must provide transparent access to data and protect the integrity of the data. The physical database design needs to take into account data ordering, indexes, data attributes, keys, variable length data, NULL or NOT NULL data specification, and so on. The physical database design is the actual specification of the database to the DBMS. Distributing data offers the following benefits:

- Data is closer to where it is needed most, which improves response times.

- Network traffic lessens.

- Data distribution balances resources more efficiently.

- Multiple copies of data lessen the impact of system failures.

As with application distribution, the important thing to remember when you are deciding how to distribute data is that you must try to determine the effects of placing the data before the application is constructed and implemented. You can readjust data distribution once you have implemented your application, but you cannot completely redistribute the data.

The obvious concern when you are distributing an application and data between a client and server is: how are requests linked from the client to the server, or between servers? On a client and server that run on the same platform, there is no problem. However, if you are using multiple platforms, gateways can provide the connectivity you require (see fig. 4.7).

Fig. 4.7
Gateways can
be used to link
applications and
databases on
different platforms
or networks.

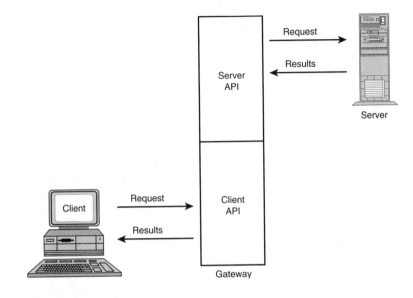

Gateways convert and translate data formats, types, and naming conventions.
However, even though gateways provide transparent access to data on multi-
platform servers, the trade-off is processing speed.

Questions

During the design stage of the software development life cycle, you should
ask yourself the following questions:

- Against what standard are you going to design your application?

  Standards are significant when designing client/server applications
  because they aim for normalization, which lets you design portable,
  interoperable systems. The International Standards Organization (ISO)
  developed the Open Systems Interconnection (OSI) model to address
  these issues.

- What hardware, software, and communications technology is going to
  be used?

  You might have an idea of what platform you want your application to
  run on, but what happens if the technology changes? What happens if
  you decide to move to another platform? Deciding to design an open
  systems application now is much easier than trying to revamp your
  application later.

- How will you functionally partition the client/server application?

  You must plan ahead and modularize your code accordingly if you want to split the application between client and server. Optimizing cost-effectiveness by improving performance should be one of your primary goals.

- How do the various parts of the application (the client, the server, and the network) work together?

  You need to pay close attention to the relationships between each component of the application. Designing each component is the easy part of the development process—designing them so they work together seamlessly is the critical part.

- How will you partition data between the client and the server?

  Planning the functional partition is not enough—you must also consider the data passing over the network. Write your code so you reduce request and reply processing.

- What security measures are needed?

  Depending on the data and the application, you may need to authenticate credentials to see if the requesters are who they claim they are.

- What access control policy is needed?

  Some functions can be available to many authenticated users, like browsing information. Some functions, particularly those that manipulate or change data, must be limited to certain authorized users. You must be able to validate identities and assign access as needed.

- What network protocols are you going to use?

  Make protocol decisions early. One of the goals of client/server computing is to make the network and server aspects of the application transparent to the users.

- How are you going to handle error reporting and error recovery?

  You must be able to trace errors when they occur. RPC libraries provide error reporting at the RPC level, but you must also address errors that happen as a result of the network and hardware.

■ What will happen if a connection is dropped?

If a connection is dropped, you need a contingency plan in the application. Perhaps the application attempts to reconnect, looks for another connection, or stops and reports the error.

■ Should processing be synchronous or asynchronous?

Multitasking, or asynchronous processing, at the server level only makes sense when one or more clients are sending multiple requests that require different times to process or processing priority. Remember that multitasking servers are generally slower than single-threaded, or synchronous, servers.

Performance

If you are developing a large application (and possibly even if you are developing a smaller application), you will have to address data volume, processing volume, network traffic, and data growth, or your application may not meet the performance requirements. Addressing performance issues like these lets you create a "leaner and meaner" application, regardless of its size.

Specific considerations that affect performance include the following:

■ Identifying whether each function, or module, will be executed often or occasionally

■ Identifying peak periods of processing

■ Identifying what types of data will be needed, and what minimum amount of data is sufficient to complete the task

■ Making sure that data access is efficient

■ Dividing large functions into smaller, more modular functions

To sum up, the outputs are defined interfaces and logically structured processes.

Construction

If you have thoroughly analyzed and designed the application, you should now only have to translate the design into code and compile the code.

When choosing a tool to help you develop client/server applications, the tool should support the following features:

■ A variety of common operating systems

■ A variety of GUIs

Tip
Performance capabilities include not only how quickly the application processes a request or transfers data, but also how much volume the application can handle.

- Standard SQL specifications

- A variety of network protocols and operating systems

- Object-oriented programming

- Windows-based code generation and debugging

- A variety of class libraries

- A powerful programming language or the ability to generate code

- Transparent interoperability of multiple-platform clients and servers

- Portable applications

- Various standards for GUIs, network protocols, and so on

Also, try to use a tool that is supported fully by a reliable, established vendor—many client/server programmers have been left out in the cold when their particular software vendors failed or were taken over by other companies.

The output is a quickly developed, easily maintained, client/server application that meets the requirements determined during the analysis stage.

Testing

To be able to effectively test client/server applications, you must do the following:

- Understand client/server technology

- Use one or more automated testing tools that are designed specifically for client/server applications

- Have copies of the analysis and design documents so you understand how the application is supposed to work

- Secure the testing environment so only authorized users can test the application

- Have access to the platform that the application runs on

Client/server applications need to be tested using well-defined test plans. GUI programs are more complicated than character-based applications, which makes testing more difficult. Each screen provides many more options and more complex navigation. Each GUI element must be tested in combination with each of the other elements. Your application must be tested to make sure the server provides referential integrity, data recovery, and concurrency. Each stored procedure on the server must be tested with each type of potential input from the client. Your application should also follow the standards determined in the design stage, which should include error handling requirements, screen navigation, naming conventions, style guidelines for GUI elements, and so on.

When developing your test plans, make sure you address the following issues:

- Network security
- Application distribution
- Performance limits
- Response times
- Processing times
- Network recovery
- Data recovery
- Interfaces with other systems
- Help screens
- Verification of user manuals
- Quality of code
- Conformity to defined standards
- Transparency
- Special conditions

When you complete the tests, you should have a reliable, efficient, client/server application, ready for execution.

Implementation

Implementation means more than just getting the application into production. Implementing a single platform client/server application means actually distributing the logic and data across the client and server, integrating the application with the system, and getting the application to run successfully. There really is no "output" from this step—but the goal is certainly to get the whole system—client, server, and network—running satisfactorily.

Maintenance

The maintenance stage of the process begins as soon as the application is implemented. Because this stage has no defined scope and never really ends, it is difficult to control. You maintain the application by correcting or modifying the application, not by redesigning it or changing the basic functionality. The types of maintenance changes include the following:

- Emergency fixes to correct problems

- Configuration changes to compensate for changes in the network, hardware, or software

- User requests for enhanced functionality

- Changes to improve performance

How Do You Develop an Application for Multiple Platforms?

Developing an application for multiple platforms is similar to a single platform application, yet more complex, as you might expect (see fig. 4.8). However, as I stated earlier, all complexities can be addressed—and need to be addressed—in the analysis and design stages of development.

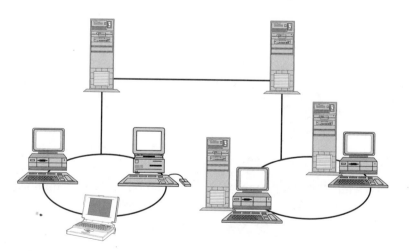

Fig. 4.8
Multiple platforms add complexity to the development process.

Analysis

When you go through the analysis stage for multi-platform client/server applications, you use the same process as you would for a single platform application. That process, summarized, is as follows:

1. Get user input.

2. Conduct JAD session.

3. Examine related existing applications.

4. Collect all bits of potentially useful data.

5. Translate requirements into tasks and categorize the tasks into related modules.

Before you exit the analysis stage of the SDLC, make sure you are confident that you have done the following:

- Defined the user requirements as clearly as possible

- Categorized the requirements

- Made sure that the requirements do not conflict with each other

Design

As with the analysis stage, you go through a similar, though more complex, process when developing a multi-platform application:

1. Determine what technology is available.

2. Develop presentation logic—specifically, the GUIs.

3. Distribute application logic.

4. Distribute the data.

5. Address performance issues.

6. Ask yourself the following question in addition to the ones outlined for single-platform development:

   If you are using multiple servers, why are you distributing the processing?

   To be able to create an efficient client/server application across multiple servers, you must understand why you are partitioning the application the way you are. Using multiple servers usually means you must implement some sort of multitasking on the client.

To sum up, the outputs are defined interfaces and structured processes.

Construction

If you have thoroughly analyzed and designed the application, you should now only have to translate the design into code and compile the code. The output is a quickly developed, easily maintained, multi-platform, client/server application that meets the requirements determined during the analysis stage.

Testing

One side effect of the complexity of multi-platform client/server architectures is that testing and debugging applications can be very difficult. Because of all the possible scenarios due to multiple states and process paths, test cases often do not replicate conditions the end user may run into or reproduce problems that have already been encountered.

To be able to effectively test multi-platform client/server applications, you must:

■ Understand client/server technology.

■ Use one or more automated testing tools that are designed specifically for multi-platform client/server applications.

■ Have copies of the analysis and design documents so you understand how the application is supposed to work across platforms.

■ Secure the testing environment so only authorized users can test the application.

■ Have access to all the platforms that the application runs on.

In addition to the questions listed for testing a single-platform application, make sure you address the following issues in your test plans:

■ Multi-platform network security

■ Application distribution across the platforms

■ Performance limits of the multi-platform application

■ Interfaces with other systems

- Conformity to the defined standards

- Transparency between platforms

- Portability

- Interoperability

- Special conditions

When you complete the tests, you should have a reliable, efficient, multi-platform, client/server application.

Implementation

When you bring a multi-platform client/server application into production, you technically face similar challenges (distributing the logic and data, integrating the application with the system, and getting it to run successfully) but with the added complications that multiple platforms present: compatibility, interoperability, and transparency. There really is no tangible "output" from the implementation step—but the goal is certainly to get the entire system not just running satisfactorily, but running across all platforms successfully.

Maintenance

The types of maintenance changes you see with multi-platform client/server applications are quite similar to the ones you see with single platform applications. Once again, the complicating factor is the fact that you now must distribute updates to multiple clients and servers across multiple platforms, and then reintegrate the system so the entire application runs successfully again. And you need to be able to do all this without impacting processing and, ultimately, your users' productivity. Developing specific maintenance procedures is the key to remaining organized and maintaining your systems with as little disruption as possible.

The output from this stage is an improved application that runs across multiple platforms successfully.

From Here...

You probably noticed that emphasis in this chapter was on analysis and design—and for good reason. If you invest the time to do a thorough job on analysis and design, your code will practically write itself.

For more information on the topics in this chapter, please refer to the following chapters:

- Chapter 5, "Responsibilities of a Client," discusses what makes up a client, what the role of the client is in the client/server process, and what responsibilities the client has.

- Chapter 6, "Responsibilities of a Server," explains what makes up a server, what the role of the server is in the client/server process, and what responsibilities the server has.

Introduction

Chapter 5

Responsibilities of a Client

In the last chapter, you learned that a client/server application is an application in which logic and data are partitioned between a client (the requester of services) and the server (the provider of services). In other words, the client asks the server to perform an action or provide information, and the server responds.

Before you design your client, you need to understand what your users expect from the client with regard to functionality and usability, what processes the client needs to initiate, and how the client requests information from the server.

In this chapter, you learn the following:

- What exactly is a client?

- What is the client's role in the client/server process?

- What responsibilities does the client have?

What Exactly Is a Client?

To design the client portion of an application, also known as the *front end*, you need to understand the various components that make up the client (see fig. 5.1). The hardware, the operating system, the network, the user interface, and the software all need to support and work with your application. A Windows application, for example, may consist of a Pentium connected to a server via a local area network running a client/server application on Windows 95.

Fig. 5.1

The client consists of hardware, the operating system, the network, the user interface, and the software.

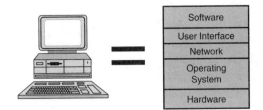

Hardware

The client hardware can be a personal computer or a workstation (see fig. 5.2). A personal computer is a microcomputer—usually an IBM-compatible or Macintosh machine. Workstations generally run some flavor of UNIX. However, keep in mind that other machines, such as minicomputers and mainframes, can make client requests of other servers.

Fig. 5.2

A client's hardware can be a personal computer or a workstation.

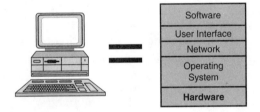

Tip

The term *client* is used in this chapter to refer to any machine that your end user interacts with directly.

The client must be physically able to handle the application. In other words, the client must have enough power to request, present, and manipulate the data. For example, to run a simple program in Windows 95, you must have at least an 80486/33 mHz processor with 8 MB to 16 MB of RAM and VGA color support. Notice that there are four important considerations when determining hardware needs:

- Processor power (for Windows 3.1, at least an 80486 processor).

- Processor speed (at least 33 mHz).

- Amount of random access memory (RAM) (at least 8 MB to 16 MB).

- Color support (VGA).

The processor is known formally as the central processing unit (CPU). The CPU controls the operation of the computer and performs the data processing. More specifically, the processor reads instructions, interprets those instructions, reads data, manipulates data, and writes data. Most client/server applications require at least a 32-bit 80486 system. The speed of the processor refers to how quickly the CPU carries out its tasks. Most client/server applications require at least 33 MHz.

The amount of RAM you have affects the performance of your application. RAM lets the CPU both read data from memory and rapidly write data to memory. The more RAM you have, the more data can be accessible to the CPU at a particular time—which translates into faster processing and better performance. Most client/server applications require at least 8 MB of RAM. 12 MB to 16 MB is usually preferred.

Color support simply means whether or not color is supported on the machine, and to what degree. Although a few client/server applications still have a command-line interface, most are designed for VGA color support.

The actual values required by your application depend on the size and complexity of the application. The more logic that resides on the client, the fatter the client. The fatter your client, the more power you need. You should ask yourself the following questions when determining what hardware needs your application will have:

- How fast does the client platform, as a whole, have to be to meet the needs of the user? Will your application require more than 8 MB of RAM? Will your application run on an 80486? A Pentium?

- What will be the minimum hardware support required? What will be the recommended hardware support?

- Does the platform support the operating system or systems your application is going to run under?

- Does the platform conform to industry standards? In other words, is the platform *open* (compatible with hardware and software from other vendors)?

- Is the platform cost-effective for your end user? If you are developing a small-scale data entry application, it doesn't make any sense to purchase a client machine that costs tens of thousands of dollars. However, if you are developing an enterprise-wide management and tracking system, a higher cost might well be justified.

Operating System

The operating system (OS) hides the details of the computer hardware from both you and your end user (see fig. 5.3).

Fig. 5.3

A client's operating system can be UNIX, Windows, or System 7.5, for example.

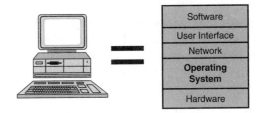

Operating systems are programs that manage the computer's resources, control the application's execution, and act as an interface between the user and the computer hardware itself. Operating systems make the computer more efficient and convenient to use, even though they are really nothing more than programs themselves.

The operating system performs the following functions:

- Controls the management of the resources that move, store, process, and control data.

- Loads instructions and data into main memory, initializes files and I/O devices, and prepares resources.

- Controls access to files, including the data format and availability, as well as access to shared resources.

- Provides the instructions and control signals for various I/O devices.

- Controls access to the system as a whole.

Operating systems are characterized by the following three basic abilities:

- The ability to address RAM.

- The ability to "simultaneously" load and execute applications.

- The ability to support or provide a standard user interface.

The ability to address RAM is not the same as how much RAM a particular piece of hardware supports. The amount of RAM that can be used is limited by the operating system. For example, DOS cannot use more than 1 MB of RAM, even if there is 32 MB of RAM on the machine. The more memory the operating system can address, the more powerful applications running under that operating system can be.

Note that *simultaneously* is in quotations. That is because computers with one CPU can only execute a single instruction at a time. However, by splitting processing time among multiple tasks, the CPU can create the illusion that multiple processes are executing simultaneously. For example, a communications program can be downloading information from a server while your user continues working in another program. Loading and executing multiple applications at a time is called *multitasking*.

Multitasking operating systems can be preemptive or non-preemptive. In a preemptive system, the operating system controls the amount of time spent on each task. In a non-preemptive system, the application controls the amount of time spent on each task—which means the application does not give up control until it has finished running its own tasks. Preemptive systems prevent one task from dominating the system, which is very important in client/server systems because if a client process is hung up waiting for an answer to a request, your user cannot move on to other tasks.

Multitasking within an application, called *multi-threading*, in conjunction with a preemptive multitasking OS, may well be the most efficient method of processing. Multi-threading lets the application set priorities and complete the tasks in order of priority.

The GUI provides the user with the look and feel of the application. The GUI can be part of the operating system itself or an extension to the operating system.

In some cases, the application is built for a particular operating system. However, sometimes the operating system is chosen after the user-interface environment is chosen. For example, OpenWindows (a GUI) runs under UNIX. Therefore, if you decide you want to use OpenWindows for your GUIs, by default you will have to choose UNIX as your operating system.

The most common operating systems used on client machines are the following:

- DOS
- Windows
- OS/2
- System 7
- UNIX

DOS is a 16-bit, single-tasking operating system. However, when DOS is used in conjunction with Windows 3.x, you get improved memory management, simulated multitasking, and data linking.

DOS-based applications can usually only access 640 KB of memory (unless aided by outside products), while Windows lets applications access more. Virtual memory even lets Windows applications use more memory than physically exists. Virtual memory is a software "trick" that lets your computer use part of your storage space on your hard drive as RAM. However, two things to remember before you rely on virtual memory are: performance is slower, and the hard disk space used for RAM cannot be used for storage.

Windows can link data in various applications, so changes made to the data in one application are updated in all other applications that use that same data. For example, you are designing a newsletter in a desktop publishing (DTP) program. Instead of importing the text into the DTP file, you can link text files to the DTP file. Now, when you make a change to the text file, the DTP file is automatically updated.

The following three things make linking possible:

- Dynamic link libraries (DLLs) allow routines to be coded as modules and linked as needed.

- Dynamic data exchange (DDE) exchanges data between applications.

- Object linking and embedding (OLE) creates a collection of objects that are linked to the software tool that created it.

Windows 95 and Windows NT are 32-bit operating systems with built-in networking capabilities. They look similar to Windows 3.x and have the base functionality of Windows 3.x, which means you don't have to learn a brand-new operating system. However, 95 and NT are much more powerful, and were designed for compatibility and portability. Since Windows 95 and NT use a more efficient memory model, they can manipulate large amounts of data. System performance increases significantly.

OS/2 is a 32-bit operating system that also provides multitasking support. Because OS/2 uses a more efficient memory model, as Windows does, OS/2 can manipulate large objects in memory. System performance increases significantly. OS/2 can run multiple DOS, Windows, and 16-bit and 32-bit OS/2 applications at the same time. DDE also lets OS/2 applications exchange data between applications. OLE is supported only between Windows applications.

OS/2 lets the user have transparent access to the data stored on the server by providing icon views of servers, which can be used just like any other desktop resource. Network directories appear simply as desktop folders.

System 7 is the system currently used by Macintosh. It is a 32-bit operating system similar to OS/2 that offers multitasking, virtual memory, and network support. System 7 also allows linking data between applications using Edition Manager and Inter-Application Communication (IAC).

UNIX also operates in a multitasking, multi-user environment, and it is far more powerful than the other operating systems discussed here. The major difference between UNIX and all other operating systems is that UNIX can run on any machine, while the other operating systems are processor-dependent.

Note

Several GUIs are available for UNIX, including OpenWindows and Motif.

Table 5.1 compares the main features of each of these operating systems.

Table 5.1   What Do You Need From Your Operating System?

Required of OS	DOS	Windows	Windows NT	OS/2	System 7	UNIX
32-bit Addressing (flat)	Y	Y	Y (flat)	Y (flat)	Y	Y
Virtual Memory	N	Y	Y	Y	Y	Y
Multitasking	N	N	Y	Y	Y	Y
GUI Support	N	Y	Y	Y	Y	Y
Data Linking	N	Y	Y	Y	Y	Y
Processor Independence	N	N	Y	N	N	Y

As you can see, Windows NT and UNIX satisfy all the requirements. Since the UNIX operating system is often too powerful as a client operating system to justify the cost, it's more likely to be installed on a server than on a client. Windows NT and OS/2 provide similar support on a smaller scale, and are usually the more cost-effective choices.

Network

A network is an interprocess communication system that allows the transfer of data between processes. The network has rules, or protocols, that determine how data is transferred. By using standard protocols and data formats, different hardware and software platforms can communicate with each other.

Networks have operating system software just as clients and servers do (see fig. 5.4). The network operating system (NOS) shields the client applications from direct communication with the server. Even though the NOS is installed on the server, part of it must run on each client.

Fig. 5.4
Novell NetWare is the most popular network operating system today.

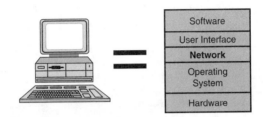

The NOS connects the client operating system with the network, which means applications can access the network through the client operating system. For example, you could save a file directly to a logical drive on the network server. The process would be transparent to you—as the user, you wouldn't have to do anything different from when you were saving the file to your hard drive.

Tip
If your client application is designed well, the only awareness the user should have of the server is entering the logon ID and password.

User Interface

Graphical user interfaces (GUIs) provide the user with an easy-to-use interface (see fig. 5.5). With GUIs, your users don't have to do much more than "point-and-click" to do their jobs. People can interact with graphical images faster and more easily than they can when presented with just text.

Fig. 5.5
User interfaces are generally tied to the operating system used on the client.

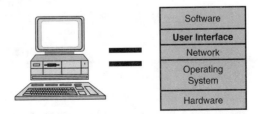

Your users are probably already familiar with GUIs from their desktop software. The interface defines how the user enters data and how the application displays data back to the user. For a more detailed discussion of the user interface, go to the following section, "What is the Client's Role?".

Software

Software can also reside on the client. Here, software means the client logic of the client/server application, as well as other software such as spreadsheets, graphics, and desktop publishing programs that may or may not be used in conjunction with the client/server application (see fig. 5.6).

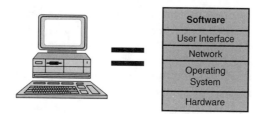

Fig. 5.6
The client portion of client/server applications usually lets you request, add, or modify data.

Usually, the client application logic provides query, data modification, and reporting services so your user can request information, receive information, change that information, and get reports that summarize or detail that information. The next section provides a more detailed discussion of the client application logic.

What Is the Client's Role?

The client/server process can be simplified into the following steps:

1. The user creates a request or query.

2. The client formats the query and sends it to the server.

3. The server checks the user's access privileges.

4. The server processes the query and returns the results.

5. The client receives the response and formats it for the user.

6. The user views and manipulates the data.

Out of these six steps, the client plays four major roles. The client is, in fact, the focus of the client/server application. The user interacts with the client, the client initiates most of the application processing, and the server exists to answer the needs of the client.

Introduction

The client performs the following functions:

- Provides an easy-to-use user interface.

- Sends requests.

- Accepts responses.

- Lets the user view and manipulate data.

Providing an easy-to-use interface consists of two primary tasks: accepting input, and displaying output. For example, the client accepts input by letting a store clerk place a special order for a customer. The client can also display the customer's information to the clerk.

Sending requests involves formatting a request and sending it to the server. If our sales clerk wants to display all outstanding special orders, the client formats the request into the SQL used by the server database management system (DBMS) and sends it out over the network to the server.

> **Note**
>
> Structured Queried Languages (SQLs) are standardized languages used to request data from database servers.

The server checks the user's access rights, processes the query, and returns the requested data. At that point, the client receives the results and interprets them in a format that the client can use. In our example, the returned database rows are translated into the list of outstanding special orders.

The final role is letting the user view and manipulate the data. The client takes the list of outstanding special orders and displays it to the store clerk. Depending on the clerk's access rights, the clerk can then add, update, or delete particular orders.

So now we know what the client does—at least at a high level. But let's get more specific. Within each of those four roles, what does the client have to do?

What Responsibilities Does the Client Have?

There is no predefined "split" in responsibilities for client/server applications. You can decide where to divide the application, depending on your needs.

The *fat client* model places more function on the client, and the *fat server* model places more function on the server, as figure 5.7 shows. Fat clients are more common among client/server applications.

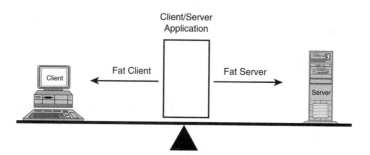

Client/Server
Application

Fat Client   Fat Server

Client

Server

Fig. 5.7
Where you distribute your applications determines whether or not you have a fat client or a fat server.

For each of the four roles—providing an easy-to-use interface, sending requests, accepting responses, and letting the user display and manipulate data—the client has certain responsibilities.

Providing an Easy-to-Use Interface

The user interface is one of the most critical pieces of your client application. No matter how many bells and whistles your application has, your user has to be able to use them!

User interface standards control the look (the screen elements) and feel (the way the user makes requests and gets feedback) of the program. A consistent interface is essential when your user interacts with multiple applications across multiple platforms.

Responsibilities

Development of the client is based on user-centered design principles. The common user access (CUA) standards describe these design principles well:

- Keep the interface consistent, so users get a familiar look and feel across applications and platforms.

- Remember that the computer serves the user. The user should control the order of tasks. The computer should never ignore the user, but rather keep the user informed and provide immediate feedback.

- Use metaphors, both verbal and visual, to help users develop conceptual images. For example, storing files in folders on the desktop is an easy-to-understand metaphor.

- Make the interface intuitive, so the user can concentrate on working rather than figuring out how the computer works.

Tip
The great majority of client/server applications are GUI-based because the older command line interfaces are antithetical to the goals of client/server applications—easy-to-use applications.

■ Don't ask the user to remember commands. Commands should be available for the user to select, so the user can rely on recognition instead of memorization.

■ Make the interface forgiving of user errors. Destructive actions should require confirmation, and users should be able to undo or cancel the last requested action.

Standards

An established interface standard provides assurance that the guidelines have been tested for consistency and easy, efficient use. IBM, Microsoft, and Macintosh are among the available standards.

On the desktop, applications and objects are visually represented by *icons* (small graphic images). The icon is manipulated to start the program, which then displays its own window in which application-specific tasks can be performed. For example, a print monitor program can be represented by a small picture of a printer. By using a *pointer* to double-click the icon, the application can be started. The print monitor application opens a *window* in which the print queue can be viewed. Objects in the print queue can then be manipulated, for instance, canceling a print job. Icons, pointers, and windows are some elements of the graphical user interface.

When following GUI standards, the main elements to focus on are the following:

■ Icons

■ Windows

■ Scroll bars

■ Pointers and cursors

■ Controls

■ Cues

■ Help

Icons can represent the application on the desktop, a container that holds files, or the files themselves. The user can manipulate the icons directly to start applications, move and store files, or open files.

Windows display views of files and objects that can be manipulated. Windows also display messages and help information, and present choices that can be made. More than one window can be open at a time.

Several types of windows allow the most control over applications. The active window is the window in which work is being done. Sometimes the system needs more information to complete a requested action, so the system displays a secondary window. For example, if you are working in a word processing file and you select the Save action, another window pops up, asking you to name the file and specify where you want to store it. Other windows give you messages to let you know that something has happened (for example, an error occurred) or that some action is in progress.

Sometimes displayed information doesn't fit in the window. In those cases, a scroll bar can be used to page up or down through the window. For example, if you have a list of one hundred names, they most likely will not all be visible at once in the window. However, you can use the scroll bars to look at the names both above and below the names that are visible in the window.

Pointers and cursors show the user where the action will be. Objects are selected by identifying them—usually by highlighting with a cursor or choosing with a pointer (such as a mouse). Once an object is selected, you can decide whether or not you want to apply an action against it. For example, you can select an application icon on the desktop by clicking it once with a pointer. Then you can decide whether or not you want to start the application.

Controls allow the selection of choices. For example, a menu is a control. You can display the menu and select one of the choices—for instance, the Print command. Some controls allow the option of making choices by either using a pointer or typing information, which allows the most efficient work method to be used.

On-line help is a standard feature of most applications now, and yours should be no exception. Help tells the user more information about a choice, or a field, or how to perform a task. Help is usually accessed through the menu bar, although it can also be accessed through a push button or key.

So what does that mean? In application-driven programming, the application logic has predefined processing paths and can offer only limited choices to users within those paths. In event-driven programming, the application logic has no predefined paths, because there is no way to anticipate what the user will want to do. An event-driven application consists of miniprograms called

Tip
In addition to the look of the application, the client controls the feel of the program. One of the CUA standards states that users are in control of the application (event-driven programming), rather than applications controlling the users (application-driven programming).

scripts that handle possible user actions within a window. The user actions that cause events are dependent on the specific options available in the window. There are multiple events that the user can trigger at any one time. You write a script for each possible action that processes an event.

The interface options discussed so far are only a handful of the options available. By using a good standards guide, you can make sure that you offer your users the easiest, most efficient way for them to complete their work, and that your interface is consistent.

What to Watch Out For

Keep these questions (adapted from IBM's *Guide for Evaluating Applications*) in mind when you are designing the client portion of your application:

- Is your application's interface attractive, yet transparent?

- Does your application display descriptive and helpful messages?

- Does your application let you undo an action?

- Does your application address users with different skill levels?

- Does your application let you customize the user interface?

- Does your application use interface elements consistently (icons, windows, choices, controls, menus, cursors, and pointers)?

- Does your application use user input options consistently (selecting, copying, moving, creating, entering text, and scrolling)?

- Does your application provide shortcuts?

- Does your application provide contextual help?

Sending Requests

When the client sends requests to the server, the client has to format the request and send it in a way the server can understand (see fig. 5.8). But what specifically does the client have to do? What standards are available to help you? And what do you need to watch out for?

Responsibilities

The main advantage of client/server systems is that the application logic and the database are separated. Splitting the application and database logic offers the following five distinct advantages:

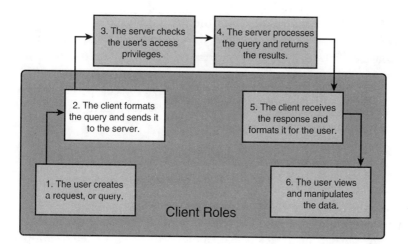

Fig. 5.8
Usually, the client requests data from a database server.

I

Introduction

- Since the bulk of the processing is done on the server, the client does not need as much power, and resources are not tied up after a request is made.

- Splitting the logic also lessens the load on the network, because the network no longer needs to transmit entire files back and forth. Using SQL reduces network traffic to queries and responses. This reduction in network traffic can be tremendous, especially on large networks with many clients.

- Users aren't limited to one client platform. SQL standardizes the queries so the data can be transferred from one platform to another transparently.

- Having the database on the server helps preserve the integrity of the data. DBMSes can provide services such as securing and protecting data, backing up data, and disk mirroring or duplexing (where data is written to two identical databases in different locations for protection). This level of data protection becomes more difficult as control becomes less centralized (as with a more distributed system).

- Transaction processing logs all the changes made to a database over a period of time to ensure that modifications are being properly recorded. The log can also be used to recover the database in the event that the system crashes.

Tip

Separating the application logic and the database gives you more flexibility when designing your application.

Tip

The database access interface essentially puts your request in an envelope, addresses it, puts a stamp on it, and mails it for you.

The database access interface is how the application submits and verifies database access requests and receives server responses. The database access interface is really made up of two parts: the actual application programming interface (API) and the stub. The application makes an SQL request, which the API prepares for the network by adding any protocol-specific statements (named pipes, for example). The stub then packages the request into a packet, ready for transmission to the server.

How the user makes the request depends on the client. Generally, the client prompts the user to enter the fields to search on, then creates the actual SQL request behind the scenes. For example, a store clerk wants to generate a list of current customers who are expecting to receive special orders that were placed over thirty days ago. The criteria for the query would include current customers expecting to receive special orders that were placed over thirty days ago.

Most likely, the application will prompt the clerk to enter something like this in the query fields:

```
Customers = Current, Status = Expecting, Date > 30 Days.
```

Remote procedure calls (RPCs) control the actual sending of the clerk's request. RPCs make designing client/server applications easier, because they make many of the network details transparent not only to the user, but also to the client operator.

> **Note**
>
> Applications that use RPCs are inherently distributed because RPCs consist of a client process and a server process.

How the data itself is distributed also affects how the data is accessed by the client. By anticipating the read and write interactions, you can determine how best to locate data so you minimize network traffic.

Data can be placed in three primary ways:

- Centralized on the server
- Placed in multiple identical copies in different locations
- Divided among several locations

Centralizing the data on the server offers the most control, because there is only one copy to access and maintain, and it contains all the necessary information. However, if the server crashes, the data is unavailable. Also, by centralizing the data, network activity increases, because everyone has to access the same data in the same area.

The main benefits of having multiple identical copies are the improvement in performance and the safety of having more than one copy in case a server crashes. When two groups of users at different nodes in the network regularly access the same information, it can improve performance significantly to have two copies of the information: one at each node.

There are two main options when there are multiple copies:

- The users can copy the required data to their own machines and work on it there.

- A database management system (DBMS) can distribute updated copies of the data at regular intervals.

Using the DBMS is more reliable than letting the users work with multiple copies of the data, because the DBMS handles the synchronization of the multiple copies of data. Letting the users copy the data they need is not adequate when you need to be sure your users are working on updated, synchronized copies of information.

Dividing data among several locations is more complex, and also less reliable. Dividing data between several locations, creates several potential problems that must be addressed. The fragmented data must be transparent to the user—in other words, the table that is divided up into segments must look like a single, whole table to the user. As a result, processing time increases, because each segment must be retrieved and put together. The table would have to be reconstructed every time the user needed more information than was available at that particular node. If one node were down, the system could not reconstruct the entire table.

Standards

Standards help design the way the client sends requests to the server. The development of the structured query language (SQL) provides a standard method for data access—in fact, SQL is the only standard method currently available. RPCs provide transparent communication between programs. Interprocess communications protocols (IPCs) provide the standards to make client/server interactions transparent to the user, and also to the client and server themselves.

> **Note**
>
> Most networks are made up of many different types and sizes of computers that have to act as a single, transparent system.

SQL lets users on client platforms develop queries to be processed on server platforms, without having to learn anything about the server operating system or DBMS.

SQL allows the following:

- A common data access method across multiple platforms.

- A common data access method across multiple applications.

- Reduction in network traffic, because instead of transferring entire files, only the requested data is returned.

SQL enforces certain database standards to enforce data integrity and protect the data. SQL also separates the database from the application, which allows partitioning of the database and application logic more easily, and also allows working with the data and the application independently.

RPCs are designed to look just like local procedure calls to the application. Once the call is made, the runtime library is responsible for finding the remote process, establishing the session, and handling the communication.

The Open Systems Interconnect (OSI) model defines an overall architecture for the complex software and hardware that make up networks. The architecture describes how machines can communicate with each other in a standardized and highly flexible way by defining layers of software that should be implemented in each communicating machine. The OSI model does not define the software itself, nor even detailed standards for that software; it simply defines the broad categories of functions that each layer should perform.

IPCs let any two applications running in the same or different environments to send and receive requests and responses.

IPCs are critical to the client because they perform the following:

- Coordinate how the client sends requests to the server and receives responses from the server.

- Control the data transfer speed between the client and the server.

- Make the server's network location transparent to the client.

In terms of the OSI model, the IPCs are responsible for the OSI transport and session layer functions of formatting, addressing, and passing outgoing packets of information. They are also responsible for receiving, verifying, and passing incoming packets of information.

A common example of an IPC used today is *named pipes*. Named pipes provides transparent communication between programs. "Named pipes" are like files that many processes can use at once. They can be write-only, read-only, or write-and-read.

> **Note**
>
> Named pipes let processes pass information to each other, and don't depend on a particular platform.

What to Watch Out For

When you are designing your application, you should pay attention to several issues. Make sure you do the following:

- Split your application wisely, so neither your client nor your server is too "fat."

- Distribute your data in the most efficient way possible. Remember that splitting data can lessen the load on the network and improve reliability, but that it increases maintenance efforts.

- Put SQL to work, creating standardized queries to your server and enforcing data integrity.

- Use RPCs to make calls to a remote procedure transparent to the user and to the client itself.

- Use an IPC like named pipes to make communication between client and server applications even more transparent.

Accepting Responses

The server checks the user's access rights, processes the query, and returns the requested data (see fig. 5.9). At that point, the client receives the results and interprets them to a format that the client can use.

The process of accepting responses is similar to the process the client uses to send requests, but in reverse. When the server responds with a return packet, the stub unpackages the results. The API then extracts the requested data and passes it to the application. In other words, instead of formatting the request and sending it to the client, the client receives the response and formats it for the user. It's that simple! The final step is letting the user view and manipulate the data (see fig. 5.10).

Fig. 5.9
Once the client receives the results from the server, it unpackages the results and translates them for the user.

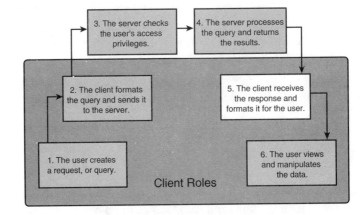

Fig. 5.10
After the user receives the requested information, the user can then view it or make another request.

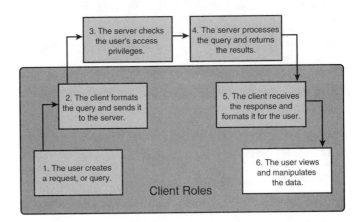

Once the data is returned, the odds are that the client is going to want to take some action. At that point, the application re-adopts its first role: providing an easy-to-use interface to accept input and display output.

From Here ...

Now that you know what a client is and what to watch out for when you create one, you need to know what a server is. In the next chapter, you'll learn what a server is, what the different types of servers are, what responsibilities a server has, and what makes a good server.

For more information on the topics in this chapter, please refer to the following chapters:

- Chapter 6, "Responsibilities of a Server," discusses what makes up a server, what the role of the server is in the client/server process, and what responsibilities the server has.

- Chapter 11, "Techniques for Developing RPC Clients and Servers," helps you develop powerful client code and shows you how to handle all types of client and server errors.

- Chapter 15, "Techniques for Developing DCE Clients and Servers," discusses binding a client to a server and how to customize the client/server interface.

Introduction

Chapter 6

Responsibilities of a Server

In the last chapter, you learned what components make up a client, what the client's role is in the client/server process, and what responsibilities the client has. In this chapter, you come to understand the client/server process from the server's point of view: what the client expects from the server, what processes invoke the server, and how the server responds to the client.

In this chapter, you learn the following:

- What exactly is a server?

- What is the server's role in the client/server process?

- What responsibilities does the server have?

Understanding Server Components

While the client takes most of the credit, since that is what the user interacts with, the server is the heart of the client/server system. Servers are where data is stored and shared tasks are performed. Today, a server can be any kind of computer—from a PC to a minicomputer to a mainframe. However, the increase in power and decrease in cost of PCs and minicomputers generally make them the more cost-effective choice. Even if the server is a standard PC or a minicomputer, what makes it different from a standard system is that it is specialized and has certain responsibilities.

Servers can be divided into six types:

- File servers

- Application servers

- Data servers

- Compute servers

- Database servers

- Resource or communications servers

> **Note**
>
> Servers can be considered to be event-driven, because essentially the server is in a waiting state until it gets a request from the client.

The type of server used depends on the task requested. Also, remember that these six roles can be combined on one system or divided among several. For example, the same machine might serve as an application server and a database server.

Most servers used in businesses today are file servers (see fig. 6.1). File servers let clients access files and share data and software. These servers are most often PCs or one-processor UNIX systems. Many people can access the file server at a time, which means the server should have multiple disk drives and network adapter cards, but only one person should access a particular file at a time.

Fig. 6.1
File servers provide storage and data services for non-database applications.

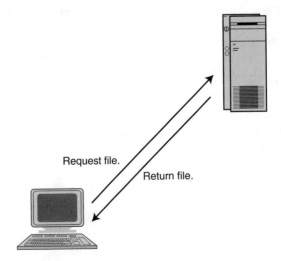

Request file.

Return file.

Application servers run application software, which is crucial when you are distributing application logic between your client and server (see fig. 6.2). Putting applications on the server means they are available to many clients. Multiple clients can then use remote procedure calls (RPCs) to invoke a process on the server. Several application servers may even work together to answer the client's request. Each server might run a different operating system on a different hardware platform, but these details are transparent to the client—the client can make requests without considering the type of machine that will respond.

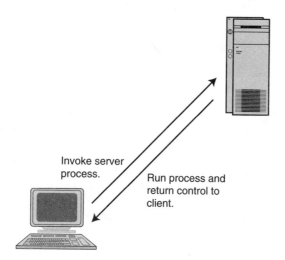

Fig. 6.2
Application servers run the server part of your client/server application.

Invoke server process.

Run process and return control to client.

Data servers are used only for data storage and management, and are used in conjunction with compute servers. These servers search and validate data, but generally don't transmit large amounts of data over the network. Compute servers pass client requests for data to data servers, and then forward the results of the requests back to the client.

Database servers are typical of client/server systems, and they have the same job as the data and the compute server put together (see fig. 6.3). Database servers run database management system (DBMS) software and most likely some of the client/server application logic—which means that this type of server needs the most power. The DBMS provides specialized services required of database products: the ability to roll back and recover data, manage space, reorganize tables, lock records, and manage the data. Servers that combine the functions of the database server and the application server are also known as *transaction servers*.

Tip
Of all the servers, the database server needs the most power.

Fig. 6.3
Database servers
are managed by
database manage-
ment systems such
as Sybase and
Oracle.

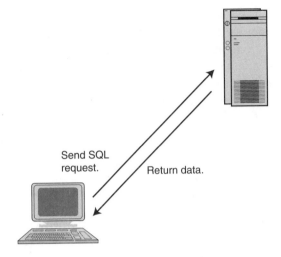

Send SQL
request.

Return data.

An easy way to distinguish between an application server, a database server, and a transaction server is how the client makes requests of the server. Servers receive the following types of requests from clients:

- Application servers take some kind of non-database-centered action in response to a client request.

- Database servers return data in response to a single SQL request from the client.

> **Note**
>
> Relational databases introduced the Structured Query Language (SQL). SQL lets you perform searches without having to know anything about the structure of the data. SQL has been accepted by the computer industry as the standard data-access language because of its capability to make databases transparent.

Tip
Client/server
applications that
use transaction
servers are called
*on-line transaction
processing* (OLTP)
applications, and
tend to have
stringent security
and data integrity
requirements.

- Transaction servers return data in response to a message that consists of a group of SQL statements. The group is called a *transaction*, and the transaction succeeds or fails as a unit.

Resource servers, which include communications servers, let many clients access particular resources that are typically too expensive to dedicate to one client (see fig. 6.4). For example, print servers connect many clients to several printers. Communications servers connect remote systems. Other resource servers might connect clients with other devices, such as multimedia resources. Usually, since resource servers are dedicated to a particular device, they don't need as much power as servers providing more complex services.

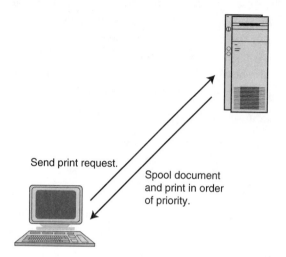

Fig. 6.4
Resource servers
let clients access
shared resources
such as printers.

Of the six types of servers, client/server applications usually use application, database, or transaction servers—or some combination of the three—the most. For our purposes, we will concentrate on those two.

To design the server portion of an application, also known as the *back end*, you need to understand the various components that make up the server (see fig. 6.5). The hardware, the operating system, the network, the database, and the software all need to support and work with your application.

Tip
The term *server* is
used in this chap-
ter to refer to any
machine that
responds to a
client request.

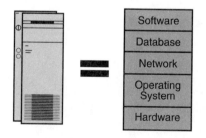

Fig. 6.5
The server consists
of hardware, the
operating system,
the network, the
database, and the
software.

Hardware

No special hardware turns a machine into a server, although particular servers do have certain requirements. You should choose the server platform based on the applications you are running and the cost-effectiveness of the machine.

In traditional computing, the "server" was the mainframe host and the "clients" were nonprogrammable terminals (NPTs). All functionality and data was kept on the host. I put the terms *server* and *clients* in quotes in this case because they were not true client/server systems. The NPT did not actually request services of the host, because all functionality, including the requesting and responding processes, were on the host. The NPT simply presented an interface to the host application. With true client/server systems, the server can be on one of any number of platforms.

The primary characteristics of the server are the following:

- The server can respond to simultaneous requests for service from multiple clients.

- The server is reliable, because the clients depend on it.

- The server is upwardly scalable, because client/server applications tend to need more and more memory and processing power.

Until recently, PC technology has been considered sufficient only for simple file servers or device servers. The more complex servers were either midrange or mainframe servers. Now, however, PCs rival the more expensive machines with fast, powerful systems.

A good configuration for a small PC server might be a tower that includes the following:

- 100 mHz CPU

- 32 MB RAM

- 2 GB of storage on two or more drives

- Multiple network adapters

- Six bus slots

A larger PC server might include the following:

- Multiple processors

- Error checking and correcting (ECC) memory

- Bus parity checking

- Performance and systems management features

- Twelve bus slots

- 64-bit interprocessor bus

- 28 to 280 GB of disk space

- Disk mirroring capabilities

When you recommend to your users what kind of server they need, don't underestimate their need. You don't want to recommend something and then find that they need to upgrade right after they set up the system. Because servers are the heart of the client/server system, they require more thought than the clients.

You need to consider some specific issues:

- Processor speed

- Number of processors

- Memory

- Storage

- Reliability

- Scalability

- Support

Ask yourself the following questions:

- How fast a processor does the application need? What is the optimum processor speed for performance? What type of processor does the application run on, a Pentium or RISC?

- What operating system is being written for support of multiple processors? Does the application need them?

- What amount of data is the application capable of handling? The user is the only one who can decide how much storage space is needed, but you should recommend that they get three times the amount they think they will need. Servers tend to be greedy. Also, multiple disks improve both performance and reliability.

- What happens if the server fails? Do the users need disk mirroring capabilities or redundant servers?

- How easy is it to upgrade the hardware? How much upgrade is possible? For example, what is the maximum amount of RAM supported—32 MB?

Operating System

Server operating systems manage the computer's resources, control application execution, and act as shields between the server applications and the clients.

You'll remember from the last chapter that operating systems:

- Control the management of the resources that move, store, process, and control data.

- Load instructions and data into main memory, initialize files and I/O devices, and prepare resources.

- Control access to files, including the data format and availability, as well as access to shared resources.

- Provide the instructions and control signals for various I/O devices.

- Control access to the system as a whole.

Servers for client/server applications work best when their operating system (OS) supports preemptive multitasking, prioritizing, interprocess communications, multi-threaded processing, memory management, application isolation, and extended services.

Each of these features is described as follows:

- *Preemptive multitasking* prevents a single task from taking over the server by letting the server operating system handle the task switching. If the server does not control the amount of time used for processing a client request, one client could monopolize the resources and prevent the server from responding to other clients.

- *Prioritizing* lets the server assign priority levels to tasks, and take care of the most important tasks first. For example, a bank teller requesting confirmation of a customer's account has a higher priority than a daily batch report request.

- *Interprocess communications* (IPCs) are what allow independent processes to share and exchange data, whether or not those processes are local (on the same machine) or remote (on other machines). IPCs make local and remote calls transparent to the application.

- *Multi-threaded processing* lets the server process more than one request at a time by setting up different paths, or *threads*, that the server can manage. By managing these threads, the server can process requests almost concurrently.

- *Memory management* determines how the server uses memory efficiently, and lets the server swap large programs and data objects in and out of memory.

- *Application isolation* keeps applications separate, so an action or error in one application does not affect any other application.

- *Extended services* provide advanced system software that can really exploit the potential of client/server systems. Some of these services include enhanced communications, binary large object (BLOB) support, network directories, authentication and authorization abilities, transaction monitors, object broker services, and more.

All four of the main operating systems in the server market are serious competitors. They all are 32-bit or higher systems that run on PCs and other hardware. The four main server operating systems are as follows:

- NetWare
- Windows NT
- OS/2
- UNIX

You might ask why I am bringing up NetWare here, when it's a network operating system. Well, NetWare isn't necessarily only a network operating system. NetWare is self-contained, which means it does not require another OS to run. You can use NetWare alone on file servers, print servers, and other device and communications servers. However, for client/server systems, NetWare alone does not have all of the features you need. However, keep an eye on Novell, because NetWare and UNIX are teaming up.

> **Note**
>
> Although NetWare has its own widely supported protocols, IPX/SPX, NetWare now also supports TCP/IP.

Here are three problems you'll encounter with NetWare 3.x that have been resolved in NetWare 4.x:

- NetWare doesn't have preemptive multitasking or prioritizing capabilities. A relatively unimportant client request can tie up the server for a long time, preventing the server from addressing the requests of other clients.

- NetWare does not support multi-threaded processing, which is a must for remote procedure calls and for multitasking.

■ Memory management capabilities are not sufficient for client/server applications. NetWare does not support virtual memory and, as a result, running out of memory and encountering memory conflicts are realistic threats.

We talked about OS/2 as a client operating system in the last chapter, but OS/2 can also be an effective server operating system. OS/2 can create a totally compatible LAN, where clients and servers run the same family of operating systems: OS/2, DOS, and Windows. And, as we discussed in the last chapter, OS/2 supports preemptive multitasking, prioritizing, interprocess communications, multi-threaded processing, memory management, application isolation, and extended services.

Windows NT (NT for short) is the "new kid on the block" and challenges all the existing operating systems. NT is a preemptive multitasking operating system that supports multi-threaded processing. NT uses a flat memory model, and can support up to 4 GB of RAM. NT runs DOS, 16-bit and 32-bit Windows, and 16-bit OS/2 applications. (However, NT does not run NetWare, which is a big drawback.)

Other features include:

■ Support for large amounts of storage

■ NT file system (NTFS), DOS, FAT, and HPFS (NTFS maintains a transaction log of all file accesses, which allows the recovery of lost data)

■ A variety of protocols, including TCP/IP, IPX/SPX, NetBios, named pipes, and more

■ Remote procedure calls (RPCs)

■ Resource sharing, including printers and files

■ System management, including statistics gathering and network configuration

■ A fault-tolerant system

■ Processor independence

■ Support for POSIX

■ LAN Manager and remote access services

As these features show, NT is a good operating system with lots of functionality. However, the true test of its success will be time.

UNIX is a multitasking operating system that was developed in the early 1970s by AT&T. Its advantage over the other systems is its power—a UNIX server can handle four to five times the number of users per server that a PC server can handle. UNIX, along with Windows NT, fully supports symmetrical multiprocessors on multiple platforms.

UNIX claims to be the only truly platform-independent operating system, and that would make a great operating system for client/server applications. However, as good as that sounds, UNIX has run into one problem that does not affect DOS and OS/2: prepackaged, or "off-the-shelf," software is not available for UNIX. The software must be compiled and linked for the specific target platform, which means that a company would have to buy a version of the software for each target platform—and continuing support for less popular platforms is not guaranteed. However, plans for a unified UNIX are in the works, which may make prepackaged UNIX software possible.

Table 6.1 compares the features of the operating systems discussed so far.

Table 6.1   Requirements of Your Operating System

Required of OS	NetWare 3.x/4.x	Windows NT	OS/2	UNIX
Preemptive Multitasking	N/Y	Y	Y	Y
Prioritizing	N/Y	Y	Y	Y
IPCs	N/Y	Y	Y	Y
Threads	N/Y	Y	Y	Y
Memory Management	N/Y	Y	Y	Y
Application Isolation	N	Y	Y	Y
Off-the-Shelf Software Available	Y/Y	Y	Y	N

Windows NT, OS/2, and UNIX are all very powerful operating systems. Currently, OS/2 and UNIX are the two most popular OSes, but Windows NT is generating a great deal of interest.

Network

The network operating system (NOS) is installed on the server, although part of it does run on the client. The NOS connects the server operating system with the network, which means the client accesses the server through the NOS without being "aware" that the server is a remote process. In other words, the remote process appears to the client to be just like a local process.

The two major network operating systems are:

■ NetWare

■ LAN Manager

Novell NetWare is a self-contained operating system, which means that it does not need another operating system, such as OS/2 or UNIX, to run on a server. While it is an excellent file and print server operating system, NetWare has needed external database server software from companies like Sybase and Oracle to function as a database server. However, by operating in conjunction with the server operating system—usually Windows, OS/2, UNIX, VMS, or MVS—NetWare can provide most of the necessary database server functionality.

Microsoft's LAN Manager NOS is good for file and print servers, but does not handle the same degree of complexity as NetWare. LAN Manager does require a native operating system—usually OS/2, UNIX, or Windows NT. Because the servers are transparent to clients, clients may access data from both NetWare and LAN Manager servers at the same time.

Database

Databases have evolved through several stages since the 1960s: from flat files to hierarchical databases, relational databases, and finally object-oriented databases (see fig. 6.6).

Fig. 6.6
DB2 and Sybase are two examples of database management systems.

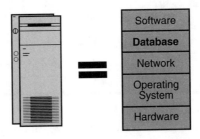

The original flat files provided data through punch cards or disk files that simulated punch cards. Records were physically stored in the same order the user viewed them. Sorting records meant copying records from one location to another, eliminating unnecessary columns, and presenting a new view for the user. Many large organizations, primarily financial institutions, still use flat files to run batch reports and batch processing.

Hierarchical databases were able to store records either physically or logically next to each other. Related data was usually stored physically close together, and index pointers allowed navigation from one record to the next. Indexes were the tool that allowed access to data in logical, rather than physical, order. However, indexes still relied on the physical location of the data. If you wanted to change the structure of the data, you had to manually change the index. If you changed the index, you had to manually update all the applications that referred to the index. The more complicated data access became, the more difficult it became to navigate through the database.

Relational databases are the standard database used today. They allow access to data using extracted indexes, which eliminate the need for navigating that database or re-sorting flat files. For performance reasons, related data is still stored close together as much as possible.

Object-oriented databases are the next logical step from relational databases. They allow even more complex data to be manipulated simply by using encapsulating processing logic.

Software

Where the client may very well run applications in addition to yours, the server most likely will not. The software on the server will be the server OS, the NOS, and the server portion of the client/server application (see fig. 6.7).

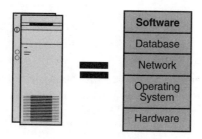

Fig. 6.7
The software portion of the client/server application is the final component that makes up the server.

Usually, the server application logic provides search, calculation, and prioritization services so that the server can respond to clients' requests for data appropriately. See the following section for a more detailed discussion.

Understanding the Server's Role

The client/server process can be simplified into the following steps:

1. The user sends a request, or query, through the client to the server.

2. The server listens for the client's request.

3. Once the server hears the request, it checks the user's access privileges.

4. The server processes the query.

5. The server returns the results to the client.

6. The client receives the results and displays them to the user.

Tip

Any process that
provides a service
in response to a
request is a server.

Out of these six steps, the server plays four major roles. The server is the heart of the client/server application, as we've said before. The server exists to answer the needs of the client, and the client depends on the reliability and timely response of the server.

The server must perform the following functions:

- Listen for the client's request.

- Check a user's privileges.

- Process the request.

- Return the results.

The server doesn't initiate any action. Instead, the server waits passively and listens for client requests to arrive over the network. The server must always respond to clients, even when multiple clients are making simultaneous requests.

Once the server hears from the client, the server must make sure the client is authorized to receive the data or response. If the client is not authorized, the server rejects the request and sends a message to the client. If the client is authorized, the server goes ahead and processes the request.

Processing the request involves receiving the client's request, converting the packet into a form the server can use, and processing the request itself.

When processing is complete, the server packages the results, and sends them back to the client. The client can then translate and use the data.

Now that we know what the server does—at least at a high level—let's get more specific. Within each of those four roles, what does the server have to do?

Understanding Server Distribution

There is no predefined "split" in responsibilities for client/server applications. You can decide where to divide the application depending on your needs. The *fat client* model places more function on the client, and the *fat server* model places more function on the server (see fig. 6.8). Application and transaction servers tend to be fat servers, while database and file servers tend to have fat clients.

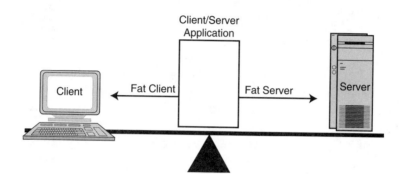

Fig. 6.8
Where you distribute your applications determines whether or not you have a fat client or a fat server.

> **Note**
>
> Fat servers are easier to maintain because most of the code is centralized on the server, instead of distributed among the clients. Also, fat servers are faster than fat clients.

No matter how you split your application, the server's basic responsibility remains the same: serve the clients that make requests.

Listening for the Client's Request

The server doesn't initiate any interaction with the client—the server simply waits for the client to make a request (see fig. 6.9). When the client does make a request, the server responds as quickly as possible.

The network adapter card physically connects the server to the network, and determines whether or not incoming packets are meant for the adapter's node. If they are, the protocol accepts them and decodes the packets so the server can process the request.

Fig. 6.9
The server waits
passively for client
requests.

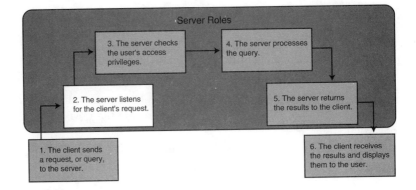

Checking a User's Privileges

Once the server hears from the client, the server must make sure the user is
authorized to receive the data or response from the server (see fig. 6.10). If
the user isn't authorized, the server rejects the request and sends a message to
the client. If the user is authorized, the server goes ahead and processes the
request.

Fig. 6.10
The server has to
make sure the user
is authorized to
make the request.

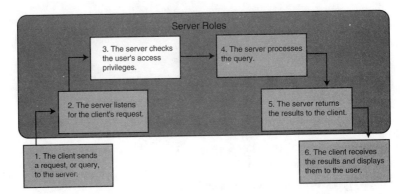

Processing the Request

The server must be able to respond to the client's request immediately. If
multiple clients are making requests simultaneously, the server needs to be
able to prioritize client requests and process multiple requests at the same
time (see fig. 6.11). But what specifically does the server have to do? What
standards are available? And what do you need to watch out for?

Once the server confirms that the user is authorized to make requests of the
server, the server can unpack the request and process it.

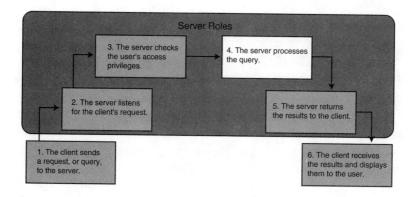

Fig. 6.11
The server
processes the
client's request.

The request could be any one of the following four types:

■ A remote request is a single data request from a single client.

■ A remote transaction contains multiple data requests from a single client.

■ A distributed transaction contains multiple data requests from a single client for data residing on multiple servers.

■ A distributed request is a transaction made up of multiple data requests from multiple clients for data residing on multiple servers.

These requests must pass what's called the ACID test: Atomicity, Consistency, Isolation, and Durability. Atomicity means the entire transaction must succeed or fail—it cannot be partially completed. Consistency means the system goes from one steady state to another steady state. Isolation means that, until a transaction completes successfully, its effects are not evident to other transactions. Durability means that once a transaction completes successfully, it is permanently committed to the system and subsequent failures will not affect it. If the transaction fails, the system is rolled back to the state it was in before it tried to process the transaction.

Tip
All requests that are part of a simple transaction must complete successfully, or none should.

This transaction management is controlled by either the DBMS or the transaction processing manager (TPM). Transaction managers protect the integrity of the data—which is an absolute requirement. The server is responsible for protecting and maintaining the accuracy of the data.

Let's get back now to the client's request. The request may simply ask for data, or it may also invoke a stored procedure. Stored procedures improve performance because they are already compiled on the host and are ready to execute. Also, they reduce network traffic. An example of a stored procedure is a trigger: if a sale is entered in a store's database, that action might trigger the server process to add the amount of the sale to a "total amount sold" value.

In terms of the Open Systems Interconnect (OSI) model, interprocess communications protocols (IPCs) provide the standards to make client/server interactions transparent to the client and server themselves. The IPCs are responsible for the OSI transport and session layer functions of formatting, addressing, and passing outgoing packets of information. They are also responsible for accepting incoming packets from the network, verifying the format and accuracy of their contents, and passing the resulting request to the session layer.

The standardized query language (SQL) is the standard data access method in client/server applications. SQL includes the following components:

- Data definition language

- Data manipulation language

- Data control language

The data definition language defines data structures, the data manipulation language moves and updates data, and the data control language defines access and security restraints. SQL processes data in sets. That way, the server can send multiple records to satisfy the client's request. SQL can also filter, transform, or combine data before sending it to the client.

Two standards govern relational databases and remote data access: IBM's Distributed Relational Database Architecture (DRDA), and ISO's Remote Data Access (RDA). DRDA provides a common protocol, and uses SQL as the common access language for connecting applications and DBMSes. The RDA protocol uses a subset of SQL as a common transfer syntax, and creates an environment that focuses on heterogeneous interoperability. Phew!

Returning the Results

When the server finishes processing the results and is ready to return the results to the client, it has to format the results and send them in a way the client can understand (see fig. 6.12).

The server hands the data over to the protocol, which addresses a packet, formats the data to put into the packet, and passes the packet to the network. The network then makes sure that the packet goes to the client.

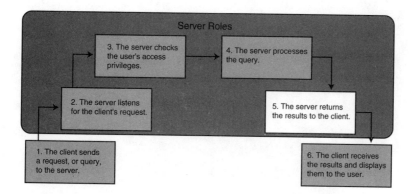

Fig. 6.12
The server returns
the results to the
client.

Introduction

From Here...

Now that you know what a client is, what a server is, and how client/server applications work, you are ready to get into the specifics.

For more information on the topics in this chapter, please refer to the following chapters:

- Chapter 11, "Techniques for Developing RPC Clients and Servers," helps you develop powerful client code and shows you how to handle all types of client and server errors.

- Chapter 15, "Techniques for Developing DCE Clients and Servers," discusses binding a client to a server and how to customize the client/server interface.

Part II

Introduction to RPC

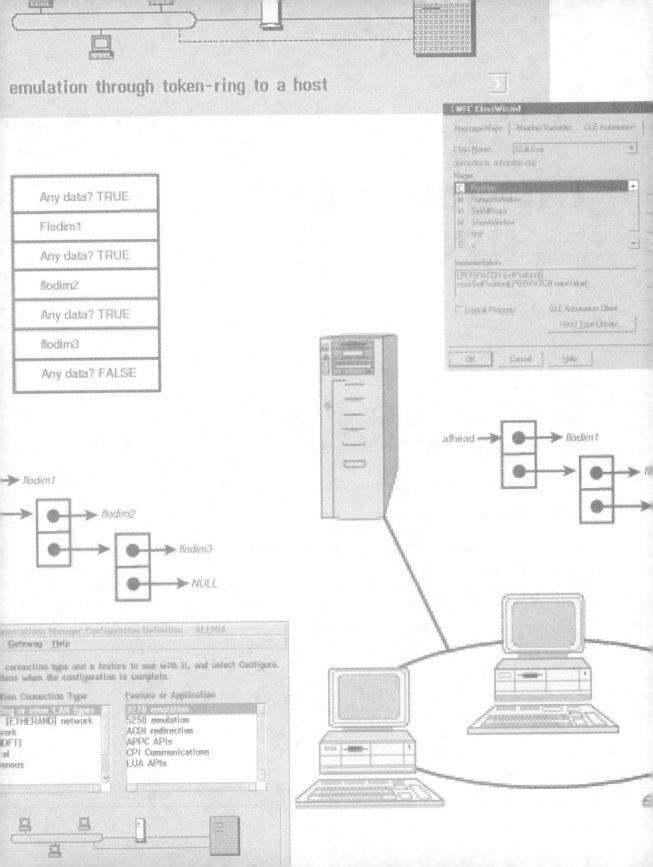

Chapter 7

What are Remote Procedure Calls?

Remote procedure calls, also known as *RPCs*, allow a client to communicate with a server in order to execute procedures. RPCs are used in distributed system utilities like NIS and NFS. RPC is also a user programming tool that is easier to program than low-level network sockets. They make the client/server model more powerful.

> **Note**
>
> Network File Service (NFS) was one of the first services built on top of the ONC RPC. It uses the Network Information Service (NIS), formerly known as Yellow Pages. NFS is a facility for sharing files in a mixed environment of operating systems, computers, and networks. NIS is a network service which provides access network wide data regardless of the location of the client or server.

This chapter contains a general discussion of RPCs. When creating applications that use RPCs, you will typically use a specific set of RPC tools—for example, Open Software Foundation's Distributed Computing Environment (OSF DCE) RPC, Sun Microsystems Open Network Computing (ONC) RPC, or Microsoft RPC. Some vendors, like Microsoft, have designed their RPCs to be compatible with OSF's DCE RPC.

The most important properties of a remote procedure call, as defined by OSF, are the following:

- Simplicity—RPCs follow the local procedure call model used in traditional applications.

- Transparency—RPCs are independent of network protocols.

- Performance—Use of RPCs shouldn't cause any performance loss in your system.

This chapter talks about how RPCs fit in with distributed computing and the client/server model and describe basic RPC concepts. You will find these concepts are useful when you begin using specific vendor RPC tools. In this chapter, you learn about the following:

- Distributed computing and the client/server model

- How RPCs are used in the client/server model

- Typical parts of an RPC application

RPCs, Distributed Computing, and the Client/Server Model

RPCs and the client/server model really fall under the broad category of *distributed computing*. In order to understand the model and the communication technologies, you need to look at the overall structure of the distributed computing paradigm. Before I talk more about RPCs, let's briefly go over what distributed computing and client/server mean, and what they do for you.

Distributed Computing

Distributed computing refers to two or more computers, communicating over a network, which accomplish some computing task. The machines can have the same operating system and processor, or a combination of operating systems and CPUs. The network can connect computers sitting side-by-side, or halfway around the world from each other.

By using distributed computing, you can more efficiently use your computing resources. Data and resources can be shared among many users, enhancing productivity. Special purpose functionality can be centralized, eliminating the need for duplication on all machines. For example, users can share access to a printer, extract data from a network database and process it locally, or distribute the load of computationally complex problems across several computers.

Connecting workstations to a network also allows for more flexibility and reliability. If more resources are needed, they can be added without the need for replacing the whole system. Greater reliability can be gained by selectively duplicating functionality and data. For instance, if you have multiple printers, and one needs to be taken off-line, the other printers can still be used by users. Similarly, if data is available on more than one computer, users will still be able to access the data even if one or more machines is unavailable.

Client/Server

Client/server is a popular model for distributed processing (see fig. 7.1). In this model, two different sets of code, known as the *client* and the *server*, are produced. These parts are typically located on different systems connected by a network, although the parts may exist on the same computer.

Fig. 7.1
This is a diagram of the client/server model.

The client part of the application makes a distributed request and receives an answer. The server part of the application receives and executes the distributed request. In this method of computing, a server controls access to resources which can be requested by a client. The resource(s) controlled by a server can be any computing resource—for example, a database, a program, or some other type of service.

A typical client/server example involves a print server. If you are running on a network and decide you want to print your latest program, the editor or word processor you are using sends a request (client) to the print server (server). The print server then controls having your text printed.

You should note that client and server can be in relative rather than absolute terms. A server can also be a client. For instance, the print server is a client when sending a request to a file server to have your file downloaded to a printer. Another example of a client/server environment is a Novell NetWare and LAN Manager network. In these networks, the file server provides storage and security services to client workstations.

The server which the client accesses is usually a continuously running daemon process. A *daemon process* is a background process that is dedicated to a particular task. It waits for a request, executes it, returns an answer, and waits for another request. This allows the server to continuously scan for client requests. The client makes a request to the server and the server sends a response back to the client (see fig. 7.2).

Fig. 7.2
A distributed request and reply client/server model.

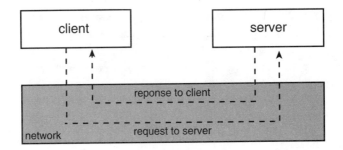

The client is usually implemented as a library. This library is usually linked directly into the application, or in the case of OS/2 or Microsoft Windows, as a dynamic link library (DLL). It consists of a call to a routine that executes, by sending a request over the network to a server and then receiving the result. The client then goes on with the rest of the program.

Writing an application that works in a client/server environment usually requires a knowledge of network communications and interprocess communication (IPC) mechanisms. IPCs are a way of sharing data between processes. For example, in a Novell environment, you use the IPX/SPX protocols to talk to a file server. In a multiplatform network, things quickly get complicated as you will most likely have to work with incompatible protocols.

RPCs and the Client/Server Model

So how do RPCs fit in with the client/server model? Well, one way of implementing communications between the client and server sides of an application is to use remote procedure calls (RPCs). Using RPCs, the client makes a procedure call which looks like a local call from the client's perspective. The procedure call is translated into network communications by the underlying RPC code, and the server receives the request. Once the server receives the request, it executes the procedure and the server returns the results to the client.

> **Note**
>
> RPCs provide a simple way for the programmer to handle network communication details in a client/server model. By using RPCs, most of the details of the network communications portion are hidden from the programmer.

RPC provides you with a network-independent IPC mechanism and frees you from having to deal with low-level sockets. This means you can keep network communication details out of application code, making it more portable. Each side behaves, as much as possible, as it would in a traditional application.

The client programmer issues a call, and the server programmer writes a procedure to carry out the desired function. To convey the illusion you are working in a single address space, hidden code handles the networking. This code handles the details relating to network protocols and transport mechanisms. RPCs can also provide the code to handle error causing conditions such as lost connections, time-outs, and network failures.

IPC and Sockets

Interprocess communication (IPC) is simply a way for processes to communicate, either locally or on networked computers. RPC makes use of IPC mechanisms; in fact, IPC mechanisms alone are enough to implement network applications. In some cases, such as when services are available locally, it makes sense to develop a simple socket-based client/server rather than a full RPC application. Some disadvantages of IPCs are that they can be hard to use, and communication can occur in potentially machine-dependent fashions.

A *socket* is an IPC channel of communication. The endpoints of a socket communications link are referenced by descriptors, similar to the way file descriptors allow access to a file. Once connected via a socket, processes can read and write information through these communication channels.

RPC Applications

Now that you've seen how RPCs fit in with distributed computing and client/server, lets talk more about RPC details.

RPCs provide the ability to call procedures outside of a local address space. This means a client can execute procedures on other networked computers or servers. In other words, the client and server run as two separate processes; therefore, they do not have to run on the same machine (although they can). To you, making an RPC call looks like a local procedure call.

In a *local procedure call*, code segments are usually in the same address space on the same machine. Arguments and return values can be passed on the process's stack.

In a remote procedure call, the procedure runs in a different address space, usually on a different computer. Arguments and return values must be packaged into messages and sent over the network. RPCs transparently handle the network details. The net effect of this is that the remote procedure call looks a local procedure call when you are coding the client application.

Stubs

RPCs use a request and reply communication model. The client sends a request message to the server procedure, which then returns reply messages. The actual mechanism for accomplishing communication is via *stubs*. Stubs contain functions mapping simple local procedure calls into a series of network RPC function calls. They are the communication interface implementing the RPC protocol and also specify how messages are constructed and exchanged.

Both client and server communicate via stubs; one for the client, the other for the server. To create stubs, a protocol compiler (like OSF's ONC RPCGEN) or interface definition language (IDL) compiler (like Apollo/HP's NCS NIDL or Microsoft's MIDL) is typically used. The generated stubs are then linked with the client and server programs.

The client stub calls procedures using the RPC library to find a remote process. It packages, or *marshals*, the arguments to the call, transmits the data to the server, and waits for the server's reply. The client stub can also find an appropriate server for the client. The remote process listens to the network via the server stub. The server stub unpacks, or *unmarshals*, the arguments, calls the required procedure, marshals the results, and sends the reply to the client. The server stub can also take care of differences in data representation by performing conversions. Let's look at this process in detail:

1. The client sends a request to the server. In the client application code, this looks like a local procedure. It looks like a local call because it's actually a call to a client stub.

2. The client stub communicates with the server stub using the RPC runtime library. The RPC runtime library is a standard set of runtime routines that handles the actual transport of data.

3. The server's RPC runtime library receives the RPC and sends the information to the server stub.

4. The server stub then activates the remote procedure in the server application.

5. When the remote procedure finishes execution, the server stub sends a reply to the client stub, again by using the RPC runtime library.

6. Finally, the client stub returns to the client application code.

Figure 7.3 shows how the RPC processes communicate via stubs.

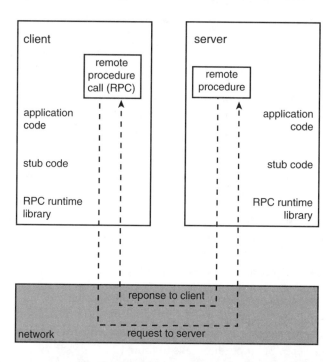

Fig. 7.3
RPC communication via stubs.

II

Introduction to RPC

Marshaling

During a remote procedure call, marshaling is the process of packaging data for transmission to a remote process. When the data arrives at the remote process, it undergoes an unmarshaling process to unpackage the data. If the data format of the sender and receiver are different, the receiver's stub converts the data into the correct format for that system and passes the data to the application.

For example, in the OSF DCE RPC, marshaling converts data into a byte stream format and packages it for transmission using a Network Data Representation (NDR). NDR enables you to share data between systems with different data formats. It handles differences in character representation (ASCII vs. EBCDIC), byte order (big-endian vs. little-endian), and other potential incompatibilities.

Clients and servers must be able to communicate using machine-independent data representation. Otherwise, you are bound to a single operating system. For example, the ONC RPC uses a standard data representation format known as *External Data Representation*, or *XDR*. In XDR, the client and the server stubs translate data into and out of this format. If you are using a protocol or interface definition compiler, you can specify the service procedures and data structures to be exchanged and leave the translation processing to the stubs.

Binding

How does a remote procedure call on a client find the server it needs? To find the right server, the client must create a binding, and load it with the information that lets the RPC runtime library find the server. A *binding* is logical association between a client and a server.

There are several types of binding methods, including the following:

- *Automatic binding*—where the client stub automatically manages bindings after a remote procedure call is made. It is the easiest type of binding because it handles the complexity of binding management for you. However, if a particular server is not needed, or security is an issue, you will need to use another type of binding.

- *Explicit binding*—where you write application code to obtain binding information and set the binding handle with RPC runtime calls. Each remote procedure call is handled separately. It is useful when you need to make remote procedure calls to more than one server.

- *Implicit binding*—where you write application code to obtain binding information and set the global binding handle with RPC runtime calls. The binding handle is in the global area of the client stub. This method gives you control over binding management without it being visible in the remote procedure call. It is useful when you need a particular server for most remote procedure calls.

Binding information typically includes the following:

- A *protocol sequence*—which is an RPC specific name. This name describes the combination of network of network communication used between the client and server. For example, a name could contain values that specify whether the connection is connection-oriented or connectionless, and the type of network and transport protocols.

- A *server host*—which is the network address or name of the host on which the server application resides. This allows the client to identify a server system.

- An *endpoint*—which is a number representing a specific server process running on a server host system. This allows the client to identify a server process running on a particular system. With TCP/IP, the actual value of the endpoint is typically a port number.

Developing an Application

When creating RPC clients and servers, one advantage is that the underlying IPC is hidden. Unless you want to, you don't have to deal with how the sockets are being used, or any network or host databases. All you need to know are the host and procedure names. The following is an overview of steps needed to create an RPC-based application:

1. Develop the interface definition. In this step, you need to decide how the client and server are going to communicate and what functions and data types will be used.

2. Specify the protocol to be used for client/server communication. This step defines the interface between the client and the server and establishes a framework for application development.

   If you use a protocol compiler (such as NIDL for OSF/NCS, ONC RPCGEN, or Netwise RPCTOOL), you identify the name of service procedures and the data types of parameters and return arguments in a protocol definition. The protocol compiler reads the definition and automatically generates the client and server stubs.

3. Develop the client and server programs.

4. Compile the programs.

5. Link the generated stubs and libraries.

6. Test and debug the programs. To test, launch the server on a remote machine and run the client application locally.

A Debugging Tip

Debugging a distributed application can be difficult. Exactly where does the problem come from? It can be difficult to tell. Using the similarity between local and remote procedure call models, you can do some initial testing. By linking the service procedures directly with the client side of your application, you can test and debug parameter passing and overall functionality without RPC calls or the network. This enables you to discover and fix bugs before you distribute the application. You can also narrow down problems faster once the application is distributed, because you've already tested a portion of the code. However, you may need to use preprocessor directives in your client and server code to make the linking possible.

To develop an RPC application, you need to write and compile an *interface definition*. It is similar to a module or library in a conventional programming language. Like selecting functions from a library, client application programmers use interface definitions to figure out how to call remote procedures. Server application programmers use interface definitions to figure out the data type of the remote procedures return value and the data types, number, and order of its arguments.

The interface is typically written in an *Interface Definition Language* (IDL). Many IDLs use a syntax similar to C, with additional attributes for network communication. *Attributes* are special keywords which provide information that helps distribute an application. The interface definition also includes a *universal unique identifier* (UUID). A UUID is a unique number that identifies something, like an interface, across all network configurations. The same UUID is used in both the client and the server, allowing them to locate one another. For example, a UUID attribute allows a client to locate a specific remote procedure on a particular server. Once the interface definition is created, it's then compiled to generate header and stub files. These files are then linked with the client and server application code.

The interface definition contains the data type definitions and procedure declarations that are shared between the client and the server. It specifies the operations a server *exports*, or makes available, to clients. Each procedure declaration contains the name of a procedure, the data type of the value it returns (if any), and the order and data type of the remote procedure. It contains the procedure declarations and data types which both client and server can use.

An interface definition file makes it easier to scale up development to multiple servers and clients for those servers because notable features of the distributed application are located in a single file.

After the interface definition file is created, it is compiled to generate the following files:

- A header file containing definitions needed by the client and server stubs, as well as for the application code (to be included in the client and server code)

- A client stub file to be linked with the client portion of the application

- A server stub file to be linked with the server portion of the application

- Client and server auxiliary stub files to be linked with the client and server portions of the application (for example, these files might convert complex data structures like pointers to and from a data stream suitable for transmission over the network)

Figure 7.4 shows typical pieces in the RPC programming process. You should note that a number of these pieces are generated for you when using an IDL or protocol compiler. Pieces you would need to write include the interface definition, client application code, and server application code. Other code pieces—like the client stub files, the server stub files, and the header file—can be generated for you.

If you develop client and server code on different systems, copies of the interface definition and interface compiler (IDL in OSF's DCE, MIDL in Microsoft RPCs) must be present on both the client and server systems. To generate code correctly for different kinds of systems, compile the interface definition for the client stub on the client system and the server stub on the server system.

Fig. 7.4
An overview of the steps in the RPC programming process.

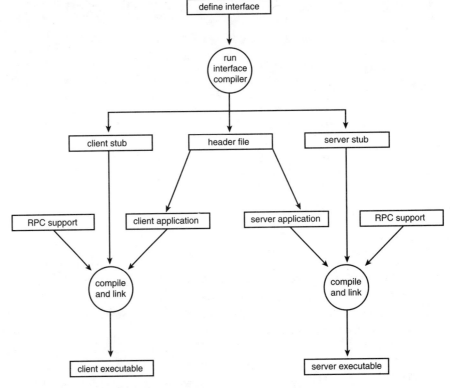

Creating the Client

To develop a client, you write application code that makes calls to operations in the interface definition file. Client stubs are linked with the application code. Along with the RPC runtime library, what looks like a procedure call is turned into network communications with the server side of the application. The client side of the application usually contains a relatively small amount of RPC code.

To find the server, the client must have some way of knowing with what server it needs to talk. This process is called *binding*. The level of control you need over binding information depends upon the needs of the client application. Binding information can be obtained automatically and be invisible to the client application code, or by calling RPC runtime routines and using a *binding handle* as a parameter in a remote procedure call. A binding handle is a pointer to information for a possible binding.

Creating the Server

To develop a server, you must know the interface definition file and some RPC runtime routines. The server side of the application usually contains most of the RPC code that needs to be written. Two distinct portions of code must be created:

- The actual remote procedure

- The code to initialize the server

Calls to the RPC runtime routines are mainly made in the server initialization, where the server is prepared to listen for remote procedure calls.

When a client makes a remote procedure call, a binding relationship is established with a server. Binding information is network communication and location information for a particular server.

Questions to Think About

The following are a few questions you might want to consider when selecting an RPC system and developing your application. These are just a sampling of the issues you might want to consider before coding your application:

- What type of error reporting and recovery do you need? Like a local procedure call application, a remote procedure call application needs a well defined error reporting scheme. For instance, the DCE RPC library provides error reporting at the RPC and communication protocol levels.

- What security and access control measures are needed? Standard operating systems security may not be enough to guarantee client and server authenticity across a network. Even when you have an adequate client/server authenticity scheme, you will still have to decide on the type of access protocol you'll need. Before coding, you may want to decide on what will happen if insufficient authentication occurs.

  Other issues, such as user access to functions, should also be considered. Some functions might be available to all users, while others might be restricted to certain users, whose identities must be validated.

- What happens when a connection is lost? If the client or server connection is cut off during an RPC, what should happen? You might choose to stop, automatically reconnect, or look for another connection.

II

Introduction to RPC

■ Do you have procedures that may not be called more than once, without changing the state of the server (known as a *non-indempotent procedure*)? For these types of procedures, you need either a reliable transport or request and reply queuing on an unreliable transport. TCP (connection-oriented) requests are reliable, executing the procedure exactly once but require more overhead. UDP (connectionless) transmissions are unreliable; they may never get to the server, or may get to the server multiple times.

■ Are global variables or objects used in your application? Memory address spaces between the client and server are different. With many RPCs, variables get to the server via request messages. This isn't a roadblock, but you may need to program around the globals. For instance, you could create an additional RPC to share global parameters between the client and server. You could also encapsulate the globals as just another outgoing request argument for each procedure.

From Here...

You now have a high-level view of where RPCs fit in with distributed computing and client/server, what RPCs are, what the major pieces of an RPC based application are, and how these pieces interact. For more information, refer to the following chapters:

■ Chapter 4, "Client/Server Development Overview," gives an introduction to the processes of developing a client/server application.

■ Chapter 11, "Techniques for Developing RPC Clients and Servers," for information on how to develop RPC-based client/server applications.

■ Chapter 13, "What is DCE?," provides an introduction to the Distributed Computing Environment.

Chapter 8

Authentication

Today's distributed computing systems require a new type of security model to address the challenges of secure, enterprise-wide computing. As opposed to the traditional host-based, multi-user systems, security for distributed applications is inherently more complex and difficult to design, implement, and maintain. To make matters worse, a number of inconsistent and incompatible security mechanisms are available from a number of providers, thus making for an integration nightmare. Last but not least, there are, as of yet, no formal standards for distributed security.

This chapter contains a discussion of authentication systems and authenticated RPCs, with emphasis on the OSF DCE RPC. Topics include the following:

- Overview of distributed security

- Types of authentication mechanisms

- Requirements for a distributed security model

- Authentication systems

- Mutual authentication mechanisms

- Authentication services

Overview of Distributed Security

Distributed computing provides a means to share data and resources from various nodes on the network. However, the capability of providing a free flow of information over insecure or unverified networks carries with it the threat of unwanted intrusion or security breaches. Among these is the capability of assuming the identity of another valid user and masquerading as that user to gain access to information, and the capability to modify and/or read sensitive data in transit.

In a distributed environment, there are different types of security mechanisms that have to be considered as part of the overall security infrastructure. Among these mechanisms are the following:

- Native Operating System Security (Host-Based)—Traditional or legacy systems require each user to provide a user identity (ID) and password to gain access to a particular platform and its services. Once users are defined, they're assigned various types and levels of privileges, which are maintained by a centralized security manager. At login time, the user's identity is checked by the host system's security component to verify whether access should be granted and what resources he or she has access to.

- Network-Level Security—Networks, like TCP/IP, have their own security requirements for users and machines (hosts). Network operating systems such as Novell NetWare also have a security mechanism for authentication and authorization of users and server hosts.

- Client/Server Component-Level Security—Designers and developers of client/server and distributed applications usually need to implement application-specific security for presentation, logic, and data components based on user identities or roles.

Each computing environment has a unique implementation based on a set of disparate, independent security mechanisms. Although the mechanisms mentioned previously are vitally important in completing the overall security requirements demanded in a distributed security model, we will focus more specifically on a distributed security model based on DCE.

Requirements for a Distributed Security Model

The goal of a security system is to provide valid users the access they need to networked computing resources and also to protect these resources against misuse. Therefore, a distributed security model needs to provide these capabilities:

- *Authentication*—This is a process that verifies the identity of some reliable entity (a human user or machine). These entities are usually referred to as *principals*. Each principal needs to have a preestablished identity stored in a secure location to be used in the authentication process.

- *Data Integrity*—This is the process of ensuring that data doesn't change between the sender and the receiver.

- *Confidentiality*—This is the process of ensuring that data can't be read except by the intended receiver.

- *Cryptography*—Encryption mechanisms such as the Data Encryption Standard (DES) with Message Digest 5 (MD5) can be used to provide data integrity and confidentiality for communications over a network. DES is based on 64-bit keys, with only 56 bits actively used, but with the 64-bit key length, it would take *n* times (two to a power of 56) for an exhaustive key search attach. MD5 is a non-invertible (i.e., the ordering is not reversible) function that produces a message digest (or checksum, and so forth) of 128 bits as output. Unlike DES, MD5 is not used for encryption and decryption since it's a one-way-only function.

Authentication Systems

Secure computer systems require authentication. It is not acceptable to send passwords in the clear, nor is it advisable to carry on a sensitive exchange of information without knowing that the identity of users and machines can be trusted. Distributed security requires a trusted chain of traceable relationships based on the capability to prove that you are who you say you are. There are many types of authentication systems in use including the following:

- Password Systems—Many authentication systems are based on the idea of a secret password known only to the user. Passwords are typically sent in clear text over the network, thus making it possible for someone to eavesdrop on the wire and read the password associated with the user identity. The interceptor can now use the password to impersonate the original user. This is the major reason why password-based authentication systems are not acceptable for distributed computing (or cellular phone networks).

- Network Address Systems—This authentication scheme uses the network address to determine the identity of the sender. In UNIX, each computer that wants to allow access to its resources can store the addresses of the valid computers in a file such as `/etc/hosts.eqiv` file.

UNIX users can choose to allow access to other users by creating account entries in the `.rhosts` file in their home directory.

Although network address-based authentication is preferable to password-based authentication, it's not foolproof. With IP source routing, for example, it's not only possible to send a network packet that impersonates a sender's address but to specify a series of route destinations for return packets.

■ Authentication Tokens (Smart Cards)—*Smart cards* are portable physical devices that individuals use to authenticate themselves. The card, which is about the size of a typical credit card, is inserted into a reader attached to the computer.

There are several types of smart cards, but they all have an embedded processor and storage capacity. The card is used to initiate a conversation with the reader and performs authentication using a PIN or some form of cryptographic key. Although using smart cards is a better mechanism than simple password authentication, smart cards do not protect against interception while being transmitted over the wire.

The authentication systems mentioned here can be quite useful in providing some level of protection against security intruders. However, each of these has inherent limitations and is open to attack (i.e., password guessing, network id impersonation, etc.). In addition, these authentication systems do not provide for the protection of data while in transit over the network. For these reasons, mutual authentication systems have been developed.

Mutual Authentication Mechanisms

Mutual authentication systems enable participants to engage in secure communication exchanges based on a trusted (authenticated) relationship with each other. There are two main types of mutual authentication systems in use today; those based on trusted third party technology, especially private key (Kerberos), and those based on public key technology, especially RSA public key.

A trusted third party is an entity that provides a trust mechanism used to store the external principal identities. A key responsibility of the trusted third party is to certify a principal's security based on its credentials. These credentials can then be used to determine whether to grant access to a particular principal.

Private Key (MIT Kerberos V4 and V5)

Kerberos, developed by MIT, is a secret key authentication service based on DES. The Kerberos service enables a client process running as a principal (user) to authenticate itself to a third-party verification server process without sending sensitive information over the wire in clear text.

Kerberos consists of a Key Distribution Center or Service (KDS) located on a physically secure network node and a set of library subroutines. There are two widely used commercial Kerberos versions: version 4 and version 5. Kerberos V5 contains a number of enhancements, including delegation of rights, unlimited ticket lifetimes, and renewable and postdated tickets.

The Kerberos KDS distributes certificates consisting of session keys and tickets (TKTs). Session keys are short-term by design and are used to authenticate clients with servers, and vice versa. Tickets contain protected information, including the client principal name, the server principal name, the session key, the ticket lifetime timestamps (start and expiration time), and the transit path of the KDS servers that vouch for the TKT.

The KDS holds the secret or master key that's shared between one instance of user and requested resource principals. Only the holder of the second half of the shared secret key can read the first half of the shared secret key. The KDS TGS grants either a Ticket Granting Ticket (TGT) or a Service Ticket (STKT). Typically, an authenticated user requests a TGT that contains a session key and ticket for presentation to a registered server for verification.

Kerberos is one of the best mutual authentication systems available today for diverse distributed environments. Remote procedure calls (RPCs) are one of the common programming paradigms, along with message passing, used to pass data over the network. Authenticated RPCs are used to ensure that secure and trusted communications can be used to communicate between clients and servers. This particular topic will be discussed in more detail in a later part of this chapter.

RSA Public Key

RSA is a public key, cryptographic algorithm for authentication, encryption, and decryption named after its inventors Ron Rivest, Adi Shamir, and Leonard Adelman.

Public key cryptography uses a pair of asymmetric keys to encrypt and decrypt. Where x and y represent two large prime numbers, $p = xy$ where p is the product or modulus. Select a number, z, that is less than p but relatively prime to $(x-1)(y-1)$ and find its inverse, q, mod $(x-1)(y-1)$ or zq = 1 mod (x-1)(y-1) where (p,z) represents the public key and q represents the private key. This assumes that factors x and y will be kept secret or destroyed immediately after use.

There is one public key and one private key per key pair. The private key is kept secret, while the public key—as implied by the name—is disseminated widely. For example, a user can send a message encrypted by the public key that will be received and decoded by the one user using the corresponding private key.

Data can be encrypted with either the public or private key. However, the data can be decrypted only by using the other member of the key pair.

In practice, RSA public key is combined with a secret key cryptographic system like the Data Encryption Standard (DES) to produce an encrypted message using an RSA digital "envelope."

As an example, if Tom wants to send Joan an encrypted message, he must first encrypt his message using a randomly selected DES key. Tom then looks up Joan's public key and uses it to encrypt the DES key. The message is sent to Joan as a digital envelope containing both the RSA encrypted DES key in conjunction with the DES encrypted message. When Joan receives the message, she opens the digital envelope and decrypts the DES key with her private key. Finally, Joan uses the decrypted DES key to decrypt the actual message that Tom sent to her.

Authentication and the DCE RPC

Clients and servers often use authenticated RPCs to ensure that their network communications are secure. OSF's DCE provides a security service that supports authenticated RPCs. The diagram in figure 8.1 shows an overview of the DCE Authentication Service.

The DCE Authentication Service is part of the overall DCE Security Service and consists of the following:

- Client's authentication runtime

- Security daemon (secd) process running on a physically secure Security server

- Registry database

- RPCs used by the security client to interact with the Security server to request information and to perform operations

DCE Authentication Service

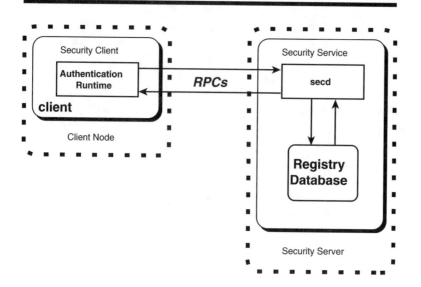

Fig. 8.1
DCE authentica-
tion service.

Physically Secured System

The primary role of the Security server is to access the Registry database in order to validate user logins and perform queries and updates to the Registry.

DCE provides several types of authentication service, as well as different protection levels using authenticated RPCs. To communicate, the client and server principal names must be registered with the security service and then must agree on the type and level of service that will be used.

The name of the client's principal, the authentication service type, and the level of authentication must be known. The name of the server's principal and the authentication service type must be known. Notice that, unlike the client, the server does not need to know the authentication level to be used.

DCE supports four types of authenticated RPC service:

■ `rpc_authn_none`—which provides no authentication. The client and server decide not to perform authentication checking.

■ `rpc_c_authn_default`—which provides a default that's based on `rpc_c_authn_dce_secret`.

- `rpc_c_authn_dce_secret`—which provides the DCE-shared secret key authentication based on Kerberos and DES.

- `rpc_c_authn_dce_public`—which provides DCE RSA public key authentication (may be part of DCE 1.2).

The developer decides what authentication service types will be used by the client and server for authenticated RPC based on their principal identities. Also, DCE-authenticated RPC supports seven different protection levels, ranging from `rpc_c_protect_level_none`, which, as implied, performs no protection, to `rpc_c_protect_level_privacy`, which encrypts all the RPC's arguments (data) in each call.

Overview of Authenticated DCE RPCs

By using the DCE Security Service's mutual authentication mechanism, DCE principals (clients and servers) can have confidence that their communications are secure. All principals register themselves with the DCE Registry Service and establish an agreed-on type of authentication.

Once the secure, trusted relationship is established between a client and server, no further interaction with the DCE Security Service is required in regards to authenticated RPCs unless the context changes or a ticket expires requiring a refresh from Kerberos. However, developers need not concern themselves with the underlying details of passing tickets and credentials and the process of encryption and decryption, because these occur as part of the authenticated RPC processing.

The sequence of steps for an RPC operation are as follows (see fig. 8.2):

1. The client issues an RPC and passes input arguments to the client stub.

2. The client stub prepares (*marshals*) the input arguments for transmission and dispatches the call to the client RPC runtime.

3. The client RPC runtime dispatches the call with any input arguments to the appropriate server stub via the server RPC runtime.

4. The server RPC runtime receives the call from the client RPC runtime and passes it to the appropriate server stub.

5. The server stub unmarshals the input arguments and passes them to the called remote procedure.

6. The remote procedure is executed and any results are sent back to the server stub.

7. The server stub marshals the results and passes them back to the server RPC runtime.

8. The server RPC runtime transmits the results to the client RPC runtime.

9. The client RPC runtime receives the call results from the server RPC runtime and dispatches them to the client stub.

10. The client stub unmarshals the results and passes them to the calling client program for further evaluation.

Overview of RPC Operation

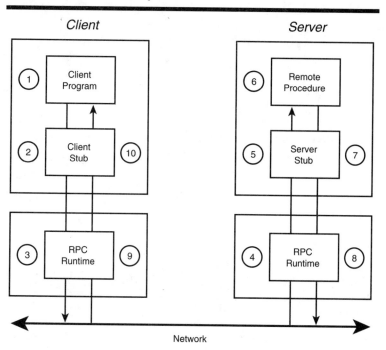

Fig. 8.2
The sequence of steps for an RPC operation.

Authentication Services

Currently, there are several major types of authentication services available to the application programmer. For discussion purposes, we will focus primarily on the DCE Security Service with brief references to other major security services (e.g., Sun Microsystems RPC, Novell NetWare, relational database management systems, and Microsoft Windows 95 and Windows NT).

The DCE Security Service

DCE uses Kerberos V5 as an authentication mechanism. Future DCE releases will likely provide support RSA Public Key, initially for DCE login. In DCE terms, every user and machine is registered as a principal within a DCE *cell* (a group of DCE machines that are registered to a Security server's trusted computing base).

In DCE, the trusted computing base is comprised of a cell's master Security service (SEC) in conjunction with the Distributed Time Service (DTS). The DTS is used to ensure that the timestamps required by Kerberos are consistent within a given Universal Time Coordinate (UTC) across all DCE platforms within the particular DCE cell (or across multiple DCE cells). Every DCE principal, whether a person or a machine, has a password, and this password is one of the components of the encrypted key. Each DCE principal is also associated with a universal, unique identifier or UUID. UUIDs are bit strings generated by DCE that are unique in time and space (a UUID can never be regenerated). In DCE, group and user UUIDs are 128 bits long and are contained within Access Control Lists (ACLs) based on POSIX.

The DCE authentication process includes logging in to the DCE cell, setting up a trusted identity based on Kerberos, and obtaining privileges with which to perform authenticated RPCs between trusted principals.

The following are the sequence of steps required for a DCE client to be authenticated and receive its privileges (see fig. 9.3):

1. Client authentication starts with a user's login to the DCE cell. The DCE Login facility takes the user's identity (user name) and transmits it in clear text over the wire to the Security Service. (For discussion purposes, it's assumed that the DCE runtime facility is used to execute requests between client and server machines.)

2. The DCE Security Service daemon (secd) takes the login request, extracts the user's name, and looks up the principal name in the Registry Service.

3. If there's a match, a secret key is derived from the user's password and is placed into a Ticket Granting Ticket (TGT) along with the principal (user) name, the current time, the requesting client machine name, and the first DES encrypted session key.

4. The ticket is then encoded with the Ticket Granting Service's secret key, and the first session key is appended.

5. The encoded ticket along with the first session key is then encoded with the user's secret key. The resulting TGT is sent back to the client process containing the current login context of the user.

6. The client workstation receives the TGT as a challenge and prompts the user for his or her password.

7. The user's password is used to decrypt the challenge TGT by converting the password to a DES key.

8. If the two passwords match, the DES key is used to extract the ticket and first session key from the TGT.

9. The client workstation then creates an authenticator using the principal (user) name, the current time, and the client workstation address.

10. It then encrypts this authenticator by using the first session key. The request for a Ticket Granting Service Ticket (TGST) is sent via RPC to the Security Server's Ticket Granting Service.

11. The TGS decrypts the ticket and extracts the first session key.

12. It also decrypts the authenticator constructed by the client workstation.

13. The timestamps are checked, and the ticket is compared with the authenticator data.

14. If they match, the TGS creates a new ticket and a (new) second session key.

15. The TGS then looks up the Security Service's secret key, encodes the new ticket with it, and appends the second session key.

16. The new ticket and the appended second session key are then encoded with the first session key (nested encryption). The new TGT is then sent back to the client's machine using the RPC as a transport.

17. The client machine takes the TGT it just received and uses its first session key to extract the ticket and the second session key.

18. The client machine's login process next requests a Privilege Service Ticket (PST). The PST is used to request a Privilege Ticket Granting Ticket (PTGT) from the TGS in order to access the Privilege Service. Obtaining the PST entails that the client machine creates a new authenticator again by using the principal name, current time, and client machine address.

Fig. 8.3

The many steps of client authentica-tion.

Client Authentication (1)

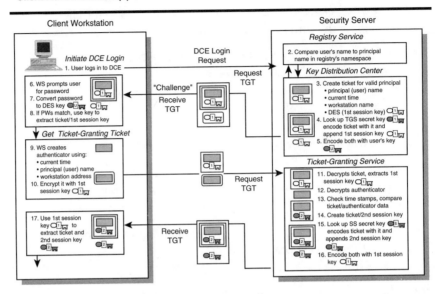

19. It then encrypts this authenticator with the second session key and sends it to the TGS.

20. The TGS decrypts the ticket and extracts the second session key.

21. It then decrypts the authenticator.

22. The timestamps are checked, and the ticket is compared with the au-thenticator data.

23. If they match, the TGS creates a new ticket and a (new) third session key.

24. The TGS then looks up the Privilege Service's secret key, encodes the new ticket with it, and appends the third session key.

25. The new ticket and the appended third session key are then encoded with the second session key and sent to the client as before.

26. The client machine takes the TGT it just received and uses its second session key to extract the ticket and the third session key.

27. To obtain the principal's privileges, the client machine's login process creates a new authenticator and encrypts it with the third session key and sends it to the Privilege Service (PS).

Client Authentication (2)

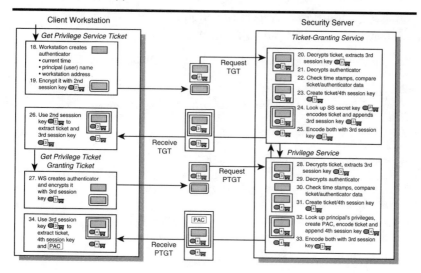

28. The PS decrypts the ticket and extracts the third session key.

29. The authenticator is decrypted.

30. The timestamps are checked and the ticket is compared with the authenticator data.

31. If they match, the PS creates a new ticket and a (new) fourth session key.

32. The PS then looks up the principal's privileges and creates a Privilege Attribute Certificate (PAC). It then encodes the new ticket and appends the fourth session key.

33. The new ticket containing the PAC and the appended fourth session key are then encoded with the third session key and sent to the client as a Privilege Ticket Granting Ticket (PTGT).

34. The client machine takes the PTGT and uses the third session key to extract the ticket, the fourth session key, and the principal's PAC. Now the client is ready to make an application-specific request—for example, to call a remote procedure on an application server.

Introduction to RPC

Requesting a DCE Application Service. When developing DCE applications, programmers need to implement the steps required to set up mutual authentication. Servers must perform the following major steps to participate in an authenticated RPC with a client:

1. The server must establish its principal identity.

2. The server must register the type of authentication service it wants to use with the RPC runtime's authentication component.

3. The server listens for client requests.

4. The server's runtime authentication responds to RPC requests and examines the client's authentication level and authorization to determine what resources, if any, the client has access to.

5. The server examines the client's PAC, if authorization is based on certified credentials, or to a principal's string name, if non-certified credentials are used.

6. The server decides whether the client can access the requested objects/resources by checking the following:

   ■ The authentication type

   ■ The authentication level

   ■ The requested server's authorization level and principal identity

   ■ The client's principal name

If the client passes all of these checks, the server allows the (application-specific) access request to take place—the RPC is completed successfully.

After obtaining a binding handle, a client must perform the following steps to participate in an authenticated RPC with a server:

1. It must modify the binding handle for the security parameters to be used by the authentication runtime.

2. It must get a handle to the current DCE login context using `sec_login_get_current_context (*login_context, *status)`.

Once all the server and client authentication setup steps have been performed, the client program is ready to send an authenticated RPC to, for example, an application server.

Other Security Services

Although we have focused on the DCE Security Service, it is by no means the only choice available to the programmer. Other security services are in common and widespread use (e.g., Sun RPC, NetWare 4, and relational database management systems), while still others (e.g., Microsoft's Windows 95 and Windows NT) are making inroads into commercial and non-commercial areas. Each is explained in further detail:

■ Sun RPC Security—RPC is widely used in the Sun ONC+ and the Network File System (NFS) that uses ONC+. There are two versions of Sun RPC: transport independent RPC (TI-RPC) and the socket-based API using TCP and UDP as a network transport. NFS provides support for authenticated RPCs in the Secure NFS product.

■ NetWare 4 Security—NetWare 4 Directory Services (NDS) provides an enterprise security mechanism for NDS objects and their attributes. The NetWare 4 authentication service uses RSA public and private key encryption mechanisms.

   Novell also provides the NetWare Core Protocol (NCP) that is used to counteract package forgery. In NCP Phase I, servers and clients are required to verify or sign each NCP packet sent over the network (the signature is never repeated—it changes with each packet). NCP Phase II provides the capability to encrypt the data portion of the NCP packet for increased security.

■ Relational Database Management Systems (RDBMS) Security—Database vendors such as Oracle, Informix, and Sybase have announced support for authenticated RPCs based on the DCE. These services are in addition to those provided by the SQL vendors themselves. For example, Oracle's Secure Network Services (SNS) 2.0 offers support for external authentication systems, including Kerberos and Sesame (an outgrowth of a European security collaboration effort).

■ Windows NT and Windows 95 Security—The Microsoft RPC, based on OSF's DCE RPC specification, provides support for Windows NT and Windows 95 specific security mechanisms for authenticated RPCs. Also, Microsoft has indicated its support for Kerberos authentication in upcoming versions of Windows NT and Windows 95.

   Microsoft's RPC can communicate with DCE-compliant servers from a number of system vendors and ISVs. Microsoft has made the DCE-compliant RPC one of the key technologies in support of its Component Object Model (COM), the basic service infrastructure for Microsoft's object linking and embedding (OLE).

II

Introduction to RPC

From Here...

This chapter covered authentication systems and mechanisms regarding authenticated RPCs, with emphasis on the OSF DCE RPC.

As stated at the beginning of the chapter, authentication of users, machines, and processes is a critical security component of distributed systems. There are a number of ways to provide for authentication, ranging from simple password-based schemes to robust and complex systems based on mutual authentication systems such as Kerberos and RSA Public Key. The DCE Authentication Service was highlighted as an example of a commercially available implementation of a mutual authentication system.

Distributed security is a relatively new field that presents a number of challenges in regards to security. Authenticated RPCs is a good example of a mechanism that addresses the need to verify the true identity of computer system users in order to properly protect data and information accessed across a network.

For more information about DCE Security and the DCE Services, see the following chapters:

- Chapter 14, "DCE Security," discusses the components of DCE Security and how they interact with each other.

- Chapter 16, "Understanding the OSF DCE Services," discusses the DCE services and how they are used.

Chapter 9

External Data Representation

If you have ever programmed with data structures, you know that they are quite easy to deal with in most cases. You can access them, modify them, do almost anything with them except export or import them from your application.

If you have ever tried to save a data structure to a file, for example, you have probably had to come up with an application specific save-and-restore format. This can be very convenient, but is often not very extensible or flexible. Whenever you add a new member to your data structure, you will probably need to add more complexity to your save/restore format. When you add the problem of creating a format that is compatible with several different types of machines, suddenly the task is much more difficult. You now have to worry about byte order, data alignment, the binary representations of mathematical quantities such as floating point numbers, and other gory details. All this is probably secondary to your application development.

The *External Data Representation* (XDR) is both a data representation standard and also a set of library routines which implement that standard. XDR allows you to easily save and restore structured data. XDR also allows you to transport data portably between any set of machines which support it.

This chapter gives you all the information you'll need to understand and use XDR in real-world applications. You will learn how to do the following:

- Use XDR's numerical conversion routines
- Use XDR's pointer conversion routines

■ Write your own XDR routines for complex data types

■ Use both XDR memory blocks and XDR file streams

■ Squeeze performance out of XDR in tight loops

■ Diagnose and overcome common XDR problems

Introducing XDR

When you deal with variables and data structures in your programs, you typically think about them in terms of what they do for you. This field might represent an account balance, while some other field might be a flag for a questionable transaction. Your approach is application oriented.

XDR is data oriented, however. The key word in External Data Representation is "External." If you want to make the data of your application available to another application—as you often do in a client/server system—or if you want to save your data to files, and later restore it, you must somehow externalize it. XDR is the tool which does this for you.

What Does XDR Do For You?

To understand why XDR is necessary and how it works, let's consider a situation which doesn't work. Suppose you are developing a network height server. Remote applications connect to your application and you send them back a numerical quantity indicating your height.

Initially, you provide a stingy amount of information, a single byte giving height in inches:

```
unsigned char ht = (unsigned char)73;
(void)write(s, &ht, 1);
```

where s is the network socket (we'll ignore network programming details in this example). Gradually, feedback from your immense user base tells you that more accuracy is called for, so you decide to send a float, indicating height in centimeters. You try the following:

```
float fht = 185.49;
(void)write(s, (char *)&fht, sizeof(float));
```

Initially, you try this by making a height request from your own machine (a Sun), and it works just fine. Shortly after you release it, however, one of your Vax users calls your customer service line and reports that your height is coming over the wire as 5,010,827,921,422,405,700,000,000,000,000,000,000. Isn't that entertaining?

The problem is very easy to understand, but not very easy to fix. Your Sun stores floating point numbers in the IEEE short floating point format (an international standard defined by the IEEE organization). It also stores the four bytes of a float in big-endian byte order, meaning that the most significant bytes of a multibyte quantity are first. Your user's Vax is probably representing floats in its native F-Float format (a DEC specific format), and using little-endian byte order, in which the most significant bytes of a multibyte quantity come last. What you thought would be a simple upgrade to your server has turned into an ugly data transportation problem.

The problem illustrated here could actually have been worse. The size of C data type `float` was referenced in the `write()` call using the `sizeof()` macro. It is possible that two different machines might use a different number of bytes to represent a `float`. This is not the case with the Sun and Vax, both of which use four bytes to represent a C float, but this is just pure luck.

This type of data representation problem can easily arise even with identical machines. Consider the case where you were transporting an `int`, instead of a `float` or a `char` (when used without qualification, terms such as `int`, `char`, `float`, and so forth will always refer to the corresponding C data types). What would happen if your server was compiled on a PC using a compiler with 32-bit `int`s, but some clients used a compiler with 16-bit `int`s?

This is the primary goal of XDR. You almost certainly do not want to have to care about machine level representations of data. You simply want to move the data in and out smoothly. XDR allows you to cease to care in almost every situation.

How Does XDR Help?

In order to use XDR to solve this problem, an additional step is needed. The producer of the data must convert that data to the XDR representation. This is you, since you are moving the data out of your server. The consumer of the data must also do more work. These are your clients, since they are moving the data into their applications.

In XDR, your server code would look something like what is shown in Listing 9.1.

Listing 9.1   A Simple XDR Encoding Example

```
#include <rpc/types.h>    /* always include these */
#include <rpc/xdr.h>
...
static char themem[42];   /* 42 is a random number */
static XDR htXdrout;
float fht = 185.49;
xdrmem_create(&htXdrout, &themem[0], 42, XDR_ENCODE);
xdr_float(&htXdrout, (char *)&fht);
(void)write(s, &themem[0], sizeof(float));
```

This code fragment is meant to illustrate the basics of XDR. First, you create an XDR memory stream using the routine xdrmem_create(). You give it memory large enough to hold the converted data (themem). The constant XDR_ENCODE marks the stream as "encoding," meaning that it will convert your data to XDR's own format. The variable htXdrout is a data structure of type XDR, which is used internally by the XDR routines to maintain state (such as how many of those 42 bytes have been used so far). You then convert the data using the conversion routine xdr_float(). The converted data is then sent out.

Of course, it is also necessary that your users' code change. If one side is using XDR to encode, then the other side should use XDR to decode. Your users' code should be highly symmetrical to your code, as shown in Listing 9.2.

Listing 9.2   A Simple XDR Decoding Example

```
static char themem[42];   /* 42 is a random number */
static XDR htXdrin;
float fht = 0.0;
xdrmem_create(&htXdrin, &themem[0], 42, XDR_DECODE);
(void)read(s, &themem[0], sizeof(float));
xdr_float(&htXdrin, (char *)&fht);
```

This code first creates an XDR whose purpose is to "decode"—that is, convert data from XDR's representation to the native representation of the user's machine. This is indicated by the XDR_DECODE token in the call to xdrmem_create(). The call to xdrmem_create() must come first, as it is used to initialize the XDR structure htXdrin. Your users then perform this conversion after they have read in the XDR data. After the xdr_float() statement, fht will contain the native float value which your application sent, in the users' local floating point format.

While this code will probably work exactly as written, it is not an example of good XDR programming style. Later, in "Managing XDR Streams," you will see how to modify these two code fragments so that they are more robust.

This example should give you the basic flavor for XDR. XDR gives you a universal, transportable data format, and it gives you the conversion routines to and from this format. The XDR library functions completely hide the gory details of the underlying data format, so that you do not actually need to understand it. The next section shows you these conversion functions and how to use them.

Using the XDR Library Functions

This section introduces all the important and commonly used XDR functions. The basic way you set up XDR is described first. The numerical conversion functions are then discussed. Pointer functions follow, with some detailed guidelines on how to recognize and avoid common errors. You will then see how you can put together these basic XDR conversion functions into larger and more complex functions of your own.

Getting Started

Since XDR is a set of data conversion tools, there must be someplace where the XDR representation is stored. XDR provides for three types of storage areas: XDR memory streams, XDR I/O streams, and XDR record streams. These are collectively referred to as *XDR streams* or just *XDRs*. There are functions for creating and using each type of XDR.

For the moment, you will concentrate on memory streams. (You'll learn more about the other XDR streams later in this chapter.) Memory areas can be thought of as flat, unstructured blocks of memory containing data in XDR format.

An XDR memory stream, which I will call a "block," is created using the following XDR library function:

```
void xdrmem_create(XDR *xdrs, caddr_t addr, u_int sz,
                    enum xdr_op op)
```

XDR blocks are based on the memory that you allocate. `addr` is the address of the base of this memory and `sz` is its size in bytes. `xdrs` is the address of a variable of type XDR, which is the name of the basic data structure used in all XDR functions. The code fragment in Listing 9.3 shows a typical situation.

Listing 9.3 XDR Memory Allocation

```
#define MYMEMSIZE   (unsigned)64*1024          /* 64k */
...
XDR     myExdr;
caddr_t mymem = (caddr_t)NULL;
...
mymem = (caddr_t)calloc(MYMEMSIZE, sizeof(char));
if ( mymem == (caddr_t)NULL ) fail();  /* error */
xdrmem_create(&myExdr, mymem, MYMEMSIZE, XDR_ENCODE);
```

There are several things to note in this code fragment. First, you must allocate the memory, and you must check that it was successfully allocated. Most implementations of the XDR stream functions do not check the validity of their arguments, or perform only minimal checking. Second, the `xdrmem_create` function returns nothing, so that you will only discover an error in creating the block at some later time when something crashes because the contents of `myExdr` are damaged or peculiar. Third, a relatively generous block of 64k bytes has been allocated. None of the examples in this chapter will come close to using this much memory, but it is always better to allocate more memory than you will ever use, rather than less. Unfortunately, there is no precise way to predict how much memory you will actually need.

In this Listing, the function `calloc()` was used to allocate and zero the memory to be given to XDR. Your platform may not provide this function, or you may prefer to use a different function for memory allocation. Whatever method is used must provide a pointer to a contiguous block of memory, which will become the sole property of XDR. If it zeroes that memory, as a further example of defensive programming, so much the better. This ensures that XDR operations, at least initially, will take place to and from blank memory. This is often very useful in tracking down problems due to wild pointers and misplaced record positions.

Caution

Always initialize any memory you are giving to XDR. Always validate XDR function arguments and check their return codes. The XDR library does not do a lot of internal error checking, partially for performance reasons. Program defensively when using XDR.

The final and critically important point to note is the fourth argument `op`, given as `XDR_ENCODE`. What is this parameter, anyway? When you are XDRing, you are either converting from a data structure of your own *to* the XDR representation, or converting *from* the XDR representation into yours. The to process is known as *encoding, serialization,* or *marshaling* (ah, technology). The from process is known as *decoding, deserialization,* or *unmarshaling.* op can also be XDR_FREE, to create a freeing stream. You will see how this is used in the section, "Constructing Your Own XDR Functions."

When myExdr was initialized, it was marked as an encoding XDR. This means that all conversion operations go into XDR. The capital E in the name was used to remind myself that this is an *encoding* XDR.

From now on, assume that you have an encoding XDR named myExdr and a decoding XDR named myDxdr, both sitting on top of nice healthy chunks of memory. The encoding XDR is initialized exactly as shown in Listing 9.3, while the decoding XDR is initialized as shown in Listing 9.4.

Tip

Give all your XDRs names that will remind you of their direction. If you mix up encoding and decoding XDRs, it will lead to endless memory faults and other pains.

Listing 9.4 XDR Memory Allocation (Decoding)

```
#define MYMEMSIZE   (unsigned)64*1024          /* 64k */
...
XDR     myDxdr;
caddr_t mymem = (caddr_t)NULL;
...
mymem = (caddr_t)calloc(MYMEMSIZE, sizeof(char));
if ( mymem == (caddr_t)NULL ) fail();  /* error */
xdrmem_create(&myDxdr, mymem, MYMEMSIZE, XDR_DECODE);
```

Note that these two code fragments are identical, except that the first uses XDR_ENCODE as the third argument to xdrmem_create(), while the second uses XDR_DECODE. All XDR functions either encode or decode (with one very important exception, which you'll meet shortly). Perhaps surprisingly, the functions for encoding are the same as the functions for decoding. That is, a function like xdr_int() can be used to encode an int (convert a native int to the XDR representation), or decode an int (convert from the XDR representation to a native int). This type of symmetry might be a little hard to get used to at first, but it leads to some interesting economies.

In the next two subsections, I have divided the basic XDR library functions for encoding and decoding into two categories: *numerical functions* and *pointer functions.* The numerical functions handle basic numeric data types, such as int, bool_t, and float. The pointer functions handle everything which is referred to by its address, such as strings and arrays.

You won't find a discussion of every single function in the XDR library here, mostly because some functions are of such limited utility that most programmers will never have occasion to use them. Once you have completed this chapter, none of these exotic functions should present any difficulty to you. Consult your subroutine library documentation section (section 3 of the UNIX man pages, for example) under XDR for more information.

Numerical XDR Functions

All the basic numerical types of the C language have XDR functions. The following are their declarations:

```
xdr_char(XDR *xdrs, char *cptr);
xdr_u_char(XDR *xdrs, u_char *ucptr);
xdr_short(XDR *xdrs, short *sptr);
xdr_u_short(XDR *xdrs, u_short *usptr);
xdr_int(XDR *xdrs, int *iptr);
xdr_u_int(XDR *xdrs, u_int *uiptr);
xdr_long(XDR *xdrs, long *lptr);
xdr_u_long(XDR *xdrs, u_long *ulptr);
```

Each of these functions returns a status code of type bool_t. Also notice that each of these functions takes exactly the same set of formal arguments: a pointer to an XDR and a pointer to the quantity being XDRed. The direction of the XDR determines the operation being performed. If you use the following:

```
short myshort = (short)5;
xdr_short(&myExdr, &myshort);
```

then myshort would be encoded into the XDR representation. While if you use the following:

```
short myothershort;
xdr_short(&myDxdr, &myothershort);
```

then a chunk of memory in myDxdr is decoded from its XDR representation, and the resulting short value stored in myothershort. This explains why the numerical data is passed in as a pointer. For an encode operation, the data (myshort, or 5 in the first example) could have been passed directly; but for decode, a pointer is required to accept the decoded value.

Notice also that each of these functions has a return type of bool_t. This is the Boolean type used by XDR. It can have the values (no surprise here) of True or False. In XDR land, True is 1 and False is 0.

This simple example gives us our first significant insight into how XDR works. When XDR is encoding, it converts the value to some common internal representation, stores it in its internal memory (which you gave it during initialization with xdrmem_create()), and performs some data alignment so that values of different sizes can be stored. It also maintains an internal *record position* which gives the location of the first piece of unused memory in this case.

When XDR is decoding, it does these operations in reverse. It looks at its current record pointer, extracts the correct amount of data based on the size of the type, converts that amount of data from its internal representation to the external representation, and then gives the value back to you (in myothershort, as it happens). It also adjusts its internal record pointer so that the next XDR decode operation will be properly aligned. Figure 9.1 illustrates both sides of the XDR process.

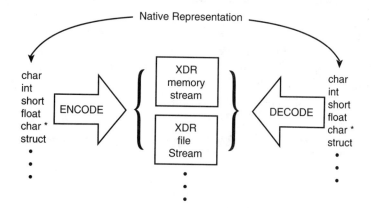

Fig. 9.1
XDR converts data to and from its internal format.

II

Introduction to RPC

Caution

In each of the XDR functions, you must supply valid pointers. The second argument to each of these functions may not be NULL or an error will occur. In general, XDR functions are extremely unforgiving of argument errors. They won't simply return False, they will most likely crash your application.

In addition to the basic integral functions, you also have XDR library calls for floating point conversion:

```
xdr_float(XDR *xdrs, float *fptr);

xdr_double(XDR *xdrs, double *dptr);
```

Each of these functions returns a status code of type bool_t. These functions work in the same way as the previous ones do. However, they differ in one very important way. If you XDR decode an integer, for example, and some-how you are at the wrong place in the memory buffer, you will probably just get a strange, but still valid, integer. If you XDR decode a `float` or a `double` at an invalid position, however, the resulting quantity might not be a valid floating point number; therefore, subsequent references to it may produce violent results (see Listing 9.5).

Listing 9.5   An XDR Floating Point Decoding Example

```
float myfloat;
float fval;
if ( xdr_float(&myDxdr, &myfloat) == FALSE ) fail();
...   /* much code */
fval = myfloat + 1.0;
```

Even though the `xdr_float` statement might succeed and return True, the final statement may produce a floating point exception. This happens be-cause `myfloat` has gotten some random collection of bits that do not corre-spond to a valid floating point number on this machine. The fact that the exception can happen many lines below the actual error makes this vicious to debug.

Caution

If you get a floating point exception on a seemingly safe floating point operation, the reason may be that you are not using a valid floating point number. If one of the operands of the statement that is causing the exception was obtained from an XDR decode operation, that is probably the original cause of the error.

You need to ensure that you are decoding what you are encoding, and vice versa. If your encodes and decodes don't match, you can easily misposition the XDR stream and get this problem. This is particularly nasty in the case of floating point quantities, since arbitrary binary data may not correspond to a valid `float`. A much safer way of writing the previous code fragment would be like what is shown in Listing 9.6.

Listing 9.6   A Safer XDR Floating Point Decoding Example

```
float myfloat = 0.0;
float fval;
if ( xdr_float(&myDxdr, &myfloat) == FALSE ||
```

```
          is_nan(myfloat) != 0 )
                  fail();
   ... /* much code */
   fval = myfloat + 1.0;
```

The initialization of myfloat to 0.0 ensures that it starts out as a valid floating point quantity. The function is_nan() is a function which returns nonzero if its argument is not a valid float (*nan* is an IEEE term which stands for "not a number").

Your system may not have the is_nan() function, but it almost certainly has some form of floating point validation function, such as finite(), fp_class_f(), or fpclass(), which can be used to perform the same type of checking as is_nan(). You made need to write a matherr() handler function to catch floating point exceptions. There may be a different set of functions for checking doubles. In any case, you will need a function that validates floating point type quantities. Find it and use it. In addition, a more comprehensive procedure for finding XDR stream misalignment and recovering from it is given in a following section, "Managing XDR Streams."

There are also two other numerical functions that handle types that look like integers:

```
   xdr_bool(XDR *xdrs, bool_t *bp);
   xdr_enum(XDR *xdrs, enum_t *ep);
```

Each of these functions returns a status code of type bool_t. The first function looks like it XDRs the Boolean type. It does, but it also does a little more. If bp points to any nonzero value, it is encoded as True. Zero is encoded as False. With decoding, the reverse logic applies. If the value in the XDR block is nonzero, then bp gets True; otherwise, it gets False.

The second function XDRs enumerated types. The XDR type enum_t is an implementation specific typedef, often an int, which XDR uses to hold any C enum.

Caution

xdr_enum() is the source of a subtle type of bug. xdr_enum() does not check to make sure that it is decoding (or encoding) a member of an actual enum; it just deals with the underlying value.

For example, look at Listing 9.7.

Listing 9.7   XDR Operations on *enum*

```
enum odds { one = 1, three = 3, five = 5 } ;
enum odds myodd = three;
enum odds myotherodd;
xdr_enum(&myExdr, (enum_t)&myodd);
...
xdr_enum(&myDxdr, (enum_t)&myotherodd);
```

The first call to `xdr_enum()` will encode `myodd`, whose numerical value is 3, into `myExdr`. The second call to `xdr_enum()`, in a decode block, of course, decodes whatever is at its current block position as an `int`. This means that even if this value is 4, it will get stored into `myotherodd`. What you subsequently do with `myotherodd` will determine how serious of an error this is.

> **Note**
>
> Your XDR applications should always check decoded `floats` and `doubles` for validity. If your XDR application is not performance limited, it is also worthwhile to check all decoded enums to ensure that they are valid members of their underlying enumerated types.

It might seem like I'm making a great fuss about XDR misreading data while decoding. This is one of the most common XDR errors, however. XDR blocks are accessed by their stream positions, and it is all too easy for the stream position to become misaligned. This usually happens because your encodes and decodes don't match, or because of wild XDR pointers. The actual error may only show up much later, far from the XDR function itself. The moral of this story is, when decoding, a little paranoia goes a long way. You can always remove the extra checks when you are sure your application is robust.

At this point, you have seen all the numerical functions of importance in XDR. You have not yet seen how to handle anything composite (like a `struct`) or any pointers (like strings or arrays). The next sections show you how to deal with these more complex data types.

Pointer Functions

C programmers are well aware of the fact that a pointer can, in fact, refer to many different types of things. The set of XDR functions available for handling the many different types of C pointers reflect this diversity in a potentially confusing way. (I was certainly confused when I first encountered them.) By realizing which functions to use in each situation, however, one can XDR much more interesting quantities than the numerical types of the previous section.

For the purposes of this chapter, we will consider three types of pointers:

- Array pointers, which point to a contiguous set of things of the same size. The array functions are xdr_vector() and xdr_array().

- String pointers, which point to an array of characters terminated by the NUL character (the character whose numerical value is zero). The string functions are xdr_string() and xdr_wrapstring().

- References, which are pointers to other data types. The reference functions are xdr_pointer() and xdr_reference().

There are special rules for using these functions which we'll see shortly.

Figure 9.2 gives a road map for deciding which XDR pointer function to use. You may want to review this figure again at the end of this section.

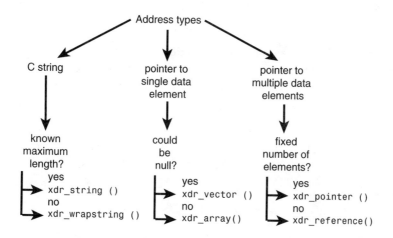

Fig. 9.2
XDR has several interrelated pointer functions.

The XDR pointer functions differ from the XDR numerical functions in three important ways. First, many of them will actually allocate memory for you during a decode operation. This can be extremely convenient if used properly. Second, these functions often allow you to specify a conversion function, so that they can act as building blocks for XDRing more complex types. Third, some of them have a little bit of error checking, mostly to prevent memory of outrageous size from being allocated. However, bad arguments still cause disastrous results.

XDR Array Functions

To start out, let us consider a fixed length array of integers:

```
#define ILEN    20
int         theints[ILEN];
```

You could easily write a for loop which would XDR this array, but it is much easier to use the library function xdr_vector(). The function is declared as the following:

```
bool_t xdr_vector(XDR *xdrs, char *vbase, u_int nelem,
                  u_int elemsize, xdrproc_t xdrone);
```

and would be used in our case as:

```
xdr_vector(&myExdr, (char *)&theints[0], (u_int)ILEN,
           sizeof(int), xdr_int);
```

xdrs is the usual XDR block, vbase is the base of the array, nelem is the number of elements in the array, elemsize is the size of each element, and xdrone is an XDR routine which can be used to XDR a single element of the array. The type xdrproc_t is declared as follows:

```
typedef bool_t xdrproc_t(XDR *, char *);
```

which means that it is a pointer to a function of two arguments; these arguments are an XDR block and a pointer to some type to be encoded or decoded. All the functions which you saw in the previous numerical functions section qualify as xdrproc_t.

This function will not allocate memory on decode. This function is a building block; once you have defined a function for XDRing the elements of an array, you can then use xdr_vector() to XDR the array itself.

The previous example was a little contrived, since arrays are typically allocated dynamically. Consider this code fragment:

```
int *iarr;
u_int ilen;
iarr = (int *)calloc(ilen, sizeof(int));
```

To XDR iarr, use the library function xdr_array() like in the following:

```
xdr_array(&myExdr, (caddr_t)&iarr, &ilen, ilen,
          sizeof(int), xdr_int);
```

The prototype for this function is as follows:

```
bool_t xdr_array(XDR *xdrs, caddr_t *arrp,
                 u_int *lenp, u_int maxlen,
                 xdrproc_t xdrone);
```

This function is similar in appearance to xdr_vector(), but differs from it in several important ways. xdrs is the usual XDR pointer, but the next argument, arrp, isn't the base of the array (which would be iarr itself in your example), but the address of the base of the array. The next argument, lenp, is likewise the address of an unsigned integer holding the number of elements in the array.

The second and third parameters are addresses because this function will allocate memory on a decode operation. It does this if the memory pointed to by the second argument, (*arrp), is NULL. Thus, the statements in Listing 9.8 will not only XDR decode the array, but they will also make iarr point to the newly allocated memory holding the array, and set ilen to the number of elements.

Listing 9.8   An Example Using *xdr_array()*

```
iarr = (int *)NULL;
ilen = (u_int)0;  /* some more paranoia */
bool_t res;
res = xdr_array(&myDxdr, (caddr_t *)&iarr, &ilen,
               (u_int)16384, xdr_int);
```

This is why the second and third arguments must be pointers, unlike xdr_vector(). After doing this, of course, you should always check everything like in the following:

```
if ( res != TRUE || iarr == (int *)NULL ||
     ilen == (u_int)0 ) fail();
```

The fourth parameter to xdr_array(), maxlen, is also an important check on decode. It is the maximum number of elements that can be expected in the array. On encode, you saw that I gave this parameter the value ilen, since I know that the number of array elements to be encoded is equal to ilen. On decode, however, if I am asking XDR to allocate the memory for me, then maxlen serves as a sanity check on the number of elements which might appear. When decoding, I don't necessarily know how many elements might appear, but I should be able to specify what the maximum number of such elements might be. I used the rather large and conservative value of 16,384 above, under the assumption that in my application, an iarr would never have more than that number of elements. The actual value is not important, so long as it is never exceeded.

You will have to decide if there is some application specific meaningful limit which you can use. If there isn't, you can always use (u_int)(-1) to bypass the size check. Note that the size check is applied on both encode and decode.

xdr_array() is another building block function, since it takes an XDR function as its parameter. Several examples of this will be given in the next section.

This routine has two interesting features which are shared by all the XDR routines that can allocate memory. First, all such routines have a size check parameter. If the size check fails, your XDR block will almost certainly be mispositioned; therefore, the rest of your XDR operations should be abandoned. This is, in fact, a general feature of XDR.

Tip
Once any XDR operation returns False, the current XDR block should not be used any further

Second, these XDR routines have a nasty habit of doing a direct fprintf() of an error message if memory allocation fails. This can be very annoying, particularly if your application is running in a windowing environment. There is not much you can do about this unless you get the XDR source and recompile the XDR library yourself. The very end of this chapter tells you how to get the XDR source if you are on the Internet.

Freeing XDR Memory

You are probably wondering what you can do with the memory that was allocated for you by XDR. Is it safe to call the following:

```
free((char *)iarr);
```

as in the case where you allocated iarr yourself? The answer is almost always, no. Fortunately, there are two simple ways to safely free such memory, by using the library routine xdr_free() (the standard way), or by using a freeing stream (the occasionally convenient way). A complete discussion of xdr_free() can be found in a following section "The Function xdr_free()." For the moment, consider the following:

```
XDR myFxdr;
xdrmem_create(&myFxdr, (caddr_t)NULL, (u_int)0,
              XDR_FREE);
```

This statement creates the third and last type of XDR memory stream: a *freeing stream*. Unlike XDR_ENCODE, which is associated with moving data into XDR, and XDR_DECODE, which is associated with moving data out of XDR, a freeing stream is used to free XDR allocated memory. To free your last iarr, use this code:

```
xdr_array(&myFxdr, (caddr_t *)&iarr, &ilen,
          (u_int)16384, xdr_int);
```

This will free the memory in a platform-independent manner. Most implementations ignore the `maxlen` parameter when using a freeing stream, but it is good practice to include it anyway. Note also that freeing streams may be safely passed to any XDR library function, but that they will not do anything unless that function can allocate memory. So, passing `&myFxdr` to `xdr_int()` is safe, but worthless.

XDR String Functions

The primary XDR string function is `xdr_string()`, like in the following:

```
bool_t xdr_string(XDR *xdrs, char **strp,
                  u_int maxlen);
```

A `string` is a C string, meaning that it ends in the NUL character `\0`. `strp` is a pointer to the base of the string, and `maxlen` has the same meaning as in `xdr_array()`. It specifies the maximum length of the string permitted, *not* including the terminating NUL character. This routine will allocate memory on decode if (`*strp`) is a `NULL` pointer.

This example shows how you encode, where I have used a random large number for the `maxlen` parameter:

```
static char *str = "He stopeth one of three";
xdr_string(&myExdr, &str, (u_int)2048);
```

To decode with memory allocation, where I have told XDR that the string cannot be longer than 2,048 characters (2,049 with the NUL), you would use the following code:

```
char *hisstr = (char *)NULL;
xdr_string(&myDxdr, &hisstr, (u_int)2048);
```

To subsequently free the memory, you would use the following statement, noting that the third argument is actually ignored:

```
xdr_string(&myFxdr, &hisstr, (u_int)2048);
```

The convenience function `xdr_wrapstring()` has the following function prototype:

```
bool_t xdr_wrapstring(XDR *xdrs, char **strp);
```

This function is exactly equivalent to the following use of the `xdr_string()` function:

```
xdr_string(xdrs, strp, (u_int)(-1));
```

In this statement, the string length is being given as the quantity `(u_int)(-1)`, which is some absolutely enormous value (about four billion on

Tip

Never ask XDR to free your memory which *you* have allocated. Always ask XDR to free memory which *it* has allocated.

II

Introduction to RPC

platforms with thirty-two bit integers). When you use xdr_wrapstring(), you are telling the XDR system to process the given string no matter what its length. The primary use for xdr_wrapstring() is because it is an xdrproc_t, since it has the appropriate two arguments (an XDR * and a pointer). xdr_string() cannot be an xdrproc_t, since it has three arguments. This means that you can use xdr_wrapstring() as an argument to xdr_array(), for example, in order to encode or decode an array of strings; while you cannot use xdr_string() for this purpose.

XDR Reference Functions

In C, whenever you have a data type which contains some information, you can also have a reference (pointer) type derived from that type, which points to that information. You can also have NULL pointers of that pointer type, which point to nothing. So, for any type mytype, you can have the following:

```
mytype v;
mytype *tp1 = (&v);              /* actual reference */
mytype *tp2 = (mytype *)NULL;   /* NULL reference */
```

More concretely, for the float type, you can have the following:

```
float  myfloat = 14.3;
float *myfptr1 = (&myfloat);
float *myfptr2 = (float *)NULL;
```

The myfloat variable actual has the storage for the bit pattern that represents 14.3, and myfptr1 points to that storage. myfptr2 points to nothing. Both myfptr1 and myfptr2 are actually address variables, or variables whose values are the addresses of something interesting.

The reason I am belaboring this fact of elementary C, is that in C, it is possible to be quite sloppy with pointers and still be successful. In XDR, it is not. It is critical to understand who is the pointer, who is the pointee, and who owns the memory.

The primary XDR reference function is the following:

```
bool_t xdr_pointer(XDR *xdrs, char **tpp,
                   u_int tsize, xdrproc_t xdrit);
```

The basic idea of this function is that if you can XDR something (such as a float), and then you can XDR a pointer to that thing. Consider the XDR encoding of myfptr1. This statement would do it:

```
xdr_pointer(&myExdr, (char **)&myfptr1, sizeof(float),
            xdr_float);
```

> **Note**
>
> The address of the pointer to be XDRed is passed (&myfptr1 in the previous example) as the second argument to the function xdr_pointer(), but the actual length (not a pointer to it) is passed as the third argument.

This code will work equally well on myfptr2. xdr_pointer() knows how to handle a NULL pointer. If you want to decode and have the XDR library allocate the memory for you, the following code would be used:

```
float *myotherfptr = (float *)NULL;
xdr_pointer(&myDxdr, (char **)&myotherfptr,
            sizeof(float), xdr_float);
```

There is a subtlety here: myotherfptr will point to allocated memory, which will contain the floating point value itself. Thus, while xdr_float() won't allocate memory for a decoded float which was encoded as a float, xdr_pointer() will allocate memory for a decoded float which was encoded as a float reference using xdr_pointer().

There is another "pointer" style function in the XDR library, called xdr_reference(). It is identical to xdr_pointer(), except that it cannot handle NULL pointers. It is occasionally useful in situations where you know the pointer cannot be NULL, since it is slightly more efficient in both time and data storage space.

xdr_pointer() and xdr_reference() really come into their own when dealing with pointers to complex types, such as structs. This is discussed next.

Constructing Your Own XDR Functions

Up to this point, you have seen only the component functions of the XDR library. It is time to tie these together with a full-fledged example of how to use XDR to accomplish something complete. You will also see in the section, "rpcgen's Output Files," of Chapter 10 that the rpcgen compiler can be used to automatically generate substantial and useful XDR functions.

Suppose that your application manipulates dynamically sized arrays of floating point numbers. These arrays are described by the data structure shown in Listing 9.9.

Listing 9.9   A Data Structure Representing a Variable Length Array

```
struct flodim {
  u_int  fl_arrlen;
  float *fl_thearr;
  } ;
typedef struct flodim flodim;
```

In this data structure, the member `fl_thearr` is a pointer to an array of floating whose length is given by the member `fl_arrlen`. There must be at least one element in the array (`fl_arrlen > 0`), and the pointer must point to valid storage (`fl_thearr != (float *)NULL`).

The total collection of all `flodims` is described by a forward linked list. This data structure will be appropriately named `allflodim` (see Listing 9.10).

Listing 9.10   A Linked List of Variable Length Arrays

```
struct allflodim {
    flodim          *af_flodim;
    struct allflodim *af_next;
    } ;
typedef struct allflodim allflodim;
```

There is a global variable which holds the head of this list:

```
static allflodim *afhead = (allflodim *)NULL;
```

The end of the list is, of course, indicated by `af_next == NULL`. Now, you're going to build XDR routines which will encode, decode, or free an individual `flodim` and also the complete list of `allflodims`.

The first step is to construct an XDR routine which will handle a single `flodim`. Since the member `fl_thearr` is a variable length array, you should use `xdr_array()`. The routine for XDRing a `flodim` structure is shown in Listing 9.11.

Listing 9.11   An XDR Function for the *flodim* Type

```
bool_t xdr_flodim(XDR *xdrs, flodim *fdp)
{
    if ( fdp == (flodim *)NULL || xdrs == (XDR *)NULL )
        return(FALSE);
    if ( xdrs->x_op == XDR_ENCODE &&
```

```
         ( fdp->fl_arrlen == (u_int)0 ||
           fdp->fl_thearr == (float *)NULL ) )
                 return(FALSE);
      return(xdr_array(xdrs, (caddr_t *)&fdp->fl_thearr,
           &fdp->fl_arrlen, sizeof(float), xdr_float));
   }
```

There are three things to note about this routine. First, fdp is not allowed to be NULL, since it must be dereferenced to get the arguments to xdr_array(). Second, you must validate that the array pointer fl_thearr is not NULL only when you are encoding, since you want the routine to allocate memory for you on decode. The x_op member of the XDR data structure is used to determine the direction. This member was set by the initial call to xdrmem_create(). Third, this routine automatically handles encoding, decoding, and freeing by making xdr_array() do all the work.

The routine xdr_flodim() XDRs a struct flodim. You are now able to XDR a struct flodim * as well, using your routine xdr_flodim() together with the XDR library routine xdr_pointer(), which will allocate the memory for the struct.

The routine that handles afhead, the list head pointer, must be either explicitly recursive or iterative, since it must traverse down the entire list structure until it hits the terminating NULL. We will look at the recursive implementation, in which the XDR function repeatedly calls itself in order to traverse the list. This is the most common implementation, and the one which you will see in rpcgen XDR code.

You will actually need two routines: one for an allflodim structure and one for an allflodim structure pointer. The second routine, which handles the structure pointer, can be easily written in terms of the first routine, which handles the structure itself. The code which handles the XDRing of the allflodim structure pointer is given in Listing 9.12.

Listing 9.12   The XDR Routine for the *allflodim* List Pointer

```
bool_t xdr_allflodim(XDR *, allflodim *);
bool_t xdr_allflodimp(XDR *xdrs, allflodim **afdpp)
{
    if ( xdrs == (XDR *)NULL ||    /* 1 */
        afdpp == (allflodim **)NULL ) return(FALSE);
    return(xdr_pointer(xdrs, (char **)afdpp,
         sizeof(allflodim), xdr_allflodim));
}
```

II

Introduction to RPC

The routine for XDRing an `allflodim` structure itself, and following the pointers contained within it, is shown in Listing 9.13.

Listing 9.13 The XDR Routine for an *allflodim* List

```
bool_t xdr_allflodim(XDR *xdrs, allflodim *afdp)
{
    if ( xdrs == (XDR *)NULL ||
        afdp == (allflodim *)NULL )
        return(FALSE);                    /* 2 */
    if ( xdrs->x_op != XDR_DECODE &&
        afdp->af_flodim == (flodim *)NULL )
            return(FALSE);                /* 3 */
    if ( xdr_reference(xdrs, (char **)&afdp->af_flodim,
                    sizeof(flodim), xdr_flodim)
        != TRUE ) return(FALSE);          /* 4 */
    return(xdr_allflodimp(xdrs,           /* 5 */
                    (char **)&afdp->af_next));
}
```

Let's work through this statement by statement. At the very top of the application, you want to XDR the quantity `afhead`. `afhead` is an `allflodim` pointer, so you must XDR it using the `xdr_pointer()` function (since the pointer might be NULL). You create the function `xdr_allflodimp()` to do this. At statement one, you sanity check the arguments. Note that while `afhead` may be NULL, `&afhead` is never NULL—so that if statement one fails, something is seriously wrong. The next statement of your function uses `xdr_pointer()` as expected. If `afhead` is NULL, this fact will be handled directly; if it is not, `xdr_pointer()` will call `xdr_allflodim()`.

Statement two of `xdr_allflodim()` does its own sanity check. Note again that `afdp` cannot be NULL, because `xdr_pointer()` would never have called it in that case.

Statement three is an application specific sanity check. You stated in your application assumptions that the `flodim` pointer in an `allflodim` can never be NULL. If you are encoding or freeing, you make this test to see if that is the case. If you are decoding, then the `flodim` pointer has not yet been filled in, and might have any value, including NULL.

At statement four, you XDR the `flodim` pointer using the function `xdr_reference()` to call the `xdr_flodim()` routine given previously. You can use `xdr_reference` since you have just checked for a NULL pointer. `xdr_reference()` will allocate the memory on decode. If this call fails, you return False.

At this point, you want to XDR the next pointer in the `allflodim` structure. Now you see why you needed the function `xdr_allflodimp()`. It makes it very easy to do this.

Now your application can use the following single statement:

```
xdr_allflodimp(xdrp, &afhead);
```

This will encode, decode, or free the entire listed headed by afhead. `xdrp` will be `&myExdr`, `&myDxdr`, or `&myFxdr`, respectively.

Suppose you are encoding and `afhead` points to a list with three elements. What happens? The top level call to `xdr_allflodimp()` detects a non-`NULL` pointer, notes that fact, and then calls `xdr_allflodim()`. This function encodes the `flodim` pointer, and then calls `allflodimp()` again. This happens twice more until the `NULL` pointer at the end of the list is seen. `xdr_pointer()` notes that and then finally returns, unwinding all the recursive calls. The XDR is complete. The top part of figure 9.3 illustrates how the list looks in memory, and the bottom part is a representation of how XDR stores it. Figure 9.4 shows how the various XDR `flodim` functions call one another in order to perform the encoding.

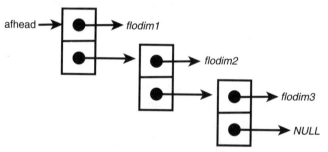

The allflodim list in memory

| Any data? TRUE |
| Flodim1 |
| Any data? TRUE |
| flodim2 |
| Any data? TRUE |
| flodim3 |
| Any data? FALSE |

The XDR representation of the allflodim list

Fig. 9.3
XDR stores a list structure in memory as a tagged linear array.

Introduction to RPC

Fig. 9.4
The XDR function
`xdr_allflodim()`
calls itself
repeatedly to
encode a `flodim`
list.

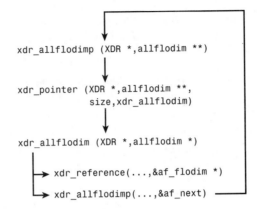

```
xdr_allflodimp (XDR *,allflodim **)

xdr_pointer (XDR *,allflodim **,
                  size,xdr_allflodim)

xdr_allflodim (XDR *,allflodim *)

        xdr_reference(...,&af_flodim *)
        xdr_allflodimp(...,&af_next)
```

The reader is encouraged to go through this code step-by-step in the case of decoding and freeing this same three member list, and convince him or herself that it actually allocates or frees all the associated memory.

The Function *xdr_free()*

Note that `xdr_allflodimp()` is a function which matches the `xdrproc_t` prototype. This means that to free the XDR memory in this example, you can also use the `xdr_free()` function which was mentioned previously. `xdr_free()` is declared as the following:

```
void xdr_free(xdrproc_t xdrthing, char *thingp);
```

`thingp` is a pointer to the memory to be freed, and `xdrthing` is the corresponding XDR routine. The difficulty with using `xdr_free()` is that you must have an `xdrproc_t` around. `xdr_free()` will work on `afhead`, but will not work on `iarr` from the previous example. The first statement below will free the memory allocated by XDR, while the second is in error, and will even compile on most systems:

```
xdr_free(xdr_allflodimp, (char *)&afhead); /* GOOD */
xdr_free(xdr_array, iarr);                 /* BAD */
```

The reason is that `xdr_array()` is not an `xdrproc_t`. It requires several more arguments which are unknown to `xdr_free()`. `xdr_allflodimp()` is perfect, however.

You will probably rarely use `xdr_free()` in your own XDR code, but it comes up constantly when using XDR routines generated by `rpcgen`.

Understanding XDR in Detail

This section will complete your knowledge of XDR. At this point, you should be familiar with how to use XDR to accomplish most tasks. This section will fill in some missing pieces and extend your repertoire. Some common problems with XDR are also discussed in greater detail.

Managing XDR Streams

Up until this point, you have been using XDR memory blocks created with xdrmem_create() exclusively. Such memory blocks are the most common type of XDR that you will encounter. There are two other XDR stream types: I/O streams and record streams. Typically, record streams are only used internally (by the higher levels of RPC), but I/O streams can be quite useful.

XDR I/O streams are created with the following function:

```
void xdrstdio_create(XDR *xdrs, FILE *fp,
                     enum xdr_op op);
```

And they are destroyed with the following function, which can actually be used to destroy any type of XDR stream:

```
void xdr_destroy(XDR *xdrs);
```

When you create an XDR I/O stream, you provide the FILE pointer associated with the file in question as the second argument. Don't be fooled by the name. The xdrstdio_create() function can be used with any FILE *. It does not have to be used with the standard I/O streams stdin, stdout, and stderr (although it can).

xdrstdio_create() uses fwrite() and fread() internally to move data into and out of the file, so that you benefit from the internal buffering of these functions. You can always extend the buffer size being used by calling setbuf() or one of its relatives before you create the FILE stream. Do not call setbuf(), or any other FILE functions, such as fseek(), on the FILE pointer after you have given it to XDR. This will interfere with XDR's internal bookkeeping.

File streams provide a direct interface to your file system. While you could do all XDR operations to and from memory streams, and then read and write these memory streams to and from files, the XDR I/O stream construction makes this unnecessary.

> **Note**
>
> xdr_destroy() is the exact inverse of the xdrxxx_create() functions. If you allo-
> cate the memory for xdrmem_create(), you must also deallocate it. If you open the
> FILE for xdrstdio_create(), you must also close it. xdr_destroy() will not
> perform these actions for you.

There are two more extremely important XDR stream functions that you
need. They are the following:

```
u_int  xdr_getpos(XDR *xdrs);
bool_t xdr_setpos(XDR *xdrs, u_int where);
```

At the very beginning of this chapter, I discussed the height server, and gave
two code fragments for XDRing the float in both the server and client applications. There was an enormous flaw in that code. How did I know what
would happen to the float after I encoded it in the server? The write() call
made two enormous assumptions—that the float data started at the beginning of themem, and that the XDRed float was the same size as the native
float.

Using these position functions, you can rewrite that code correctly. The
xdr_getpos() function takes an XDR stream and returns an offset indicating
that stream's current position. xdr_setpos() takes an XDR stream and an
offset and attempts to set the XDR stream position to that position.

To see how xdr_getpos() is used, we will rewrite the height server from the
beginning of this correctly, as shown in Listing 9.14.

Listing 9.14 A Robust Version of the Height Server

```
static char themem[42];   /* 42 is a random number */
XDR htXdrout;
float fht = 185.49;
u_int xstartpos;
u_int xendpos;
xdrmem_create(&htXdrout, &themem[0], 42, XDR_ENCODE);
xstartpos = xdr_getpos(&htXdrout);
xdr_float(&htXdrout, (char *)&fht);
xendpos = xdr_getpos(&htXdrout);
(void)write(s, &themem[(int)xstartpos],
            (xendpos - xstartpos));
```

xstartpos gives you the beginning position of the stream. xendpos gives you
the position of the stream after encoding the float. So the difference of these

two tells you how many bytes were used in the XDR representation of the `float`.

You should actually check the return code of `xdr_getpos()`, since it can fail and return `(u_int)(-1)`; although, this is almost impossible on memory streams, and unlikely on I/O streams unless the underlying `FILE` cannot `fseek()`.

You can also use `xdr_getpos()` and `xdr_setpos()` as a powerful troubleshooting tool.

Troubleshooting

I've just started using XDR in my scientific application. I have used `floats` *for a long time without any problems. Now I am getting floating point exceptions seemingly at random. The only thing I have changed recently is the addition of XDR, but the floating point exceptions seem to happen far from the XDR code. What is wrong?*

The problem is not XDR itself, but the way it is being used. You are undoubtedly decoding some `float` or `double` at the wrong position. Check to make sure that your sequence of encodes and decodes is identical by putting a call to `xdr_getpos()` after each XDR call, in both encode and decode sections, and printing out its return value:

```
xdr_double(&myExdr, &myd);
(void)fprintf(stderr, "After double myd: %x\n",
              xdr_getpos(&myExdr));
```

When you find a mismatch between the encode and decode streams, you have probably found your bug. In general, it is also possible for a wild pointer in the application to overwriting XDR memory. This is probably not happening in your case, however, since your application worked before you added XDR.

Earlier, I advised you to abandon XDRing whenever any XDR function returned `False`. You can also use `xdr_getpos()` and `xdr_setpos()` to recover from such an error if you must (see Listing 9.15).

Listing 9.15 Recovering From an XDR Error

```
u_int posbeforeugly;
posbeforeugly = xdr_getpos(&myExdr);
if ( xdr_ugly(&myExdr, &theugly) == FALSE ) {
    xdr_setpos(&myExdr, posbeforeugly);
    ... /* do the rest of the error recover */
}
```

Handling Lists, Graphs, and Multiple References

One of the most common problems in using XDR on reference/pointer constructs is the problem of multiple references. Suppose, for example, that the `allflodim` list structure previously given was a circular list, rather than a NULL terminated one. This would mean that the `af_next` pointer of the last `allflodim` structure would point to the first member of the list, rather than being NULL.

What would happen in this case if you tried to use the function `xdr_allflodimp()` on afhead? In your example with three members on the list, the termination condition would not be met. The third call to `xdr_allflodimp()` would call into `xdr_pointer()`, which would see the pointer to the first element of the list and would proceed to XDR it again. An XDR encode or decode attempt would just circulate around and around the circular list until memory was exhausted. An XDR free operation would crash very quickly, since it would keep trying to free the same memory over and over.

If `allflodim` had been a double-linked list, with `af_next` and `af_prev` pointers, then each member of the list would be visited twice—once as `af_next` is XDRed from the previous member, and once as `af_prev` is XDRed from the subsequent member.

The problem here is not limited to circular lists or double-linked lists. It is shared by queues, rings, directed graphs (DGs), and many other pointer structures. The problem is that if there is more than one way to reach the same element (a "multiple reference"), then XDR will visit that element more than once. This is never what you want. Even if XDR does not crash your application, the data will be hopelessly corrupted.

Unfortunately, there is no single easy solution to this problem. The solution depends on the pointer structure. In the case where `allflodim` is a double-linked list, for example, you could still use the code given previously for encode and free operations. For decode, you would have to do what is shown in Listing 9.16.

Listing 9.16   Recreating a Doubly-Linked List After an XDR Operation

```
allflodim *work;
allflodim *worknext;
allflodim *workprev = (allflodim *)NULL;
xdr_allflodimp(&myDxdr, &afhead);
work = afhead;
while ( work != (allflodim *)NULL ) {
```

```
        worknext = work->af_next;
        work->af_prev = workprev;
        workprev = work;
        work = worknext;
    }
```

The encode and free part of `xdr_allflodimp()` simply ignore the `af_prev` member. No attempt is made to examine the value of `af_prev` in any of the list elements; it is always treated as `NULL`. The code for the decode direction manually reconstructs the backward list pointers after the XDR decode operation is done, replacing the `NULL`s which were put there by the encode operation with the actual back pointers. I have used the fact that the back pointers are redundant to rebuild them after the decode.

Had `allflodim` been a circular list, I could have employed a similar strategy. The links between the last list member and the first list member would be deliberately broken before an XDR encode or free. The forward pointer from the last member to the first would be encoded as `NULL`, as would the back pointer from the first member to the last. These two pointers would be manually rebuilt after a decode.

More complicated structures will require more complicated approaches. You will either have to write custom XDR routines with care, so that multiple references are avoided or destroyed before encode/free and recreated after decode; or, you will have to transform your pointer representation so that multiple pointer references are replaced with something less harmful.

In a DG, for example, each node can be given a node name (an integer or string), and the array of successor pointers for a node can be replaced by an array of node names representing the successor nodes. In this approach, each node has a dual identity: as a name (node index) and as a pointer destination. The data structure shown in Listing 9.17 illustrates the type of organization which you might use. When you are encoding, you only encode the (integer) node names; all the pointers become `NULL`. When you decode, you reconstruct the pointers by matching node addresses with their names.

Listing 9.17 An XDR Friendly Directed Graph Structure

```
    struct dgnode {
    /*
      This is my node name.  It is XDR encoded
    */
       int      dg_mynodename;
    /*
```

(continues)

```
Listing 9.17   Continued

       This is the number of successors to this node.  It is
       XDR encoded.
   */
      int      dg_nfollowers;
   /*
       This is the array of successor pointers.  It is XDR encoded
       as NULL.
        struct dgnode *dg_followers;
   /*
       This is the array of successor names (which are integers). It
       is XDR encoded.
   */
      int      *dg_nameoffollowers;
   /*
       Similar elements for predecessors go here.
   */
       ...;
      } ;
```

Performance and Data Representation

After seeing the multi-layered way in which XDR works, cascading down
from complex routines like xdr_allflodimp() to simple ones like xdr_float(),
you are probably wondering what the lowest level of XDR is. Accessing XDR
at its lowest level *can* improve the performance of your application.

In the very first example of this chapter, you saw that trying to blindly transmit a float from one machine architecture to another was a recipe for disaster. XDR avoids such problems by specifying a universal format for data.

This universal data scheme guarantees that the data appears the same to all
machines, but it is also the source of potentially unnecessary overhead, since
the translation may not be necessary. XDR is also doing data alignment operations as it loads and unloads data, which can also be eliminated by careful
programming. There are two ways in which you can eliminate some of XDR's
overhead: by avoiding the data translation and by *inlining*, which is described
in the following pages.

The following two XDR library routines are used to load data directly into or
out of an XDR block:

```
bool_t xdr_opaque(XDR *xdrs, caddr_t ptr, u_int sz);
bool_t xdr_bytes(XDR *xdrs, char **ptrptr, u_int *szp,
                 u_int maxsz);
```

The first routine XDRs sz bytes of data at location ptr, and will not allocate
memory for you; while the second routine XDRs (*szp) bytes of data—not to
exceed maxsz—at location (*ptrptr), and will allocate memory for you.

These two routines basically just copy bytes and ensure data alignment. They do not convert data in any way. If you are going to use these routines, you should be sure that all possible consumers of the data use exactly the same representation for that data as all possible producers.

One possible application for these routines might be to transfer the machine representation of another application's executable code. Since this data is just a vast array of uninterpreted bytes with no intrinsic meaning, there is no point in converting it to XDR's representation. For large blocks of such "opaque" data, the savings can be substantial.

The other method of performance improvement is *inlining*. Inlining is used when you have a significant amount of data which is integral, meaning that it is one of the types short (*unsigned short*) int (*unsigned int*) long (*unsigned long*) enum, or bool_t, such as in a data structure like that shown in Listing 9.18.

Listing 9.18   A Data Structure Containing Only Integral Types

```
struct tinydata {
    short  mys;
      u_long myl;
      int    myi;
} mytiny;
```

Floats and all pointer types require special handling, and may not be inlined. Inlining also only works on memory based XDR streams in most implementations.

To use inlining, you first need to get an inline buffer, which is done using the following routine (almost always a macro):

```
char *XDR_INLINE(XDR *xdrs, u_int bytecount);
```

(The return type might be a long *—check your xdr.h header file.) Once you have a buffer, you can inline your data using one of the type macros with a corresponding set for the unsigned types named IXDR_GET_U_type and IXDR_PUT_U_type (see Listing 9.19).

Listing 9.19   The XDR Inline Macros

```
long   IXDR_GET_LONG(char *buf);
void   IXDR_PUT_LONG(char *buf, long Tel);
short  IXDR_GET_SHORT(char *buf);
void   IXDR_PUT_SHORT(char *buf, short thes);
bool_t IXDR_GET_BOOL(char *buf);
void   IXDR_PUT_BOOL(char *buf, bool_t theb);
```

To XDR encode the structure in Listing 9.19, you would use the code shown in Listing 9.20.

Listing 9.20   Using the XDR Inline Macros to Encode an Integral Structure

```
char *buf;
int   nby;
nby = 3 * sizeof(long);
buf = XDR_INLINE(&myExdr, nby);
if ( buf != (char *)NULL ) {
    IXDR_PUT_SHORT(buf, mytiny.mys);
    IXDR_PUT_U_LONG(buf, mytiny.myl);
    sizeof(int) == sizeof(short) ?
        IXDR_PUT_SHORT(buf, mytiny.myi) :
        IXDR_PUT_LONG(buf, mytiny.myi) ;
}
else ...;  /* use xdr_short() ... */
```

nby must be large enough for three longs, since the basic XDR unit for all numerical types is a long. The ugly conditional code in which the size of an int is tested to see if it is the same that of a short is necessary because there is no IXDR_xxx_INT; you can easily define one yourself.

To XDR decode using inlining, use the code in Listing 9.21.

Listing 9.21   Decoding Using the XDR Inline Macros

```
char *buf;
int   nby;
nby = 3 * sizeof(long);
buf = XDR_INLINE(&myDxdr, nby);
if ( buf != (char *)NULL ) {
    mytiny.mys = IXDR_GET_SHORT(buf);
    mytiny.myl = IXDR_GET_U_LONG(buf);
    mytiny.myi =
        ( sizeof(int) == sizeof(short) ?
            IXDR_GET_SHORT(buf) : IXDR_GET_LONG(buf) );
}
else ...;  /* use xdr_short() ... */
```

The advantage to inlining is that it is faster than using the standard XDR routines. Its disadvantage is that it has more code, since it is usually not possible to write a single routine for both encode and decode (there is no inline free). Another disadvantage is that you must keep track of data size and data location yourself, and do so symmetrically in the encode and decode stages. Inlining does not save data space.

Other XDR Routines

There are several XDR routines which you can find in the reference documentation, such as xdr_union(), xdr_void(), and the xdrrec_xxx() functions. You will only use these functions once in a blue moon, if ever. These routines exist because they are used by higher levels of RPC libraries, and not by typical user code.

Tip
Don't use inlining unless your application is spending most of its time in the XDR library routines.

Getting the XDR Source Code

If you have FTP, Mosaic, Netscape, or some other means of transferring files, and can get on the Internet, you can get the XDR source code from several different sites, including:

- bcm.tmc.edu (as part of RPCSVC4.0)

- titan.rice.edu (as part of RPCSVC4.0)

- ftp.uu.net (in the comp.sources.unix archive)

From Here...

To learn more about XDRs, refer to these chapters:

- Chapter 4, "Client/Server Development Overview," acquaints you with the client/server model.

- Chapter 10, "Language Specification," teaches you the rpcgen data description language and shows you how it can be used to generate XDR code.

- Chapter 11, "Techniques for Developing RPC Clients and Servers," shows you actual XDR routines in action in clients and servers.

II

Introduction to RPC

Chapter 10

Language Specification

If you have ever created a library of functions, then you know that an extremely important aspect of library design is the specification of its external interfaces. This interface specification will be the only thing which most, if not all, of your library users will see. This specification defines which functions are available in the library, how they are called, and what they return.

The situation is quite similar in client/server development. Since the client applications are completely separate from the server application, the definition of the client/server interface serves a similar purpose. It defines the services (remote functions) that the server provides, how they are called, and what they return.

There is an important difference between these two situations, however. If you are developing a library of C functions, the external interface will also be specified in C (using ANSI prototypes, for example). In the client/server case, a special interface definition language is used. This language has its own interface compiler, known as rpcgen. This chapter will teach you how to develop rpcgen interface definitions, and how to use them. You will learn how to do the following:

- Define structures and unions
- Specify constants, typedefs, and enumerated types
- Create the all important "program" directive
- Customize rpcgen's output
- Avoid the most common rpcgen pitfalls

Introduction to *rpcgen*

This section presents a goal-oriented introduction to rpcgen, the remote procedure interface compiler. rpcgen is an application which was created as a labor-saving tool for people developing client/server applications. If you are in this position, you will immediately realize that what you do for the client, you must also do for the server. If you arrange to transmit a set of things from the client to the server in some format, then the client must know how to create that format and the server must know what that format means.

What this really means is that when you are developing a client/server application, the first thing you must develop is the interface. The *interface* is the set of data formats which the client and server use to talk to one another. A *remote procedure* is nothing more than a way of taking the procedure arguments, sending them somewhere, executing the procedure at the remote destination, capturing the result, and sending it back.

Developing remote procedures is very similar to developing local C procedures. You define the calling sequence, the return value, and what the procedure does; and then you make it perform. Remote procedures, however, involve two extra steps. For the client, these steps are:

- Packaging the arguments and sending them.

- Receiving and interpreting the return.

For the server, these steps are:

- Receiving and interpreting the arguments.

- Packaging up the return and sending it.

▶ See "Client Calling Conventions," p. 294

▶ See "Server Functions," p. 302

▶ See "Client-Server Rendezvous," p. 316

rpcgen exists to simplify the "package up" and "interpret" parts of these steps. It takes an interface definition in its own special language, very similar to C, and does a lot of the work in creating standard transmit and receive wrappers. You have probably already guessed that it does this work by using XDR as the basic encode/decode tool (for more information on XDR, see Chapter 9). In the next two chapters, you will see how the transmit and receive parts are handled, and how everything is tied together into a working application.

How *rpcgen* is Used

Using rpcgen is very similar to using a compiler. You develop an input file and then apply rpcgen to it. Your input file will consist of a set of type definitions, such as structs and unions, and a set of remote procedure declarations. Your file is written in rpcgen's own input language.

In a typical client/server development, you will first ask yourself, "What does the server do?" The answer to this question leads you to a detailed description of the server's services. These services will be accessed through a set of external interfaces. When you have defined these down to a level of individual procedures—what arguments each one takes, and what it returns—you will then have completed the procedure definition stage.

In order to use these procedures, you will, of course, need data structures. Defining these data structures defines the service requests which flow from the clients to the server, and the service responses which flow from the server back to the clients. When you have completed the data structure definitions, you will have a fully specified rpcgen input file.

You no doubt noticed that no mention was made of any code or algorithms in this description. That's because rpcgen handles only the interfaces between remote applications—it does not handle any of the actual work. You must still write the server code that carries out the services and the client code that construes the user's wishes into requests. An rpcgen input file is therefore much more like a C .h file than a .c file. It defines how to do things, but does not actually do them.

rpcgen's Output Files

> **Note**
>
> rpcgen input files traditionally have the suffix .x on UNIX systems and .X on DOS and VMS systems. Many automated build procedures, such as "make," have built-in rules for files with these suffixes.

Suppose you have done the work I just described for a client/server application. You have an rpcgen input file called deffile.x. If you apply rpcgen to it as shown below, what happens?

```
rpcgen deffile.x
```

II

Introduction to RPC

This is the default use of rpcgen, with the interface file as the sole command line argument. It will generate four output files: a file of data structure definitions and function declarations called deffile.h, a file of XDR routines called deffile_xdr.c, and two files of client and server interface code called deffile_clnt.c and deffile_svc.c, respectively.

> **Note**
>
> The default output files always end in .h, _xdr.c, _clnt.c, and _svc.c.

The include file deffile.h contains the standard C definitions of all the interface data types that you declared in deffile.x. rpcgen converts them from its own compact representation to a more wordy form suitable for your C compiler. This file is included in the three .c files.

◀ See "Constructing Your Own XDR Functions," p. 243

The file deffile_xdr.c is a complete implementation of all the code necessary to XDR any data types defined in deffile.x (or deffile.h). This illustrates another important use for rpcgen. Even if you are not developing a client/server application, you can use rpcgen to write XDR routines for you automatically. If you have read Chapter 9, "External Data Representation," you will appreciate that this can be a tremendous savings in time and effort. You will still have to hand code your XDR routines if you want to take advantage of certain features such as inlining.

The two files deffile_clnt.c and deffile_svc.c are symmetric. They provide common interface routines for the client side and the server side of your application. Clients call routines in deffile_clnt.c in order to exercise remote procedures. Servers are called by routines in deffile_svc.c to implement these procedures. Both sides make use of the XDR routines of deffile_xdr.c to encode and decode data. The overall effect is very similar to a local procedure call. In fact, as we will see in the next chapter, you can merge the client and server routines into a single local application for debugging purposes. Figure 10.1 shows how the client, server, and intermediate routines generated by rpcgen are wired together.

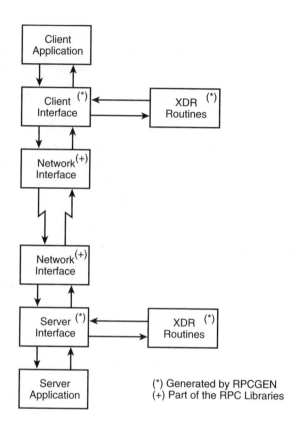

Fig. 10.1

rpcgen generates routines used by clients and servers.

(*) Generated by RPCGEN
(+) Part of the RPC Libraries

Why use *rpcgen*? An example...

Why should you use rpcgen? It is a (slightly) new language, after all, so what are its advantages? A simple example should illustrate how much time and effort rpcgen will save you.

Suppose you would like to develop a simple network database server. This server will accept two types of requests. Clients can ask the server for the value of an entry, and can attempt to set an entry. When clients ask for an entry, they must select which entry is desired, and can request the value in one of several formats. When they attempt to set an entry, they must again specify which entry, and can provide the value in one of several formats. They can also specify an expiration interval, or *age delta*. This is used to prevent entries from being changed too rapidly. If the entry had been changed within that number of seconds, then the set request will fail.

This is a very simple interface. It has only two requests, and the amount of data being transmitted on either side is small. However, if you try to sit down and write such an application from scratch, it will very quickly become clear that the coding is time-consuming and tedious. You have to invent a way of encapsulating the arguments, transmitting them, handling errors, and so on. The mind can boggle, even for something this simple.

With rpcgen, the interface definition is a few minutes work. Once you have created a very brief rpcgen input file for this interface, you run rpcgen on it and all your XDR, client interface, and server interface routines are created for you, automatically. This is the power of rpcgen. You will see this example fully developed at the end of the next section.

A Note on Versions

Unfortunately, there are several versions of rpcgen floating around. You may find that your system has rpcgen, rpcgen.new, and perhaps even rpcgen.tli. Some of these versions produce better (or worse) code than others. Some have extended features and more numerous command line arguments.

This chapter describes the features that are common to all rpcgens, and the defects that many of them share. You may discover to your great joy that some of the bugs or deficiencies that I cite are not present on your system. More power to you.

The *rpcgen* Input File

Tip
If you are using rpcgen to develop XDR routines only, you may skip this subsection.

The basic language tools that you will need to develop your interface definition will be covered first. The five top level statement types (const, enum, struct, union, and typedef) will be described, as well as the melange of special syntax rules needed.

The final topic will be the rpcgen "program" statement. The program statement is almost always the focus of your rpcgen development, because it defines your interfaces.

C Syntax and *rpcgen* Syntax

If you were to compare an rpcgen input file with a C header file (.h file), you might not notice any immediate difference. This is both a strength and a weakness of rpcgen. Many statements that are valid C will be rejected by rpcgen, and a few of rpcgen's constructs will infuriate any C compiler.

With your knowledge of C and a few simple guidelines, however, it is very easy to write `rpcgen` input.

The greatest difference between C and the `rpcgen` language stems from the fact that the `rpcgen` language is an interface definition language. An `rpcgen` input file is not the place for shared data structure definitions, global variables, interesting macros, or any of the other common purposes of a C `include` file. All the statements in an `rpcgen` file are there to help define the interfaces of your remote procedure calls.

An immediate consequence of `rpcgen`'s single-mindedness is that it will only accept five types of statements. That is, every *top level statement* (i.e., a statement not contained inside any other statement) in an `rpcgen` input file must begin with these five "definition keywords:"

- `const`
- `enum`
- `struct`
- `typedef`
- `union`

Note

The keyword "program" and the special symbol % are special cases which will be treated separately.

When you look at this list, you might ask, "What about `int`? What about `float`?" All the standard C data types are certainly allowed, but only inside one of these statements (in a structure definition, for example). You cannot have the following as a top level statement in an `rpcgen` input file:

```
static int myqlim = 5;
```

Indeed, you cannot really have global variables, or any kind of variables at all. Think of an `rpcgen` input file as a set of type definitions.

The next set of sections describe each of these statements in detail, with several diversions to discuss typical situations that you will encounter. Throughout the descriptions of the various keywords, assume that you are working with an `rpcgen` input file called `deffile.x`.

The *const* keyword

The const statement is the simplest type of rpcgen statement. A const statement defines a constant, almost always an integer:

```
const     myval = 10;     /* a */
```

Note that, unlike ANSI C, it is not a const something, like a const int or a const float, it is just a const. This also exposes the first subtlety of rpcgen. Why not just use a #define?

The reason is part of the way that rpcgen works. rpcgen converts its input into C output file(s). If you had a statement like the following:

```
#define myval    10      /* b */
```

in your file deffile.x, then this define would be seen within deffile.x, but would never make it to any of rpcgen's output files. This is because rpcgen runs the C preprocessor before parsing its input. So, in order to obtain statement b (the define) in the output files, you must put statement a (the const) in deffile.x.

You may, in fact, have a const anything, so that the following is quite legal, although rare:

```
const mystr = "this is MY string";
```

If you find that you need a constant defined in a system include file, your best bet is usually to simply create a local copy of that constant, such as the following:

```
const MAXHOSTNAMELEN = 64;     /* good */
```

Do not try this:

```
#include <sys/param.h>      /* MAXHOSTNAMELEN is here */
const MHNL = MAXHOSTNAMELEN;
```

This is an excellent idea that will not work. The problem is the include file. rpcgen will object to many things in the include file.

The *enum* keyword

An enum statement has the same syntax as in C. You write it as the following, where ENAME is the name of your enumerated type, and MEMBER1, MEMBER2, and so forth are the names of its members:

```
enum ENAME { MEMBER1, MEMBER2, ... } ;
```

Note that members may optionally have an initializer, as in:

```
enum myenum { ceci, nest, pas, une = 1, pipe } ;
```

There is one major difference between most versions of rpcgen and C, which arises in enums and any other declarations involving symbolic names. rpcgen does not check for name conflicts! The following would be accepted by many rpcgens the world over, while almost every C compiler would complain bitterly:

```
enum fr { ooh, la, la } ;
```

The only way to detect such errors is to compile the C output files from rpcgen. If you are generating the .h file, then check that as well.

Troubleshooting

I have been writing an rpcgen interface definition for my file and directory deletion module. My input file, deleteme.x, passes through rpcgen fine; but when I compile the client file, I get an amazing number of errors. Is rpcgen generating incorrect code?

When you are developing an rpcgen input file, you should not assume that everything is fine just because rpcgen does not complain. Sadly, rpcgen does not do comprehensive error checking on the input file. Your input file may have problems which rpcgen propagates to its output files. Therefore, every time you rpcgen your input file, you should always check the .c and .h output files it generates. Execute the following:

```
rpcgen      deleteme.x
```

Then, try to compile your outputs with the following:

```
cc -c deleteme*.c
```

Make a dummy program dum.c containing the lines:

```
#include <stdio.h>
#include "deleteme.h"
void hiya(void) {}
```

Now, try to compile that, too, with the following:

```
cc -c dum.c
```

Always double-check rpcgen's output. It is very unlikely that rpcgen is generating code incorrectly. The most likely source of your problem is a name conflict or other error in your input file. When you compile dum.c above, you should get the same type of error messages, which will point you to problems in your deleteme.h file. Look at the problem lines and trace them back to the rpcgen statements from which they came. This will be the source of the errors.

It is always wise to have a short edit—rpcgen—compile cycle so that duplicate name errors can be caught quickly.

There is one more thing to note about enums. Like many C compilers, rpcgen will assign values to uninitialized members in the most direct (and often the least convenient) way. The members of myenum mentioned previously will get the following values:

```
enum myenum { ceci=0, nest=1, pas=2, une=1, pipe=2 } ;
```

Notice that both nest and une have the value 1, and both pas and pipe have the value 2—probably not what you wanted.

The *struct* keyword

The struct keyword introduces a structure definition. You will find that you will use structs to transmit almost all of your RPC argument lists.

The struct statement is almost exactly the same as in C. A struct is a list of members, which may contain any standard C data types and any data types that you have defined within your rpcgen input file. It may also contain forward references to pointer types that are not yet defined, just as in C. Listing 10.1 shows a sample struct definition.

Listing 10.1   Examples of *rpcgen struct* Statements

```
struct firstone {
      int fone;
      struct secondone *sptr;
      } ;
struct secondone {
      int sone;
      int sone2;
      } ;
```

You may even use data types that are not defined in your rpcgen input file. You must be prepared to define them elsewhere, of course. This is one way to provide hooks for getting at your custom XDR or client/server routines.

Unfortunately, there are several things with which rpcgen is not happy. You may not have bitfields in rpcgen structs. You may not have anonymous structures. You may not define structures within other structures. Listing 10.2 will not please rpcgen at all.

Listing 10.2   Nested *rpcgen structs* Are Not Permitted

```
struct {                         /* first error: anonymous */
    int one;                     /* ok */
    unsigned two : 16;           /* second error: bitfield */
    struct three {               /* 3rd error: nested defn */
        float four;              /* ok */
        } ;
} ;
```

When you define a `struct`, `rpcgen` will perform a special courtesy for you. It will also create a `typedef` for that structure, of the same name. For the two structures in Listing 10.1, the following statements will appear in the `.h` file after the definitions of `struct firstone` and `struct secondone`:

```
typedef struct firstone firstone;

typedef struct secondone secondone;
```

From this point forward, you can and should use `firstone` instead of `struct firstone`. This helps to separate structure definition from structure use. You should also not include a `typedef` in your `struct` declaration. The `typedef` keyword is allowed by `rpcgen`, as you will soon see, but it should not be combined with `struct`.

`Struct` processing suffers from the same defect as `enum` processing—name conflicts are not noticed by `rpcgen`. It is quite possible to have members with identical names, two `structs` with the same name, or even two different types (a `struct` and an `enum`, for example) with the same name. Always compile your outputs as a cross-check.

System Structures and *include* Files

You may constantly struggle with `include` files when you write C programs. It often seems hard to get the right ones, and in the right order. Where, you might ask, is `struct timeval` defined on this system, anyway? Happily, you will almost certainly never have that problem in `rpcgen`, because it is almost impossible to include any of the standard system files in an `rpcgen` input file!

This is because few of the standard `include` files obey the potpourri of restrictions which `rpcgen` imposes. Their main offense is to define or refer to globals or functions—`stdio.h` is an excellent example of this. Any system `include` file that contains `extern`, for example, is hopeless. If your system has a well-written `<sys/types.h>`, you *may* be able to use it, but don't bet on it.

Tip
You can easily get include files into one or more of your output files using the % directive; see the section "Special Rules" later in the chapter for more information.

This means that if you really need a data structure definition in your rpcgen input, such as a struct timeval, then you have two choices. The simplest solution, of course, is to copy the definition; this is an ugly practice, but it will work. Your second choice is to create an automated extraction tool to get the structure definitions out of the system files. I almost always choose the first approach.

Pointers and Arrays

There is another, more subtle stumbling block with structures. Consider the slight modification in Listing 10.3 to your previously successful definition.

Listing 10.3 A Dangerous Example of Mutually Referential *structs*

```
struct firstone {
    int fone;
    struct secondone *sptr;
    } ;
struct secondone {
    int sone;
    struct firstone *fptr;
    } ;
```

This is perfectly legal input. It will pass rpcgen with flying colors, and all the output files will compile without a problem. When you attempt to use the XDR routines that are generated, or send or receive such a structure, you may encounter the "multiple reference" problem which was discussed in Chapter 9, under the section "Handling Lists, Graphs, and Multiple References."

> **Caution**
>
> If you have not read this section in Chapter 9, I strongly suggest you do so before you attempt to put any structures containing pointers in your rpcgen files. Multiple reference errors are the most common rpcgen semantic errors by a wide margin.

Tip
Think of your structure pointers as dynamic links. If possible, design them so that you can never reach the same link in more than one way.

It is always a good idea to take great care with pointer members in any structure. rpcgen will generate code which will always attempt to dereference any pointer except the NULL pointer.

This is usually what you want. However, there are two types of pointers which merit special treatment—arrays and strings. If the array is of fixed size, then a standard is used. If you have a pointer to a dynamically allocated array of items, however, then you use the special rpcgen notation <> for a variable length array.

The declaration in Listing 10.4 defines various types of integer pointers.

Listing 10.4   Four Types of Pointer in *rpcgen*

```
struct someptrs {
        int     *oneptr;
        int     iarray[20];
        int     ivarray<128>;
        int     ivqarray<>;
} ;
```

oneptr is a simple pointer to a single integer. If it is not NULL, then a single int at the location it points to will be accessed. iarray is an array pointer. Twenty elements at its base address will be accessed. ivarray is a pointer to a variable length array of integers, whose length is at most 128 integers. ivqarray is a pointer to a variable length array of integers, whose maximum length is not known.

> **Caution**
>
> An rpcgen declaration of THING * is always interpreted as a pointer to exactly one THING. If you want an array or string, make sure you use [ ], <>, or string.

The value inside the <> (called the *length field*) must be an integer literal, or an integer defined as a const. It may also be blank, which stands for "unknown length."

In terms of XDR, the routine xdr_pointer() is used for oneptr, xdr_vector() for iarray, and xdr_array() for ivarray and ivqarray. The length field is used for the maxlen argument in the calls to xdr_array().

◀ See "Pointer Functions," p. 236

You are probably wondering how you actually use a variable length array. There has to be some way to dynamically set the length of such an array. If you use rpcgen on struct someptrs and look at the .h file that it generates, you will find the following inside the definition generated for struct someptrs:

```
struct {
        u_int           ivarray_len;
        int             *ivarray_val;
        } ivarray;
```

rpcgen has turned the variable length array into a structure declaration very similar to the one you might have created yourself. The ivarray_len member is used to set the number of elements pointed to by the ivarray_val pointer.

There is one troubling aspect of `ivarray` structure which `rpcgen` created. It is an anonymous structure (no structure tag) inside the definition of `struct someptrs`. There is no way to use this structure definition elsewhere. How do you create a new type that represents a variable length array of integers? You cannot do it within a structure member declaration. The answer is a clever use of `typedef`, as you will soon see.

Strings

None of the pointer methods previously described will work with a C string, because a C string has special semantics—its endpoint is denoted by the NUL character. To refer to a C string, use the special `rpcgen` keyword "string" together with the <> notation. The following declarations refer to two C strings:

```
string      shortstring<20>;
string      somestring<>;
```

The first will not be longer than twenty characters, not counting the terminating NUL. The second has an unspecified length, up to some system specified maximum (often 65,535 bytes).

It is an error to use just plain `string`. The following declaration just won't work:

```
string      badstring;          /* quite bad */
```

Also, if you use just a `char *`, it will be treated as a pointer to a single character.

Note that `rpcgen` does not generate a special structure for a `string`. There is no equivalent to the `ivarray struct` that you saw previously. Instead, it just converts a string into a `char *` in its `.h` output file.

The *union* Keyword

`rpcgen` unions are quite different from their C counterparts. They are much more similar to variant records in Pascal or Ada. An `rpcgen` union looks like a cross between a standard C union and a switch statement. It consists of a series of *arms*, which are the various ways in which the contents of the union may be viewed, and a *discriminator*, which selects which arm to use. For this reason, it is often called a *discriminated union*.

A typical `rpcgen` union looks like what is shown in Listing 10.5.

Listing 10.5   An *rpcgen* Union Using an *enum* Discriminator

```
enum heighttype { ENGLISH = 1, METRIC = 2 } ;
union Height switch ( heighttype whichheight ) {
     case ENGLISH:
            int     feetinch[2];
     case METRIC:
            float   cm;
     default:
            void;
} ;
```

The whichheight parameter is the discriminator. When it has the value ENGLISH, the field feetinch is used. When it has the value METRIC, the field cm is used. When it has neither of these values, the union is void—no value at all is used.

More formally, an rpcgen discriminated union must look like Listing 10.6.

Listing 10.6   Formal Definition of an *rpcgen* Union

```
union UNAME switch ( INTorENUM DISCRIMNAME ) {
     case CVALUE1:
            DECLARATION;              /* arm 1 */
     case CVALUE2:
            DECLARATION;              /* arm 2 */
     ...
     default:
            DECLARATION;
     } ;
```

All the mandatory keywords are shown in lowercase. UNAME is the name of the union. INTorENUM declares the type of the discriminant, whose name is DISCRIMNAME. The discriminant must be either an integer or an enum. After this are one or more cases, as in a C switch statement. Each of the case statements must contain a literal integer, a const whose value is an integer, or a member of an enum. Each case must be followed by exactly one member declaration, which may be the special statement void indicating "no value." Any member declaration which is legal in a struct is also acceptable in a union. The default arm, while not strictly necessary, is strongly encouraged, and should be the last arm given. The usual warning about name collisions applies.

II

Introduction to RPC

One extremely common form of discriminated union is shown in Listing 10.7.

Listing 10.7   An *rpcgen* Union Discriminated by an Error Word

```
union dataorerror switch ( int errno ) {
    case 0:
        struct mydata     *theactualdata;
    default:
        void;
    } ;
```

This union says "if errno is zero, then my actual data is present; otherwise, there is no data, and errno tells you why." When you are building up client/ server routines, you will realize that this is extremely useful, because it saves you the trouble of creating a dummy version of the theactualdata data in case an error occurs.

When you pass the declaration of dataorerror through rpcgen, you will get what is shown in Listing 10.8.

Listing 10.8   The C Code Generated from Listing 10.7

```
struct dataorerror {
    int       errno;
    union {
        struct mydata *theactualdata;
        } dataorerror_u;
    } ;
typedef struct dataorerror dataorerror;
```

The name of the internal union always has the suffix _u. If there were five arms in the rpcgen union, there would be five members in the dataorerror_u union. As with variable length arrays, this new union is created within an enclosing structure, so dataorerror_u cannot be used elsewhere. You can use dataorerror, however, since it is globally declared.

The *typedef* keyword

The typedef keyword is used in just the same way it is used in C, except that it should not be used with structs and unions, since rpcgen automatically generates typedefs for them. typedef has one special use in rpcgen: it enables you to declare variable length arrays as top level items.

To define a global structure for a variable length array of floats (with no specified maximum length) use the following:

```
typedef      float              farray<>;
```

This is expanded by rpcgen to become:

```
typedef struct {
     u_int           farray_len;
     float           *farray_val;
     } farray ;
```

This trick is necessary in order to have the type farray available for subsequent statements in your rpcgen input file. If you now had the following, this would declare a structure with a single int myint and a variable length array of floats myfarray:

```
struct iandf {
     int        myint;
     farray     myfarray;
     } ;
```

farray can now be used just like any other C data type.

Special Rules

There are just three special constructs left and your tour of rpcgen syntax will be finished. These constructs are the bool keyword, the opaque keyword, and the % directive.

rpcgen has a built-in Boolean type, called bool. It is not bool_t, as you might expect from Chapter 9, but is converted into bool_t by rpcgen. Why create a new name for the same thing? Nobody knows.

rpcgen has a built-in type for opaque data, called opaque. Opaque data is an array of uninterpreted bytes which is encoded and decoded using the XDR routine xdr_opaque(). The designations opaque or uninterpreted are because the XDR system passes these bytes without any encoding or decoding.

◀ See "Performance and Data Representation," p. 254

Because opaque always refers to an array, you must use it with either an explicit or variable length declaration. If you are dealing with the raw byte stream of an executable program with a fixed header and variable length machine code, you could use these declarations:

```
opaque      ProgramHeader[32];
opaque      ProgramBytes<65536>;
```

The final topic is the % directive. The % symbol is processed specially by rpcgen. Anything after a % is copied by rpcgen into its output—in fact, it is copied into all the output files that rpcgen generates. In most cases, you will only want the statement copied into one of the output files, such as into the .h file (the .h file in included in any .c files generated).

rpcgen provides a set of special preprocessor symbols that can be combined with % to select where the statements are to go. Table 10.1 shows the preprocessor symbols and the output files to which they correspond, assuming an input file named deffile.x.

Table 10.1   Preprocessor Symbols and the Files They Select

Preprocessor Symbol	Output File
RPC_HDR	deffile.h
RPC_XDR	deffile_xdr.c
RPC_CLNT	deffile_clnt.c
RPC_SVC	deffile_svc.c

For example, if you want to make sure that the include files <sys/types.h> and <sys/param.h>, as well as a definition for MAXHOSTNAMELEN, are included in the .h file, you could use the code in Listing 10.9 in the rpcgen input file.

Listing 10.9   Using % for Conditional Preprocessing

```
#ifdef RPC_HDR
%#include <sys/types.h>
%#include <sys/param.h>
%#ifndef MAXHOSTNAMELEN
%#define MAXHOSTNAMELEN   64
%#endif
#endif
```

Notice that the outer #ifdef RPC_HDR ... #endif is processed by rpcgen before the C preprocessor ever sees it, while the inner % statements are passed unchanged (without the %, of course) into the deffile.h output. This approach has a drawback, however; you have no control over where this code will be placed in the output file. You will need to experiment with your rpcgen to see if % suits your needs.

The *program* statement

When you write an application in C with more than one source file, you will also typically create one or more header files that define those functions which must be externally visible. If you are using ANSI C, you will go further and put full function prototypes in your header files. This helps catch common syntax errors, such as calling functions with too few or too many arguments.

The `rpcgen` `program` statement serves a very similar purpose. In order to make a remote procedure call truly remote, it is necessary to transmit the arguments of the procedure to the machine on which it will execute, execute it, and collect and transmit the result. The program statement defines the remote procedures, their arguments, and their return codes.

The program statement has the form shown in Listing 10.10.

Listing 10.10   An *rpcgen program* Statement Template

```
program PROGNAME {
     version PROGVERS {
          remote-procedure-definition;
          ...
          } = VNUMBER ;
     /* more version blocks can go here */
     } = PNUMBER ;
```

`PROGNAME` is the name of this interface definition. This should be a string and is traditionally a short but descriptive name entirely in uppercase. The `PROGVERS` is another string which provides a symbolic name for the version of this interface definition. You are allowed to provide multiple versions within the program, although typically you will have only one. This is done by adding another block beginning with the `version` keyword, as shown in Listing 10.11.

Listing 10.11   An *rpcgen program* Statement with Two Versions

```
program PROGNAME {
     version PROGVERS1 {
          remote-procedure-definition;
          ...
          } = VFIRST ;
     version PROGVERS2 {
          another-remote-procedure-definition;
          ...
          } = VSECOND ;
} = PNUMBER ;
```

VNUMBER in Listing 10.10, or VFIRST and VSECOND in Listing 10.11, are the actual numerical values of the current version(s). Version numbers may be any positive value. You are permitted to include any version number without including its predecessors, so that a single version block at version 3 is quite acceptable. Typically, your protocol number will start at 1. As your interface develops, you may find it necessary to change the protocol, and therefore the protocol's version number. You may also find it necessary to support more than one version, leading to multiple version blocks within your program statement.

PNUMBER is a relatively arbitrary number which serves to uniquely identify your interface. It is typically a very large number, written in hex with a 0x prefix. By convention, program numbers should be in the range 0x20000000 to 0x3FFFFFFF, although this restriction is never seriously enforced. All that matters is that it is unique across all machines which you will be using. Under UNIX, you can check the files /etc/rpc and /etc/services for program numbers used by system services, or you can issue the command rpcinfo -p to get a dynamic list of port numbers in use.

> **Note**
>
> If you keep your program numbers in the range 0x20000000 to 0x3FFFFFFF, you will almost certainly avoid a conflict with the system services, which almost always used very small program numbers.

Within each version block are the actual remote procedure definitions. They look like the definition of a function with one argument (with some extra stuff at the end), and have the following form:

```
RETURNTYPE          PROCNAME(ARGTYPE) = NUMBER;
```

RETURNTYPE is the type returned by the procedure PROCNAME. ARGTYPE is the type of the argument—note carefully that only one argument is allowed by most versions of rpcgen. You are not allowed to have a comma-separated list of arguments as you are in C. Traditionally, procedure names are given in uppercase, while the return types and argument types are given as you have defined them. Note also that both the argument and the return types are allowed to be void on most systems. If your C compiler can handle void *, then your arguments or returns can also be void in rpcgen.

Each of your procedures must have an identifying number, which is given after the procedure definition itself. The numbers must start at one, and should always be consecutive. If you have more than one version block, the procedure numbers should restart at one within each one.

The *rpcgen* Example Concluded

Let's revisit the network database server which was discussed at the start of this chapter. You now have the tools to develop the complete rpcgen input file, including the program definition. Suppose you choose to pass entry values in two forms: unsigned long integer array and printable string. You can encapsulate the variable entry value definition as shown in Listing 10.12.

Listing 10.12   An *rpcgen* Database Interface: the *entry* Type

```
const IENTRY = 1;
const SENTRY = 2;
const MAXSTRLEN = 64;
union someentry switch ( int how ) {
    case IENTRY:
            unsigned long    intentryval[4];
    case SENTRY:
            string           stringval<MAXSTRLEN>;
    default:
            void;            /* some error stored in "how" */
    } ;
```

For the get operation, you need to wrap the format selector with the entry name, which you will pass as a string. For the set operation, you need to wrap an entry name with an entry value and the additional age parameter (see Listing 10.13).

Listing 10.13   An *rpcgen* Database Interface: *get* and *set* Operand Types

```
struct egetter {
        string        entryname<>;
        int           how;
    } ;
struct esetter {
        string        entryname<>;
        someentry     entryval;
        u_int         age;
        } ;
```

You also want to ensure that the appropriate database files get included in the .h file that rpcgen outputs, so you add the following:

```
#ifdef RPC_HDR
%#include "mydatabase.h"
#endif
```

The result of a get operation is the entry, or an error code stored in the how field. The result of a set operation is an error or success code. You can thus define the interface as displayed in Listing 10.14.

Listing 10.14 An *rpcgen* Database Interface: *program* Statement

```
program NETDBPROG {
    version NETDBVERS {
        someentry        GETDB(egetter)    = 1;
        int              SETDB(esetter)    = 2;
        } = 1;
    } = 0x21000012 ;          /* a palindrome */
```

If you pass this definition through rpcgen and observe the outputs, you will see two functions that look something like the following:

```
someentry        *getdb_1(egetter *);
int              *setdb_1(esetter *);
```

The GETDB and SETDB remote procedures have been converted into client and server functions named something like getdb_1() and setdb_1() (the names may be slightly different for different rpcgens). The _1 suffix comes from the version. Also, all of the arguments and return codes have been converted into pointers; this is because the underlying XDR operations must have pointers. This extremely important conversion will be discussed extensively in the next chapter.

This interface definition is also easily extensible. If you subsequently determine that you also need to transmit the entry value as a struct dbentry, you only need to do the following steps:

1. Define the struct dbentry in the input file.

2. Add another arm to the union (and another const for the discriminant).

3. Bump the version number to 2 to indicate that this is a newer version of the interface.

As was promised, these 29 lines of code provide the complete remote database server interface. More detail, such as the definition of possible error codes, should, of course, be added to make this a full-fledged interface definition. Even so, this example illustrates one of the greatest benefits of rpcgen: its compactness.

The *rpcgen* Command Line

To complete your understanding of rpcgen, a few more words need to be said about the outputs of rpcgen. Most client/server developers use rpcgen in its default form. There are situations, however, in which you may need finer control over the output generated. This section covers all the major command line options to rpcgen and tells you what they do.

In all the examples previously given, rpcgen was always being asked to generate the .h output file and the three C interface files, as well. In some situations, you only need one of these files. Figure 10.2 shows the rpcgen command line switch that you use to generate only one of these outputs.

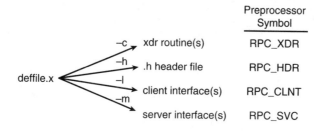

Fig. 10.2
rpcgen command line options can be used to select which output files are generated.

If you use one of these switches, then you must use only one. It is not possible to generate exactly two output files; if you use -c, for example, you cannot also use -m. If you are using one of these output selectors, as they are called, then you will almost certainly want to use the following as well:

```
-o outputfile
```

This option can only be used with one of the selectors. When rpcgen is generating only a single output file, it insists on putting its results to stdout, so you can also redirect the output to a file of your choice. If your goal is to create XDR routines, all of the following will work:

```
rpcgen deffile.x
rpcgen -c deffile.x > deffile_xdr.c
rpcgen -c deffile.x -o deffile_xdr.c
```

The first command will generate more, of course.

rpcgen has several other command line options which are related to its interface to the network. (For more information on how these are used, refer to the sections "Initialization" in Chapter 11 and "Server Startup and the inetd" in Chapter 12.) The networking command line options are the following:

- ■ `-s transname`

- ■ `-I`

- ■ `-K timeout`

- ■ `-L`

The `-s` option is used to specify the type of underlying network transport which the clients and server will use. `transname` is a string, such as `tcp`, representing a transport type. You may be able to give more than one `-s` option to enable support for multiple transports. `-s` is the only option which applies to client code as well as server code.

The next three command line options apply to server code only. `-I` generates code for servers which can be activated by the UNIX server-of-servers, the `inetd`. If `-K` is also given with `-I`, then `timeout` specifies the number of seconds which the server will wait for a client request before exiting. `-K 0` means "service one request, then exit." `-K -1` means "wait forever for a request." `-L` indicates that the server should divert its standard error output, `stderr`, to the system log file using the operating system's networked logging facility `syslog()`.

Finally, `rpcgen` will also respond to any number of `-Dname=val` options, just like most C compilers. This is equivalent to the statement `#define name val`. For some strange reason, most implementations of `rpcgen` do not support `-Uname`. There are a few other `rpcgen` options that you may encounter in the `rpcgen` documentation. I have never used them, and you probably will not either.

From Here...

To learn more about the topics covered in this chapter, refer to these chapters:

- ■ Chapter 4, "Client/Server Development Overview," acquaints you with the client/server model.

- ■ Chapter 9, "External Data Representation," teaches you the inner workings of the XDR code that `rpcgen` generates and uses.

- ■ Chapter 11, "Techniques for Developing RPC Clients and Servers," shows you how to effectively integrate `rpcgen`'s outputs into the client/server application development process.

- ■ Chapter 12, "RPC Under UNIX," gives you the UNIX-specific information you will need to create and manage remote procedure call code.

Chapter 11

Techniques for Developing RPC Clients and Servers

Writing a client/server application might seem like a lot of work. You have to write the client and you have to write the server. Although you are probably convinced of the benefits, even the necessity, of the client/server approach, it still might seem a daunting and time-consuming task.

My mission in this chapter is to demonstrate the ease and efficiency of developing client/server applications through a series of straightforward techniques using RPC. In fact, it is more efficient to create a server and then write one or more clients that use it than it would be write a monolithic program for each potential application.

There are certain conventions that must be obeyed when developing RPC clients and servers. These conventions are related to the way in which arguments and replies are passed back and forth across the network interface. As you have seen from Chapter 10, "Language Specification," arguments must be packaged up and encoded, and then sent. Replies undergo the same process in reverse. Both clients and servers must follow their respective conventions.

Of course, there are also special RPC functions that clients and servers must use in order to contact one another, send and receive information, handle errors, ensure security, and the like. I will show you all you need to know to quickly get your client and server up and running, chatting away fluently with one another.

This chapter will cover generic client/server programming using RPC. This material will be (mostly) platform independent, and leads directly into the UNIX-specific information of Chapter 12. This chapter is not meant to be an exhaustive review of every possible RPC function. Rather, it is intended as a thorough and practical discussion of the main design and implementation concepts that underlie RPC.

In this chapter, you will discover how to:

- Develop robust client code

- Create efficient server functions

- Handle all types of client and server errors

- Perform nonblocking execution of server functions

- Customize your server

Introduction to RPC Clients and Servers

The RPC client/server model is a special case of the general client/server model that was discussed in Chapter 4, "Client/Server Development Overview." In RPC, we assume that all of the clients' needs may be satisfied by executing one or more function calls. The client specifies its desire by executing a procedure. The arguments are transmitted (over the network) to the server, which does the actual work. The server then returns any results to the client (also over the network).

This division of labor also implies a certain type of partitioning between the client and the server. Since each request will usually translate to a single procedure call, the type of work being done must be amenable to being divided this way. If you find that you cannot easily map requests to functions in a more or less one-to-one fashion, then your application may not be suitable for the RPC approach. The X Window System is a major set of clients and servers that do not fit the RPC model, for example.

The client program and the server program tend to be very different beasts. Since the server is doing the actual labor, most of the actual "algorithms" will be in the server program. Since the client is typically interacting with the outside world, most of the "user interface" will be in the client program. We will now take a closer look at each half of the client/server pair, in order to better understand how each is developed.

Client Design Considerations

The client application is the bridge between the requests themselves and the worker performing the requests—the server. The client must take each request and turn it into a function call that is actually executed elsewhere, in an entirely different process. The fact that the remote procedure is executed in an environment that is distinct from the client's has a number of implications.

If the client and the server were a monolithic application, all of this application's internal resources, or *state*, would be localized. Global variables known to one function would be known to all. There would be no issues of synchronization or resource contention. In a monolithic application, for example, a work function would be able to say to itself "well, I know that the log file has already been opened, so therefore…"

> **Note**
>
> The concept of *state* will be used frequently in this chapter. Unfortunately, it is hard to define precisely. For our purposes, think of state as global or persistent information. Global variables retain their value until changed, unlike local variables, and so are part of the application's state. Open files, semaphores, and anything else that requires assistance from the operating system, are also part of an application's state. In these cases, the operating system itself is storing part of the state for you, such as the current read/write position of an open file.

None of these things apply in the client/server environment. If the client wants the value of a server global variable, it must ask for it. If the client wants exclusive access to a resource, it may well have to reserve it in one RPC call, use it in a second call, and then release it in yet a third call. It must also be mindful that other clients may be waiting impatiently for that resource.

In short, the client must be aware that the server very often has state, and it must manage its manipulation of that state through very well-defined operations. It cannot make any of the assumptions that a monolithic application may make. In the ideal client, each request is atomic and orthogonal. *Atomic* means it does exactly one thing, and *orthogonal* means that that thing is completely independent of all other requests from this or any other client. Such abstract perfection may be impossible to achieve in a real application. Client developers must be aware of this as a goal, however.

In practice, the potential interaction between requests means that each request function must be considered in relation to all other request functions. If you find that a particular function depends on assumptions about other functions that have already been executed, then you may need to do more work on your interface definition.

Let us take a concrete example. Consider a remote pager server and its clients. The server will accept messages for any registered user and will distribute the messages of a registered user to her on request. There are two clients. The sender client sends a single message to the server. Its interface looks like the following:

```
SendOne(from_me, to_person, message);
```

where each of the arguments is a string. The receiver client gets the messages of a designated person. Its interface looks like the following:

```
ReceiveAll(to_me)
```

where its single argument is also string. This seems like a phenomenally simple set of interfaces. What can go wrong?

Imagine a situation in which you are the receiver. Your pager has just vibrated, and you hit the transmit icon. Someone has sent you a vast number of junk messages. When the function ReceiveAll() is executed, you will be blocked for the entire time the message text is being transmitted. In addition, the server is also blocked. Not only can it not receive or transmit messages for anyone else, it also cannot receive any additional messages for you. This is bad client design. Fortunately, there are straightforward methods for avoiding blocking in both the client and the server.

▶ See "Client Batch Requests," p. 336

▶ See "Server Callbacks," p. 340

Suppose you add the following client interface:

```
NumberOfMessages(to_me)
```

If you do this, you must modify your receive function. The reason for this is that if you call NumberOfMessages() and get back five, for example, when you call ReceiveAll(), you may not get back five messages, because more messages might have arrived between the call to NumberOfMessages() and the call to ReceiveAll(). If memory had been allocated based on five messages, but seven are incoming, this could be a nasty shock.

Suppose you modify the receive interface to the following:

```
ReceiveSome(number_of_messages, to_me)
```

You should also consider that the number of messages you get back might be *less* than the number requested. This might happen if the server imposes a limit on the size of text it will transmit at one time, for example.

Clearly this interface is not as simple as it seemed initially. The server has state, namely the number of messages and the messages themselves, and the client must always take that state into account. I encourage you to ponder this example a little further, by adding messages subjects and password protection, for example. Every piece of additional state can, and probably will, increase the logical complexity of the server. If you have passwords, then you must, of course, ensure that a user has supplied the correct password before access to any messages is permitted. If you are going to provide the convenience of message subjects, then you will almost certainly want an additional client interface that retrieves only the subjects. Even a small increase in the amount of state can lead to a large increase in server logic.

The two fundamental rules of RPC client design are the following:

- Ask the server for the best-defined, simplest things possible.

- Be prepared for any possible results; make no assumptions.

Simplicity must be balanced against selfishness, however. `ReceiveAll()` is simple, but it is also resource intensive and it is not well defined—since `all` can and will change as the sender client interacts with the server.

Server Design Considerations

The server application is the application that does the work. It gets work requests from one or more clients and must carry out that work if possible, delivering to each client all of, but only, what it requested. Even if your client/server design involves only one client that will ever interact with the server, the server may still have to store large amounts of information between requests. This is its state.

What is part of this state? Every file that is open is part of the server state. A remote database server will almost certainly have an enormous amount of state, for example (open records, locked records, record position, and so on). Every data structure that persists between remote procedure calls is state. In the remote pager service I described previously, the messages themselves are the state. Every interaction with an external device is state. In a remote print server, the server should keep track of how much of each print request has been fulfilled, as well as information on which printers are available and their state. Deciding how much state to keep, if any, is one of the critical issues of server design.

The other issue you will encounter immediately once you start trying to develop an RPC server is the work—when is the work to be done? This is an issue because the typical RPC server operates as a dispatcher. It waits for a request to arrive, and when one does, it calls the corresponding procedure. When that procedure returns, it takes the results and returns them to the client, and then goes back into its wait loop.

This means that in a generic RPC server no work can be done before a request arrives, nor can any be done after the reply is issued. To see why this is a problem, consider the remote print server. A client asks it to print a file. You would like the print server to take the request, queue it up to the printer, tell the client that it is being printed, and then poll the printer for status. If the client comes along later and asks for status, you can supply it. The problem with this formulation is the statement "and then poll the printer for status." There is no "and then"—once the server has returned a reply to the client, the typical RPC server will go back to its top level wait loop.

If you are constructing an RPC server, there are generally four strategies you can use, individually or in combination, to get around this difficulty:

- Make the work small enough that it can be accomplished entirely within the server's work procedures.

- Decompose the work so that the current call to a work procedure does some or all of the work requested by the previous call(s).

- Customize the server so that its top level loop looks for requests and calls a `DoWhenIdle()` procedure when there are no requests pending.

- Customize the server so that its top level loop interleaves request processing with work processing.

Note that this difficulty arises in RPC server design precisely because RPC servers are quite often *single-threaded*: while a server is processing one request it cannot do anything else. Other client/server systems, such as DCE, remove this restriction by allowing multiple client requests to execute simultaneously. It is also possible to make multi-threaded RPC servers on some operating systems, such as Sun's Solaris. Multi-threaded servers tend to be more complex than single-threaded servers, however.

Figure 11.1 shows the flow of execution in the server for each of the first three strategies. The first approach, the "synchronous" approach, is the simplest. In this synchronous approach, every client is blocked while any remote procedure is being executed, so that the work must be "small" or the clients must expect to be blocked. Most clients would probably become extremely impatient with a remote print server that printed all files synchronously.

SYNCHRONOUS

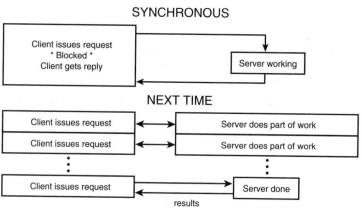

Fig. 11.1
An RPC server can
perform its work in
several different
ways.

NEXT TIME

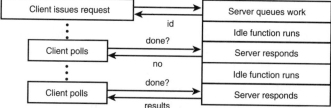

IDLE PROCESSING

> **Caution**
>
> You must design your RPC server so that clients are never blocked unexpectedly.
> The server must be prepared to refuse or modify client requests that might lead
> to lengthy or infinite blocking, unless the client is designed to accommodate that.

The second approach, the "next time" approach, can be very useful for
cleaning up internal state. For example, almost all RPC servers arrange that
whenever a remote procedure is executed, it frees any memory that had been
allocated the last time that particular procedure was called. In this case, it
does not matter if that remote procedure is called once a second or once a
year. This approach is not very useful for executing client work unless the
server expects the client to call in frequently, or if the result is itself optional.
The remote print server could be implemented such that it only asked the
printer hardware for status if the printing client asked the server for status.

The second approach is also used when the client is willing to poll. For
example, a remote database server could be implemented with two query
functions:

```
id    LaunchThisRequest(query-description)
result  AreYouDone(id theid)
```

The first client request simply sets up the query. The server puts the query on a work list and returns an id. Every subsequent client call to AreYouDone() executes a portion of the query, as shown in figure 11.1, and returns No, via a discriminated union (discriminated unions were described in the section entitled "The union keyword" in Chapter 10). This No indicates that the server has not yet fully processed the query. When it is finally done, it sets the done field in the discriminated union to Yes and returns the query result itself. Polling is often combined with the third approach.

My personal favorite is the third approach, the "idle processing" approach, when suitably combined with the first two. Customizing the server is not as fearsome as it sounds. It is, in fact, quite straightforward. All it really means is modifying the server top level. If you are using rpcgen (discussed in more detail in Chapter 12), then the server top level containing main() is created for you automatically. It must be edited, preferably by an automated procedure that can be put in your makefile. I use a one-line script to do this. At the end of this chapter, I will discuss server customization in detail. For the moment, your DoWhenIdle() function can be thought of as a background task that can do anything you want it to, provided it does not take too long. No new requests are received or processed while DoWhenIdle() is executing, so you must take care to avoid long delays.

When polling is combined with an idle function, the resulting strategy is sometimes known as a *collector*, or *mailbox*. In the remote database example above, the LaunchThisRequest() server function would put the query on an internal work queue, as figure 11.1 shows. Each call to the DoWhenIdle() function from the server top level would advance the query, doing a little more of the required word. The clients still need to call AreYouDone() periodically to collect the results of the query. The difference here is that AreYouDone() itself is not executing any part of the work; it is merely looking for completion. Once again, when the server has completed the work, it sends back the results of its processing to the client. Collectors must also be able to save error information. Naturally, the collector approach implies a lot of server state.

The fourth approach is the "asynchronous" approach. Anything can happen, in any order. Since new requests are intermixed with your work function(s), this approach is more like a multitasking operating system than a server. It can be done, but I would recommend that you avoid it until you have thoroughly mastered the first three approaches. This approach is not shown in figure 11.1, as it would look like a set of crossed arrows careening wildly around the page.

There is one more factor which the RPC server designer must consider: execution order. In a monolithic application, you would never arrange that term() be called before init(). You would never deliberately write() to a file that had never been opened, or that had already been closed. RPC procedure calls can be executed in any order whatsoever, so that each server procedure must make no assumptions (you have heard this before) about the sequence of execution of its procedures. If you have an init() and term(), then you should have a state variable called has_been_inited. The init() function sets has_been_inited to True, term() sets has_been_inited to False, and every procedure that depends upon init() having been executed (or not) *must* test the value of has_been_inited and ensure that it is True. Out-of-order execution can be caused by multiple clients, confused clients, network issues, or other causes.

The following are the three fundamental rules of RPC server design:

- Save as much state as you need in order to satisfy any reasonable request.

- Decide how the server is going to work based on when it is going to do that work.

- Be prepared for all possible requests in any order; make no assumptions.

Server rule 3 is the mirror image of client rule 2, which said "be prepared for any possible result."

The Client Application

In this section, I will describe the basic client functions you will need in order to create a functional and robust client. I will also discuss the conventions clients should follow in order to make the best use of the server. From this point forward, I will assume that your client/server interface definition has been developed using rpcgen. You may certainly use your own custom functions, but they should obey the same calling sequences as functions generated by rpcgen.

◀ See "Understanding Server Distribution," p. 187

Structure of the Client

An RPC client consists of three pieces: the client top level, the client interface, and the client XDR routines. The client top level contains the main() function, and is responsible for translating user and/or external requests into remote procedure calls. These remote procedure calls are contained within the client interface, which makes use of the client XDR routines and the RPC library functions to contact the server over the network.

◀ See "The rpcgen Input File," p. 264

If you have defined the client/server interfaces in an RPCGEN file named myint.x, for example, then the client interface portion will be contained in the file myint_clnt.c, created for you by RPCGEN, and the client XDR routines will be in the file myint_xdr.c, also made by RPCGEN. Your job is thus to create the top level of the client.

Consider a very simple example client and look at the issues that arise from implementing it. Our client will be an interface to a "remote file manager." The remote file manager permits only the following three operations. The client may ask if a file exists by name, it may attempt to read from a file, or it may try to delete a file.

First, put the RPCGEN interface definition in a file named fmgr.x. It will have the definitions as shown in Listing 11.1.

Listing 11.1 *rpcgen* **Interface Definition for the File Manager**

```
const MAXTOREAD = 4096;
 /* maximum number of bytes read in one shot */
typedef opaque bstrm<MAXTOREAD>;
/* an opaque rpcgen type to hold the bytes */
struct readrequest {        /* read some bytes from a file */
    u_int           bytestoread;
/* number of bytes to be read */
    string          thefile<>;   /* name of the file */
    } ;
union readresult switch ( int serverr ) {
/* result of a readrequest operation */
    case 0:                 /* if no error, then return... */
        bstrm           thebytes; /* the file contents */
    default:                        /* otherwise, return ... */
        void;                   /* nothing */
    } ;
program FMPROG {                    /* program definition */
    version FMVERS {                /* version definition */
        bool            FILE_EXISTS(string)         = 1;
/* "exists" operation */
        readresult          FILE_READ(readrequest)      = 2;
/* "read" operation */
        void            FILE_DELETE(string)         = 3;
/* "delete" operation */
        } = 0x1;            /* version 1 */
    } = 0x24002400;            /* random program number */
```

Initialization

The first thing the client must do is to contact a server. The function that is used to open a connection to a server is:

```
CLIENT *clnt_create(char *hostname, u_long progno,
            u_long versno, char *transportname);
```

A server is identified by hostname, the name of the machine on which it is running, its program number progno, and its version number versno. The transportname specifies how the client and the server converse. It must be the name of a valid network protocol (see Chapter 3, "Communications Protocols"). RPC servers understand tcp and udp by default.

In your file manager, use the first command line argument, argv[1], to specify the server's hostname. The other command line arguments will be used to specify what operation you want the file manager to perform, and provide any arguments needed. The initialization sequence is shown in Listing 11.2.

Listing 11.2 Opening a *CLIENT* Connection to the File Manager

```
#include <stdio.h>
#include <rpc/rpc.h>                /* fundamental rpc definitions */
#include "fmgr.h"   /* file manager data structures */
int main(int argc, char **argv)
{
    CLIENT *fmgrc;          /* a pointer to the client connection*/
    if ( argc < 2 ) error(...);
/* can't connect without the server name in argv[1] */
    ...
    fmgrc = clnt_create(argv[1], FMPROG, FMVERS,
/* try to connect */
        "tcp");                 /* using the tcp protocol */
    ...
}
```

The first two include files may or may not be already included in fmgr.h—it depends on your version of rpcgen. Take a peek and find out. You must include the fmgr.h file, however. It contains all the definitions generated by the protocol compiler. In particular, it contains the actual values of FMPROG and FMVERS which are used in contacting the server. These were defined symbolically in the rpcgen input file shown in Listing 11.1, and appear as constants defined in the fmgr.h file created by rpcgen. CLIENT is a data type which contains all the information needed to maintain contact with the server, and is used in all subsequent calls to the remote functions. Note that there is a companion function to clnt_create() called clnt_destroy(); we will consider this function at the end of this section.

If fmgrc is not (CLIENT *)NULL, you have established a server connection. If it is NULL, something has gone wrong. In the next subsection, we will see how

Tip
The second and third arguments to clnt_create() are always the program name and version name of the interface.

II

Introduction to RPC

to handle this type of failure. If your client absolutely must contact the server, the code should loop until fmgrc is not NULL. Otherwise, this is a fatal error and the client application should terminate.

Client Calling Conventions

Now that there is a connection to the server, we should do something with it. Presumably, this involves parsing the command line to determine the user's intentions in invoking the file manager client. The exact manner in which this is done is an application-specific user interface issue, not an RPC issue, so we will not specify it further. Let's just assume that this has been done, and we have discovered that the desired operation is "does the file exist?" Let us also suppose that the filename is stored in a local variable fname. What now?

We know from Chapter 10 that RPCGEN has created a function for us named file_exists_1 (or perhaps file_exists_0x1; 1 is the version, FMVERS). If we examine fmgr_clnt.c, where this function is implemented, we discover that its prototype is:

```
bool_t    *file_exists_1(char **, CLIENT *);
```

This illustrates the primary convention that clients must bear in mind. Arguments are passed by reference, and results are returned by reference. Recall from the "Pointer Functions" section of Chapter 9 that this is necessary in order to interface to XDR. Since the string that holds the filename is a char *, the first argument to file_exists_1() is the address of the string, and is a char **. The second argument is the CLIENT pointer, which we got during initialization. We call this function as shown in Listing 11.3.

Listing 11.3 Calling the File Manager Function *file_exists_1()*

```
bool_t *adr_of_exists;       /* the address of the return code */
bool_t it_exists = FALSE;
/* the return code itself - assume failure */
adr_of_exists = file_exists_1(&fname, fmgrc);   /* invoke the RPC */
/*
  If the remote procedure did not return a NULL pointer...
*/
if ( adr_of_exists != (bool_t *)NULL ) {
/*
  then dereference that pointer to get the actual return code
*/
    it_exists = (*adr_of_exists);
    xdr_free(xdr_bool, adr_of_exists);
/* and then free the memory */
    }
```

This code fragment almost completely ignores the necessary error checking, which will be taken up below. If the return code from the `file_exists_1()` function is `NULL`, then something in the RPC chain failed. Whatever the reason, the server has not returned anything meaningful, so we assume in this case that the file does not exist (the variable `it_exists` was initialized to `False`, and remains `False` in this case). If the return code from `file_exists_1()` is not `NULL`, then that return code is the address of the value we want. The actual existence or nonexistence of the file named in `fname` is obtained by dereferencing the pointer returned by `file_exists_1()`.

The second statement within the `no error` block is a call to `xdr_free()`, which frees any memory allocated when the return value was constructed. Many clients omit this step. Indeed it may be safely omitted for all primitive types, such as the `bool` used here, since XDR only allocates memory for nonprimitive types. Unless you are transmitting massive amounts of data or looping many times, you may follow the sloppy but common client practice of not calling `xdr_free()` at all. If you do use it, recall that its first argument is its XDR procedure, and the second argument is the return value itself (the pointer, not its contents).

The other two remote procedures are defined in exactly the same way. Their prototypes will be:

```
readresult *file_read_1(readrequest *, CLIENT *);
void *file_delete_1(char **, CLIENT *);
```

The second of these is worthy of note for two reasons. The functions `file_exists_1()` and `file_read_1()` both return a result, and thus represent a server "round-trip." Data travels across the network twice, from the client to the server and back. The function `file_delete_1()` returns nothing. It represents a server one-way trip. Data travels in only one direction, from the client to the server. This is clearly more efficient, but it is not an efficiency that you will often be able to exploit. In almost every case, you will want status or information back from the server, so that a round trip will be mandated.

The second thing to note is that some older implementations will have a C compiler that cannot handle a `void *` type. In this case, you will have to modify the interface to return a dummy value, such as an `int`. This will then result in an unnecessary server round trip.

Once your client top level is developed, it is a simple matter to build the client application. If the file manager client top level is called `Cfmgr.c`, then under UNIX this compile command will do the trick:

```
cc -o Cfmgr Cfmgr.c fmgr_clnt.c fmgr_xdr.c -lrpc -lm
```

On some systems, the RPC library is called RPC, while on others it is called RPCSVC, so that you may need to replace -lrpc with -lrpcsvc. For non-UNIX systems, a similar command must be invoked to link together the object files from the client top level (Cfmgr.o), the client stubs (fmgr_clnt.o), the client XDR routines (fmgr_xdr.o), the RPC library, and the math library.

Error Handling

Remote procedures can fail in several different ways. Each of the links in the client/server chain can fail, and is a potential source of error. RPC clients must thus be alert to possible failures and handle them appropriately.

When clnt_create() fails, the following two functions may be used to get diagnostic information on the reason for the failure:

```
void  clnt_pcreateerror(char *msg);
char *clnt_spcreateerror(char *msg);
```

The first function is very similar to perror(). It prints a message on the standard error output containing the argument msg and an additional string describing the reason for the failure. The second function does not print this combination; it returns it as a pointer into an internal string space. This string should be copied or used immediately.

The failure of a remote procedure call has a variety of possible manifestations, and great care must be taken to test for all of them. Let us look at the most interesting and diverse situation in the file manager client, the failure of a call to file_read_1(). Consider this code:

```
readresult *rrval;
readrequest SomeReadRequest;
...
rrval = file_read_1(&SomeReadRequest, fmgrc);   /* try to read a /*
/* file using the File Manager */
```

What are the failure modes?

```
len = rrval->readresult_u.thebytes.bstrm_len;
/* number of bytes read */
buf = rrval->readresult_u.thebytes.bstrm_val;
/* pointer to the bytes read */
```

All the following represent an error of some kind:

```
rrval == (readresult *)NULL     /* the server returned nothing */
rrval->serverr != 0        /* the server had an error */
len == 0 && buf != (char *)NULL /* good buffer pointer,
but zero bytes */
len > 0 && buf == (char *)NULL/* bad buffer pointer,
but nonzero bytes */
```

The first error is a serious one. It can mean that the server, or the server's machine, has crashed; that a network failure has occurred; or that local memory has been exhausted. It can also indicate a slightly softer failure in the server, in which it has chosen to return nothing rather than something, perhaps because it ran out of memory. It can also indicate serious internal corruption in the RPC data structures, in the client, or in the server.

The second failure is a message from the server indicating that it could not carry out the request. The server should set the value of `rrval->serverr` to an error code giving the cause of the failure. This could be a state-related failure. Suppose your client calls `file_exists_1()` for a given file, and the server says that it exists. Your client then calls `file_read_1()` on that file, hoping for some data. Between your call to `file_exists_1()` and your call to `file_read_1()`, another client has called `file_delete_1()` on that very file. If the server is well written, `rrval->serverr` should be an error code for `file does not exist` in this case. The client must be prepared for such results. Note also that if `serverr` is not 0, the contents of the `thebytes` member of `readresult` are undefined, and should not be accessed, since the union definition gave this case as `void`.

The third and fourth errors are also worrisome. RPC has given us back a structure, but its contents make no sense. In case three, we are given back a pointer to the file contents which the server read, namely `buf`, but also told that the length of that buffer is zero. It is possible that this means that the remote file exists, but has zero length. In that case, however, the server should really set `serverr` to an appropriate and unambiguous code alerting us to that fact. In the fourth case, the pointer is `NULL`, but the length is nonzero. Neither case is self-consistent. Either the server has generated a bad structure (server software bug), or it has been corrupted in transmission or reception.

The following functions are available to clients for error diagnosis:

```
void   clnt_perror(CLIENT *, char *msg);
char *clnt_sperror(CLIENT *, char *msg);
```

These functions are the exact analogs of the previous `clnt_create()` error functions. The first prints a message to the standard error output describing the error, prefixed with `msg`. The second returns the composite error string instead. There is also a much more detailed error reporting function called `clnt_geterr()`.

The first argument is the client pointer, and the second is a pointer to a local `struct rpc_err`. This structure is defined in the file `<rpc/clnt.h>`. For most purposes, it has one member of interest, namely `re_status`. This member is of

Tip
Client should always perform all possible error checks on RPC results.

II

Introduction to RPC

type `clnt_stat`, which is also defined in that same file. This enumeration contains a long list of reasons for RPC failure. It is important to note that if this member has the value zero, RPC has not detected any error. If you have detected an error and RPC has not, then memory has almost surely been corrupted, probably as a result of some mismatch between the server's and the client's ideas of the arguments or return values. Clients should exit immediately in this case.

Other Client Functions

There are two other RPC functions that clients will often use, namely `clnt_control()` and `clnt_destroy()`. The first is used to achieve finer control over the client interface, and the second is used to gracefully shut down the connection to a server.

The prototype for `clnt_control()` is:

```
bool_t  clnt_control(CLIENT *clnt, int request,
            char *requestdata);
```

The first argument is the current client handle. The second argument is a selector for the type of control operation you want to perform. The third argument is a generic pointer to information that qualifies or is set by the request. The interface is parallel to the `ioctl()` system function. The most useful requests and the corresponding data type of the third argument are shown in Table 11.1.

Table 11.1 Client Control Requests and Their Data Types	
Request	**Data Type**
CLSET_TIMEOUT	struct timeval *
CLGET_TIMEOUT	struct timeval *
CLGET_FD	int *
CLGET_SERVER_ADDR	struct sockaddr *

In each case, the third argument must be a pointer to actual memory; `clnt_control()` will not allocate memory for you.

The first two requests set and get the timeout that is imposed on every network operation. The default timeout imposed by RPC is twenty-five seconds. If the timeout is exceeded, the current remote procedure will return an error and set the re_status part of the rpc_err struct to RPC_TIMEDOUT, indicating that a timeout occurred.

The existence of a timeout is another reason why it is important that the client and server arrange that the server never block any client for a long period of time. If it does block for longer than the timeout, the client will receive a timeout error, even if the server is fine. Of course, you are free to set the timeout to any value you wish. If both members of the struct timeval are zero in a CLSET_TIMEOUT call, the timeout becomes infinite.

Unfortunately, many implementations have a bug in timeout handling. The bug is that CLSET_TIMEOUT requests have no effect. If your site has classic RPC, your RPCGEN will be called rpcgen and you probably have this bug. If your RPCGEN is called rpcgen.new or rpcgen_tli, you probably do not have this bug.

> **Note**
>
> To test for the timeout bug, create a simple RPC function in your rpcgen interface file that says:
>
>   int   sleep_for_ten_second(void) = ...
>
> Set the client timeout to five seconds and then call this function in the client. In the server, implement this function so that it calls sleep(10) and then returns 42. If the client call times out, you do not have this bug. If the client call does not time out, and you get back 42, you do have this bug.

If you do have the bug, you will have to complain to your vendor, or experiment. If you are on the Internet, you can get the full RPC source from several locations, which are listed in a section in Chapter 9, "Getting the XDR Source Code" (XDR and RPC come as a package). Sadly, I have never found a site that has a one-file patch for the timeout bug, so you will need to dig around. A slightly painful workaround is also given in a section in Chapter 12, "clnt_call() and NULLPROC."

The third and fourth client control requests allow you to get access to the underlying file descriptor of the socket connecting the client and the server, as well as the server's network address. When you are not executing RPC calls, the socket sits idle and can be used for arbitrary network communication. You can thus conduct two completely independent conversations with the server, one using RPC and another using your own protocol over the same communication channel.

Needless to say, this approach is for experienced network programmers only, as it is somewhat perilous. If the server fails to read all the data on the socket that the client sent in the private protocol, the next RPC call will find a buffer filled with garbage, and ugly events will occur. The RPC library will almost certainly return an error message such as `cannot decode result`, or it may simply generate a memory fault. I have found one extremely good use for this back door, however.

If you are familiar with network programming at the socket level, you are also aware of the concept of "urgent data." Urgent data are special, very short messages that can be processed out of sequence by the recipient. All RPC messages travel by the normal, nonurgent route, so you can use the third and fourth control calls to get enough information to send urgent data to the server, using an interface something like the following:

```
int   ssock = (-1);      /* socket file descriptor */
struct sockaddr_in  saddr;
/* network representation of a socket address */
clnt_control(fmgrc, CLGET_FD, &ssock);
/* get the socket underlying the connection */
clnt_control(fmgrc, CLGET_SERVER_ADDR, &saddr);
/* get the socket's address, too */
sendto(ssock, "!", 1, MSG_OOB, &saddr,
/* send one byte of urgent data */
         sizeof(struct sockaddr_in));
```

I have omitted error checking; you should not. The return values of both calls to `clnt_control()` should be checked to ensure that they are equal to `TRUE`, and the return from `sendto()` should be checked to make sure that it is equal to one, the number of bytes sent. Note that many implementations permit only one byte to be sent as urgent data (some allow 16 or more). This type of interface can be used as a special "drop everything" or "reset yourself" call to the server. In particular, if a server is written such that it processes RPC requests after they arrive using a `DoWhenIdle()` function and some kind of work queue, this type of message can be used to get the server's attention immediately. The server must then be expecting urgent data, so that you must be following server strategy number three or four, which is to say you must have a modified server top level that is looking for urgent data and knows how to handle it.

The final client function to consider is `clnt_destroy()`. It has the following prototype:

```
void clnt_destroy(CLIENT *);
```

Its purpose is to cleanly shut down the connection to the server opened with `clnt_create()`. It also deallocates any internal memory that `clnt_create()`

allocated. You might expect that you would use this function often in clients. After all, when you open() a file, is it not prudent to later close() it?

In fact, I recommend that you use this function with care. The reason is that if any RPC error has occurred, a subsequent call to clnt_destroy() can crash your client application in some implementations. If no error has occurred, then it is quite safe to use this function, but if any of the "memory-corrupting" errors which I described previously has occurred, it is better to simply exit().

Caution

If you think that you have memory corruption in an RPC client, you should exit() immediately, unless this is impossible. Do not call any function that allocates memory before you exit().

The only situation in which you need to use this function is when you are opening and closing many server connections in the same application. For example, if your client connected to a server on every machine on your local network in order to collect local disk utilization statistics, for example, then you clearly must call clnt_destroy() for each clnt_create(). Otherwise, you might eventually run out of open file descriptors.

The Server Application

This section describes the creation of an RPC server. This discussion will closely parallel the RPC client discussion previously, and will make use of the same examples. The reader is urged to familiarize him- or herself with the client side of RPC before delving into the server side.

Structure of the Server

An RPC server consists of three pieces: the server top level, the server procedures or work functions, and the server XDR routines. The server top level contains the main() function and is responsible for initializing the server and making it known to the network, and also for executing the main loop that waits for RPC requests and then dispatches them. The server top level dispatches to the remote procedure calls, which are the means by which the server accomplishes work. The server top level also collects the return values of the work functions and transmits them back to the client. The server top level makes use of the server XDR routines and the RPC library functions to interface with the network.

Following the previous file manager example, the server top level is contained entirely within the file `fmgr_svc.c` created by RPCGEN. The server XDR routines are identical to the client XDR routines, through the miracle of XDR symmetry, and are contained with the RPCGEN'ed file `fmgr_xdr.c`. Your job as a server developer is to write the middle piece, the server remote procedures.

Server Conventions

The server developer's task is the inverse of the client developer's task. The client developer writes the client top level and calls the RPC procedures, which are already implemented in the file `fmgr_clnt.c`. The server top level is already written by RPCGEN, and the server developer must implement those procedures. To develop the file manager server, you must therefore implement these three functions:

```
bool_t          *file_exists_1(char **fnamep)

readresult       *file_read_1(readrequest *rrp)

void             *file_delete_1(char **fnamep)
```

Notice that these prototypes are identical in their first arguments and return values to the corresponding client functions. On the client side, each of these functions took a second parameter, a CLIENT *. On the server side, each of these functions is also called with a second argument, not shown above. This second parameter is of type SVCXPRT *. Just as a CLIENT data structure describes a client's interface to the server through the network, a SVCXPRT ("service transport") data structure describes a server interface to the client through the network. We will see more about this parameter in the next chapter. Many servers can ignore it.

It is important to realize that the entire job of developing the file manager server consists of writing these three functions. There is no initialization or termination that must be handled explicitly. The automatically generated server top level handles that, setting up ports for both TCP and UDP connections by default.

Server Functions

Now consider how a good server would implement these functions, starting with the quite simple `file_exists_1()`. Listing 11.4 shows what the code for this function would look like.

Listing 11.4 Server Code for the File Manager *exists* Function

```
#include <stdio.h>
#include <rpc/rpc.h>          /* RPC definitions */
#include "fmgr.h"        /* essential File manager definitions */
...
bool_t *file_exists_1(char **fnamep)
{
    static bool_t itexists;      /* 1, must be static */
    char *fname;             /* name of requested file */

    xdr_free(xdr_bool, &itexists); /* 2 */
    itexists = FALSE;             /* 3, assume failure */
    if ( fnamep == (char **)NULL ||
        ( fname = (*fnamep) ) == (char *)NULL ||
        fname[0] == '\0' )       /* 4, server rule 3 */
            return(&itexists);
    if ( access(fname, F_OK) >= 0 )
/* ask operating system if file exists */
            itexists = TRUE;      /* 5, success */
    return(&itexists);
}
```

Even this extremely short example illustrates all the basics of server programming, albeit in a somewhat contrived manner. Statements 1 and 2 display the most important practical rule of server programming, namely the "rule of delayed free."

The variable `itexists` is static, because it will hold the result that is passed back to the client, by reference, as a reply. Any memory allocated by the XDR system cannot be freed within the body of this function, since to do so would destroy the reply. Therefore, it must be freed on the next call into this function. That is why statement 1 declares the variable to be static, so that its value is saved from one call to the next. The call to `xdr_free()`, which takes the corresponding XDR function and a pointer to the value, actually frees the memory. This is a perfect illustration of server work strategy number two, in which work left over from the previous call to a remote procedure is accomplished in the current call to that same procedure.

At this point, you are probably jumping up and down and screaming, "But `itexists` is a local variable! There can't be any memory allocated by XDR for it, and `xdr_free()` never frees anything with primitive types, anyway!" You are absolutely correct; in this particular function, these statements are not strictly necessary. However, when we implement the function `file_read_1()`, they will be absolutely necessary. As an RPC server writer, you are strongly encouraged to get into the habit of always following these two rules, even if they seem pointless.

II

Introduction to RPC

> **Caution**
>
> Every RPC server function must declare all result variables as static. Every RPC server function must also call xdr_free() on the address of the result as the first statement of the function. Failure to do so will result in a *memory leak*, in which memory is allocated but never freed. The server must free all memory it allocates, or it will eventually run out of memory.

Failure to follow one of these rules is the single most common server programming error. The server allocates memory, either directly or via XDR, and passes it back to the client. The server never frees it because xdr_free() is never called, or, even worse, the result variable is not static, so that xdr_free() is called on a wild pointer. The server will either slowly consume all memory on its machine, if you are lucky, or will crash, because it has freed stack memory and is now executing somewhere random, such as in its copyright notice.

Statement 3 initializes the result to FALSE. In statement 4, I am following server rule number three, which instructs us to expect anything. This translates into defensive programming in which every possible error situation is tested. If the argument fnamep is NULL, or if it does not look like the valid address of a valid string, the default return value, FALSE, set in statement 3, is returned (by reference, of course).

Statement 5 calls the system function access() to determine if the file actually exists. The tag F_OK asks for just that. If the access() call passes, the return value is set to TRUE; otherwise it remains as FALSE. Note that your platform may not have this particular function, but will undoubtedly have some method for determining if a file actually exists. Figure 11.2 illustrates the entire sequence of events from the call to file_exists_1() on the client side, through server processing, and back to the ultimate reply checking by the client.

There is an obvious defect with this interface. FALSE is returned for three distinct reasons. FALSE is returned if the argument was an invalid string pointer (fnamep == NULL, possibly an RPC error), if the underlying string was invalid, or if the file did not exist. A better interface would not return a bool_t; it would return an int or enum with the possible values BADARG, BADFILENAME, DOESNOTEXIST, and EXISTS (defined as consts in fgmr.x) in order to distinguish these cases. In particular, the client should be clearly notified about BADARG (fnamep == NULL), since that is the most potentially serious of these errors.

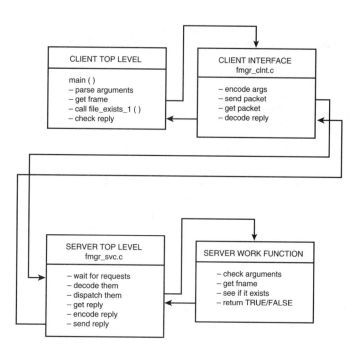

Fig. 11.2
An RPC server
executes a remote
procedure call on
behalf of its client.

With this simple example under our belts, let us consider the more involved
function file_read_1(). The code in Listing 11.5 shows an implementation of
this function.

Listing 11.5 Server Code for the File Manager Function

```
readresult *file_read_1(readrequest *rrp)
{
     static readresult theres;      /* must be static */
     char *fname;                /* name of the requested file */
     char*bufr = (char *)NULL;    /* a local buffer for data */
     u_int lentoread;            /* number of bytes to read */
     int   fd;                   /* file descriptor of file */
     int   lenread;              /* number of bytes actually read */

     xdr_free(xdr_readresult, &theres);         /* 1 */
     (void)bzero(&theres, sizeof(readresult)); /* 2a */
     theres.serverr = BADARG;                   /* 2b */
     if ( rrp == (readrequest *)NULL )          /* 3 */
          return(&theres);    /* always return by reference */
     lentoread = rrp->bytestoread;       /* how many bytes does
client want? */
     if ( lentoread == (u_int)0 ||                    /* 4 */
          lentoread > MAXTOREAD ||
          ( fname = rrp->thefile ) == (char *)NULL ||
          fname[0] == '\0' ) {
          theres.serverr = BADREQUEST;  /* something is wrong
```

(continues)

Listing 12.5 Continued

```
with client's request */
        return(&theres);
        }
    bufr = (char *)malloc(lentoread);      /* allocate memory for
file contents (platform specific !) */
    if ( bufr == (char *)NULL ) {   /* could not get memory */
        theres.serverr = SERVEROUTOFMEM;      /* 5 */
        return(&theres);
        }
    fd = open(fname, O_RDONLY);   /* open the file, read only */
    if ( fd < 0 ) {               /* file open failed */
        theres.serverr = CANTOPENFILE;           /* 6 */
        free(bufr);        /* free the memory (platform specific)*/
        return(&theres);
        }
    lenread = read(fd, bufr, lentoread); /* read the file */
    (void)close(fd);                     /* close the file */
    if ( lenread <= 0 ) {   /* could not read file, or file had
zero length */
        theres.serverr = SOMEREADERROR;        /* 6 */
        free(bufr);  /* always free that memory, prevent leaks */
        return(&theres);
        }
    theres.readresult_u.thebytes.bstrm_len =
        (u_int)lentoread;        /* tell the client how many bytes
were actually read */
    theres.readresult_u.thebytes.bstrm_val = bufr; /* tell the
client where the bytes are */
    theres.serverr = 0;                            /* 7 */
    return(&theres);                 /* successful return */
    }
```

Tip
Server functions should always initialize their return value to a sensible default and set any error code to a default error value. Error codes should not be set to no error by default.

The implementation of this function is very similar to that of `file_exists_1()`; there is simply more work to do here. Statement 1 is the mandatory freeing of previously allocated memory.

In statement 2, which has two parts, I ensure that if I ever inadvertently return from this function, the contents of the return value will be sensible, and will indicate an error. Statement 2a zeroes out the returned structure. Statement 2b sets up a default error code. You might argue that statement 2b could be placed right after statement 3 in that clause. This is true, but the purpose of having statement 2b first is to guard against programming bugs in which the client seems to get a success code but the contents of the reply are trash. If statement 2b were not present and the code returned at statement 3, for example, the client would get a zero value for serverr. However, the buffer point in the readresult would be NULL and the buffer length would be zero (because I zeroed out the entire reply structure). A poorly written client might only check serverr, see that it indicated success, dereference the NULL pointer in the readresult, and then crash.

Statement 3 is the usual check for a bad RPC argument. Statement 4 is an exhaustive check for every possible set of inappropriate arguments. The subsequent code tries to allocate local memory, open the named file, and read the indicated amount of data. Recall that the maximum permitted data request size was defined to be the constant MAXTOREAD, whose value is 4,096 bytes. This means that we do not need to worry about asking for gigantic amounts of memory, or reading gigantic amounts of data. We are also protected against problems that might arise on platforms on which an int is only 16 bits. Statement 4 tests to make sure that the value of lentoread does not exceed MAXTOREAD, so that the previous code shown will work for 16-bit ints and 32-bit ints. In statement 5, I return an error code indicating out of memory (all these errors codes should be consts in fmgr.x, of course).

> ### Caution
>
> Never use any function that allocates memory on the stack, such as alloca(), in RPC server functions for memory that is part of the reply. Memory corruption in the server will almost certainly result, and the client may be compromised as well, since invalid data will probably be transmitted.

Both statements labeled 6 could actually return two error codes: the error code shown, indicating what failed, and also the value of the global errno, which might tell the client more about why the failure occurred. After all, the open() call could have failed because the file does not exist, or because the server does not have permission to read the file. The code also does not distinguish a read() failure (bytes read < 0) from an end-of-file condition (bytes read == 0)—and it should. The interface for file_read_1() should be modified to allow both the application error code serverr and the system error code errno to be returned to the client.

If we reach statement 7, the code has read something. Don't forget to set the error code to zero to indicate this. Note that there is no way to free bufr in case of success, except by waiting until the next time this function is called.

The code for file_delete_1() is shown in Listing 11.6. The only unique thing to notice about file_delete_1() is that it returns void *, namely nothing. As a result, there is no declaration of a static variable to hold the result, nor is there need to call xdr_free().

Listing 11.6   The File Manager Function *file_delete_1*()

```
#include <stdio.h>
#include <rpc/rpc.h>          /* RPC definitions */
#include "fmgr.h"        /* essential File Manager definitions */
...
void *file_delete_1(char **fnamep)
{
    char *fname;              /* name of requested file */

    if ( fnamep == (char **)NULL ||
        ( fname = (*fnamep) ) == (char *)NULL ||
        fname[0] == '\0' )       /* sanity check the argument */
            return(&itexists);
    (void)unlink(fname); /* ask operating system to delete the
file*/
    return((void *)NULL);
}
```

Once your server work functions are developed, it is a simple matter to build the server application. If the server functions are in a file called Sfmgr.c, use this compile command under UNIX:

```
cc -o Sfmgr fmgr_svc.c Sfmgr.c fmgr_xdr.c -lrpc -lm
```

Other platforms should compile fmgr_svc.c, Sfmgr.c, fmgr_xdr.c, and link the resulting object modules with the RPC and math libraries. On some systems, -lrpc may need to be replaced with -lrpcsvc, as with the client.

Client/Server Debugging

Troubleshooting
I am having mysterious problems with my RPC client/server application. How do I know what the source of my problems is? Is it the network, RPC itself, or my code? Where do I begin?
Debugging client/server applications does take some work. Standard debugging techniques are often not applicable. If your server is started at boot time, or is started asynchronously (that is, by inetd), your debugger may not be smart enough to be able to attach to it. Furthermore, your server may not have any standard output or standard error output, so that even debugging printf()s in the server may not work. There are three special techniques I often use that make for very effective debugging.
The first approach is to debug the application code without the RPC library calls. You can link the client top level directly to the server work functions and then debug the resulting monolithic application. The second approach is to add logging to both the client and the server. Make them write the arguments and return values for each

remote procedure call to separate debug files (one for each client, and one for the server). The final approach is to create a maintenance client. This client has a single server request, which asks the server to dump its entire state. This can be used to repeatedly ask the server, "How are you doing now?" to track down when things first went wrong.

The issue of debugging a client/server application is worth some further explanation. Let us consider each of the three techniques mentioned above in greater detail.

In the first technique, we want to create a monolithic application that does not use RPC and does not access the network. If the client top level in the file manager is called Cfmgr.c and the server work functions are in a file called Sfmgr.c, then we can compile and link these two files, together with fmgr_xdr.c, and have a monolithic application. There is one small problem with this, however. Any calls your client makes to clnt_() functions, clnt_create() in particular, must not use the real versions in the RPC library. You should make a file in which all the clnt_() functions the client uses are stubbed out, such as the following:

```
static CLIENT dummy;
CLIENT *clnt_create(char *h, u_long pn, u_long pv,
                    char *xptr)
{ return(&dummy); }
void clnt_destroy(CLIENT *c) { }
...
```

You will also have to comment out any code in your server that uses the second server argument SVCXPRT *rqstp. Once you have made these two modifications, and compiled and linked those three files (without the RPC library, or the files fmgr_svc.c or fmgr_clnt.c), you will have a fully integrated application that you can debug as a single process. Once this application is fully functional, you can be confident that it is not your code that is failing.

The second debugging step is logging. You can easily arrange that your client log every RPC request and reply to a file. Make sure you do this with timestamps, since the client and the server execute independently. In the server, you can arrange that a log file be opened when the server is started, through a minor server customization. After this is done, you should modify every server function to log all its requests and replies to that file (which should be different from the client log file!), again with timestamps. It may be necessary to add a sleep(1) to each server function to ensure that its timestamps are not so close together that you cannot match them with the corresponding client timestamps. You should also check to make sure that the client's machine and the server's machine agree on what time it is, so that the timestamps are reasonably close.

Once you have these two log files, you can compare the sequence of events in client and server and look for anomalies. Once you see a mismatch, such as `client sent request with filename motd` alongside `server received request with filename an^T30^]x9`, then you may have pinpointed the problem. A peek back at the debugging advice in Chapters 9 and 10 would now be advisable, since you may have violated one of the rules of interface construction. In particular, if a client makes a simple RPC call, hangs around for minutes, and then crashes, you are almost certainly faced with a case of "multiple reference" (see the "Handling Lists, Graphs, and Multiple References" section in Chapter 9).

Finally, whenever I am developing a fairly large client/server application, I always take the time to create a maintenance client. A maintenance client has one or two interfaces to the server. It can ask the server to describe all its current state, or it can optionally reset all or part of the server's state to some nice initial condition. This is certainly extra work, but if you are going to put weeks or months into the development of a server and one or more clients, then it is time well spent to put in a few extra days and add these one or two extra RPC functions. Even the first "dump" function alone can be of enormous utility.

Server Customization

One difficulty with using RPCGEN to generate the server top level is that it gives you no flexibility in adding your own initialization functions or in changing the wait-then-dispatch loop. If you are a careful and thoughtful programmer, you have an automatic build procedure, such as a makefile, which re-creates the _svc.c file every time the .x file changes. This means that you cannot manually edit the _svc.c file or your changes will be lost the next time you edit the .x and then build.

The solution is simple. If you examine a server top level, such as our fmgr_svc.c, you will find that the last thing its main() does, after much highly interesting code, is call svc_run(). svc_run() is the internal RPC function that implements the server dispatch loop. It is designed to run forever. If your system has a noninteractive text-processing tool such as sed, the UNIX "stream editor," you can modify your build procedure to run that tool on the _svc.c file. My makefile looks like this for the _svc.c file:

```
fmgr_svc.o:        fmgr_svc.c
  - rm -f tmp.c
  sed -f serversed fmgr_svc.c > tmp.c
  mv tmp.c fmgr_svc.c
  $(CC) -c $(CFLAGS) fmgr_svc.c
```

This little trick runs the automatically generated server top level source through a script serversed, which makes two small changes to it. This script is one line long:

```
s/main()/main(a,v) int a;char **v;/g;s/svc_run()/mysvc_run(a,v)/g
```

It is not important to understand how this cryptic sed statement works. What it does is to perform two replacements in the file fmgr_svc.c. It replaces main() with main(a,v) int a; char **v, and it also replaces the final call to svc_run() with a call to mysvc_run(a,v).

The implementation of the mysvc_run() function is the key to server customization. If you are relentlessly curious, then you probably have already consulted the system documentation, so you know that it gives you the source for svc_run(). My implementation of mysvc_run() just builds on that. The version I use looks like that shown in Listing 11.7.

Listing 11.7   A Replacement for the Function *svc_run()*

```
FILE *serverlog = (FILE *)NULL;     /* logging FILE pointer */
extern int errno;          /* global C library error code */
int mysvc_run(int argc, char **argv)
{
   fd_set readfds;  /* a bitfield of file descriptors to examine */
   int dts;  /* total number of file descriptors supported by OS */
    int sl;                /* return code from select() */

    ProcArgs(argc, argv);      /* custom func #1 */
    dts = getdtablesize();      /* Ask OS how many file descriptors it
supports */
    while ( 1 ) {   /* loop forever looking for client requests */
        readfds = svc_fdset;   /* may be changed by RPC library,
so must be set each iteration */
        errno = 0;         /* clear global error code */
        sl = select(dts, &readfds, (int *)NULL, /* ask OS if any
fds may be read */
            (int *)NULL, (struct timeval *)NULL);
        if ( sl == 0 ) DoWhenIdle();    /* custom #2 */
        else if ( sl > 0 ) {    /* If there is data to be read
then ... */
            CheckForUrgent();       /* custom #3 */
            svc_getreqset(&readfds);   /* call RPC library
function to handle client requests */
            }
        else    {    /* sl < 0, system error or interrupt */
```

(continues)

```
Listing 11.7   Continued
                  if ( errno == EINTR ) continue;   /* if the error was
      an interrupted system call, try again */
                  return(-1);   /* any other error is serious, so quit
      looping and return */
              }
          }
      }
```

Without going into the precise gore of how this works, notice that it does
provide three types of customization. The command line arguments to the
server are passed into `myxvc_run()`, where they are processed by the first custom function, `ProcArgs()`. You write this function, so it can do anything you
want. In particular, it can open a logging file (perhaps named on the command line) and store its FILE pointer in `serverlog`. Every server function can
then using this code to log diagnostic messages:

```
if ( serverlog != (FILE *)NULL )
    (void)fprintf(serverlog, "Some diagnostic...");
```

The local variable `sl` is the return code of the system function `select()`. If it is
zero, this means that there are no incoming requests to this server. In this
case, the second custom function `DoWhenIdle()` is called, which you also
write, and which does whatever you want (such as checking the printer to see
if it is out of paper, for example). Make sure that your `DoWhenIdle()` does not
take too long or clients may be blocked.

If `sl` is positive, there is something incoming. The above code takes this opportunity to call the third custom function `CheckForUrgent()`. If you have
followed the "private protocol" strategy described previously, and are using
urgent data as a private message from the client telling the server to do something special, then this function should check for urgent data, peel it off the
socket, and do that special thing (or save the urgent data for the server functions to handle later). This call must be before the call to `svc_getreqset()`, so
that the urgent data is gone before the RPC library looks at the socket. If you
are not using urgent data, this customization may be omitted, of course. If
you do use urgent data, the function `CheckForUrgent()` should also execute
quickly.

As you might guess, the function `svc_getreqset()` is the main dispatch function that decodes incoming RPC requests, arranges to call the appropriate
server function, and sends back its reply too.

With this level of customization, you will find that almost every server task
that does not fit into the generic server can be accommodated.

Multiple Clients and Server State

The simple file manager client/server application developed in the previous two subsections really does not involve any server state. It is true that the client may be surprised if a `file_exists_1()` call succeeds and a subsequent call to `file_read_1()` fails, but that is a really not a server issue.

If we were to make the file manager a little more realistic, however, it would become immediately apparent that the server must have state. The `file_read_1()` call is quite inefficient. If a client is reading a large file 4,096 bytes at a time, each call to the server involves an `open()` and a `close()`. It would be much more reasonable to provide an interface with client `file_open()`, `file_read()`, and `file_close()` calls.

Once we do this, however, the server must have state. It cannot permit one client even to attempt to delete a file which has been `open()`ed by another client (the operating system and/or file system may or may not give an error when attempting to delete an open file). If more than one client is reading the same file, the server may choose to open it only once, but maintain a set of file position indicators for each file, and use `seek()`, a relatively inexpensive system call, to move around in the file whenever a call to `file_read_1()` is executed.

Any solution involves keeping some set of information about what files are open, which client has them open, and what that client is doing to them (such as the `seek()` position). The server must now have a provision for garbage collection as well. If a client exits or crashes, the server will want to decrement the reference count on the files it has open, and close any that now have no active clients accessing them. If we also add the ability to `write()` files, the complexity increases vastly.

Most RPC servers that you will write will permit multiple simultaneous clients. Even if that is not your original design, useful servers, like useful applications in general, tend to be used in ways which were not envisioned at the onset of development. Even if the second client is only the maintenance client I described in the previous Troubleshooting section, there may still be multiple clients running about, interleaving their calls to the server in quite random ways.

This is why I have stressed the importance of considering what state the server should keep as a vital part of the server design. If the server cannot keep track of its internal state, it cannot hope to sort out requests from multiple sources arriving in an arbitrary order.

From Here...

At this point, you been exposed to the fundamental design principles for both RPC clients and servers. You have seen how to write client and server code, and you know many of the challenges inherent in making that code bulletproof. You have also seen a number of more advanced topics, such as server customization, which you can use to enhance your application's functionality. To learn more about the topics discussed in this chapter, refer to the following chapters:

■ Chapter 9, "External Data Representation," acquaints you with the XDR routines that are at the heart of data transmission under RPC.

■ Chapter 10, "Language Specification," teaches you the RPCGEN data description language, and shows you how it can be used to automatically generate large parts of the client and server code.

■ Chapter 12, "RPC Under UNIX," provides much greater platform-specific detail on how all levels of RPC work in a UNIX environment.

■ Chapter 15, "Techniques for Developing DCE Clients and Servers," shows you the DCE way of creating clients and servers, and contrasts it with RPC.

Chapter 12

RPC Under UNIX

Even a cursory glance at the UNIX system documentation for the client and server functions immediately demonstrates their underlying complexity. RPC under UNIX contains many functions named clnt_xxx() and svc_xxx(), as well as several other prefixes. Several sets of functions seem to be only slightly different from one another. This is a reflection of the fact that the hierarchy of RPC functions is both deep and rich. There are many directions in which one can go.

This chapter focuses on a set of important topics in client/server development using RPC in a UNIX environment. This chapter assumes that you have already familiarized yourself with the contents of Chapter 11, "Techniques for Developing RPC Clients and Servers." That chapter gave you all the basic information that enabled you to get a client/server application up and running. It also provided you with some hints for how to go beyond the strictures of RPCGEN output.

In this chapter, I will go much further and add several critical RPC techniques that you can use to adapt and improve your clients and servers. These tools will let you do the following:

- Find a server with specific capabilities

- Selectively accept or reject requests within a server

- Broadcast messages from a client

- Handle multiple versions in both client and server

- Perform callbacks from the server to the client

- Batch client requests

- Configure a server to run under the inetd

Client/Server Rendezvous

When I discussed initialization in Chapter 11, I examined the client function `clnt_create()`, which takes a hostname parameter to select which server to contact, based on the host on which it is running. I did not discuss server initialization, except in a brief peek at the top level of a typical server, when I reviewed methods for server customization.

One important part of client and server initialization is a step that is sometimes called *rendezvous*. This is the step in which a client and a server agree that they will communicate with one another and establish how they're going to do it. It is implicit that if a client and server are to talk then they must first discover one another.

Simple clients may well be satisfied to find a particular server, or any server, that serves its particular set of requests. Complex clients often seek specific capabilities, however, rather than specific servers or hosts. If I am running a distributed ray tracing client, I almost certainly am looking for a server on a machine with a fast CPU that is not very busy at the moment. I really won't care if it is on host A or host B.

Unfortunately, there is no obvious way to realize this type of selectivity short of using the tedious go-fish approach of connecting to each server in turn and asking for that capability. Having the hostname as the only free parameter at my disposal is quite inconvenient. In general, clients would like to have the ability to discover information about potential servers. Servers can also benefit from the ability to be able to discover information about their clients and perhaps use that information to select, reject, or prioritize requests.

This subsection covers four loosely related methods for discovery or rendezvous. The three client techniques permit them to discover if a server has crashed, send a request to all servers, and identify all servers on a particular machine. The sole server technique is one by which a server may know its client more intimately. I will sneak in a variety of information about lower-level RPC functions throughout these discussions.

clnt_call( ) and NULLPROC

The simplest question that a client can ask a server is, "Are you there?" If the client has already called `clnt_create()`, then it can, of course, invoke any of its remote procedures and then check for an error. This approach violates the principle of orthogonal design, however, since it would be using one procedure to mean two things. Is it then necessary to incorporate an "are you there" procedure into every remote protocol?

If you have used RPCGEN to create your server (or part of it), the answer is no. RPCGEN automatically creates a procedure that provides precisely this capability. It is procedure number zero, hence it is often called the *NULL procedure*, or NULLPROC. Unfortunately, RPCGEN does not automatically create a high-level function for the NULL procedure as it does for the ones that you define in your interface file. Therefore, it must be called by resorting to a lower-level RPC function:

```
enum clnt_stat clnt_call(CLIENT *clnt, u_long procno,
    xdrproc_t argx, char *argp, xdrproc_t resx,
    char *resp, struct timeval tmo);
```

The clnt argument is the CLIENT pointer obtained from clnt_create(). argx and resx are the XDR function pointers used to encode the outgoing argument, whose address is given in argp, and to decode the incoming result, which will be stored where resp points. The argument procno is the all important procedure number, which in the case of the NULL procedure is simply zero.

The argument tmo specifies a timeout, in seconds and microseconds within the system type struct timeval, that will be used to determine how long to wait for the call to return. Note that this argument is passed by value, not by reference. The return type is an enum clnt_stat, which you saw in Chapter 11, "Techniques for Developing RPC Clients and Servers." For the purposes of this call, you need only look for the case where the function returns RPC_SUCCESS. Anything else indicates that the server is dead—or in bad shape.

The clnt_call() functions sit just below the set of functions generated by RPCGEN. If you look in any clnt.c file, you will see that each of the functions that the client calls immediately makes use of clnt_call(), with the value of procno equal to the various symbolic constants of the procedures defined in the corresponding .x file. For example, if you look back at the simple file manager from the previous chapter, the FILE_READ procedure looks like Listing 12.1 (TIMEOUT is a global struct timeval).

Listing 12.1 The Implementation of the *FILE_READ*

```
readresult *
file_read_1(readrequest *argp, CLIENT *clnt)
{
    static readresult res;          /* place to hold the result */
    bzero((char *)&res, sizeof(res));    /* initialize it to all
zero bytes */
    if (clnt_call(clnt, FILE_READ, xdr_readrequest,   /* call the
RPC */
```

(continues)

Listing 12.1   Continued

```
        argp, xdr_readresult, &res, TIMEOUT)
        != RPC_SUCCESS)
        return(NULL);                    /* if it failed return NULL */
    return(&res);    /* otherwise return a pointer to the result */
}
```

When you use `clnt_call()` to call the `NULLPROC`, you pass in no data and expect no results. I often encapsulate this call within a much simpler function, as shown in Listing 12.2.

Listing 12.2   Determining if the RPC Server is Alive

```
bool_t serverok(CLIENT *cli, int sec)
{
    struct timeval tmo;              /* Unix timeout structure */
    enum clnt_stat sta;             /* RPC result code */

    tmo.tv_sec = sec;               /* timeout in seconds */
    tmo.tv_usec = 0;                /* no microseconds */
    if ( clnt_call(cli, NULLPROC, xdr_void,
        (char *)NULL, xdr_void, (char *)NULL, tmo) ==
        RPC_SUCCESS ) return(TRUE); /* server responded -
it is alive */
    else return(FALSE);  /* no response or bad response -
it is dead */
}
```

This function may be put in a utility library and called by any client to determine if its server connection is alive with a timeout of sec seconds. Note that even though no client data is sent, nor any reply received, the client and server are still exchanging a small amount of information. Thus, you do not want to make the timeout too small—certainly don't make it zero.

There is one other very important thing to notice about this function. Recall that in the "Other Client Functions" section of Chapter 11, I told you about the notorious timeout bug that prevents `clnt_control()` from correctly setting the default timeout. With `clnt_call()`, however, you can individually set the timeout on every remote procedure call. This involves editing the default `clnt.c file` created by RPCGEN, of course, but if you must change the timeouts of various RPCs then this is the way to do it.

Client Broadcast

Suppose that you are writing a distributed printing system. Each machine on your network has a server that manages the print jobs for all local printers. There is also a client application that can request that a file be printed on a specific printer (given by name) on a specific machine (also given by name). This client would clearly be much more useful to the average user if it had a bit more intelligence.

There are several types of more specific jobs that this client could do. If the user has a short file then he might like to request that it be printed on "the printer that is least busy." If there are only two printers on the network that can handle *OPL* (*Obscure Printer Language*), then it would be nice to be able to say "print this file on either of the OPL printers," without their actual printer names or the names of the machine(s) to which those printers are connected.

This illustrates the need for a second type of selection by the client: the ability to find out if a server has a certain capability without tediously questioning each server in turn.

The function that you use to do this has this formidable prototype:

```
enum clnt_stat clnt_broadcast(u_long prno, u_long vno,
u_long pcno, xdrproc_t argx, char *argp,
xdrproc_t resx, char *resp, selproc choosethem);
```

Here prno and vno are the program number and version number of the RPC interface shared by the client and server. The next five parameters are the remote procedure number procno, the XDR encoding procedure argx, the outoing argument pointer argp, the XDR decoding procedure resx, and the XDR incoming pointer resp. These are exactly the same as in the clnt_call() prototype given at the very beginning of this section. The final parameter is a selection procedure, which must have this prototype:

```
typedef bool_t selproc(char *resp,
                       struct sockaddr_in *saddr);
```

The purpose of clnt_broadcast() is to make a remote procedure call on all servers and arrange that when each server replies to the client, the function choosethem will be called with the decoded results (in resp) from that particular server. The parameter saddr will contain the network level address of the responding server. If the selection procedure returns FALSE, then clnt_broadcast() will continue to seek other servers. If it returns TRUE, then the broadcasting will stop.

Tip
All the individual timeouts in the lower-level clnt_xxx() functions work, even if setting the timeout with clnt_control() does not.

Introduction to RPC

How would you use this in the distributed printer example? Define an interface procedure that asks the server if it supports a given printer description language, something like the following:

```
const PS = 1;
const HPGL = 2;
...
const OPL = 14;        /* The Obscure Printer Language */
...
bool           PR_SUPPORTS(int) = 5;
```

These RPCGEN definitions generate a function pr_supports_1() that can be used to ask a single server if it supports a particular printer language. They can also be used for a client broadcast. The code in Listing 12.3 will generate the broadcast.

Listing 12.3   Sending a Client Broadcast

```
static int    want = OPL;  /* the integer parameter specifies */
                           /* the type of printer desired */
static bool_t has = FALSE; /* initialize - assume failure */
clnt_broadcast(PRPROG, PRVERS, PR_SUPPORTS,
    xdr_int, (char *)&want, xdr_bool, (char *)&has,
    choosethem);            /* perform the broadcast */
```

Note that I have assumed that the program number is PRPROG and its version is PRVERS for the sake of this call. The argument parameter is an int so that the output encoding function is xdr_int. The output argument's address is &want, where want has the value OPL since you are seeking a printer that supports that language. The input decoding function is xdr_bool since the result parameter is of type bool_t. You provide the address of storage for a bool_t as the next parameter. This is where each server's response will be placed. The choosethem() function looks like Listing 12.4.

Listing 12.4   The Selection Procedure for the Broadcast in Listing 12.3

```
#include <sys/types.h>
#include <sys/socket.h>
#include <netdb.h>

char servnam[MAXHOSTLEN+1];  /* this global holds the name of
the server */

bool_t choosethem(char *resp, struct sockaddr_in *sad)
{
```

```
        bool_t really = FALSE;          /* initialize - assume failure */
        if ( resp != (char *)NULL ) { /* if the response was not the
NULL pointer then ... */
                really = *(bool_t *)resp; /* dereference the pointer to get
the server's reply */
                if ( really == TRUE )     /* if the server said "YES"
then ... */
                        addrtoname(sad);        /* convert the network address
to a name */
                }
        return(really);              /* return a success/failure code */
}
```

This function first verifies that the result pointer resp is not NULL. In this case, it will just be the address of the static has from Listing 12.3. It then dereferences what the server returned, and sets really to that value. If the server returned TRUE, then the selection function will also return TRUE and the broadcasting will end. If the server has returned FALSE, or some other error has occurred causing the server to not return anything, then the broadcast will continue.

Note that in the case of success, I have also made a call to a function named addrtoname, which will convert the network address to a server name. This is necessary since the client creation function clnt_create() wants a string for the server's hostname. The code for this utility is in Listing 12.5.

Listing 12.5 Converting a Network Address to a Hostname

```
void addrtoname(struct sockaddr_in *sad)
{
    struct hostent *hen;                /* host database pointer */
    hen = gethostbyaddr(&sad->sin_addr, /* ask the host database
if it knows this address */
            sizeof(struct in_addr), AF_INET);
    if ( hen != (struct hostent *)NULL ) /* if it does, then copy
then ... */
            (void)strcpy(servnam, hen->h_name); /* copy the hostname
to the global servnam */
    endhostent(); /* close the host database opened by
gethostbyaddr() */
}
```

Note that I have had to resort to a global string variable, servnam, in order to get the result back into the routine that actually called clnt_broadcast(), since the selection function itself is only permitted to return a Boolean. Evil, but necessary.

There is a very important design consideration for selection procedures: they should know when to terminate. The reason is that the selection procedure must eventually return TRUE or the broadcasting will continue. In the previous example, this was easy: you were looking for a particular response and when you got it, the selection procedure returned TRUE.

In general, client broadcast is not a good way to try to gather information from every server. As an example of how not to use a selection procedure, suppose that you decided to use clnt_broadcast() with the NULLPROC and use the selection function to build a list of all servers. In principle, this is a very clever idea, but in practice it will be extremely slow. The reason is that the selection function can never know if all servers have responded. It can only keep returning FALSE and hoping for some additional action.

What will happen is that eventually clnt_broadcast() will timeout waiting for a reply. Be aware that it sets its timeout to larger and larger values as it becomes more and more frustrated waiting for a reply. This use of the NULLPROC will work, but it will not complete quickly. I tried this experiment on a single host network, and it took almost a minute to get the (correct) reply.

> **Caution**
>
> You should always use clnt_broadcast() with the expectation that it might take a long time, even if your selection function is well designed. If no servers are running, for example, then it will take many seconds before a timeout occurs.

Note that you can specify that the selection function be a NULL function pointer. In this case, the broadcast message is sent out, but no results are expected (and there is no timeout delay). This is one method of sending a one-way message to every server. This might be very useful for a global reset operation, for example.

There are several things to be aware of when performing client broadcast. First, clnt_broadcast() uses the UDP protocol. This means that it will not have the reliability of a TCP connection. Some packets may be lost so that you do not necessarily get a response from every server, particularly on a large network. Second, only those servers that support UDP will reply. Of course, default servers built by RPCGEN automatically support both UDP and TCP; but you also saw in the "The rpcgen Command Line" section of Chapter 10 that you could use an RPCGEN command line to build in support for only TCP.

Another restriction is that the size of the outgoing message is limited to a relatively small number of bytes; in many implementations, this is just over 1K (a restriction imposed by `clnt_broadcast()` itself, not UDP). In practice, I have never encountered this limitation, and I question the wisdom of attempting to send this much data via UDP anyway.

Tip
UDP is cheap. Include it in all of your servers.

Finally, a word about server support for client broadcast is in order. In general, a server does not have to do anything special. It is invoked from a broadcast operation in the same way as from a standard client RPC. However, `clnt_broadcast()` may retransmit its requests (particularly with poorly designed selection procedures). Therefore, the server must anticipate that it may be entered multiple times as a result of a single `clnt_broadcast()`.

Troubleshooting

I have written a client broadcast function. Whenever I execute it, nothing happens. The server does not get any packets. If I examine the return code of `clnt_broadcast()`, it is the most uninformative RPC_CANTSEND. I know it can't send, but why?

The `clnt_broadcast()` function uses RPC_CANTSEND to indicate some problem in creating its UDP socket. This is almost always an indication that your network is misconfigured (an all too common problem for "out of the box" systems). On a UNIX system, the command `ifconfig` can be used to obtain information about a network interface. It can usually be invoked as `ifconfig -a` to get information about all network interfaces, or as `ifconfig Ifacename` to get information about an interface named `Ifacename`, which will be some obscure string describing your network device (`le0`, `ne0`, `qe0`, ...).

If an `ifconfig` tells you that your broadcast address is 255.255.255.255 or 0.0.0.0, or if it does not declare that broadcasting is enabled on one or more of your network interfaces, then `clnt_broadcast()` will always fail with this error. Talk to your system administrator, or examine the system documentation for `ifconfig` yourself. Network administration is a life's work, so I cannot, unfortunately, give you more specific advice if your network is misconfigured.

Other return codes from `clnt_broadcast()` are usually indications of something much more serious than network configuration problems. Note that RPC_TIMEDOUT means just what it says and can be safely ignored.

Client Selection and Identification

The server has two ways to handle client requests selectively: it may choose to accept only connections from certain clients, or it many select which requests to process on each RPC call.

When a server starts up, it advertises itself as available for communication. In general, it is not particularly easy to interfere with this process and include or exclude specific clients. It is much simpler to add an OPEN RPC, which each client must execute to gain access to the server. The information gained by the server during the OPEN call can be used in subsequent RPC calls to select what to process and at what priority.

The way I usually do this is to define an OPEN call in which the client passes whatever information is needed to help the server choose if it wishes to serve this client. This information could be a priority flag, for example, indicating how much of the server's resources it wants. In a distributed computer server, for example, the client might say "I need three of your CPUs." The server can then decide if it has that many free at the moment, and return success or failure.

If the OPEN call succeeds, then the server returns an identifier to the client. This identifier becomes part of the client's subsequent interface calls. If the OPEN call fails, then the server should return some unique value indicating that the OPEN was refused. A well-behaved client should then terminate. If the server was started by inetd (more below), then the server can also simply terminate, which the client will perceive as an RPC error. It is not advisable for the server to attempt to close its side of the connection by force. The burden of responsibility is on the client.

In the file manager example from the last chapter, you might thus add this interface (and bump the version number to two):

```
typedef u_int          id;
const    BADID = 0;
id              FILE_SERVEROPEN(string) = 4;
```

in which the client is passing its identifying information as a string. Each of the other client interfaces must also be modified to include the id as part of the argument. For example, the readrequest struct should become that shown in Listing 12.6.

Listing 12.6   A Newer Form of the *readrequest* Structure

```
struct idreadrequest {
      id          myid;        /* identifier from OPEN call */
      u_int       bytestoread; /* number of bytes to read */
      string      thefile<>;   /* name of the file from which to
read those bytes */
      } ;
```

The first thing a client should do is to call the `FILE_SERVEROPEN` procedure, and if the result is `BADID`, it should then exit (see Listing 12.7).

Listing 12.7   Using the File Manager's *OPEN* Procedure

```
static int *idp;          /* pointer to returned id */
static int  id = (id)BADID;  /* returned id itself - initialize
to a known bad id */
idp = file_serveropen_2("stuff", cli);  /* execute the server OPEN
procedure */
if ( idp == (id *)NULL ||  /* if the server returned nothing, or ... */
     ( id = (*idp) ) == (id)BADID ) { /* the id is not good then ... */
     print error message and exit      /* bail out (nicely) */
     }
```

The server should do whatever application-specific operations are required to determine if it will initiate a dialog with a client identifying itself as "stuff." This is the parameter that the server will get when line three of Listing 12.7 is executed. If it will talk to such a client, it should then return some kind of valid `id`; if it won't, it should return `BADID`. If it does accept this client, then your server probably should add the `id` to an internal list of acceptable `ids`. For each subsequent RPC, it can then check the `id` part of that RPC interface and reject the request if the `id` is not on the list. So, in a `FILE_READ` request, there will be code in which `rrqp` is the incoming `idreadrequest` * argument and `rrep` is the static `readresult` whose address is returned as the result (see Listing 12.8).

Listing 12.8   The File Manager Server Spurns an Unregistered Client

```
if ( rrqp != (idreadrequest *)NULL ) { /* if the read request is not
invalid */
     if ( ! onlist(rrqp->id) ) { /* but the client's id is not on
the list then ... */
          rrep.errno = BADID; /* refuse to client's read request */
          return(&rrep);       /* declare a bad id error and return */
          }
     }
```

Here, `onlist` is a Boolean function that checks to see if the `id` is on the list of valid `ids` kept by the server. Note that this use of `ids` is no substitute for authentication or other forms of security. It is merely a simple mechanism by which servers can track individual client requests back to the client from which they came.

There is another mechanism that the server can also use to get network information about the client, such as its host address. In the "Server Conventions" section of Chapter 11, I briefly mentioned that each RPC call in the server actually receives two parameters: the address of the client argument and a parameter of type SVCXPRT. Thus, the file manager server function file_read_1() is actually called as the following:

```
readresult *file_read_1(readrequest *rrqp,
                        SVCXPRT *rqstp)
```

A SVCXPRT (*service transport handle*) is an opaque server data structure containing information about the current client connection. It is parallel to the client side CLIENT data structure. Most of the contents of a SVCXPRT are inaccessible—and uninteresting—but the following call:

```
struct sockaddr_in *svc_getcaller(SVCXPRT *rqstp);
```

can be used to recover the network address of the client making the current request. You can use the addrtoname() function that I gave above to convert this address into a hostname, for example. Note that svc_getcaller() isn't really a function—it's a macro.

Tip

svc_getcaller() can be used in server logging to record the hostname of each client-making RPC.

A distributed compute server, for example, could keep track of which hosts have made compute requests and prioritize requests on the basis of past selfishness. Greedy hosts could be put on the end of a request queue. This approach is obviously more coarse-grained than the per-client id idea, and is probably only appropriate when the server expects only a single client per host.

Caution

Manipulating a SVCXPRT can be hazardous since most implementations have a nasty habit of invalidating its contents if RPC errors have occurred. In particular, if you have read the system documentation, you might be tempted to try a call to the following to get status on your connection:

```
SVC_STAT(SVCXPRT *rqstp);
```

This call can crash your server if RPC errors have occurred. Even svc_getcaller() can return garbage. Usually the addrtoname() function will just fail in that case and not crash. The following unbelievably ugly code will often select out bad SVCXPRTs:

```
if ( (int)rqstp < (int)main )
        beware...
```

The *portmapper*

If you have written UNIX interprocess communication programs (IPC) or are somewhat familiar with network programming, then you know that part of the way a network application identifies itself is by way of a *port*. A port is just a number that an application uses as part of the network address used to contact another application. Standard UNIX port numbers are stored in the file /etc/services. For example, whenever you use the file transfer protocol (FTP) to transfer files, you are almost certainly using port number 21.

This is a completely static, file-based mechanism. In addition, port numbers are very often limited to 16 bits. By contrast, RPC uses a dynamic mechanism for port assignment. Undoubtedly, you've already noticed that the program number defined by your interface is a u_long, which is typically 32 bits. The program number is not a port number; rather, it is a key by which clients and servers can rendezvous with one another on a dynamically assigned port, using a separate application known as the portmapper.

When a server starts up, it must make itself known to the portmapper. In particular, it must register its program number and version number(s). To do this, it goes through a series of registration steps. During this process, the server allocates one or more ports and then tells the portmapper that it is a server for program MYPROG, version MYVERS, and that it can be found on port 7154, for example.

When the client starts up, it will generally call the clnt_create() function to try to contact a server. Of course, you already know that two of the arguments to this function are the program number and version number of the desired server. What clnt_create() does is to contact the portmapper also and ask, "Do you have a server registered for MYPROG, MYVERS?" In this case, the portmapper will answer, "Yes, and it is located on port 7154." The remaining part of the clnt_create() code then makes the direct connection to that server, using the hostname argument and this port number to build a complete server network address. This method of rendezvous is illustrated in figure 12.1.

One immediate practical application is that a client may contact the portmapper directly and ask about the available program numbers, versions, and ports, known collectively as *mappings*. There are two ways of doing this. From the UNIX command line, you can use the application program rpcinfo to get a list of all known mappings. It can also be used to perform a call to the NULLPROC of a given server and to perform a broadcast to the NULLPROC. These options are accessed as follows:

```
rpcinfo -p { host }
rpcinfo -u host programnumber { version }
rpcinfo -t host programnumber { version }
rpcinfo -b program version
```

The first invocation probes the portmapper and prints out all registered information. If the optional argument host is given, then the portmapper on that host is probed; otherwise, the portmapper on the current host is probed. The output from this command will look something like Listing 12.9.

Fig. 12.1

Clients rendezvous with servers via the portmapper.

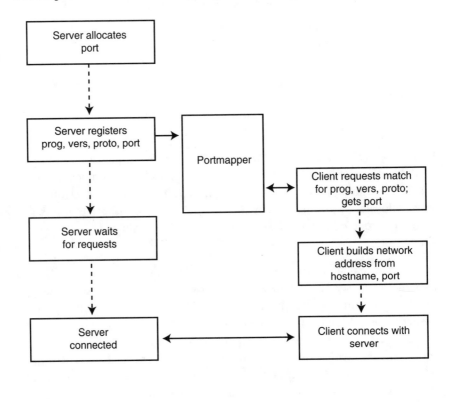

Listing 12.9 | Sample Output from *rpcinfo -p*

100000	2	udp	111	portmapper
100005	1	udp	1030	mountd
100017	1	tcp	1061	rexd
... .				
603988992	1	udp	1060	
603988992	1	tcp	1081	

The first column of the output is the program number—sadly given in decimal. The second column is the version, the third is the name of the network protocol supported, and the fourth is the numerical value of the port number. The fifth column will be blank except for those servers that have made their names known through the process described later in the "Server Startup and the `inetd`" section.

You will notice that all the system services have relatively small numbers, although there is a set of very large numbers at the end. If you translate 603988992 into hex, you get 0x24002400—the program number of our favorite file manager server. Notice that it is registered twice—once for UDP and once for TCP. This is to be expected since servers created by RPCGEN register themselves under both protocols by default.

> **Note**
>
> Take the `portmapper` mapping list with a grain of salt. It contains the list of all registrations ever performed and not deleted, as well as all system services. A server may have died, exited, or be otherwise unavailable even if it is registered with the `portmapper`.

The invocation `rpcinfo -u` makes a UDP call to the `NULLPROC` of the server with the named `programnumber` on the named host and reports the results. Giving the version number is optional. `rpcinfo -t` does the same thing using TCP, while `rpcinfo -b` makes a `clnt_broadcast()` to the `NULLPROC` of the named program, version pair. These latter three calls can be used to see if a given server is alive. The last call will be time consuming for reasons you have already seen.

Within the client application, you already know how to do a `clnt_broadcast()` and how to invoke the `NULLPROC` for a connected client using `clnt_call()`. How do you get the `portmapper` mapping information programmatically? Use the function shown in Listing 12.10.

Listing 12.10   Retrieving *portmapper* Information

```
struct pmaplist *
pmap_getmaps(struct sockaddr_in *sad); /*where a struct pmaplist is
defined as the following */
struct pmap {
    unsigned long pm_prog;          /* program number */
    unsigned long pm_vers;          /* version number */
    unsigned long pm_prot;          /* protocol number */
    unsigned long pm_port;          /* port number */
```

(continues)

II

Introduction to RPC

```
Listing 12.10   Continued
        } ;
    struct pmaplist {
        struct pmap      pml_map;     /* one mapping */
        struct pmaplist *pml_next;    /* pointer to the next mapping */
        } ;
```

This is just a linked list of maps, each of which has the four elements of a
pmap. Note that in most implementations, the pm_port, which gives the port
number, will actually contain only 16 bits of information. Note also that the
pm_prot field gives the network protocol and will almost always be equal to
one of the constants IPPROTO_UDP (for UDP) or IPPROTO_TCP (for TCP).

I do not know why the pmap_getmaps() function insists on a network address
rather than a hostname—after all, the point of the RPC abstraction is to make
distributed programming accessible to people without forcing them to be
network programmers also. The piece of code in Listing 12.11 will get you the
list of portmapper mappings on a given host by name.

```
Listing 12.11   Getting portmapper Mappings from a Hostname
    #include <stdio.h>
    #include <sys/types.h>
    #include <sys/socket.h>
    #include <rpc/rpc.h>
    #include <rpc/pmap_prot.h>              /* 1 */
    #include <netdb.h>
    extern struct pmaplist *
        pmap_getmaps(struct sockaddr_in *);    /* 2 */
    struct pmaplist *getmaps(char *hname)
    {
        struct pmaplist *pp;      /* mapping linked list */
        struct hostent  *hen;     /* host database pointer */
        struct sockaddr_in sa;    /* network address */
        (void)bzero((char *)&sa,    /* zero out the network address */
            sizeof(struct sockaddr_in));
        hen = gethostent(hname); /* get the host database entry for
    the given host */
        if ( hen == (struct hostent *)NULL ) { /* if no such host was
    found then ... */
            endhostent(); /* close the host database opened by
    gethostnen() */
            return((struct pmaplist *)NULL); /* return failure */
        }
        (void)bcopy(hen->h_addr, &sa.sin_addr,
            hen->h_length); /* copy the network address of the host */
        sa.sin_family = hen->h_addrtype;      /* also, record the
```

```
address family */
    endhostent(); /* close the host database opened by gethostent() */
    return(pmap_getmaps(&sa));   /* call the pmap function */
}
```

The statements marked 1 and 2 will be needed in some implementations because the `rpc.h` file does not include the `portmapper` include files, and also because no prototype for `pmap_getmaps()` is given in those files. As a client, you can now determine all the servers that might be running on a given machine. You can determine exactly which versions are supported by those servers and exactly which protocols. While the mapping list might well contain dead entries, it is guaranteed that any RPC servers running on the named machine will be registered with the `portmapper` on that machine, so the `pmap_getmaps()` function is a very powerful way of determining exactly whom to contact in advance.

If you call the `pmap_getmaps()` function, then you should dispose of the memory that it allocates for you when you are done. Note that I have passed the address of pp to the function `xdr_free()`, not pp itself:

```
struct pmaplist *pp;
pp = getmaps("myhost");
....
xdr_free(xdr_pmaplist, &pp);
```

Multiple Versions

Multiple versions are a fact of programming life. As soon as you have deployed a piece of software, your users will begin to provide you with feedback. Eventually, you will need to add new features, fix bugs, disable security holes, or just make general changes. Some of your existing clients may not want to upgrade, however, so that you will be stuck with having to support several versions of client code, server code, or both.

Even if your installed base is small (one, for example), it may not be worth the effort for you to rewrite existing software when the interface changes. This still puts you in a situation of having older applications running older versions and brand-spanking-new applications running the most up-to-date versions.

Fortunately, it is straightforward to add support for multiple versions in client/server applications using RPC. RPCGEN supports it quite nicely, and the client and server modifications are simple. In fact, it is almost never necessary to write a separate server for each version—one set of server code can suffice for all versions. In the next section, I will consider an example in which the file manager from Chapter 11, "Techniques for Developing RPC Clients and Servers," is upgraded to version 2.

RPCGEN Support

Suppose you leave your file manager version 1 interface exactly as is, but add a new set of features and functionality and call that "version 2." I will add the FILE_SERVEROPEN interface that I described previously, which will mean that all my version 1 data structures will have to be changed. There are two choices for doing this modification: I can either make the data structures into discriminated unions and use the version number as the discriminant, or I can declare separate data structures for the different versions. Since the file manager version 1 interface is very simple, I will choose the latter approach. This means that I will add the id and idreadrequest data types that you have already seen. I will also need one for an id plus a string:

```
struct idstring {      /* id + string */
     id          theid;
     string      thestring<>;
     } ;
```

The "program" part of the interface will now have two version clauses, one for each version. It will look like Listing 12.12.

Listing 12.12 Two Versions of the File Manager

```
program FMPROG {
    version FMVERS {
        bool               FILE_EXISTS(string)        = 1;
        readresult          FILE_READ(readrequest)     = 2;
        void               FILE_DELETE(string)        = 3;
        } = 1;
    version FMVERS2 {
        bool               FILE_EXISTS(idstring)       = 1;
        readresult          FILE_READ(idreadrequest)       = 2;
        void               FILE_DELETE(idstring)      = 3;
        id               FILE_SERVEROPEN(string)      = 4;
        /* the rest of the version 2 RPCs ... */
        } = 2;
    } = 0x24002400;
```

The first part is absolutely identical to the original. All the arguments and return types are the same, as are the procedure numbers. The second version clause declares the same set of procedure names for the first three RPCs with differing arguments. After that, everything is new for version 2.

If you now run this input through RPCGEN, it will do its standard work for you. If you investigate the contents of fmgr_clnt.c or fmgr_svc.c, you will see that they now refer to functions with both _1 and _2 suffixes, namely:

```
file_exists_1(), file_exists_2(), file_read_1(),
file_read_2(), file_delete_1(), file_delete_2(),
file_serveropen_2(), ...
```

This is the method used for preventing conflicts in function names for different versions. Each version clause is thus associated with a unique set of functions for that version. Since FILE_EXISTS is an interface in both versions, you see both file_exists_1() and file_exists_2(). Since FILE_SERVEROPEN only exists in version 2, you only see file_serveropen_2() with no corresponding _1(). Further, if you look in fmgr_xdr.c and fmgr.h, you will see that all the data types are represented there.

Client Support

What work needs to be done on the client side? Amazingly, the answer is almost none. Older client code that only supports the version 1 interface may be recompiled and relinked with the new fmgr.h, fmgr_clnt.c, and fmgr_xdr.c without change. Similarly, a client written explicitly for version 2 never needs to even think about the version 1 interface. It just calls the _2() functions with their respective arguments.

Of course, if you have an existing version 1 client that you want to upgrade to the version 2 interface, then you have work to do. Not only must you change all your file_read_1() calls to file_read_2() calls, but you must also change the logic of the client to support the new interface by calling file_serveropen_2() first to get an id, for example. But this is nothing more than the work you would have to do anyway to write a new version 2 client.

There is also one very entertaining optimization that clients can perform. It is possible for a client to be written so that it will look for and then use the highest possible version that a server supports. You may need to do this if older servers exist, for example. If your interface has three versions, then you might like to find a server that supports version 3, but the reality may be that at your site, the highest version supported by any server is two. Your client then needs to be adaptable and find the best version fit. This unlikely sounding scenario is quite common if your server comes from a vendor, but your clients are written internally. The fact that version 3 servers exist does not necessarily mean that you have bought one.

The following function may be used by clients written to accept a range of version numbers:

```
CLIENT *clnt_create_vers(char *hname, u_long progno,
    u_long *gotvers, u_long lovers, u_long hivers,
    char *proto);
```

The parameters `hname`, `progno`, and `proto` are exactly as in `clnt_create()`. `lovers` is the lowest version number that this client will accept, and `hivers` is the highest. On success, the actual version number obtained is stored in `gotvers`, and a `CLIENT` pointer returned. On failure, `NULL` is returned and the contents of `gotvers` are undefined.

Of course, you can also use `pmap_getmaps()` to find the version numbers supported on a given host, and do it yourself. The advantage of `clnt_create_vers()` is that it not only searches the version range, but it also makes the server connection as well. Naturally, you must now use the value of `(*gotvers)` to decide which client version functions to call.

This function also has another use. In some older versions of RPC, it is possible for a `clnt_create()` to return a `CLIENT` pointer even if the version number specified in the call to `clnt_create()` is not supported by the server. If your implementation has this bug, then you will learn of it the first time you make a client remote procedure call. The call will return a `NULL` pointer, and the error code in the `cf_stat` member of the extern `rpc_createerr` struct will be `RPC_PROGVERSMISMATCH`. If you must have the version `thevers` and you want to detect this error immediately, then use `clnt_create_vers()` with `lovers` and `hivers` both set equal to `thevers`. If it succeeds, then you will have a connection to a server that supports that version. If that version is not available, it will return `NULL`.

If `clnt_create_vers()` fails with `RPC_PROGVERSMISMATCH`, then you can also use the `rpc_createerr` struct to find out which versions are supported, using something like the code in Listing 12.13.

Listing 12.13   Determining Client Version Limits

```
CLIENT *cli;               /* CLIENT pointer */
u_long  gv = 0L;           /* version used for CLIENT connection */
cli = clnt_create_vers("myhost", MYPROG, &gv,
    MYPROGV1, MYPROGV2, "tcp"); /* try to connect to the server */
if ( cli == (CLIENT *)NULL &&      /* if it failed due to version
mismatch */
        rpc_createerr.cf_stat == RPC_PROGVERSMISMATCH ) {
            (void)printf("Low %d, high %d\n",
            rpc_createerr.cf_error.re_vers.low, /* minimum version */
            rpc_createerr.cf_error.re_vers.high); /* maximum version */

        }
```

Server Functions

Server support for multiple versions involves a different set of choices than it does in the client. Usually, a client will be targeted for one version (although it may have to support more than one). As the interface evolves and new versions are created, the server functions for the later versions may well be built upon those of earlier versions. The main choice is to decide if the changes warrant writing a whole new server or attempting to make a single server support multiple versions.

For the case of the file manager (and for every other case with which I have been personally involved), the correct design choice is to write a single server. The new data structures have not changed that much, and the core file operations themselves have not changed at all. Since the RPCGEN output file fmgr_svc.c has calls to all the _1() and all the _2() functions, your two-headed server must resolve all those calls. This can be done very easily without tediously duplicating code.

To see how, consider the functions file_exists_1() and file_exists_2(). Their return types are the same, but their arguments are different and their semantics are different. The _2() version wants a valid id, while the _1() version hasn't a clue about ids. But you can easily implement the _2() function in terms of the _1() function, as shown in Listing 12.14.

Listing 12.14   The Second Version of the *EXISTS* RPC

```
bool_t *file_exists_2(idstring *idsp)
{
    static bool_t bval;                    /* static result value */
    static char  *fname = (char *)NULL; /* filename */
    xdr_free(xdr_bool, &bval);             /* free previous result */
    bval = FALSE;                          /* assume failure */
    if (idsp == (idstring *)NULL || !onlist(idsp->id))
        return(&bval);          /* if the argument is invalid or
client unregistered, then fail */
    fname = idsp->thestring; /* get the filename from the argument */
    return(file_exists_1(&fname)); /* call the version 1 procedure */
}
```

This trick worked because the version 2 argument was a superset of the version 1 argument. I can use this same approach with the other two interface functions that are shared between version 1 and version 2 of the file manager. Another very common approach is to have each of the various version-dependent functions perform their version-specific processing, and then arrange that they all call a single common function that does the work.

> **Caution**
>
> If you are using shared code in a server that supports multiple versions, you must make sure that you always return the address of a static variable from every version function.

Notice that every possible return pathway in the previous example returns the address of a static. I know that the old code in file_exists_1() does, and all the new code in file_exists_2() does so explicitly.

Once you have implemented all the _1() and _2() version functions in the server, your work is done. The fmgr_svc.c file generated by RPCGEN has arranged to register the server with both versions. It knows this because you included both versions within a single "program" statement in the fmgr.x file. It also knows how to distinguish which versions are expected by different clients. It knows this because the different versions are registered with the portmapper under different port numbers. There is a port for version 1 and another for version 2. Therefore, when a request arrives on a particular port, it is routed by the top level server code to the correct version-specific server function.

Suppose you had chosen the other design strategy and decided to leave your version 1 file manager server alone while writing a version 2 server from scratch. If you do this, you certainly do not want to leave the two interfaces within the same RPCGEN .x file. The reason is twofold. First, if you do leave them in there, you will need to write stubs for all the _1() version functions in your _2() server since the fmgr_svc.c generated by RPCGEN will reference them. Second, if you compile and link to the unmodified fmgr_svc.c, then it will register both versions. This is confusing to clients since your new server does not actually support version 1. It is better in this case to have one .x file for each version's interface. The common data structure definitions can be put in their own file, and #include-d within both .x files, since RPCGEN runs the C preprocessor for you.

Client Batch Requests

You have already seen a number of cases in which the client makes a remote procedure call to the server and does not expect any reply. Information is sent on a one-way trip, which is itself a performance enhancement since one half the network traffic is missing. It is possible to group a set of such client requests together and transmit them all at once, thereby reducing the network traffic even further. This process is known as *client batching.*

When you perform client batching, you have little control over when the actual requests are sent. You can be certain that they are sent in order, however. You can also count on the fact that whenever you invoke an RPC that does require a reply, any outstanding batch requests will be sent. As a result, you can use any such RPC as a "flush" command. You are also restricted to using TCP as the transport protocol.

Consider a contrived example in order to illustrate client batching. Suppose I define two interface procedures:

```
void      SENDINT(int)       = 10; /* 10 is random */
int       GETINTSUM(void)  = 11;
```

The SENDINT procedure will send an integer to the server, which will add it to a running sum. Since it does not return a result, this procedure is a candidate for batching. The GETINTSUM procedure will be used to retrieve the running sum in the server and reset that sum to zero. Since this procedure does return a result (the sum), it will flush any outstanding requests, which is quite appropriate, since it will come after all the SENDINT requests.

On the client side, I have these invocations (see Listing 12.15).

Listing 12.15   Client Batch Processing

```
static int iter;              /* loop counter */
static int *ires;             /* RPC result pointer */
enum clnt_stat cf;            /* RPC status code */
static struct timeval zerotmo = { 0, 0 };      /* zero timeout */
cf = RPC_SUCCESS;             /* no errors yet */
for(iter=0;iter<128 && cf == RPC_SUCCESS;iter++) {    /* while no
errors ... */
      cf = clnt_call(cli, SENDINT, xdr_int, &iter,
          xdr_void, NULL, zerotmo); /* send an integer (128 times) */
      if ( cf == RPC_TIMEDOUT ) cf = RPC_SUCCESS; /* 1 */
      }
if ( cf == RPC_SUCCESS ) {              /* if no errors occurred */
      ires = getintsum_1(NULL, cli);              /* 2 */
      if ( ires != (int *)NULL )         /* if the server returned
something then ... */
          (void)printf("Sum is %d\n", (*ires));   /* print it */
      }
```

Introduction to RPC

This code illustrates the fact that you must set the timeout to zero in order for client batching to work. This makes perfect sense, but it also means that you cannot just call sendint_1(), since the only reliable way to set the timeout is by using clnt_call().

The statement labeled 1 is also worth examination. Since the timeout is zero, most implementations will return RPC_TIMEDOUT from the clnt_call(). This is not at error—it is what you want. Set it to RPC_SUCCESS in this case so that the for loop is not exited. Any other error will cause an exit. Since you are not getting any information back from the server, however, it is not possible that cf will have any value associated with a server error. This is the primary drawback with client batching—errors are not seen when they occur. Of course, you can always arrange to fetch the error later.

You might, for example, define a GETERROR interface that clients can use to get information on errors that occurred during batch processing. This interface, which is an excellent example of the collector form of interface design that was discussed in the "Server Design Considerations" section of Chapter 11, might look like Listing 12.16.

Listing 12.16 RPC Declarations for a Generic Error Structure

```
struct nrerror {         /* error in proc with no return */
    u_long  procno;  /* proc where it happened */
    int     ecode;   /* the error code itself */
    } ;
nrerror GETERROR(void) = 12;
```

Tip

When you are using client batching, make sure that you have a mechanism for retrieving errors from the server. Define an error retrieval interface function or use server callback.

The statement labeled 2 serves two purposes: it will flush out any of the batched calls in the for loop, and it will get the result from the server. In this case, the result will be the sum of all the integers from zero to 128, inclusive. When I ran this code and used a network sniffer program, it detected exactly one network transfer to the server and one back. The one transfer to the server consisted of the 128 SENDINT calls and the single GETINTSUM call. If I had not used client batching, but simply called sendint_1() 128 times, there would have been 129 transfers to the server and one back. Client batching can result in an enormous savings in execution time, particularly if there are large data transfers or if the network is very busy or slow.

On the server side, very little needs to be done to support client batching. The server will see batched requests no differently than straight-line requests. The only change that you might want to make is to ensure that errors that occur in processing remote procedure calls, and that do not themselves have return values, are saved.

With this definition, the server code for the SENDINT, GETINTSUM, and GETERROR operations would look like Listing 12.17.

Listing 12.17   Server Implementation of the Integer Sum Functions

```
static int thesum = 0;        /* initialize the sum to zero */
static nrerror theerr = { 0L, 0 } ; /* no error */
void *sendint_1(int *iptr)
{                    /* if the argument is valid, add it to the sum */
    if ( iptr != (int *)NULL ) thesum += (*iptr);
    else {          /* set the error structure members to ... */
         theerr.procno = SENDINT;        /* a symbol denoting this
procedure */
         theerr.ecode = BADPTR; /* const in .x file */
         }
    return((void *)NULL);      /* return nothing - this is a batched
function */
}
int *getintsum_1(void *dum)
{
    static int ns;            /* static result value */
    xdr_free(xdr_int, &ns);   /* free previous results */
    ns = (-1);                /* assume failure */
    if ( theerr.procno == 0L ) { /* ok */
         ns = thesum; /* set the return code to the current sum */
         thesum = 0;          /* reinitialize the sum */
         return(&ns);         /* return the sum */
         }
    return(&ns);    /* error case - return ns, whose value is -1 */
}
nrerror *geterror_1(void *dum)
{
    static nrerror locerr;    /* static error value */
    xdr_free(xdr_nrerror, &locerr);   /* free previous results */
    locerr = theerr; /* set the return code to the current error */
    theerr.procno = 0L;       /* reinitialize to NO ERROR */
    theerr.ecode = 0;         /* reinitialize error code to zero */
    return(&locerr);          /* return the error code */
}
```

In this implementation, an error that occurs during execution of the sendint_1() function is recorded in the global theerr. This is appropriate since sendint_1() has no mechanism for sending back an error code. When getintsum_1() is entered, the global error structure is checked. If there were no errors, then the sum (also stored in a global, thesum) is returned and that global is cleared. If there was a prior error, then X1 is returned. This is a clue to the client, which was expecting a non negative sum to be returned, that some prior error occurred. If this happens, then the client should call geterror_1(), which gets the stored error information from the server and clears it as well.

The next section will describe another method that the server can use to tell the client something it might not otherwise have known.

Server Callbacks

Up to this point, the servers that you have considered have been the handmaidens of their clients. They accept requests, process them in various ways, and provide the results. The results may come back immediately, or they may be collected later. The server never initiates communication; it merely provides results or perhaps status on the results. There are situations in which this is not convenient, however. The client may not want to poll for an asynchronous result. The client may not be able to wait because the data is time-critical. Certain server processing errors may require immediate client attention.

All of these situations can be addressed by the method of *server callback*. In server callback, the server initiates communication: it effectively becomes a client while the client acts as the passive recipient, as if it were a server.

Design Considerations

Server callback should be used sparingly. It is much too easy and too tempting to set up multiple threads of control with the client calling and the server calling back in what becomes a very confusing and hard to follow sequence of events. Callbacks should be used only when the server must provide information to the client that cannot be provided any other way, or for situations in which the information is of sufficiently high priority that it cannot wait.

I recommend that you consider server callback for the following situations only:

- Completion notification for asynchronous processing

- Error notification with no direct error pathway

- Any high priority event in the server's processing

In the collector processing, which you saw in the "Server Design Considerations" section of Chapter 11, the client had to poll to see if the processing was done. This polling can be quite wasteful, particularly if the server processing will take a long time. As you have already seen, there are cases in which an error occurs in the server, but it has no way of returning that error. Such errors may be collected (as you saw previously), but if they are sufficiently important, then a server callback is justified.

Finally, the server itself is an application program and is subject to all sorts of unexpected events, even if it is idle. If the server has been running for a long enough time, it may receive the UNIX signal SIGXCPU (CPU usage quota exceeded). If the server is the single-point interface to a device or resource, and the state of that device or resource unexpectedly changes (the array processor died, the database is backing itself up and won't be available for an hour, the colliding metal plates stopped colliding, and so forth), then future client operations may be compromised or impossible. In such situations, the server probably wants to let its client know that such an event has occurred rather than just brutally and unexpectedly exiting or crashing. This is particularly true for client applications that are interacting with the user. This is an ideal use for a server callback.

The Client Becomes a Server

The client must do four things to be available for callbacks: it must create a service, it must obtain a portmapper mapping for that service, it must associate a dispatch function with that mapping, and it must tell the real server how it may be contacted. Normally, the first three parts of this operation are performed in the code generated by RPCGEN for the server. Since you are doing them in the client, they must be done manually. Fortunately, these three steps can be encapsulated in a single function (see Listing 12.18).

Listing 12.18 Creating a Callback

```
struct cbinfo {          /* callback info */
     u_long progno;      /* program number */
     u_long versno;      /* version number */
     u_long loproc;      /* minimum procedure number used */
     u_long hiproc;      /* maximum procedure number used */
     } ;                 /* this goes in the .x file */
const CBPROC = 1;        /* so does this */
cbinfo *makecallback(void)
{
     static cbinfo cbi = { 0L, 0L, 0L, 0L } ;    /* initialize
callback info */
     SVCXPRT *xprt;      /* Service Transport pointer */
     u_long      tra = 0x40000000;      /* beginning of transient
program numbers */
     u_long    proto = IPPROTO_TCP;  /* use TCP protocol */
     u_short    port; /* the callback's port */
     bool_t resu = FALSE;    /* assume failure */
     int i = 0;
```

(continues)

```
Listing 12.18   Continued
        xprt = svctcp_create(RPC_ANYSOCK, 0, 0);    /* create TCP service
handle, 1 */
        if ( xprt == (SVCXPRT *)NULL ) return(&cbi); /* if it failed,
return zeroed cbinfo */
        port = xprt->xp_port;           /* get the port number of the
transport, 2 */
        while ( ( resu = pmap_set(tra, 1L, proto, port) )
             == FALSE && ( i++ < 128 ) )      /* try to give to
portmapper, 3 */
             tra++;              /* increment program number on failure */
        if ( resu == FALSE ) {          /* if all 128 tries failed */
             svc_destroy(xprt);         /* destroy transport, 4 */
             return(&cbi);              /* return zeroed cbinfo */
             }
        if ( svc_register(xprt, tra, 1L, dsp, proto)  /* got portmapper
mapping, try to register */
             == FALSE ) {               /* if it failed, 5 */
             (void)pmap_unset(tra, 1L); /* remove mapping, 6 */
             svc_destroy(xprt);         /* destroy transport */
             return(&cbi);              /* return zeroed cbinfo */
             }
     cbi.progno = tra; /* success! set program number ... */
     cbi.versno = 1L;  /* version number ... */
     cbi.loproc = 0L;  /* minimum procedure number = NULLPROC ...*/
     cbi.hiproc = (u_long)CBPROC; /* and maximum procedure number  */
     return(&cbi);     /* return successful callback info */
     }
```

Consider what this function does. First, I have defined a data type, struct cbinfo, that contains all the relevant information about the callback that is being created. The progno and versno members will be the program number and version number, respectively, of the callback interface; loproc will be the number of the lowest acceptable callback procedure; and hiproc the highest. Remembering that you are now acting as a server; these are the pieces of information that identify your services. The definition of cbinfo should be in the .x file since the real server will be sent this information.

In statement 1, I create a service transport using TCP. The first argument specifies that I want a socket to be created for me, while the next two say that I want the default send and receive buffer sizes. If this fails, then the function returns the zeroed version of the static cbinfo structure. In statement 2, I extract the port number from the SVCXPRT created. I have now accomplished the first of the three stages of server creation.

Statement 3 is a loop that attempts to find an unused `portmapper` mapping. It begins at the value `0x40000000`, which is the start of the so-called transient mapping range. By convention, callback services are registered there. The function `pmap_set()` actually does the work of trying to create a mapping. Its second argument is the version (1 here), while the third and fourth are the protocol (TCP) and the port number.

Since it is inconceivable that 128 transient port numbers are actually in use (unless someone was very careless), if the bottom of the loop still has `resu` equal to `FALSE`, then I destroy the service (freeing network and process resources) in statement 4 and return. On success, I have completed step two of service creation. I now have a valid transport handle (`SVCXPRT`) and a valid mapping. Statement 5 completes the process. It registers the function `dsp` as the dispatch function for program number `tra`, version 1, which uses protocol `proto = TCP`. If this step fails, I release the mapping in statement 6, destroy the transport, and return. `pmap_unset()` is a function that takes the program number and version number of a mapping and removes that mapping from the `portmapper`.

On success, the `cbinfo` structure is filled in with the service information, which is returned to the caller. The `cbinfo` structure pointer is the ideal type of information that a client may pass a server in an `OPEN` interface call. This tells the server how to call back to the client by giving it all the appropriate information. You will see below how the server does this. Figure 12.2 illustrates the client callback initialization process.

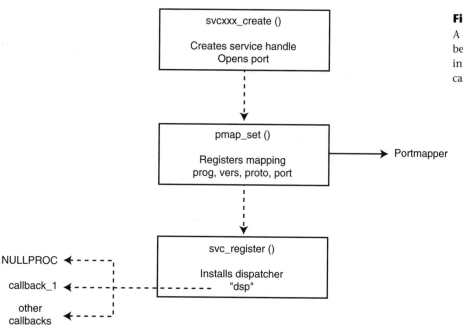

Fig. 12.2
A client must become a server in order to receive callbacks.

> **Caution**
>
> If you obtain a `portmapper` mapping using `pmap_set()`, you should always arrange to delete it later with `pmap_unset()`. Mappings are generally not deleted automatically when a client application exits and are also not garbage collected by the `portmapper`. If you fail to unset your mapping explicitly, it cannot be reused. You can verify that mappings have been unset using `rpcinfo`.

The dispatch function is the function that is called whenever an incoming service request arrives. It should be declared as the following:

```
void dsp(struct svc_req *rq, SVCXPRT *xprt);
```

It is called a dispatch function because it is just a switch statement that calls the appropriate function based on the request number. Note that in the previous `makecallback()` function, I declared that the function `dsp` supports procedures 0 (`NULLPROC`) and also 1 (`CBPROC`), which is presumably my real callback function. To understand how the dispatch function works, suppose that the callback function itself is called `callback_1()`, that it expects a `u_long`, and that it will return a `bool`. The callback itself looks like Listing 12.19.

Listing 12.19 Template for a Callback Function

```
bool_t *callback_1(u_long *ulptr)
{
    static bool_t bres;            /* static result value */
    xdr_free(xdr_bool, &bres);     /* free previous result */
    /* process ulptr here */
    return(&bres);       /* return a pointer to the result */
}
```

This function follows the semantics of a server function exactly. It declares its return to be static, passes it through `xdr_free()` on each entry, and returns the address of its result. It looks like a server function because it is a server function—the client callback function is entered when the client is acting as a server and the server as a client.

The dispatch function will have the form in Listing 12.20.

Listing 12.20   A Callback Dispatch Function

```
void dsp(svc_req *rq, SVCXPRT *xprt)
{
     static u_long uarg;      /* static result value */
     bool_t *bres;            /* return code from callback_1() */
     switch ( rq->rq_proc ) {      /* decide what to do based on
procedure number */
        case NULLPROC:            /* if its the NULLPROC then ... */
           (void)svc_sendreply(xprt, xdr_void, NULL);   /* send a
reply without data */
           break;
        case CBPROC:              /* if its an actual callback then ...*/
           if ( svc_getargs(xprt, xdr_u_long, &uarg) ==     /* get
callback arguments */
              FALSE ) {         /* argument get failed, 1 */
              svcerr_decode(xprt); /* decode the error */
              return;          /* and give up */
              }
           bres = callback_1(&uarg, xprt);   /* argument get succeeded:
call the callback function, 2 */
           if ( bres != (bool_t *)NULL ) {  /* result was OK */
             if ( svc_sendreply(xprt, xdr_bool, bres) ==    /* try to
send a reply */
               FALSE )                 /* if it failed, 3 */
                svcerr_systemerr(xprt); /* declare a system error */
              }
           (void)svc_freeargs(xprt, xdr_u_long, &uarg);      /* free
memory allocated during argument processing */
           return;
        default:        /* invalid procedure number */
           svcerr_noproc(xprt);   /* a "no procedure" error */
           return;
        }
     }
```

Without becoming enmeshed in unimportant detail, examine what the dispatch function does, concentrating on the case when the request procedure is CBPROC, your callback. The first thing it does, at statement 1, is to try to decode the argument into a local u_long, the argument type of the call-back_1() function. If this fails, it calls an appropriate error function and returns.

At statement 2, the dispatch function calls the callback with the address of its argument. If the callback function returns a NULL pointer, then the next clause is bypassed. Otherwise, its return pointer is passed into a function that tries to send a reply at statement 3. If that fails, another error handling function is called. Any storage allocated for the argument is then freed. Note that you didn't really need to make uarg static since it is set and freed in the body of the dispatch function.

II

Introduction to RPC

The dispatch function also has two other switch branches. The NULLPROC branch just sends an internal reply that tells the client (the real server in this case) that it is OK. The default case of the switch calls yet another error handling function to indicate that a procedure number was received that is not handled. This dispatch template may be easily extended to handle multiple callback functions. Simply define their procedure numbers as consts in the .x file, and add a case statement that uses the appropriate XDR functions for decoding the arguments and encoding the results. In fact, if you look at any _svc.c file generated by RPCGEN, you will see a dispatch function that looks very similar to the previous.

At this point, the client has registered itself as a server with the portmapper. It has declared that if any requests arrive, they should be routed through the dispatch function dsp, which will arrange to call the appropriate callback. The client still has to arrange to receive these requests somehow. In short, it must run some version of the server top level in order to get requests. Naturally, it does not wish to block perpetually while doing so. The function in Listing 12.21 does the job nicely.

Listing 12.21 Nonblocking Replacement for the Server Top Level

```
void getrequests(void)
{
     static int dts = 0;      /* maximum number of file descriptors
permitted */
     fd_set readfds;   /* bit array of descriptors able to be read */
     if ( dts == 0 ) dts = getdtablesize();     /* set dts if not
already set */
     readfds = svc_fdset;      /* set readable descriptors to those
owned by our SVCXPRT */
     if ( select(dts, &readfds, NULL, NULL, NULL) > 0 )   /* if there
are RPC requests then ... */
          svc_getreqset(&readfds);  /* process them */
}
```

If you look back at the "Server Customization" section of Chapter 11, "Techniques for Developing RPC Clients and Servers," you will see a slightly more elaborate version of this function. What getrequests() does is determine if there are any outstanding network packets on any of the file descriptors associated with your callback service. If it finds any, then it calls the function svc_getreqset(), which will ultimately call your own dsp. Figure 12.3 shows the calling sequence when a callback arrives.

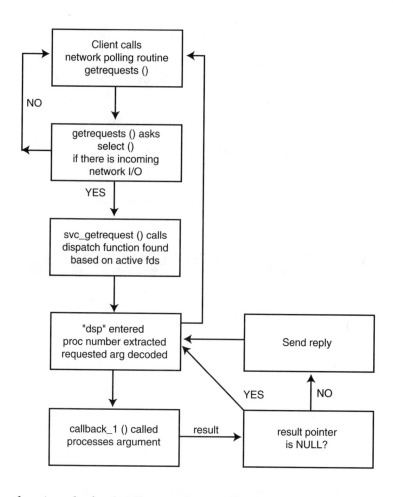

Fig. 12.3
A client receives a callback.

Therefore, in order for the client to obtain callbacks, it must periodically call getrequests() and expect to be blocked for the duration of the callback's execution. "Isn't this just another form of polling?" you might well ask. The answer, of course, is yes. However, this form of polling is much less expensive than collection polling.

In collection polling, the client is actually sending a request over the network to the server and then processing the server's reply, so that a network round-trip takes place for each poll operation. In getrequests(), you are asking the operating system, via the select() system call, if any I/O is possible on the service file descriptors. No data is sent and the overhead is minimal. The execution time of the select() will be much faster than the corresponding network round-trip time of the explicit poll interface call.

Tip
Make your callback functions fast. Your client is blocked while they are executing.

To summarize, a client that wants to receive callbacks should perform the following operations:

- On *initialization,* create a transient service using a function such as `makecallback()` and then send that information to the server.

- Periodically, call `getrequests()` in the top level client application.

- On *termination,* call `pmap_unset()` to remove any `portmapper` mappings it has created.

The structure of such a client's main program will look something like Listing 12.22.

Listing 12.22   Client Top Level Using Callbacks

```
CLIENT *me;          /* CLIENT pointer */
cbinfo *cbptr;       /* callback information */
int    id, *idp, done = 0;
me = clnt_create("serverhost", MYPROG, MYVERS, "tcp");   /* open main
client connection */
cbptr = makecallback();  /* make client a transient server */
idp = serveropen_1(cbptr, cli);      /* tell real server our
callback info */
id = (*idp);         /* save the open identifier for future use */
/* other init goes here */
while ( done == 0 ) {   /* while there is work ... */
    /* clients main work goes here */
    getrequests();      /* get & process callback requests */
    }
if ( cbptr && cbptr->progno )     /* if we had a callback mapping,
clean it up*/
    (void)pmap_unset(cbptr->progno, cbptr->versno);
/* other exit processing goes here */The Server Becomes a Client
```

When the server wants to become a client, its job is easy. All the information it needs is contained in the `cbinfo` structure described above. When it needs to make a callback, it simply makes a `clnt_call()` using that information. To see how this is done in detail, implement the `serveropen_1()` function that I mentioned in the previous client section. This function takes a `cbinfo` pointer and returns an `id`. This function could be implemented as in Listing 12.23.

Listing 12.23   Server Open Procedure That Records Callback

Information

```
static char chost[128];    /* client's hostname */
static cbinfo thecb = { 0L, 0L, 0L, 0L };       /* client callback
information */
static CLIENT *cli = (CLIENT *)NULL; /* client pointer for callbacks */
id *serveropen_1(cbinfo *cbptr, SVCXPRT *xprt)
{
    static id theid;       /* static result value */
    xdr_free(xdr_id, &theid);   /* free previous results */
    theid = (id)0;      /* assume failure - initialize the id to an
invalid value */
    if ( cbptr == (cbinfo *)NULL ) return(&theid);    /* invalid
callback info - return the invalid id */
    thecb = (*cbptr);      /* save the callback info */
    if ( thecb.progno != 0L ) {      /* if the client is giving us
actual callback information then ... */
        addrtoname(svc_getcaller(xprt));   /* convert the client's
network address to a hostname */
        cli = clnt_create(chost, thecb.progno,
                    thecb.versno, "tcp");        /* open a callback
connection to the client */
        if ( cli == (CLIENT *)NULL ) return(&theid); /* open failed
return invalid id */
    }
    /* id creation code goes here */
    return(&theid);   /* return the valid id */
}
```

This function does not send a callback, but it does set up the server so that it can later send a callback. It also uses a number of the techniques that you have seen already. If the `cbinfo` pointer is not `NULL`, then the information in that pointer is copied into a global variable. This is necessary since you will need that information later. `svc_getcaller()` is then used to extract the client's network address, which is passed into your `addrtoname` function. Assume in this case that the `addrtoname` function puts the client's hostname in the global `chost`.

The server now becomes a client by calling `clnt_create()`, using the client's hostname, and the program and version number passed in via the `cbptr`. The TCP protocol is assumed; you could have also made the protocol a field in the `cbinfo struct`. `cli` is now a valid client handle that can be used at any later point to make a callback to the real client. Of course, you did not actually need to create a client handle here—this could have been deferred until the point at which the server wanted to make the callback.

The server's invocation of the callback will take the form shown in Listing 12.24.

Listing 12.24   The Server Makes a Client Callback

```
bool_t *callback_1(u_long *uval)
{
     static bool_t bres = FALSE;          /* callback result - assume
failure */
     static struct timeval t = { 5, 0 } ; /* a five second timeout */
     if ( cli != (CLIENT *)NULL &&        /* if the client pointer is
valid, and ... */
         CBPROC >= thecb.loprog &&         /* the callback procedure
number is ... */
         CBPROC <= thecb.hiprog )          /* within the valid range,
then ... */
             clnt_call(cli, CBPROC, xdr_u_long, uval,
                 xdr_bool, &bres, t);  /* make the callback */
         return(&bres);                    /* return the result */
}
```

Notice that I have used the low and high procedure numbers passed in during the serveropen_1() to verify that my callback procedure number CBPROC is actually a supported callback. I could have just let the dispatch loop in the real client handle this, but by checking it here, I have avoided an unnecessary network access in the event that it is not supported. I could have also made this check during the serveropen_1() procedure itself. Of course, I should also check the return code of clnt_call() and have better error reporting. The five second timeout is completely arbitrary.

Server Startup and the *inetd*

Up to this point, I have not said anything about how a server application is actually started. Client applications are typically started by the user, but how are servers started? There are three answers to this question. Simple servers, like clients, may be started by the user and are typically placed in the background since they will often run forever. Under UNIX, you place a process, such as the myserver process, in the background as follows:

```
myserver &
```

The user who starts it assumes responsibility for running it, shutting it down, and so forth. Servers that perform privileged operations, or that need to be started shortly after the operating system is booted, are often started from the local system initialization file, which is named something like /etc/rc.local on most UNIX machines. The Network File System server processes, nfsd and biod, are excellent examples of this.

In both of these cases, the server is started under fixed circumstances and is probably eternal. There is a third method that allows you to arrange that the server will be started only when requests for that server are issued. If your server will be running on a heavily loaded machine or processing requests infrequently, it is worthwhile to consider this approach as it conserves system resources.

This approach makes use of a server of servers known as the inetd. The inetd uses two sets of files to deal with servers: a configuration file, usually known as /etc/inetd.conf, and a subsidiary file that contains only RPC information, usually known as /etc/rpc. These two files are privileged, so you will need to find a system administrator or root user to perform modifications to these files.

If you want your server to be started by the inetd, you must create the server top level using the RPCGEN flag -I. This causes RPCGEN to arrange that the server top level inherits its startup network socket from the inetd. Another RPCGEN option that you might want to use in conjunction with -I is -K. The default behavior of servers started by inetd is to exit after two minutes of inactivity. If you give a -K argument to RPCGEN followed by a number, that number becomes the length of the inactivity timer in seconds.

Once you have created an inetd-compatible server, you must then modify the /etc/rpc file to statically declare its portmapper mapping. This file contains a series of one line entries, each of which looks like the following:

```
servicename          programnumber     { alias ... }
```

The first field is the official name of your server's service. This name should be the same as the name of the server executable; so that for the file manager server, it would be fmgr. The second field is the program number that this service will use—in decimal (groan). After the second field, one or more optional fields may be given. These act as aliases for your official service name so that the file manager might declare that it can also be known as filemanager.

Once you have made the change to the /etc/rpc file, you will suddenly notice that the output from rpcinfo will include the official name of your server (when your server is running and registered). This is because rpcinfo scans this file to get the name information.

The final change that you must make is to add a line to /etc/inetd.conf telling the inetd how and when to start your server. Note that many sites have a global inetd.conf for the system services and a local inetd.conf (perhaps called /etc/inetd.conf.local) for local services. You will need to discover which actual file needs to be modified, or have it done for you. Each entry in inetd.conf is again a single line. For RPC servers, this line will have six or seven fields.

The first field consists of the official service name, a slash (/), and the set of versions supported. If there is only a single version, just give that. If there is a range of versions, then give them in the form LOVERS-HIVERS. The second field is the word stream for TCP servers and dgram for UDP servers. If your server supports both, then you can either split it into separate executables and create inetd entries for both, or you can list it under its primary protocol. The third field will be one of the two strings, rpc/tcp or rpc/udp. The same rule applies to this field.

The fourth field tells inetd what to do if a service request comes in while a server is running. If this field says wait, then inetd will wait until the existing server terminates before it will start another. If the field says nowait, then inetd will blithely fire up another server to serve the new request. wait is your power choice.

At the fifth field, things get a little tricky. On some UNIX platforms, the fifth field will be the name of a user, often root. When the server is started, inetd will start it as if that user had started the server in the background, i.e., it will make the server process owned by that user. On other UNIX platforms, this field is absent, and all servers started by inetd are owned by the user that owns inetd itself—usually root. If your inetd.conf entries have seven fields, then you are in the former category; if they have six, you are in the latter. For the purposes of this discussion, assume that the fifth field is present. If so, put the name of a valid user there.

The sixth field must be the full path name of the server executable. The seventh field is the list of command line arguments to be passed into the server when it starts up. Traditionally, this will start with the last component of the executable's path name and will be followed by the real arguments. You could use these arguments to enable logging, for example.

Once the modifications have been made, then the inetd will need to be sent a signal that causes it to reread its configuration file. The UNIX magic of kill -HUP pid, where pid is the UNIX process identifier of the inetd, will usually do it (this must be done by a privileged user, of course).

The following are my entries for the file manager in /etc/rpc and
/etc/inetd.conf, respectively:

```
fmgr   603988992  filemanager
fmgr/1-2        stream rpc/tcp wait mark /usr/mark/fmgr fmgr
```

From Here...

In this chapter, you've been thoroughly exposed to many of the finer points
of client/server programming under UNIX. You've learned how to locate
specific servers and to communicate with more than one server using client
broadcast. You now understand how to improve client/server performance
using batching. And the powerful callback technique has become part of your
repertoire. To learn more, refer to these chapters:

- Chapter 3, "Communications Protocols," teaches you about TCP, UDP,
  and other lower-level network protocols.

- Chapter 16, "Understanding the OSF DCE Services," is the DCE counterpart to the information contained in this chapter.

- Chapter 18, "Client/Server Development with OLE," shows you the OLE
  way to write client and server applications.

II

Introduction to RPC

Part III

Introduction to DCE

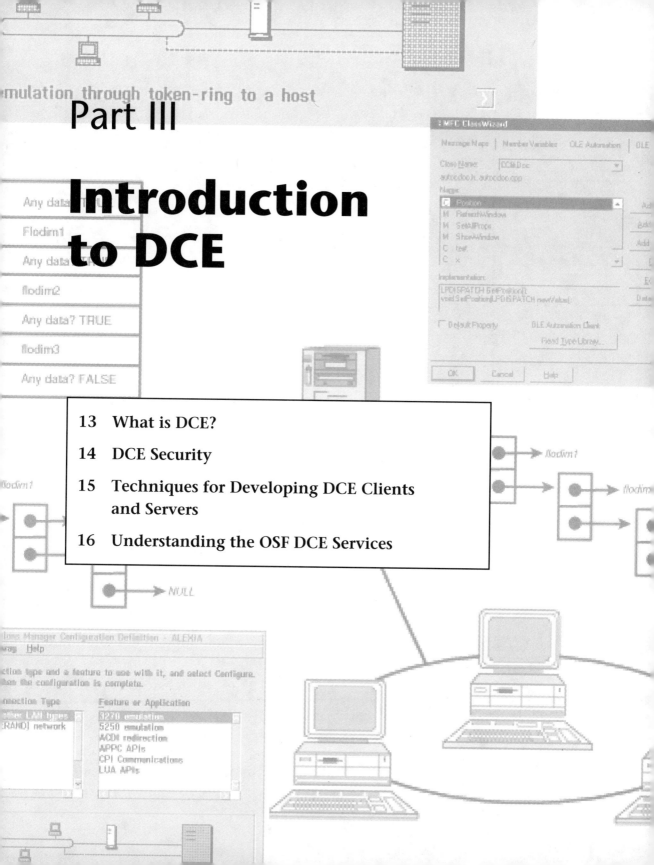

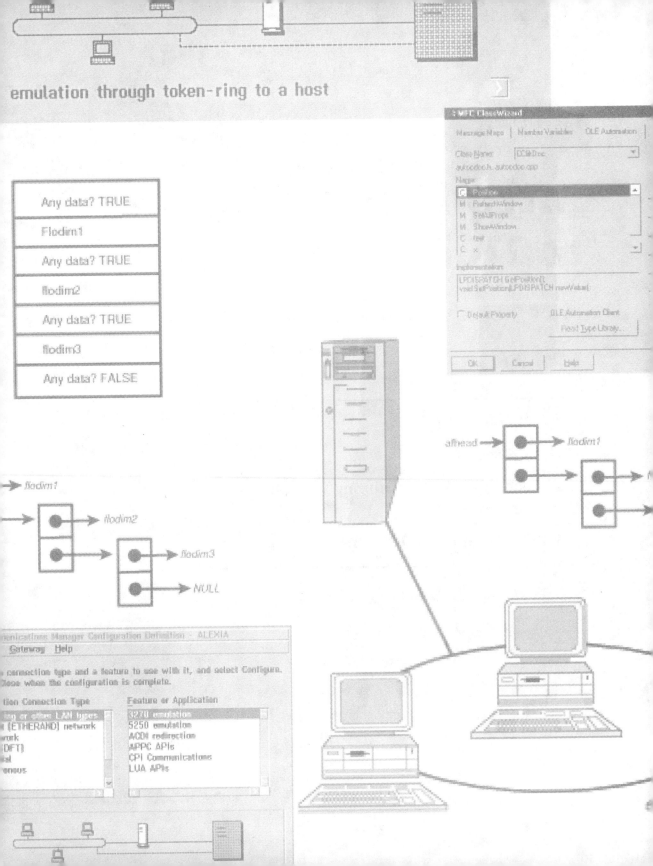

Chapter 13

What is DCE?

DCE is the commonly used acronym for the Open Software Foundation's (OSF) *Distributed Computing Environment*. It provides a set of operating system independent interfaces and facilities that ease the process of developing and maintaining distributed applications, and for administering a distributed environment. DCE is a set of software services layered above the operating system which provides a uniform set of interfaces for developers of distributed applications.

While other distributed computing environments exist, most of the major system vendors have announced support for OSF's DCE. The X/Open Company, Ltd. has adopted the Application Environment Specification (AES) portions of DCE as part of their Common Application Environment (CAE) specification. X/Open is a vendor and end user consortium whose goal is to identify and specify system independent services, interfaces, and system profiles for portable applications.

This chapter discusses the general architecture and components of DCE. The majority of the chapter will survey the individual components of DCE, with attention to their features and how the tight integration of the components allows the separate components to support one another. Some of the specific topics to be covered are the following:

- Threads in DCE

- RPC (remote procedure calls) in DCE

- The DCE security service

DCE Architecture and Components

OSF's DCE provides a set of common *Application Programming Interfaces* (*APIs*) and services for client/server applications. It is best viewed as a software layer between the operating system and the application. The primary benefit of DCE is that application developers have a uniform, publicly defined set of distributed programming APIs and distributed system services available for a variety of operating systems and hardware platforms.

> **Note**
>
> In general, DCE is supported by most flavors of UNIX and several non-UNIX platforms (Cray Unicos and OS/2, to name two). A significant number of other non-UNIX platforms support DCE for client usage only, meaning that you will need a server somewhere on your network that can provide the server applications.

DCE itself is a modular, layered, integrated framework of technology components, with place holders for future technologies. The DCE technologies are as follows:

- Threads Interfaces

- RPC Interfaces and Service

- Directory Service

- Distributed Time Service

- Distributed Security Service

- Distributed File Service

- Diskless Support Service

These DCE components are fully integrated within DCE. Full integration means that they all make use of the components layered below them, and provide services to the components above them. The Threads, RPC, CDS, Security, and DTS components are the minimum required components of a DCE installation. This required component set is often referred to as a "secure core." The other components are optional or administrative in nature.

DCE Threads

Threading allows for a process to be subdivided into multiple single-sequence flows of control within that single process.

DCE Threads is a user level threads library that provides APIs for thread creation, synchronization, scheduling, exception handling, and destruction. Thread creation is explicitly done via the `pthread_create()` routine, and results in the creation of a new thread of control.

> **Note**
>
> DCE Threads complies with the Posix Threads draft standard (draft 4).

What are Threads?

Threads are individual flows of control within a single program. Traditionally in multitasking, multi-user operating system environments, each program runs as a process in its own address space. Process creation is usually via the `fork()` system call, and tends to be an expensive operation in most implementations.

Threads solve this problem by providing multiple control flows within a single process address space. Threads within the operating system can also result in more efficient utilization of multiple processors. Thus, there are two categories of threads:

- User-level threads that execute within a single address space and let applications programmers avoid expensive `fork()` operations

- Kernel-level threads that can make more efficient use of multiprocessing system resources

DCE Threads is a user-level threads library that makes use of kernel level threads when available. Since processes as a whole tend to become blocked when they invoke a blocking system level operation, DCE also provides a set of wrapper or jacket routines for the most commonly used blocking system routines.

Although threads provide strong benefits to the applications programmer, they have their disadvantages as well. Chief among these are the following:

- Added complexity for the programmer

- Shared state between threads

- Need for additional synchronization to maintain shared state

III

Introduction to DCE

Let's examine each of these in turn. First, since there are now multiple flows of control within a single process address space, the applications programmer is faced with a new concept: deadlock. Earlier, this was of concern only to the systems programmers. The programmer now also has to contend with a whole new complex set of APIs.

Secondly, since all the threads share a single address space, they can all access the global state variables within the program, leading to inconsistent values for these variables. This potential for race conditions requires that the programmer use mutual exclusion and condition variables to serialize access to these state variables.

Thirdly, the transformation of a single-threaded program into an multi-threaded application results in a combinatorial explosion in the number of possible application states. The programmer must add synchronization between the different flows of control to make sure that illegal states are never entered. To illustrate, consider a single-threaded program that has six possible states. When it is separated into two threads each having three states, there are altogether nine possible states that the application can be in. The programmer must take care to ensure that only the six original states can be entered under all conditions of inputs.

DCE Thread Synchronization

DCE Threads provides three mechanisms for synchronizing multiple threads. They are as follows:

- Mutual exclusion objects (mutexes)

- Condition variables

- The `pthread_join()` routine

Mutual exclusion objects are used to control or serialize access to shared resources such as variables. The DCE Threads component includes APIs, which you can use to create, initialize, lock, unlock, and destroy mutexes. A mutex is created and initialized, in association with a shared resource. When a thread needs to access the resource, it tries to lock the mutex. If the lock succeeds, the thread has exclusive access to the shared resource. Once the thread is finished with the resource, it can unlock the mutex. When a thread tries to lock an already locked mutex, the thread is blocked until the lock is released. As long as all threads follow this protocol of trying to lock a mutex before accessing the associated shared resource, accesses to the shared resource are safely serialized.

Note that the mutex approach does not allow any communications between the different threads, it only serializes access to shared resources. When multiple threads need to communicate or synchronize with one another, a condition variable is used in conjunction with a mutex.

This mechanism works in the following manner: A thread waits for another thread to reach some point in its processing by waiting on a condition variable. When the second thread reaches that point in its processing, it signals the condition variable. This results in the first thread being woken up. This communication is anonymous; thread A does not know or care whether it is thread B, or thread C, or both, that are waiting on the condition variable. Similarly, the awakened thread does not know that it was thread A that woke it up from its wait on the condition variable.

DCE Threads provides APIs for the creation, initialization, waiting, signaling, and destruction of condition variables. They also allow explicit synchronization between two specific threads by means of the `pthread_join()` routine. However, synchronization can occur only after the thread being joined has completed execution. For example, a thread A would block on a call to `pthread_join()` with an argument of thread B. When thread B completes execution, thread A will return from the `pthread_join()` routine, and continue execution.

DCE Thread Scheduling

DCE Threads allows the applications programmer some control over the scheduling of threads in the application program. DCE Threads provides APIs for two intertwined scheduling mechanisms:

- Scheduling priorities
- Scheduling policies

Every thread has a priority associated with it, and threads with higher priority take precedence over threads with lower priority. However, the exact manner in which threads are scheduled depends on the scheduling policy in effect. There are three scheduling policies allowed in DCE Threads:

- FIFO—where the highest priority threads are run in a first-in, first-out order until they block or complete. When all the highest priority threads are blocked or have completed execution, the threads of the next lower priority are run. This process is repeated for all scheduling priority levels.

III

Introduction to DCE

■ Round robin— where the highest priority threads are time-sliced until they all block or have completed execution. Then the threads in the next lower priority level are run in the same manner.

■ Time-slicing—which is the default scheduling policy for DCE Threads, runs every thread by time-slicing. Higher priority threads get a larger time-slice than lower priority threads. Unlike FIFO and round robin scheduling, however, there is never any starvation, i.e., every thread is guaranteed to run, and a low priority thread cannot be locked out by higher priority threads.

DCE Thread Exceptions

DCE Threads provides two different fault reporting and handling mechanisms. One is an asynchronous, UNIX-style status and return code approach (using an errno global variable and the given function's return value). The other is a synchronous exception mechanism. Status codes require the programmer to insert code after every call to check the return value of the procedure. Exceptions allow the programmer to insert localized code for certain classes of failures at a single point within the program. The exception handling code is invoked only when an exception occurs. The exception mechanism supplies the programmer with the following verbs:

■ TRY

■ CATCH

■ CATCH_ALL

■ FINALLY

■ ENDTRY

■ RAISE

■ RERAISE

These verbs can be used in one of two styles. When an exception is raised, the first handler associated with the exception is invoked. This can be the code in either the CATCH block or the FINALLY block. If no exception handler exists at a particular level within the program, the exception is passed up to the next higher level in the program.

In the first form of exception handling, code to recover from specific exceptions is installed in the CATCH blocks. In the second style, the code in the FINALLY block is always executed, regardless of whether or not an exception was raised.

The RAISE verb allows for the delivery of a specific exception. The RERAISE verb is used to propagate exceptions up through the various levels in the program. This is usually done when exception handling at a particular level is not complete, as is the case with FINALLY blocks. Since any one of a number of exceptions may or may not have occurred, exceptions are RERAISE'd as the final step in a FINALLY block.

DCE Threads and DCE's Component Integration

The use of threads in DCE is an example of the tight integration of DCE's components. Although many newer operating systems support threading, not all operating systems in use today do. While user-level threads may not make as efficient use of multi-processor environments, many components of DCE require threading. These components are as follows:

- RPC
- Security Service
- Directory Service
- Distributed Time Service

The DCE Threads library is therefore present to support use of DCE in environments that do not natively support threading.

DCE RPC

RPC stands for *remote procedure call*. RPCs are based on the function call mechanism available in procedural languages. For example, procedure A calls another procedure B, transferring control to B until B returns. In the local procedure call case, both A and B are in the same process address space. In the RPC case, A and B are in separate process address spaces, usually on different machines.

This characteristic of RPCs requires that the arguments pass and values return between the two procedures differently from the local case. In the local case, arguments and return values are passed on the process stack. In the remote case, since the two procedures are in different processes and possibly on different machines, the arguments and return values must be marshaled into network packets on the sender side, and unmarshaled on the receiver side. The term *marshaling* is used to refer to the following two actions:

- The conversion of data from one host format to another (for instance, EBCDIC to ASCII, or 32-bit integers to 16-bit integers)

- The deflation and inflation of program abstract data types into a stream of bits that can be transmitted and received over a network

This complexity (namely, the marshaling and unmarshaling of application data, and the details of the network transmission) is hidden from the applications programmer. An RPC interface compiler generates the code on the basis of an interface specification provided by the programmer. Most RPC implementations also access two other services: a binding service and a security service. The binding service allows for the runtime association of server names with server locations, so that locations do not need to be hard-coded into the application. Since networks are notoriously insecure, the transmitted data may need to be encrypted and the sender must be authenticated. Most RPC implementations usually provide some default behavior with respect to binding and security transparent to the programmer.

RPCs serve to help disguise remote actions as local procedure calls. In spite of everything that RPC systems do, there are three glaring differences between local and remote procedure calls that cannot be hidden from the programmer:

- A remote procedure call can take over an order of magnitude longer to execute than local procedure calls, due to network latencies.

- Disguising the remoteness doesn't make the call a local procedure call; it just resembles one. RPCs expose programmers to such non-local problems as remote site failures. The programmer must take explicit actions to handle the new failure modes introduced by RPCs.

- The programmer has to be aware of execution semantics. When a local procedure call is made, the programmer is sure that the called procedure will be invoked exactly once. Many RPC implementations do not provide this "exactly-once" guarantee. They tend to provide "at-most-once" or "at-least-once" semantics, since the execution semantics are often very closely tied to the network transport protocol used.

DCE RPC is an RPC implementation that is used by all the DCE technology components above it. It actually consists of a number of distinct programming facilities and services:

- DCE RPC Interface Definition Language (IDL) Compiler

- DCE RPC runtime libraries

- DCE RPC endpoint mapper

- Universally Unique Identifier (UUID) facility

- Name Service Independent (NSI) interfaces to the Directory Service

- Interfaces to the Security Service

The mechanics of a DCE RPC call at runtime are usually as follows. The server process starts up, and as part of its DCE initialization sequence, performs the following actions:

- It registers its service interface with the RPC runtime.

- It registers its network endpoint address with the local endpoint mapper (called `rpcd` in DCE 1.0, and `dced` in DCE 1.1).

- It registers its service name and interface with the DCE Directory Service.

- The server then waits, listening for client requests.

The client, upon startup, communicates with the DCE Directory Service to locate the host that the server is available on. The client then queries the endpoint mapper on the server host to find the dynamic network endpoint address that the server is registered at. It then begins to communicate directly with the server, making requests and waiting for responses.

> **Note**
>
> While most of the server-side actions listed previously need to be coded by the programmer, the reverse is true on the client side. Most of the client side actions are automatically generated by the IDL compiler from the IDL specification file provided by the programmer.

DCE Directory Service

In the context of computer systems, a directory service names all the objects or entities present in the system in order to provide a global naming scheme within the system. Names serve two purposes in computer systems:

- Names allow the unique identification of system resources.

- Names provide a level of indirection, abstracting objects from their location information.

Names allow multiple computations or processes in UNIX to share references to the same object(s). For instance, two different processes in an UNIX system can both refer to `/usr/bin_file`, and you can assume that both processes are referring to the same file. Naming schemes traditionally fall into two categories:

III

Introduction to DCE

- Flat, or single-level—where there can be only one instance of a named object within the whole system. Flat naming schemes imply that there is only one context for a name.

- Hierarchical—which are more common in computer systems and allow different names to be associated with the same object in different contexts. For example, /tmp/temp_file and /temp_file from the /tmp directory both refer to the same file object (or resource).

  Hierarchical naming schemes also allow the reuse of names in different contexts. For instance, different processes in the UNIX world can simultaneously read from and write to /dev/console. This name maps onto different objects for each of the processes.

This gets us to the second purpose of names: to abstract objects from their location. Users must be able to refer to and access system resources by name, without having to know their location.

The Directory Service component of DCE consists of four subcomponents:

- The DCE Cell Directory Service (CDS)

- The DCE Global Directory Service (GDS)

- The DCE Global Directory Agent (GDA)

- The X/Open Directory Service (XDS)

The CDS stores names and attributes of resources within a single DCE cell. A *cell* is defined as a set of computers which have frequent communication between the members. Members of a cell tend to be, but are not always, geographically close. At least one CDS must be present in every cell. The GDS is a higher-level directory to connect cells, and is compatible with the X.500 worldwide directory service. The GDA passes identifiers it cannot find in the CDS to the GDS. In addition to X.500, the GDA provides for compatibility with the *Domain Name Service* (*DNS*) addressing scheme widely used on the Internet. The fourth component, XDS, allows application programmers to write adhering to a single standard, which is compatible with both X.500 (through GDS) and DNS.

Distributed Time Service

The Distributed Time Service (DTS) supports several other components of DCE which require a consistent time stamp, such as the security module and the *Distributed File System* (*DFS*). The DTS divides all servers on the network into four types:

- Clerks—which are any servers that do not provide time services to another server.

- Local servers—which synchronize with other servers on the same LAN (local area network).

- Global servers—which provide time services to an extended LAN or a WAN (wide area network).

- Couriers—which are specific local servers acting as a links to a global server.

DTS may be set to synchronize all local servers at periodic intervals. To synchronize the DCE LAN or WAN with the rest of the world, Universal Coordinated Time may be acquired from such locations as the National Bureau of Standards or the U.S. Naval Observatory in any of three methods—dial-up lines, short-wave radio, or satellite link. For compatibility, DTS may interoperate with the Internet's *Network Time Service* (*NTS*).

DCE Security Service

Like all of the other distributed system services, the problem of security in a distributed environment is more complex than that in a centralized computing environment. Computer networks are notoriously insecure, and eavesdropping or impersonation can be easy. Yet in a distributed environment, different computers, services, and users all need to interact with one another in a secure manner. This means that any confidential information has to be encrypted before being transmitted across the network. Both the sender and receiver must be able to encrypt and decrypt the information successfully.

Security is fundamentally a means of providing controlled access to system resources. A security service must provide the following features:

- Confidentiality/privacy of user data

- Integrity of system resources

- Availability of system resources

Users must be able to keep their data confidential. They must be able to prevent other users from viewing private data and ensure that any data they provide is used only for the purpose for which it was intended. Integrity of system resources implies that system resources must not be corrupted. While integrity is a requirement of the system as a whole, it just means that the system behavior must not be corrupted by malicious attacks in the security context. Similarly, the availability of system services or resources must not be compromised by malicious attacks.

III

Introduction to DCE

These requirements imply that the security service must be able to answer the following two questions:

- Is user X who they claim to be? (authentication)
- Is user X allowed to perform operation Y on resource Z? (authorization)

Authorization is usually provided via two intertwined mechanisms:

- Access Privileges, associated with each resource user
- Access Control Lists, associated with each resource

The DCE Security Service provides both authentication and authorization. It actually consists of the following three services:

- Authentication Service
- Privilege Service
- Registry Service

All three services are implemented within a single daemon, the DCE Security Server. The DCE Security Service also provides the following four facilities:

- Login Facility
- Access Control List (ACL) Facility
- Key Management Facility
- ID Map Facility

The DCE Authentication Service is based on the Kerberos Version 5 network security protocol. It works as follows:

1. When the user logs in to DCE, the security runtime on the login host sends the username in plain text to the Authentication Server.

2. The Authentication Server encrypts the user ID and a conversation key with its secret key. It then places these together with the conversation key into an envelope encrypted with a key derived from the user's password.

3. The security runtime on the client uses the password entered from the keyboard to decrypt the packet returned by the Authentication Server.

4. The client runtime requests a ticket to the Privilege Service from the Authentication Service, encrypting this request with the conversation key obtained from step 3 (conversation key #1).

5. The Authentication Service returns a *Privilege Ticket Granting Ticket* (*PTGT*) and a new conversation key (conversation key #2), both encrypted together with conversation key #1. The PTGT contains the user id and conversation key #2, encrypted together with the Privilege Service key.

6. The security runtime on the client decrypts the response, and "discovers" conversation key #2.

7. The security runtime on the client sends off the PTGT in a request to the Privilege Service.

8. The Privilege Service decrypts the PTGT using its private key. It then prepares a *Privilege Attribute Certificate* (*PAC*) based on the user information in the Registry Service. The PAC and a new conversation key (conversation key #3) are encrypted into a PTGT using the Authentication Service's key. The PTGT and the conversation key #3 are encrypted using conversation key #2, and returned to the client.

9. The security runtime on the client host decrypts the response using conversation key #2.

   At the end of this sequence of actions, both the security server and the user are authenticated to one another. When the user (client) needs to communicate with an application server, the following steps are gone through.

10. The client sends its PAC to the Authentication Server along with the principal name of the application server. This request is encrypted with conversation key #3.

11. The Authentication Server decrypts the request, re-encrypts the PAC and a new conversation key (conversation key #4) using the application server's key. This is then encrypted along with conversation key #4 using conversation key #3, and returned to the client.

12. The client security runtime decrypts the response. It then encrypts the application request with conversation key #4, and sends it off to the application server.

III

Introduction to DCE

13. The application server security runtime sees from the request header that the message is encrypted, and sends a random number in clear text to the client.

14. The client security runtime encrypts the random number using conversation key #4, and sends it back to the application server with its PAC for the application server.

15. The application server security runtime decrypts the server ticket using its secret key, getting the client's PAC and conversation key #4.

16. The application server security runtime then decrypts the encrypted random number returned by the client. If it matches the number it sent out in clear text, the client is authenticated.

17. The application server security runtime then decrypts the client request using conversation key #4, which is now used as a session key for all communications between the client and the server.

18. The application server then checks the client's PAC, and it's own *Access Control List (ACL)* to see whether the client is authorized to request the operation. If the client is authorized, the request is processed and the results are returned to the client. Otherwise, an authorization failure message is returned to the client.

DCE Distributed File Service

DFS is not actually a component of DCE as much as it is a distributed client/server application built using the "lower" layer components of DCE. DFS is a "super-directory" system that takes the file and directories of more than one file server, and makes the file system appear to be on a single, bigger file system.

The primary goal of DFS is user transparency with scalability and performance. The tradeoff of increased user transparency in a robust distributed file service is significant administration costs. DFS has the following several components:

- Cache Manager
- Local File System (LFS)
- Fileset Server
- Replication Server
- Scout
- Fileset Location Server
- File Exporter
- Token Manager
- Basic OverSeer Server (BOS Server)
- Update Server
- Backup Server

These DFS components may be divided into three groups: the client, the File Server, and the administrative server.

DFS Client

The only component needed for a DFS client machine is the Cache Manager. When a user requests a file, the Cache Manager first looks for the file locally. If the file is not present, the Cache Manager sends a request to its designated File Server to retrieve the file and cache the file on the client machine. Local caching improves user-perceived performance. Local caching also reduces network load, as opposed to having to access the remote file at either the original storage location, or if the file was cached on the local File Server. By reducing network load and therefore reducing dependence on the network, local caching also improves availability of files and overall robustness of the system.

DFS File Server

The File Server components are the File Exporter, the Local File System (LFS), and the Token Manager. The File Exporter responds to RPC calls for local files and retrieves the requested file using either the LFS or the *UNIX File System* (*UFS*), if present. UFS is supported, but does not provide as much functionality as using LFS. LFS features not part of the UNIX File System include integrated support for DCE cells (remember, a cell is a group of associated computers), authorization using DCE Access Control Lists (ACLs) from the Security Service, and the ability to back up and relocate parts of the file system without loss of service or downtime. The Token Manager prevents accidental corruption of files by maintaining synchronization of updates to files, using the Time Service for chronology.

DFS Administrative Server

The Administrative Server components may reside on the same machine as the File Server components. The following are the Administrative Server components of DFS:

- Fileset Server—which gives the administrator the ability to define a fileset. A logical collection rather than a physical grouping, filesets do not reference local file naming practices, but are subgroups using the global Directory Service.

    Accordingly, members of a fileset do not have to reside on the same physical partition, and the entire fileset or any of its members may be moved without loss of association with that fileset. Filesets make administration of the network easier by allowing movement of filesets to other nodes of the network.

- BOS (Basic Overseer) Server—which monitors DFS processes running on a given server.

- Replication Server—which allows automatic updates of fileset copies on another server at specified intervals.

- Update Server—which is used to distribute administrative information across DCE nodes.

- Scout—which collects local file information from File Exporter components in order to monitor file and directory information for all DFS nodes.

- Backup Server—which backs up file server data and maintains records of its activity. Incremental backups are possible.

- Fileset Location Server—which records the location of filesets on file server machines.

- The Fileset Server—which provides another layer between the user and the file, allowing files and filesets to be moved to other machines or nodes with no effect visible to the user.

DCE Diskless Support Service

Some nodes of a network may lack a disk for storage of a local file system. The four functions a network must provide for a diskless node to work in the DCE network are booting, configuration, remote file access, and (optionally) swapping support. DCE allows a diskless system to obtain a copy of the kernel over the network. Configuration information is provided by a Diskless Configuration (DLC) Server. The global naming and logical (as detached from physical) partitioning provided by the Directory Service and the Distributed File Service allow for the diskless system to use files stored on other servers in the LAN or WAN. Swapping, if implemented, is provided for in the same manner as booting and configuration—by designating another machine's disk as the swap server for the diskless system. While the boot and configuration servers are required to reside on the same server, the DFS File server and the swap server may be defined as the same machine as the boot/configuration server, a second node, or a second and third server.

From Here...

This chapter's goal was to give a basic introduction to the structure and components of DCE. Now that you have the overall concepts, the rest of this section of this book can help you make use of these features in a DCE environment. For more information on the topics covered in this chapter, refer to the following:

■ Chapter 14, "DCE Security," provides more explanation of how to configure the Kerberos-based authentication and permission security module of DCE.

■ Chapter 15, "Techniques for Developing DCE Clients and Servers," goes into more detail about the design and implementation of client/server software in a DCE environment.

■ Chapter 16, "Understanding the OSF DCE Services," discusses how DCE works with several varieties of the UNIX operating system.

III

Introduction to DCE

Chapter 14

DCE Security

In virtually any computer system, security is an important issue. Most computer environments provide measures to control access to data and system services. In most cases, users must identify themselves with a password and are given certain sets of access rights to different files, programs, and data areas.

Security is a very important issue in a distributed environment. Users can be in different locations and client programs can operate outside the immediate control of a server. The environment must provide support for identifying users, making sure that they are who they say they are, and granting them appropriate privileges and access rights. This chapter examines the DCE security service and its component parts. Specifically, it describes the following things:

- Authentication and authorization

- The registry database

- Access control

- Network security and Kerberos

- Programming with the DCE security service

Security in a Distributed Environment

Consider for a moment the "normal" security aspects of an operating system. Users log in with a username and password, are given some sort of identifiers that mark them as belonging to certain groups, and are granted access rights to some portion of the file system. The specifics of these security features will vary from system to system, but most multi-user systems implement some security service that is similar.

Now, consider what happens when you move to a distributed computing environment. The security service now has to contend with client programs wanting access from many different computers, both local and remote. Users will attempt to log in from computers that are not under your control. How can you verify their identity? Can you trust that they are really who they say they are? You will want to restrict access from various locations and possibly change the access rights of users depending on their location.

It gets worse. How can you protect your data that is being transferred via the network? What about your passwords and authentication mechanisms? Someone could read them off the network and then use them to access your system. You have to protect them from attack.

As you can see, a distributed environment drops a whole new set of security problems in your lap. When you have to deal with clients and servers that are in different locations, and under different administrative control, the security issues are complex to say the least.

Authentication

Authentication deals with the problem of verifying that an entity, be it a user or a computer, is really who it claims to be. In DCE, this entity is known as a *principal*. In order for a principal to prove its identity, it must provide some sort of secret key that the authentication server can verify. If the principal is a person, the key is the person's password.

As part of the login process, DCE converts the user's password into a secret key and checks it against the key in the registry database. If they match, DCE considers the user to be *authenticated*. The keys are sent over the network in encrypted form.

> **Note**
>
> It is important to remember the differences between *authentication* and *authorization*. An authenticated user has convinced DCE that it is who it claims to be. It may or may not have the necessary authorization to access any data.

Once a principal has authenticated itself with the authentication service, the principal's process is given a very important piece of data known as a *ticket*. Just as a ticket in an amusement park allows you to ride different rides and see different shows, a DCE ticket allows a process to request different services. This ticket is presented to the *Privilege Server,* which gives the process a data structure that defines that process' authorization information. This data structure is known as a *Privilege Authorization Certificate (PAC).*

A ticket allows a process to access specific services under DCE. Different tickets are good for different services. The ticket that is granted to a user as part of the login process is known as the *ticket granting ticket.*

In order to keep tickets from being used to attack a DCE system, tickets are only valid for a specific period of time. After that period, they expire and are not honored by a DCE server. The principal will have to reauthenticate in order to get new tickets.

The Registry

In order for DCE to properly identify and authenticate principals, it has to keep records that describe the users of the system and their organizational structure. This information is critical: it tells DCE what principals are allowed access, which groups they belong to, and what accounts they can use for access. This collection of information is known as the *registry* database.

The registry maintains principal account and membership information. It also maintains policy information about the registry itself. For example, the registry might maintain information about the valid lifespan of an account or a password. It might also maintain information about the acceptable length or format of passwords.

> **Note**
>
> The collection of all the principals, groups, accounts, and organizations that a particular registry database controls is known as a *cell.*

In the registry, principals have IDs and belong to *groups* and *organizations*. A principal's ID is similar to the user ID (UID) under UNIX. It is used to uniquely identify a principal. A *group* is a collection of principals that are logically related. A company department or a product development team

III

Introduction to DCE

might be a good choice for defining a group. Groups are denoted by a group ID, which corresponds to the UNIX group ID (GID). An organization is usually used to define higher-level divisions that might contain several groups. A principal may be a member of several different groups but is usually a member of only one organization. An organization has an ID that uniquely identifies it as well.

Group membership is an important concept in DCE security. Quite often, groups are used to allow, control, and deny access to system and network resources. For that reason, it is important that the groups in a DCE environment be set up in a way that makes sense for security purposes.

> **Note**
>
> Group IDs are used for access control; organization IDs are not. Organization IDs are usually used for maintaining account policy information.

Access Control

DCE provides accounts and groups for identifying principals, and mechanisms for authenticating them. But how does it actually control access to system resources?

DCE uses a concept known as an *Access Control List (ACL)* to grant and restrict access to system resources. An ACL is a list of entries that describe the types of access that principals have to a resource.

ACLs provide a robust mechanism for controlling access, much more so than most other operating systems. Under UNIX, for example, access to files is controlled by three categories: owner permissions, group permissions, and everybody else. DCE ACLs provide much more selectivity and much more control over the levels of access that you can grant or deny. Table 14.1 shows the UNIX access permissions.

Table 14.1 UNIX Access Permission Entities	
Entity	**Meaning**
Owner	The owner of the resource
Group	A group member
Other	Anyone else

Compare these to the entities that can be specified in a DCE ACL. Table 14.2 shows the valid ACL entities.

Table 14.2   DCE ACL Access Permission Entities

Entity	Meaning
user_obj	The owner of an object
user	An object's user from the local cell
foreign_user	An object's user from a foreign cell
group_obj	The owner of a group
group	A group from the local cell
foreign_group	A group from a foreign cell
other_obj	Anyone else from the local cell
foreign_other	Anyone else from a foreign cell
any_other	Anyone that does not fall into one of the previous categories
mask_obj	Permissions to be disabled automatically
unauthenticated	Permissions given to unauthenticated users

Just as ACLs provide more ways to specify *who* can access an object, they also give more ways to say *what* can be done to the object. Table 14.3 lists UNIX's access permissions.

Table 14.3   UNIX's Access Permissions

Permission	Definition
r	Read access
w	Write access
x	Execute access

By contrast, Table 14.4 lists some of the permissions that can be specified in an ACL. ACLs support up to 32 different permissions that can be defined for an object.

III

Introduction to DCE

Table 14.4 Some ACL Access Permissions	
Permission	**Definition**
a	Can modify authentication information
c	Controls an object; can modify ACLs on an object
d	Delete permission for an object
D	Can delete an object from the registry
i	Can add information to a directory
n	Can change the name of a directory
r	Read permission for objects
u	Can modify user information

Network Security and Kerberos

Network security is a major concern. We've briefly discussed the issues surrounding authentication, but there are also problems guaranteeing the integrity and privacy of data. What is to prevent someone from tapping your network and capturing packets as they zip around your Ethernet? If someone manages to capture a login session, it would be pretty easy to replay it into the network and gain access.

The obvious solution to most of these problems is to encrypt the data. This in itself causes problems. How do the client and server share the same key to encrypt and decrypt the data, without sending the key through an insecure channel? These problems are handled by the DCE security service via a mechanism known as *Kerberos*.

Kerberos acts as a trusted third-party arbitrator during authentication. All sides must trust Kerberos for the authentication process to work. Each party deposits a secret password with Kerberos. This password converts a principal's private key into a key that is known to both the principal and Kerberos.

When a client makes a request to Kerberos, Kerberos generates a random session key. It then encrypts the session key with the server's key to make a *ticket*. The ticket and a second copy of the session key are then encrypted with the client's key and sent back to the client. This basically makes a two-part envelope—one part that is readable by the client and one part that is readable by the server. When the client receives the encrypted packet from Kerberos, it uses its own key to decrypt it. Once decrypted, the packet turns into a session key and an encrypted server ticket. At this point, the client trusts the Kerberos server because the packet was encrypted with the client's private key, known only to the client and Kerberos.

At this point, the client sends the session key along with the encrypted ticket to the server. The server uses its private key to decrypt the ticket. The ticket contains the random session key that Kerberos generated. The server compares the two session keys—the unencrypted one and the one that was encrypted—and checks for a match. If they match, the server now trusts the client, because the only way the client could send the encrypted packet was to get it from Kerberos. Now, the client and server have a session key that was randomly generated and known only to them and Kerberos. They can use this key to encrypt data to ensure its integrity and privacy.

Programming with the DCE Security Service

DCE security allows clients and servers to authenticate each other and communicate securely by making authenticated RPC calls. It is up to the client and the server to decide how much authentication they will require, as well as how much security they will use in communicating their data.

Levels of Security

DCE security allows clients and servers several different levels of authentication and data security. Some situations might require no authorization, while others may require secret key authorization. Table 14.5 shows the different authorization levels available from the DCE security service.

Table 14.5 DCE Security Authorization Levels

Level	Meaning
rpc_c_authn_none	No authentication
rpc_c_authn_default	Default level of authentication
rpc_c_authn_dce_secret	DCE secret key authentication
rpc_c_authn_dce_public	Reserved for future use

III

Introduction to DCE

Of these different types, the most common is `rpc_c_authn_dce_secret`, DCE secret key authentication.

Just as with authentication, DCE security supports different levels of data security during the authenticated RPC transaction. Table 14.6 lists the different data security levels that are available.

> **Note**
>
> As a general rule, as the data security level is increased, more CPU resources are required and there is a greater impact on system performance.

Table 14.6   DCE Data Security Levels

Level	Meaning
`rpc_c_protect_level_none`	Use no data protection.
`rpc_c_protect_level_connect`	Use an encrypted handshake during the connect with the server process.
`rpc_c_protect_level_call`	Verify each client and server response.
`rpc_c_protect_level_pkt`	Verify that all data is from the expected source process.
`rpc_c_protect_level_pkt_intg`	Check for modification of the data by using a cryptographic checksum.
`rpc_c_protect_level_privacy`	Encrypt all user data.
`rpc_c_protect_level_default`	The default level for a particular cell. This level is determined by the DCE administrator.

The Authenticated RPC Call

DCE security services take place in the context of an authenticated RPC call. An authenticated RPC call is an RPC with an authentication and data protection level selected. This allows each party in the RPC transaction to be sure of the identity of the other party, as well as the integrity of the data.

Several steps must be completed in order to use authenticated RPC. Some steps are completed on the server side of the transaction, while others are performed by the client. When the server process starts, it establishes the particular principal that is to be used as its identity. This principal may be different from the user that started the server process. Next, the server registers its authentication information with the registry. This sets the level of authentication that the server will use when a client makes a request.

From the client side, the client sets up a binding handle for the RPC call and configures it with the client's security information. This security information is contained in a data structure that holds the name of the server, the client's binding handle, the requested data security level and authentication level, the client's Privilege Authorization Certificate (PAC), and the server's authorization service. If a client does not set the security information for its RPC call binding handle, all RPC calls made with the handle will be unauthenticated.

> **Note**
>
> From a resource point of view, it is rather time-consuming and expensive to create a secure binding handle. A process should reuse the handle if more than one authenticated RPC call is to be made.

Once the client has successfully configured its binding handle and associated the security information with it, the client can now initiate an authenticated RPC call.

When the server side of the authenticated RPC call is invoked, the server makes a call to retrieve the client's PAC in order to check the client process's privileges. If the client has requested access to an object with an ACL, the server must also check the ACL to see if the client has access. At this point, the server must make a decision. If the client has the correct authorization and privileges, the server will allow the RPC call to complete. The exact set of authorization decisions that the server performs is specific to each RPC server.

Servers and ACLs

If a client wants to access an object that is protected by an ACL, the server must check and verify that the client has the right to access this object. How does the server do this? It interacts with an entity known as an *ACL Manager*. Basically, an ACL Manager is responsible for checking an access request against an object's ACL, and granting or denying access according to the ACL permissions. Different components of DCE have different ACL Managers that are responsible for their ACLs.

A set of function calls exists that allow programmers to access the ACL Manager interface. These calls are prefixed with `sec_acl_mgr`. Table 14.7 lists the most common ACL functions and their actions.

III

Introduction to DCE

Table 14.7   DCE ACL Management Function Calls

Function	Description
sec_acl_mgr_configure	Returns a handle to an ACL database. Can also be used to create an ACL database.
sec_acl_mgr_replace	Used to replace an ACL in the ACL database.
sec_acl_mgr_is_authorized	Compares an object's ACL with a process' PAC and grants or denies access.
sec_acl_mgr_lookup	Returns a pointer to an object's ACL.
sec_acl_mgr_get_access	Finds the total level of access granted by a process' PAC.

The most common ACL management function call is probably
sec_acl_mgr_is_authorized. This call takes a process' PAC and checks for
access to an object. The server in an authenticated RPC call will use this function to check the client's PAC against the ACL of the requested object.

From Here...

Security is an important consideration in a network environment, and it
encompasses several different concepts. In this chapter, we have looked at the
basic components of the DCE security services, how they interact with each
other, and how they provide support for processes to make authenticated
RPC calls. For more information about DCE and authenticated RPC, see the
following chapters:

- Chapter 8, "Authentication," discusses the role of authentication in
  RPC.

- Chapter 13, "What is DCE?," gives an introduction to the Distributed
  Computing Environment.

Chapter 15

Techniques for Developing DCE Clients and Servers

The DCE developer has many tools in his toolbox. With them, he or she can build a large number of different items in a large number of different ways. The approach to a software construction project is rarely as straightforward and procedural as building a new deck, however. You can go out and buy plans which will tell you how much wood to purchase, how to cut it, and how to assemble it, with every detail of the construction spelled out minutely. Unfortunately, you cannot do quite the same thing with DCE client/server development.

At the lowest level, every one of the hundreds of functions in the DCE system serves a clearly defined purpose. You must come up with the grand scheme for your applications, and develop that scheme in enough detail that you can then choose the set of tools and materials to use in your implementation. While your application goals might be clear, the linkage between them and the facilities that DCE provides can be murky.

The purpose of this chapter is to provide a set of roadmaps for using DCE in client/server development. In the process of describing DCE's various methods of meeting your needs, I will also go into some detail about the design decisions you will face in using DCE. My goal is to help you make your deck turn out to be a deck, rather than a haphazard collection of lumber stuck to the side of your house.

This chapter discusses these important topics:

- Using the DCE global name service in clients and servers

- Binding a client to a server

- Designing and customizing the client/server interface

- Choosing the server architecture

- Handling errors

Creating the Interface

The interface is the language by which the client and server communicate. Establishing this language is a critical part of client/server application design and should be the first thing you undertake. The interface governs which operations are executed by the server on behalf of the client, what data is transmitted, and what results are returned. The interface doesn't do anything itself, but it does specify what may be done by the applications.

If you develop a program consisting of several files using ANSI C, you will undoubtedly create one or more header files. These header files will define the data structures shared among the various files, and will also provide protototypes for all the externally visible functions. These files define the interfaces between the various sets of functions in the different files. They are written in standard C syntax.

In a single process application, one can have global context such as global variables, shared file descriptors, common heap memory, and so on. In any client/server application, the client and the server will be separate processes so that global context is not possible. The functional interface between the client and the server is their sole means of communication, and everything which the client wishes to send to the server, or receive back from it, must be defined in their interface.

In DCE, the interface definition process is basically the same as the creation of a common header file, with a few twists. DCE breaks this process down into two steps. The basic interface, consisting of the globally known constants, shared data structures, typedefs, and, of course, the all important remote operation definitions themselves, is defined in an interface definition file using the Interface Definition Language (IDL). DCE also provides an auxiliary file, the Attributes Control File (ACF), which may be used to customize or specialize the interface for special situations or special clients.

The IDL syntax and the ACF syntax are both similar to standard C. They incorporate additional constructs to specify things that C, with its typical terseness, leaves out. The next two sections, "Defining the Interface with IDL" and "Customizing the Interface with ACF," review the use of the IDL and ACF files in defining the client/server interface. These sections are not meant to be a comprehensive treatment of either IDL or ACF; rather, they will describe some of the prototypical, and often confusing, issues that arise in DCE interface development. The third section, "Naming and the Role of the CDS," discusses a topic that is not usually lumped with "interface definition"—the topic of global naming. DCE provides a rich global name service that is used by clients to locate their servers. It is something that is outside both the client and the server but is critical to both of them, and is an integral, though mostly hidden, part of their interface with one another.

Defining the Interface with IDL

The interface definition for a DCE client/server application is stored in an IDL file. This file will consist of an interface header, whose primary purpose is to define a symbolic name for the interface, and an interface body, which defines the set of data types and procedure definitions shared between the clients and the server. The header specifies "who" the interface is, while the body says "what" the interface does. The header contains a very small number of very specific parts with the sole function of uniquely identifying the interface. The body contains the data types and remote procedure prototypes that you would expect in a standard .h file, as well as IDL specific attributes that control how the interface data is interpreted.

The contents of the IDL file, which should be named something.idl, are processed by a tool called idl (no surprises here) to create a set of .c files that are linked to the client and the server, and that act as the glue code between them and the DCE lower level library functions. idl also creates an .h file that is included by both client and server code, and contains somewhat modified versions of the data type and function declarations of the IDL file. Figure 15.1 shows the inputs and outputs to the idl compiler.

The IDL header takes this form:

```
[
     uuid(347A2376-4720-03AC-00819D000000),
     version(2.0)
]
```

III

Introduction to DCE

Fig. 15.1

The idl compiler converts interface definitions into C code.

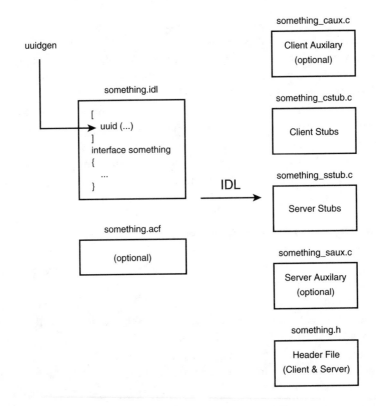

It contains two components that make up what I refer to as the "symbolic name" for the interface: the UUID and the version number. The UUID, or Universal Unique IDentifier, is a quantity with a large number of bytes, which you see written above as a set of hex numbers separated by dashes. The exact format of the UUID is not relevant; you will almost always obtain it automatically, by running a utility called uuidgen (or uuid_gen), which generates a new UUID for you. It is guaranteed to be unique across all other UUIDs anywhere because it encodes both the unique network identifier of your machine, the time at which it was created, and a steadily incrementing serial number.

The UUID should be thought of as the symbolic name of the interface. When a server declares itself as available and ready to serve, it advertises the UUID(s) of its interface(s). A potential client must have one of the same UUIDs in order to be compatible with that server. All other considerations, such as matching network protocols, are subordinate to first finding a matching interface as given by the UUID of that interface.

The version number is also an important qualifier. It is written as a decimal number with the integer part denoting the major version and the decimal part denoting the minor version. The version number is also significant since clients may only converse with servers with the same major version number and with a minor version number that is at least as large as the client's. While the header portion of the IDL file might seem like a minor detail of book-keeping, it is, in fact, the primary identification for an interface. We will return to the issue of the interface name and how the client finds the server several times in subsequent sections.

> **Note**
>
> DCE matches clients and servers on an all-or-nothing basis. UUIDs, protocols, and versions must all match or DCE will not make the connection.

It is also possible to put a small number of attributes in the header portion of the IDL file. These attributes control the default form for a pointer (the `pointer_default` attribute), as well as allow one to specify the precise network address at which a client and server are to connect (the `endpoint` attribute).

Pointers are, in fact, our next topic of discussion. They are also probably our most important topic of discussion, both in terms of developing a DCE interface and developing the client and server programs themselves. If you have read any of the chapters on RPC then you are already aware of the issues involved with using pointers in a networked environment. DCE provides a very consistent (and only slightly confusing) way of treating pointers. The syntax of IDL is particularly well suited to uncovering bugs or poor design involving pointer manipulation.

IDL defines two types of pointers: reference pointers and full pointers. A reference pointer is a pointer to existing storage with a known data type—and therefore a known size. A reference pointer is never NULL. A full pointer may or may not point to allocated storage. The amount of data stored at the location to which it points may not be known in advance. A full pointer may be NULL. IDL also provides a string type, indicating an array of characters terminated by the NUL character (a zero byte, ASCII '\0'). A string may be given as a reference pointer or a full pointer. The [ref] attribute is used for reference pointers, [ptr] for full pointers, and [string] for strings of either flavor.

◀ See "Handling Lists, Graphs, and Multiple References," p. 252

In C, the distinction between reference pointers and full pointers also exists, but it is often blurred. It is also one of the most common sources of error in C programs—referring to storage that does not exist. IDL strongly encourages you to consider carefully the distinction between the two types of pointers, and provides a syntax to indicate which is which. It also enforces certain rules for pointer utilization in order to prevent common errors. The distinction is not only important for semantic reasons, it is also important for performance reasons. While full pointers provide the greatest functionality, they do so at some cost in execution time.

In IDL, you will encounter pointers at two places within the body of the interface definition: in data type definitions (as a member of a data structure, for example), and in procedure definitions (as either parameters or as the return type). There are two approaches to dealing with these pointers. The first is to annotate every occurrence of every pointer with either a [ref] attribute or a [ptr] attribute. Those pointers which will always point to allocated storage may be [ref]; all other pointers should be [ptr]. The second approach is to use the pointer_default attribute in the IDL header file. You can easily modify the header given above, adding a comma after the version declaration, and then this line:

```
pointer_default(ptr)
```

which says that every ambiguous pointer should be considered to be a full pointer. If the expression had been given as pointer_default(ref), this would have indicated that every ambiguous pointer should be considered to be a reference pointer. (I say "ambiguous pointer" because there are certain situations in which only one type of pointer is possible. We will see examples of this shortly.)

Tip
Label all IDL pointers with a [ref] or [ptr] attribute, even if it is not required by IDL.

Which approach should be used? I recommend that you use both. In fact, I recommend that you annotate all IDL pointers, whether you need to or not. Not only does this provide an excellent means of documenting your design, it also helps to expose errors. IDL will catch certain erroneous combinations and warn you.

Let us take some concrete data structure examples. The following IDL data structure declaration:

```
typedef struct {
        int       myint;
    [ref]    int  *myotherint;
    } twoints;
```

defines a data structure with two members: an integer and a reference to an integer. Such a structure must be accessed in such a way that myotherint always refers to valid storage. Here are two initializations for such a structure, one good and one bad:

```
static int theint = 14;
twoints thetwo;
thetwo = { 10, &theint } ;   /* Good */
thetwo = { 10, NULL } ;      /* Bad */
```

The second is bad, of course, because it causes myotherint to point to invalid storage by making it a NULL pointer. If it is desired to support both these initializations then the [ptr] attribute should be used in the structure declaration.

One subtle situation in which it is essential to use full pointers is when there are two or more ways of reaching the same element by following pointers. One classic example of this is the following doubly linked list:

```
typedef struct {
        int         myint;
    [ptr] struct list_o_ints *next;         /* forward pointer */
    [ptr]      struct list_o_ints *prev; /* reverse pointer */
    } list_o_ints;
```

In this case, the embedded next and prev structure pointers must be given the [ptr] attribute because there will be two ways to reach each structure member on the list: by following the next pointers forward, and by following the prev pointers backward, next and prev will also be NULL at the end and beginning of the list, respectively.

Note

Whenever you have lists, queues, or trees of data structures, apply the traversal test. If it is possible to reach the same element in more than one way by following pointers, then the IDL [ptr] attribute must be used.

When declaring procedures and their parameters in IDL, care must again be taken with pointers. Procedure parameters in IDL must be given a direction attribute, either [in], [out], or [in,out] indicating how the data is to flow. [in] refers to data flowing into the server, [out] to data flowing out of the server, and the composite [in,out] to data going in both directions. IDL has two sets of rules for handling pointers for [in] and [out] parameters.

Chapter 16, "Understanding the OSF DCE Services," will explore these rules in more detail. For our purposes, we need only look at the restrictions that IDL imposes and the impact these have on the interface design. In the case of [in] parameters, there is little difference between [ref] and [ptr]. If there is data present, then it is transmitted. If the pointer is NULL and it was given the [ptr] attribute, then no data is sent. If it is NULL and the [ref] attribute was

III

Introduction to DCE

given, then you will either get an error, or whatever trash is at location 0 will be sent to the server. Both results are bad.

If the parameter is an [out] parameter, indicating that data is coming from the server, then it must be a [ref] pointer. Any attempt to combine [out] with [ptr] will result in an idl error. How do you get data back from the server in this case? Can DCE be so primitive as to not perform memory allocation in this case? No, of course not. The solution is to use the same type of construct as you would in C. If you have a value in a C function and you wish to have a called function modify that value, then you must pass in a pointer to that value. If you wish the called function to modify a pointer, then you must pass in a pointer to a pointer, as follows:

```
int *iptr1 = (int *)NULL;   /* always initialize pointer variables */
int *iptr2 = (int *)NULL;
badmodifyiptr(iptr1);       /* bad */
okmodifyiptr(&iptr2);       /* good */
```

In the first case badmodifyiptr gets int * as its argument, value NULL. It can modify that value to its heart's content, but it will not be reflected in the caller's value of iptr1. In the second case, okmodifyiptr gets int ** as its argument. It does not modify its argument, it modifies what it points to, as follows:

```
okmodifyiptr(int **iptrptr)
{
     (*iptrptr) = (&some_global_integer);
}
```

thereby modifying the caller's value of iptr2. In IDL, you would declare a procedure such as the following:

```
void intproc(
     [in]       int    various;
     [out, ref] int **iptrptr;
     );
```

and then call the procedure in this manner:

```
int  five = 5;
int *realoptr = (int *)NULL;
intproc(five, &realoptr);
```

It is important to understand that iptrptr is a true reference pointer. It is a pointer to an integer pointer. Its storage is already allocated in the variable realoptr. It is also important to understand that (*iptrptr), which is an integer pointer, is a *full* pointer. If this were not the case, then it could not be modified, and the above would not work. How does IDL know what type of pointers to use for the inner pointers in the case of multiple dereference? It uses the `pointer_default` attribute, which should have been set to `ptr` in this case.

Caution

Always declare `pointer_default (ptr)` in your IDL header when you are using multiple pointers (pointers to pointers).

In the case of parameters which are [`in,out`], the behaviors of [`in`] and [`out`] are combined. In the case of [`ref`] pointers, the value at the pointed-to location is sent to the server, and the server return is written into that same location, destroying its previous contents. In the case of [`ptr`] pointers, any data present at the pointed-to location is transmitted, and any server result written at a potentially different address. DCE performs the necessary memory allocation in the client stubs in the case of [`ptr`] pointers.

Note

If the return code of an interface procedure is a pointer then it is always a full pointer. You do not need to use the [`ptr`] attribute in this case because there will never be any ambiguity. Use it anyway.

You might ask why the [`ref`] attribute should ever be used. It seems like [`ptr`] provides all of the features of [`ref`] with none of the restrictions. As I indicated previously, one reason is performance. When you use a [`ptr`] pointer, it may be necessary for the server, and also the client, to allocate memory. Since memory allocation can be expensive (particularly if it is done very often), this can be undesirable.

Pointer usage is an area where careful interface design really pays off. Consider the case of asking for an array of integers to be returned, and you do not know in advance how many integers will be in the array. You might argue that this case requires a full pointer. It might, but if you can bound the problem then you can obtain a performance improvement. For example, if the constraints of your application dictate that there will never be more than ten integers in that returned array, then you can make the pointer a [`ref`]. Declare a fixed array of ten integers, and have the remote procedure tell you how many it returned. We could modify `intproc()` in the previous code fragment to do this using the following IDL declaration:

III

Introduction to DCE

```
int intproc(
     [in]       int  various;
     [out, ref] int *staticptr;
     );
```

and then calling it as follows:

```
int tenints[10];
int howmanyi;
howmanyi = intproc(five, &tenints[0]);
/* use tenints[0] ... tenints[howmanyi-1] */
```

There is another reason for preferring reference pointers to full pointers: robustness. Because a [ref] pointer may not be NULL if it turns out to have the value NULL, then this probably points to an error in the application itself. If you are quite certain that a pointer should always reference a valid value, then you should make it a reference pointer. If such a pointer goes NULL then you know that you have a problem.

Customizating the Interface with ACF

Tip
Always initialize all pointers. Make certain that every pointer is set to NULL or points to valid memory before any DCE functions are used.

The IDL file for a particular server and its various clients defines the interface between those applications. There is also another file, the Attributes Control File (ACF), which can be used to customize how a particular client works, or even how a particular server works, without changing the interface itself. I have found this to be useful in two specific cases: implementing a subset of the interface and error handling.

Very often you will start down the road of client/server development with one particular client/server combination in mind. After you have implemented them, however, other clients will probably suggest themselves. Most of these clients will have almost identical interfaces. The similarities will outnumber the differences. It would be unproductive, as well as a poor maintenance decision, to generate several slightly different versions of the original interface to handle this. You can use one or more ACF files, in combination with a single IDL file, to generate the code for more than one client.

Suppose, for example, that I have implemented a fairly sophisticated server which is serving several copies of the same client on different client machines. I have decided (wisely) to instrument the server to see where it is spending its time so that I can improve its performance in critical routines. To this end the server is gathering statistics. Rather than have the server log vast amounts of statistics data in text form to a log file, I implement a very simple query client. It will have only a few operations—perhaps an open and close routine, a "get statistics" routine, and maybe a "reset statistics" routine as well.

Naturally, I want to reuse the existing open and close routines from the IDL file. However, the IDL file also defines all the routines of the main client. I have two obvious choices, both of which seem bad. I can copy the overlapping routines from the main IDL file to a new one, add the "get statistics" and "reset statistics" routines, and then build a new client; or I can add these two routines to the main IDL file. The first choice is very bad since I now have the same set of routines in two places. (I could also abstract the common routines into a separate file and use an IDL "import" directive, but that lacks visibility.) The second choice is better, but my maintenance client will now have stub code for all the routines which it does not care about.

This might seem like a contrived example, but when you have several clients sharing slightly different copies of the same interface, it can become very tedious. Fortunately, there is a very simple solution. Create two ACF files, one for the main client and another for the maintenance client. The ACF files will use the attributes [code] and [nocode] to selectively declare which interface procedures are being used in each client. The first says that code for the procedure to which it is attached should be generated; the second says that it should not. Thus, the main client would have the ACF shown in Listing 15.1...

Listing 15.1   The ACF File for the Primary Client

```
interface myserver     /* main_client.acf */
{
    [code] server_open();              /* necessary open routine */
    [code] server_close();             /* necessary close routine */
    [code] server_difficult_operation(); /* another necessary */
    /* routine and so on for all procedures, except */
    [nocode] server_getstatistics();     /* not needed by primary */
    /* client */
    [nocode] server_resetstatistics();   /* ditto */
}
```

...while the maintenance client would only use the [code] attribute with those procedures which it needed. Its ACF is shown in Listing 15.2.

Listing 16.2 The ACF File for the Maintenance Client

```
interface myserver    /* maintenance_client.acf */
{
    [code] server_open();        /* every client needs this */
    [code] server_close();              /* this too */
    [nocode] server_difficult_operation();     /* only needed by */
    /* primary client and so on for all procedures, except */
    [code] server_getstatistics();  /* needed by maint. client */
    [code] server_resetstatistics();      /* ditto */
}
```

There is one slight inconvenience. The idl compiler expects the .idl file and the .acf file to have the same basename, so if your main client's IDL is main_client.idl then you must link it to maintenance_client.idl in order for it to be able to successfully process the second definition. Your makefiles for these two clients will, of course, have to be in different directories as well, to avoid the client stubs of one from being accidentally overwritten by the client stubs of the other (since the interface name, myserver, is the same).

Tip
ACF is often very useful in specifying different error handling methods for different clients.

This semitrivial application of the ACF file should give you some idea of its overall utility. It is possible to extract different behaviors for different clients from the same interface using ACF.

DCE provides a mechanism known as "exceptions" that provides for asynchronous notification of two types of errors: communication errors and "faults." An exception is very much like (and may well be implemented as) a UNIX signal. It strikes without warning and will cause your client to exit abruptly unless it is dealt with in some way. DCE provides two approaches:

- Use a (mostly) convenient set of macros specifically for that purpose

- Arrange to convert these asynchronous notifications into synchronous error codes

You can, of course, mix these two approaches.

I will talk more about client design issues associated with exceptions and error handling in general in a following section, "Client Components." For the moment, let us consider how to generate synchronous error status when we want it. The ACF provides these two attributes: [comm_status] and [fault_status]. These may be attached to a procedure itself, or as the attributes of a parameter to a procedure. It is conventional, but not mandatory, to use both attributes together.

For example, suppose my `server_open()` procedure returns an identifier that I would normally store in an unsigned long. My IDL file contains an entry like the following:

```
unsigned long server_open(/* its parameters/);
```

Now it just so happens that the C data type `unsigned long` and the IDL data types `unsigned32` and `error_status_t` are all identical. Thus if I create an ACF entry which says the following:

```
interface mainiface
{
    [comm_status, fault_status] server_open();
    /* other operations and their attributes */
}
```

I have now arranged that if either type of error occurs during the execution of this procedure, the error status will be delivered as the return code of `server_open()`. Of course, this only works if I can distinguish valid returned IDs from DCE error codes. In this case, it also depends on the amazing coincidence that the procedure's return type matches the error type.

It is usually much more useful to attach these two attributes to a parameter of a procedure rather than to the procedure itself. This parameter must also show up in the IDL file, of course. If we now suppose that the `server_open()` routine actually returns a string, then we might have an IDL entry like:

```
[ptr, string]
        char *server_open(
            /*other parameters*/,
            [out, ref] unsigned32 *ovlstatus
            );
```

and a corresponding ACF entry of the following:

```
server_open(
        [comm_status, fault_status] ovlstatus
        );
```

There are several things to notice in this example. First, the status parameter must be last in the IDL declaration, and it must be of type `unsigned32` or `error_status_t`. Second, it must be `[out]` and therefore `[ref]`. Third, the corresponding ACF entry does not need to include all the parameters of the `server_open()` procedure—merely the one to which the attributes apply.

The `ovlstatus` parameter can now be used in two ways. The server may use it to send back any kind of status that is appropriate for this particular procedure. DCE is also allowed to use this same parameter to indicate if a communication error or fault occurred. You now have to distinguish the two types of

III

Introduction to DCE

errors, which you can do by calling the utility routine `dce_error_inq_text()` (which will fail on a non-DCE error code). You could also use two parameters—one for your error codes and one for DCE's error codes, of course. Notice, finally, that if I omit the ACF entry, then the parameter is simply another status parameter for the server to use as it wishes.

Caution

Error handling is one of the most complex issues in client design. Do not enforce a narrow error policy on all clients, such as forcing them to always exit on any error. Give individual clients as much flexibility as possible.

There is one more critical ACF directive which has to do with binding methods. We will cover this in the "Using DCE's Binding Methods" section.

Naming and the Role of the CDS

One of the most important questions in the design of distributed applications is how clients locate their servers. In network programming at the lowest level, the client must concoct an address for the server from a relatively magic combination of seemingly arbitrary numbers. In RPC, as we saw in Chapter 11, "Techniques for Developing RPC Clients and Servers," the client usually locates the server by specifying the server's host and a pair of identifying numbers. DCE provides a very high-level approach to this problem through the medium of a separate facility known as the Cell Directory Service (CDS).

I consider the CDS to be part of the client/server interface, since some coordination scheme must be agreed upon in advance by clients and servers in order to use any such "name service." The CDS implements such a name service by associating interfaces with symbolic names that appear in the form of filenames, organized hierarchically. Servers make their existence known by registering their interface specification(s) with the CDS in connection with a string that looks like a filename. Clients locate servers by doing a search for such an interface/name pair. Since the CDS is itself a distributed application, it is possible to perform this type of lookup without reaching across the network to the server's host.

CDS provides three types of entries: individual entries, group entries, and profile entries. Individual entries are like files. A typical CDS entry for a remote temperature server might be the following:

```
"/.:/applications/thermistor"
```

which looks an awful lot like a UNIX filename, except for the peculiar .: base "directory." Once a server has registered its interface under a specific name, clients may then search the CDS using that name. The result of such a search does not provide a complete description of the server's network address, but it does provide enough information to determine if a compatible match is possible.

A group entry is a higher level construct. Servers may not only register their individual filenames, they may also join groups, which are also described by filenames. This provides a second way in which clients may contact servers. A client can ask for all the servers in a particular group, given by its CDS filename, and then examine each for an appropriate match. Every server that provides some form of read-only weather information might want to advertise its services by joining a group named /.:/weather_group. This group entry would point to a set of individual entries, which might all be located in a subdirectory of .:/applications. DCE provides an administrative application called rpccp, which can be used to create new CDS directories.

Finally, CDS contains entries known as *profile entries*. Profile entries allow you to set up completely general pointers to other entries. Your software department might create a profile entry that contains pointers to all the various server groups containing all the various servers (temperature, barometric pressure, stock quotations, and so on) that it has written, as well as pointers to servers implemented by other departments. Profile entries are yet another place for a client to begin a server search.

I recommend the following approach to creating CDS entries. First, use the DCE administrative tools to discover any existing profile, group, or individual entries. Choose your server CDS name in accordance with whatever schemes are already in place, or invent a logical naming scheme if none exists. Second, create an individual entry for the server. Third, put your server in an appropriate group. If no appropriate group exists, create one. Finally, find a logical profile entry and make it point to your group. If none exists, create one.

Why go to all this trouble, you might ask? When you first started programming, you started accumulating files. If you are anything like me, in the beginning you had all your files in a single directory. Over time, you grew more sophisticated (or more compulsive), and you began making logical subdirectories. Of course, your first directory schemes were never permanent, and have probably evolved with you to this day. But at least there is a prayer that if you are looking for a memo it will be in the memos directory, not in bin.

Tip
Servers should have a single CDS individual entry, be a member of one CDS group entry, and be reachable from at least one profile entry.

III

Introduction to DCE

The threefold rule of DCE naming ensures that any client that follows at least one consistent search strategy (by profile, by group, or by individual entry name) will have a chance of finding a compatible server. Servers that follow the "object model" are often exceptions to this "rule of three." We will discuss this model more at the end of this chapter.

Understanding the DCE Client

This section discusses two of the primary areas that you, as the client developer, must address. First, it reviews the components that make up a DCE client—both those that are automatically generated and those that you must create yourself. The section "Using DCE's Binding Methods" discusses the various ways in which a client may connect to one or more servers, and how the DCE name lookup routines may be used to facilitate this. Because of the great flexibility that DCE offers you, this is an area that you should consider carefully in your client design. "Error Handling" then covers the very important topic of the DCE exception mechanism and the ways it can be made to work for you. The nitty-gritty details of actually implementing a client are covered in Chapter 16, "Understanding the OSF DCE Services."

Client Components

A DCE client consists of four components. The client top level (called simply the "client" in the OSF documentation) is the main program of the client. It contains whatever code implements the logic of the client, which actually makes the remote procedure calls defined in its interface to the server. These remote procedure calls are contained within the second and third components of the client: the client stubs and the client auxiliary. Both these files are generated by idl from the IDL file, as well as the client's ACF file, if there is one. If the interface is named ifx, then the stub file will be called ifx_cstub.c, and the auxiliary file ifx_caux.c. The client stub file acts as the glue between the client top level and the DCE RPC libraries, the fourth component of the client. Figure 15.2 shows how the components of a DCE client work together.

Note that the client stub file will always be generated by the idl compiler, but the auxiliary file will only be generated under certain circumstances (idl bases its decision on whether there are multiple pointer pathways, and also on ACF attributes, which I have not discussed). For the most part you need not concern yourself with the contents of any of these four components other than your own top level. Of course, you will be making a few explicit (and many implicit) calls to DCE RPC libraries. The overwhelming majority of your direct interaction with DCE will be in binding to a server.

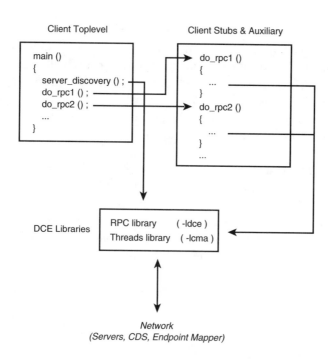

Client Toplevel

```
main ()
{
    server_discovery () ;
    do_rpc1 () ;
    do_rpc2 () ;
    ...
}
```

Client Stubs & Auxiliary

```
do_rpc1 ()
{
    ...
}
do_rpc2 ()
{
    ...
}
...
```

DCE Libraries

```
RPC library      ( -ldce )
Threads library   ( -lcma )
```

Network
(Servers, CDS, Endpoint Mapper)

Fig. 15.2
Much of the work in a typical DCE client is performed in the `cstub` and `caux` files.

Using DCE's Binding Methods

Binding is the process by which a client establishes communication with a server. As with many other things in DCE, there are several ways in which clients can bind to servers, each of which is tailored to different client needs. There are, in fact, three binding methods in DCE, known as automatic binding, implicit binding, and explicit binding. Before we discuss how to bind, it is worthwhile to understand a little bit about what a binding is.

In order to make a network connection, you must build up a complete network address. The two components of such an address are the host part and the network port number(s) at which the server is located. In the DCE abstraction, almost all the details of building this address are hidden from you. DCE abstracts the process of discovering which hosts are running a particular server using its CDS name service. Once you have the host information, it is then possible for your client to contact a process running on that host known as the *endpoint mapper*, which will give you the network port information and allow you to complete the connection to the actual server process. The first stage gives you a *partial binding handle*, and in the second step you have a *complete binding handle*. The three different binding methods represent increasing levels of control over this process.

III

Introduction to DCE

In automatic binding, all the steps of the binding process are completely hidden from the client, including the binding handle itself. In implicit binding, the binding handle is contained in a global variable, which the client must set using one of the search methods that I described previously. In explicit binding, the client can manage as many binding handles as it wishes, and must explicitly include the binding handle as a parameter to each remote procedure call. Let's look at each of these a little more closely.

Automatic Binding

In automatic binding, the DCE libraries consult the environment variable RPC_DEFAULT_ENTRY the first time a remote procedure call is used by the client. A search is instituted for that particular server using the CDS search rules that I described previously; if it is found, that server is used for all subsequent RPCs. In automatic binding, you have no control over which server you will get. If more than one server is registered with the given interface, the client will get whichever one it encounters first during the CDS name search.

You specify automatic binding by using the auto_handle attribute in your client's ACF file. Automatic binding is obviously only useful if your client does not care which particular server executes its RPC requests. If your client is looking for an array processor server so that it can perform billions of floating point computations, for example, it will probably be happy if it can find any such machine available; which one it uses is not important.

Implicit Binding

In implicit binding, the binding information is stored in a global variable that must be set by the client before it calls any remote procedures. This statement must be placed in the header portion of the client's ACF file:

```
[
    implicit_handle(handle_t my_bind)
]
```

This statement will be transformed by the idl compiler into a declaration of the global variable my_bind, which has the DCE data type handle_t (it actually comes out in the .h file as being of type rpc_binding_handle_t, which is really the same type). It is the client's responsibility to set this global variable to some appropriate value at startup. The usual way that this is done is to use the DCE routines whose names begin with rpc_ns_binding. There are begin(), next(), and done() routines. If you have ever programmed with the UNIX getxxxent() routines then you know the drill: the begin() routine initializes things, the next() routine fetches an entry, and the done() routine cleans things up.

This pseudocode in Listing 15.3 shows a typical sequence that a client using implicit binding might use to find a server. I call this the server discovery (or server rendezvous) loop.

Listing 15.3   Using Implicit Binding

```
idl_boolean foundserver = FALSE;    /* Assume failure */
unsigned32 status = 0;              /* always initialize */
unsigned_char_t *startentry = "/.:/applications/hiya"; /* place to
/* start looking */
rpc_ns_binding_import_begin(.., startentry, Iface,..); /* init
binding search loop */
while ( foundserver == FALSE ) { /* until one is found */
     rpc_ns_binding_import_next(.., &my_bind, &status); /* get a
binding */
     if ( status != rpc_s_ok ) break; /* if error, break out of
the loop */
     foundserver = usethisbinding(my_bind,..); /* application
specific test for compatible server */
     }
rpc_ns_binding_import_done(..);    /* end binding search loop */
```

The _begin() function is called first. It actually takes five arguments, the two most important of which are the startentry argument, which specifies a CDS entry at which to start looking for the server, and the Iface argument. The Iface argument is a data type containing the symbolic name of the interface created by the IDL compiler from your UUID and version number. The variable name would look something like myiface_v2_3_c_ifspec for an interface named myiface at version 2.3. The actual contents of this data structure are defined in the .h file created by idl. This parameter is critical, since only servers that have registered themselves under this interface will be found.

Tip

Always initialize error status parameters to zero.

The _next() function inside the while loop retrieves one binding and stores it in my_bind (this function actually takes three arguments). If there are no more matching bindings left then status will be set to an appropriate error code. At this point, the client has a binding handle and can now call usethisbinding to perform whatever application specific operations are required to decide if this binding is the one it wants. For example, the client can use DCE utility routines to obtain a string representation of the binding and then tease out information such as the hostname of the server from this string. This is only a partial binding; there is no server connection yet.

Finally, when a server has been found, when all matching CDS entries have been exhausted, or when some error occurs, the loop is exited and the _done() function is called. This performs the necessary cleanup. If a binding

III

Introduction to DCE

has been set in the `my_bind` global variable, then the client may call any of its RPC procedures now. The first RPC call will actually convert the partial binding into a complete binding. Each of the client RPC routines implicitly uses the global binding `handle my_bind`.

Tip

The first RPC a client makes to a server is often special. Maximize your error checking and error recovery accordingly.

Because the first client RPC is actually fully resolving the binding handle, there are a number of additional reasons why it might fail. The following is a partial list of some of these reasons:

- The CDS namespace is out of date, and the server is not actually running.

- The server has (erroneously) failed to register its endpoint(s).

- The client is not authorized to connect to the server (security failure).

Explicit Binding

The explicit binding method offers the client the greatest possible control over server communication. In explicit binding, you put the `explicit_handle` attribute in the client's ACF file. Alternately, each RPC procedure can be explicitly declared in the IDL file with a first parameter of type `handle_t` and direction `[in]`:

```
interface myiface
{
    void myproc1(
        [in] handle_t thisbinding,
        ...              /* other parameters */
        );
    /* every other procedure also takes this param */
}
```

If you use the ACF method, the `idl` compiler automatically adds a binding handle parameter to each RPC procedure definition. This method is more general, although less explicit, since it allows you to use the same IDL file for other clients that do not use explicit binding. After you have added the parameter in the IDL file, you are stuck with it for every client, all of which must now use explicit binding.

The most obvious difference between implicit binding and explicit binding is that every RPC routine now has an additional parameter that the client must provide. The top level client loop in the case of explicit binding is essentially identical to the one I showed in Listing 15.3 for the case of implicit binding. Note that in the explicit binding case your client may well want to keep more than one server binding so that it can talk to multiple servers. The previous code could be modified to save several binding handles rather than just the single one in my_bind.

There is one other subtle difference in how you might implement the server discovery loop. In the code of Listing 15.3, I called an application specific function usethisbinding to decide on the acceptability of a given handle. In the case of explicit binding, where it is quite possible to have several fully bound handles in the client application, this function may actually call client RPC routines to ask the server if it supports certain features. The function could then return TRUE or FALSE based on the server's reply.

To see how this might work, consider the array processor server example which I gave earlier. A client searching for array processor servers might set its initial CDS entry to the array processor servers' group:

```
unsigned_char_t *startentry = "/.:/ap_group";
```

The client interface could also explicitly define query procedures that ask the server if it has certain features, then call one or more of the query routines during server discovery, as shown in Listing 15.4.

Listing 15.4   An Example of a Server Query Procedure

```
/* This is the IDL declaration. "Rolled BLAS" is important in
numerical processing */

boolean gotrolledblas(
    [in] handle_t thisbinding,
    [out, ref] rpc_error_status_t *status;
    ) ;

/* This is the client code used to select specific servers */

idl_boolean
usethisbinding(rpc_binding_handle_t ubind)
{
    rpc_error_status_t mysta = rpc_s_ok;   /* always initialize */
    idl_boolean locbool = FALSE;          /* assume failure */
    locbool = gotrolledblas(ubind, &mysta);    /* ask the server:
"Do you have rolled BLAS?" */
    if ( locbool == TRUE && mysta == rpc_s_ok )
        return(TRUE);        /* If server says yes, and no error
then use this server */
    else
        return(FALSE);  /* Otherwise, do not use this server */
}
```

Choosing a Binding Method

How do you choose the binding method for a particular client? There is a very basic rule of thumb that I use to choose a binding method. Even though this rule is a gross oversimplification, it works for a surprisingly large number of cases, at least until you become proficient with DCE.

- If the client is willing to talk to *any* server, use automatic binding.

- If the client needs to talk to *one specific* server, use implicit binding.

- If the client needs to talk to *more than one* server, use explicit binding.

There are several factors that modify this rule. As you have already seen in Chapter 14, "DCE Security," you cannot use automatic binding and also use the DCE security features. Also, if you use context handles, which will be described in Chapter 16, "Understanding the OSF DCE Services," you must use the explicit method. Context handles are useful when using threads, which I will discuss later in this chapter.

It is even possible to mix and match between the different methods, using implicit binding for all but a few server calls that need to talk to a different server. These calls would use explicit binding. As your knowledge of DCE grows you will become more comfortable with binding issues, and the criteria for choosing a binding method will become clearer.

Error Handling

I feel that error handling is the most important area in distributed application development. It is impossible to overestimate the amount of time, effort, and grief you will save yourself and your users if you design good error handling in your clients and servers. In distributed applications, there is much more that can go wrong. Not only can you have application specific errors in the client and server, but you can also have communication errors between them. The use of a "compiled" interface definition with its own syntax and semantics can also lead to errors, particularly when you confuse the [ptr] and [ref] attributes.

DCE provides two mechanisms for error notification, a synchronous one and an asynchronous one. Earlier in the chapter, I discussed the use of the [comm_status] and [fault_status] attributes, which are used when you desire synchronous notification. In this section, I will talk a bit more about what these mean, and also review the asynchronous "exception" mechanism.

Note

Debugger technology for distributed applications, particularly those using threads, is much less developed than it is for monolithic applications. Design your DCE applications with extensive error reporting and tracing capabilities.

Synchronous Error Handling

The purpose of the [comm_status] and [fault_status] attributes is to give your client visibility into errors that happen within the DCE portions of its code. There are many possible things that can go wrong with a client/server connection: the server application may crash, or the server's machine may crash or go off the network. There are also more subtle failure modes. For example, the server's memory may become corrupted because some routine wrote 129 bytes into an array that only holds 128, for example. Server memory corruption can result in the client receiving a garbled result packet from a remote procedure call.

Naturally, the client wants to know about all such conditions. If the server connection is broken, the client may be able to take action to connect to a different server. This occurs frequently if the server is using the object model (see "Using DCE Objects," later in this chapter). Using the [comm_status] attribute on a procedure return or a status parameter permits the client to detect these conditions and take direct action. DCE provides many error codes (too many to summarize) and error print facilities to help with this task.

There are two other special attributes that clients may attach to procedures in the IDL file and that may be used by the DCE libraries in cases of communication failure. The [idempotent] attribute tells DCE that a procedure may be retried without changing the semantics of the result. A getstatus routine would probably fall into this category. If it took three tries to get the status, your client would still have it, and, presumably, reading the status on the server three times would be the same as reading it once. Anything that changes the server state or some external state should probably not be given the [idempotent] attribute. A routine that adds a command to a queue, issues a database write transaction, increments the reference count on an object, or modifies a file would not be idempotent since it would be harmful or confusing to execute such a request more than once.

III

Introduction to DCE

> **Caution**
>
> Use the [idempotent] attribute with care. Even if a procedure can be retried, that does not mean that it should be retried. In particular, this attribute should be avoided in applications in which performance is critical because every retransmission will take additional time.

The other useful IDL attribute is [maybe]. A procedure that has the [maybe] attribute may actually not be executed at all—due to communication problems or other errors—when it is called. This attribute may also be used to indicate that no response is really required for this procedure. Both [maybe] and [idempotent] let your application be casual about error checking and should be used with care.

Fault status errors are a more serious concern than communication status errors. A "fault" usually means a memory fault, often involving an attempted access to an invalid memory location. Accessing location zero (by reading a NULL pointer) or attempting to write to an uninitialized location will usually result in fault errors. The following is a typical example:

```
unsigned32  status = 0; /* always initialize */
unsigned32 *statusp;
somereffunc(&status);   /* OK */
somereffunc(statusp);   /* probable memory fault! */
```

The function somereffunc() is expecting a [ref] pointer, which must be a pointer to allocated storage. The first call works nicely because it is passing in the address of a local variable, which has the required storage. The second call passes in an uninitialized address variable, which is probably either pointing at zero or at whatever harmful location just happens to be on the stack. When somereffunc() tries to write there, a memory fault will probably occur, just as if you had written the following:

```
*(unsigned32 *)0 = value_being_written;
```

If you are careless, you can get a fault in the first statement as well. If somereffunc() is expecting a reference pointer to an idl_long_float, which takes up 64 bits, but you pass it a pointer to storage for only 32 bits, as shown in the first line of code, you will either get a memory fault or you will corrupt some part of your memory space.

If you get a fault_status error code as a result of any DCE library function or remote procedure call, your application should almost certainly clean up and exit as quickly as possible. You have no way of knowing if your local memory is corrupt, or where. Your chances of recovering from a fault are usually slim.

Troubleshooting

I've followed your advice for handling fault-type errors. I have a very simple cleanup routine. Even so, this routine behaves very strangely, and sometimes the application crashes anyway. What should I do?

If your application's local memory has been corrupted, then very few operations are safe. Any function that allocates memory should be avoided. Unfortunately, some functions such as `fprintf()` may allocate memory internally, and may not properly document their behavior. Your cleanup routine should not make any further RPC calls, nor should it allocate memory. System calls should be used sparingly. If you must print a message to the user or to a log file, I strongly encourage you to use `sprintf()` function into a static string, followed by a `write()` function.

If you already have FILE pointer, then you *might* try to `fflush()` it, get its underlying file descriptor with `fileno()` and then `write()` to that. Depending on your implementation, `fflush()`, `fclose()`, and `exit()` might all be unsafe, so you may need to resort to `exit()` if you have such a routine. Check your system documentation to see how much cleanup your `exit()` routine does. In particular, find out if it calls any application defined, and potentially dangerous, `atexit()` or `onexit()` handlers. Try to locate an exit function that refrains from any cleanup. On many systems there is a function called `_exit()` which may be used for this purpose

---

Exceptions

Exceptions are the default mechanism by which communication errors and faults are communicated to a client or server application. An exception is like a UNIX signal. It arrives asynchronously, interrupting the normal flow of control, and is associated with a tag describing the exception, like a UNIX signal number. A timeout error on an RPC call could result in the delivery of an `rpc_x_call_timeout` exception, for example. Like signals, the arrival of an exception will usually cause the application (client or server) to terminate. If you are not using the synchronous error approach described in the previous section, you must make explicit provisions for handling exceptions.

There are two ways to handle exceptions. The first is to explicitly register one or more exception handlers very early in your application code. These work a lot like UNIX signal handlers. A set of `pthread()` routines is used to do this; please consult the OSF documentation for more information. The more common (but less flexible) approach is to use a set of exception handling macros defined in the include file `<pthread_exc.h>` (some systems may have a shorter name for this file). The exception mechanism is actually a part of DCE `pthreads`, which are discussed in the "Threads and Server State" section later in this chapter.

A block of code is protected from exceptions by adding the TRY macro at the very beginning of that block. Typically, this would be at the very start of your server or client main() routine. At the end of the block that you wish to protect, put the macro FINALLY. This macro is followed by your cleanup code, at the end of which you place the ENDTRY macro. Note that these three macros must all occur within the same code block. You may not cross routine or { } boundaries. You may go down (into functions) but not up (out of the current function). This exception handling mechanism is very similar to the "catch/throw" paradigm, which occurs in other programming environments, such as lisp, Ada, and Tcl.

For example, the main routine of your client might look like Listing 15.5.

Listing 15.5   A Client Template Using the Exception Handling Macros

```
void main(int argc, char **argv)
{
     /* declarations */
     TRY
          /* server discovery code */
          /* application code */
     FINALLY
          /* cleanup code */
     ENDTRY
}
```

If an exception occurs between the TRY and FINALLY macros, control will be immediately transferred to the first statement of the FINALLY block. If no exceptions occur, the code in the TRY block will someday terminate, and should fall off the end of the TRY block. When this happens, the code in the FINALLY block is also executed. In fact, the exception macros do not provide you with any way of determining whether or not an exception occurred. If you want this information you must provide a mechanism for doing it yourself. My favorite technique is to use a sequence variable, which is set in the body of the application, and which is checked in the FINALLY block in order to determine what to do.

Consider a client that asynchronously prints a file from a spool directory, polls for completion on the server, and deletes the spool file on success. Listing 15.6 gives the basic code for this client.

Listing 15.6   A Detailed Example of Exception Handling

```
typedef enum { STARTUP, GOTSERVER, SENTFILE, PRINTOK,
               PRINTBAD } where ;  /* client state indicating how
/* far it got */
void main(int argc, char **argv)
{
     /* declarations */
     where whereami = STARTUP;    /* client is in STARTUP state */
     rpc_error_status_t statu = rpc_s_ok; /* always initialize */
     TRY
          /* server discovery code */
          whereami = GOTSERVER;     /* client has a SERVER */
          /* open spool file, sent it to server */
          whereami = SENTFILE;      /* client has sent a file */
          statu = rpc_s_ok;         /* reinitialize status to OK */
          /* poll for completion, set statu */
          if ( statu == rpc_s_ok ) whereami = PRINTOK;
          /* file printed OK */
          else whereami = PRINTBAD; /* file failed to print */
     FINALLY
          if ( whereami == PRINTOK ) {    /* if file printed OK, */
          /* then... */
               delete spool file and exit(0);
               }
          else {                          /* some failure */
               print message using "whereami"; /* print message
          /* based on state */
               if ( statu != rpc_s_ok) { /* if status wset, */
               then ... */
                    print "statu" as well;
                    }
               exit(some_error_code);
               }
     ENDTRY
     _exit(-1);  /* paranoia */
}
```

In this case, the sequence variable whereami is used to keep track of where the application is in its processing. It would obviously be bad for the cleanup code to always delete the spool file, or even to rely on the value of statu in choosing to do so. An exception could have happened during the poll-for-complete RPC, which left statu = rpc_s_ok, but which indicated that the file was not printed after all. By setting whereami to a good value only after the successful completion of the poll-for-complete call, we ensure that the spool file is not deleted erroneously.

III

Introduction to DCE

We have only discussed the simplest form of exception processing. There are more involved forms in which CATCH macros can be used to catch specific exceptions. There is also a CATCH_ALL macro, which will catch all exceptions and other variations on the theme. I personally find the approach above to be sufficient for most cases.

Choosing an Error Handling Approach

The key question for the client/server developer is which form of error handling is to be used. The synchronous form of error processing applies only to the client, so in the server you are restricted to the exception mechanism. The question, therefore, applies only to the client.

The exception mechanism allows you to concentrate much of your error handling code in the FINALLY (or CATCH_ALL) block. The synchronous mechanism gives you much finer control, however, and permits you to attempt recovery strategies that would be harder to implement with exceptions. DCE will also let you do both in the same application, if you wish.

In some ways, the simplicity of the exception mechanism is deceptive. Certainly, your exception handler code does allow you to process all exceptions neatly in one place. However, your application has to deal with other forms of error. Your client startup procedure may encounter errors, your remote procedures may encounter errors, and any external interaction which the client has (such as reading a file) is another source of error. A large portion of your client application code is going to be checking for these errors, so it is misleading to say "all my error handling code is in the exception handler." I'm also a believer in the general principle that synchronous design is intrinsically simpler in many cases.

I therefore recommend two simple rules:

- Always use exception handling in the server.

Tip
If you are using the synchronous error mechanism for any RPC routine, use it for all RPC routines.

- Use the synchronous error mechanism in the client unless every error is fatal, or the client spends less than 25 percent of its time on error checking and recovery.

A database interface would undoubtedly want to be compulsively robust and should therefore use synchronous error handling. A client that checks to see if the soft drink machine is empty (yes, there are such clients) can probably do so without complex error recovery and can use the exception mechanism.

Understanding the DCE Server

This section discusses the development of a DCE server. I will first review the components that go into the server, and then discuss the typical sequence that a server uses when starting up. I will then review the two models for server binding, the service model and the object model, and try to provide some guidelines for choosing between them. I will also take a brief peek at the topic of threads and their impact on server design.

Server Components

A DCE server contains five components:

- The server top level

- The DCE libraries

- The server stub functions

- The server auxiliary functions

- The actual remote procedures

The server top level is the main program of the server. It contains the code that the server uses to register itself with the Cell Directory Service and also with the endpoint mapper. Once this has occurred, most server top levels simply call a `listen()` routine, which waits for incoming network packets. These network packets are partially handled by the DCE libraries (the second component) and partially by glue routines in the server stubs and the server auxiliary files (the third and fourth components). These latter two files are generated by the `idl` compiler from the IDL file defining the interface, and also from any ACF file used. The remote procedures themselves are the fifth component. Figure 15.3 shows the components of a DCE server.

The server stub and auxiliary files are very similar to the corresponding client files. For an interface named `iface` these files will be named `iface_sstub.c` and `iface_saux.c`. Once again, the auxiliary file is only generated in certain cases.

The remote procedures are the core of the server. Every procedure that the interface defines must be implemented by the server. The remote procedures do the actual work specified by the client: printing files, loading the array processor, updating the database, or whatever is called for by the interface.

III

Introduction to DCE

Fig. 15.3

The DCE libraries convert network requests into RPCs in a DCE server.

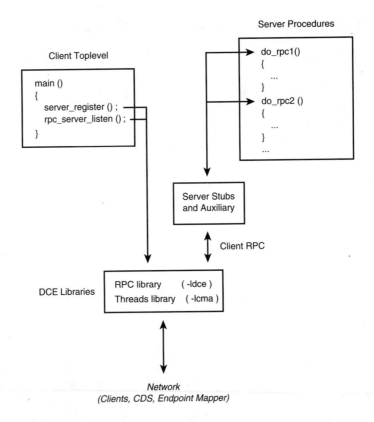

Server Startup

We have already seen the steps that a client uses to find a server. It usually initiates a CDS search to obtain a binding handle, and then makes RPC calls to access the server's services. We have also seen that the CDS name service only does part of the job. It only provides enough information to locate the server's host, resulting in a partial binding. A complete binding is only obtained when the client actually contacts a server. The details of this are almost always buried in the RPC library, which uses the endpoint mapper to get the server's endpoints (network port numbers). In order for a server to start up, it must make itself known to both CDS and the endpoint mapper.

The pseudocode in Listing 15.7 shows how a typical server does this. (Once again I have omitted all error checking and many of the calling parameters in order to illustrate the basic concepts.) This code is geared toward the service model rather than the object model. Chapter 16, "Understanding the OSF DCE Services," provides complete details on how to perform the server startup.

Listing 15.7   Typical DCE Server Startup Code

```
void main(int argc, char **argv) /* server toplevel */
{
     unsigned_char_t *ename = "/.:/applications/serv";
     /* my entry name */
     unsigned_char_t *gname = "/.:/myservgroup";   /* my group name */
     rpc_binding_vector_t *bvptr = NULL;                /* binding
vector pointer */
     rpc_server_register_if(Iface,..);   /* register interface, 1a */
     rpc_server_use_all_protseqs(..);    /* use all possible net
protocols, 1b */
     rpc_server_inq_bindings(&bvptr,..); /* ask for possible
bindings, 1c */
     rpc_ns_binding_export(..,ename, Iface,
          bvptr,...);                    /* register our entry with
CDS , 2 */
     rpc_ns_group_mbr_add(..,gname,..); /* join our CDS group,
3,  optional */
     rpc_ep_register(Iface, bvptr,...); /* register our endpoint 4 */
     rpc_server_listen(..);             /* wait for requests, 5 */
}
```

This might seem like a lot of work just to register the server, but in fact this is relatively simple. The first three statements, all labeled 1, do not communicate with CDS—they just interact with the DCE libraries. Statement 1a says that the server is going to use the interface `Iface`. This is the symbolic name for the interface, generated from the IDL file, including the UUID and version information. It is exactly like the `Iface` argument to `rpc_ns_binding_import_begin()` which we saw in the client bindings section earlier. Statement 1b says that the server is going to use all possible protocol sequences. We could just as well have called a different routine to say that the server was only going to support TCP, but it is considerate and inexpensive to use them all. Statement 1c asks the DCE libraries what bindings have been constructed so far based on the interface and protocol information and returns those bindings in `bvptr`. This is a binding vector, which is just an array of bindings.

Statement 2 actually registers the server with the CDS name service. It is registered by its bindings (`bvptr`), by its symbolic interface descriptor (`Iface`), and is also given a name by which CDS will know it in the parameter `ename`. This is a CDS individual entry that a client may use to find this server. The server may optionally add itself to a CDS group named gname using statement 3. If you follow the "rule of three," which I gave in the "Naming and the Role of the CDS" section, you should include this step so that clients may find you by the group entry as well. You could also add a profile entry pointer entry here, but I'm assuming that a profile already exists and points to your group, so this step is not needed.

Statement 4 registers the server with the endpoint mapper. The endpoint mapper is sent the symbolic interface descriptor Iface and the binding vector bvptr. You might well ask, "Why distribute the information this way; why not have the endpoints stored in the CDS entry as well?" The rationale for this subdivision of labor is that CDS entries change much less frequently than endpoints, so it makes sense to keep the endpoint information local, while distributing the naming information globally.

> **Note**
>
> It is possible to give your server a "well-known" endpoint, which corresponds to a fixed network address, and store that information in the CDS entry, but this is not recommended. Fixed network addresses are typically associated with servers that are part of the operating system or DCE itself.

At this point, the server is fully registered. It is now ready to listen for client remote procedure calls, which it does in statement 5. The function will never return under normal circumstances. We will look at this function again when we discuss threads in the next section.

Using DCE Objects

The clients and servers that we have discussed so far have been bound together by their interface. An interface is developing and documented in the IDL file. The header information of that file is transformed by the idl compiler into an abstract interface specification, which is the primary piece of information by which a client and a server know that they are compatible. When the server registers itself, it registers the interface and effectively declares, "I am a print server," or "I am an array processor server." This is the *service model* of binding. It corresponds to the way in which almost all distributed applications using any form of RPC are implemented.

DCE provides another binding model, the *object model* of binding, which can be of great utility in certain situations. The best way to understand this model is to consider a prototypical example in which it would be used. Suppose we are implementing a server that provides distributed read-only access to a small set of critical files—much like NIS provides access to the password, group, and other files on a UNIX machine.

In the service model, we provide a set of services that would operate on one particular file from the set of files that are being managed. The server registers the interface's descriptor. The open() procedure opens one of these files and returns an identifier to the client. The client then uses this identifier in subsequent access operations, such as readoneentry(), forward(), back(), and so on. The close() procedure releases the resources associated with the identifier and closes the connection. One aspect of this service approach is that the client does not know if the server is managing the file it wants until it tries the open() call. If the server is, it gets an identifier. If the server is not, it gets an error of some kind. In a large system with many such servers, it might be time consuming to locate a server that is managing a specific file.

This issue is easily addressed in the object model of binding. Each file being managed is construed as an object. In practical terms, this means that each file being managed is associated with a UUID. The server managing files PWD and GRP, and ETHRS registers the object UUIDs of these three files. A client wanting a server managing ETHRS can now ask CDS for such a server by conducting a search for the ETHRS entry. The object model is even more useful when there is more than one server serving a particular object. It is often the case that critical resources are assigned a primary server and a backup server, in case the primary server fails. If a client is communicating with the primary server for ETHRS and that server fails, then it simply conducts another CDS search to locate the backup server for the ETHRS entry. Since only the primary and backup servers for ETHRS would have registered this entry, this should be much more efficient than sorting through the potentially large number of servers that provide a compatible interface.

Thus, the object model of binding can be used in cases where discrete resources are being managed by the server, as opposed to the situation where services are being offered. Unfortunately, it also takes a little more work, particularly in server startup, to implement this model. Chapter 16, "Understanding the OSF DCE Services," provides more information about using the object model of binding.

Threads and Server State

Threads are an enormous topic. An entire book could easily be written about threads. I can only scratch the surface in this section. My goal here is only to introduce the concept and alert you to its potential implications in server design.

A thread is a generalization of the concept of a process. If we consider the UNIX process model, each process is more or less a world unto itself. It has its own virtual memory, its own file descriptors, and its own set of unique operating system resources. When you create a new process, by typing a command at your command interpreter, for example, an immensely complex and time-consuming sequence of events happens, which initializes all those resources, carves out a hunk of virtual memory, and does many other things which you probably never think about (and shouldn't). In short, there is a lot of context to a process.

There are many situations in which it is undesirable to have a lot of context or "state" information. More global context usually translates into more code complexity, larger memory requirements, and poorer performance. If you have ever tried to work on a system with hundreds or thousands of other processes running, you have had firsthand experience with this. There are many situations in which you would like to have many independent streams of control, each with only a tiny amount of local context. Massively parallel computers can do such things in hardware, but it is often desirable to be able to do similar things in software on machine with only a single CPU.

Threads were created to permit many small, independent streams of control, and have now become a standard part of many operating systems. Some implement threads in the OS itself, while others implement them in a user library. In fact, some operating systems, such as Mac and Windows NT, use threads rather than traditional "processes" to schedule most user activity. Threads are sometimes called lightweight processes. The basic features of threads include the ability to create many of them quickly, to have at least the illusion of independent, concurrent execution, and to provide a small local context while still allowing an access mechanism for a shared, global context.

Threads are an intrinsic part of DCE. In DCE, they are called pthreads, since they originally came from a public domain implementation of a proprietary thread-like library. We have already seen that DCE's exception mechanism is built on pthreads. DCE also supports multithreaded servers. This means that it is possible for a DCE server to be constructed so that server operations are executed concurrently, rather than sequentially.

As you are already aware, client RPC calls to a server are executed in a nondeterministic manner. If two clients are connected to the same server and both execute an RPC, it cannot be predicted which one will execute first; so a good server must be designed in such a way that it does not have to rely upon any particular sequence of operations. It is quite possible for a server to get a `close()` RPC before an `open()` RPC because the `close()` could be coming from the second client, while the `open()` is coming from the first. Chapter 11, "Techniques for Developing RPC Clients and Servers," has an extensive discussion of the importance of orthogonal design and server state, most of which applies to DCE as well.

In DCE, client remote procedure calls can become completely concurrent, thanks to threads. If a traditional RPC server is executing one procedure on behalf of a client, it is completely blocked from doing anything else. In particular, it cannot process other clients' requests. In a DCE server, it is possible to arrange that each incoming client request create a separate thread, which exists only for the duration of its execution. Since threads execute concurrently, this means that a DCE server may receive and process a request from one client while it is servicing another. In fact, the first argument to the `rpc_server_listen()` is the number of simultaneous threads that the DCE libraries will allow. If this value is given as 1, then a traditional, single-threaded, blocking server is created. If this number is anything else, then a multi-threaded server results.

The difficulty with threads revolves around the question of state. If the server has any state, then it must be managed in a way that prevents thread collisions. Just as two UNIX processes that have access to a piece of shared memory can collide if they both attempt to write to that memory at the same time, two threads can collide if they attempt to access some part of the server state at the same time.

There are several tools that may be used to avoid this type of collision. The server may send some or all of its state back to the client, using a context handle. A context handle is nothing more than a data structure that has been designed into the interface and that contains the application specific context that a particular client needs to maintain between calls to the server. In the file access example that I gave in the last section, the identifier returned from the `open()` procedure is an example of the type of state information that must be preserved from call to call within the client. Context handles also include binding information, so that explicit binding becomes mandatory.

Even with context handles the server may still need to keep some information in global variables. DCE threads provide a rich set of data protection functions that can be used to protect global data against multiple access. These are used just as you would use a file or record lock to coordinate access to some shared resource. Chapter 16, "Understanding the OSF DCE Services," covers DCE semaphores, mutexes, and condition variables in more detail.

III

Introduction to DCE

You will probably want to start out with single-threaded servers. This will simplify your development and debugging, and will also help you focus on the design issues inherent in your application. Once you have an operational server with more than one client, you should begin to consider how threads might be used. Even if you think that you will never implement a multithreaded server, it is still a good idea to design your server data structures and state so as not to preclude using threads in the future.

From Here...

You have now been thoroughly exposed to all the major components of DCE. You know how to design a well-constructed and robust client, how to write a server tailored to your application's needs, and how to bind the two together. You have also had a glimpse of some of the more advanced aspects of DCE. To learn more about DCE and client/server design in general, refer to these chapters:

- Chapter 11, "Techniques for Developing RPC Clients and Servers," discusses client/server design issues within the context of the simpler, but more limited, RPC approach.

- Chapter 14, "DCE Security," describes the robust security facilities of DCE.

- Chapter 16, "Understanding the OSF DCE Services," gives you detailed information on actually implementing DCE clients and servers.

Chapter 16

Understanding the OSF DCE Services

This chapter contains a discussion of the Open Software Foundation's Distributed Computing Environment (DCE) release 1.0x and 1.1. It describes the DCE services and how to use them in a distributed heterogeneous enterprise-wide computing environment.

This chapter discusses the following concepts:

- RPC facility

- Threads facility

- Directory service

- Security Service

- Distributed Time Service

- Distributed File Service

- Common DCE facilities

DCE Overview

DCE provides a set of integrated tools, facilities and services that enable the creation, implementation, and support of distributed applications in a mixed (heterogeneous) hardware, software, and networking environment. DCE's services are well-integrated and comprehensive in scope and functionality. DCE also supports data sharing through its directory service and distributed file service. In addition, DCE provides connectivity and interoperability with the world outside DCE by providing Global Directory access to both X.500 and the Internet Domain Naming Service (DNS).

The DCE Cell

DCE has the notion of a cell—a collection of machines running DCE are part of a cell or domain if they share the same Security, CDS (Cell Directory Service), DTS (Distributed Time Service), and, optionally, DFS (Distributed File Service) servers. The DNS/X.500 are separate domains or namespaces and are not strictly speaking part of a DCE cell. In DCE 1.0.x, the cell had one name only—DNS or X.500. In DCE 1.1, cells can have both a DNS and a X.500 name (with differing syntax) at the same time, as well as a primary name and any number of cell name aliases.

> **Note**
>
> The RPC and Threads services are not considered to be confined to a specific cell; they are the underlying services the cells and the cell-specific services (DSS, CDS, DTS, and optionally, DFS) use.

DCE Packaging, Tools, Facilities, and Services

DCE contains packages for DCE application development and the DCE Runtime (also known as the DCE Runtime Executive). DCE provides different types of tools for application development and DCE cell administration. DCE components consist of facilities and services. DCE facilities are of the following two types:

- Application programming facilities—These include the DCE RPC and Threads and their associated libraries and application programming interfaces (APIs).

- Common facilities that support multiple service components—These include the DCE Control Program (dcecp), DCE Host Services, the Application Message Service, Serviceability, and the Backing Store Databases.

DCE services are long running processes or daemons that reside on one or more machines in a DCE cell and include the following:

- Directory Service

- Security Service

- Distributed Time Service

- Distributed File Service

DCE and Distributed Computing Models

DCE is standards-based and provides three types of distributed computing models: client/server for application distribution, the remote procedure call to enable clients to find servers, and the data sharing model. In a traditional, host-based system, all of the computing capabilities and services are memory resident ones, typically on one platform with a single CPU. Distributed computing extends the host-based service model to nodes located across the network, each with its own CPU, memory, and storage.

On a host-based system, there is no need for a remote procedure call. Instead, the system facilities and services communicate between each other using some form of interprocess communications (IPC). The distributed computing model extends the host-based paradigm by allowing some or all of the various facilities and services to run remotely on separate processors connected by a network. To some degree, DCE can be thought of as a network operating system that consists of a number of processes running on a number of hosts or nodes. DCE is designed to fulfill the requirements of a distributed model of computing. At the same time, DCE is engineered to be scaleable, extensible and portable, while providing a high degree of reliability, availability, and serviceability (RAS) from a software perspective.

To summarize, DCE threads based on a POSIX draft are designed to be an efficient and flexible mechanism for providing concurrency within a process. DCE threads are used by other DCE components including the RPC and the OSF Distributed File System (DFS). Using threads causes changes in the way programs are designed, coded, and tested because the ability to have concurrency in both clients and servers opens up a whole new, and hopefully better, way of programming distributed applications.

RPC Facility

At the heart of the DCE model resides the Remote Procedure Call, or RPC. The RPC is used as the communication vehicle among the various DCE facilities and services. The RPC can be thought of as the equivalent of a dial tone

III

Introduction to DCE

on a telephone because it is used to establish and verify connectivity to a network. However, unlike a simple dial tone, the RPC provides key capabilities including:

◀ See "Network Protocols in General," p. 81

◀ See "Stubs," p. 200

◀ See "Binding," p. 202

■ Data marshalling and data conversion as part of the RPC stub routines

■ The high-level transport mechanism over one or more network protocols

■ The mechanism for clients to bind to (locate) one or more servers across the network

Figure 16.1 shows how RPCs function within DCE.

Fig. 16.1
A DCE RPC function travels from a client to a server and back.

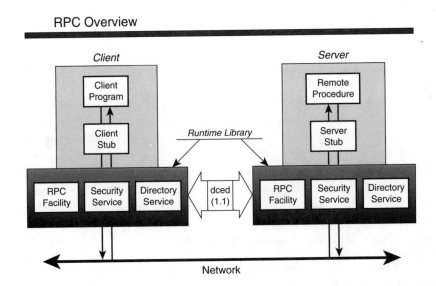

Fundamentally, the DCE RPC is a high-level transport that is network protocol transparent (for example, from the OSI transport layer of the OSI network architecture). Another popular high-level transport is the message-passing mechanism—sometimes referred to as "messaging," but this can be confused with store and forward mechanisms like e-mail.

Both RPC and message-passing transports are important, and each has its unique benefits and limitations. In an RPC, you send a packet, wait, and receive a packet back. In a message-passing system, you send a packet, and that's it. However, RPCs and message-passing are complements of each other (they are both based on sockets). Both have a place in building distributed applications. It is up to the application designers and programmers to decide when to use either RPCs or message-passing mechanisms (DCE 1.0x-1.1 supports the RPC only). It is likely that a future version of DCE will support both the RPC as well as the message-passing transports.

> **Note**
>
> Chapter 2, "OSI Network Architecture and Objectives," explains the OSI seven-layer model of network architecture.

Threads Facility

The DCE threads facility is a user space or kernel space, library implementation based on the POSIX 1003.4a (draft) standard. The use of threads allow a program to perform tasks in parallel, if desired (see fig. 16.2). For example, each time a client issues a new RPC call, a thread is created and attached to the RPC during its life span. When the RPC terminates, the thread is released. Threads execute and progress independently within a single address space (no additional malloc is requested; there is no additional process overhead). Multithreaded processes have multiple points of execution at an instance of time. Unlike other DCE components, threads are a local (non-networked) facility that are application- and platform-specific.

Using Threads with RPCs

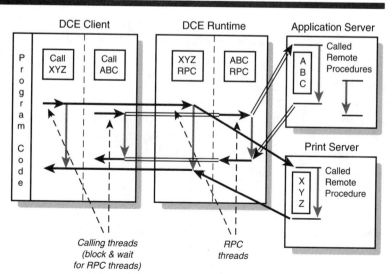

Calling threads
(block & wait
for RPC threads)

RPC
threads

Fig. 16.2

Threads allow RPCs to operate in parallel and not have to operate sequentially.

Unlike the single-threaded programming model, the use of threads allows a developer to have multiple RPCs in progress simultaneously that may or may not have synchronization dependencies on each other. For example, one thread may be reading a record from a remote database, while another may be spooling output to a printer, and a third thread may be awaiting I/O from an input device. It should be noted that the DCE runtime itself uses threads. The implication is that DCE clients and servers are already multithreaded. The decision to write applications that use threads is determined by the designer and/or the developer. Using threads in a program will add complexity and will require programmers to think about concurrent processes instead of the traditional single, sequential line of program execution.

Programmers must manage threads, make choices about thread scheduling and priorities, synchronize the global resources accessed by threads, and handle error conditions. In short, writing multi-threaded programs requires a new set of practices that are not intuitive to traditional programmers. End users should not be aware that threads are being used in an application except that an application with threads properly implemented should run faster than the same application without threads (this is very application-specific and will have to be ascertained on a case by case basis).

DCE threads are used by the other DCE components and may be based on user-space threads that the DCE library provides, or on operating system level kernel threads (this is a vendor implementation determination). That is, if DCE is ported to a modern, kernel threads-based operating system, DCE will be able to use that operating system's threads libraries. For operating systems that do not support kernel-level threads, the DCE threads library can be used. For a minimal diagram of how threads operate, see figure 16.3.

Another important note about the use of threads is that the libraries provided by system vendors and third parties, ISVs have to be thread-safe, or reentrAnt. That is, these libraries need to support concurrent multi-threaded access. If they do not, DCE provides a compatibility feature known as "wrapper routines" that essentially result in single threading an operating system or library call. DCE threads call the jacket routines which, in turn, issue the calls to the non-threaded resource. This mechanism prevents threads from blocking an entire process that uses interrupts or signal mechanisms.

Access to shared variables must be synchronized in order to prevent "race" conditions (when two or more threads attempt an operation on a shared variable and each thread is trying to complete before the other thread can start). DCE threads communicate through the use of sharable synchronization objects that are either mutual exclusion (mutexes) or condition variables.

Simple Threads Example

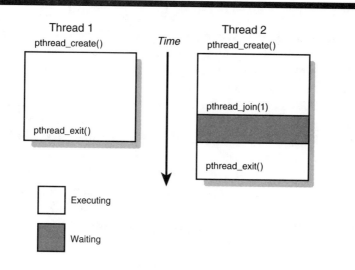

Fig. 16.3
A diagram of a
simple thread.

A mutex is a variable that is used to ensure the integrity of shared resources accessed by multiple threads. A mutex is either locked or unlocked and is purely advisory (for example, all threads using the shared resource must follow the same rules). A thread locks its corresponding mutex before accessing a shared resource. When it has completed its operation, the thread unlocks the mutex so that another thread can use it. If another thread requests to lock the mutex that is already locked, the calling thread must wait.

A condition variable enables a thread to block itself from executing pending an event interrupt (for example, non-UNIX wake-up signal) from another thread indicating that shared data is in a particular state. Programmers must associate a mutex with each condition variable used.

Directory Service

In a distributed computing environment, network transparency and location independence are two highly useful capabilities. Network transparency refers to the ability of users to not have to know or care where their servers (service providers) physically reside. Location independence refers to the ability to separate the location of the object (or thing) from the object itself. Unfortunately, most distributed or client/server systems in use today rely on the notion of a configuration file or hard-coded addresses to point their clients to the desired servers (databases, fileservers, print servers, etc.). In DCE, network transparency and location independence are provided by the Directory Service (also sometimes referred to generically as a naming service).

The DCE Directory Services is composed of the Cell Directory Service (CDS), the Global Directory Service, either the Internet Domain Naming Service (DNS) or an implementation of OSI's X.500. The Cell Directory Service contains a secure and replicated namespace or database and supports name-based queries from clients attempting to locate servers. CDS is designed to contain data that doesn't change frequently. As a result, CDS uses caching of binding information at the DCE client which is not dynamically updated when a server deregisters itself from CDS in a controlled manner, or when it terminates abnormally. Replication of CDS partitions within a DCE cell permit a high degree of availability and to some extent, load balancing (although this is not built in to CDS). Partitioning allows information to be stored in different servers' physical disk locations. CDS has a sophisticated update propagation mechanism that allows changes to the CDS master to be sent to CDS replicas within a single cell.

DCE applications and DCE components (Security Service, Distributed Time Service, DFS) use CDS as their location information repository in order for clients to obtain binding information for available servers. The DCE Directory Service allows both name-based and network-based identification information to be stored, queried, and to have relevant associated attributes and data retrieved for use by the client process. It also provides a global, unified namespace. For example, named resources in one cell can be accessed from other cells. A client process in cell A can find and use (security permitting) an application server in cell B. Part of the reason this can be accomplished is that the DCE Name Service Interface (NSI) puts a fully qualified name including the cell name into CDS. As mentioned earlier, the DCE Directory Service is a two-level (tier) naming architecture (see fig. 16.4). Junctions are used by DCE to connect its various namespaces together.

Fig. 16.4
DCE uses a two-tier directory structure to allow processes in one cell to see resources in another cell.

Two Tier Directory Service Architecture

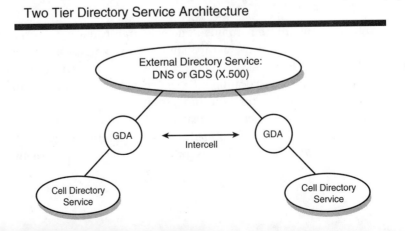

The first tier is composed of CDS servers that run within a particular cell. When an RPC is sent from the client process, the local CDS server in cell A attempts to resolve the reference within its own namespace based partly on the cell name prefix. If the name resolution is successful, no external directory service RPCs are made. If unsuccessful, an RPC request is sent via the DCE Global Directory Agent (GDA) process to the external directory service (either DNS or X.500) for resolution. DNS/X.500 looks into its namespace for the pathname of the external cell name's CDS server in cell B. The CDS server in cell B's role is to look into its namespace to resolve the application server location request and return the binding information back to the requesting client in cell A. All of this is done automatically by DCE once the cell relationships have been established through DNS/X.500 and CDS.

In DCE 1.0x releases, CDS had a single level (or flat) namespace. DCE 1.1 extends this structure by enabling cells to have a hierarchy of cells as related sets of parent/child cells. A cell's root can now be placed within another cell instead of being restricted to a DNS/X.500 global namespace (see fig. 16.5). With the hierarchical cell capability in DCE 1.1 comes the security mechanism of transitive trust that will be described in the DCE Security section later.

DCE 1.1 Namespace

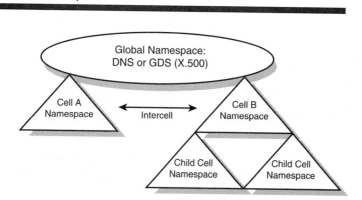

Fig. 16.5
In DCE 1.1, cells are not required to descend directly from the global namespace.

DCE 1.1 also added cell aliasing capabilities to CDS. Cell aliasing enables, for the first time, DCE cell names to be changed. It also provides a mechanism for multiple cell aliases where the cell has a single primary name with any number of alias names that can be used to refer to it.

CDS is composed of several components (see fig. 16.6):

III

Introduction to DCE

■ CDS Server—A server process (cdsd for CDS daemon) that runs on one (or more using replication) physical node on the network. CDS contains a namespace built on top of one or more database clearinghouses.

■ CDS Clerk—A client process that typically runs on a client-only node whose role is to act as the intermediary between DCE client applications and CDS servers regarding binding information. The CDS clerk maintains a local cache of binding information that is incrementally built via CDS queries. The design goal is for DCE client applications to look in the local cache before going over the wire to CDS, which is relatively expensive and time-consuming. The CDS client writes the cache to disk periodically to provide some backup in the event of a local system failure.

■ .CDS Advertiser—A client facility that works with the CDS Clerk whose role is to act as the intermediary between the CDS Clerk and the CDS Server. The CDS Advertiser maintains the network address of the CDS Server so that the CDS Client can find it.

■ CDS administration programs (detailed in the following section).

Fig. 16.6
CDS is composed
of several
interrelated
components.

Cell Directory Service Components

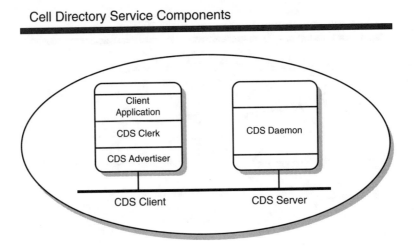

The DCE CDS is accessible interactively using four command line interfaces, or programmatically using APIs. Interactive access to CDS includes:

■ dcecp (part of DCE 1.1)—The DCE control program based on the Task Control Language (Tcl) that provides a single administrative shell for managing DCE.

- `cdscp`—The CDS control program that manages CDS clerks and servers.

- CDS namespace browser—OSF's Motif-based tool for viewing (but not updating) the structure and content of CDS namespaces.

- `acl_edit`—The DCE Access Control List editor, used across DCE components, manages access to CDS clearinghouses and their contents.

Programmatic access to DCE's Directory Service includes:

- Name Service Interface (NSI) API—Used by DCE principals to import and export binding information for clients and servers (part of the DCE RPC). The NSI works with three types of entries within the Directory Service database:

    Server entry—Interface and binding information used by a client to access a particular server.

    Group entry—Contains names of server entries or other group entries that have a common interface and/or object.

    Profile entry—Contains specified search paths through the database for server entries, group entries, or other profile entries that have a particular interface and/or object. Profiles contain priority attributes that specify the order in which entries are searched (clients use these to access entries first by their priority number then by their sequential ordering within each priority).

- X/Open's Directory Services (XDS) API—Used by applications to access X.500 services and advanced CDS capabilities. XDS provides facilities for creating, modifying, deleting, and looking up names and attributes.

CDS Database Structure

Each DCE cell must have at least one and preferably more CDS servers. The Directory Service (for example, CDS) maintains three types of data elements or entries:

- Clearinghouses—One or more physical CDS databases that manages a collection of directories assigned to it. It should be noted that the tree-structured naming hierarchy is independent of the directories' locations. Copies of directories can be held in different clearinghouses but one clearinghouse must be designated as the master with one or more designated as read-only replicas. CDS has mechanisms for maintaining consistency across replicas.

■ Directories—A logical grouping of CDS information usually consisting of directory entries and directory replicas.

■ Directory Entries—Consists of an entry name and its attributes.

Services Related to the DCE Directory Service

In DCE, there are two services that relate to the Directory Service—search paths and unique names for objects. The ability to specify a search path is provided by the DCE RPC and is used for looking up names in the CDS namespace. This is accomplished through the use of RPC profiles (discussed earlier). Depending on how the RPC profiles are set up, they can be used to designate search priority or to logically associate a resource name to a particular location. The common example of this is to set up profiles for network printers based on their physical location (by building, floor, and so on).

The second related service, unique names for objects, is provided by a DCE Universal Unique Identifier (UUID) facility. Virtually all DCE objects have a UUID assigned to them. This association takes place either when DCE creates an object or, for application development, through an interactive utility called uuidgen. Each instance of a UUID is guaranteed to be unique in time and space (a UUID can never be duplicated). UUIDs are one of the key aspects of DCE that assist in naming DCE objects in a distributed environment and provide the basis of object-orientation for DCE.

However, DCE's object-orientation should not be confused with object-oriented standards and/or object frameworks like OMG's CORBA and Microsoft's COM. In the future, DCE itself may be extended to include a full object model based on either or both of these emerging object frameworks. In the meantime, DCE today can provide the interoperability layer for either CORBA or COM based products from various vendors.

Security Service

A distributed computing environment is designed to encourage the free-flow of data and/or information as well as the sharing of resources and services in the network by secure, trusted parties. However, it is well known that computer networks and the nodes attached to them are vulnerable to security threats from unknown and potentially unfriendly intruders. Some of these threats include the following:

■ Impersonation or masquerade—An entity pretends to be someone else (assumes its identity).

- Data modification—An entity intercepts and modifies, at some point, data being sent over the wire between the sender and the intended receiver.

- Data privacy or confidentiality—An entity intercepts and reads sensitive data being sent over the wire between the sender and the intended receiver.

The DCE Security Service provides a series of mechanisms designed to ensure that distributed resources are only accessible by properly identified and authorized users. These mechanisms are:

- Authentication—Proving to DCE that you are who you claim to be. DCE requires clients and servers to have their identities mutually authenticated via a trusted third party (the DCE Security server).

- Authorization—Authentication answers the question of who I am. Authorization answers the question of what, given my identity and associated privileges, I am allowed to do when I request access to a given server. In DCE, the server decides whether or not to grant access to a requester of its resources (program processes, files, directories, etc.). The DCE authorization checking mechanism is based on the POSIX 1003.6 (draft) Access Control Lists (ACLs). DCE ACLs are a superset of POSIX that provide extensions designed to make them more useful in a distributed security environment.

- Data integrity and data privacy—Are features provided in authenticated DCE RPCs (see Chapter 8, "Authentication"). Data integrity ensures that, while data can be read, it may not be modified in transit over the wire between the sender and the intended receiver. Data privacy ensures that sensitive data may not be read by an eavesdropper on the network. When data privacy is specified, full encryption is used to protect every data packet sent over the wire. In DCE the current cryptographic mechanism used is the Data Encryption Standard (DES).

DCE's underlying security mechanisms for authentication and data integrity/data privacy are based on the Kerberos 5 network authentication service from MIT's Project Athena. The DCE implementation is modified to use the DCE RPC facility as the communication mechanism between components of the Security Service. The structure of DSS (Distributed Security Service) is shown in figure 16.7.

III

Introduction to DCE

Fig. 16.7

The components
of DSS use RPCs
(not shown) to
work together.

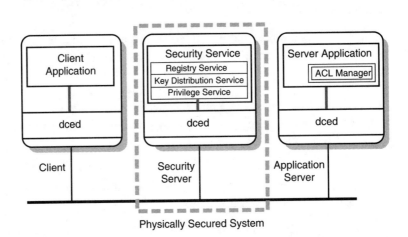

DCE 1.1 Security Components

Physically Secured System

All of the DCE Services are designed to make use of DSS' discretionary controls. Application designers and developers can choose the level of security that meets their requirements. The DCE Security Service, like the Cell Directory Service, uses the concept of a cell and has its own namespace. Furthermore, CDS is used to establish, via a junction in its namespace, the Security Service's definition of the cell (the unit and scope of the DCE Security Service). Every DCE cell contains one master Security server (shown in the center of figure 16.7) with one or more read-only replicas or slaves. DCE supports the notion of a trusted computing base and implements this via the Security Service in conjunction with the DCE Distributed Time Service (discussed later). The DCE Security Service's Registry contains a database of the following:

- *Principals*—An entry used to define a human user or machine/process by name and UUID.

- *Groups*—An entry used to define a collection of associated principals by name and UUID (groups can be logically associated with virtually anything that makes sense for your organization).

- *Organizations*—An entry used to associate a set of principals to a real department, cost center, etc. The organization entry is currently used primarily for documentation purposes.

- *Accounts*—An entry used to associate principals with local as well as foreign cell accounts.

- *Policies*—An entry that defines the cell security policies.

Principals, groups, and organizations (PGOs) are defined in the Security Registry by the Cell Administrator. Every principal (a human user or a server machine/process) must be defined to a local or home cell. Principals and groups can also be defined as foreign entries within other DCE cells, if DCE intercell communication and security has been set up to allow this access to occur. Once a principal has been authenticated, the DCE Security Service's authorization mechanism is used to determine what actions or operations that principal (local or foreign) is allowed to perform on a particular resource (DCE ACLs provide a very fine level of access control within a cell). Every DCE object is associated with an ACL, and each ACL consists of a list of entries that define who has what permissions for a particular object.

In order for an application server to perform authorization, an ACL Manager must be used (DCE's CDS and DFS implement ACL managers as well). The role of the ACL Manager is to extract the UUIDs of the client wishing to access a particular resource from the Privilege Attribute Certificate (PAC) and compare them to the UUIDs stored in an object's ACL. If the permissions match, the client can proceed with its requested operation, otherwise the server rejects the request because the client is not authorized.

> **Note**
>
> In DCE 1.1, an Extended PAC or EPAC is used in place of the PAC (the data structure of an EPAC is different from a pre DCE 1.1 PAC). In a mixed DCE 1.0x and DCE 1.1+ environment, the EPAC may be effectively truncated due to the data structure differences. More to the point, new security features introduced in DCE 1.1, like delegation, may not work in a mixed DCE release configuration.

The DCE RPC facility is fully integrated with the DCE Security Service. All of the Security Service's features are available to the programmer so that the best use of authentication, data integrity and data privacy and authorization become design considerations during distributed application development. DCE clients choose the type and level of security services required, and the DCE server (CDS, DFS) and/or the DCE application server determines whether or not to grant access to a resource depending on what was specified by the client as part of its RPC setup routines.

In order for an authenticated client to access a server, that server must first have exported its binding information (for example, a name) into CDS. The authenticated client performs a CDS search in order to locate and import the server's binding information from one or more CDS entries (an interface may be supported by one or more servers). One or more (if replication is used)

III

Introduction to DCE

CDS servers in the cell may be searched before the specified entry is located and returned to the requesting client. Assuming that the client has a valid ticket from the appropriate security server, the client can issue an authenticated RPC to request service from a particular server that supports the desired interface(s).

The DCE 1.0x Security Service established the functional baseline for supporting the requirements of a distributed security environment. DCE 1.1 adds some significant new capabilities to this framework including:

- *Extended Registry Attributes*—The Registry database's attribute schema has been expanded to include both user specified attributes that can be used to store legacy system security attributes (e.g., for single sign-on), as well as DCE client credentials to support secure delegation.

- *Secure Delegation*—A client's identity and credentials can be passed to a server that, in turn, acts as a client to a second server. Each time there is a delegation along a security trust chain, all of the identities and credentials of every participant is appended into the Extended Privilege Attribute Certificate (EPAC) by using the ERA schema.

- *Hierarchical Cells*—Allow parent/child relationships to be defined within a cell as well as the ability to have transitive trust within the relationships. In DCE 1.0x, the cell namespace is flat. This changed in DCE 1.1 by allowing child cells to be rooted in the parent cell namespace. This new structure simplifies the exchange of security keys by enabling a parent's trusted siblings to communicate securely without performing an additional key exchange.

- *Support for X/Open's Generic Security Service API (GSSAPI)*—Allows non DCE RPC based clients to access the DCE Security Service for authentication and credential issuing purposes. GSSAPI is a programmatic interface that allows various security mechanisms to access DCE Security without having to use the DCE RPC as a transport (although the GSSAPI does convert the non DCE RPC request into a DCE RPC in order to comply with the DCE RPC access to the DCE Security Service).

- *Extended Login Capabilities*—DCE 1.0x introduced the DCE Login Facility that is used to login and initialize a user's DCE Security Service environment. When a user login has been authenticated, the DCE Security Service returns the user security credentials that are used to access other DCE services such as the Distributed File System (DFS). DCE 1.1 added new capabilities to the DCE Login process including: pre-authentication, password management (strength-testing, re-use, and so on), and the ability to require that servers be accessed only from trusted machines.

■ *ACL Manager Support*—In DCE 1.0x, it was very difficult for developers to implement an ACL Manager for authorization checking. In DCE 1.1, an ACL Manager library coupled with a general ACL backing store database greatly simplifies the writing of application-related ACL Managers.

■ *Audit Facility*—In DCE 1.0x, there were no audit capabilities. In DCE 1.1, an audit facility is provided to detect and record changes to the Security Service Registry database as well as changes to the Distributed Time Service (DTS). DCE application programmers can also build auditing into their DCE servers by specifying code points within security related operations where auditing is required. The Audit API is used to enable auditing to take place on designated operations. DCE cell administrators can tailor and fine-tune the recording of events using event class and filter mechanisms to produce audit trails (for example, files).

The DCE Security Service is accessible interactively using several command line interfaces or programmatically using APIs. Interactive access includes the following:

■ dcecp (part of DCE 1.1)—The DCE control program based on the Task Control Language (Tcl) that provides a single administrative shell for managing DCE services.

■ rgy_edit—The DCE Security Registry editor used for adding, modifying and deleting principals, groups, etc.

■ sec_admin—The DCE Security administration program.

■ kinit, klist, and kdestroy—DCE supported Kerberos user commands. The Kerberos API is used internally by DCE Security but is not exposed to developers. The Authenticated RPC API is used to programmatically access Kerberos features.

■ acl_edit—The DCE Access Control List editor, used across DCE components, that manages access to Security service-based objects.

Distributed Time Service

In a traditional host-centric system, there is one concept of time (the host's internal clock). In a distributed system, each node on the network has its own concept of time based on the internal clock. As a result, each node has a different concept of what the common notion of time is (each node is self-referencing and doesn't talk to other systems to coordinate its time). In a query-based information access system like a data warehouse, the processor's notion of time may not be relevant. However, as soon as data and information can become dynamically updated, a common notion of time is critical. Timestamps need to be generated for system and application level objects (records, files, transactions, and so on). In order to achieve synchronization of time-sensitive events occurring across different nodes, it is required that every node agree on the same concept of the current time.

DCE addresses this problem through the use of the Distributed Time Service (DTS). DTS provides time synchronization mechanisms to allow:

- Distributed hosts to periodically synchronize their internal clocks.

- The synchronized time to be relatively and reasonably accurate with Universal Time Coordinate (UTC), a worldwide standard.

It is impractical to have continuous time synchronization across distributed host nodes in the network. There are two reasons for this. First, there is some processing overhead and network traffic required when synchronization occurs. Second, there is a network propagation delay or latency from the point of the master time server to all of its dependents. As a result, DTS contains an inaccuracy factor that is reasonably close to the actual time. This requires DTS or similar mechanisms in a distributed environment to not only perform synchronization but to introduce a new timestamp format that includes a range or interval of inaccuracy.

DTS is composed of a number of components including:

- *DTS Time Format*—DTS uses 128-bit binary timestamps that include: inaccuracy value, time zone difference, daylight savings indicator, etc.

- *DTS Clerks*—A process that runs on DCE client machines. The DTS Clerk's role is to keep track of the node's time based on the UTC. The Clerk requests time synchronization on a periodic basis from DTS Servers.

- *DTS Servers* of the following types:

    Local—DTS servers within a single DCE cell that synchronize UTC time with each other (preferably three instances).

    Global—DTS servers that are located (using the Directory Service) across DCE cells (connected via LANs or WANs).

    Courier—A designated DTS server that acts as the time synchronization "agent" between the Global and Local DTS servers.

- *DTS Backup Courier Servers*—Alternate DTS Couriers that provide high availability for Local and Global time server communications and time synchronization.

- *The DTS API*—Allows programmers to code applications that work with the DTS timestamps.

- *The Time Provider Interface (TPI)*—Describes how a time provider (e.g., using the Network Time Protocol or NTP) can pass time values to a DTS server.

- *Time Provider Servers*—A designated DTS server that connects to the UTC Time Provider (e.g., an Internet link to NTP) using the Time Provider Interface. The TPS imports the true UTC time value and uses this to synchronize all associated DTS servers (Local, Global, and Courier).

The DCE Distributed Time Service is accessible interactively using several command line interfaces or programmatically using the DTS API. Interactive access includes the following:

- `dcecp` (part of DCE 1.1)—The DCE control program based on the Task Control Language (Tcl) that provides a single administrative shell for managing DCE services.

- `dtscp`—The DTS control program.

- `acl_edit`—The DCE Access Control List editor, used across DCE components, that manages access to DTS-based objects.

DTS server configuration is highly site-dependent and varies depending on the network architecture. The DTS server topology is hierarchical in nature with the top of the tree being responsible for determining and propagating the UTC time values down to the DTS Clerks. DTS is closely integrated with the DCE components, most notably the Security Service. DTS uses the DCE RPC facility as well as the Directory Service (to locate DTS servers).

Distributed File Service

The DCE Distributed File Service (DFS) is a DCE application that manages various information (for example, the file system structure) within its namespace. DFS is built on and uses the DCE services (Security and Directory) and facilities (RPC and Threads). DFS provides a real-time, highly available service structure for creating, maintaining, and propagating file system entities across heterogeneous systems. DFS manages files and directories, and provides access to them from authorized DFS (and NFS) clients. The components of DFS are shown in figure 16.8.

Fig. 16.8

The Distributed File Service provides a level of abstraction within the file system, making distributed file requests transparent to the user.

DFS Components

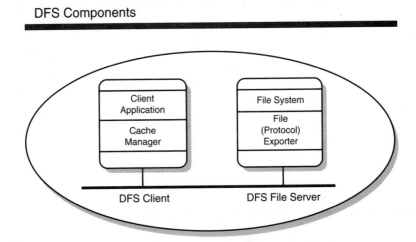

DFS is comprised of several components including:

- *Cache Manager*—Part of the DFS client whose role is to take a user-submitted file system request from a client application and look within the local cache for a copy of the requested data. If the Cache Manager doesn't locate the cached copy, it sends a request to the DFS File Server. By using local caches, network traffic as well as the load factor on DFS servers can be significantly reduced.

- *File Exporter*—A process that runs on the DFS File Server machine whose role is to handle client requests for files that it manages.

- *Token Manager*—A process that also runs on the DFS File Server machine whose role is to synchronize access to various files by multiple clients by issuing (typically read or write) tokens.

- *DCE-Based Local File System* (*LFS*)—The physical file system provided as part of DCE that manages file storage on disk. Although similar to the UNIX File System (UFS), LFS provides greater capabilities such as: replication, DCE ACL support, log-based fast re-start file system recovery, on-line back-up, and last but not least, DCE cell support and integration. The DCE LFS also complies with the POSIX 1003.1 standard.

> **Note**
>
> Replication of the DFS copies the filesets, which associate files and directories that may not reside on the same physical server, or within the same DCE cell, to other servers. Replication of filesets prevents one hardware failure from incapacitating the directory structure for an entire cell.

- *Fileset Server*—Allows DCE/DFS administrators to perform various fileset operations (create, move, update, delete, etc.).

- *Fileset Location Server*—Provides a fully replicated directory service whose role is to keep track of the File Server machine and the unit of disk storage (aggregate) where each DFS fileset resides. Users access filesets by name without knowing or caring where the fileset physically resides (provides location transparency).

- *Replication Server*—Handles the replication of filesets to provide high availability of DFS filesets on multiple systems.

- *Backup Server*—Used for backing up data (for example, filesets) located on the Fileset Server machines.

- *DFS/NFS Secure Gateway*—Provides authenticated access from NFS clients to DCE DFS. NFS users (who have DCE accounts) can use their DCE identities to have authenticated access to DFS data using a DFS client acting as a Secure Gateway.

The DCE Distributed File Service is accessible to administrators interactively using command line interfaces or programmatically using APIs. DFS administration is a non-trivial task due to the various processes that need to be set up and maintained for DFS. There is no standard DFS configuration—each setup is flexible and site-variable requiring a degree of planning and design on the part of the administrator. The typical tasks in administering DFS include fileset administration (relocation, on-line backup, and so on) and editing DFS ACLs. Fortunately, DFS has a set of administrative tools to aid in this process including the following:

- Scout—Provides DFS usage monitoring by collecting and displaying status information concerning the File Server machines' File Exporters.

- `dfstrace`—Allows DFS processes to be traced either in user-space or in the kernel and contains a set of commands for low-level debugging and diagnostics.

■ `acl_edit`—The DCE Access Control List editor, used across DCE components, which manages access to DFS-based objects.

Developers typically access DFS utilizing POSIX 1003.1 calls to the file system. Using DFS, programmers can write distributed applications without using the DCE RPC.

DFS supports information access and sharing on a worldwide basis, providing a single system image of the files and directories that it manages (see fig. 16.9).

Fig. 16.9
DFS allows access to other cells to appear as local activities.

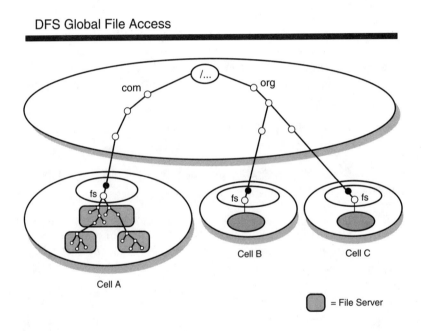

DFS Global File Access

Cell A

Cell B

Cell C

= File Server

Remote files are treated no differently than locally-resident files. This provides location independence, data transparency and user mobility. DFS can be thought of as the next generation NFS with its ability to provide real-time access to a real-time image of the file system. DFS can truly be considered a "killer" application for DCE.

Common DCE Facilities

Within DCE, certain facilities are used by or across a number of DCE services and are considered as common facilities. As mentioned previously, DCE 1.0x contains `acl_edit`, the DCE Access Control List editor which is used across

DCE components and manages access to the DCE Services' objects. DCE 1.1 provides additional DCE facilities including the DCE Control Program (dcecp), and DCE Host Services.

DCE Control Program (*dcecp*)

The DCE 1.1 Control Program (dcecp) was developed in response to DCE users' requests for improvements in administering DCE cells and components. The dcecp is built on the Berkeley Task Control Language (Tcl, pronounced "tickle"). Tcl is a portable command language that is the basis of the dcecp (the Tcl command interpreter is also provided so that users can write their own scripts). The dcecp uses an object-operation style syntax (object followed by an operation) that is combined with the DCE component tools (such as rpccp, cdscp, rgy_edit, sec_admin, acl_edit, and dtscp) to provide one seamless, DCE administrative shell. In short, dcecp's command-line interface is a much needed and very useful tool for administering and maintaining DCE cells and their components.

DCE Host Services

DCE 1.1 Host Services provide remote DCE system administration and management capabilities. In DCE 1.1, every DCE defined node runs a DCE daemon (dced) that provides the interface to Host Services. The dced provides services for the following:

- *Security Validation Service (SVS)*—Maintains a secure DCE login context for identifying DCE hosts. Provides certification for distributed applications that the DCE Security Daemon is legitimate and can therefore be trusted.

- *Endpoint Mapper Service (EMS)*—Maintains a local RPC database (for the endpoint mapper). The DCE RPC runtime facility uses this service to resolve binding information between DCE clients and servers.

- *Server Configuration and Execution Service (SCES)*—A DCE server control service that is part of dced. SCES enables DCE servers to be started and stopped either manually or automatically (will start a DCE server automatically, if it is not running, in order to fulfill an RPC request for service).

- *Key Table Management Service (KTMS)*—Allows for remote management of DCE server key tables and is used to add, change, and remove keys and the key table itself.

■ *Host Data Service* (*HDS*)—Used to manage the DCE node's hostdata objects. Typical hostdata operations include: adding, changing, listing and removing data items on DCE hosts. An additional hostdata operation, named catalog, allows you to list the names of all of the objects on the specified host.

From Here...

As was stated at the beginning of the chapter, DCE provides a set of integrated tools, facilities and services that enable the creation, implementation, and support of distributed applications in a mixed (heterogeneous) hardware, software, and networking environment. DCE's services are well-integrated and comprehensive in scope and functionality.

DCE is the vendor-neutral, de facto standard for building enterprise-wide distributed applications. Most system vendors, many ISVs, and end-user organizations have endorsed and adopted DCE, and DCE products and services are becoming widely available.

For more information on the topics discussed in this chapter, refer to the following:

■ Chapter 8, "Authentication," provides more information on authenticated RPCs.

■ Chapter 13, "What is DCE," gives you an introduction to DCE.

■ Chapter 14, "DCE Security," provides a more detailed examination of DCE's DSS (Distributed Security Services).

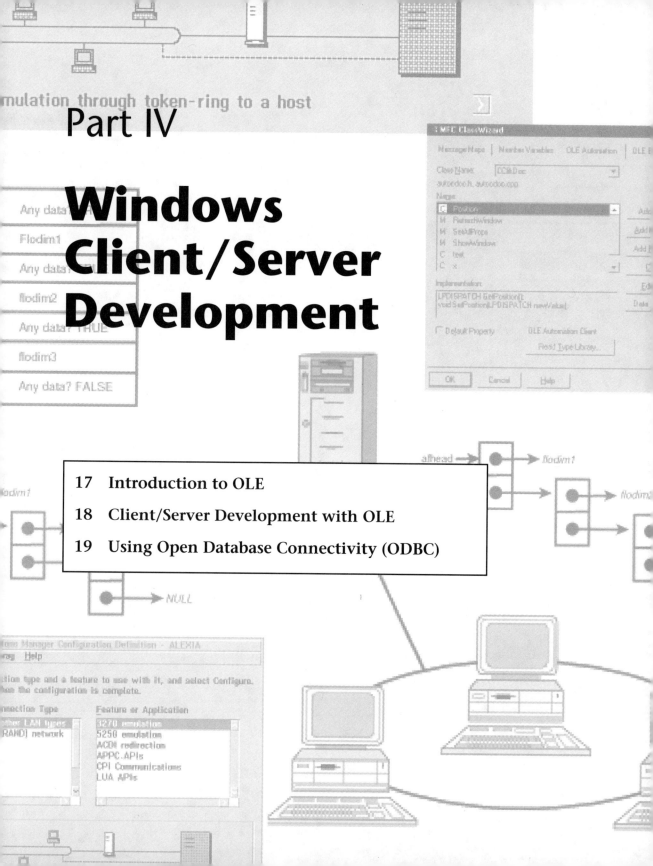

Part IV

Windows Client/Server Development

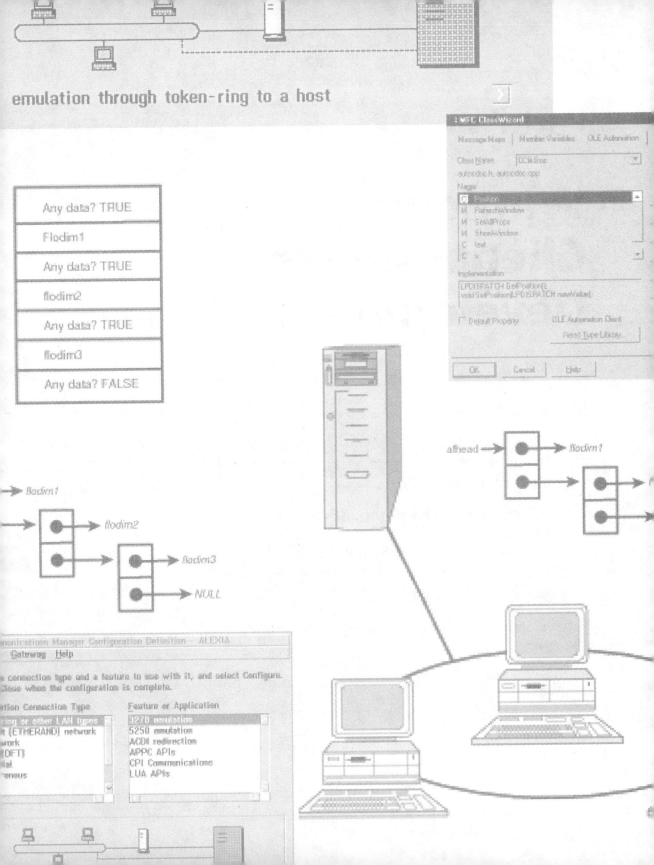

Any data? TRUE

Flodim1

Any data? TRUE

flodim2

Any data? TRUE

flodim3

Any data? FALSE

Chapter 17

Introduction to OLE

Microsoft's OLE technology is a major communication and interaction paradigm under Windows. It provides mechanisms for the exchange of data and
for application communication and interaction, as in a client/server model.
You will probably find that OLE is substantially different from the other
client/server paradigms that you have looked at so far.

While there is no way that one chapter can cover everything that OLE encompasses, this chapter will provide an introduction to OLE and cover its key
features. Specifically, you will look at:

- A brief history of OLE

- Overview of key features

- Document-oriented architecture

- Introduction to the Component Object Model

- OLE automation

Brief History of OLE

The primary idea behind the development of OLE was the desire for applications to easily integrate and interoperate. Microsoft made a first attempt at
application integration when it provided the *dynamic data exchange* (*DDE*)
specification. DDE was not a specific product or feature, but rather was a
protocol specification for how applications could communicate and share
data. Unfortunately, it proved to be rather difficult for both developers and
users.

In 1991, Microsoft released OLE 1.0, which was an attempt to provide an object-oriented application communication model for Windows. OLE 1.0 introduced the concepts of *compound documents*, and *linked* and *embedded* objects. These concepts provide a basis for application integration.

As with everything in a 1.0 release, there were problems with the OLE 1.0 libraries. There was little documentation and few code samples for developers. In addition, the OLE 1.0 system was built on top of DDE, so it inherited all the problems that were associated with DDE. In 1993, Microsoft released OLE 2.0. This release introduced many new features and fixed most of the problems associated with OLE 1.0.

Overview of OLE Features

The current release of OLE provides several mechanisms that are used for application integration. Some of these concepts have been around since OLE 1.0, while others were added when OLE 2.0 was released. Since the OLE paradigm is a bit different from other types of client/server communication systems, it is important that you understand these concepts.

Compound Documents

Under OLE, documents take on a new meaning. You're used to thinking of a document as being some data for a particular application, such as a letter written in a word processor. However, when using OLE, it makes more sense to think of a document as a storage repository for different types of data objects. You see, OLE provides the capability to store multiple data objects from different applications within the same document. A document that contains data objects from different applications is called a *compound document*.

There are two different ways of storing data objects with a compound document. The data can actually be completely stored within the document, in which case it is known as an *embedded* object. In addition to embedding an object, OLE allows you to just store path information that indicates the original source of the data. An object that has only path information stored is known as a *linked* object.

To activate an embedded or linked object from within the main document, you simply double-click the object. Windows will activate the OLE server application that is associated with the object, and allow you to edit the object.

Structured Storage

In order to manage the multiple data objects that can exist within a document, OLE 2.0 provides a structured storage mechanism for persistent objects.

> **Note**
>
> A *persistent object* is a data object that continues to exist after the application terminates. Under OLE, such an object would be the data that you created or modified with your application.

The OLE structured storage mechanism for compound documents provides an environment that looks much like a file system. It stores actual file data, known as *streams*, and directory information, known as *storages*. The compound document structured storage mechanism also keeps data objects from being written to the file until an application actually commits them. This feature is known as *transacted storages*.

In-Place Activation

OLE 2.0 provides an enhanced method of interacting with embedded objects via *in-place activation*. Also known as *visual editing*, in-place activation allows a user to double-click an embedded object and work with that object without having to use a different application program.

When an embedded object is activated in-place, the application that is needed in order to interact with the OLE object temporarily takes control of the document window. The various menus and controls of the object's application will temporarily replace the controls of the document window. See figure 17.1 for an example of in-place activation.

The obvious advantage to in-place activation is that objects created by different applications can easily be used and modified from a single location. There is no need for the user to switch between application windows in order to interact with different data objects.

IV

Windows Development

Fig. 17.1
This is an example
of in-place
activation of an
Excel spreadsheet
inside a Word for
Windows
document.

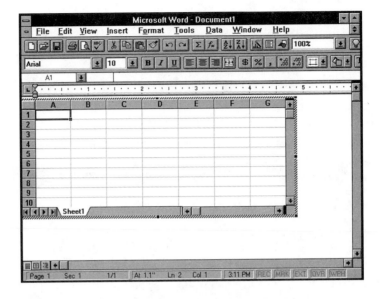

Lightweight Remote Procedure Calls

As you would expect, OLE provides a way for objects to communicate with
each other. The *Lightweight Remote Procedure Call (LRPC)* provides the object
communication mechanism. LRPC is designed to communicate between OLE
objects on the same server. It handles marshaling parameters and interprocess
interface calls, as well as translating calls and parameters between 16- and 32-
bit environments. Under the Distributed OLE environment, the LRPC system
has been replaced with a real remote procedure call subsystem. This allows
true RPC communication between client and server processes distributed on a
network. Figure 18.2 shows how the RPC and LRPC systems fit into the OLE
object system.

Fig. 17.2
LRPC and RPC
in the OLE
environment.

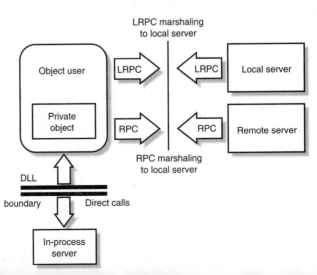

The Component Object Model

OLE is based on an object model known as the *Component Object Model* (*COM*). This model defines the basis for how OLE's components work and interact. While there are a lot of details to the Component Object Model that are beyond the scope of this chapter, we will try to give you an overview that will help you understand the COM and how it affects OLE's behavior (see fig. 17.3).

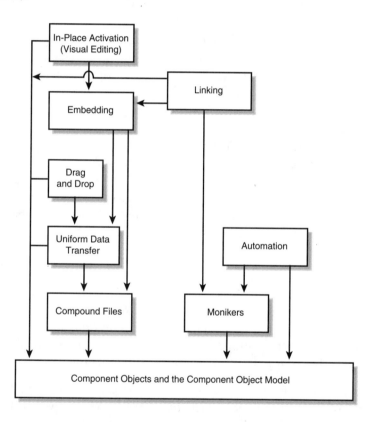

Fig. 17.3
OLE technologies and the Component Object Model.

Object Communication Interfaces

In OLE terminology, objects use *interfaces* to communicate with each other. An interface is basically a set of related functions that provide interobject communication. They provide a stable, published way for users to interact with OLE objects.

OLE objects are conceptually similar to C++ objects, except for a few important differences. Under OLE, all methods in an interface are public. There are no protected or private interface methods. Also, OLE objects don't allow direct data manipulation, nor do they support normal C++ style inheritance. OLE provides its own mechanisms for reusing objects.

In order to qualify as an object under the Component Object Model, an interface must support at least one special interface, known as IUnknown. In a manner similar to a C++ object, an interface has a definition header. The following code shows the interface definition for IUnknown:

```
interface IUnknown
{
      virtual HRESULT    QueryInterface(IID& iid, void **ppbObj)=0;
      virtual ULONG          AddRef()=0;
      virtual ULONG          Release()=0;
}
```

As you can see, all methods in this interface definition are virtual. The QueryInterface() method allows a user to query an object to see if it supports a particular interface. The AddRef() and Release() methods increment and decrement the object's reference count, respectively.

Reference Counting

Under OLE, a single object can be accessed by multiple clients. In order to keep track of how many clients are using an object, OLE uses *reference counting*. The idea behind reference counting is simple: when you start using an object, you increase the reference count of the object by one to indicate that another process is using the object. When you are finished with an object, you decrease its reference count by one. When an object's reference count reaches zero, the object can safely be destroyed.

The object itself is responsible for managing its own reference counts. The reference count value for an object is manipulated by a set of function calls. It is important that all processes that access OLE objects manage their reference count information correctly. If reference count information is not correct, objects may not be destroyed when they are supposed to, or they may inadvertently be destroyed while processes are still using them.

When you get a pointer to an interface via QueryInterface(), the object increments its own reference count by calling AddRef(). However, if you make a copy of this pointer, you will have to call AddRef() yourself to increment the counter again. When you finish with the pointer, you then call Release(), which decrements the reference count. Remember this basic rule: call AddRef() for each new copy of a pointer and Release() to destroy each pointer.

Aggregates and Delegates

In an object-oriented programming environment, programmers will typically want to reuse objects in the most effective way. A common way of achieving this is via *inheritance*. In inheritance, a primary object known as a *base class* implements a significant portion of the default behavior of an object. Programs then create new classes that are derived from the base class. These derived classes will inherit the default behavior defined in the base class and will either add new functions or override existing functions from the base class.

OLE takes a different track with regard to inheritance. The OLE environment attempts to make it possible to reuse objects between different organizations on different platforms. In order to do this, Microsoft provides two mechanisms for handling composite objects: *aggregation* and *delegation.*

Under aggregation, an object can actually contain more than one object. An aggregate object is a composite of multiple objects. To the object's user, the aggregate appears to have an interface that consistsa of the interfaces from all its internal objects. The object's user does not need to know how an object is actually constructed. Aggregates are typically used when an object wants to provide the default interfaces from more than one object.

In order to change the default behavior of an object, you need to resort to delegation. Under delegation, one object creates an internal version of another object, and overrides all its methods. It then makes these overridden methods visible. In this way, an object can change or supplement the methods of the overridden object.

Marshaling

In order to send parameters between OLE processes, OLE uses *marshaling.* Essentially, marshaling is the process of validating and converting the data, packaging the data, and sending it to a remote process. Under OLE, there are three basic types of servers: in-processes servers that are part of the current OLE process, local servers that are a different process on the same machine, and remote servers that are on a different machine on the network. Both local and remote servers require marshaling support.

By using marshaling, OLE hides the details of interprocess communication from the user. LRPC calls are used if the called OLE process is on the same machine. If you are calling a procedure in an OLE process that is on a different machine, OLE is designed to support network RPC calls.

When an interface method for an OLE object is called, in reality a call to a *proxy* object is made. This proxy object, which is created by OLE, validates the parameters and performs any necessary conversion. It then calls the actual procedure, the true function that you intended to call, via an LRPC. When the called procedure is activated, OLE does another bit of trickery. Before the routine that you wanted is activated, the actual call invokes a *stub* routine that recreates the original parameters. At this point, the real procedure is called.

This is probably a bit confusing at first glance. The good news is that whenever you use the standard Component Object Model interfaces, marshaling is completely implemented in the OLE libraries.

OLE and MFC

Like most application development projects under Microsoft Windows, most developers find it easier to use the Microsoft Foundation Classes (MFC) to provide support for OLE applications. MFC is a set of classes that provides a development framework around which applications can be built.

A framework provides a whole application development philosophy, not just some reusable libraries. As you would guess, frameworks are not really designed to be used for bits and pieces of an application. Typically, you have an "all or nothing" situation with regard to framework development.

Having said all this, frameworks are not bad. In fact, they can save a significant amount of time in the development process by encapsulating a lot of common functionality. A complete discussion of the MFC framework is far beyond the scope of this book, however MFC does provide a large set of classes that support OLE applications. You will probably find that these classes will make life as an OLE developer much easier for you.

OLE Automation

OLE automation is a powerful method that allows for programs to interact and integrate. For years, developers have recognized the need to allow users to customize applications and to provide scripting language support. Unfortunately, you need to learn multiple scripting languages and interfaces in order to work effectively.

Microsoft originally saw OLE automation as a mechanism for a global Windows macro language. However, they decided to allow software developers to write their own macro languages instead. In order to provide macro capability for Windows, Microsoft extended Visual Basic to include OLE automation support, so as to provide an easy route for users to control Windows applications.

One of the major problems with the design of any software product is deciding the exact set of features to include. It is not possible to include every feature, or make the application be all things to all people. However, by including OLE automation support in your application, you can make it possible for your user to completely customize your application to suit his or her environment. By designing in a good set of features that can be used in different ways, and making these features available via OLE automation, you can provide a much more comprehensive application to your users.

Exposing Automation Objects

To use OLE automation, a programmer defines a set of operations and makes them accessible (*exposes* them) by other applications. These exposed operations form an Application Programming Interface (API) for the automated OLE object. Operations that have been exposed for automation use can have parameter lists, and appear similar to normal procedure calls. In addition to application-specific OLE objects, Microsoft provides a list of objects that OLE automation applications should support. These objects are aimed at an application that uses documents as its basic data element, so they may not be appropriate for every circumstance (see Table 17.1).

Table 17.1   Microsoft Standard Objects for OLE Automation Applications

Object	Description
Application	The root object
Document	The primary object that supports printing, retrieving, and saving data
Documents	A collection object that represents a set of Document objects
Characters	The text-formatting object
File	An OLE object that handles file access
Files	A collection object that represents a set of File objects
Font	An object that describes the document font
Menu	An OLE object that represents a menu
Menus	A collection object that represents a set of Menu objects

(continues)

Table 17.1 Continued	
Object	**Description**
MenuBar	An OLE object that represents a menu bar
MenuBars	A collection object that represents a set of MenuBar objects
Window	The display area of the application
Windows	A collection object that represents a set of Window objects

Each of these standard objects has several different methods that must be implemented in order to provide its full behavior. A complete discussion of these issues is beyond the scope of this chapter. For a thorough exploration of Microsoft's recommended objects and OLE automation in general, see *Using OLE 2.x in Application Development* from Que.

Understanding Distributed OLE

Distributed OLE allows the client and server objects to be located on different physical machines. Distributed OLE also allows access to data from non-Windows based machines, provided the non-Windows machine supports OLE.

> **Note**
>
> Currently Microsoft does not provide an operating system that supports Distributed OLE. MS has stated that their next generation OS, particularly Windows NT and Windows 95, will at some point in the future (not with initial release, however), support Distributed OLE. Windows NT OLE uses RPCs instead of LRPCs and Windows 95 is also suspected to use RPCs instead of LRPCs. Beta versions of Distributed OLE are being tested on Windows NT and Digital Equipment Corp. machines.

Distributed OLE provides a new server called the Service Control Manager (SCM). This new server satisfies the request of an OLE client by finding and running the requested OLE server.

In normal OLE, the client requests a class ID from a particular server and uses the class factory to create the required object. This is typically done using the CoGetClassObject function. In Distributed OLE, the client does the same to create the requested object. The difference between Distributed OLE and

OLE 2.0 exists within the OLE system itself. Basically Service Control Managers exist on each machine linked by the network. The SCM located on the client's machine searches the registry for the location of the server requested. If this server resides on another machine, the client's SCM contacts the SCM residing on the server's machine, asking it to start the server. The server's SCM then starts the server and, if successful, alerts the client's SCM that the server is available. Now to the client, the client's SCM appears to be the server. And the server's SCM appears to be the client for the server's services. Thus, neither the client nor the server know they are working across the network. All network traffic is handled by the Service Control Managers using RPCs.

As discussed in Chapter 7, "What Are Remote Procedure Calls?," an RPC enables two applications to exchange data across a network. The calling application is not aware of the location, operating system, or even machine type running the procedure called. All machine, OS, and network parameter conversions are handled by the RPC by using a standard uniform data format. This conversion of data is called marshaling and is similar to OLE's marshaling interfaces such as IStdMarshal. In RPCs, there is a client application and a client stub, which is similar to Distributed OLE's Service Control Manager. There is also a server stub on the server's machine when using RPCs. The marshaling of data between the two stubs takes care of various machine, OS, and application specific conversions.

> **Note**
>
> One of the conversions done during the marshaling of data includes the swapping of bytes in multi-byte objects. This is sometimes necessary because different CPUs order their bytes in memory in different orders. On Intel machines, for example, the bytes are stored with the low order byte at the starting address. This is called *little-endian* and thus all Intel CPUs are little-endian machines. Other CPUs, such as the 68000 series manufactured by Motorola, store the high order byte at the starting address. This is called *big-endian*.

The stub provided in RPCs is equivalent to a proxy in OLE. The proxy is responsible for marshaling the data to the server and for communicating with the client. The stub in OLE is the same as the server stub in RPCs. The OLE stub is responsible for unmarshaling the data and communicating with the server. OLE 2.0 provides default proxies and stubs, but in Distributed OLE you may need to create your own proxies and stubs plus provide an interface, using Imarshal, to marshal the data between your client and server. The best news is that if you use COM then, when Distributed OLE becomes available, your applications will be able to use Distributed OLE without even recompiling the code! You will gain access to Distributed OLE for free.

From Here...

The OLE environment provides mechanisms for applications to exchange data and interoperate on that data. By using compound documents, OLE objects created by different applications can be stored within the same file structure. The object linking and embedding technologies allow objects of different types to be linked together or physically stored within other objects.

In-place activation allows the creating application of an object to be activated from an embedded object. This allows a user to interact with an OLE object without having to switch to a different application. By using OLE automation, you can advertise a set of operations and allow applications to interact with each other without human intervention.

OLE provides an interesting base for client/server application development. For more information on OLE and Windows client/server application development, see the following:

- Chapter 4, "Client/Server Development Overview," introduces various client/server mechanisms.

- Chapter 18, "Client/Server Development with OLE," shows how to use the OLE environment to create client/server applications.

- Que's *Using OLE 2.x in Application Development* provides a detailed look at OLE development with numerous code samples.

Chapter 18

Client/Server Development with OLE

OLE is a complex technology, one in which a single chapter cannot hope to provide all the answers. Thus, this chapter will strive to provide a general overview of implementing OLE in your application to provide both client and server services on a single system.

Unfortunately, the current OLE 2.0 technology does not support true remote procedure call type network operation; that is, the client and server must run on the same machine. Microsoft is currently developing a version of OLE, called Distributed OLE, that provides a true network-capable client/server technology. This new technology uses RPCs as defined by the Open Software Foundation (OSF) in its Distributed Computing Environment (DCE) model.

Since OLE is a complex technology, using a straight Windows SDK approach requires a very large learning curve for the OLE 2.0 API. Using an application framework, such as Microsoft's Foundation Classes (MFC) or Borland's Object Windows Library (OWL), is highly recommended. So for this chapter, MFC will be used whenever possible to illustrate sample code; otherwise, straight OLE SDK code will be used when the framework does not provide sufficient wrappers for OLE functionality.

This chapter provides an overview of OLE, and looks at the following:

- The various components of an OLE application

- Implementing an OLE client using MFC

- Implementing an OLE server using MFC

- A discussion of implementing OLE Automation

- A brief introduction to Distributed OLE

A Brief History of OLE Technology

OLE is not a single technology, but a number of technologies supporting integration of various components within and between applications. At one time, components were simply other documents or spreadsheets, but the OLE technology has matured and expanded, and compound documents are only a small part of OLE today. OLE is quickly approaching the ability to integrate whole applications within other totally unrelated applications, even those from different vendors. Most of this functionality is available today with OLE 2.0, thus bringing the promise of the client/server paradigm to the Windows desktop.

> **Note**
>
> The term OLE at one time was an acronym for Object Linking and Embedding, which described how components could be integrated into an application. They could be either linked or embedded. Today Microsoft uses the term OLE as a word by itself, and does not consider it to be an acronym.

Microsoft introduced OLE 1.0 in 1991 as an object-oriented technology addition to Dynamic Data Exchange, or DDE. OLE was originally developed to allow Microsoft application developers, specifically those working on the Microsoft PowerPoint Presentation application, to use the services of Microsoft Graph. Programming in OLE 1.0 proved difficult for developers for a variety of reasons, the largest difficulty being with the use of DDE, which is inherently asynchronous and thus very error-prone and system resource-intensive, especially if requests are sent to an application that is not currently loaded. Other difficulties developers faced were the lack of documentation and example programs.

In 1993 Microsoft introduced OLE 2.0 after an exhaustive design cycle and beta tests. OLE 2.0 fixed many of the problems associated with DDE and OLE 1.0, including the following features:

- Interapplication drag-and-drop which allows users to drag data, or other objects, from one application to another.

- In-place editing of embedded and linked objects, so that users do not have to leave the current application and switch over to the embedded application. All menus and tools become available within the current application.

■ Uniform Data Transfer, which describes the data and its transfer. This method is much more robust than the two previous methods of using the Clipboard or using DDE.

■ Structured Storage for objects that mimic an operating system's file system within an application. This provides easy access to an application's data both from within the application and from external applications.

The main technologies behind OLE are a set of layered, independent technologies. Among them are Objects, Interfaces and the Component Object Model (COM), Link Tracking and Management, Compound files and structured storage, Uniform Data Transfer, and OLE Automation.

Developing OLE Containers

An MFC-based OLE container (in fact, any MFC OLE program, whether it is a container, is a server, or deals with automation) has to initialize the OLE libraries (DLLs). This is done by calling the MFC function afxOleInit, as shown in Listing 18.1.

Listing 18.1   Initializing the OLE System with MFC

```
BOOL SampleApp::InitInstance()
{
    // Initialize OLE libraries
    if (!AfxOleInit())
    {
        AfxMessageBox(IDP_OLE_INIT_FAILED);
        return FALSE;
    }
}
```

The menu identifier to use for in-place activation must also be specified. This ID will specify to MFC where to place the server's menu item when it is loaded. You must specify this ID. MFC also provides several other built-in services for your application, such as the standard OLE insert object dialog. See Listing 18.2 for an example of the code generated by AppWizard to supply other OLE built-in services.

Listing 18.2 Defining the Application Class Behavior

```cpp
// ocontain.cpp : Defines the class behaviors for the application.
//

#include "stdafx.h"
#include "ocontain.h"

#include "mainfrm.h"
#include "ocontdoc.h"
#include "ocontvw.h"

#ifdef _DEBUG
#undef THIS_FILE
static char BASED_CODE THIS_FILE[] = __FILE__;
#endif

/////////////////////////////////////////////////////////////////
// ContainApp

BEGIN_MESSAGE_MAP(ContainApp, CWinApp)
    //{{AFX_MSG_MAP(ContainApp)
    ON_COMMAND(ID_APP_ABOUT, OnAppAbout)
        // NOTE - the ClassWizard will add and
        // remove mapping macros here.
        // DO NOT EDIT what you see in
        // these blocks of generated code!
    //}}AFX_MSG_MAP
    // Standard file-based document commands
    ON_COMMAND(ID_FILE_NEW, CWinApp::OnFileNew)
    ON_COMMAND(ID_FILE_OPEN, CWinApp::OnFileOpen)
END_MESSAGE_MAP()

// Constructor
ContainApp::ContainApp()
{
}

/////////////////////////////////////////////////////////////////
// The one and only ContainApp object

ContainApp theApp;


BOOL ContainApp::InitInstance()
{
    // Initialize OLE libraries
    if (!AfxOleInit())
    {
        AfxMessageBox(IDP_OLE_INIT_FAILED);
        return FALSE;
    }

    // Standard initialization
    Enable3dControls();
```

```
        // Load standard INI file options (including MRU)
        LoadStdProfileSettings();

        // Register the application's document
        // templates.  Document templates
        //   serve as the connection between
        // documents, frame windows and views.
        CSingleDocTemplate* pDocTemplate;
        pDocTemplate = new CSingleDocTemplate(
            IDR_MAINFRAME,
            RUNTIME_CLASS(ContainDoc),
            RUNTIME_CLASS(CMainFrame),        // main SDI frame window
            RUNTIME_CLASS(ContainView));
        pDocTemplate->SetContainerInfo(IDR_CNTR_INPLACE);
        AddDocTemplate(pDocTemplate);

        // Enable DDE Execute open
        EnableShellOpen();
        RegisterShellFileTypes();

        // simple command line parsing
        if (m_lpCmdLine[0] == '\0')
        {
            // create a new (empty) document
            OnFileNew();
        }
        else
        {
            // open an existing document
            OpenDocumentFile(m_lpCmdLine);
        }

        // Enable drag/drop open
        m_pMainWnd->DragAcceptFiles();

        return TRUE;
}

/////////////////////////////////////////////////////////////////
// ContainApp commands

// cntritem.cpp : implementation of the ContainCntrItem class
//

#include "stdafx.h"
#include "ocontain.h"

#include "ocontdoc.h"
#include "cntritem.h"

#ifdef _DEBUG
#undef THIS_FILE
static char BASED_CODE THIS_FILE[] = __FILE__;
#endif
```

(continues)

Listing 18.2 Continued

```
/////////////////////////////////////////////////////////////////////
// ContainCntrItem implementation

IMPLEMENT_SERIAL(ContainCntrItem, COleClientItem, 0)

// Constructor
ContainCntrItem::ContainCntrItem(ContainDoc* pContainer)
    : COleClientItem(pContainer)
{
    // Initialize rectangle
    m_rect.SetRect(10, 10, 50, 50);

}

// Destructor
ContainCntrItem::~ContainCntrItem()
{
}

void ContainCntrItem::OnChange(OLE_NOTIFICATION nCode, DWORD
dwParam)
{
    ASSERT_VALID(this);

    COleClientItem::OnChange(nCode, dwParam);

    // When an item is being edited (either in place or fully open)
    //  it sends OnChange notifications for changes in the state of
    //  the item or visual appearance of its content.

    switch (nCode)
    {
       case OLE_CHANGED :
          InvalidateItem();
          UpdateFromServerExtent();
          break;

       case OLE_CHANGED_STATE :
       case OLE_CHANGED_ASPECT :
          InvalidateItem();
          break;
    }

}

BOOL ContainCntrItem::OnChangeItemPosition(const CRect& rectPos)
{
    ASSERT_VALID(this);

    // During in-place activation
    // ContainCntrItem::OnChangeItemPosition
    // is called by the server to change
    // the position of the in-place
    // window. Usually, this is a result of the data in the server
```

```
    // document changing such that the extent has changed or as a
    // result of in-place resizing.
    //
    // The default is to call the base class, which will call
    // COleClientItem::SetItemRects to move the item
    // to the new position.

    if (!COleClientItem::OnChangeItemPosition(rectPos))
        return FALSE;

    InvalidateItem();
    m_rect = rectPos;
    InvalidateItem();

    // Mark document as dirty
    GetDocument()->SetModifiedFlag();

    return TRUE;
}


void ContainCntrItem::OnGetItemPosition(CRect& rPosition)
{
    ASSERT_VALID(this);

    // During in-place activation,
    // ContainCntrItem::OnGetItemPosition
    //   is to determine the location of this item. The default
    //   implementation created from AppWizard simply returns a
    //   hard-coded rectangle. Usually, this rectangle would reflect
    //   the current position of the item relative to the view used
    //   for activation. You can obtain the view by calling
    //   ContainCntrItem::GetActiveView.

    // Return rectangule relative to client area of view
    rPosition = m_rect;
}


void ContainCntrItem::OnDeactivateUI(BOOL bUndoable)
{
    COleClientItem::OnDeactivateUI(bUndoable);

    // Close an in-place active item whenever it removes the user
    //   interface.  The action here should match as closely as
    //   possible to the handling of the escape key in the view.

    Deactivate();  // nothing fancy here—just deactivate the object
}


void ContainCntrItem::Serialize(CArchive& ar)
{
    ASSERT_VALID(this);
    // Call base class first to read in COleClientItem data.
    // Since this sets up the m_pDocument pointer returned from
    //   ContainCntrItem::GetDocument, it is a good idea to call
    //   the base class Serialize first.
    COleClientItem::Serialize(ar);
```

(continues)

Listing 18.2 Continued

```
        // now store/retrieve data specific to ContainCntrItem
        if (ar.IsStoring())
        {
            ar << m_rect;
        }
        else
        {
            ar >> m_rect;
        }
}

void ContainCntrItem::InvalidateItem()
{
    GetDocument()->UpdateAllViews(NULL, HINT_UPDATE_ITEM, this);

}

void ContainCntrItem::UpdateFromServerExtent()
{
    CSize size;
    if (GetExtent(&size))
    {
        // OLE returns the extent in HIMETRIC units
        //   however, we need pixels.
        CClientDC dc(NULL);
        dc.HIMETRICtoDP(&size);

        // Only invalidate if it has actually changed
        if (size != m_rect.Size())
        {
            // Invalidate old, update, invalidate new
            InvalidateItem();
            m_rect.bottom = m_rect.top + size.cy;
            m_rect.right = m_rect.left + size.cx;
            InvalidateItem();

            // Mark document as modified
            GetDocument()->SetModifiedFlag();
        }

    }

}

/////////////////////////////////////////////////////////////////
// ContainCntrItem diagnostics

#ifdef _DEBUG
void ContainCntrItem::AssertValid() const
{
    COleClientItem::AssertValid();
```

```
    }

    void ContainCntrItem::Dump(CDumpContext& dc) const
    {
        COleClientItem::Dump(dc);
    }
    #endif
```

///

Developing OLE Servers

The OLE server is an application that provides services for a client application. Typically, the server is embedded/linked into an OLE container/client that resides on the same system as the server.

There are two types of OLE servers you can build with MFC: full servers and mini-servers. The difference is that a full server is a stand-alone application such as MS Excel, while a mini-server can be embedded only within an OLE client. MS Graph is an example of a mini-server.

A server application also has to register itself with the system registration database. You could do this with a utility called REGEDIT and use the REG file created by AppWizard, but this is unnecessary, because the framework dynamically registers your server at run time. AppWizard also generates a class identifier for your application, called the CLSID. This is a unique number generated for your program so as to distinguish it from other objects in the system.

The Sample Code

A server application must initialize the OLE system, register itself with the system, and associate its document and views with the system, as shown in Listing 18.3.

Listing 18.3   The Main OLE Server Application Files

```
// Initialization
BOOL CServerApp::InitInstance()
{
    // Initialize OLE libraries
    if (!AfxOleInit())
    {
        AfxMessageBox(IDP_OLE_INIT_FAILED);
```

Listing 18.3 Continued

```
            return FALSE;
        }

        // Standard initialization
        Enable3dControls();

        // Load standard INI file options (including MRU)
        LoadStdProfileSettings();

        // Register the application's document templates. Document
        //  templates serve as the connection between documents,
        //  frame windows, and views.
        CSingleDocTemplate* pDocTemplate;
        pDocTemplate = new CSingleDocTemplate(
            IDR_MAINFRAME,
            RUNTIME_CLASS(CServerDoc),
            RUNTIME_CLASS(CMainFrame),          // main SDI frame window
            RUNTIME_CLASS(CServerView));
        pDocTemplate->SetServerInfo(
            IDR_SRVR_EMBEDDED, IDR_SRVR_INPLACE,
            RUNTIME_CLASS(CInPlaceFrame));
        AddDocTemplate(pDocTemplate);

        // Connect the COleTemplateServer to the document template.
        //  The COleTemplateServer creates new documents on behalf
        //  of requesting OLE containers by using information
        //  specified in the document template.
        m_server.ConnectTemplate(clsid, pDocTemplate, TRUE);

// Note: SDI applications register server
        // objects only if /Embedding
            //   or /Automation is present on the command line.

        // Parse the command line to see if launched as OLE server
        if (RunEmbedded() || RunAutomated())
        {
            // Register all OLE server (factories) as running. This
            //   enables the OLE libraries to create objects from other
            //   applications.
            COleTemplateServer::RegisterAll();

            // Application was run with /Embedding or /Automation.
            //   Don't show the main window in this case.
            return TRUE;
        }

        // When a server application is launched stand-alone, it is a
        //   good idea to update the system registry in case it has
        //   been damaged.
        m_server.UpdateRegistry(OAT_INPLACE_SERVER);

        // create a new (empty) document
        OnFileNew();
```

```
            if (m_lpCmdLine[0] != '\0')
            {
                // You can add command line processing here
            }

            return TRUE;
        }

        /////////////////////////////////////////////////////////////////
        // CServerApp commands

        // oservdoc.cpp : implementation of the CServerDoc class
        //

        #include "stdafx.h"
        #include "oserv.h"

        #include "oservdoc.h"
        #include "srvritem.h"

        #ifdef _DEBUG
        #undef THIS_FILE
        static char BASED_CODE THIS_FILE[] = __FILE__;
        #endif

        /////////////////////////////////////////////////////////////////
        // CServerDoc

        IMPLEMENT_DYNCREATE(CServerDoc, COleServerDoc)

        BEGIN_MESSAGE_MAP(CServerDoc, COleServerDoc)
            //{{AFX_MSG_MAP(CServerDoc)
                // NOTE - the ClassWizard will add and
                // remove mapping macros here.
                //    DO NOT EDIT what you see in
                // these blocks of generated code!
            //}}AFX_MSG_MAP
        END_MESSAGE_MAP()

        // Constructor
        CServerDoc::CServerDoc()
        {
        }

        // Destructor
        CServerDoc::~CServerDoc()
        {
        }

        BOOL CServerDoc::OnNewDocument()
        {
            if (!COleServerDoc::OnNewDocument())
                return FALSE;
```

(continues)

Listing 18.3 Continued

```
        return TRUE;
}

/////////////////////////////////////////////////////////////////
// CServerDoc server implementation
COleServerItem* CServerDoc::OnGetEmbeddedItem()
{
    // OnGetEmbeddedItem is called by the framework to get the
    //  COleServerItem that is associated with the document. It is
    //  only called when necessary.

    CSrvrItem* pItem = new CSrvrItem(this);
    ASSERT_VALID(pItem);
    return pItem;
}

/////////////////////////////////////////////////////////////////
// CServerDoc serialization
// No code to serialize with this application
void CServerDoc::Serialize(CArchive& ar)
{
    if (ar.IsStoring())
    {
    }
    else
    {
    }
}

/////////////////////////////////////////////////////////////////
// CServerDoc diagnostics

#ifdef _DEBUG
void CServerDoc::AssertValid() const
{
    COleServerDoc::AssertValid();
}

void CServerDoc::Dump(CDumpContext& dc) const
{
    COleServerDoc::Dump(dc);
}
#endif //_DEBUG

/////////////////////////////////////////////////////////////////
// CServerDoc commands
```

When a container application activates a server, the server creates an object based on the MFC OLE class COleServerItem to provide an interface between the server document and the calling application. To display the server's information, you must override the OnDraw member function, as shown in Listing 18.4, to display the information.

Listing 18.4 The OLE Server's View Class, Including the *OnDraw* Member Function

```cpp
// oservvw.cpp : implementation of the CServerView class
//

#include "stdafx.h"
#include "oserv.h"

#include "oservdoc.h"
#include "oservvw.h"

#ifdef _DEBUG
#undef THIS_FILE
static char BASED_CODE THIS_FILE[] = __FILE__;
#endif

/////////////////////////////////////////////////////////////////
// CServerView

IMPLEMENT_DYNCREATE(CServerView, CView)

BEGIN_MESSAGE_MAP(CServerView, CView)
    //{{AFX_MSG_MAP(CServerView)
        // NOTE - the ClassWizard will add
        // and remove mapping macros here.
        //    DO NOT EDIT what you see in
        // these blocks of generated code!
    ON_COMMAND(ID_CANCEL_EDIT_SRVR, OnCancelEditSrvr)
    //}}AFX_MSG_MAP
END_MESSAGE_MAP()

// Constructor
CServerView::CServerView()
{
}

// Destructor
CServerView::~CServerView()
{
}

/////////////////////////////////////////////////////////////////
// CServerView drawing
void CServerView::OnDraw(CDC* pDC)
{
    CServerDoc* pDoc = GetDocument();
    ASSERT_VALID(pDoc);
```

(continues)

Listing 18.4 Continued

```
    CRect r;
    GetClientRect(&r);


    // By adding code here, you can control what type of informa-
tion
    //  is viewed in the server while it is being edited.
    pDC->DrawText("This is the Sample Server Application", -1,
                  &r, DT_CENTER | DT_WORDBREAK);

}

/////////////////////////////////////////////////////////////////
// OLE Server support

// The following command handler provides the standard keyboard
//  user interface to cancel an in-place editing session.  Here,
//  the server (not the container) causes the deactivation.
void CServerView::OnCancelEditSrvr()
{
    GetDocument()->OnDeactivateUI(FALSE);
}

/////////////////////////////////////////////////////////////////
// CServerView diagnostics

#ifdef _DEBUG
void CServerView::AssertValid() const
{
    CView::AssertValid();
}

void CServerView::Dump(CDumpContext& dc) const
{
    CView::Dump(dc);
}

CServerDoc* CServerView::GetDocument() // non-debug version is
inline
{
    ASSERT(m_pDocument->IsKindOf(RUNTIME_CLASS(CServerDoc)));
    return (CServerDoc*)m_pDocument;
}
#endif //_DEBUG

/////////////////////////////////////////////////////////////////
// CServerView message handlers
```

Implementing OLE Automations

OLE automation provides a way for application developers to make their application's functionality available to other applications. Think of it as a way for a user to use your application within a form of a macro language. OLE Automation defines a standard way to export the functions and controlling methods useful to other applications using OLE objects. To fully understand OLE Automation, you should be familiar with the terms described in Table 18.1.

Table 18.1 OLE Automation Nomenclature	
Term	**Definition**
Automation Controller	Any application, such as Visual Basic or Access, which can control Automation objects or servers.
Automation Object	`IDispatch`—controlled objects.
Automation Server	Same as Automation objects.
Method	An exposed Automation function.
Property	A variable exposed to other applications.

An application can be both a server and a controller, which means such applications can control other applications or be controlled from other applications. Microsoft's Excel and Project applications are examples. Microsoft Word is an example of an Automation server, but it is not an Automation controller since it cannot control other applications.

To use OLE Automation, the developer must define a set of operations and objects, and make them accessible to other applications. The exposed operations and OLE objects are available from any macro language or developer tool that supports OLE Automation.

Using Visual C++ to Create an OLE Automation Server

Using Visual C++ to create OLE Automation servers allows you to use the Microsoft Foundation Class library. Using MFC makes adding OLE Automation server support to your application very easy. You can use MFC to provide most of the OLE functionality, thus insulating you from the OLE SDK. You can also use the ClassWizard tool to automate much of the programming work needed.

MFC uses a series of macros, as shown in Listing 18.5 between the code lines surrounded by the `BEGIN_DISPATCH_MAP` / `END_DISPATCH_MAP`. This macro map is called the *dispatch interfaces*. The framework uses these macros to expose the server's functionality to the world. It is possible to expose the functionality—that is, the properties and methods provided by the server—in one of two ways: by using `get` or `set` functions, or by exposing the variable directly to the calling application.

The preferred method is to use a pair of `get` and `set` functions rather than exposing the variable directly, for much the same reasons you use `get` and `set` functions in C++ rather than making a variable public—to provide data hiding and encapsulation. By hiding the variable from other applications, it becomes possible in the future to change how the variable is implemented without changing how others use the function.

You can use ClassWizard to expose a function. Invoke ClassWizard and switch to the OLE Automation tab to expose a function. Select your document's class name from the Class Name combo box. Then click the Add Property button to activate the Add Property dialog box.

Adding Properties

From the Add Property dialog box, you can set the external name of the property. This is the name other applications will use to access this property. You also set the method of how the property is accessed, whether with a pair of `get` or `set` functions, or directly via a member variable. Finally, set the data type of the property using the Type combo box.

When you have provided the needed information and pressed the OK button, ClassWizard places new function definitions, member variable declarations, and dispatch map entries into your document's class definition files. ClassWizard also updates the ODL (Object Description Language) file to reflect your application's new property.

Adding Methods

To add methods to your program, simply click the Add Method button in ClassWizard, which displays the Add Method dialog box. From the Add Method dialog box, you can set the external name of the function, specify the function's return type, and specify any parameters.

A Sample MFC-based OLE Automation Server

Listing 18.5 provides the basic modules of an MFC OLE automation application. It is based on the sample provided with Visual C++, and simply displays text in a window. The properties and methods provided by the server are items such as the x and y positions of the text and the text itself.

Listing 18.5   A Sample OLE Automation Server

```cpp
// autocdoc.cpp : implementation of the CClikDoc class
//

#include "stdafx.h"
#include "autoclik.h"

#include "autocdoc.h"
#include "dialogs.h"
#include "autocpnt.h"

#ifdef _DEBUG
#undef THIS_FILE
static char BASED_CODE THIS_FILE[] = __FILE__;
#endif

/////////////////////////////////////////////////////////////////
// CClikDoc

IMPLEMENT_DYNCREATE(CClikDoc, CDocument)

BEGIN_MESSAGE_MAP(CClikDoc, CDocument)
    //{{AFX_MSG_MAP(CClikDoc)
    ON_COMMAND(ID_EDIT_CHANGETEXT, OnEditChangetext)
    //}}AFX_MSG_MAP
END_MESSAGE_MAP()

BEGIN_DISPATCH_MAP(CClikDoc, CDocument)
//{{AFX_DISPATCH_MAP(CClikDoc)
    DISP_PROPERTY(CClikDoc, "text", m_str, VT_BSTR)
    DISP_PROPERTY_EX(CClikDoc, "x", GetX, SetX, VT_I2)
    DISP_PROPERTY_EX(CClikDoc, "y", GetY, SetY, VT_I2)
    DISP_PROPERTY_EX(CClikDoc, "Position",
                     GetPosition, SetPosition, VT_DISPATCH)
    DISP_FUNCTION(CClikDoc, "RefreshWindow",
                     Refresh, VT_EMPTY, VTS_NONE)
    DISP_FUNCTION(CClikDoc, "SetAllProps",
                     SetAllProps, VT_EMPTY, VTS_I2 VTS_I2

VTS_BSTR)
    DISP_FUNCTION(CClikDoc, "ShowWindow",
                         ShowWindow, VT_EMPTY, VTS_NONE)

    //}}AFX_DISPATCH_MAP
END_DISPATCH_MAP()

/////////////////////////////////////////////////////////////////
// CClikDoc construction/destruction

CClikDoc::CClikDoc()
{
    EnableAutomation();

    m_pt = CPoint(10,10);
```

(continues)

Listing 18.5 Continued

```
      m_str = _T("Automation!");

      AfxOleLockApp();
}

CClikDoc::~CClikDoc()
{
      AfxOleUnlockApp();
}

BOOL CClikDoc::OnNewDocument()
{
      if (!CDocument::OnNewDocument())
          return FALSE;

      // TODO: add reinitialization code here
      // (SDI documents will reuse this document)

      return TRUE;
}

void CClikDoc::Refresh()
{
      UpdateAllViews(NULL);
      SetModifiedFlag();
}
/////////////////////////////////////////////////////////////////
// CClikDoc serialization

void CClikDoc::Serialize(CArchive& ar)
{
      if (ar.IsStoring())
      {
          ar << m_pt << m_str;
      }
      else
      {
          ar >> m_pt >> m_str;
      }
}


/////////////////////////////////////////////////////////////////
// CClikDoc diagnostics

#ifdef _DEBUG
void CClikDoc::AssertValid() const
{
      CDocument::AssertValid();
}

void CClikDoc::Dump(CDumpContext& dc) const
{
      CDocument::Dump(dc);
```

```
}
#endif //_DEBUG

///////////////////////////////////////////////////////////////
// CClikDoc commands

void CClikDoc::OnEditChangetext()
{
    CChangeText dlg;
    dlg.m_str = m_str;
    if (dlg.DoModal())
    {
        m_str = dlg.m_str;
        Refresh();
    }
}

short CClikDoc::GetX()
{
    return (short)m_pt.x;
}

void CClikDoc::SetX(short nNewValue)
{
    m_pt.x = nNewValue;
    Refresh();
}

short CClikDoc::GetY()
{
    return (short)m_pt.y;
}

void CClikDoc::SetY(short nNewValue)
{
    m_pt.y = nNewValue;
    Refresh();
}

void CClikDoc::SetAllProps(short x, short y, LPCTSTR text)
{
    m_pt.x = x;
    m_pt.y = y;
    m_str = text;
    Refresh();
}

void CClikDoc::ShowWindow()
{
    POSITION pos = GetFirstViewPosition();
    CView* pView = GetNextView(pos);
    if (pView != NULL)
    {
        CFrameWnd* pFrameWnd = pView->GetParentFrame();
        pFrameWnd->ActivateFrame(SW_SHOW);
        pFrameWnd = pFrameWnd->GetParentFrame();
```

(continues)

Listing 18.5 Continued

```
            if (pFrameWnd != NULL)
                pFrameWnd->ActivateFrame(SW_SHOW);
    }
}

LPDISPATCH CClikDoc::GetPosition()
{
    CClikPoint* pPos = new CClikPoint;
    pPos->m_x = (short)m_pt.x;
    pPos->m_y = (short)m_pt.y;

    LPDISPATCH lpResult = pPos->GetIDispatch(FALSE);
    return lpResult;
}

void CClikDoc::SetPosition(LPDISPATCH newValue)
{
    CClikPoint* pPos = (CClikPoint*)
                CCmdTarget::FromIDispatch(newValue);
    if (pPos != NULL && pPos->IsKindOf(RUNTIME_CLASS(CClikPoint)))
    {
        m_pt.x = pPos->m_x;
        m_pt.y = pPos->m_y;
        Refresh();
    }
}


// autoclik.cpp : Defines the class behaviors for the application.
//

#include "stdafx.h"
#include "autoclik.h"

#include "mainfrm.h"
#include "autocdoc.h"
#include "autocvw.h"

#ifdef _DEBUG
#undef THIS_FILE
static char BASED_CODE THIS_FILE[] = __FILE__;
#endif

/////////////////////////////////////////////////////////////////////
// CClikApp

BEGIN_MESSAGE_MAP(CClikApp, CWinApp)
    //{{AFX_MSG_MAP(CClikApp)
    ON_COMMAND(ID_APP_ABOUT, OnAppAbout)
            // NOTE - the ClassWizard will add
            // and remove mapping macros here.
            //    DO NOT EDIT what you see in
            // these blocks of generated code!
```

```
    //}}AFX_MSG_MAP
    // Standard file based document commands
    ON_COMMAND(ID_FILE_NEW, CWinApp::OnFileNew)
    ON_COMMAND(ID_FILE_OPEN, CWinApp::OnFileOpen)
    // Standard print setup command
    ON_COMMAND(ID_FILE_PRINT_SETUP, CWinApp::OnFilePrintSetup)
END_MESSAGE_MAP()

/////////////////////////////////////////////////////////////////
// CClikApp construction

CClikApp::CClikApp()
{
    // TODO: add construction code here,
    // Place all significant initialization in InitInstance
}

/////////////////////////////////////////////////////////////////
// The one and only CClikApp object

CClikApp theApp;

// This identifier was generated to be statistically unique for
your
// app. You may change it if you prefer to choose a specific
// identifier.
static const CLSID BASED_CODE clsid =
{ 0x0002180b, 0x0000, 0x0000, { 0xC0, 0x00, 0x00,
            0x00, 0x00, 0x00, 0x00, 0x46 } };

/////////////////////////////////////////////////////////////////
// CClikApp initialization

BOOL CClikApp::InitInstance()
{
    // Initialize OLE libraries
    if (!AfxOleInit())
    {
        AfxMessageBox(IDP_OLE_INIT_FAILED);
        return FALSE;
    }

    // Standard initialization
    // If you are not using these features and wish to reduce the
    //  size of your final executable, you should remove from the
    //  following the specific initialization routines you do not
    //  need.

    Enable3dControls();

    LoadStdProfileSettings();  // Load standard INI
                               // file options (including MRU)
```

(continues)

Listing 18.5 Continued

```
// Register the application's document templates. Document
//  templates serve as the connection between documents, frame
//  windows and views.

CMultiDocTemplate* pDocTemplate;
pDocTemplate = new CMultiDocTemplate(
     IDR_ACLIKTYPE,
     RUNTIME_CLASS(CClikDoc),
     RUNTIME_CLASS(CMDIChildWnd),   // standard MDI child frame
     RUNTIME_CLASS(CClikView));
AddDocTemplate(pDocTemplate);

// Connect the COleTemplateServer to the document template.
//  The COleTemplateServer creates new documents on behalf
//  of requesting OLE containers by using information
//  specified in the document template.
m_server.ConnectTemplate(clsid, pDocTemplate, FALSE);

// Register all OLE server factories as running. This enables
// the OLE libraries to create objects from other applications.
COleTemplateServer::RegisterAll();
      // Note: MDI applications register all server objects
      //  without regard to the /Embedding or /Automation on the
      //  command line.

// create main MDI Frame window
CMainFrame* pMainFrame = new CMainFrame;
if (!pMainFrame->LoadFrame(IDR_MAINFRAME))
     return FALSE;
m_pMainWnd = pMainFrame;

// Enable DDE Execute open
EnableShellOpen();
RegisterShellFileTypes();

// Parse the command line to see if launched as OLE server
if (RunEmbedded() || RunAutomated())
{
     // Application was run with /Embedding or /Automation.
     //  Don't show the main window in this case.
     return TRUE;
}

// When a server application is launched stand-alone, it is a
//  good idea to update the system registry in case it has
//  been damaged.
m_server.UpdateRegistry(OAT_DISPATCH_OBJECT);
COleObjectFactory::UpdateRegistryAll();

// simple command line parsing
if (m_lpCmdLine[0] == '\0')
{
     // create a new (empty) document
```

```
#ifndef _MAC
        // On the Macintosh, this call isn't required, since the
        // Finder is already sending the app a message to open a
        // new document.
        OnFileNew();
#endif
    }
    else
    {
        // open an existing document
        OpenDocumentFile(m_lpCmdLine);
    }

    // Enable drag/drop open
    m_pMainWnd->DragAcceptFiles();
    // The main window has been initialized, so show and update it.
    pMainFrame->ShowWindow(m_nCmdShow);
    pMainFrame->UpdateWindow();

    return TRUE;
}

/////////////////////////////////////////////////////////////////////
// CAboutDlg dialog used for App About

class CAboutDlg : public CDialog
{
public:
    CAboutDlg();

// Dialog Data
    //{{AFX_DATA(CAboutDlg)
    enum { IDD = IDD_ABOUTBOX };
    //}}AFX_DATA

// Implementation
protected:
    virtual void DoDataExchange(CDataExchange* pDX);
    //{{AFX_MSG(CAboutDlg)
        // No message handlers
    //}}AFX_MSG
    DECLARE_MESSAGE_MAP()
};

CAboutDlg::CAboutDlg() : CDialog(CAboutDlg::IDD)
{
    //{{AFX_DATA_INIT(CAboutDlg)
    //}}AFX_DATA_INIT
}

void CAboutDlg::DoDataExchange(CDataExchange* pDX)
{
    CDialog::DoDataExchange(pDX);
    //{{AFX_DATA_MAP(CAboutDlg)
    //}}AFX_DATA_MAP
}
```

(continues)

Listing 18.5 Continued

```cpp
BEGIN_MESSAGE_MAP(CAboutDlg, CDialog)
    //{{AFX_MSG_MAP(CAboutDlg)
        // No message handlers
    //}}AFX_MSG_MAP
END_MESSAGE_MAP()

// App command to run the dialog
void CClikApp::OnAppAbout()
{
    CAboutDlg aboutDlg;
    aboutDlg.DoModal();
}

/////////////////////////////////////////////////////////////////////
// CClikApp commands

// autocpnt.cpp : implementation file
//

#include "stdafx.h"
#include "autoclik.h"
#include "autocpnt.h"

#ifdef _DEBUG
#undef THIS_FILE
static char BASED_CODE THIS_FILE[] = __FILE__;
#endif

/////////////////////////////////////////////////////////////////////
// CClikPoint

IMPLEMENT_DYNCREATE(CClikPoint, CCmdTarget)

CClikPoint::CClikPoint()
{
    EnableAutomation();

    // To keep the application running as long as an OLE automation
    //  object is active, the constructor calls AfxOleLockApp.

    AfxOleLockApp();
}

CClikPoint::~CClikPoint()
{
    // To terminate the application when all objects created with
    //  with OLE automation, the destructor calls AfxOleUnlockApp.

    AfxOleUnlockApp();
}
```

```
void CClikPoint::OnFinalRelease()
{
    // When the last reference for an automation object is released
    //  OnFinalRelease is called. This implementation deletes the
    //  object. Add additional cleanup required for your object
    //  before deleting it from memory.

    delete this;
}

BEGIN_MESSAGE_MAP(CClikPoint, CCmdTarget)
    //{{AFX_MSG_MAP(CClikPoint)
        // NOTE - the ClassWizard will add
        // and remove mapping macros here.
    //}}AFX_MSG_MAP
END_MESSAGE_MAP()

BEGIN_DISPATCH_MAP(CClikPoint, CCmdTarget)
    //{{AFX_DISPATCH_MAP(CClikPoint)
    DISP_PROPERTY(CClikPoint, "x", m_x, VT_I2)
    DISP_PROPERTY(CClikPoint, "y", m_y, VT_I2)
    //}}AFX_DISPATCH_MAP
END_DISPATCH_MAP()

/////////////////////////////////////////////////////////////////////
// CClikPoint message handlers

// autocvw.cpp : implementation of the CClikView class
//

#include "stdafx.h"
#include "autoclik.h"

#include "autocdoc.h"
#include "autocvw.h"

#ifdef _DEBUG
#undef THIS_FILE
static char BASED_CODE THIS_FILE[] = __FILE__;
#endif

/////////////////////////////////////////////////////////////////////
// CClikView

IMPLEMENT_DYNCREATE(CClikView, CView)

BEGIN_MESSAGE_MAP(CClikView, CView)
    //{{AFX_MSG_MAP(CClikView)
    ON_WM_LBUTTONDOWN()
    //}}AFX_MSG_MAP
    // Standard printing commands
    ON_COMMAND(ID_FILE_PRINT, CView::OnFilePrint)
    ON_COMMAND(ID_FILE_PRINT_PREVIEW, CView::OnFilePrintPreview)
END_MESSAGE_MAP()
```

(continues)

Listing 18.5   Continued

```
/////////////////////////////////////////////////////////////////
// CClikView construction/destruction

CClikView::CClikView()
{
     // TODO: add construction code here
}

CClikView::~CClikView()
{
}

/////////////////////////////////////////////////////////////////
// CClikView drawing

void CClikView::OnDraw(CDC* pDC)
{
     CClikDoc* pDoc = GetDocument();
     ASSERT_VALID(pDoc);

     pDC->TextOut(pDoc->m_pt.x, pDoc->m_pt.y, pDoc->m_str);
}

/////////////////////////////////////////////////////////////////
// CClikView printing

BOOL CClikView::OnPreparePrinting(CPrintInfo* pInfo)
{
     // default preparation
     return DoPreparePrinting(pInfo);
}

void CClikView::OnBeginPrinting(CDC* /*pDC*/, CPrintInfo* /*pInfo*/
)
{
     // TODO: add extra initialization before printing
}

void CClikView::OnEndPrinting(CDC* /*pDC*/, CPrintInfo* /*pInfo*/)
{
     // TODO: add cleanup after printing
}

/////////////////////////////////////////////////////////////////
// CClikView diagnostics

#ifdef _DEBUG
void CClikView::AssertValid() const
{
     CView::AssertValid();
}

void CClikView::Dump(CDumpContext& dc) const
```

```
{
    CView::Dump(dc);
}

CClikDoc* CClikView::GetDocument() // non-debug version is inline
{
    ASSERT(m_pDocument->IsKindOf(RUNTIME_CLASS(CClikDoc)));
    return (CClikDoc*)m_pDocument;
}
#endif //_DEBUG

/////////////////////////////////////////////////////////////////////
// CClikView message handlers

void CClikView::OnLButtonDown(UINT nFlags, CPoint point)
{
    CClikDoc* pDoc = GetDocument();
    pDoc->m_pt = point;
    pDoc->Refresh();

    CView::OnLButtonDown(nFlags, point);
}

// dialogs.cpp : implementation file
//

#include "stdafx.h"
#include "autoclik.h"
#include "dialogs.h"

#ifdef _DEBUG
#undef THIS_FILE
static char BASED_CODE THIS_FILE[] = __FILE__;
#endif

/////////////////////////////////////////////////////////////////////
// CChangeText dialog


CChangeText::CChangeText(CWnd* pParent /*=NULL*/)
    : CDialog(CChangeText::IDD, pParent)
{
    //{{AFX_DATA_INIT(CChangeText)
    m_str = _T("");
    //}}AFX_DATA_INIT
}

void CChangeText::DoDataExchange(CDataExchange* pDX)
{
    CDialog::DoDataExchange(pDX);
    //{{AFX_DATA_MAP(CChangeText)
    DDX_Text(pDX, IDC_EDIT1, m_str);
    //}}AFX_DATA_MAP
}
```

(continues)

Listing 18.5 Continued

```cpp
BEGIN_MESSAGE_MAP(CChangeText, CDialog)
    //{{AFX_MSG_MAP(CChangeText)
        // NOTE: the ClassWizard will add message map macros here
    //}}AFX_MSG_MAP
END_MESSAGE_MAP()


/////////////////////////////////////////////////////////////////////
// CChangeText message handlers


// mainfrm.cpp : implementation of the CMainFrame class
//

#include "stdafx.h"
#include "autoclik.h"

#include "mainfrm.h"

#ifdef _DEBUG
#undef THIS_FILE
static char BASED_CODE THIS_FILE[] = __FILE__;
#endif

/////////////////////////////////////////////////////////////////////
// CMainFrame

IMPLEMENT_DYNAMIC(CMainFrame, CMDIFrameWnd)

BEGIN_MESSAGE_MAP(CMainFrame, CMDIFrameWnd)
    //{{AFX_MSG_MAP(CMainFrame)
        // NOTE - the ClassWizard will
        // add and remove mapping macros here.
        //    DO NOT EDIT what you see in
        // these blocks of generated code !
    ON_WM_CREATE()
    //}}AFX_MSG_MAP
END_MESSAGE_MAP()

/////////////////////////////////////////////////////////////////////
// arrays of IDs used to initialize control bars

// toolbar buttons - IDs are command buttons
static UINT BASED_CODE buttons[] =
{
    // same order as in the bitmap 'toolbar.bmp'
    ID_FILE_NEW,
    ID_FILE_OPEN,
    ID_FILE_SAVE,
        ID_SEPARATOR,
    ID_EDIT_CUT,
    ID_EDIT_COPY,
    ID_EDIT_PASTE,
        ID_SEPARATOR,
```

```
        ID_FILE_PRINT,
        ID_APP_ABOUT,
};

static UINT BASED_CODE indicators[] =
{
        ID_SEPARATOR,              // status line indicator
        ID_INDICATOR_CAPS,
        ID_INDICATOR_NUM,
        ID_INDICATOR_SCRL,
};

/////////////////////////////////////////////////////////////////////////
// CMainFrame construction/destruction

CMainFrame::CMainFrame()
{
        // TODO: add member initialization code here
}

CMainFrame::~CMainFrame()
{
}

int CMainFrame::OnCreate(LPCREATESTRUCT lpCreateStruct)
{
        if (CMDIFrameWnd::OnCreate(lpCreateStruct) == -1)
            return -1;

        if (!m_wndToolBar.Create(this,
              WS_CHILD | WS_VISIBLE | CBRS_TOP |
              CBRS_TOOLTIPS | CBRS_FLYBY) ||
            !m_wndToolBar.LoadBitmap(IDR_MAINFRAME) ||
            !m_wndToolBar.SetButtons(buttons,
              sizeof(buttons)/sizeof(UINT)))
        {
            TRACE0("Failed to create toolbar\n");
            return -1;      // fail to create
        }

        if (!m_wndStatusBar.Create(this) ||
            !m_wndStatusBar.SetIndicators(indicators,
              sizeof(indicators)/sizeof(UINT)))
        {
            TRACE0("Failed to create status bar\n");
            return -1;      // fail to create
        }

        // TODO: Delete these three lines if you don't want the
        //   toolbar to be dockable
        m_wndToolBar.EnableDocking(CBRS_ALIGN_ANY);
        EnableDocking(CBRS_ALIGN_ANY);
        DockControlBar(&m_wndToolBar);

        return 0;
}
```

(continues)

Listing 19.5 Continued

```
/////////////////////////////////////////////////////////////////
// CMainFrame diagnostics

#ifdef _DEBUG
void CMainFrame::AssertValid() const
{
    CMDIFrameWnd::AssertValid();
}

void CMainFrame::Dump(CDumpContext& dc) const
{
    CMDIFrameWnd::Dump(dc);
}

#endif //_DEBUG


/////////////////////////////////////////////////////////////////
// CMainFrame message handlers
```

From Here...

As stated in the beginning of this chapter, whole books have been written on implementing OLE programs. OLE is a complex technology that requires further study. While this chapter has presented a brief introduction to using OLE technologies in a client/server paradigm on a single computer system, from here you should investigate the following resources for further information:

- Chapter 4, "Client/Server Development Overview," offers a discussion of the pros and cons of client/server development in Windows.

- Chapter 7, "What Are Remote Procedure Calls?," provides a more in-depth discussion of RPCs and how they are used in client/server applications.

- Chapter 17, "Introduction to OLE," introduces the basic building blocks of OLE and how they form a client/server environment.

Chapter 19

Using Open Database Connectivity (ODBC)

Open Database Connectivity (ODBC) is a uniform interface standard used to access databases. ODBC is a database access library. The same thing that can be done by Sequiter's CodeBase, Borland Paradox Engine, Informix ESQL, or dozens of other libraries can be done by ODBC. It allows your applications to manipulate data in a database.

ODBC does have one major distinction. It can manipulate almost any database. It can access DB2 on an AS/400. Btrieve files on a laptop can be manipulated. It can access files that you might not even consider to be databases, like Excel spreadsheets or ASCII data. This chapter assumes that you're using one of Microsoft's Windows ODBC implementations; either the 16-bit Windows 3.x, or the 32-bit Windows 95 or Windows NT. With little or no change in source code, applications can use the ODBC Applications Programming Interface (API) on either platform.

One might wonder how ODBC can manipulate such diverse databases. The vast majority of databases conforms, in whole or in part, to the relational database concepts of E. F. Codd, the person who is credited with creating the relational model, developed in the '70s. ODBC looks at databases for what they have in common, not how they differ.

ODBC is based on the Structured Query Language (SQL). Using SQL greatly simplifies the API. It is the calculus of the relational database. However, using ODBC does not make your application instantly and completely database-independent.

Some of the topics that will be covered in this chapter are ODBC's workings, the requirements for running ODBC, the relational model, client/server interfaces, ODBC structure, and so on.

How Does ODBC Work?

Through the use of drivers, ODBC provides a considerable degree of database independence. Drivers are specific to a database: a Paradox ODBC driver is used to manipulate a Paradox database, a FoxPro ODBC driver to manipulate a FoxPro database, and so on.

A driver is a module (usually a DLL) written to support ODBC function calls. By calling these functions inside the driver, your application manipulates the database. If you want to manipulate a different type of database, you dynamically link to a different driver. The interface between ODBC and the driver varies little. There is a specific set of functions, known as the core, which is supported by all ODBC drivers. ODBC support by a driver is judged by the number of other functions that it provides.

Another component of ODBC is the *driver manager,* which is contained inside ODBC.DLL, and is linked to all ODBC applications. It loads the desired drivers and manages the binding of ODBC function calls in your application to functions in the DLL.

ODBC drivers for large, client/server database management systems (DBMSes) such as Oracle or Informix do not directly manipulate a database. Instead, these drivers provide an interface to the network communication protocol that these databases use for remote operation. In some cases, ODBC drivers for client/server DBMS speak to the database engine through the proprietary interface provided by the DBMS's manufacturer.

Where Did ODBC Come from?

If you have used a client/server DBMS's native library, or embedded SQL, you will notice that there is a strong resemblance to the equivalent components of the ODBC API. The basic design for ODBC was provided by the X/Open Consortium and the SQL Access Group. Microsoft, the implementor of ODBC, has positioned it as a major part of WOSA, the Windows Open Systems Architecture. WOSA is Microsoft's vision of enterprise computing along with Telephony Application Programmer's Interface (TAPI), the Messaging API (MAPI), and others.

Why You Should Use ODBC?

There are several reasons—some good, some technical—to use ODBC. Much of the motivation for using ODBC stems from its relative database

IV

independence. Changing databases is usually easy, and often trivial. It's often just a matter of changing drivers.

Let's say, for instance, that you are doing a downsizing. Your company is shopping for a client/server system to replace its aging mainframe. If you use ODBC, your development effort need not wait until a platform and database management system has been bid and delivered. You can develop on your PC with a database whose behavior is similar to a true client/server environment.

Another good reason to use ODBC is to avoid using a different database API for each type of database that you use with an application. These database libraries usually take from a few weeks to several months to learn, even though they all operate in a similar manner.

What Do You Need to Use ODBC?

There are several ways to use ODBC. The most convenient way is to purchase one of the following:

- Microsoft Visual C++ 2.0

- Microsoft Visual Basic 3.0 for Windows Professional edition

- Level II of the Microsoft Developer's Network: the Development Platform CD-ROM

Any of these will provide you with the basic tools necessary to use ODBC. Each of these methods will be discussed in the following pages.

Visual C++ 2.0

Most of this chapter has been written assuming that the user will be working closely with Microsoft's Visual C++ 2.0. Visual C++ should include the libraries and headers for ODBC 2.0. It also includes the ODBC on-line help reference and various other items.

Note

Currently, Microsoft has released Visual C++ 2.2 as the minor upgrade for Visual C++ 2.0. By buying the Visual C++ subscription package from Microsoft, one is guaranteed to get the next 3 major upgrades in a year. It also provides other information, any minor upgrades, and so on.

Visual C++ also includes the Microsoft Foundation Classes (MFC 3.0). MFC is a Windows application framework that includes extensive database classes based on ODBC. It also supports Windows 95 and NT. At present, Microsoft is scheduled to release the next version of Visual C++ (4.0) that should provide additional MFC support for ODBC.

Visual Basic Professional Edition

Visual Basic can access ODBC data sources through the JET Database Engine, a common interface used to access ISAM files and ODBC data sources. This interface provided the model that the MFC class designers used to implement the MFC database classes. This provides a simple, high-level interface to ODBC functionality. Visual Basic 4.0, which includes an enterprise edition, offers additional tools to support client/server work.

The MSDN-II CD-ROM: The ODBC 2.0 SDK

The CD-ROM contains the following:

- The ODBC libraries and headers
- Several example programs
- Several utility programs
- ODBC application setup tools and examples
- Extensive on-line help
- The Desktop Database Driver Set
- All the redistributable components of ODBC

If you are serious about ODBC, you should really get the SDK. In particular, the ODBCTest utility program can be of great help when exploring the API or testing queries during development. ODBCTest allows you to fully test the API and discover any hidden anomalies that would otherwise escape testing during development.

The Desktop Database Driver Set

The Desktop Database Driver Set is a suite of ODBC drivers for the most common PC databases. The databases supported are:

- Microsoft Access
- FoxPro
- dBASE

- Paradox

- Excel Spreadsheets

- ASCII delimited and fixed-length files

What You Need to Learn to Use ODBC

In order to learn ODBC, a plan is required. Without this, it becomes a hard task. Using ODBC requires a working knowledge of the following:

- Relational operations and terminology

- SQL grammar

- ODBC architecture

If an honest effort is made to learn these three items, learning the API will pose little problem.

The Relational Model

You already know something about relational databases if you know how to use PC databases. The relational model will be briefly described in the following section.

The relational model is the foundation on which RDBMs are implemented. It consists of the following:

- **Constructs**, which are the objects on which the model operates

- **Integrity rules**, which must be satisfied for a database to be valid

- **Operators**, which specify how we manipulate the objects of the model

One of the objectives of the relational model is to make the database understandable by both end users and programmers. In order to achieve this and produce stable systems, it is important that attention is paid to the design of the database. The process that leads to a simple and stable database consists of the following three steps:

- Defining the entities

- Defining the relationships

- Defining the attributes

Once the fundamentals of the relational model are known and its terms and basic operations are understood, one might be interested in learning more about database design.

Structure Query Language Grammar

SQL grammar defines the operations that may be performed on databases and tables. Some of the commonly used SQL statements are:

- CREATE—Permits the creation of tables and indexes

- DROP—Allows the destruction of tables and indexes

- INSERT—Adds new rows to a table

- UPDATE—Changes values in one or more rows in a table

- DELETE—Removes rows from a table

One statement in particular merits greater study than the above. It is the SELECT statement, used to query a table. Its grammar is much more complete than for any of the others. The SELECT statement is used quite extensively. It can be used to perform a join, or multi-table inquiry. This operation, a powerful concept, makes it possible to show the relationships in tables directly.

ODBC Architecture

ODBC architecture is explained in a broad sense in the following section of this chapter. Every effort was made to provide enough information wherever deemed necessary so that a better understanding of the general architecture can be obtained. ODBC online help also goes a long way in providing key information about usage, requirements, and so on.

SQL: The Client/Server Language

ODBC specifies *Structured Query Language* (*SQL*) as its database language. It is used by databases supporting other models, and is also used for file, network, and object-oriented database access.

SQL has been extended by database vendors far beyond a database language. Some dialects include logic flow constructs (such as IF-THEN-ELSE or DO-WHILE). In certain cases, SQL can be used as a full-fledged programming language. These SQL extensions offer opportunities to partition client/server applications in an optimal fashion.

ODBC Data Types

Each data source defines the SQL data types that it handles. The names used by each data source may vary. Use the function SQLGetTypeInfo() to get the names of the data source types.

> **Note**
>
> Some of the function calls mentioned here and in other areas of the book are to give the user an idea of the capabilities of ODBC. In order to get to know these function calls and other calls better, using the actual software is best.

The ODBC SQL defines three levels of conformance: *minimum, core*, and *extended,* which also apply to the data types. All of the data types may not be supported at a conformance level by a data source.

Data Definition Language

A *data definition language (DDL)* is a language or a subset of a language that makes possible the defining of objects. SQL uses three verbs for the definition of SQL objects:

- CREATE

- ALTER

- DROP

Data Control Language

A *Data Control Language (DCL)* is the subset of a database language that makes possible the defining of privileges or restrictions placed on the users of the database:

- Granting Privileges: The GRANT statement is used to grant privileges to users. The following statement allows you to grant privileges to more than one user:

      GRANT SELECT, UPDATE ON Book TO Tom. Stewart, Brett

- Revoking Privileges: The REVOKE statement is used to revoke privileges from a user:

      REVOKE SELECT, UPDATE ON Book FROM Tom. Stewart, Brett

Data Manipulation Language

The *Data Management Language* (*DML*) portion of SQL is the set of statements that makes possible the manipulation of data in tables. The statements described under DCL were regarding the administration of your database. SQL's DML contains only four verbs:

- DELETE—Deletes rows from a table

- INSERT—Allows adding of rows to a table

- SELECT—Used to execute queries against ODBC data sources. It is a powerful statement with many features and allows the performance of all the relational operations

- UPDATE—Used to update rows of a table

SQL Functions

A data source may support a number of functions in SQL. The functions are broken down into the following categories:

- String

- Numeric

- Time and data

- System

- Data type conversion

An Overview of the Structure of ODBC

While the design of ODBC is innovative, it is not difficult to understand. At this stage, if you have read the past few pages in this chapter, you can begin to understand some of the design principles and capabilities of ODBC API and its data source drivers.

For a better understanding of the ODBC interface, other run-of-the-mill, database-specific interfaces need to be described first. As you may know, every database management system and vertical database application requires some way to talk to its native data format. This connection is known as the interface. This interface can be as simple as direct file access or several layers removed.

Database interfaces fall into two categories:

- Local

- Client/Server

Local Database Interfaces

Local DBMSes have been around since the beginning of computing. Data access is as shown in figure 19.1. As indicated in the figure, the local database management system is storing its data on a local hard drive. The DBMS accepts commands from the user or from a user-supplied program. The commands are translated into simple disk access commands, which are passed on to the file system.

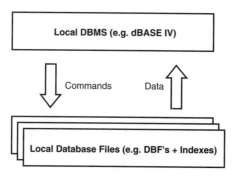

Fig. 19.1
Local DBMSes access their data directly.

In a network situation, a few more layers are involved. This is shown in figure 19.2. In this case, when the files where data is stored are located on a server across the network, the DBMS behaves in exactly the same manner as explained earlier. The network operating system has the responsibility of making sure that its server volumes emulate local drives, so that the DBMS will get the data it needs.

Fig. 19.2
Even across a
network, local
DBMSes work in
the same way.

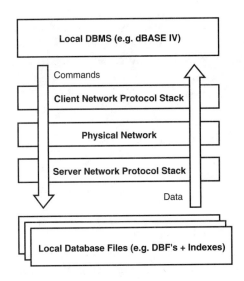

Client/Server Database Interfaces

A client/server DBMS distributes the workload between the workstations and server machines. Due to tremendous advances made in hardware, this technology has become very affordable. The server is used not just for storing and retrieving database data to be passed across the net, but also to process the data before the workstation ever receives it. The success of a client/server system depends a lot on the quality and capacity of the server hardware. Speed and access are also important issues.

The database interface between the client and server is obviously more complex in nature than a local system. Figure 19.3 shows a client/server database interface in great detail. The front-end application sends commands to the server-based database engine, which takes over the task of reading data from the physical disk, processing it, and passing it to the front-end application. The database interface between the client and server is necessarily more complex than in a local system. Several layers of translation as shown are necessary to convey commands and result sets between the workstation and the server. In this case, communication is the key.

Client/server systems are to some extent closer to ODBC in principle than are local DBMSes. The main difference is that each client/server system manages the communication between its workstation and server portions in a proprietary manner by which it becomes incompatible even with other client/server systems. This is the same problem as with many local DBMSes: the lack of ability to get data from various types of data sources.

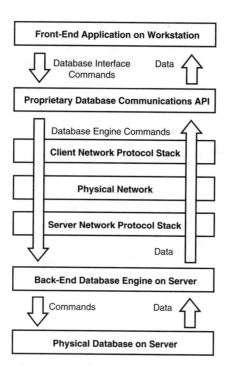

Fig. 19.3
In a client/server system, the server does the database work while the workstation manages the user interface.

Several companies had thoughts along the same lines as ODBC, before it was adopted as the most popular database interface standard. Tools that provided some of the same benefits were developed in their own products. A good example is the "PowerKeys" that work with the Approach end-used DBMS, now owned by Lotus (Lotus was bought out by IBM).

The ODBC Alternative

ODBC uses a layered approach to data management. At each layer in the database communication structure where there's a possibility of product-specific differences, ODBC gets in between the potentially incompatible components and provides a common interface. From a structural point of view, there are two types of ODBC drivers:

- Single-tier

- Multiple-tier

Single-tier drivers do more work than multiple-tier drivers, but multiple-tier drivers are typically more complex because normally they must support higher levels of API and SQL grammar functionality.

Single-Tier Drivers

In ODBC terminology, single-tier drivers are the approximate equivalent of the local DBMS. They sit between the application requesting the data and the database itself. Figure 19.4 indicates how a single-tier ODBC driver acts as the database engine.

Fig. 19.4

A single-tier ODBC driver acts as a database engine.

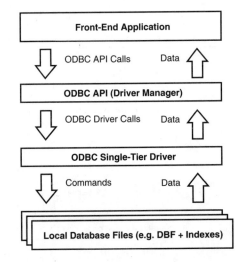

When the user performs some action in the application that results in a need for data or other database operations, the application passes an ODBC function call to the Driver Management component of ODBC. The Driver Manager, which is responsible for managing communications between the application and the ODBC drivers it uses, determines what needs to be done. If it's something the Driver Manager can handle directly (such as certain types of cursor operations), it will do so, and will pass any results (return codes, for example), back to the application. If the Driver Manager needs to call a function in the driver (such as an SQLExecute() call to obtain a result set), it will do that, and will ferry the results back to the application.

Multiple-Tier Drivers

Multiple-tier drivers pass commands and data back and forth between the database engine and the client application. Figure 19.5 indicates how a multiple-tier ODBC driver fits into the overall database communication structure.

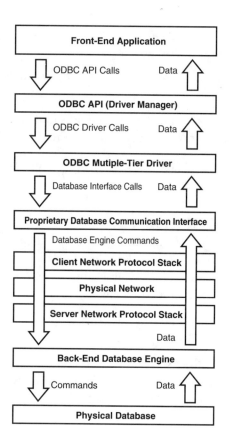

Fig. 19.5
A multiple-tier ODBC driver sits between the client application and the database server.

IV

Windows Development

In a multiple-tier driver configuration, the flow of requests and results goes like this:

1. The front-end application issues a request for data or for some other type of database processing; this request goes to the ODBC driver manager.

2. The driver manager either fulfills the request or (usually) passes it on to the driver.

3. The multiple-tier driver translates the request into terms that the vendor-specific database communication interface (such as SQL Server's DB-Library) can understand, and passes it to the interface.

4. The interface sends the request over the network to the database engine on the server.

5. The server processes the request and sends the results, if any, back to the database communication interface.

6. The database interface forwards results to the multiple-tier ODBC driver.

7. The multiple-tier driver forwards the results to the application, usually directly into buffers where the data is expected.

8. The front-end application presents the data to the user in the appropriate fashion.

A Typical ODBC Session

In the following sections, I will go into detail about the things required to get an application to work with ODBC. First, let's talk about the steps an ODBC-capable application takes during a typical running, and the things that ODBC has to do to fulfill each request. The steps are as follows:

1. The application starts up and creates an ODBC environment, establishing a workspace for future ODBC function calls to utilize.

2. The application either creates an ODBC connection automatically, or first asks the user for a login, password, and possibly the name of the data source. The information provided by the application or by the user is passed to the ODBC API, which uses it in establishing a connection to the data source.

3. When the connection handle has been established, the application needs to create a statement handle through which it will execute ODBC commands.

4. Once the statement handle is available, the application will probably need to obtain information about the structure of the database with which it will be working. It may not need all the details at once, but it will probably need at least some of this information immediately. The application can issue "catalog and statistics" function calls to inquire about table structures and other database-specific details.

5. When the user activates a feature that requires information from the database, the application must formulate a query in proper ODBC SQL grammar. This looks a lot like a standard SQL statement, although special items such as functions and procedure calls can alter its appearance a little. The application sends the request to ODBC and then ODBC passes it to the data source driver.

6. When the application is closed, it first needs to free the statement
handle, then release any database connections that have been made,
and then release the ODBC environment itself. A single-tier driver will
ensure that all local database files are closed correctly; a multiple-tier
driver will close its sessions with the server database.

Data Sources and Drivers

Applications written in ODBC obtain data by connecting to data sources. In
this section, installation and the use of the ODBC Administrator will be discussed. In addition, the different drivers, how to choose them, and the role
played by ODBC drivers for applications will also be discussed.

Installation and the Use of the ODBC Administrator

The ODBC Administrator is a Control Panel applet essential to the use of
ODBC. It handles installed drivers and assists in managing data sources. Access to call-tracing of ODBC function calls is also provided. The Administrator
can also be executed from the Windows program manager.

Installing the Administrator and its support files enables you to add sections
of the registry needed for ODBC operation. The Administrator can be obtained from several sources.

Two of these sources are:

- Microsoft Visual C++ 2.0
- ODBC 2.0 Software Development Kit

Configuring Logging

ODBC gives you a logging facility through the Administrator. This facility
logs the ODBC function calls and the SQL statements passed to the driver. In
many cases, this is more accessible than using a full debugger, especially just
to get an overview. In many cases, trying to get an overview using a full
blown debugger can bog things down.

ODBC Driver—What Is It?

ODBC does not give direct access to a database. Instead, applications communicate with a driver through the ODBC driver manager. In turn, the driver
manager passes SQL statements and other information from the application

to a driver. The driver, in turn, passes the result sets from these statements back to the application.

ODBC Drivers are DLLs that provide an interface from your application to the data inside a specified database. This is not unlike the database library you may have used before, however, with one major difference: ODBC provides a nearly *uniform* interface to all databases supported by a driver.

Different Types of ODBC Drivers

Drivers differ widely, both in capability and modes of operation. They are classified by the ODBC standard based on three criteria: API conformance levels, SQL grammar conformance, and driver type.

API Conformance

The API conformance level of a driver places limits on the functions that your application can call. While driver developers do not implement every ODBC function, they are encouraged to conform to one of three levels of functionality.

These levels are the following:

- Core API conformance

- Extension Level 1 API conformance

- Extension Level 2 API conformance

These levels are general guidelines. Some drivers omit several functions from their claimed level of support. Almost all drivers implement functions belonging to a higher conformance level.

Core API conformance is a bare minimum of functionality sufficient for very basic applications. The twenty-three functions that make up the core involve allocating and freeing environments, database connections, and SQL statements. They provide basic support for passing parameters into statements and assessing the results returned. Limited cataloging functions and error-message retrieval are available as well.

Extension Level 1 adds 19 additional functions for your use in applications. One of things provided is the ability to learn what conceptual data types are available and what each is called. This capability is indispensable if your program is to work with several different drivers. The majority of drivers conform to this level.

Extension Level 2 extends Level 1 with 19 more functions. Among other additions, you can get information about both primary and foreign keys, about table and column permissions, and stored procedures in the database.

SQL Grammar Conformance

The SQL conformance level of a driver determines what structured query language grammars may be used in ODBC statements. It also specifies what data types are available.

The conformance levels defined for ODBC are the following:

- Minimum SQL grammars

- Core SQL grammars

- Extended SQL grammars

The minimum SQL grammar contains most of the features that you need. Things like CREATE and DROP tables, SELECT, INSERT, UPDATE records are provided. This minimal set of features is probably enough for most developers.

The core grammar adds a number of useful features. Some of the grammars provided are ALTER tables, CREATE and DROP indexes and views, and so on. Several new data types such as Integer types for both short and long, floating point types of both single and double precision are also provided.

To this set, the Extended grammar introduces some very sophisticated new grammars. The concept of cursor control is added.

This measure of a driver is complicated by the nature of SQL. It seems that no two DBMS vendors use the same grammars. Any two DBMSes may use two different SQL grammars to implement the same feature.

Driver Type

Driver type is a characterization of the division of labor between the driver and the associated DBMS.

There are two basic types:

- Single-tier drivers

- Multiple-tier drivers

Single-tier drivers process both the ODBC function calls and the SQL statements. For example, the dBASE driver can manipulate dBASE tables and indexes like a stand-alone DBMS. It also contains an SQL parser to translate into function calls the strings passed to the driver.

Single-tier drivers are most often compliant with Core or Extension Level 1 API. Multiple-tier drivers have a separate DBMS. The driver must still process function calls from ODBC applications; however, it does not have to process the SQL statements. That is a job for the DBMS.

Choosing Drivers and Approaches

Developers cite several reasons for using ODBC. Before choosing the drivers your applications support, you should examine your motivations. Some of the reasons for choosing ODBC are listed below.

Single Targets

There is no reason to avoid using ODBC if you are targeting a single DBMS, and there are several advantages in using ODBC. ODBC developers can avoid wasting time learning yet another database API. Client/server developers don't have constant access to the actual system they are targeting. You certainly do not want to bring your company's mission-critical computer system to its knees while developing an application. You should find a local DBMS with compliance characteristics similar to your target system. The worst that can happen is a reboot.

Multiple Targets

The most popular reason to use ODBC is that it enables support of all databases with one application. If a product is to be used with every type of DBMS imaginable, ODBC is probably the best option.

ODBC Environment and Connection

ODBC applications are written to issue SQL statements and perform queries. In order for this to happen, the environment and connectivity have to be set up. Prior to this, the appropriate header files and libraries need to be added for making the necessary ODBC function calls. These header files and libraries vary from vendor to vendor and may have to be added depending upon the compiler in use.

System requirements also need to be met before writing any application. A word of caution: since the environment for ODBC can have the same lifetime as the application, it is important to remember to free the environment before the application terminates. Likewise, it is imperative that error-checking is strictly followed and applied as far as an ODBC API is concerned.

> **Caution**
>
> Failure to do so might result in unpleasant situations, such as system crashes for apparently mysterious reasons.

Initializing and Freeing a Connection

A connection gives an ODBC access to a data source. In this case, before freeing the environment when the program is exited, all connections that may have been established should also be freed. This order is also significant because resources may be lost if you fail to observe this order, and other applications may not be able to function.

Connecting to and Choosing a Data Source

Typical applications tend to allow choosing and connecting to any data source. This is especially true for applications that emphasize connectivity. Providing the capability of choosing a data source by the end user also means that the application must support all associated drivers. The `SQLConnect()` function can be used to connect to a data source. It connects your application to a specific data source and links the connection handle (HDBC) with that connection. The parameters for `SQLConnect()` supply the information needed to connect to a data source. The preconditions for using `SQLConnect()` are simple. A valid connection handle is required. The connection handle must have been allocated with a valid environment handle (HENV).

Disconnecting from a Data Source

On completion of all operations with the database by the application, you should disconnect from the database before the ODBC environment is freed. For the ODBC environment and connection, the order of events is very important. A given application should typically follow these steps:

1. Start your application.

2. Allocate an environment handle.

3. Allocate a connection handle.

4. Connect to a data source.

IV

Windows Development

5. Perform all necessary functions.

6. Disconnect from the data source.

7. Free the connection handle.

8. Free the environment handle.

9. Terminate your application.

> **Note**
>
> ODBC also provides what are known as catalog functions to help extract information from databases during run time.

An Introduction to the ODBC Statement

The *statement* is the workhorse of the ODBC API, enabling you to execute SQL statements and perform queries. ODBC statements also perform most of the manipulation on databases. A statement is more than just a command to be sent to the database engine; it is a construct that is allocated in memory and that has a number of other constructs connected to it.

How to Create and Free a Statement

Before a statement can be executed, you must create a statement handle or HSTMT. The statement handle is one of the most basic ODBC object types. It is similar to statement handles such as the environment (HENV) and connection (HDBC) handles. The HSTMT handle is created and destroyed in much the same manner as the HENV and HDBC handles.

The lifetime of a statement handle is limited to its parent database connection handle. A simplified order of events around the creation of the statement handle is as follows:

1. Start the application.

2. Create the environment handle (HENV).

3. Create the connection handle (HDBC).

4. Connect to a data source, using the connection handle.

5. Create a statement handle (HSTMT).

6. Use the statement handle to execute statements.

7. Free the statement handle.

8. Disconnect from the database.

9. Free the connection handle.

10. Free the environment handle.

11. Terminate the application.

No more than one ODBC environment handle should be created. Since the environment manages your connection to the ODBC DLLs, your application can have only one copy of an application in memory. Allocating a second environment is pointless.

Allocating and using more than one connection handle is perfectly permissible and sometimes very useful. Some drivers support only one connection. Others may support only one statement handle. Both of these limitations are infrequent, but they are quite annoying. If you are writing to a single target driver or a small number of drivers, you should read the driver documentation to see if it is subject to either limitation.

You also can connect to and disconnect from a data source as often as you desire, but there is a downside. Connections to local, single-tier, data sources may take only a fraction of a second. True client/server sources that run in a separate task from the application may take several seconds, leaving your application dead in the water (at least in synchronous execution). Connect to and disconnect from a data source only when necessary.

Creating a Statement Handle

Before you can create a statement, you must have a valid connection. In turn, to be valid, your connection must be created after the creation of an ODBC environment. A statement is initialized by calling the SQLAllocStmt() function. The prototype is the following:

```
RETCODE SQLAllocStmt(HDBC hdbc, HSTMT* phstmt);
```

where hdbc is a handle to a valid connection and phstmt is a pointer to an unused statement handle (HSTMT).

Freeing a Statement Handle

After you finish with a statement handle, you should free it before freeing the connection associated with the statement. Failing to do so causes a memory leak in your program and error messages when you try to free your connection. A statement handle is freed by passing it to the SQLFreeStmt() function. The prototype for SQLFreeStmt() is:

```
RETCODE SQLFreeStmt(HSTMT hstmt, LWORD nOption);
```

where hstmt is a valid statement handle and nOption is an integer constant.

Execution of a Statement

The real substance of an ODBC statement is the text of an SQL statement. ODBC parses this text and translates the SQL grammar into actions. These actions can be performed immediately, or stored for later execution. If you want to perform an action once, you probably want to use direct execution. If the statement performs an action repeatedly, you want to use prepared execution.

Synchronous and Asynchronous Execution

As in other programming environments, there are two modes or methods of execution, depending upon the number of tasks that can be accomplished at a given time.

Synchronous Execution

The default mode of statement execution is *synchronous*. A statement executed synchronously does not relinquish control of program flow until all processing has been completed. The time required to execute some statements, such as the deletion of all records from a huge table, can be lengthy. If your application has a single thread of execution, it may be prevented from doing important processing.

Asynchronous Execution

Some drivers support *asynchronous execution*. When first called, the SQLExecute() function returns a value of SQL_STILL_EXECUTING. At this point, your application is free to do other processing.

Periodically, your application should call SQLExecute() with the same statement handle as the original call. The other parameters should be valid but are ignored. The return value is SQL_SUCCESS if the statement has finished processing. If statement processing is still in progress, the function return value is SQL_STILL_EXECUTING.

Asynchronous execution may free your application to do other things, but it is not without problems. Certainly, the complexity of your code increases. This is especially true if you are writing an interoperable application that must also be prepared to operate synchronously. Performance will probably suffer as well.

Creating Tables with the DDL

SQL is one part of a complete database management language. While it lets you perform queries on your data and tables, another necessary area of database syntax is the DDL, or Data Definition Language. This part of the language lets you define tables and other aspects of your database.

Although creating a table is usually an administrative task performed during the initial establishment of a database, there are a few different situations in which an application might need to create a table during a session. Some of the functions or processes that ODBC allows you to perform are:

- Creating, dropping, and altering tables.

  Creating a table is a simple operation. The CREATE TABLE command can be used. The statement can be issued as follows:

  ```
  retcode = SQLExecDirect(hstmt, "CREATE TABLE mytable (id
  INTEGER, field2 CHAR(20); field3 VARCHAR(200))", SQL_NTS);
  ```

  To drop a table, the syntax is follows:

  ```
  retcode = SQLExecDirect (hstmt, "DROP TABLE mytable", SQL_NTS);
  ```

- Creating indexes on tables.

  The CREATE INDEX statement can be used to create an index on a table. It looks like this:

  ```
  retcode = SQLExecDirect(hstmt, "CREATE INDEX id ON mytable
  (id)", SQL_NTS);
  ```

- Dropping indexes.

  To get rid of an index, the DROP INDEX command can be used as follows:

  ```
  retcode = SQLExecDirect(hstmt, "DROP INDEX index1", SQL_NTS);
  ```

- Creating and dropping views.

  To create a view, the following syntax can be used:

```
retcode = SQLExecDirect(hstmt, "CREATE VIEW myview (field2,
field3) AS (SELECT field2, field3 FROM mytable)", SQL_NTS);
```

To dispose of a view, simply drop it:

```
retcode = SQLExecDirect(hstmt, "DROP VIEW myview", SQL_NTS);
```

Inserting, Updating, and Deleting Rows

Although querying is the operation that gets the most publicity, it is really only half the picture. Invariably, users will spend almost as much time in changing the data in their databases as they will in examining it. The methods and aspects of data manipulation include the following:

- Inserting, updating, and deleting rows in a database

- Finding out what sections of a database have been affected by updating

- Maintaining referential integrity

- Returning meaningful data from a trigger, such as an error message

- Misleading read-only mode potential

Queries and Result Sets

Querying is the core of an ODBC program. All of the initialization, preparing statements, and parameter and option setting leads up to the complicated task of querying. This is followed by managing the retrieving results and presenting them to the users. In any program, the real meat is its querying capability, which also happens to be the heart of ODBC. The following concepts and functions of querying are of importance:

- Defining how queries are done: the SQL SELECT statement

- Ordering of operations: the components of a query

- Setting up for a query

- Determining the number of result columns

- Getting information about a result column

- Counting the number of rows returned

- Binding columns to facilitate easy retrieval

- Working with the data

- Cleaning up after queries

Users judge a program more on its query results than on any other component, as queries are often performed at crucial moments in business processes. This being the case, the sequence of events or operations that need to take place while querying a database through ODBC are as follows:

1. First, using either `SQLPrepare()`/`SQLExecute()` or `SQLExecDirect()` preformulated SQL statements are sent to the database through ODBC. At this stage, various options can be set to direct the behavior of the statement.

2. When the statement is issued, the application does not actually receive the data. Instead, the command is simply presented to the database engine, which formulates a plan for its execution.

3. Find out the number of columns present in the result set to help decide how to deal with the results. This can be obtained by the `SQLNumResultCols()` function.

4. To find out the attributes of the columns you have retrieved, you can use the `SQLDescribeCol()` and `SQLColAttributes()` functions.

5. Next, find out the number of rows retrieved or affected by the statement by using `SQLRowCount()`.

6. By calling `SQLBindCol()` for each column, you can provide a place for ODBC to put the results where your program or application can get them.

Setting Parameters with Prepared Statements

There may be need to execute the same statement more than once. Rather than having to set up all the options each time you want to run a statement, you can put it together once and run it over and over. In fact, you can set up several statements in memory at once, and call the right one for a particular purpose each time a common task needs to be done.

There is, however, a slight flaw in this concept. How often do you execute exactly the same command more than once? Maybe in the case of SELECT statements, which are used to fill grids or input screens, but what about in data modification statements? Almost never—although you'll often execute very similar commands with slightly different data.

Fortunately, ODBC provides a reconciliation between the desire to save time preparing statements and the fact that some aspects of the statements are likely to be different every time. The solution lies in the concept of ODBC parameters.

Obtaining Parameter Information

Several different functions are used to obtain various levels of information and statistics about the parameters the application has set up. These functions include the following:

- Getting detailed information about parameters

- Finding out the number of parameters

- Getting a list of parameters

Passing and Accepting Procedure Parameters

There are certain issues involving parameters when they're passed to procedures on which you need to focus. The differences in sending parameter values to procedures revolve around the fact that a procedure can actually return changed values in parameters. In other words, parameters may not be just for input; they can also be used to hold output. Also, a procedure called at the database engine level can directly return a status value, similar to an ODBC function's retcode, and that value can be captured and returned to your ODBC application.

> **Note**
>
> SQLProcedureColumns() is an ODBC function call that can be used to find out the nature of each column/parameter that a procedure uses or returns.

Clearing Parameters

To "unbind" parameter definitions from a statement, call the SQLFreeStmt() function with option set to SQL_RESET_PARAMS. This will reset all parameter buffers at once.

The result will be that the statement exists in the form that it did before any parameters were bound. You will have to bind them again if you want to reuse the statement.

Cursor Library and Positioned Operations

The term "cursor" refers to a set of rows retrieved from a result set. In the other sense, a cursor is a scrollable "pointer" to the current row of a result set. In either case, a cursor can be thought of as a window on the result set. Cursors are used as a relatively convenient and efficient method for working with one piece of a result set at a time, as needed by the application (usually for display and editing purposes).

There are two general cursor attributes: block and scrollable. You may have heard these terms before; their definitions follow:

- Block—The capability to retrieve a set of rows from a result set and position the cursor on the first row of that set.

- Scrollable—The capability to retrieve a set of rows from a result set and position the cursor on a given row in that set, allowing your application to perform some functions directly on that particular row.

Cursor Library and Cursor Basics

The cursor library is a DLL that sits between ODBC's driver manager and the data-source-specific driver. It contains a variety of functions that are used by other ODBC functions, or which can be called directly by the application. This DLL works with drivers at or above the Extension Level 1 API conformance level.

Driver's Support for Cursors

In order for your application to work with a specific ODBC driver, you need to know in advance, from the documentation provided by the driver, whether the level of cursor support is being provided. This can also be accomplished by the `SQLGetInfo()` function. There are 12 `fInfoType` values that relate explicitly to cursor and these are:

- `SQL_CURSOR_COMMIT_BEHAVIOUR`

- `SQL_CURSOR_ROLLBACK_BEHAVIOR`

- `SQL_FETCH_DIRECTION`

- `SQL_BOOKMARK_PERSISTENCE`

- `SQL_LOCK_TYPES`

- SQL_POS_OPERATIONS

- SQL_POSITIONED_STATEMENTS

- SQL_MAX_CURSOR_NAME_LEN

- SQL_ROW_UPDATES

- SQL_SCROLL_CONCURRENCY

- SQL_SCROLL_OPTIONS

- SQL_STATIC_SENSITIVITY

Releasing a Cursor

By making a call to SQLFreeStmt() function, a cursor can be released. Specifying SQL_CLOSE in the fOption argument will close the cursor and release the result set, like in the following:

```
RETCODE SQLFreeStmt( hstmt, SQL_CLOSE);
```

In this case, SQL_CLOSE is the fOption parameter, that closes the cursor but does not destroy the statement handle.

Optimizing ODBC

There are many rationalizations from developers attempting to explain why they don't work with ODBC, but the most significant and credible one is that the extra functionality carries with it a performance hit. Here are the ways by which you can improve the speed of your ODBC-enabled application:

- Reduce all kinds of problems by designing your database right in the first place

- Make yourself look good by choosing optimized drivers

- Minimize overhead by checking each driver capability only once

- Trim down application and feature initialization times by disconnecting/reconnecting as little as possible

- Make judicious use of synchronous/asynchronous modes

- Minimize execution preparation times by choosing between SQLExecute() and SQLExecDirect()

- Make your queries efficient by retrieving results judiciously

- Streamline your cursor operations by always binding the primary key column

- Avoid extra work by turning off bookmarks if not needed

- Tailor the application to your load expectations by selecting the lowest usable transaction isolation level

- Look for inefficiencies by testing your code with the tracing facility

By following all or some of the steps outlined here, most of the aches and pains in slowing down a system or application can be avoided.

From Here...

ODBC, from its initial concept to its present-day form, has practically taken over as the de facto standard of choice for database communications. While its success can be attributed to several factors, immense support from Microsoft has helped it a great deal. We can expect to see further support from Microsoft in the future, because of its continued drive to be a market leader in this area, and we should see Microsoft providing enhancements that users need.

For more information on the topics discussed in this chapter, refer to the following:

- Chapter 4, "Client/Server Development Overview," for a discussion of the pros and cons of client/server development in Windows.

- Chapter 23, "Multiplatform Applications," gives an expanded view of using different platforms to create a client/server system.

- Chapter 24, "A Survey of Commercial Client/Server Products," discusses in more detail other remote databases and their relationship to ODBC.

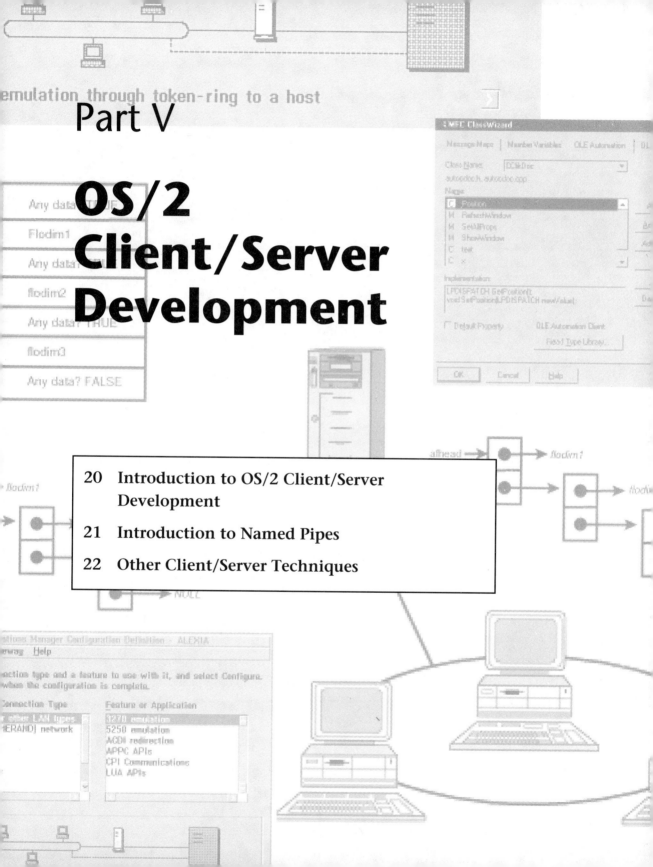

emulation through token-ring to a host

Part V

OS/2 Client/Server Development

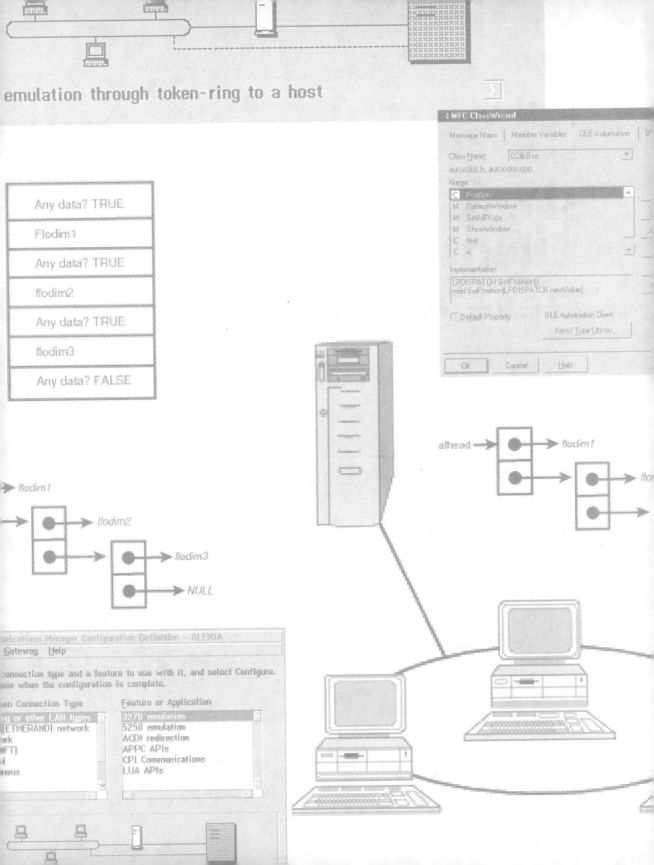

Any data? TRUE

Flodim1

Any data? TRUE

flodim2

Any data? TRUE

flodim3

Any data? FALSE

MFC ClassWizard

Message Maps | Member Variable | OLE Automation |

Class Name: CCtrlDoc

autocdoc.h, autocdoc.cpp

Name:
- Position
- M RefreshWindow
- M SetAllProps
- M ShowWindow
- C test
- C x

Implementation

LPDISPATCH GetPosition();
void SetPosition(LPDISPATCH newValue);

☐ Default Property   OLE Automation Client
                          Read Type Library...

OK   Cancel   Help

flodim1

flodim2

flodim3

NULL

afhead → flodim1

flo

Communications Manager Configuration Definition - ALEXIA

Gateway Help

connection type and a feature to use with it, and select Configure.
se when the configuration is complete.

Connection Type   Feature or Application

[ETHERAND] network   3270 emulation
ork   5250 emulation
FT]   ACDI redirection
                             APPC APIs
neous   CPI Communications
                             LUA APIs

Chapter 20

Introduction to OS/2 Client/Server Development

Businesses and organizations all over the world are looking for improved ways to do business and remain competitive—and that competitive edge is provided by information. The power of computers to manage this unbounded stockpile of facts and figures is what makes the computer a necessary resource to a successful organization. Why are these facts important to developers? Because the world of computing is continually going through changes that affect the way developers work and the skills required to meet these demands. Among the best choices to meet these demands is OS/2. OS/2 provides one of the best client/server platforms available for your PCs and workstations.

Many organizations start out with a single computer to keep track of all information pertinent to its operation. As an organization and its requirements grow, its methods for the management of information will change. OS/2 provides many ways to manage information and provide solutions when changes are necessary. The single computer that once served so well now severely limits the way an organization operates. A more powerful computer will be needed to handle the processing requirements. A larger storage medium may be needed to handle an increasing client demand or retain a historical reference of daily operation. OS/2 is designed to take advantage of advanced equipment and to handle changes in its configuration to meet client demand. Multiple sites of operation or accounting purposes will make a single central computer obsolete, inefficient, and unmanageable.

The problem of increasing information requirements, combined with the economic factors of budget constraints, organization security, and equal departmental access to the proper information, makes choosing a hardware and software solution a difficult proposition. These difficulties make OS/2 in the client/server model a cost-efficient and scaleable solution to a growing organization's informational requirements.

Overview of Client/Server Concepts

OS/2 fits well into many of the changes that are needed to create or extend a client/server system. As a client, OS/2 enables the user to use a vast amount of existing software in the computing environment and connects to a lot to the software that can not be run native on OS/2. As a server, OS/2 is just as capable of allowing many clients access to information and providing services to varying platforms.

Client/Server Rational

Changes in a computing environment come slowly, and OS/2 can help by providing the compatibility of running most of a business' older DOS and Windows software. The older software may provide a level of comfort for the users, but it still must fit into the ideas of a client/server environment. By allowing all software run on OS/2 to gain access to services provided by OS/2, this makes OS/2 an excellent choice in the client/server system.

Upsizing

Upsizing is the effect of bringing a series of personal computers together and allowing them to share information, resources and services. Upsizing is the conceptual opposite of downsizing because you are trying to get individuals and departments on a network to remove redundancy. Upsizing is more cost-efficient for an organization. A single resource, such as a laser printer, shared among a group or a work site is easier to manage and maintain. The sharing of a single resource can also benefit the individuals involved because the single resource can be faster, bigger, and better. Why is upsizing important? Is it effective? Are there any financial benefits? The problem with ignoring the need to upsize your systems is that an organization will continue to function and individuals will make adjustments to their jobs to finish tasks. Unfortunately, in business time is money—these individuals are doing tasks that the proper system can do for less money and time.

A laser printer in a centralized location can give a large group of individuals the use of a high-quality printing device. The cost equivalent of this centralized resource could be individual dot matrix printers. This solution suffers not only from lower print quality, but also from the added maintenance expense of having to monitor, supply, and repair equipment at each individual workstation.

OS/2 works well for upsizing because as a client platform it can connect to most server platforms and works in the smaller peer-to-peer networks providing services via each person's PC. OS/2's multitasking ability gives it a key advantage for server applications and providing remote services.

Downsizing

Once an organization came to terms with the reality that it needed a centralized repository for information, this was answered in the past by using a multi-user mainframe. The mainframe, or "legacy system," was the only solution until the personal computer was adopted by business as a standard computing environment. This migration from mainframes to personal computers is called "downsizing." Many of the advantages of downsizing revolve around the growing information services that mainframes served. Many businesses want to take advantage of downsizing but cannot afford to restructure their information systems. The mainframe may have been too large an investment or the cost of migrating the data to a server was prohibitive; then the mainframe became an information server. The capability of a mainframe to become an information server is dependent on the producer of the mainframe to extend the mainframe operating system to handle the required communication and data requests from clients.

Why is downsizing important? Is it effective? Are there any financial benefits? These are questions that many organizations ask themselves, only to find that they cannot afford to remain locked onto the mainframe for their information services. Personal computers, as low-cost standard hardware, allow an organization to distribute the processing power to the individual in the organization and make the individual responsible for his or her own queries and reports. Information on the mainframe was retrieved by reports generated on a daily, weekly, monthly or yearly basis. Individuals and departments that needed the reports would have liked the information immediately, but were restricted by the mainframe's process load as a limited resource.

The organization couldn't afford to have the information available on immediate request from the mainframe. The problem with specialized requests for information is that, though necessary, they could not be filled quickly enough to make the newly acquired information useful. The amount of time that it took for a programmer to understand the problem, write code, test, and debug the program became too expensive and time-consuming. The problem was that not only was the data centralized, but all other services were centralized as well.

OS/2 works for downsizing because the same computer system and operating system software can be extended with minor additions of server software to become an effective and useful server. An OS/2 client is created by allowing connection to the server. The server can still be a mainframe, but the OS/2 client has taken the processing burden off the mainframe. OS/2 can also run tasks in the background, so the client station is not rendered useless by other tasks.

Coexistence

Coexistence is the ability to perform operations across platforms regardless of vendor or hardware. The concept of an "open" system is the driving force behind this form of client/server architecture. Historically, an organization would buy only from one or two providers of hardware and software. This was not a problem, because there were very few alternatives. In the modern era of computing, an organization cannot afford to be "locked into" a single service or provider. The coexistence of systems and services allows an organization to purchase the right system for the right job for the best price. OS/2 coexists better than any other platform. Not only does it run DOS and Windows 3.x software, but it can also display X Windows seamlessly on the desktop.

Client/Server Characteristics

We have discussed why we want to move towards a client/server model and how OS/2 meets these requirements. This is an important part of understanding the scope of problems we are going to encounter in making system choices. We know that we need to strike a balance between centralization and distribution. The exact balance is based on the organization's informational needs and budget. We now know the problems with what we currently have—we need to know what we are trying to achieve. The name client/server denotes a separation of duties that work in conjunction to achieve a goal. This separation of duties is not enough to distinguish a system as a client/server system. The following will help clarify and solidify elements that make up a minimal definition of client/server characteristics.

Location Independence

The server aspect of a system does not have to reside on a separate machine. It will normally, but does not have to. In the client/server model, the location of the service should not be a concern to the client. The client/server model works exceedingly well on a single machine that can run multiple processes. The service needs to be able only to serve clients, independent of their location. In many cases, the location of the server is hidden from the user or can be selected so that different sets of data can be used interchangeably. In most cases, OS/2 does not have to change access methods for local or remote data. OS/2 named pipes will work on the local machine or use remote data on machines that supports named pipes.

Loose Coupling

The delivery mechanism for services is message-based. This allows interaction based on a minimal independent communication. A service provider can be removed and replaced by another provider, as long as the new provider responds to the messages in the same way. OS/2 handles many different forms of communication requests and conforms to industry standards for these services.

Service Independence

The server has very specific tasks to perform. How it accomplishes these tasks is the concern of the server, not the client. Just like the rationale for using loose coupling, service independence encapsulates changes without affecting the client process.

Shared Resources

The management of a single or a series of resources must be handled to allow the servicing of multiple clients with the required access rights. In a system with a print server, the server will allow the spooling of documents from the local machine and will store them in a priority queue. This will allow the client to continue processing while the print server manages the printing of the documents.

Asymmetric Service Requests

A client/server system allows the requesting of services from a client, which allows the server to wait for requests and process previous requests instead of being required to poll all the known clients. The client will be able to make a request and not be forced to wait for a response. OS/2 can handle many different forms of service requests and in some cases can handle multiple forms. OS/2 systems set up with NetWare and LAN Server can provide services for both.

System Scaling

System Scaling is the measurement of performance when a hardware aspect of a system is modified. System scaling is divided into two types: vertical and horizontal. Vertical scaling is when server hardware is improved or is attached to another system for performance gains. Horizontal scaling is the modification of the number of clients with little or no performance change. The use of system scaling will allow an organization to make decisions on performance changes based on the current configuration and the best way to improve the performance. OS/2 uses industry standard PC hardware and handles the addition of new hardware with little difficulty. Server software for OS/2 can be as simple as peer-to-peer services to LAN Server handling hundreds of clients.

The client/server characteristics described here will give a system the capability to operate in a loosely coupled environment, but do not meet everybody's ideal situation. Client/server, like many new aspects of computers, suffers from many different definitions and ideals. Do not let any one belief change your organization's perspective of your system. The proof is in the doing.

Server Types

Many different companies have tried to claim that their product is "the true client/server" product. The distinguishing characteristic between each product is the nature of the servers.

File Servers

The earliest form of client/server interaction is the file server. The client makes requests of the server for file records over a network. This is a basic and primitive form of data service. A file server's prime consideration is to share files across a network in the form of large data objects. File servers suffer performance limitations due to the multiple messages that are transferred to emulate the client's file system. OS/2 can handle many of the industry standards for Network File Systems. All that is needed is the correct software and the file system driver for OS/2. OS/2 provides a method to extend the file system by using an Installable File System (IFS).

Database Servers

Clients that need a specific subset of information pass a request to a database server. A common format for a database request is an SQL (Structured Query Language). Using an SQL request allows the code processing and the data to reside on the same machine, the server. The results of the SQL request are returned to the client. SQL gives the client software the advantage of a flexible request method, while the results are in a standard format that can be used by many different forms of software. The remote processing of the SQL and the subsequent database query release the client to continue other processing. Advanced use of SQL allows queries on multiple databases on the same command. This allows multiple databases to appear as one source of information to the client. Many native products exist for OS/2 including Oracle, Informix, Watcom SQL, IBM DB2/2 and SQL Server.

Transaction Servers

Clients that have a static request for a server, and also have other requirements based on security and speed, call a remote procedure on the server system. A remote procedure is a group of SQL statements triggered by a single client request. The remote procedure, known as a transaction, will return a success status for the entire transaction. The applications written for the transaction server are known as OLTP, or Online Transaction Processing. This kind of application normally requires high security and rapid response time.

Groupware Servers

Servers with the specific task of managing varying information formats to allow interaction between individuals on the network handle a new form of client/server system called groupware. The most predominant example of groupware is Lotus Notes. OS/2 has both client and server products for Lotus Notes. Groupware deals with e-mail, text, images, sound and other forms of work flow information. Groupware is also characterized by an additional level of client/server APIs used in the generation of applications using a scripting language or a visual forms tool. Groupware communication between the client and the server tends to be vendor-specific.

Object Servers

The design of software objects with OOD (Object Oriented Design) and OOA (Object Oriented Analysis) is leading to a software revolution of OOP (Object Oriented Programming). This approach to software development has shown that separating data into its own operable units leads to code reuse, flexible libraries, and an improvement in program reliability.

This same approach to software development is giving us object servers. Object servers communicate with client applications using communication objects. These communication objects are layered over the system's communication protocols. This allows objects to be written that are not concerned with the method of communication and that bind directly into the operating system's services and operations.

The remote object that a client establishes communications with is an ORB (Object Request Broker). The ORB finds the requested object, calls the method requested by the client, and returns the information to the client from the object. This technology has been implemented in various forms by companies now shipping commercial programs. Among the best known is IBM's DSOM (Distributed System Object Model). The model that DSOM is based on is called SOM (System Object Model) and is what gives OS/2's Workplace Shell its consistent feel and advanced object-oriented user interface. OS/2 software for object-oriented databases include Versant, Objectivity, and Poet.

Advantages of OS/2

Choosing a platform for a client/server project is not a simple task, many platforms promise a wealth of tools, connectivity, and stability. OS/2 delivers on every aspect and consideration that a client/server platform needs. IBM's unwavering commitment to this operating system and its tools, software, and service make it a prime example of what a client/server machine can be.

OS/2 as a Platform

It is unfortunate that many of the choices that are made for a platform are made based on a single factor: either existing hardware, current versions of development tools, or marketing hype. When an investigation of all the factors that should be taken into account for a client/server platform is completed, OS/2 normally stands out as an operating system that supports many of the necessary components for a client/server system.

Hardware

IBM's OS/2 is a 32-bit, multitasking, single-user operating system designed for the Intel 80X86 family of microprocessors. This targeting of a popular hardware platform gives OS/2 a performance advantage over cross-platform operating systems by coding for efficiency in critical subsystems. The hardware requirements of OS/2 are higher than that required of DOS machines, but it will become clear as we describe the operating systems features why this is necessary.

Microprocessors. OS/2 2.0 and later require an Intel 32-bit microprocessor chip. This means that the 80386, 80486, Pentium, or the 80X86 clones are required. This is by no means a difficult requirement because the Intel family of computers holds the largest share of the business and home computer market.

Memory. Minimum memory requirements for OS/2 2.1 are 8 megabytes but, as with all operating systems that can take advantage of large amounts of memory, it is highly recommended that you run the operating system in more than its minimum. I have found that OS/2 2.1 will run multiple applications in a responsive manner in 12 megabytes. OS/2 3.0, known as OS/2 Warp, has dropped the minimum memory requirements to 4 megabytes, but experience once again says that if you want the operating system to respond then you probably should not use less than 6 megabytes of memory.

Disk Drive Space. All versions of OS/2 allow configurable installation by selecting options during installation. A minimal system can be installed using only 33 megabytes, but this will not allow the use of system features that make OS/2 the most versatile and stable operating system available for personal computers. Options such as seamless Microsoft Windows support, multimedia support and media files, advanced power management for laptop computers, PCMCIA devices, tools and games, REXX batch language and optional bitmaps can be omitted, but leaving these out will be a hindrance to your functionality and enjoyment of the operating system. A full install will take up over 55 megabytes. A minimal system installation can be expanded later by using the OS/2 install program to add system features not detected by the install program.

OS/2 Warp also comes with the OS/2 BonusPack. These programs will require up to 30 additional megabytes, but the addition of 32-bit versions of CompuServe Information Manager for OS/2, IBM Works, Personal Information Manager, FaxWorks for OS/2, IBM Internet Connections for OS/2, a multimedia viewer, and a system information tool makes the BonusPack a minimal investment in drive space for useful applications.

The Operating System

Individual platforms each have their advantages and disadvantages, and OS/2 has many of the advantages necessary for an operating system to succeed in the client/server arena. Many of OS/2's abilities are not unique but are combined on a single platform that allows many of the features that users want in their software and developers want to make their software perform at the computer's best level.

Multitasking. OS/2 multitasks preemptively. This means that if special precautions are not taken, then any running task will be stopped, its current state stored, and another task will be started. It is not advised to prevent an operating system from swapping out a task. This will lead to task starvation, and all other tasks will fail to perform their duties. *Task starvation* is when a task cannot multitask because of the way an operating system decides which task is to be run next. Tasks that have higher priority can cause the starving task to not get enough resources. There are reasons to prevent a task from swapping out, but these can normally be worked around using Interprocess Synchronization methods. OS/2 implements this swap prevention using a Critical Section. While in a Critical Section the task can not be put on hold. A Critical Section will be used if the overhead of semaphores is unacceptable and the protected area is very short and does not make calls outside the code area. A semaphore placed in a strategic place will prevent other tasks from going through until the semaphore is released.

Preemptive multitasking is one of the distinguishing characteristics of a true operating system. Microsoft Windows 3.1 runs on top of DOS (Disk Operating System), forcing compromises in the way the system performs basic services. Microsoft Windows 3.1 uses cooperative multitasking to work around the non-preemptive structure of DOS. Cooperative multitasking allows a running task to monopolize the system until it voluntarily gives up control. This means that a poorly running application or a corrupted application can lock up the system, causing the user to force a shutdown of the system. This "forced shutdown" can cause the loss of information from other running tasks.

A process in OS/2 is the equivalent of a running program. A process consists of its own memory, system resources, and at least one running task. A process can start up other tasks that share the parent processes' memory and resources. This is the advantage that true multitasking operating systems have over "operating shells." A process can start up multiple child tasks to perform a job for the parent process, without the parent process suffering significant slowdown from being dedicated to the job. Traditional child tasks are calculating long and complicated math routines and submitting a print job. In both of these jobs, it must be considered that the information being used cannot be modified during the operation. This is a small price to pay for the continued use of the parent process.

OS/2 can use a total of 4,096 threads in the system. Each application, including its child threads, is run in protected-mode for the safety of the system. The protected mode requirement is not only for OS/2 applications; it extends to DOS and Microsoft Windows applications. The protected mode of operation does not allow memory access outside the thread's memory boundary. If any system services are needed, the operating system must be asked to perform this task by using OS/2 kernel API calls. This memory constriction is part of what makes OS/2 a stable and error-resistant operating system.

OS/2 assigns a thread a priority for scheduling. Scheduling is the order that tasks are placed in while waiting to be run. Giving a thread a priority lets the user tell the operating system an order of importance for tasks. A thread can be assigned one of four priority classes. A priority class can be:

- Idle—This is a very low-priority thread which is used for non-visual non-critical threads that spend most of their time asleep waiting for free processor time. A client polling daemon that will occasionally prompt a server for low-priority information is good example of a idle class thread.

- Regular—A user-interactive or calculation-directed thread will be assigned a regular class priority. This priority allows rapid preemption of the thread due to the program waiting for user input or user-requested calculations. Liberal use of regular class treads allows multiple threads to be multitasked with minimal visual delay, and allows a fair and efficient use of system resources. Idle class threads must wait for regular class threads to finish their tasks.

- Server—A thread that runs on a system that is waiting for a client request must be allowed high scheduling over lower threads. Somewhere there is a client waiting for a request that this machine has been set up to service. Regular and idle class threads must wait for server class threads.

- Time Critical—An assignment of this priority class makes the need of the thread the system's highest priority. Threads that must have responsiveness and an immediate response would benefit from using this priority class. Real-time and communication applications are the normal use of this priority class.

OS/2 has an elaborate task-queuing system that deals with priority classes and priority levels. A priority level is a number from 1 to 31. Tasks inherit priority levels from their parent process. This priority level can also be set by the programmer using the `DosSetPriority` API call. A thread's priority level is the dynamic part of its priority state. The more time a thread spends away from an execution time-slice, the higher the priority level becomes, until the thread gets a share of execution time. After the task has used its share of processor time, the priority level is set back to the original priority level. The scheme prevents starvation (a thread getting no execution time) while still ordering thread execution to honor the priority-level requests.

V

OS/2 Development

OS/2 manages multitasking by using time-slices. A given thread will execute until its time-slice is over and is preempted by the operating system, or until it voluntarily transfers control to the operating system. OS/2's default minimum time-slice is 32 milliseconds, but this can be set up to 65,536 milliseconds by setting the TIMESLICE variable in the CONFIG.SYS file.

Interprocess Synchronization—Semaphores. OS/2 provides the ability to run multiple programs at the same time, so the next logical step is to get these programs to operate independently of each other while still working together to complete a task. With interprocess synchronization, programs can also communicate with other programs on other machines. This is the natural progression towards a client/server environment. Interprocess synchronization has technical difficulties that must be resolved before it can be implemented. The major consideration is that any two communicating programs do not know when they will be running, and therefore do not know when and how much data makes up a synchronization attempt. Restricting the programs to run in a limited time frame is unacceptable. This would violate some of what we have gained by having a multitasking system, and would not map well across the network. We must still allow a thread to execute in a natural way, but we can set up operating system mechanisms to allow us to write programs that will obey set conventions.

An operating system mechanism that allows interprocess synchronization is semaphores. OS/2 semaphores are atomic services that allow programs to synchronize operation. An atomic service is a service that cannot be interrupted or tasked out. Without atomic services, a thread that is ready to proceed and tries to send a message to another thread, but is interrupted in the middle of that message, could cause the other thread to continue when that thread needs to wait for the completion of the synchronization message.

Semaphores under OS/2 are part of the operating system's protected memory space, and can be used only via handles (a numeric ticket telling the operating system which part of a service to use) or names and API calls. The following code fragment demonstrates the API call to create an unnamed Event Semaphore and the handle set by the call:

```
if( DosCreateEventSem( NULL, &semHandle, 0, 0 ) )
{
        printf( "The number value of the handle is %lu\n", semHandle
);
}
```

In this example, you should note that the address of the handle (&semHandle) was passed in. This is so the API call can set the value of the handle. Handles are simply magic numbers to the operating system that allow the correct API call to tell the operating system which element of the repeated type is being addressed.

OS/2 supports three types of semaphores—mutual exclusion semaphores, event semaphores, and multiple wait (MuxWait) semaphores. All semaphores can be addressed in two ways, by handle or by name. If addressed by name, the semaphore is always shared. If a semaphore is created with no name, it must be addressed using the returned semaphore handle. A semaphore addressed only by its handle is known as an anonymous semaphore, and is almost always used for process synchronization of child threads.

OS/2 allows control of semaphore visibility by creating semaphores as either shared or private. Shared semaphores are available to all threads on the operating system and are usually accessed using a name given to the semaphore. Private semaphores are accessed by using a magic number identifying the semaphore to the operating system. There are over 64,000 shared semaphores in the operating system. Private semaphores are used to synchronize threads in a process. There are over 64,000 private semaphores available per process.

Mutual Exclusion Semaphore. This semaphore is used to serialize access to resources. If a thread wants access to a resource, it requests ownership of the semaphore. If a thread requests ownership and the semaphore cannot grant the thread's request, the state of the thread is determined by a parameter on the request. A parameter of the semaphore request is the number of milliseconds to wait for another thread to release the semaphore. If this request times out, the request will return a return code telling the thread of the failure. A request of 0 milliseconds will cause the thread to block and be suspended by putting it on a suspended thread list. The thread will be reactivated when the semaphore becomes available and can receive ownership of the semaphore. This reactivation of the thread is on a FIFO (First In First Out) basis. The capability of an operating system to put a thread asleep is critical for system efficiency. If the operating system could not suspend the requesting thread, each and every thread would then have to go into a "wait then test" loop. This not only wastes processor time, but would also cause the loss of the FIFO behavior of the waiting threads.

Event Semaphore. This semaphore is used as a signaling device to another thread. The receiving thread will commonly give up a resource or cause an operation to be done. The blocking behavior of the waiting thread is the same as that of a mutual exclusion semaphore, but the waiting thread does not get ownership of the semaphore. It is the duty of the waiting thread to

V

OS/2 Development

Tip
The nature of semaphores relies on the creation of a single semaphore, the request of ownership, the release of ownership, and the deletion of the semaphore. In most cases the thread that creates the semaphore is responsible for its deletion.

reset the event semaphore. The event semaphore has a counting behavior such that multiple posts will allow multiple releases of waiting threads. The creation, use, and deletion cycle of the event semaphore is the same as a mutual exclusion semaphore.

Multiple Wait Semaphore. A thread may be waiting not on a single, but on multiple, semaphores or any of a group of semaphores. In this way, a multiple wait semaphore is not a true semaphore, but is a semaphore container and manager for dealing with more than one semaphore. A multiple wait semaphore can only contain a series of one kind of semaphores, either mutual exclusion semaphores or event semaphores. The multiple wait semaphore behaves differently for each type of collected semaphores. A multiple wait semaphore can be named or anonymous, just like any other semaphore.

A thread can be told to suspend or time-out for waiting on a multiple wait semaphore. The wait command can be requested to wait for one of the contained semaphores, or it can be told to wait for all of the contained semaphores. If the thread is to respond to a single contained semaphore, the thread must also release the multiple wait semaphore once. This one-to-one correlation is just like every other semaphore we have discussed, but if the thread is to wait for all of the contained semaphores, the release must be called the same number of times as there are semaphores in the multiple wait semaphore. This behavior also makes perfect sense, but is not intuitive to the developer using the multiple wait semaphore.

Why is such a complicated semaphore necessary? Can't we just use a series of nested test commands? The multiple wait semaphore is necessary because we cannot use multiple nested test commands and achieve the required effect in the thread. If we use a series of nested test commands, the first test will suspend the thread until the semaphore is released. While the thread is suspended, one or all of the other semaphores may have been released, but the thread cannot respond or continue because it is suspended. A multiple wait semaphore allows us to use any or all of the contained semaphores, independent of order, via one specialized semaphore.

Interprocess Communication (IPC). OS/2 has built into the operating system the mechanisms for interprocess synchronization. This allows the operating system to build interprocess communication protocols from these atomic parts. Interprocess synchronization is a form of communication, but is limited to a boolean state or the state of multiple booleans. We will distinguish interprocess synchronization and interprocess communication by the amount of data that can be transferred between threads and processes. OS/2 provides four forms of interprocess communication protocols (IPC).

Shared Memory. Shared memory, as the name implies, is not a sophisticated form of IPC, but can implement most forms of data exchange in a simple way. This is the earliest form of IPC for operating systems, because the operating system must have the ability to allocate areas of memory to programs. Shared memory is then just an extension of the operating system to allocate and allow access to the memory allocated. There are no synchronization abilities built into shared memory IPC, so coordination must be done using semaphores.

A Queue. When blocks of data need to be received from multiple processes by a single process, a queue provides both synchronization and multiple ordering formats of the received data. The ordering of the blocks of data can be in one of three forms: First In First Out (FIFO), Last In First Out (LIFO) and by priority. Information in the queue can be retrieved by the receiving process in sequential order or randomly. Queues add efficiency by not transferring all the data during every communication step. Queues give access to the information put on the queue but does not make a copy of the information for the developer.

Anonymous Pipes. When data transfer using file access methods is necessary, an anonymous pipe provides access to a fixed size data area via separate read and write handles. An anonymous pipe uses the data area as a circular buffer to reuse the data area. Overloading the pipe or trying to read from an empty pipe will cause an error similar to normal file I/O failures. Anonymous pipes are normally used as a data transfer method between parent and child threads. It also gives the developer the familiarity of using file access methods. When anonymous pipes are created, they are not given a name; this limits the access to the pipe to usage from the pipe handle returned during the pipe's creation.

Named Pipes. Named pipes are the most used and most powerful IPC available. They allow data transfer between unrelated processes using the standard file I/O operations. Named pipes can provide two-way communication across machine boundaries, making them ideal for client/server applications. They also provide a lowest common denominator for client/server development, letting programmers design their own API layer above the named pipe, and providing the most flexibility in what can be sent or received. A named pipe also has the added feature of servicing multiple clients from the same server-created named pipe. Development using named pipes under OS/2 will be covered in a separate chapter in this book. When Named pipes are created they are given a name local to the server that creates it. Access to the named pipe from remote access clients requires the addition of the network host name to the pipe's name.

Memory Management. The ability to multitask multiple application grinds to a complete halt if your machine runs out of memory. This is a major flaw with DOS. The ability to use more memory on a machine under DOS became such an issue that many companies wrote their own memory management schemes to allow DOS to use all of the available memory. Why was this necessary? Why was DOS incapable of accessing all of a machines memory? It has to do with the size of the machine word and addresses.

DOS was built using 16-bit addressing which could address only the first 640K of memory. This decision was made to work with the first microprocessors from Intel, the 8086. This chip's registers are 16-bits wide. The opinion of the engineers at the time was that we would never need any more memory than that. The ability to add 32-bit addressing was also considered too expensive in both machine cycles and memory. This addressing scheme brought the IBM PC to the largest installed base of computers in the world, but its success also showed the importance of the computer to the world. When more was needed from the same PC architecture, the operating system was not able to help. Memory management schemes were created to allow access to memory above one megabyte, but this access could only allow swapping of blocks of data into lower memory areas where it could be directly accessed. This form of memory addressing worked, but carried heavy penalties for the developer and the user. The industry created extended memory management standards, but like many standards, everybody had their own. Later on, 32-bit chips were developed which could directly address up to 4 gigabytes of memory, but DOS still could not do 32-bit addressing.

What makes OS/2's memory management so important? Each process under OS/2 receives its own virtual address space. Each process, regardless of its platform origin, can receive an addressable space of 512 megabytes. Each virtual address space is protected from every other, and is prevented from accessing areas outside of its given address space. This protection is provided for each OS/2, Windows and DOS application. If an application attempts to address an area outside its address space, a page fault is generated by the hardware and OS/2 terminates the process, preventing the corruption before it does damage.

Each process, regardless of platform origin, uses the same memory management scheme. OS/2 supports many of the DOS memory extenders seamlessly, without modification to the program. OS/2 memory management supports Expanded Memory Specification (EMS), Lotus-Intel-Microsoft (LIM), Extended Memory Specifications (XMS), and the DOS Protected Mode Interface (DPMI). The support for DPMI has been upgraded to support both standard and enhanced memory models for Microsoft Windows. Some of these memory modes can be more stressful to the operating system. OS/2 allows each process to configure its memory requirements individually. If a DOS program does not need a memory extender, then the overhead of loading that extender for that process is skipped. A Microsoft Windows session can be started using the same address space as other sessions to increase loading speed and lower memory requirements, or each can have its own address space. Opening multiple Windows sessions will exhaust system resources quickly, but opening a separate session for a special purpose can have benefits of its own. A separate Windows session for debugging an application can protect other Windows programs running in a separate session.

OS/2 uses the Intel 32-bit class machine's paging feature to give the operating system demand-paged virtual memory. OS/2 gives each process a table of memory blocks called pages. Each of these pages is 4 kilobytes and matches the memory allocation size of the Intel microprocessor. An operating system does not have to use the microprocessor's paging size but the microprocessor works best with this page size, and OS/2 takes full advantage of this feature. Demand-paged virtual memory is one of the key reasons why OS/2 2.0 and above will only run on an Intel 80386 or better. Each process's memory is managed by its allocated paging table. The paging table allocates 512 megabytes of paged memory to each process, but will only commit memory for the pages that are in use by the process. This allows more memory to be acquired at the time of use. When physical memory is exhausted, then the least-used pages in memory will be swapped automatically by OS/2. Memory swapping is the act of removing a page of memory from the operating system's memory and storing it on a hard drive. Swapping will occur when more physical memory is required or a page of memory is needed that has been swapped to the hard drive. Using demand-paged virtual memory will let OS/2 use all of the physical memory and as much drive space available on the drive that holds the swapper file as the total system memory available.

OS/2 uses the Intel 80386 architecture to allow system code to access any address boundaries, while user code has more restrictions in its addressing range. The Intel 80386 has four rings of protection. The OS/2 core operating system runs at ring zero, which is required to allow the system efficiency and unlimited access for system calls. Ring zero allows code to be run without checking for its right to do so. OS/2 does not use ring one. I/O devices, such as device drivers, run in ring two. Ring two does not allow as much free access as the lower rings but is less restrictive or guarded than ring three. This is why beta device drivers tend to destabilize and lock-up the operating system. All other programs run in ring three. This is where the most protection from errant processes is supported by both the hardware and the operating system. Ring three operations are checked by the system and will cause a shutdown of the offending task.

Dynamic Linking (DLLs). OS/2 allows the creation of run-time sections of code that are not part of an executable's code. Dynamic linking to independent sections of code and resources allows more than one program to use the code and resources without taking up more memory. System extensions of OS/2 are implemented as DLLs. This allows the system to be modified or repaired without relinking the object code. The use of DLLs also allows the DLL to be loaded if and when it is needed. This on-demand loading will help speed up program execution because a given DLL may never be used and the given DLL may already be loaded by another application.

Exception Handling. OS/2's multitasking abilities also require that it be able to handle serious errors without corrupting and jeopardizing the entire system's stability. When OS/2 detects an exception, it will usually terminate the offending program unless the program has registered its own handler for the exception. OS/2 has API calls to allow developers to design their own exception handler for every thread.

File Systems and IFS. OS/2 supports two hard drive file systems, High Performance File System (HPFS) and File Allocation Table (FAT). The FAT system is the default built into OS/2. HPFS can be set up during system installation as an Installable File System (IFS). Both FAT and HPFS support file representation as a hierarchy of files and subdirectories.

FAT is the file system used by DOS, and is fully supported by OS/2. OS/2 needs extra abilities from its file systems to support Extended Attributes (EA). The Extended Attributes allow the operating system to store extra file-related information on each file. The Extended Attributes are necessary to store and extend the functionality of the file system, so OS/2's Workplace Shell will have an area to store system- and user-defined information about files. This helps OS/2 use FAT as an object-oriented file system necessary to run an object-oriented graphical interface. IBM has improved FAT under OS/2 to be a 32-bit file system. DOS FAT is a 16-bit file system. The 32-bit FAT system has proven performance benefits. Many programs, especially disk I/O intensive applications, will run faster under OS/2 with a low-process load. If a high-process load is applied to the system, the resulting elapsed time will appear longer, but the amount of time used by the system to complete the task will be less than under DOS.

HPFS has many advantages over FAT. It supports a larger maximum file size of 2 gigabytes and a maximum partition size of 512 gigabytes. It supports long files names, and is not restricted to the eleven-character file name (the 8.3 format) that FAT uses. HPFS can handle fully qualified path names (x:\dir\subdir\filename.ext) of up to 260 characters. The key advantage that HPFS has over FAT is that it is optimized for handling large files and file systems and is fairly resistant to file fragmentation—not immune, but resistant.

OS/2 supports Installable File Systems (IFS). An IFS is a driver that requires a common application interface to use the supported file system. An IFS that many OS/2 users have is the Compact Disk File System (CDFS). If your OS/2 system has a CD-ROM drive, the OS/2 installation program sets up an IFS in your CONFIG.SYS using a system file called CDFS.IFS. The format of a compact disk is different from FAT and HPFS and, by using an IFS driver, OS/2 will see the compact disk as just another file system. If your machine has a NetWare network connection then the NetWare install program would have installed an IFS name NWFS.IFS.

Multimedia. OS/2 2.1 shipped with Multimedia Presentation Manager/2 (MMPM/2) and OS/2 then became the leading-edge general purpose multimedia operating system in the world. This is not just a boast of IBM, OS/2 has the best multimedia engine available for the PC. Developing both small and large multimedia applications for OS/2 has proven to be relatively simple, scalable with minimal error introduction and, given the stable system that supports it, I have found no system-running standard hardware that can compare. Many other systems require special hardware to match MMPM/2 capabilities. The MMPM/2 product consists of three subsystems, described below.

Multimedia I/O Programming Interface (MMIO). The core of MMIO is the MMIO manager. The MMIO manager is a controller for handling and synchronizing the use of multimedia data files. All recognized multimedia files use a standard manipulation interface and a consistent way to open, query file data, write data, read data and close multimedia files. Other services provided by MMIO are installable I/O systems for MMIO to read your own or unsupported media format, handlers to extend the MMIO interface for additional functionality, memory file extensions to allow a block of memory to appear as a MMIO-recognized data format, and buffering of file I/O for performance gains. In a client/server environment, this allows remote storage and access to multimedia data with less burden on the network.

Tip

On drive partitions of less than 100 megabytes, HPFS will not show much difference from a FAT partition, but on larger partitions the performance of HPFS will become more evident.

V

OS/2 Development

Synchronization/Streaming Programming Interface (SPI). The synchronization/streaming programming interface provides a low-level interface used by applications to move data quickly between source and target areas with high priority. This guarantees that multimedia playback has no hesitations. SPI has a synchronization mechanism to easily combine multiple data sources for playback. The SPI synchronization is accomplished by a controlling data stream that sends out periodic timing messages to the rest of the data streams; the timing messages keep all data streams on time. The use of OS/2 makes the management of data streams easier on the synchronization controls by using threads to keep accurate control of the data streams, and the flat memory model to give simple access to large data streams. The simplified synchronization of multimedia data streams allows networks to better manage the delivery of information to clients. The receiving of multimedia data is time critical, so the streaming of data on the network is critical.

Media Control Interface (MCI). The media control interface was a joint development effort of IBM and Microsoft. It provides a simple consistent device independent interface to media devices. MCI uses logical device interface to control video, videodisc, MIDI, compact disc, and waveform audio. A logical device supports simple VCR-type controls, including play, pause, stop, open, close and seek. Other logical devices support specific commands for the device. MCI consists of two API calls, a send command and a send string. The send string call allows the developer to design a cumulative series of text commands dynamically. The MCI has no performance impact on networks but allows a familiar control interface on all platforms regardless of the server platform.

OS/2 as a Client

Choosing a client platform depends on the requirements of the users. If you listen to any specific vendor of operating systems, their perspective of what is required for a client platform will conform to their product. This is not to say what the vendor is trying to say is incorrect, but sales are made by making the customer think that the offered product is the best value for his or her money. Perceiving the needs of the client's operating system will allow a customer to make the correct choice for today's and tomorrow's requirements. OS/2 offers an almost ideal platform for a client operating system.

Platform Resources

OS/2 runs on the Intel family of 32-bit microprocessors. The memory and disk requirements of OS/2 allow use on most networked machines.

Multitasking

Client machines do not perform the same tasks as servers. A server machine will be dedicated to being a server, doing the same kind of operations day in and day out. A client machine needs to do all the operations and tasks that an individual does in a job. This means that a client machine will run many applications not related to the client/server process. Word processors, spreadsheets and multimedia all need to run in harmony with each other. All the daily work requires preemptive multitasking to allow all programs to run together, and system protection so an errant application will not lock or crash the entire system, doing possible damage to the file system in the process. OS/2's preemptive multitasking and system protection answer this need.

Integrated Environment

A client machine needs to remain as comfortable and intuitive as possible for the user. OS/2 provides seamless integration of all applications on the same desktop. DOS applications can be run full-screen or in a DOS window. Windows applications can be run in a full-screen Windows desktop or can be placed seamlessly on the OS/2 desktop with no change in the program's appearance. OS/2 applications can be as primitive as their Windows counterparts, or they can be integrated into the work environment using desktop objects to manipulate and report on local and remote information.

Installation Support

The job of keeping all clients' software updated and installing new software can be difficult and time-consuming. OS/2 provides unattended network installation support. Software can be installed from a remote system, including the OS/2 operating system.

Multimedia Support

Organizations can use MMPM/2 as a multimedia base for the presentation of graphics, network use of video conferencing and remote repositories of sound, digital video and text. OS/2's ability to easily synchronize multimedia presentations while still protecting other applications makes it an excellent choice for handling multimedia.

Software Support

The ability of OS/2 to run the largest base of software is a convincing argument for its choice. Most DOS, Microsoft Windows, and OS/2 applications can be run on the same system. People do different jobs in different ways. OS/2 allows users to choose the software platforms they work best in or to use platforms that are currently available or required by employers.

V

OS/2 Development

Seamless Client Access

Many of a client's services can be provided to the user as graphical symbols or icons. File servers will appear as another drive icon, printers will appear as another print object, and e-mail service boxes and note creation will appear as service icons and template objects to be manipulated. Network services are accessed by clicking on icons. The more familiar a user becomes with interaction with objects instead of programs, the more natural these actions become. OS/2's Workplace Shell has support for these seamless client/server abilities.

OS/2 as a Server

A server running OS/2 presents a client/server system with the same advantages as a minicomputer. OS/2 can match or surpass any operating system in many of the critical server requirements.

Server Power

A well-equipped server station using the 32-bit OS/2 has both the raw microprocessor speed and the operating system support to maintain a dedicated and stable server. A 32-bit processor will be able to transfer large blocks of data in 32-bit sections instead of smaller amounts that 16-bit software and 16-bit microprocessors are limited to. An OS/2 server has the protected memory capability to prevent errant tasks from corrupting memory and crashing the system.

Installation, Support, and Management

OS/2 is easier to install, support, and maintain than comparable 32-bit operating systems. Many of the tools for server modification have graphical or object-oriented interfaces, making tasks simpler to understand and accomplish. IBM's support centers exist in most industrial centers of the world, with a long history of useful customer support.

Add-On Services

OS/2 provides the base server functions and system hooks to allow other server software to be selected at the administrator's discretion. The OS/2 system design allows varying services to fit in seamlessly and work as interchangeable pieces. Other servers are bundled with extended services provided with the system as part of the cost of the server software. These bundled services are often the administrator's only choice, are of questionable value, and do not allow for modular replacement of selected pieces.

Scalability

As a child of the Intel 32-bit hardware, OS/2 can easily support hardware changes as long as supported drivers are provided. IBM produces OS/2 SMP, a version of OS/2 that supports symmetric multiprocessing (SMP). A version of OS/2 SMP will support Intel's APIC chip. A beta of this system was demonstrated using a 16-microprocessor configuration. Multiservers can support the workload that a powerful single server has trouble with. Multiservers must be supported with operating system extensions such as Distributed Computing Environment (DCE) or Transaction Processing Monitors, which OS/2 fully supports

Communication Stacks

OS/2 supports many communications stacks that allow OS/2 to communicate with most clients and servers on most types of networks. Supported stacks are APPC, NetBIOS, IPX/SPX, Named Pipes and TCP/IP. These stacks coexist as well as or better than any in the communication industry.

Distributed Computing

Industry standards for distributed computing service have been implemented for OS/2. A full implementation of OSF Distributed Computing Environment (DCE) as well as different vendors' implementation of messaging, queuing and event notification can reside on OS/2. The software giants, LAN Server and NetWare, can exist and be run together on the same system.

Database Support

Implementations of major industry databases such as DB2/2, Oracle, Sybase and Gupta exist for the OS/2 platform. Transaction Processing is also supported on OS/2 with CICS.

Groupware Support

Person to person communication and cooperative work is finding a market in today's workplace. Lotus Notes server for OS/2 is a major groupware platform. OS/2 supports other specialized groupware formats for workflow, document imaging, and real-time multimedia human interaction.

Communications for OS/2

Client/server systems require a way for the applications on the client side to talk to the applications on the server side. The goal of any communications software is to allow the client transparent access to the server. Transparency is

V

OS/2 Development

achieved by layering multiple levels of software over the hardware. Developers will use the appropriate level in the communications software to gain the required access to communicate with the networking hardware.

Transparency

Setting up a seamless system for the client presents many causes for concern. Concepts that we take for granted on a client's local system must be managed by networking software. Not all levels of transparency are implemented due to the real-world concerns of security, efficiency and cost. Different aspects of transparency that are used tend to make up the defining characteristics of a communication method.

Forms of transparency implemented by communication methods are:

- Namespace transparency, for consistent naming conventions of resources on the network.

- Logon transparency, so that a single logon will allow the client access to all servers that it is allowed to use.

- Time and Date transparency, so that all services think they are doing operations at the same consistent time.

- Failure transparency, so that a network failure will not cripple or crash the client system, session reconnection will be invisible, and multiple retries of a request will not cause errors or failures.

- Location transparency, so that the user does not know the server name or address.

Stacks

The multiple levels of software that are available to the application to allow communication to the server are called stacks. The lowest level of stacks is the device drivers, which provide access to communication hardware. As you go up the stack different layers represent various levels of abstraction to communicate with the hardware. The upper level provides the simplest access, but is also the most restrictive and inflexible. The further down the level is, the more flexible it is, but also more complicated to use. Stacks provide a multitude of access options for any kind of development plans. In theory, vendors provide stacks that are designed to work with other vendors' stacks. Multiple stacks allow development at a single layer without being concerned about what lower layers and hardware are available. But the reality of the situation is a little different from the conceptual design. Not all vendors' stacks work with other vendors' stacks. OS/2 has the industry standard stacks implemented for the platform and has a reputation for having stacks work well together. Not all stacks use all the layers, so drawing parallels between stacks is not always a one-to-one concept.

TCP/IP

Interest in TCP/IP stems from the protocol's use on UNIX systems and the Internet. The Internet provides a networking service across the United States and many other nations. OS/2 is not left out of this global network. Many traditional TCP/IP services are provided for OS/2, including web browsing using IBM's WebExplorer. These services require TCP/IP protocol services. TCP/IP is important enough to OS/2 that we will be covering TCP/IP Socket programming in Chapter 22, "Other Client/Server Techniques."

TCP/IP Advantages. Implementations of TCP/IP for OS/2 are provided by multiple vendors, but we will focus on IBM's TCP/IP for OS/2. This product provides a 32-bit implementation of the TCP/IP protocol stack and services, and a rich set of related products. IBM's product design philosophy has been to allow a customer to purchase the basic services, and then extend services from that base package to serve a specific need. TCP/IP for OS/2 does not waiver from this design objective.

Services. Application services provided by TCP/IP for OS/2 include many of the industry standard TCP/IP applications with some applications extended to take advantage of OS/2's system features.

News Reader is a multithreaded application that allows the user to read UseNet news services. UseNet news services provide access to a large selection of information posted by other users of the news service. Newsgroups can be subscribed to so that reading sessions will only read groups that the user selects. This application also allows posting of items, which is the basis of the service.

UltiMail is an application to read and send e-mail sent to a user. This product has been extended beyond normal text-based SendMail to allow the exchange of multimedia files, including bitmaps, GIF files, TIFF files, audio wave files, MIDI files, video clips, RTF files (Rich Text Format) and binary files. UltiMail implements Workplace Shell objects for mail folders, envelopes and address books. These Workplace Shell extensions allow users to work in a familiar manner with logical elements from the real world.

Talk allows users to communicate with interactive messages. The application interface will be split into two areas, the typing area and the display area.

V

OS/2 Development

Keystrokes entered while the application is in focus will be sent to the receiver's display area, while the receiver's keystrokes will be shown on the sender's display area. A talk session can be initiated by requesting an Internet address to talk to. The receiving Internet address will display a message on the screen requesting a talk session with the sender's Internet address.

Domain Name System (DNS) is a database system designed to convert symbolic (logical) names to Internet addresses. This allows users to use names instead of numbers to express the address of another machine. Local services keep a small subset of conversions that are used most frequently. The address of a Name Server is given to the DNS so that names that are not found locally can be resolved by a series of remote name services. This delegation of conversions allows a series of name servers to find a name if it has been entered in a name table. Name Servers also save the local name table from becoming too large and being inaccurate when remote names change.

Telnet is the TCP/IP remote terminal connection protocol. A terminal is a remote command line emulator. Commands typed in a telnet session will be executed on the remote machine. OS/2 can be configured to be a telnet client (to send commands) or to be a telnet server (to accept commands). OS/2 telnet includes terminal emulation for VT100, VT200, ASCII and IBM 3270.

PMANT is a Presentation Manager (Graphical) application that does IBM 3270 terminal emulation for a remote session. IBM 3270 emulation is a character-based terminal protocol that allows the placement of characters on the screen and communication of screen changes to the host.

Simple Mail Transfer Protocol (SMTP) is a protocol allowing connection to a mail server to make requests as a client. TCP/IP for OS/2 provides LaMail, a PM application to interface with SMTP, and provide a user interface for Sendmail, which uses SMTP. LaMail is a good example of a client application.

File Transfer Protocol (FTP) is a protocol for transferring files to and from a remote machine. Transfer modes for FTP are binary and ASCII. ASCII mode does end-of-line translation on text files. TCP/IP for OS/2 provides an FTP text mode application and a PM application for graphically operating FTP. FTP also provides directory listing, creation and changing, remote file deletion and multiple file transfer services. Multiple FTP client sessions can be run at the same time. TCP/IP for OS/2 also provides an FTP server. The OS/2 FTP server includes security features by maintaining and requesting named account access with password verification.

Trivial File Transfer Protocol (TFTP) is similar to FTP, but it cannot use file and directory services and does not support the security features of FTP. A TFTP session does not connect to a configured TFTP server the way that FTP does. It operates on a connectionless protocol. A connectionless protocol handles all the communication issues for each request, instead of creating and maintaining a connection.

Simple Network Management Protocol (SNMP) is the industry standard for managing TCP/IP network. SNMP uses two types of tasks to manage a network: monitors and agents. A monitor task queries the agent tasks for the status of the remote machine. Agent tasks reside on network nodes and monitor node activity, execute remote commands, and can send emergency messages called traps to the monitor task.

Packet InterNet Groper (PING) is an application that uses SNMP to prompt a remote station for its current state of operation. PING sends out a message to the remote machine; if that machine answers, it is "alive." If it does not respond in a defined amount of time after a defined number of iterations then it is "not responding."

PMPING is an application that graphically displays the status of a PING's query with multiple remote machines.

Remote printing services are provided by TCP/IP for OS/2 in both client (LPR) and server (LPD) applications. A line printer client, LPR, transfers a text file to be spooled and printed by a line printer daemon, LPD, on a remote machine. A daemon is a task that only handles requests for services.

Network File System (NFS) is Sun Microsystems-distributed file system that supports hierarchical file structures and file locks, and does ASCII file conversions in the same style as FTP text file transfers. TCP/IP for OS/2 provides a full implementation of both client and server software. NFS uses SunRPC for client/server communications.

Sun Remote Procedure Call (SunRPC) allows programs to execute remote functions on a server machine using APIs. The client first builds a message using parameters of the server address, program number, a procedure number for a remote procedure and a version number. This message is sent to the server, it is unpacked, the passed remote procedure is executed, and a response is sent back to the client. Many vendors, including IBM, offer SunRPC and NFS, because it is freely licensed by Sun Microsystems as part of the Open Network Computing (ONC) environment.

Kerberos Authentication System is a security system that provides authorization checking based on the user instead of the node. When a Kerberos server identifies a client and checks the connection for authenticity, the client is issued an encrypted key. The encrypted key is used by the client to make requests to other servers that require the key. A client must request separate keys for each service. The Kerberos Authentication System never transmits passwords across the network. Passwords are used to decode keys.

X Windows is a client/server protocol for graphical presentation of windows. The terms for client and server are reversed when talking about X Windows. An X Window client manages the presentation of windows on an X Window server. The X Window server sends mouse and keyboard events to the X Window client. This server/client scheme is an advanced version of a host/terminal arrangement. An X Window server can connect to multiple X Window clients, with each client controlling a separate window on the X Window server.

Development using TCP/IP for OS/2 is done using API calls. TCP/IP provides these multiple development kits for programming different services of TCP/IP:

- NetBIOS for TCP/IP provides connections for Internet operations using NetBIOS. This interface supports sessions, datagrams and naming services.

- The FTP API extends the command line capabilities of FTP. A program can connect to 256 FTP servers at once, or do file transfers between FTP servers without spooling the file to the local machine.

- Berkeley Sockets API provides the most flexible—and most complicated—way to write TCP/IP communications programs. The OS/2 implementation supports three socket types: raw, stream, and datagram. These sockets can provide Internet addressing information, name services, and peer-to-peer communications. New services can be added by expanding the socket interface.

- X Windows and OSF Motif API provide the standard X Windows APIs, GUI APIs, header files and OSF Motif widgets. Proper use of this development kit will allow the developer to create X Window programs on OS/2 and easily port them to and from other X Window platforms.

- Kerberos API provides calls for the management of authentication requests and ticketing services. Requests for reading and writing of encrypted and unencrypted messages can be done.

■ SNMP DPI API provides a way to dynamically modify a SNMP agent without recompilation. It also extends the OS/2 SNMP agent by creating subagents that register with the OS/2 SNMP agent.

Products. TCP/IP for OS/2 can be purchased by specific part or in grouped packages.

■ The Base Package includes the standard TCP/IP applications, daemons and the protocol stack.

■ The NetBIOS Package includes support for NetBIOS with TCP/IP.

■ The Programmer's Package includes development support tools for FTP API, Kerberos, NCS, SNMP DPI API, Sockets and SunRPC.

■ The Applications Package includes the Base Package without IBM's TCP/IP protocol stack. This allows an OS/2 system to run TCP/IP with other vendors' stacks if they are socket-based.

■ The DOS/Windows Access Package includes support for DOS and Microsoft Windows TCP/IP programs to execute in OS/2 sessions supported by TCP/IP for OS/2. The DOS TCP/IP applications must adhere to the IBM TCP/IP programming interface, and the Microsoft Windows TCP/IP applications must adhere to the WinSock API.

■ The Total Package includes the Base Package, the X Window Server Package, the NFS Package and the Extended Networking Package. This combination of packages makes up a common TCP/IP for OS/2 workstation.

■ The X Windows Client Package includes applications for running X Windows in a client environment and the X libraries.

■ The X Windows Server Package includes applications for controlling and displaying X Windows applications on a remote OS/2 Presentation Manager machine.

■ The OSF/Motif Package includes the OSF/Motif for client applications under OS/2. This package must be used in conjunction with the X Windows Client Package.

■ The NFS Package includes both client and server runtime support.

■ The Domain Name Server Package includes applications for name server support.

V

OS/2 Development

■ The Extended Networking Package includes support for both SNA, through sockets, and the X.25 interface.

■ The UltiMail Package includes the Workplace Shell applications for e-mail with multimedia.

NetWare

Novell NetWare is the most popular file server and network operating system. NetWare 4.x for OS/2 allows OS/2 to become a NetWare Server, and in turn allows NetWare clients to use NetWare OS/2 services. The NetWare Requester for OS/2 lets OS/2 clients use Novell LAN services.

NetWare on OS/2. How does a Network Operating System (NOS) operate with OS/2? It would appear that you have two operating systems running at the same time. Through the magic of OS/2 memory management, ring 0 addressing privileges and device driver management, the NetWare server (NOS) is coexisting on the same machine under OS/2. Quite an accomplishment, considering that you can get over 90% of native NetWare performance from this NOS/OS combination. The remaining performance loss is attributed to OS/2 handling hardware and device services over NetWare.

The NOS/OS combination is accomplished by having OS/2 allocate a large block of memory that is not to be managed by OS/2. NetWare is loaded into this memory space and is started. OS/2 and NetWare share resources by using special drivers that allow NetWare access without modification to NetWare. CD-ROM drives cannot currently be shared. NetWare cannot share hard drive space with OS/2, so it is given its own drive partition to manage. NetWare for OS/2 can achieve up to 95% performance of a dedicated NetWare server.

When NetWare was started it was run at ring 3 like other OS/2 application, it is run at ring 0. NetWare appears to OS/2 as a trusted application.

NetWare Advantages. One of the key advantages that NetWare has is its ability to allow different systems to see the same files in their own format. A NetWare server uses its own private format for file storage, but if a DOS FAT, OS/2 HPFS, Sun NFS, or Macintosh AFP appearance is needed, then NetWare can do the translations automatically.

NetWare can also allow you System Fault Tolerance III (SFT III), a fault tolerance using replicated servers. The creation of huge files can now be broken up across multiple drives. A single file can as big as 32 terabytes (32,000 gigabytes!). NetWare also has built-in accounting services that manage services for billing purposes, support for authentication using encrypted keys, routing capabilities for AppleTalk, TCP/IP and IPX/SPX, and fast data transfer using Wide Area Networks (WANs). This is currently only available for 3.x servers.

The NetWare Requester for OS/2 provides transparent access to all of NetWare's features. A key advantage for OS/2 is that files can be manipulated using the Workplace Shell, including OS/2 drag and drop features. A file on a NetWare server can be visually manipulated to use a NetWare printing service (drag and drop a file on a printer).

OS/2 API Groups for NetWare. Developing NetWare applications is as simple under OS/2 as any other system. There are even NetWare calls for special services required for OS/2. To use NetWare services OS/2 must have the NetWare LAN Requestor for OS/2 and for NetWare development the NetWare Development Tool Kit is required.

NetWare Services. The APIs used to provide access to NetWare services are also known as NWCalls. NWCalls cover access to login, queues directories, shared files, semaphores and printer services. NWCalls fall into these groups:

- Accounting Services are calls that allow the configuration of NetWare to keep track of resource usage by individual accounts.

- Apple File Services (AFP) are calls that use Apple Computer's AppleTalk Filing Protocol (AFP). These services allow the storage of data files that have extra attributes beyond FAT attributes.

- Auditing Services are calls that allow a history trace of NetWare system events. The filtering of an event history can be set up to test for varying conditions. These services are only available for NetWare 4.x

- Bindery Services are calls that maintain information of NetWare server access privileges. A NetWare server stores this information in a database of bindery objects. Bindery objects can be any named entity that needs to access the NetWare server. These services also allow the querying of bindery objects based on object attributes.

- Connection Services are calls that return the status of connections to a NetWare server. A NetWare server keeps a table of information on each currently connected object.

- Data Migration Services are calls that transfer requested files to be stored on an archive area. During data migrations, if special services are required of the operators, they will be prompted to load the proper device.

- Deleted Files Services are calls that can search for, recover, and purge deleted files.

- Directory Services are calls that allow operations on NetWare's X.500 directory service. NetWare's X.500 directory service is an arrangement of objects representing the directory system. These calls allow the creation, querying, and modification of the objects.

- Extended Attributes Services are calls that allow a client to modify an OS/2 extended attribute of stored files.

- File Server Environment Services are calls that allow the management of clients' connections on the server. A NetWare server must receive logon, logoff, connect, and disconnect calls to allow clients access to the server. These calls can also query the server for information about the server.

- File Systems Services are calls that allow NetWare file services. These services include the creation, deletion, and renaming of directories; the setting of file attributes; the copying, renaming, and erasing of files; and the getting, releasing, and clearing of file locks

- Message Services are calls that allow the broadcasting of a text message of no more than 265 characters to specified workstations.

- Name Space Services are calls that allow clients to create files on a NetWare server using the client's naming convention. Supported client naming conventions include OS/2 (HPFS), UNIX, Macintosh, FTAM and DOS. The access of multiple clients with different naming conventions would force the use of name spaces for each naming convention.

- Path and Drive Services are calls that allow the mapping or removal of a network drive to a directory path, the parsing of path strings and the retrieval of drive information.

- Print Server Services are calls that allow print servers to be configured, managed and resource-defined. Resource definition can be printers, print jobs, and print queues.

- Print Services are calls that allow clients to redirect data from a local machine port to a NetWare server's print queue.

- Queue Management Services (QMS) are calls that manage the creation, management, and control of FIFO jobs queues. Job queues are requests for processing that the client does not want to wait for.

■ Synchronization Services are calls that implement a network counting semaphore on the server to limit access to a resource. This counting semaphore can have an upper boundary limit of 127, but if the upper boundary is set to 1, only serial access is allowed to the resource.

■ Transaction Tracking Services (TTS) are calls that track NetWare files transactions for completion and file integrity. If a transaction is incomplete, the server will back out of the transaction. A file can be set as a transaction file by changing the file's extended attribute for transactions. NetWare servers can handle up to 200 transactions at a time, but only one per client.

■ Volume Services are calls that allow clients to get information about mounted volumes on the server.

Peer-To-Peer Communications. This service allows OS/2 to communicate with other OS/2, Microsoft Windows, and DOS NetWare Requesters at a peer-to-peer level. Protocol that this service can use includes TLI, NetBios and IPX/SPX, as defined in the following list:

■ TLI Services are calls that provide peer-to-peer services using a variation of Berkeley socket called Transport Layer Interface (TLI). TLI is a Novell standard protocol.

■ IPX Services are calls that provide datagram service using Novell's Internet Packet Exchange (IPX). Datagrams are sent with a small amount of networking overhead, but secure no guarantee that the datagram will be received. IPX is a NetWare protocol.

■ SPX Services are calls that provide Sequenced Packet Exchange (SPX) services that are more reliable than IPX. SPX is a wrapper around IPX that guarantees packet delivery. SPX is a NetWare protocol.

■ NetBIOS Services are calls that provide NetBIOS emulation using IPX/SPX. This service allows OS/2 Requester to communicate with DOS and Microsoft Windows Requester, and does not require server assistance.

Network Named Pipes. Network Named Pipes are such an important client/server mechanism for OS/2 that there will be another chapter in this book on OS/2 named pipes. Network Named Pipes do not require a NetWare server to function. They also allow up to 1000 connections. OS/2 supports both client and server Named Pipes access. DOS and Microsoft Windows support only client access to Named Pipes. Many of the Named Pipes calls are native to

V

OS/2 Development

OS/2, but the calls that are not are used to get network Named Pipes server names. OS/2 Named Pipes API and Development are covered in Chapter 21, "Introduction to Named Pipes."

LAN Server

LAN Server has its history in the Microsoft product LAN Manager. Both products make networking a key part of the operating system, support the other's client software, and use the same security system. IBM LAN Server is a 32-bit version of LAN Manager that is optimized for OS/2.

LAN Server Advantages. Testing industry benchmarks report that LAN Server is among the fastest NOS available. LAN Server simplifies network development by using the LAN Server API package. This package is consistent with OS/2 development, because it was designed to be a natural extension of the operating system. LAN Server will be based on the DCE/DME platform. The DCE Toolkit for OS/2 is available for LAN Server. LAN Server has integrated disk mirroring and duplexing, support for four LAN adapters on a single LAN segment, and object-oriented Workplace Shell applications for simple installation and configuration.

Network Functionality. Network Administration Services provide a broad range of facilities to keep a system running efficiently. LAN Server allows administrators to manage profiles of users, groups and area resources; it collects accounting information on resource usage; it allows other operators to manage subsets of the system with the permission of the system administrator; it can set up audit trails on users and groups; and it can automate the scheduling of job execution.

Network Services are a series of configurable applications managed by LAN Server. Network Services can be developed using simple specifications that allow the new programs to be an extension of LAN Server. Bundled Network Services include:

- Server Service, request management for resources.

- Netpopup Service, which causes messages to "pop-up" on the user's screen.

- Alerter Service, where specified users are notified of requested situations.

- Remoteboot Service, where diskless workstations can be started from the server.

- Replicator Service, which provides that designated files on a server can be automatically distributed to other servers and clients.

- Netrun Service, which allows remote execution on a server if the server has the application.

- Workstation Service, which allows the redirection and return of system functions from other clients and servers.

- Time Server Service, which allows all clients and servers to designate a single server to synchronize their system times.

Peer Services allow LAN Requester clients access to other LAN Requester clients. Peer Services do not have many of the features of a dedicated LAN Server, but for small offices with meager network requirements, this is a cost-effective way to share resources.

Multimedia Services allow LAN Server to reserve a high percentage of network bandwidth for multimedia use. This does crowd the network, but gives clients a central repository for large-volume multimedia files that can be accessed with minor performance issues.

Management of Network Devices allows the queuing of information to and from clients. This lets the clients shift the burden of large data management of devices to the server. Clients may then later retrieve the results of the operation.

Fault Tolerance gives LAN Server features such as disk mirroring, disk duplexing, HPFS defective sector remapping, read/write operation alerts and the ability to handle power failures with hardware support from Uninterruptible Power Supplies (UPS).

Multiprocessor Services allows LAN Server to use multiple processors on specialized hardware. One processor is the master, which farms out tasks to the other processors. This is known as asymmetrical multiprocessing.

Security Services allow the administrator to control or restrict every aspect of a user's access to the server. This is done by User Profile Management (UPM). To grant a user logon and resource rights, the user must have permission set in its UPM. Passwords are encrypted twice for extra security. Numerous other security features have been implemented for LAN Server, giving an administrator the ability to protect the server.

Remote Resource Access allows users to use resources on the server transparently on the client. Remote devices appear and behave the same as local

V

OS/2 Development

devices on the client's desktop. A Workplace Shell printer or drive icon will perform the same service, in the same way, for both local and remote use.

OS/2 APIs for LAN Server. Named pipe services are calls that provide two-way interprocess communication using normal file I/O functions calls. Named pipe calls are part of OS/2's interprocess communications scheme, not a library extension.

MailSlot Services are calls that use NetBios datagrams to perform a unidirectional interprocess communication. MailSlots are created on the server side, can perform a blocking wait, and do not need to be opened or closed.

Alert Services are calls that provide messages of network events to applications.

Network Management Services are calls that manage the server's audit log, the error log, network statistics for clients and servers, and network servers, clients and sessions. These calls can also provide information from the IBMLAN.INI file.

Resource Management Services are calls that manage connections between clients and servers and the sharing of server resources, serial devices and their queues, and monitor a server's open pipe, file and device status. These calls can also provide and modify handle-based information.

Access Control Services are calls that provide control of all types of accounts, and change or view all types of access to server resources.

Network Services are calls that provide management of messages, files and network service programs. These calls can also provide time services, and can run remote programs.

Products. There are multiple flavors of LAN Server to choose from, ranging from a simple server to specialized services for multimedia and other platforms:

- OS/2 LAN Server—Entry is a slimmed-down version of the Advanced product. The features excluded from this product are used in the enterprise and large-scale client/server sites.

- OS/2 LAN Server—Advanced is recommended for client/server environments where speed, security and functionality are needed, and a very large number of clients is anticipated.

- OS/2 LAN Server—Ultimedia is an extension product for multimedia use. This specialized product is used to enhance specific high-volume network traffic.

- OS/2 LAN Server—Macintosh is an extension product which caters to the Apple Macintosh clients on the network.

From Here...

In this chapter, you discovered the capabilities of OS/2 and how they make OS/2 an excellent choice for a client/server platform. You also learned about client/server tools and their development interface. I hope this chapter has helped prepare you for a better understanding of OS/2 as a client/server platform.

The following chapters will provide broader information on selected topics that relate to this chapter:

- Chapter 1, "What Is Client/Server?," gives an extended introduction to client/server systems.

- Chapter 3, "Communications Protocols," provides a deeper view of TCP/IP protocol stacks that is the model for TCP/IP for OS/2.

- Chapter 4, "Client/Server Development Overview," shows the steps necessary for planning and implementing a client/server project.

- Chapter 23, "Multiplatform Applications," gives an expanded view of using different platforms to create a client/server system.

Chapter 21

Introduction to Named Pipes

In our introduction to OS/2 and client/server computing, we discovered that OS/2 provides a multitasking operating system with many advanced features that gives the developer easier ways to accomplish complicated development. OS/2 gives us multitasking—what more do we need? The ability to multitask OS/2, Windows, and DOS applications and to protect these applications from each other is impressive, but it doesn't take much imagination to envision the need for these processes and threads to communicate with each other. A thread or process spawned by a parent is likely to need to transfer information.

If we take the concept of multitasking a step further, we have multiple processes on a machine needing to communicate with each other to keep the system running, in sync, and accomplishing tasks. As operating system abstractions are developed using process communication, developers can create systems that are stable and easy to upgrade. Computers do not always operate in isolation, and attaching a computer to a network can give the computer access to remote resources. Using a network implies communications between systems, but this communication is achieved through separate processes on separate machines. It is not hard to see that process communication is a parallel and necessary part of the client/server puzzle.

Interprocess communication, or IPC, is the mechanism for the transfer of information between threads and processes. OS/2 has multiple IPCs, including shared memory, queues, semaphores, and pipes. We will focus on pipes, particularly named pipes due to their ability to operate across networks. Many other systems including NetWare and Windows NT support Network named pipes.

What Are Pipes?

Pipes are a memory buffer managed by the operating system to help processes communicate. It is important to a process that the memory buffer is managed by the operating system, because the operating system can restrict and enforce access to the buffer. The working area of the memory buffer is known as the pipe size. This is the maximum amount of data that can be stored by the pipe. A pipe can handle data in two ways. First, it can treat it as a byte stream, so if the pipe becomes full, it will block the sending process until more memory becomes available. The other data transfer mode is a message. A message is an agreed-upon data structure that relays an abstract concept to the receiver. The only difference in these two data transfer methods is if a message is sent and cannot be received by the pipe, the pipe will cause a send failure and will not put any of the message in the pipe.

OS/2 has three kinds of pipes—unnamed, named, and network named. Unnamed pipes can be used only by threads and processes that are related, meaning parent and child processes and sibling child processes. Named pipes can be accessed by any process that knows the name of the pipe. Named pipes can also be network named pipes. Figure 21.1 shows all three pipes.

Fig. 21.1
An abstraction of
OS/2 pipes.

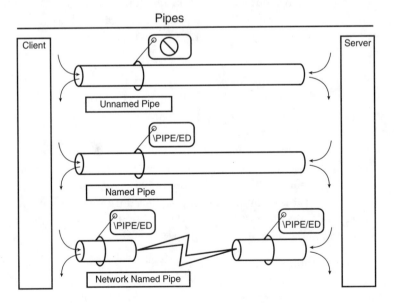

Pipes

Client

Server

Unnamed Pipe

\PIPE/ED

Named Pipe

\PIPE/ED   \PIPE/ED

Network Named Pipe

Shared memory is an early form of IPC that allowed a process to write to memory. This behavior could cause problems, because a process could overwrite unused information. The synchronization of access to the memory area had to be managed by the developer. This is an error-prone and tedious process. Pipes will not allow data to be overwritten, and shared memory cannot be shared across a network.

Queues are an IPC that can transfer only 32 bits of information. A common use of queues is to pass a pointer to a shared memory area. This forces the developer to decide where the memory allocation and reallocation are to occur, and still does not allow communication across a network. Queues can be read only by the creator of the queue, not the client of the queue.

A *semaphore* is another IPC that is primarily used to synchronize processes. This is a Boolean test normally used to allow a process to block or continue execution. If no data transfer is necessary, a semaphore is the IPC of choice. A semaphore does not provide synchronization across a network.

OS/2 APIs

The Application Programming Interface (API) is included and is a part of the OS/2 operating system. This is an important part of why pipes are fundamental and powerful under OS/2. When a pipe is opened, a handle is returned for use, much the same as with a file handle. OS/2 uses the parallel between file handles and pipe handles to simplify the use of pipes. The OS/2 API calls that provide operations on file handles also work on pipe handles. Thus, the same calls that read from a data file allow reading from a network named pipe. This behavior allows the redirection of standard I/O to different processes and basic terminal operations across the network. A program run on a remote system will simply have its input received from a remote input device and its output redirected to the remote device through pipe handles. Network named pipe drivers are available for most major networks, including Novell, IBM LAN Server, and Microsoft LAN Manager. Systems that do not have the ability to create named pipes will have client versions of named pipe drivers. This allows less-capable systems to become clients on the network and advanced systems to avoid the overhead of being a named pipe server.

To use the development features of OS/2, you should understand the APIs that make up the systems interface. Many APIs will return an error code giving a sign of success or a symbolic value for the kind of error that caused the failure. Not all of the APIs described will be used in our examples, but they will be included both for comparison with similarly structured API calls and for the reader's use in development. This chapter does not describe all of the OS/2 APIs for each group of operations. The descriptions included here are for better understanding of the development examples provided for pipes.

> **Note**
>
> The "Dos..." API calls are not strictly for FAT file system calls or Virtual DOS sessions. These calls are a catchall for operating system calls that do not fall into other specific API categories, such as "Win..." for PM Windowing functions, or "Gpi..." for Graphical Presentation. The "DOS..." naming convention is the cause of confusion for beginning OS/2 developers; the call could just as accurately have been named "Os..." APIs.

File System

OS/2 provides a family of APIs to gain access to the two file systems that come with OS/2, FAT and HPFS. A subset of these function calls also provides access to pipes. Not all OS/2 file APIs work on pipes, but the reuse of API calls allows OS/2 developers to make very little changes to the way they manipulate data using handles.

DosOpen

DosOpen creates a new file or opens an existing file, depending on parameters and the existence of the file. This API can be used on pipe handles. The syntax of DosOpen is:

```
DosOpen(
      PSZ      fileName,
      PHFILE     fileHandle,
      PULONG     action,
      ULONG    fileSize,
      ULONG    fileAttribute,
      ULONG    openFlag,
      ULONG    openMode,
      PEAOP2     eaBuffer      );
```

Parameters.

- *fileName* is a null terminated string of the path and name to the file or device.

- *fileHandle* is a pointer to the file handle opened if successful. The handle pointed to is set by the function.

- *action* is a pointer to an unsigned long. This value is the response of the open function and the action it accomplished. See actionFlags in the following section for values.

- *fileSize* is an unsigned long. This value is the byte size of the new or replaced file.

- *fileAttribute* is an unsigned long. It represents the file attributes of a new file. See `fileAttributeMask` in the following section for values.

- *openFlag* is an unsigned long. This value masks to set opening actions for given file states. See `openFlagMask` in the following section for values.

- *openMode* is an unsigned long. It flags to give access permission to the file handle.

- *eaBuffer* is a pointer to an `EAOP2`. `EAOP2` sets the file extended attributes for created files.

Flags and Masks. `actionFlags` are the following flags:

- `FILE_EXISTED`—Creation failure due to file existence

- `FILE_CREATED`—Creation successful

- `FILE_TRUNCATED`—Existing file shortened to given length

`fileAttributeMask` are the following values:

- `FILE_NORMAL`—Open for reading and writing

- `FILE_READONLY`—Open for reading only

- `FILE_HIDDEN`—File not displayed for directory listings

- `FILE_SYSTEM`—File is a system file

- `FILE_DIRECTORY`—File is a directory

- `FILE_ARCHIVED`—File archive bit set

`openFlagsMask` are the following values:

- `OPEN_ACTION_FAIL_IF_EXISTS`—File open fails if requested file exists

- `OPEN_ACTION_OPEN_IF_EXISTS`—File open succeeds if file exists

- `OPEN_ACTION_REPLACE_IF_EXISTS`—Replace file if it exists

- `OPEN_ACTION_FAIL_IF_NEW`—File open fails if file does not exist

- `OPEN_ACTION_CREATE_IF_NEW`—File open creates file if file does not exist

`openModeMask` are the following values:

- `OPEN_ACCESS_READONLY`—File can only be read

V

OS/2 Development

- `OPEN_ACCESS_WRITEONLY`—File can only be written to

- `OPEN_ACCESS_READWRITE`—File can be read and written to

- `OPEN_SHARE_DENYREADWRITE`—No file sharing

- `OPEN_SHARE_DENYWRITE`—File sharing for reading

- `OPEN_SHARE_DENYREAD`—File sharing for writing

- `OPEN_SHARE_DENYNONE`—File sharing for reading and writing

- `OPEN_FLAGS_NOINHERIT`—If set on no, child process inherits file handles

- `OPEN_FLAGS_NO_LOCALITY`—File access method unknown

- `OPEN_FLAGS_SEQUENTIAL`—File access method sequential

- `OPEN_FLAGS_RANDOM`—File access method random

- `OPEN_FLAGS_RAMDOMSEQUENTIAL`—File access method mostly random

DosRead

`DosRead` reads a given byte limit from the file into a buffer. This API can be used on pipe handles. The syntax of `DosRead` is the following:

```
DosRead(
    HFILE     fileHandle,
    PVOID     buffer,
    ULONG     bufferLength,
    PULONG    bytesRead      );
```

Parameters.

- *fileHandle* is a handle to a file. This handle gives access to the file.

- *buffer* is a pointer to a memory area. This is where the transferred data is copied to.

- *bufferLength* is an unsigned long. This number tells the `read` function the maximum number of bytes to read.

- *bytesRead* is a pointer to an unsigned long. The number written into this variable is the number of bytes read into the memory area.

DosWrite

`DosWrite` writes a given number of bytes from the memory buffer to a file. This API can be used on pipe handles. The syntax of `DosWrite` is as follows:

```
DosWrite(
      HFILE      fileHandle,
      PVOID      buffer,
      ULONG      bufferLength,
      PULONG     bytesWritten     );
```

Parameters.

- *fileHandle* is a handle to a file. This handle gives access to the file.

- *buffer* is a pointer to a memory area. This is where the transferred data is copied from.

- *bufferLength* is an unsigned long. This number tells the write function the number of bytes to write.

- *bytesRead* is a pointer to an unsigned long. The number written into this variable is the number of bytes written into file.

DosClose

DosClose closes the given file handle. This API can be used on pipe handles. The syntax of DosClose is the following:

```
DosWrite( HFILE fileHandle );
```

Parameters.

- *fileHandle* is a handle to a file. This handle gives access to the file.

DosResetBuffer

DosResetBuffer forces data written to a file to be written if it has been cached. This is commonly known as "flushing the buffers." This API can be used on pipe handles. If performed on a pipe handle, it will force the calling process to block until data has been read by the receiving end of the pipe. The syntax of DosResetBuffer is:

```
DosResetBuffer( HFILE fileHandle );
```

Parameters.

- *fileHandle* is a handle to a file. This handle gives access to the file.

Named Pipes

A named pipe allows interprocess communication using a simple naming convention. The name of the pipe gives a process the ability to query the operating system for a data connection that does not have to be in the same process. OS/2 will grant the process access to the data connection, but OS/2 has to have a way to tell which of the many pipes it is managing is the one being requested. The name of the pipe lets OS/2 know which pipe the process requires.

States

Knowledge of a named pipe's state is important to using the named pipe. Just as a file cannot be modified when it is closed, a named pipe can be modified only when it is in a connected state. Named pipes have four states: listening, connected, disconnected, and closing. When a named pipe is created, it sets to the disconnected state. This means that the system object known as a named pipe exists, but has no one local to communicate with. When the server connects to the named pipe, the named pipe is put in the listening state. This means that it is connected to the local server, but has no remote connection to work with. The named pipe is ready and is listening for a client connection.

When the client opens the named pipe, the named pipe is now ready for action and is put in the connected state. When the named pipe is in the connected state, read and write operations can be done. If the client closes the named pipe, then it is put in the closing state. When the named pipe is in the closing state, the server knows that it will be unable to send or receive information from the client. The server can now disconnect and close the named pipe.

DosCreatePipe

`DosCreatePipe` is the API used to create unnamed pipes. Unnamed pipes can be used only by related processes. Two file handles are created by `DosCreatePipe`, one a read file handle and the other a write file handle. The final parameter is the size of the pipe created. To close the handles created by `DosCreatePipe`, use `DosClose` on both file handles. The syntax of `DosCreatePipe` is as follows:

```
DosCreatePipe(
     PHFILE      readHandle,
     PHFILE      writeHandle,
     ULONG       size     );
```

Parameters.

- *readHandle* is a pointer to a file handle. This variable is set to the pipes file handle ID for reading.

- *writeHandle* is a pointer to a file handle. This variable is set to the pipes file handle ID for writing.

- *size* is an unsigned long. This value is the requested size of the pipe.

DosCreateNPipe

DosCreateNPipe is the OS/2 API used to create a named pipe. The name of the pipe must begin with a backslash, the word PIPE, another backslash, and a file name. You can name the file using 8.3 naming standards or the naming standard used by the system of the creator of the named pipe. The syntax is as follows:

```
DosCreateNPipe(
     PSZ       nameOfPipe,
     PHPIPE     pipeHandle,
     ULONG     openMode,
     ULONG     pipeMode,
     ULONG     writeBufferSize,
     ULONG     readBufferSize,
     ULONG     time          );
```

Parameters.

- *nameOfPipe* is a PSZ, a null terminated string, containing the name of the pipe being created.

- *pipeHandle* is a pointer to a pipe handle. The referenced variable is set to the handle of the pipe.

- *openMode* is an unsigned long. This value is initialized to represent the requested pipe behavior. See openModeMask under "Flags and Masks" for values.

- *pipeMode* is an unsigned long. This value is initialized to represent different requested pipe behavior. See pipeModeMask under "Flags and Masks" for values.

- *writeBufferSize* is an unsigned long. This value is the size of the write buffer. Writing is viewed from the server perspective.

- *readBufferSize* is an unsigned long. This value is the size of the read buffer. Reading is viewed from the server perspective.

- *time* is an unsigned long. This value represents the default timeout for clients of this pipe using DosWaitNPipe. If the value is zero, the system default is used.

Flags and Masks. openModeMask are the following values:

- NP_INHERIT—Pipe handles can be inherited by child processes.

- NP_NOINHERIT—Pipe handles cannot be inherited by child processes.

- NP_ACCESS_INBOUND—Information is received by the server from the client, no client information.

- NP_ACCESS_OUTBOUD—Information is sent by the server to the client, no server information.

- NP_ACCESS_DUPLEX—Information can be sent and received by both client and server. The pipe will not overwrite data in the pipe.

- NP_WRITEBEHIND—Information can be cached on the remote system.

- NP_NOWRITEBEHIND—Information cannot be cached on the remote system.

pipeModeMask are the following values:

- NP_WAIT—Operations on the pipe will result in a blocking wait if the operation cannot be done immediately.

- NP_NOWAIT—Operations on the pipe will return an error if the operation cannot be completed immediately. A write operation will return zero bytes written and a read operation will return ERROR_NO_DATA.

- NP_TYPE_BYTE—The type of the created pipe is byte.

- NP_TYPE_MESSAGE—The type of the created pipe is message.

- NP_READMODE_BYTE—Reading operations will recognize the pipe as a byte-type pipe.

- NP_READMODE_MESSAGE—Reading operations will recognize the pipe as a message-type pipe.

- Low eight bits—These bits represent the number of instances of the pipe that can exist at the same time. Valid instance numbers are from one to 254. The number 0 is invalid. The number 255 or -1 allows unlimited instances of the pipe.

DosConnectNPipe

DosConnectNPipe is the OS/2 API used to connect to a created named pipe.
After the process is connected to the named pipe, it will block wait until the
client attaches to the named pipe. The syntax is as follows:

```
DosConnectNPipe( HPIPE pipeHandle );
```

Parameters.

- *pipeHandle* is a pipe handle. The handle value is used by the function to
  connect to named pipe handle.

DosCallNPipe

DosCallNPipe is the OS/2 API that combines the opening, writing, reading,
and closing series of operations into a single function. DosCallNPipe simplifies
the process of sending and receiving a response for a single call. The named
pipe must be able to be written to and read from a duplex named pipe.
DosCallNPipe can block until a named pipe becomes available or it can time
out and return an error message. The syntax is as follows:

```
DosCallNPipe(
    PSZ        nameOfPipe,
    PVOID      writeBuffer,
    ULONG      writeBufferSize,
    PVOID      readBuffer,
    ULONG      readBufferSize,
    PULONG      bytesRead,
    ULONG      time            );
```

Parameters.

- *nameOfPipe* is a PSZ, a null terminated string, containing the name of the
  pipe being created.

- *writeBuffer* is a pointer to a memory area that contains the information to be written to the named pipe.

- *writeBufferSize* is an unsigned long that tells the function how much
  of the *writeBuffer* is to be written to the named pipe.

- *readBuffer* is a pointer to a memory area that is to be written to as a
  response to the information written to the named pipe.

- *readBufferSize* is an unsigned long that represents the maximum
  amount of bytes that can be written to *readBuffer*.

- *bytesRead* is a pointer to an unsigned long that is set by the function
  returning the number of bytes written to *readBuffer*.

V

OS/2 Development

- *time* is an unsigned long that signifies the timeout period or to block until the named pipe is opened. The values that can be assigned to this parameter are the same as the time parameter for DosWaitNPipe.

DosTransactNPipe

DosTransactNPipe is an OS/2 API that combines a write operation followed by a read operation. DosTransactNPipe is similar to DosCallNPipes behavior, but it requires a named pipe that has already been opened in duplex mode. DosTransactNPipe is commonly used for a series of synchronous requests. DosTransactNPipe does not have to be concerned with a timeout value like DosCallNPipe, because it has to be given a valid named pipe handle as a parameter. The syntax is as follows:

```
DosTransactNPipe(
    HPIPE       pipeHandle,
    PVOID       writeBuffer,
    ULONG       writeBufferSize,
    PVOID       readBuffer,
    ULONG       readBufferSize,
    PULONG      bytesRead      );
```

Parameters.

- *pipeHandle* is a pipe handle. The handle value is used by the function to perform actions to the named pipe.

- *writeBuffer* is a pointer to a memory area that contains the information to be written to the named pipe.

- *writeBufferSize* is an unsigned long that tells the function how much of *writeBuffer* is to be written to the named pipe.

- *readBuffer* is a pointer to a memory area that is to be written to as a response to the information written to the named pipe.

- *readBufferSize* is an unsigned long that represents the maximum amount of bytes that can be written to *readBuffer*.

- *bytesRead* is a pointer to an unsigned long that is set by the function returning the number of bytes written to *readBuffer*.

DosWaitNPipe

DosWaitNPipe is the OS/2 API that the client issues to wait for or check the status of a named pipe. If a process has no other tasks than to work with the named pipe, or can do nothing else until the pipe has been opened, it will issue a blocking wait. If a process has many tasks to do and has been designed to periodically poll for the named pipe, a limited timeout period should be used. The syntax is as follows:

```
DosWaitNPipe(
      PSZ       nameOfPipe,
      ULONG     time            );
```

Parameters.

- *nameOfPipe* is a PSZ, a null terminated string, containing the name of the pipe being opened.

- *time* is an unsigned long. This value lets the function block wait until the named pipe becomes available by setting time to -1 or all bits set to on. If time is set to zero, the timeout duration is defined by the named pipe when it was created. Any other value is the timeout period before returning.

DosDisconnectNPipe

DosDisconnectNPipe is the OS/2 API that a server of a named pipe will call after the client has closed the named pipe. This will set the named pipe to a disconnected state, which allows other processes or the same process to connect to the named pipe as the server. The syntax is as follows:

```
DosDisconnectNPipe( HPIPE pipeHandle );
```

Parameters.

- *pipeHandle* is a handle to the named pipe that will be disconnected from the process.

DosSetNPHState

DosSetNPHState is an OS/2 API that can change the current operation state of a named pipe using the named pipe handle. Operating state information that can be changed consists of the pipe's blocking type, and the read-mode pipe type. The syntax is as follows:

```
DosSetNPHState(
      HPIPE     pipeHandle,
      ULONG     pipeState     );
```

Parameters.

- *pipeHandle* is a handle to the named pipe that will be set for named pipe operation information.

■ *pipeState* is an unsigned long. The value is set to a maskable bit pattern for operation information. See pipeStateMask under "Flags and Masks" for values.

Flags and Masks. pipeStateMask are the following values:

■ NP_WAIT—Operations on the pipe will result in a block if the operation cannot be done immediately.

■ NP_NOWAIT—Operations on the pipe will return an error if the operation cannot be completed immediately. A write operation will return zero bytes written and a read operation will return ERROR_NO_DATA.

■ NP_READMODE_BYTE—Reading operations will recognize the pipe as a byte-type pipe.

■ NP_READMODE_MESSAGE—Reading operations will recognize the pipe as a message-type pipe.

DosQueryNPHState

DosQueryNPHState is an OS/2 API that gets the operation state from a named pipe using the named pipe's handle. State information on a named pipe consists of the maximum number of pipe instances, the pipe's blocking type, the type of the pipe, the read-mode pipe type, and ownership of the handle. The syntax is as follows:

```
DosQueryNPHState(
     HPIPE      pipeHandle,
     PULONG     pipeState     );
```

Parameters.

■ *pipeHandle* is a handle to the named pipe that will be queried for named pipe operation information.

■ *pipeState* is a pointer to an unsigned long. The value is set to a maskable bit pattern for operation information. See pipeStateMask under "Flags and Masks" for values.

Flags and Masks. pipeStateMask are the following values:

■ Low eight bits—These bits represent the number of instances of the pipe that can exist at the same time. Valid instance numbers are from one to 254. The number 0 is invalid. The number 255 or -1 says that an unlimited number of instances of the pipe can be created.

- NP_WAIT—Operations on the pipe will result in a block if the operation cannot be done immediately

- NP_NOWAIT—Operations on the pipe will return an error if the operation cannot be completed immediately. A write operation will return zero bytes written and a read operation will return ERROR_NO_DATA.

- NP_TYPE_BYTE—The type of the created pipe is byte.

- NP_TYPE_MESSAGE—The type of the created pipe is message.

- NP_READMODE_BYTE—Reading operations will recognize the pipe as a byte-type pipe.

- NP_READMODE_MESSAGE—Reading operations will recognize the pipe as a message-type pipe.

- NP_END_CLIENT—The named pipe handle is a client's handle.

- NP_END_SERVER—The named pipe handle is a server's handle.

DosQueryNPipeInfo

DosQueryNPipeInfo is an OS/2 API that gets named pipe information. Information about the named pipe at level one consists of the size of the read and write memory areas, the name of the pipe and the name length, and the maximum and current number of instances. Level two information is the client ID for each instance of the named pipe. The syntax is as follows:

```
DosQueryNPipeInfo(
        HPIPE      pipeHandle,
        ULONG      infoLevel,
        PVOID      infoBuffer,
        ULONG      infoBufferSize    );
```

Parameters.

- pipeHandle is a handle to the named pipe that this function is to get information on.

- infoLevel is an unsigned long that can be set to 1 or 2. Each level returns a different type of information to the memory area given by infoBuffer.

- infoBuffer is a pointer to a memory area. Level one information is written in a PIPEINFO structure. See PIPEINFO for details of the structure. Level two information is written as a two-byte field containing an identifier to the client attached to the named pipe.

■ *infoBufferSize* is an unsigned long that tells the function how much memory is available at *infoBuffer*.

Flags and Masks. PIPEINFO is the following format:

■ cbOut—The size of the writing buffer.

■ cbIn—The size of the reading buffer.

■ cbMaxInst—The maximum number of instances of the named pipe.

■ cbCurInst—The current number of instances of the named pipe.

■ cbName—The name of the named pipe. This will also include the systems name at the beginning of the name.

■ szName—The length of the named pipe name.

DosPeekNPipe

DosPeekNPipe is an OS/2 API that allows the process to view information from the pipe without removing the information, a non-destructive read. DosPeekNPipe will also return current state information of the named pipe. The syntax is as follows:

```
DosPeekNPipe(
    HPIPE        pipeHandle,
    PVOID        readBuffer,
    ULONG        readBufferSize,
    PULONG       bytesRead,
    PAVAILDATA   availData,
    PULONG       pipeState     );
```

Parameters.

■ *pipeHandle* is a handle to a named pipe that will be read from but will not be modified.

■ *readBuffer* is a pointer to a memory area that will be written to by the function.

■ *readBufferSize* is an unsigned long that tells the function the number of bytes available in *readBuffer*.

■ *bytesRead* is a pointer to an unsigned long that tells the calling process the number of bytes written to *readBuffer*.

- *availData* is a pointer to a structure of AVAILDATA that returns information about the amount of data in the named pipe. See AVAILDATA under "Flags and Masks" for the structure's format.

- *pipeState* is a pointer to an unsigned long that returns the state of the named pipe. See pipeStateFlag under "Flags and Masks" for values.

Flags and Masks. AVAILDATA is the following format:

- Low sixteen bits—The amount of data in the named pipe in bytes.

- High sixteen bits—The size of the next message in the pipe. The size is zero if the pipe type is byte.

pipeStateFlag are the following flags:

- NP_STATE_DISCONNECTED—Named pipe not connected.

- NP_STATE_LISTENING—Named pipe waiting for remote open.

- NP_STATE_CONNECTED—Named pipe is connected.

- NP_STATE_CLOSING—Named pipe is closing. Remote connection has closed.

DosSetNPipeSem

DosSetNPipeSem is an OS/2 API that attaches an event semaphore and an identifier to a pipe. The attaching process then can wait for the event semaphore and then poll the semaphore for the incoming data. Semaphores are not available on all machines that have named pipes, so DosSetNPipeSem can be used only on local (named or unnamed) pipes. If a semaphore attachment to a networked named pipe is attempted, an error will be returned. The syntax is as follows:

```
DosSetNPipeSem(
     HPIPE      pipeHandle,
     HSEM       semHandle,
     ULONG      keyId      );
```

Parameters.

- *pipeHandle* is a handle to a pipe that has a semaphore attached to it. When data is received, the semaphore is signaled.

- *semHandle* is a handle to a semaphore that is attached to the pipe given in *pipeHandle*.

■ *keyId* is an unsigned long that gives each created pipe a unique identifier. This allows the process to query the pipe or the semaphore for the identifier.

DosQueryNPipeSemState

DosQueryNPipeSemState is an OS/2 API that gets information from a semaphore that has been attached to a pipe using DosSetNPipeSem. The information received allows the client process to determine which pipe has available data and the status of the pipe. The syntax is as follows:

```
DosQueryNPipeSemState(
    HSEM            semHandle,
    PPIPESEMSTATE      pipeSemInfo,
    ULONG           pipeSemInfoSize    );
```

Parameters.

■ *semHandle* is a handle to an event semaphore that has been attached to a pipe.

■ *pipeSemInfo* is a pointer to a PIPESEMSTATE structure that is filled based on the status of the pipe attached to the event semaphore. See PIPESEMSTATE under "Flags and Masks" for the structure's format.

■ *pipeSemInfoSize* is an unsigned long that tells the function the size of the pipeSemInfo parameter in bytes.

Flags and Masks. PIPESEMSTATE are the following values:

■ fStatus—A state flag for pipe operations is put in this field. See fStatusFlag under "Flags and Masks" for values.

■ fFlag—The low bit of this field is set if the process on the other end of the pipe is waiting.

■ usKey—The identity key set in DosSetNPipeSem is put in this field. This identity key will allow the process to tell which pipe has data if more than one pipe is using the same event semaphore.

■ usAvail—If fStatus is set to NPSS_RDATA, this field holds the number of bytes available for reading. If fStatus is set to NPSS_WDATA, this field holds the number of bytes available for writing.

fStatusFlag are the following flags:

- NPSS_EOI—The pipe attached to the given semaphore has no more information.

- NPSS_RDATA—There is data available for reading from the pipe attached to the given semaphore.

- NPSS_WSPACE—There is empty data area available for writing to the pipe attached to the given semaphore.

- NPSS_CLOSE—The pipe attached to the given semaphore has been closed.

Semaphores

All named semaphores must begin with a backslash, the word sem32, another backslash, and a DOS FAT convention file name. An example of a named semaphore could be \sem32\mysem. In the language C, you must remember that a backslash is an escape sequence, so use two backslashes to get a backslash in a string. For example, the C string \\sem32\\cstring would be the name of a semaphore called \sem32\cstring.

Event Semaphore

Event semaphores allow processes to signal each other of events remote to the processes. Event semaphores can be either posted or set. A posted state is where the semaphore has received the required signal, and a process waiting on the semaphore will become unblocked. A set state is where the semaphore is waiting for a posting and will block or timeout any process that attempts to wait on the semaphore. Figure 21.2 shows an event semaphore and two processes using the event semaphore for synchronization.

Figure 21.2 shows that Process A runs until the requested event semaphore is reached. Process A cannot continue until the event semaphore is in a posted state. Process A will wait until Process B posts to the event semaphore. Process A does the required task that the event semaphore protected. When Process A is done with the protected area, then the event semaphore is set until a process posts to it again.

DosCreateEventSem. DosCreateEventSem is an OS/2 API that requests that OS/2 create an event semaphore. The semaphore can be created unnamed by passing a NULL pointer to eventSemName. The semaphore can be created as a private or shared semaphore, and can have an initial state of posted or set. The syntax is as follows:

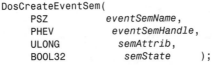

```
DosCreateEventSem(
      PSZ            eventSemName,
      PHEV           eventSemHandle,
      ULONG           semAttrib,
      BOOL32           semState    );
```

Fig. 21.2

An event sema-
phore used by two
processes.

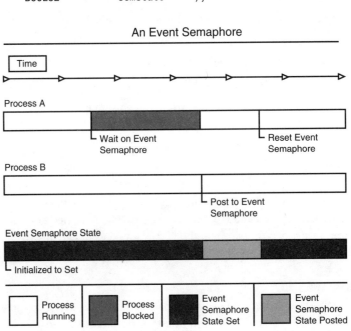

An Event Semaphore

Parameters.

■ *eventSemName* is a NULL terminated string that is the name of the event
   semaphore. If no name is given, then the event semaphore is a private
   semaphore.

■ *eventSemHandle* is a pointer to an event semaphore handle that is assigned the event semaphore handle created by calling this function.

■ *semAttrib* is an unsigned long that sets the event semaphore to be a
   public or private semaphore. Named semaphores are normally, but
   not always, public and unnamed semaphores are always private. Set
   semAttrib to 0 for a private semaphore and to 1 for a public semaphore.

■ *semState* is a 32-bit Boolean value that sets the event semaphore's
   initial state to set or posted. If *semState* is FALSE the semaphore is set.
   This initializes the semaphore for a process to post to it, and any
   DosWaitEventSem calls will block or fail. If semState is True, the
   semaphore is posted.

DosOpenEventSem. DosOpenEventSem is an OS/2 API that allows a process access to a previously created event semaphore. DosOpenEventSem does not create an event semaphore and will fail if a nonexisting event semaphore is attempted to be opened. DosOpenEventSem will only work on named semaphores. The syntax is as follows:

```
DosOpenEventSem(
    PSZ      eventSemName,
    PHEV     eventSemHandle      );
```

Parameters.

- *eventSemName* is a null terminated string that is the name of the event semaphore to open and set *eventSemHandle*.

- *eventSemHandle* is a pointer to an event semaphore handle that is set to the event semaphore handle.

DosWaitEventSem. DosWaitEventSem is an OS/2 API that checks the event semaphore for its state. If the state is or becomes posted, the function returns with no errors. If the semaphore state is set, the function call will block, based on the *timeOut* parameter. The syntax is as follows:

```
DosWaitEventSem(
    HEV      eventSemHandle,
    ULONG    timeOut      );
```

Parameters.

- *eventSemHandle* is an event semaphore handle that the process is attempting to wait for.

- *timeOut* is an unsigned long that tells the function how many milliseconds to wait for the event semaphore before failing and returning an error message. If *timeOut* is set to SEM_INDEFINITE_WAIT (0xFFFFFFFF), the process does a blocking wait until the event semaphore is posted to.

DosResetEventSem. DosResetEventSem is an OS/2 API that sets the event semaphore's state to set, gets a count of the number of postings to the semaphore, and resets the posting count to zero. The syntax is as follows:

```
DosResetEventSem(
    HEV           eventSemHandle,
    PULONG        postCount      );
```

Parameters.

■ *eventSemHandle* is an event semaphore handle for which the calling process is attempting to change so the semaphore state is set.

■ *postCount* is a pointer to an unsigned long that is set to the number of times the event semaphore has been posted to.

DosPostEventSem. DosPostEventSem is an OS/2 API that sets the event semaphore's state to posted and increments the posting count. A process blocking on the event semaphore will be reactivated. The syntax is as follows:

```
DosPostEventSem( HEV     eventSemHandle );
```

Parameters.

■ *eventSemHandle* is an event semaphore handle for which the calling process is attempting to change so semaphore state is posted.

DosQueryEventSem. DosQueryEventSem is an OS/2 API that gets the posting count from an event semaphore. The syntax is as follows:

```
DosQueryEventSem(
    PHEV            eventSemHandle,
    PULONG          postCount      );
```

Parameters.

■ *eventSemHandle* is an event semaphore handle for which the calling process is attempting to get the semaphores posting count from.

■ *postCount* is a pointer to an unsigned long that is assigned the number of times the event semaphore has been posted to and not reset.

DosCloseEventSem. DosCloseEventSem is an OS/2 API that tells the event semaphore that the calling process has finished using the event semaphore. The creation of the event semaphore sets the semaphore's usage count to one. Every open call will increment the semaphore's usage count by one. Every time an event semaphore is closed, the semaphore's usage count is decremented. When the semaphore's usage count becomes zero, the operating system will delete the event semaphore. The syntax is as follows:

```
DosCloseEventSem( HEV eventSemHandle );
```

Parameters.

■ *eventSemHandle* is an event semaphore handle that the process is attempting to close.

Multiple Wait (*MuxWait*)

MuxWait semaphores manage a list of semaphores and allow monitoring of multiple semaphores. The MuxWait semaphore is complicated, but is necessary due to the blocking nature of semaphores. If a process needs to monitor multiple semaphores, waiting on one and then the other is not acceptable if all you need is either one. The process is blocked unnecessarily. The strategy of not blocking on the semaphores and keeping track of each of the semaphores after it timesout causes an unnecessary loss of processing time. The MuxWait semaphore can handle these situations, with some limitations. All the semaphores on a MuxWait semaphore must be of the same type, either event semaphores or mutual exclusion semaphores. A MuxWait semaphore cannot contain MuxWait semaphores. All the semaphores to be put on a MuxWait semaphore must be created and opened before they are put on the MuxWait semaphore. Figure 21.3 shows the synchronization that a MuxWait semaphore and two event semaphores can have on a waiting server and two client processes.

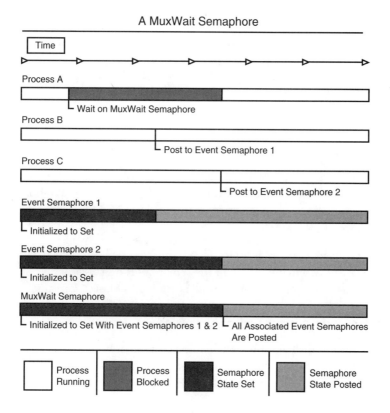

Fig. 21.3
MuxWait sema-
phore usage.

V

OS/2 Development

Figure 21.3 shows a single `MuxWait` semaphore that is dependent on two event semaphores. The `MuxWait` semaphore will not set to a posted state until both of the event semaphores are in a posted state. Process A cannot continue until the `MuxWait` semaphore is in a posted state. This does not happen until Process B and Process C post to event semaphores 1 and 2.

DosCreateMuxWaitSem. `DosCreateMuxWaitSem` is an OS/2 API that requests that OS/2 create a `MuxWait` semaphore. The semaphore can be created unnamed by passing a `NULL` pointer to `muxWaitSemName`. The `MuxWait` semaphore needs a series of event or mutex semaphores, but all the series of semaphores must be of the same type and cannot be another `MuxWait` semaphore. The syntax is as follows:

```
DosCreateMuxWaitSem(
    PSZ             muxWaitSemName,
    PHMUX           muxWaitSemHandle,
    ULONG           semRecArraySize,
    PSEMRECORD      semRecArray,
    ULONG           muxWaitSemAttribute        );
```

Parameters.

- *muxWaitSemName* is a null terminated string that is the name of the `MuxWait` semaphore to be created.

- *muxWaitSemHandle* is a pointer to a `MuxWait` semaphore handle that is set to the handle of a `MuxWait` semaphore.

- *semRecArraySize* is an unsigned long that tells the function the number of elements in *semRecArray*. This value cannot be greater than 64.

- *semRecArray* is a pointer to an array of `SEMRECORD`s that are the individual semaphores and semaphore information for the list of semaphores that a `MuxWait` manages. See `SEMRECORD` under "Flags and Masks" for details of the structure.

- *muxWaitSemAttribute* is an unsigned long that defines the behavior of the `MuxWait` semaphore for all the semaphores on `semRecArray`. See `muxWaitSemAttributeFlag` under "Flags and Masks" for values.

Flags and Masks. `SEMRECORD` has the following format:

- `hsemCur`—This field stores the handle to a semaphore that is to be added to the `MuxWait` semaphore. This semaphore must be created or opened before it is added to the `MuxWait` semaphore.

- `ulUser`—This field stores the user defined identifier for the `hsemCur` semaphore.

muxWaitSemAttributeFlag are the following flags:

- DC_SEM_SHARED—The MuxWait semaphore is a shared semaphore. This flag is only valid for unnamed semaphores because named semaphores are shared by default.

- DCMW_WAIT_ANY—The MuxWait semaphore will be released if any of the contained semaphores are released or posted.

- DCMW_WAIT_ALL—The MuxWait semaphore will be released if all of the contained semaphores are released or posted.

DosOpenMuxWaitSem. DosOpenMuxWaitSem is an OS/2 API that allows a process access to a MuxWait semaphore that has already been created. Remember that multiple threads in a process automatically have access to the MuxWait handle. The syntax is as follows:

```
DosOpenMuxWaitSem(
      PSZ      muxWaitSemName,
      PHMUX    muxWaitSemHandle     );
```

Parameters.

- *muxWaitSemName* is a null terminated string that is the name of the created MuxWait semaphore the process is trying to gain access to.

- *muxWaitSemHandle* is a pointer to a MuxWait semaphore handle that is set to the handle of the named MuxWait semaphore.

DosAddMuxWaitSem. DosAddMuxWaitSem is an OS/2 API that adds a semaphore to the list of semaphores that the MuxWait semaphore manages. The added semaphore must be of the same type of semaphore as all the other semaphores on the list. DosAddMuxWaitSem can be called even if there are processes blocking on the MuxWait semaphore. The syntax is as follows:

```
DosAddMuxWaitSem(
      HMUX          muxWaitSemHandle,
      PSEMRECORD    semRec           );
```

Parameters.

- *muxWaitSemHandle* is a MuxWait semaphore handle that is going to have another semaphore added to the MuxWait semaphore's list of semaphores.

- *semRec* is a pointer to a SEMRECORD that is the individual semaphore and semaphore information that will be added to the list of semaphores that the MuxWait semaphore manages. See SEMRECORD in DosCreateMuxWaitSem under "Flags and Masks" for details of the structure.

V

OS/2 Development

DosWaitMuxWaitSem. DosWaitMuxWaitSem is an OS/2 API that checks the MuxWait semaphore for its state. If the state is or becomes posted, the function returns with no errors. If the semaphore state is set, the function call will block the process, based on the *timeOut* parameter. The syntax is as follows:

```
DosWaitMuxWaitSem(
      HMUX          muxWaitSemHandle,
      ULONG         timeOut,
      PULONG        semId      );
```

Parameters.

- *muxWaitSemHandle* is a MuxWait semaphore handle that is the MuxWait semaphore the process is to wait for.

- *timeOut* is an unsigned long that is the number of milliseconds the process is to wait until returning an error message. If the value of timeOut is set to SEM_INDEFINITE_WAIT (0xFFFFFFFF), the function will return when the MuxWait semaphore is clear.

- *semId* is a pointer to an unsigned long that is set to the user-defined identifier that caused the MuxWait semaphore to clear.

DosQueryMuxWaitSem.

DosQueryMuxWaitSem is an OS/2 API that gets the current semaphore information that makes up a MuxWait semaphore. The syntax is as follows:

```
DosQueryMuxWaitSem(
      HMUX          muxWaitSemHandle,
      PULONG        semRecCount,
      PSEMRECORD    semRecArray,
      PULONG        muxWaitSemAttribute      );
```

Parameters.

- *muxWaitSemHandle* is a handle to a MuxWait semaphore that is queried for information on the MuxWait semaphore.

- *semRecCount* is a pointer to an unsigned long that tells the function the number of elements in *semRecArray*. This value cannot be greater than 64. The value is set by the function to the number of elements in *semRecArray* that have been set.

- *semRecArray* is a pointer to an array of SEMRECORDs that are the individual semaphores and semaphore information for the list of semaphores that a MuxWait manages. This array's memory area must be provided by the process. The function will fill in the correct number of SEMRECORDs. See SEMRECORD in DosCreateMuxWaitSem for details of the structure.

- *muxWaitSemAttribute* is a pointer to an unsigned long that is set to the value that defines the behavior of the MuxWait semaphore for all the semaphores on *semRecArray*. See `muxWaitSemAttributeFlag` in `DosCreateMuxWaitSem` for values.

DosCloseMuxWaitSem. `DosCloseMuxWaitSem` is an OS/2 API that closes an opened or created `MuxWait` semaphore. A `MuxWait` semaphore has an internal counter that tracks the number of open `MuxWait` semaphores. When the internal counter becomes zero, the `MuxWait` semaphore is deleted. The syntax is as follows:

```
DosCloseMuxWaitSem( HMUX     muxWaitSemHandle );
```

Parameters.

- *muxWaitSemHandle* is a `MuxWait` semaphore handle that is to be closed.

DosDeleteMuxWaitSem. `DosDeleteMuxWaitSem` is an OS/2 API that removes a semaphore from the list of managed semaphores. Any process waiting for the `MuxWait` semaphore will be released if the removed semaphore completes the `MuxWait` semaphore's attribute goal. This call allows the removal of the last semaphore that will release waiting processes. The syntax is as follows:

```
DosDeleteMuxWaitSem(
     HMUX     muxWaitSemHandle,
     HSEM     semHandle    );
```

Parameters.

- *muxWaitSemHandle* is a `MuxWait` semaphore handle that is the `MuxWait` semaphore that a semaphore will be deleted from.

- *semHandle* is a semaphore handle that will be removed from the `MuxWait` semaphore list of semaphores.

Development Examples

A firm understanding of the OS/2 APIs is necessary to create pipes and supporting system objects. We have described many of the pipe and semaphore calls. The knowledge we now have will help us write small coding examples.

Named Byte Pipes

Information is transferred by pipes in two modes, byte and message. Byte transfer is normally used for large blocks of data that need to be moved in sections. Byte transfer can also allow a dynamic sizing of message transfer,

V

OS/2 Development

but this tends to force the developer to design complicated subsystems for reading. The programs TKCLI11.C and TKSRVR11.C transfer string messages from the client to the server (see Listings 21.1, 21.2, and 21.3). A message that begins with the letter *Q* will end both programs.

Listing 21.1   TALK1.H   *Talk1* Header Source

```
/************************************************************
 * talk1.h
 */
#ifndef TALK1_H
#define TALK1_H
#define INCL_DOSNMPIPES
#define INCL_ERRORS
#define INCL_DOSFILEMGR
#include <os2.h>
#define PIPENAME  "\\PIPE\\NPTALK"
/* You could easily replace the local named pipe name with
 * a server constant for network named pipes.
 * \\SERVERNAME\PIPE\NPTALK instead of \PIPE\NPTALK
 */
#define SERVPIPENAME ("\\\\SERVERNAME" + PIPENAME)
#define MAXBUFFER 255

#endif   /* TALK1_H */
```

Listing 21.2   TKCLI11.C   *Talk11* Client Source

```
/************************************************************
 * tkcli11.c
 * Talk Client program using DosOpen, DosRead, DosWrite, DosClose
 */

#include <stdio.h>
#include <conio.h>
#include <string.h>
#include "talk1.h"

APIRET   retCd = NO_ERROR;    /* return code */
/*
 * main control function
 */
   void
```

```
main() {
   ULONG    quitFlag = 0;
   ULONG    resp;
   ULONG    strLength;
   UCHAR    action;
   HPIPE    pipeHandle;
   UCHAR    writeBuffer[MAXBUFFER];
   setbuf( stdin, NULL );  /* no buffering of standard input */
   setbuf( stdout, NULL ); /* no buffering of standard output */
   retCd = DosWaitNPipe( PIPENAME, -1 );  /* block wait */
   if( retCd ) {      /* error on DosWait */
      quitFlag = 1;  /* flag for exit */
   } else {
      retCd = DosOpen(  PIPENAME, /* open named pipe for write access */
                        &pipeHandle,
                        &resp,
                        0,
                        0,
                        FILE_OPEN,
                        OPEN_ACCESS_WRITEONLY ¦ OPEN_SHARE_DENYNONE,
                        0     );
      if( retCd ) {  /* error on DosOpen */
         exit( 0 );
      }
   }
   while( !quitFlag ) {     /* loop until flagged for exit */
      printf( "Type messages to send to the server.\n" );
      printf( "To quit begin the message with the letter \'q\'\n" );
      writeBuffer[0] = '\0';
      scanf( "%[^\n]", writeBuffer );  /* read text message */
      _flushall();
      strLength   = strlen( writeBuffer ) + 1;  /* message length */
      switch( writeBuffer[0] ) {     /* first char of message*/
         case 'Q':       /* if the first char is Q */
         case 'q': {
            quitFlag = 1;  /* flag for exit*/
         }
         /* no break here, even on a quit we want to send the message */
         default: {     /*  send text message*/
            retCd = DosWrite( pipeHandle, writeBuffer, strLength, &resp );
            if( retCd ) {     /* error on DosWrite*/
               quitFlag = 1;
            }
         }
         break;
      }
   }
   DosClose( pipeHandle ); /* close pipe */
}
```

Listing 21.3 TKSRVR11.C *Talk11* **Server Source**

```
/************************************************************
 * tksrvr11.c
 * Talk Server program for tkcli11.c programs.
 * Simple program to display string messages.
 */
#include <stdio.h>
#include <string.h>
#include "talk1.h"

APIRET   retCd = NO_ERROR;
/* Setup of the client program
 * This includes creating and connecting a named pipe.
 */
   void
initialize( PHPIPE pipeHandle ) {
   ULONG    direct      = NP_ACCESS_INBOUND; /* read only */
   /* blocking read/write, type byte, one pipe instance */
   ULONG    modeP       = NP_WAIT ¦ NP_TYPE_BYTE
                          ¦ NP_READMODE_BYTE ¦ 0x01;
   ULONG    timeOut     = 5000;  /* five second timeout */
   printf( "Initalize\n\n" );
   retCd   = NO_ERROR;
   /* create named pipe, read only */
   retCd   = DosCreateNPipe( PIPENAME,
                             pipeHandle,
                             direct,
                             modeP,
                             0,
                             MAXBUFFER,
                             timeOut    );
   if( !retCd ) {
      /* connect to given pipe */
      retCd = DosConnectNPipe( *pipeHandle );
   }
   if( retCd ) {
      exit( 0 );  /* exit on failure */
   }
}
/*
 * processing of client requests, includes displaying messages,
 * and shutdown of server system.
 */
   void
processing( HPIPE pipeHandle ) {
   ULONG    quitFlag = 0;
   UCHAR    readBuffer[MAXBUFFER];
   ULONG    retSize;
   ULONG    serverCount = 1;
   retCd = NO_ERROR;
   while( !quitFlag ) {
   /* blocking read from client */
      retCd = DosRead( pipeHandle, &readBuffer, MAXBUFFER, &retSize );
```

```
            if( !retCd && 0 != retSize ) {
                switch( readBuffer[0] )
                {
                    case 'Q':   /* if the first char of the string is q */
                    case 'q': {
                        printf( "Quitting because of \"%s\"", readBuffer );
                        quitFlag = 1;  /* flag for exit */
                    }
                    break;

                    default: {  /* display text message */
                        printf( "Message %d —> size = %lu \"%s\"\n",
                                serverCount, retSize, readBuffer );
                        serverCount++;
                    }
                    break;
                }
            } else {    /* invalid DosRead */
                quitFlag = 1;  /* flag for exit */
            }
        }
    }
    /*
     * Shut down the client program and its corresponding pipe.
     */
        void
    shutdown( HPIPE    pipeHandle ) {
        APIRET    retCd = NO_ERROR;
        printf( "Shutdown\n\n" );
        retCd = DosDisConnectNPipe( pipeHandle ); /* disconnect pipe */
        if ( !retCd ) {
            retCd = DosClose( pipeHandle );  /* close pipe */
        }
    }
    /*
     * main control function
     */
        void
    main()
    {
        HPIPE pipeHandle;

        initialize( &pipeHandle );
        processing( pipeHandle );
        shutdown( pipeHandle );
    }
```

The Talk1 example programs use many of what was discussed in this chapter. It is simple to get the client program to communicate with a remote server program by giving the pipe name in the header a network name. No other code changes are necessary. A client program could be written to get the remote pipe name from the command line, a file, or prompt the user for the name.

V

OS/2 Development

The `Talk2` client program is a basic looping and test for a quit condition program. The pipe is opened using `DosOpen`, just like a data file open and the pipe is closed using a corresponding `DosClose`. The main loop in the program prompts the user for a string message to send to the client and checks for the first letter of the message to be the letter Q. This stopping condition gives the user a way to exit the program and allows the client program to exit gracefully. The data communication between the programs is done using `DosRead` and `DosWrite`, but to the pipe is not a file. The only unusual call is to `DosWaitNPipe`, which blocks the client program until the named pipe exists and is ready for communication.

The `Talk2` Server program is a little more complicated, but only in the setup and shutdown of the named pipe. The server has the responsibility of creating and destroying the named pipe. The pipe is created using `DosCreateNPipe` and destroyed with `DosCloseNPipe`. The responsibility of being the server forces the server program to use other calls to open and close the pipe. The pipe serves no purpose until the server connects, so the server program does not use `DosOpen` and `DosClose`. The `DosConnectNPipe` is the server version of `DosOpen` and `DosDisConnectNPipe` is the server version of `DosClose`.

Named Message Pipes

The `talk2` series of programs uses message pipes to establish a transaction format of communication. The header file `TALK2.H` contains a structure that is the format for communication between the client and the server (see Listing 21.4). The programs `TKCLI21.C`, `TKCLI22.C`, and `TKCLI23.C` will send and respond to messages in the same way (see Listings 21.5, 21.6, and 21.7). `TKCLI23.C` is special because it opens and closes a named pipe in the same call. This requires the server to then disconnect and connect again. The server program `TKSRVR21.C` does not disconnect and reconnect after each message transaction, but is sufficient to demonstrate the ability of `TKCLI23.C` (see Listing 21.8). Trying all the client programs will result in the same communication results, but accomplished using a different method.

Listing 21.4   TALK2.H   *Talk2* Header Source

```
/**************************************************************
 * talk2.h
 */
#ifndef TALK2_H
#define TALK2_H
#define INCL_DOSNMPIPES
#define INCL_ERRORS
#define INCL_DOSFILEMGR
```

```
#include <os2.h>
#define PIPENAME   "\\PIPE\\NPTALK"
/* You could easily replace the local named pipe name with
 * a server constant for network named pipes.
 * \\SERVERNAME\PIPE\NPTALK instead of \PIPE\NPTALK
 */
#define SERVPIPENAME ("\\\\SERVERNAME" + PIPENAME)
#define MAXTEXT   255
#define TALK_QUIT 0
#define TALK_TALK 1
#define TALK_RESP 2

typedef struct tag_nptalk {
    ULONG     mode;
    UCHAR     text[MAXTEXT];
    ULONG     textLength;
} NPTALK;
typedef NPTALK *PNPTALK;

#define NPTALKSIZE sizeof( NPTALK )
#endif    /* TALK2_H */
```

Listing 21.5   TKCLI21.C   *Talk21* Client Source

```
/*************************************************************
 * tkcli21.c
 * Talk client using DosOpen, DosWrite, DosRead,
 * and DosClose. For every write there is a read.
 */

#include <stdio.h>
#include <conio.h>
#include <string.h>
#include "talk2.h"

APIRET   retCd = NO_ERROR; /* return code */
/*
 * main control function
 */
   void
main() {
    ULONG     quitFlag = 0;
    ULONG     resp;
    UCHAR     action;
    HPIPE     pipeHandle;
    NPTALK    readBuffer;
    NPTALK    writeBuffer;
    setbuf( stdin, NULL );  /* No buffering of standard input */
    setbuf( stdout, NULL ); /* No buffering of standard output */
    retCd = DosWaitNPipe( PIPENAME, -1 );  /* block wait */
    if( retCd ) {     /* error on DosWait*/
```

(continues)

Listing 21.5 Continued

```
            quitFlag = 1;   /* flag for exit */
        } else {
            retCd = DosOpen(  PIPENAME,        /* open named pipe */
                              &pipeHandle,
                              &resp,
                              0,
                              0,
                              FILE_OPEN,
                              /* reading and writing */
                              OPEN_ACCESS_READWRITE |
                              OPEN_SHARE_DENYNONE,
                              0     );
            if( retCd ) {  /* error on DosOpen */
                exit( 0 );
            }
        }
    while( !quitFlag ) {
        /* prompt for operation */
        printf( "Actions :\n\t\'S\' to send talk message.\n" +
                "\t\'Q\' to quit -> " );
        action  = _getche();   /* get a single char */
        if( !action ) {        /* if an extended char */
            action  = _getche();   /* get next byte */
        }
        printf( "\n" );
        _flushall();           /* flush all buffers */
        switch( action ) {
            case 's':        /* send a message */
            case 'S': {
                writeBuffer.text[0]  = '\0';
                printf( "Talk Message to send -> " );
                scanf( "%[^\n]", writeBuffer.text );   /* read message */
                writeBuffer.mode  = TALK_TALK;       /* message mode */
                writeBuffer.textLength = strlen( writeBuffer.text );
                /* send message */
                DosWrite( pipeHandle, &writeBuffer, NPTALKSIZE, &resp );
                /* wait to receive message */
                DosRead( pipeHandle, &readBuffer, NPTALKSIZE, &resp );
                /* print return message to client */
                printf( "\nThe Server says \"%s\".\n", readBuffer.text );
            }
            break;

            case 'q':
            case 'Q': {
                printf( "Press any key to exit -> " ); /* exit prompt */
                action  = _getch();     /* get anything */
                writeBuffer.mode  = TALK_QUIT;   /* quit mode */
                strcpy( writeBuffer.text, "Goodbye." );
                writeBuffer.textLength  = strlen( writeBuffer.text );
                /* send message */
                DosWrite( pipeHandle, &writeBuffer, NPTALKSIZE, &resp );
                /* wait to receive message */
                DosRead( pipeHandle, &readBuffer, NPTALKSIZE, &resp );
                quitFlag = 1;  /* flag for exit */
```

```
            }
            break;

            default: {
                /* invalid key pressed */
                printf( "\nThis is not a valid key, try again.\n" );
            }
            break;
        }
        printf( "\n" );
    }
    DosClose( pipeHandle );     /* close named pipe */
}
```

Listing 21.6   TKCLI22.C   *Talk22* Client Source

```
/***********************************************************
 * tkcli22.c
 * Talk Client program using DosOpen, DosTransactNPipe,
 * and DosClose. Acts just like tkcli21.c
 */

#include <stdio.h>
#include <conio.h>
#include <string.h>
#include "talk2.h"

APIRET    retCd = NO_ERROR; /* error code */
/*
 * main control function
 */
    void
main() {
    ULONG    quitFlag = 0;
    ULONG    resp;
    UCHAR    action;
    HPIPE    pipeHandle;
    NPTALK   readBuffer;
    NPTALK   writeBuffer;
    setbuf( stdin, NULL );  /* no buffering of standard input */
    setbuf( stdout, NULL ); /* no buffering of standard output */
    retCd = DosWaitNPipe( PIPENAME, -1 );  /* blocking wait */
    if( retCd ) {      /* named pipe wait error */
        quitFlag = 1;  /* flag for exit */
    } else {
        retCd = DosOpen(  PIPENAME,        /* open named pipe */
                          &pipeHandle,
                          &resp,
                          0,
                          0,
                          FILE_OPEN,
                          OPEN_ACCESS_READWRITE |
                          OPEN_SHARE_DENYNONE,
```

(continues)

Listing 21.6 Continued

```
                               0     );
      if( retCd ) {   /* error on open */
         exit( 0 );
      }
   }
   while( !quitFlag ) {
         /* prompt for action */
         printf( "Actions :\n\t\'S\' to send talk message.\n" +
                 "\t\'Q\' to quit -> " );
         action   = _getche();   /* get action char */
         if( !action ) {    /* if extended char */
            action   = _getche();   /* get next byte */
         }
         printf( "\n" );
         _flushall();   /* flush all buffers */
         switch( action ) {
            case 's':   /* send a message */
            case 'S': {
               writeBuffer.text[0]  = '\0';
               printf( "Talk Message to send -> " );
               scanf( "%[^\n]", writeBuffer.text );
               /* fill send message */
               writeBuffer.mode  = TALK_TALK;
               writeBuffer.textLength  = strlen( writeBuffer.text );
               /* combine write and read into one API call */
               DosTransactNPipe( pipeHandle, &writeBuffer, NPTALKSIZE,
                              &readBuffer, NPTALKSIZE, &resp );
               printf( "\nThe Server says \"%s\".\n", readBuffer.text );
            }
            break;

            case 'q':   /* quit client */
            case 'Q': {
               printf( "Press any key to exit -> " );
               action   = _getch();
               /* send quit message to server */
               writeBuffer.mode  = TALK_QUIT;
               strcpy( writeBuffer.text, "Goodbye." );
               writeBuffer.textLength  = strlen( writeBuffer.text );
               /* single operation for read and write */
               DosTransactNPipe( pipeHandle, &writeBuffer, NPTALKSIZE,
                              &readBuffer, NPTALKSIZE, &resp );
               quitFlag = 1;   /* flag for exit */
            }
            break;

            default: {   /* invalid action */
               printf( "\nThis is not a valid key, try again.\n" );
            }
            break;
         }
         printf( "\n" );
   }
   DosClose( pipeHandle );
}
```

Listing 21.7   TKCLI23.C   *Talk23* Client Source

```c
/***********************************************************
 * tkcli23.c
 * Talk Client using DosCallNPipe.
 * Forces server to disconnect and reconnect
 * after a single communication.
 */

#include <stdio.h>
#include <conio.h>
#include <string.h>
#include "talk2.h"

APIRET   retCd = NO_ERROR; /* return code */
/*
 * main control function
 */
   void
main() {
   ULONG     quitFlag = 0;
   ULONG     timeOut = 3000;
   ULONG     resp;
   UCHAR     action;
   NPTALK    readBuffer;
   NPTALK    writeBuffer;
   setbuf( stdin, NULL );   /* no buffering of standard input */
   setbuf( stdout, NULL );  /* no buffering of standard output */
   retCd = DosWaitNPipe( PIPENAME, -1 );   /* blocking wait */
   if( retCd ) {
      quitFlag = 1;   /* flag for exit */
   }
   while( !quitFlag ) {
         printf( "Actions :\n\t\'S\' to send talk message.\n" +
                 "\t\'Q\' to quit -> " );
         action   = _getche();
         if( !action ) {
            action   = _getche();
         }
         printf( "\n" );
         _flushall();
         switch( action ) {
            case 's':
            case 'S': {
               writeBuffer.text[0]  = '\0';
               printf( "Talk Message to send -> " );
               scanf( "%[^\n]", writeBuffer.text );
               writeBuffer.mode  = TALK_TALK;
               writeBuffer.textLength  = strlen( writeBuffer.text );
/* This line is the major difference between previous client programs */
/* DosCallNPipe connects, writes, reads, and closes in a single command */
               retCd = DosCallNPipe( PIPENAME, &writeBuffer, NPTALKSIZE,
                                     &readBuffer, NPTALKSIZE,
                                     &resp, timeOut );
```

(continues)

Listing 21.7 Continued

```
                if( !retCd ) {
                    printf( "\nThe Server says \"%s\".\n", readBuffer.text );
                } else {
                    printf( "Connection failure\n" );
                }
            }
            break;

            case 'q':
            case 'Q': {
                printf( "Press any key to exit -> " );
                action   = _getch();
                writeBuffer.mode = TALK_QUIT;
                strcpy( writeBuffer.text, "Goodbye." );
                writeBuffer.textLength = strlen( writeBuffer.text );
/* DosCallNPipe connects, writes, reads, and closes in a single command */
                retCd = DosCallNPipe( PIPENAME, &writeBuffer, NPTALKSIZE,
                                      &readBuffer, NPTALKSIZE,
                                      &resp, timeOut );
                if( retCd ) {
                    printf( "Connection failure\n" );
                }
                quitFlag = 1;
            }
            break;

            default: {
                printf( "\nThis is not a valid key, try again.\n" );
            }
            break;
        }
        printf( "\n" );
    }
}
```

Listing 21.8 TKSRVR21.C *Talk22* Server Source

```
/************************************************************
 * tksrvr21.c
 * Talk server program to be used by tkcli2?.c programs
 * Creates a single message-type named pipe and processes
 * messages until a quit message is received.
 */
#include <stdio.h>
#include <string.h>
#include "talk2.h"

APIRET   retCd = NO_ERROR; /* error code */
/*
 * Setup of the client program.
```

```
 * A single message-type named pipe will be created
 * and connected to.
 */
   void
initialize( PHPIPE pipeHandle ) {
   ULONG    direct      = NP_ACCESS_DUPLEX;  /* two way communications */
   /* the pipe will block wait for client connection */
   ULONG    modeP       = NP_WAIT ¦ NP_TYPE_MESSAGE
                         ¦ NP_READMODE_MESSAGE ¦ 0x01;
   ULONG    timeOut     = 5000;  /* 5 second timeout */
   printf( "Initalize\n\n" );
   retCd    = NO_ERROR;
   retCd    = DosCreateNPipe( PIPENAME,
                              pipeHandle,
                              direct,
                              modeP,
                              NPTALKSIZE * 4,   /* leave lots of room */
                              NPTALKSIZE * 4,   /* for reads and writes */
                              timeOut     );

   if( !retCd ) {
      retCd = DosConnectNPipe( *pipeHandle );   /* connect to named pipe */
   }
   if( retCd ) {
      exit( 0 );
   }
}
/*
 * Processing of messages.
 * This includes text communication and exit commands.
 */
   void
processing( HPIPE pipeHandle ) {
   ULONG    quitFlag = 0;
   NPTALK   readBuffer;
   NPTALK   writeBuffer;
   ULONG    retSize;
   retCd = NO_ERROR;
   while( !quitFlag ) { /* repeat until quit flag set */
      /* blocking read of named pipe */
      retCd = DosRead( pipeHandle, &readBuffer, NPTALKSIZE, &retSize );
      if( !retCd ) {
         if( retSize == NPTALKSIZE ) {
            switch( readBuffer.mode ) {   /* text message received */
               case TALK_TALK: { /* text communication with client */
                  printf( "The message is \"%s\"\n", readBuffer.text );
                  writeBuffer.mode  = TALK_RESP;
                  strcpy( writeBuffer.text, "Got it!" );
                  writeBuffer.textLength  = strlen( writeBuffer.text );
                  /* send received message back */
                  retCd = DosWrite( pipeHandle, &writeBuffer,
                               NPTALKSIZE, &retSize );
               }
               break;

               case TALK_QUIT: { /* quit message received  */
```

(continues)

V

OS/2 Development

Listing 21.8 Continued

```
                           printf( "Quitting the application.\n" );
                           writeBuffer.mode   = TALK_RESP;
                           strcpy( writeBuffer.text, "That's it, I Quit!!" );
                           writeBuffer.textLength  = strlen( writeBuffer.text );
                           /* send response to quit message back */
                           retCd = DosWrite( pipeHandle, &writeBuffer,
                                             NPTALKSIZE, &retSize );
                           quitFlag = 1;
                        }
                        break;

                        default:    /* should not receive other messages */
                        {
                            quitFlag = 1;  /* problem, quit program */
                        }
                        break;
                    }
                }
            }
            if( retCd ) {
                quitFlag = 1;
            }
        }
    }
}
/*
 * Shutdown server program.
 * This includes disconnecting and closing the pipes
 */
   void
shutdown( HPIPE   pipeHandle ) {
    APIRET   retCd = NO_ERROR;
    printf( "Shutdown\n\n" );
    retCd = DosDisConnectNPipe( pipeHandle );
    if ( !retCd ) {
        retCd = DosClose( pipeHandle );
    }
}
/*
 * main control function
 */
   void
main()
{
    HPIPE pipeHandle;
    initialize( &pipeHandle );
    processing( pipeHandle );
    shutdown( pipeHandle );
}
```

The `Talk2` programs accomplish the same tasks as the `Talk1` programs, but use a message pipe instead of a byte pipe. A message pipe reads and writes a block or record of data instead of a stream of bytes. Each of the client programs does the same task, but uses different API calls to do it. The `Talk2` series of program can only use one client program at a time.

`TKCLI21` client program uses all the same API calls used by the client program of `Talk1`, but uses a structure with a string and other information contained inside, including a mode flag for telling the server that it is quitting. `DosRead` and `DosWrite` use a size parameter to get the message size amount of data.

`TKCLI22` client program performs the same as `TKCLI21` client program, but uses `DosTransactNPipe` instead of the `DosWrite` and `DosRead` combination. `DosTransactNPipe` uses both a read and write buffer area for the API call, so in a single call, the sending of a message, the wait to receive a response, and the receiving of the message from the server program are accomplished.

`TKCLI23` client program only allows a single exchange of information instead of a repeating loop of messages. Only a single transaction is allowed because this client program uses `DosCallNPipe`. `DosCallNPipe` does the same operations as `DosTransactNPipe`, but also opens and closes the given named pipe for the calling process. This is limiting for the `TKSRVR21` server program, because it only has one exchange of information and is forced to close the connection on the name pipe. `DosCallNPipe` is not useful for prolonged conversations with a server program, but it is perfect for sending a single message without the coding overhead of opening, waiting, sending, receiving, and closing.

`TKSRVR21` server program is almost identical to the `Talk1` server program, but it handles message based communication instead of a byte stream and the message has a mode field to tell the server program that this is the last message and shut down.

Named Pipes with an Event Semaphore

The `talk3` series of programs will use the `TKCLI2?.C` client programs. The header file `TALK3.H` defines the number of pipes that the client program opens (see Listing 21.9). The server program `TKSRVR31.C` will allow multiple copies of the client programs to communicate with it (see Listing 21.10). This is the maximum number of client programs that the server program can connect to. The server program will create and connect to multiple pipes, and each of these pipes will have the same event semaphore attached to it. The server program will then wait for the event semaphore and use calls to tell which pipe posted to the semaphore. The event semaphore will be reset, the pipe will be read from and responded to. If one client sends a quit request message, the server will shut down.

Listing 21.9   TALK3.H   *Talk3* Header Source

```
/***********************************************************
 * talk3.h
 */
#ifndef TALK3_H
#define TALK3_H
#define INCL_DOSNMPIPES
#define INCL_DOSSEMAPHORES
#define INCL_ERRORS
#define INCL_DOSFILEMGR
#include <os2.h>
#define PIPENAME  "\\PIPE\\NPTALK"
/*
 * When using semaphores you CANNOT use network named pipes!
 */
#define MAXPIPES   0x00000005
#define IDOFF      100
#define MAXTEXT    255
#define TALK_QUIT 0
#define TALK_TALK 1
#define TALK_RESP 2

typedef struct tag_nptalk {
   ULONG    mode;
   UCHAR    text[MAXTEXT];
   ULONG    textLength;
} NPTALK;
typedef NPTALK *PNPTALK;
#define NPTALKSIZE sizeof( NPTALK )

#endif   /* TALK3_H */
```

Listing 21.10   TKSRVR31.C   *Talk31* Server Source

```
/***********************************************************
 * tksrvr31.c
 * Talk server program to be used by tkcli2?.c programs
 * Creates multiple named pipes and attaches a single
 * event semaphore to them. This allows the client program
 * to wait on multiple local pipes without multiple threads.
 */

#include <stdio.h>
#include <string.h>
#include "talk3.h"

APIRET   retCd = NO_ERROR;
HPIPE    pipeHandle[MAXPIPES];    /* multiple pipes */
HEV      eventSemHandle;          /* a single event semaphore */
/*
 * Setup of the server program.
 * Multiple pipes are created and connected to.
 * Each pipe has a Set event semaphore attached.
 */
```

```
      void
initialize( void ) {
   ULONG     direct      = NP_ACCESS_DUPLEX;
   ULONG     modeP       = NP_NOWAIT ¦ NP_TYPE_MESSAGE
                           ¦ NP_READMODE_MESSAGE ¦ MAXPIPES;
   ULONG     loop;
   ULONG     timeOut     = 5000;
   retCd     = NO_ERROR;
   printf( "Initalize\n\n" );
   if( !retCd ) {
      /* create a single unnamed event semaphore */
      retCd = DosCreateEventSem( NULL,                /* unnamed semaphore */
                                 &eventSemHandle, /* semaphore handle */
                                 DC_SEM_SHARED,   /* shared semaphore */
                                 FALSE    );      /* semaphore Set */
   }
   if( !retCd ) {
      for( loop = 0; loop < MAXPIPES; loop++ ) {
         retCd = DosCreateNPipe( PIPENAME,
                                 &(pipeHandle[loop]),
                                 direct,
                                 modeP,
                                 NPTALKSIZE * 4,   /* give the read and */
                                 NPTALKSIZE * 4,   /* write buffer space */
                                 timeOut    );
         if( !retCd ) {
            DosConnectNPipe( pipeHandle[loop] );
         }
         if( !retCd ) {
            retCd = DosSetNPipeSem( pipeHandle[loop],    /* pipe handle */
                                    eventSemHandle, /* attach semaphore */
                                    loop + IDOFF    );   /* pipe id */
            if( retCd ) {
               loop  = MAXPIPES;
            }
         }
         if( retCd ) {
            loop  = MAXPIPES;    /* exit for loop */
         }
      }
   }
   if( retCd ) {
      exit( 0 );
   }
}
/*
 * Processing of the messages received from clients.
 * The process will block on a single event semaphore
 * until a single client program sends a message.
 */
   void
processing( void ) {
   ULONG        quitFlag = 0;
   ULONG        retSize;
   ULONG        resp;
   ULONG        loop;
   ULONG        pipeInfoSize;
```

(continues)

Listing 21.10 Continued

```
    USHORT          pipeNumber;
    NPTALK          readBuffer;
    NPTALK          writeBuffer;
    PIPESEMSTATE    pipeInfo[MAXPIPES*3];
retCd = NO_ERROR;
while( !quitFlag ) { /* repeat until quit flag set */
    /* block wait until event semaphore posted */
    retCd = DosWaitEventSem( eventSemHandle, SEM_INDEFINITE_WAIT );
    if( !retCd ) {
        DosResetEventSem( eventSemHandle, &retSize ); /*reset semaphore*/
        pipeInfoSize  = sizeof( pipeInfo ) * 3;  /* leave room */
        /* get the state of all the pipes */
        retCd = DosQueryNPipeSemState( eventSemHandle, pipeInfo,
                                       pipeInfoSize );

        if( !retCd ) {
            pipeNumber  = 0;
            for( loop = 0; loop < MAXPIPES; loop++ ) {
                /* find pipe with data to be read */
                if( pipeInfo[loop].fStatus == NPSS_RDATA ) {
                    pipeNumber  = pipeInfo[loop].usKey; /* save pipe id */
                    loop  = MAXPIPES;
                }
            }
            if( pipeNumber != 0 ) {
                pipeNumber -= IDOFF;   /* translate id to array offset */
            }
        } else {
            exit( 0 );  /* problem getting pipe states */
        }
        if( !retCd ) {
            /* get data from correct pipe */
            retCd = DosRead( pipeHandle[pipeNumber], &readBuffer,
                             NPTALKSIZE, &retSize );
            if(   !retCd   &&
                  retSize == NPTALKSIZE ) {
                switch( readBuffer.mode ) {
                    case TALK_TALK: { /* text message received */
                        printf( "The message is from pipe %d - \"%s\"\n",
                                pipeNumber, readBuffer.text );
                        writeBuffer.mode  = TALK_RESP;
                        strcpy( writeBuffer.text, "Got it!" );
                        writeBuffer.textLength  = strlen( writeBuffer.text );
                        retCd = DosWrite( pipeHandle[pipeNumber], &writeBuffer,
                                          NPTALKSIZE, &retSize );
                        /* reset event semaphore from write */
                        DosResetEventSem( eventSemHandle, &retSize );
                    }
                    break;

                    case TALK_QUIT: { /* quit message received */
                        printf( "Quitting the application.\n" );
                        writeBuffer.mode  = TALK_RESP;
                        strcpy( writeBuffer.text, "That's it, I Quit!!" );
                        writeBuffer.textLength  = strlen( writeBuffer.text );
                        retCd = DosWrite( pipeHandle[pipeNumber],
                                          &writeBuffer, NPTALKSIZE,
```

```
                                      &retSize );
                     /* reset event semaphore from write */
                     DosResetEventSem( eventSemHandle, &retSize );
                     quitFlag = 1;
                  }
                  break;

                  default:    /* any other message is an error */
                  {
                     quitFlag = 1;
                  }
                  break;
               }
            }
         }
      }
      if( retCd ) {
         quitFlag = 1;
      }
   }
}
/* Shut down server program
 * This includes closing the semaphore and disconnecting
 * and closing all the pipes
 */
   void
shutdown( void ) {
   ULONG    loop;
   printf( "Shutdown\n\n" );
   DosCloseEventSem( eventSemHandle );
   for( loop = 0; loop < MAXPIPES; loop++ ) {
      retCd = NO_ERROR;
      retCd = DosDisConnectNPipe( pipeHandle[loop] );
      if ( !retCd ) {
         retCd = DosClose( pipeHandle[loop] );
      }
   }
}
/*
 * main control function
 */
   void
main()
{
   initialize();
   processing();
   shutdown();
}
```

TKSRVR31 server program allows us to use a single event semaphore to notify the server of an incoming request. The function initialize creates a single event semaphore using DosCreateEventSem. The event semaphore is the only way to alert the server program of messages from any of the named pipes created using DosCreateNPipe. The event semaphore is attached to each of the named pipes using DosSetNPipeSem.

After initialization, the server program processes messages from multiple client programs. The server program waits for the event semaphore to be posted to using DosWaitEventSem call. DosWaitEventSem is called with the SEM_INDEFINITE_WAIT flag to force the process to wait until a message is sent to the client program. When the client program knows that a message has been put into the named pipe, the client program uses the DosQueryNPipeSemState call to determine which client program sent the message using which named pipe. Once the server program has determined which named pipe to use, the server program processes the message in the same way our other server programs process incoming information.

Our server program processes information until any of the client programs sends a Quit message. The server program will now shutdown, but first it must deallocate the resources that it has. DosCloseEventSem is called to close the single event semaphore and DosDisConnectNPipe is called on all the named pipes to close all the resources.

Named Pipes with Multiple Event Semaphores

The last development example will use multiple pipes on a server attaching an individual event semaphore to each created pipe. After all the event semaphores are attached, we will add each event semaphore to a MuxWait semaphore. A MuxWait semaphore will enable the server program to wait for all of the event semaphores to be posted, the MuxWait semaphore then becomes posted, and the server program reads and responds to all of the pipes. Server program TKSRVR41.C uses multiple TKCLI2?.C programs as clients (see Listing 21.11).

Listing 21.11 TKSRVR41.C *Talk41* Server Source

```
/*************************************************************
 * tksrvr41.c
 * Talk server program to be used by tkcli2?.c programs
 * Create multiple named pipes and attach a different event
 * semaphore to each. All of the attached event semaphores are
 * added to a MuxWait semaphore and the process waits for all
 * of the event semaphores to be posted before posting to the
 * MuxWait semaphore. Each of the pipes are then read from and
 * the server program is shut down.
 */

#include <stdio.h>
#include <string.h>
#include "talk3.h"

APIRET      retCd = NO_ERROR;
HPIPE       pipeHandle[MAXPIPES];
```

```
HEV          eventSemHandle[MAXPIPES];
SEMRECORD    semaphoreRecords[MAXPIPES];
HMTX         muxWaitSemHandle;
/*
 * Setup the client program
 * Multiple pipes are created and connected to.
 * Multiple event semaphores are created and attached
 * to a corresponding pipe. Finally all the event semaphores
 * are added to a MuxWait semaphore.
 */
   void
initialize( void ) {
   ULONG     direct   = NP_ACCESS_DUPLEX;
   ULONG     modeP    = NP_NOWAIT | NP_TYPE_MESSAGE
                      | NP_READMODE_MESSAGE | MAXPIPES;
   ULONG     loop;
   ULONG     timeOut  = 5000;
   retCd     = NO_ERROR;
   printf( "Initalize\n\n" );
   for( loop = 0; loop < MAXPIPES; loop++ ) {
      retCd    = DosCreateNPipe( PIPENAME,
                                 &(pipeHandle[loop]),
                                 direct,
                                 modeP,
                                 NPTALKSIZE * 4,
                                 NPTALKSIZE * 4,
                                 timeOut     );
      if( !retCd ) {
         DosConnectNPipe( pipeHandle[loop] );
      }
      if( !retCd ) {
         retCd = DosCreateEventSem(
                    NULL,                    /* unnamed semaphore */
                    &eventSemHandle[loop],   /* semaphore handle */
                    DC_SEM_SHARED,           /* share the semaphore */
                    FALSE     );             /* semaphore Set for Posting */
      }
      if( !retCd ) {
         /* attach semaphores to each pipe */
         retCd = DosSetNPipeSem(
                    pipeHandle[loop],        /* pipe handle */
                    eventSemHandle[loop],    /* semaphore to attach */
                    loop + IDOFF    );       /* simple id for pipe */
/* build a list of event semaphore records for the MuxWait semaphore */
         semaphoreRecords[loop].hsemCur   = eventSemHandle[loop];
         semaphoreRecords[loop].ulUser    = loop + IDOFF;
      }
      if( retCd ) {
         loop  = MAXPIPES;    /* exit for loop */
      }
   }
   if( !retCd ) {
/* anonymous MuxWait semaphore that waits on all the added semaphores */
      retCd = DosCreateMuxWaitSem( (PSZ)NULL, &muxWaitSemHandle,
                                   MAXPIPES, semaphoreRecords,
                                   DCMW_WAIT_ALL );
```

(continues)

Listing 21.11   Continued

```
        }
        if( retCd ) {
          exit( 0 );
        }
}
/*
 * Processing of the messages received from multiple client programs.
 * The process will block wait on the MuxWait semaphore until all the
 * client programs post a message, and will then display all the messages.
 */
   void
processing( void ) {
    ULONG         retSize;
    ULONG         resp;
    USHORT        pipeNumber;
    NPTALK        readBuffer;
    NPTALK        writeBuffer;
    retCd = NO_ERROR;
    /* block wait on MuxWait semaphore */
    retCd = DosWaitMuxWaitSem( muxWaitSemHandle,
                          SEM_INDEFINITE_WAIT, &resp );
    if( !retCd ) {
       for( pipeNumber = 0; pipeNumber < MAXPIPES; pipeNumber++ ) {
          /* read a message from each pipe */
          retCd = DosRead( pipeHandle[pipeNumber], &readBuffer,
                         NPTALKSIZE, &retSize );
          if(   !retCd   &&
                retSize == NPTALKSIZE ) {
             printf( "The message from pipe %d - \"%s\"\n",
                     pipeNumber, readBuffer.text );
             writeBuffer.mode   = TALK_RESP;
             strcpy( writeBuffer.text, "Got it!" );
             writeBuffer.textLength  = strlen( writeBuffer.text );
             retCd = DosWrite( pipeHandle[pipeNumber], &writeBuffer,
                            NPTALKSIZE, &retSize );
          }
       }
    }
}
/*
 * Shut down server program
 * This includes removing all the event semaphores from the MuxWait
 * semaphore and closing each event semaphore. Disconnecting and
 * closing each pipe. Finally closing the MuxWait semaphore.
 */
   void
shutdown( void ) {
    ULONG    loop;
    printf( "Shutdown\n\n" );
    for( loop = 0; loop < MAXPIPES; loop++ ) {
```

```
        DosDeleteMuxWaitSem( muxWaitSemHandle, eventSemHandle[loop]
    );
        DosCloseEventSem( eventSemHandle[loop] );
        retCd = NO_ERROR;
        retCd = DosDisConnectNPipe( pipeHandle[loop] );
        if ( !retCd ) {
            retCd = DosClose( pipeHandle[loop] );
        }
    }
    DosCloseMuxWaitSem( muxWaitSemHandle );
}
/*
 * main control function
 */
    void
main()
{
    initialize();
    processing();
    shutdown();
}
```

TKSRVR41 server program uses multiple event semaphores attached to a
single MuxWait semaphore to wait for messages from all of the client programs, and then prints all the received messages at the same time. Multiple
named pipes and event semaphores are created using DosCreateNPipe and
DosCreateEventSem. Each of the event semaphores is attached to a single
named pipe. All of the events semaphores are attached to a single MuxWait
semaphore using the DosCreateMuxWaitSem call.

The processing of information begins after each of the event semaphores are
posted to—caused by the client programs sending a message to the client
program. When all of the client programs have sent a message, the MuxWait
semaphore is posted to, causing the call to DosWaitMuxWaitSem to release the
server program to service all of the named pipes. TKSRVR41 can only handle a
single round of messages, but by extending the provided development logic,
it could repeat the process until a Quit message is sent.

The shutdown of TKSRVR41 is more complicated than any of our previous
servers. Each of the event semaphores must be removed from the MuxWait
semaphore using DosDeleteMuxWaitSem. Then the removed event semaphores
are destroyed using the DosCloseEventSem call. Each of the named pipes must
be closed using DosDisConnectNPipe and finally, the MuxWait semaphore can be
closed using DosCloseMuxWaitSem.

From Here...

This chapter discussed pipes, semaphores, file manipulation under OS/2, and how they relate to each other on a multitasking platform. You also learned how to develop client/server applications using named pipes and how OS/2's integrated abilities to handle pipes makes OS/2 an ideal client/server platform.

The following chapters provide broader information on selected topics that relate to this chapter:

- Chapter 1, "What is Client/Server," gives an extended introduction to client/server systems.

- Chapter 4, "Client/Server Development Overview," shows the steps necessary for planning and implementing a client/server project.

- Chapter 23, "Multiplatform Applications," gives an expanded view of using different platforms and their development styles for creating a client/server system.

Chapter 22

Other Client/Server Techniques

OS/2 provides a platform for both client and server computing, and native network communications using named pipes. What more do we need to perform all our computing needs? In a perfect world, we would all use the same operating system and network communication, but different ways of accomplishing tasks has lead to different solutions. Every person, company, and organization has an individual way of getting things done. This leaves us with some interesting problems. If my computer only speaks "xyz" protocol and the information I need is on a computer that only speaks "pdq," then we are out of luck—but this is not an acceptable response to our problem. Fortunately for us, we are using OS/2, with the convenient feature of using multiple protocols, on our networking stack. OS/2 can handle a diverse range of communication needs and can participate in most networking environments.

Network named pipes is not the only solution that OS/2 offers to developers. We will explore a few of our development options and get a better feeling for what client/server solutions OS/2 can provide.

This chapter introduces and evaluates the following:

- Sockets

- Socket Calls

- Basic Socket Development

- CPI-C and APPC

- CPI-C Calls

- Basic CPI-C Development

TCP/IP Sockets

Sockets originated on the UNIX operating system as a peer-to-peer LAN protocol. Sockets allow an API-based interface to TCP/IP. Sockets have different characteristics for each network. Socket family, types, and addressing force the socket developer to be aware of the variations of sockets.

What Are Sockets?

Sockets are a network-addressable connection point that is allocated and managed by the operating system. The user does not directly manipulate a socket. The user is given a socket descriptor, which is a number that tells the operating system which socket is being used. Sockets and socket descriptors are similar to named pipes and pipe handles. Figure 22.1 shows the relation of socket descriptors, sockets, and the network.

Fig. 22.1
Abstraction of
sockets.

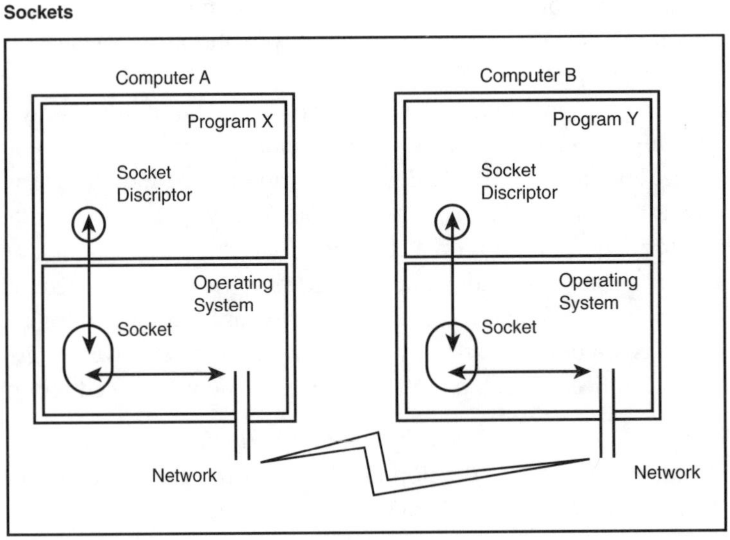

Figure 22.1 shows that a program does not contain the socket, but uses a socket descriptor and function calls to access the socket. The socket descriptor is similar to pipe handles as a way to identify the required resource to the operating system, and in the case of program failure the operating system can manage the abandoned resource.

Socket Types

There are three types of sockets: *stream sockets*, *datagram sockets*, and *raw sockets*. Each provides a different interface to TCP/IP layers. The decision of which type of socket to use should be based on the needed services, transfer efficiency, and reliability.

Stream Sockets

Many of the problems of transferring data across a network are handled for the developer, because stream sockets use the TCP transport protocol. They handle flow control and packet reordering, and are not restricted by data block size. Transfer of data is handled like file access. Traditional socket development uses the socket descriptor just like a file handle. Reads and writes are done on a socket-like file I/O and console interaction.

Datagram Sockets

If a developer requires fast data transfer with very little overhead, datagram sockets are a good choice. The UDP datagram service is interfaced for communications. This does not have automatic retransmission, packet ordering, detection for duplicated or lost data, or receipt acknowledgment. UDP datagram service also limits the size of a single datagram.

Raw Sockets

Development using raw sockets is normally reserved for new protocols. Any socket development not using stream or datagram functionality will use raw sockets as a starting point. Raw sockets provide even less services than datagram sockets, but allow the developer to only build what is considered the necessary functionality for their new socket type. The interface used allows access to the lower levels of TCP/IP, namely IP and ICMP.

Socket Families

There are four socket families to choose from using UNIX. IBM's OS/2 TCP/IP allows only one family of sockets, Internet.

- AF_INET—This is the only family supported by OS/2. This does not generally cause a problem. Most development uses the Internet family as the default.

- AF_UNIX—This socket family provides UNIX to UNIX IPC.

- AF_PUP—This socket family provides Xerox XNS.

- AF_APPLETALK—This socket family provides Appletalk network.

Socket Address

A socket address consists of the Internet address and a port number. The Internet address allows communication with a given machine, and the port number is an application service ID. The port numbers are reserved numbers that are set up on machines to provide services to the network.

A socket address is a C structure that contains the address family flag and a direct access memory block for flexible information storage. Different structures are cast or made to look like the socket address structure. This provides a single type of parameter for all the types of addresses. These structures will be described in more detail under the appropriate socket call.

Byte Order

There are two types of byte ordering, big-endian and little-endian. Big-endian is the ordering used by Motorola microprocessors, and is also known as network ordering. Big-endian is the ordering used by Intel microprocessors. It is important that network ordering is used because it gives developers a standard order to work from. It is better always to make calls to reorder information than not know. Sockets do not handle ordering for the developer. You must make the calls if it is necessary.

Socket Calls

Socket development involves 58 calls. These calls are easier to understand if they are classified by group. Unless otherwise noted, all socket calls return an int with a 0 indicating success and a -1 indicating an error. If an error occurs, the error code can be obtained by calling sock_errno().

Core Calls

The OS/2 socket calls are very similar to the standard socket calls provided on UNIX systems. The calls defined here do not cover all the socket calls, but do provide many of the fundamental calls needed to do basic development. OS/2 does not provide the socket development library as part of the operating system, but can be purchased as an additional product for development by using the OS/2 TCP/IP Development Kit.

sock_init. This call initializes socket data structures for the calling process and checks for the existence of necessary networking components. The syntax is as follows:

```
sock_init();
```

socket. This call requests that the operating system creates a socket with given characteristics, and returns a socket descriptor. If an error occurs, the error code can be obtained by calling sock_errno(). The syntax is as follows:

```
socket( int   domain,
        int   type,
        int   protocol );
```

Parameters.

- *domain*, the address domain is an `int`. This must be `AF_INIT` for OS/2.

- *type*, the socket type is an `int`. See socket types under the "Flags" section.

- *protocol*, the requested protocol is an `int`. This is normally set to `0`, the default protocol.

- `socket` returns an `int` that is a socket descriptor.

Flags. Socket types are:

- `SOCK_STREAM`—Use this flag if you want the socket to handle data transfer like file manipulation. This will also give you automatic error detection and resend.

- `SOCK_DGRAM`—Use this flag if you do not want all the overhead handled by stream sockets. Useful for transferring fixed-size blocks of data.

- `SOCK_RAW`—Use this flag if you want to design your own socket behavior and abilities. This will also allow the developer access to lower-level protocols.

bind. This call requests that the operating system binds or attaches a name to the given socket. The syntax is as follows:

```
bind(    int              s,
      struct sockaddr    *name,
      int                namelen    );
```

Parameters.

- *s*, the socket descriptor is an `int`. This is the socket that local information will be attached to.

- *name*, the socket name information is a pointer to a `struct sockaddr`. This structure is described under "Structures" as `sockaddr`. Normally the structure addressed is not of this type, but it does give a common format for other address-related structures. The structure used for the Internet address family is `sockaddr_in`, and is described under "Structures" as `sockaddr_in`.

- *namelen*, the size of the memory area addressed by the parameter *name* is an `int`.

Structures. `struct sockaddr` is the following:

- `sa_family` is an `int`. This contains the address family flag. For OS/2, this is `AF_INET`.

- `sa_data` is an array of 14 `char`. This is a binary data area that holds information that varies depending on the format of the original structure.

`struct sockaddr_in` is the following:

- `sin_family` is an `int`. This contains the address family flag. For OS/2, this is `AF_INET`.

- `sin_port` is an `unsigned short`. This is the port number in network order.

- `sin_addr` is a `struct in_addr`. This structure is described under `struct in_addr`.

- `sin_zero` is an array of eight `char`. This array needs to be set to all zeros for proper operation.

`struct in_addr` is:

- `sin_zero` is an `unsigned long`. This 32-bit number is the Internet address used by the application. This must also be in network order.

soclose. This call requests that the operating system close the socket attached to the socket descriptor and release system resources used by the socket. If the connection related to this socket is still open, it will be closed. The syntax is as follows:

```
soclose(    int    s    );
```

Parameters.
- `s`, the socket descriptor is an `int`. This is the socket that will be released.

send. This call sends data to an open socket. If the receiving socket is not ready to receive, the `send` call blocks by default. A `send` can be set to be non-blocking by using the call `ioctl`. The syntax is as follows:

```
send(    int         s,
         char        *msg,
         int         len,
         int         flags    );
```

Parameters.

- *s*, the socket descriptor is an `int`. This parameter is a reference to the socket you want to use to send data.

- *msg*, the information to transmit is a pointer to `char` buffer. This parameter references a memory area that contains the information to send.

- *len*, the amount of information is an `int`. The largest amount of data that can be sent is 32,768 bytes.

- *flags*, send options value is an `int`. This parameter is normally `0`, but can be set to a value or combined values for send options.

recv. This call receives data from an open socket. If the data is larger than the receiving buffer, the excess is discarded. The `recv` call will wait until data is available from the caller. When data is available, the caller will be blocked, if the caller can be blocked. The syntax is as follows:

```
recv(    int     s,
     char    *buf,
     int     len,
     int     flags    );
```

Parameters.

- *s*, the socket descriptor is an `int`. This parameter is a reference to the socket to get data from.

- *buf*, the memory area to read into is a pointer to a `char` buffer. This parameter references a block of memory to store received data.

- *len*, the maximum amount of data is an `int`. This parameter tells the `recv` the size of the memory area.

- *flags*, receive options value is an `int`. This parameter is normally `0`, but can be set to a value or combined value for receive options.

- `recv` returns an `int` that gives the amount of data received. If the value is `0`, the connection is closed. If the value is `-1`, an error has occurred.

writev. This call sends multiple data buffer areas to an open socket. The `writev` call does not send all of the buffers in one call. This call must be used multiple times on the same array of data buffers to send all of the data buffer areas. This looping should continue until it returns a `0` amount transferred or an error value. While writing a data buffer area, the receiver will be blocked. If the receiver cannot be blocked, the `writev` call will return an error and an appropriate error code will be set. This form of transfer is helpful when trying to handle the limitations of datagram sockets. The syntax is as follows:

```
writev(    int            s,
           struct iovec        *iov,
           int            iovcnt    );
```

Parameters.

- ■ `s`, the socket descriptor is an `int`. This parameter is a reference to the socket that `writev` will send `struct iovecs` to.

- ■ `iov`, multiple structures of data to send is a pointer to an array of `struct iovec`'s. This parameter references an array of data buffers to send to the socket. See `struct iovec` under the "Structures" section.

- ■ `iovcnt`, count of `struct iovec`'s is an `int`. This parameter tells `writev` the number of `struct iovec`'s to send to the socket.

- ■ `writev` returns an `int` that gives the amount of data sent. If the value is `0`, the connection is closed. If the value is `-1`, an error has occurred.

Structures. `struct iovec` is the following:

- ■ `iov_base` is a pointer to an array of `char`. This is an individual data area to transfer.

- ■ `iov_len` is an `int`. This is size of the corresponding `iov_base` data area.

readv. This call is designed to receive multiple `send`s from a connected socket and store the transferred information to a series of data buffers. The `readv` call is called only once to receive into multiple buffers. The array of data buffers must be allocated by the developer before the call. This form of transfer is helpful when trying to handle the limitations of datagram sockets. The syntax is as follows:

```
readv(    int            s,
          struct iovec        *iov,
          int            iovcnt    );
```

Parameters.

- ■ `s`, the socket descriptor is an `int`. This parameter is a reference to the socket that `readv` will receive data from.

- ■ `iov`, multiple structures of data to store is a pointer to an array of `struct iovec`'s. This parameter references an array of data buffers to receive data from the socket. See `struct iovec` under `writev` the "Structures" section.

■ *iovcnt*, count of struct iovec's is an int. This parameter tells readv the number of struct iovec's that can be stored from the socket.

■ readv returns an int that gives the amount of data received. If the value is 0, the connection is closed. If the value is -1, an error has occurred.

sendto. This call works like send, but sends information on a socket ignoring the sockets bind connection status. This call works on both connected and unconnected sockets. This call allows quick and temporary connect and bind. The syntax is as follows:

```
sendto(    int           s,
           char          *msg,
           int           len,
           int           flags,
           struct sockaddr  *to,
           int           tolen   );
```

Parameters.

■ *s*, the socket descriptor is an int. This parameter is a reference to the socket you want to use to send data.

■ *msg*, the information to transmit is a pointer to char buffer. This parameter references a memory area that contains the information to send.

■ *len*, the amount of information is an int. The largest amount of data that can be sent is 32,768 bytes.

■ *flags*, send options value is an int . This parameter is normally 0, but can be set to a value or combined value for send options.

■ *z*, the socket name information is a pointer to a struct sockaddr. This structure is described under bind's "Structures" section as sockaddr. Normally the structure addressed is not of this type, but it does give a common format for other address-related structures. The structure used for the Internet address family is sockaddr_in and is described under bind's "Structures" section as sockaddr_in.

■ *tolen*, the size of the memory area addressed by the parameter *to* is an int.

■ sendto returns an int that gives the amount of data sent. If the value is 0, the connection is closed. If the value is -1, an error has occurred.

recvfrom. This call works like recv, but receives information on a socket ignoring the sockets bind connection status. This call works on both connected and unconnected sockets. This call allows quick and temporary connect and bind. The syntax is as follows:

```
recvfrom(    int            s,
             char           *buf,
             int            len,
             int            flags,
             struct sockaddr    *name,
             int            namelen    );
```

Parameters.

- `s`, the socket descriptor is an `int`. This parameter is a reference to the socket you want to use to send data.

- `buf`, the information to receive is a pointer to `char` buffer. This parameter references a memory area that the call will store data to.

- `len`, the amount of information is an `int`. The largest amount of data that can be stored in `buf`.

- `flags`, send options value is an `int`. This parameter is normally `0`, but can be set to a value or combined value for send options.

- `name`, the socket name information is a pointer to a `struct sockaddr`. This structure is described under `bind`'s "Structures" section as `sockaddr`. Normally the structure addressed is not of this type, but it does give a common format for other address-related structures. The structure used for the Internet address family is `sockaddr_in`, and is described under `bind`'s "Structures" section as `sockaddr_in`.

- `namelen`, the size of the memory area addressed by the parameter `name` is an `int`.

- `recvfrom` returns an `int` that gives the amount of data sent. If the value is `0`, the connection is closed. If the value is `-1`, an error has occurred.

connect. This call performs different tasks for different socket types. For datagram and raw sockets, the `connect` call establishes the remote address as a peer. This allows these socket types to make calls restricted to sockets in a connected state. The `connect` call does two things for a stream socket. First, it will perform a bind to a local address if the socket has not already had a bind established. Second, it will establish a connection with the given remote address. A `connect` is done by a client program to establish a connection with a server. The server must be in a listen state, ready to receive a connection. If the server is not ready, the `connect` call will return an error. The syntax is as follows:

```
connect(     int               s,
             struct sockaddr   *name,
             int               namelen     );
```

Parameters.

- *s*, the socket descriptor is an `int`. This is the socket that local information will be attached to.

- *name*, the remote socket name information is a pointer to a `struct sockaddr`. This structure is described under `bind`'s "Structures" section as `sockaddr`. Normally the structure addressed is not of this type, but it does give a common format for other address-related structures. The structure used for the Internet address family is `sockaddr_in`, and is described under `bind`'s "Structures" section as `sockaddr_in`.

- *namelen*, the size of the memory area addressed by the parameter *name* is an `int`.

listen. This call is only appropriate for stream sockets. It sets up a server program for receiving connections from remote clients. First, `listen` will perform a bind on the socket if it has not already been done. Second, it allocates a queue of connections requests. This allows the server to limit the number of connections available using the server. A `listen` call must be issued by the server before any accept calls can be made. The syntax is as follows:

```
listen(     int     s,
            int     backlog     );
```

Parameters.

- *s*, the socket descriptor is an `int`. This is the socket that the server program will receive connection request from.

- *backlog*, connection limit is an `int`. This is the number of connection entries to be set up for the server.

accept. This call is only appropriate for stream sockets. It allows the server to set up different sockets for client programs, so the client will not tie up the "well-known" port. There are two ways for a server to use the `accept` call. The first is to get the client's address by passing a `sockaddr` parameter. The second is not to get the client's address immediately. The client's address can be retrieved later by using `getpeername`. The syntax is as follows:

```
accept(     int               s,
            struct sockaddr   *name,
            int               *namelen     );
```

Parameters.

■ *s*, the socket descriptor is an `int`. This is the socket that local information will be attached to.

■ *name*, the client socket name information is a pointer to a `struct` `sockaddr`. This structure is described under `bind`'s "Structures" section as `sockaddr`. Normally the structure addressed is not of this type, but it does give a common format for other address-related structures. The structure used for the Internet address family is `sockaddr_in`, and is described under `bind`'s "Structures" section as `sockaddr_in`.

■ *namelen*, the size of the memory area addressed by the parameter *name* is a pointer to an `int`. This parameter will be returned with the amount of data put into *name*.

shutdown. This call disconnects a socket. A `shutdown` does not have to be a total disconnection. Communication to or from a socket can be shut down, leaving the other direction of communication active. The syntax is as follows:

```
shutdown(    int     s,
         int     how    );
```

Parameters.

■ *s*, the socket descriptor is an `int`. This is the socket that will be shut down.

■ *how*, shutdown options flag is an `int`. This parameter tells `shutdown` how much of a shutdown is wanted on the socket. See how under "Flags" for acceptable values.

Flags. *how* is:

0—`shutdown` transfers from the socket.

1—`shutdown` transfers to the socket.

2—`shutdown` transfers to and from the socket.

gethostid. This call returns a unique ID for each host on a system. The returned value is a 32-bit number and is in network order. The syntax is as follows:

```
gethostid();
```

Parameters.

- gethostid returns an unsigned long that is a unique ID among all hosts on a system.

getpeername. This call gets the remote socket address on the given socket. This call can only be performed on connected sockets. The syntax is as follows:

```
getpeername(     int              s,
          struct sockaddr    *name,
          int                *namelen    );
```

Parameters.

- s, the socket descriptor is an int. This is the socket that information will be retrieved from.

- name, the client socket name information is a pointer to a struct sockaddr. This structure is described under bind's "Structures" section as sockaddr. Normally the structure addressed is not of this type, but it does give a common format for other address-related structures. The structure used for the Internet address family is sockaddr_in, and is described under bind's "Structures" section as sockaddr_in.

- namelen, the size of the memory area addressed by the parameter name is a pointer to an int. This parameter will be returned with the amount of data put into name.

getsockname. This call retrieves the local socket address on the given socket. This call is often used to get the port number assigned to a socket after the socket is bound. If the socket is not bound, the socket address will be cleared and given only the correct socket family value. The syntax is as follows:

```
getsockname(     int              s,
          struct sockaddr    *name,
          int                *namelen    );
```

Parameters.

- s, the socket descriptor is an int. This is the socket that information will be retrieved from.

- name, the client socket name information is a pointer to a struct sockaddr. This structure is described under bind's "Structures" section as sockaddr. Normally the structure addressed is not of this type, but it does give a common format for other address-related structures. The structure used for the Internet address family is `sockaddr_in`, and is described under `bind`'s "Structures" section as `sockaddr_in`.

■ *namelen*, the size of the memory area addressed by the parameter *name* is a pointer to an `int`. This parameter will be returned with the amount of data put into *name*.

getsockopt. This call allows the developer to get information about the given socket. Normally a socket option must be presented at the same level as the protocol layer, but OS/2 supports only the `SOL_SOCKET` level. The syntax is as follows:

```
getsockopt(      int          s,
           int          level,
           int          optname,
           char         *optval,
           int          *optlen    );
```

Parameters.

■ *s*, the socket descriptor is an `int`. This is the socket that information will be retrieved from.

■ *level*, an option level is an `int`. This parameter takes a flag to set what level to get options. Currently, the only level accepted is the `SOL_SOCKET` level flag.

■ *optname*, a socket option is an `int`. This parameter takes a `SOL_SOCKET` option. See `SockOptFlag` under the "Structures and Flags" section.

■ *optval*, a memory buffer that retrieves option information is a pointer to an array of `char`. This parameter will normally need an `int`-size buffer except for `SO_RCVBUF`, `SO_SNDBUF`, and `SO_LINGER`. See `SockOptFlag` under the "Structures and Flags" section for details.

■ *optlen*, the size of the memory area addressed by the parameter *optval* is a pointer to an `int`. This parameter will be returned with the amount of data put into *optval*.

Structures and Flags. `SockOptFlag` are the following:

■ `SO_BROADCAST`—Enables/disables the broadcasting of messages using the socket. This is not a valid option for stream sockets.

■ `SO_DEBUG`—Enables/disables the ability to get debugging information.

■ SO_DONTROUTE—Enables/disables the routing of information which will cause the information to be sent only to directly connected networks. This is not a valid option for stream sockets.

■ SO_ERROR—Enables/disables the returning of errors on the socket. Normally used for the checking of asynchronous errors.

■ SO_KEEPALIVE—Enables/disables the ability of the socket to timeout and shut down the socket automatically. This option is valid only for stream sockets.

■ SO_LINGER—Enables/disables the ability to block a socket that is trying to close, but has data waiting on it. See struct linger later in this section. This option is valid only for stream sockets.

■ SO_OOBINLINE—Enables/disables the socket's ability to get out-of-band data. This allows out-of-band data to be stored, instead of forcing another receive with an out-of-band data flag. This option is valid only for stream sockets.

■ SO_RCVBUF—Changes the size of the socket's receive buffer. The optval must be the size of a long, and specifies the size of the buffer. This is normally done for application efficiency reasons.

■ SO_RCVLOWAT—The socket will receive low-water-mark information.

■ SO_RCVTIMEO—The socket will receive timeout information.

■ SO_REUSEADDR—Enables/disables the use of local addresses in the bind operation. This option normally prevents local addresses and foreign addresses from being the same.

■ SO_SNDBUF—Changes the size of the socket's send buffer. The optval must be the size of a long, and specifies the size of the buffer. This is normally done for application efficiency reasons.

■ SO_SNDLOWAT—The socket will send low-water-mark information.

■ SO_SNDTIMEO—The socket will send timeout information.

■ SO_TYPE—Gets the type of the socket. It will be one of the three socket types.

■ SO_USELOOPBACK—Do not use hardware when able to.

struct linger is the following:

- int l_onoff—Set this data member to 0 to turn lingering off, any other value will turn lingering on.

- int l-time—Set this data member to the number of seconds to linger before closing.

setsockopt. This call allows the developer to set information about the given socket. Normally a socket option must be set at the same level as the protocol layer, but OS/2 supports only the SOL_SOCKET level. The syntax is as follows:

```
setsockopt(      int          s,
          int          level,
          int          optname,
          char         *optval,
          int          *optlen    );
```

Parameters.

- s, the socket descriptor is an int. This is the socket that information will be set for.

- level, an option level is an int. This parameter takes a flag to set at what level to get options. Currently, the only level accepted is the SOL_SOCKET level flag.

- optname, a socket option is an int. This parameter takes a SOL_SOCKET option. See SockOptFlag under getsockopt's "Structures and Flags" section.

- optval, a memory buffer for option information to be set is a pointer to an array of char. This parameter will normally need an int-size buffer except for SO_RCVBUF, SO_SNDBUF, and SO_LINGER. See SockOptFlag under getsockopt's "Structures and Flags" section.

- optlen, the size of the memory area addressed by the parameter optval is a pointer to an int. This parameter will be returned with the amount of data put into optval.

select—OS/2 Style. This call monitors a group of sockets for activity. The OS/2 format of select requires a pointer to an array of socket descriptors, followed by count information on the array. The syntax is as follows:

```
select(    int      *s,
       int      noreads,
       int      nowrites,
       int      noexcepts,
       long     timeOut    );
```

Parameters.

- *s*, an array of sockets is a pointer to an `int`. This parameter points to an array of socket descriptors to be monitored by select. If accept returns a positive value, the socket descriptors inactivated in *s* are set to -1.

- *noreads*, the number of read sockets in *s* is an `int`. This parameter tells select the number of read sockets in *s*.

- *nowrites*, the number of write sockets in *s* is an `int`. This parameter tells select the number of write sockets in *s*.

- *noexcepts*, the number of exception sockets in *s* is an `int`. This parameter tells select the number of exception sockets in *s*.

- *timeOut*, the timeout value is a long. This parameter is the amount of time in milliseconds to wait for actions on a socket. A value of 0 indicates immediate return and a value of -1 indicates indefinite wait.

- select returns an `int`, the number of sockets that activity occurred on.

***select*—BSD Style.** This call monitors a group of sockets for activity. The BSD format of select requires three special parameters that point to a mask set. These mask sets can be manipulated using the macros FD_ZERO, FD_SET, FD_INSET, and FD_CLR. All the macros take a socket descriptor and a pointer to a `struct fd_set` except FD_ZERO. FD_ZERO takes a pointer only to a `struct fd_set`. The syntax is as follows:

```
select(    int            nfds,
           fd_set         *readfds,
           fd_set         *writefds,
           fd_set         *exceptfds,
           struct timeval *timeOut    );
```

Parameters.

- *nfds*, the number of socket descriptors to monitor is an `int`. These are the total set by *readfds*, *writefds*, and *exceptfds*.

- *readfds*, the read sockets to monitor is a pointer to an `fd_set`. This parameter is the set of read sockets to monitor.

- *writefds*, the write sockets to monitor is a pointer to an `fd_set`. This parameter is the set of write sockets to monitor.

- *exceptfds*, the exception sockets to monitor is a pointer to an `fd_set`. This parameter is the set of exception sockets to monitor.

- *timeOut*, a timeout value is a pointer to a `struct timeval`. The amount of time to wait before returning.

Structures and Macros. FT macros are:

- FD_ZERO—Clears all of the fd_set

- FD_SET—Sets the bit for the given socket in the given fd_set

- FD_INSET—Tests the given fd_set for the given socket

- FD_CLR—Clears the bit for the given socket in the given fd_set

Structure name is:

- tv_sec—Number of seconds

- tv_usec—Number of microseconds

ioctl. This call changes various operating abilities of a socket. Unless otherwise noted, the data parameter takes an int-size buffer using Boolean sets and responses. The syntax is as follows:

```
ioctl(     int          s,
     int          cmd,
     char          *data,
     int          lendata      );
```

Parameters.
- s, the socket descriptor is an int. This parameter is the socket to be operated on.

- cmd, the command to perform is an int. This parameter is the command being requested. See IoctlFlags under the "Structures and Flags" section for a list of available commands.

- data, information area for data transfer is a pointer to a char buffer. This parameter points to a buffer that is read from or written to, depending on the command issued.

- lendata, the size of the information area referenced by data is an int. This parameter tells ioctl the size of the buffer pointed to by the data parameter.

Structures and Flags. ioctl flags are the following:

- FIOASYNC—Enables/disables asynchronous input/output.

- FIONBIO—Enables/disables nonblocking input/output.

- FIONREAD—Finds the number of readable bytes for the socket. The data parameter is set as ioctl's response.

- `SIOCADDRT`—Add an entry to the routing table. The data parameter takes a struct `rtentry`.

- `SIOCATMARK`—Tests for the current location being out-of-band data.

- `SIODARP`—Removes an arp table entry. The data parameter takes a struct `arpreq`.

- `SIOCDELRT`—Removes an entry to the routing table. The data parameter takes a struct `rtentry`.

- `SIOCGRAP`—Queries for an arp-table entry. The data parameter takes a struct `arpreq`.

- `SIOCGIFADDR`—Queries for the network interface address. The data parameter takes a struct `ifreq`.

- `SIOCGIFCONF`—Queries for the interface broadcast address. The data parameter takes a struct `ifreq`.

- `SIOCGIFCONF`—Queries for the network interface configuration. The data parameter takes a struct `ifreq`.

- `SIOCGIFDSTADDR`—Queries for the network interface destination address. The data parameter takes a struct `ifreq`.

- `SIOCGIFFLAGS`—Queries for the network interface flags. The data parameter takes a struct `ifreq`.

- `SIOCGIFMETRIC`—Queries for the network interface routing metric. The data parameter takes a struct `ifreq`.

- `SIOCGIFNETMASK`—Queries for the network interface network mask. The data parameter takes a struct `ifreq`.

- `SIOCSARP`—Adds an arp table entry. The data parameter takes a struct `arpreq`.

- `SIOCSIFADDR`—Sets the network interface address. The data parameter takes a struct `ifreq`.

- `SIOCSIFBRDADDR`—Sets the interface broadcast address. The data parameter takes a struct `ifreq`.

- `SIOCSIFDSTADDR`—Sets the network interface destination address. The data parameter takes a struct `ifreq`.

- `SIOCSIFFLAGS`—Sets the network interface flags. The data parameter takes a struct `ifreq`.

■ SIOCSIFMETRIC—Sets the network interface routing metric. The data parameter takes a struct ifreq.

■ SIOCSIFNETMASK—Sets the network interface flags. The data parameter takes a struct ifreq.

Utility Calls

There is a total of 37 socket utility calls, but we will describe only a few of the most immediate ones for our use. Many of these calls handle converting data into network order, so that all platforms can be assured of proper data format.

htonl. This call translates a long int into network byte order. The syntax is as follows:

```
htonl(     unsigned long          a );
```

Parameters.

■ a, binary data is an unsigned long. This parameter is the information that needs to be translated.

■ htonl returns an unsigned long, the same data as the a parameter but in network order.

htons. This call translates a short into network byte order. The syntax is as follows:

```
htons( unsigned short      a );
```

Parameters.

■ a, binary data is an unsigned short. This parameter is the information that needs to be translated.

■ htons returns an unsigned short, the same data as the a parameter but in network order.

ntohl. This call translates a network byte order long into the host's long format. The syntax is as follows:

```
ntohl( unsigned long      a );
```

Parameters.

■ a, binary data is an unsigned long. This parameter is the information that needs to be translated.

- ntohl returns an unsigned int, the same data as the a parameter but in the host's native order.

ntohs. This call translates a network byte order short into the host's short format. The syntax is as follows:

```
ntohs( unsigned short    a );
```

Parameters.

- a, binary data is an unsigned short. This parameter is the information that needs to be translated.

- ntohs returns an unsigned short, the same data as the a parameter but in the host's native order.

bswap. This call swaps the byte order of an unsigned short. This call is not dependent on the host byte ordering. The syntax is as follows:

```
bswap( unsigned short    a );
```

Parameters.

- a, binary data is an unsigned short. This parameter is the information that needs to be translated.

- bswap returns an unsigned short, the same data as the a parameter but with the bytes swapped.

lswap. This call swaps the byte order of an unsigned long. This call is not dependent on the host byte ordering. The syntax is as follows:

```
lswap( unsigned long    a );
```

Parameters.

- a, binary data is an unsigned long. This parameter is the information that needs to be translated.

- lswap returns an unsigned long, the same data as the a parameter but with the bytes swapped.

gethostbyaddr. This call gets host information based on an Internet address. The syntax is as follows:

```
gethostbyaddr(     char    *addr,
            int     addrlen,
            int     domain          );
```

Parameters.

- ■ *addr*, data area for address is a pointer to a `char buffer`. This parameter is a 32-bit Internet address in network order.

- ■ *addrlen*, size of `addr` parameter is an `int`. This parameter tells `gethostbyaddr` the size of the data area pointed to by `addr`.

- ■ *domain*, address domain is an `int`. This parameter can only be `AF_INET` on OS/2.

- ■ `gethostbyaddr` returns a pointer to a `struct hostent`. This structure contains network information about the host.

gethostbyname. This call gets host information based on the name of the host. The host name is resolved using name servers. The syntax is as follows:

```
gethostbyname( char     *name );
```

Parameters.

- ■ *name*, a string name is a pointer to a `char` array. This parameter tells `gethostbyname` the string name of the desired site.

- ■ `gethostbyname` returns a pointer to a `struct hostent`. This structure contains network information about the host.

Socket Call Steps

One of the advantages of using sockets is that the order of operation of a client and server program are similar. A client program will initialize the socket system, get a socket, bind to the socket, connect to a server, transfer and receive information, and close the socket. A server program will initialize the socket system, get a socket, bind to the socket, listen to the socket for a connection, accept the connection, transfer and receive information, and close the socket used for communication to the client. These similarities simplify the development process for the programmer.

Examples

The development of socket programs becomes simple with the understanding of socket library calls and the order of setup for communication. The following examples show client and server implementations of socket communications.

Client. The client program, Listing 22.1, will establish a connection on an agreed-upon port. After a connection has been established, we will send a message to our client program, which should be running to receive our connection. After we send a message, we will wait for a response, and then shut down the connection and the program.

Listing 22.1 Lunch Socket Client Code

```
/* A simple client program to extend a lunch
 * invitation to the server.
 */

#include <types.h>
#include <netinet\in.h>
#include <sys\socket.h>
#include <netdb.h>
#include <stdio.h>

#define  LUNCH "We are going for pizza at noon."

void main( void )
{
    unsigned short      port_number;
    char                info_buffer[100];
    struct hostent      *hostname;
    struct sockaddr_in  server_address;
    int                 cli_socket;

    /* Socket Initialization */
    sock_init();

    /* Get the server address using the logical name of the server
*/
    hostname = gethostbyname( "host.information.net" );

    if( (struct hostent *)0 == hostname )
    {
        /* Could not get host entry */
        exit( 1 );
    }

    /* The "well-known" port number on the server machine */
    port_number = 1027;


    /* Buffer a message to send */
    strcpy( info_buffer, LUNCH );

    /* Set up the socket address structure */
    server_address.sin_family      = AF_INET; /* OS/2s only option
*/
    server_address.sin_port        = htons( port_number );
                                            /* Network Byte Order
*/
```

(continues)

Listing 22.1   Continued

```
    server_address.sin_addr.s_addr = *( (unsigned long *)hostname-
>h_addr );

    /* Set up the stream socket and get a socket descriptor */
    cli_socket  = socket( AF_INET, SOCK_STREAM, 0 );
    if( cli_socket < 0 )
    {
        exit( 2 );
    }

    /* Connect to server address */
    if( connect( cli_socket, (struct sockaddr *)&server_address,
                sizeof( server_address ) ) < 0 )
    {
        exit( 3 );
    }

    /* Send information to server */
    if( send( cli_socket, info_buffer, sizeof( info_buffer ), 0 ) <
0 )
    {
        exit( 4 );
    }

    /* Receive a response to lunch */
    if( recv( cli_socket, info_buffer, sizeof( info_buffer ), 0 ) <
0 )
    {
        exit( 5 );
    }

    /* Close the socket */
    soclose( cli_socket );

    exit( 0 );
}
```

Listing 22.1 begins by calling the sock_init function. This initalizes system
software for the client program to use sockets. Host name information is
gotten using the gethostbyname call. The struct hostent pointer returned by
gethostbyname is used later by the connect call. A struct sockaddr_in is
initalized using a well-known port number and the Internet address of the
host requested by gethostbyname. A socket descriptor is gotten using the
socket call and is used along with struct sockaddr_in by the connect call. If
the connection is successful, a message is sent using send, and a response is
received using the recv call. Now that you are finished with the socket, close
the socket with the soclose call.

Server. The server program, Listing 22.2, will establish a listening position on an agreed-upon port. When a connection is requested, it will accept the connection by creating a new socket to communicate with the client. After the server receives a message, the server will respond with a message and will shut down both open sockets. In a traditional server situation, the server would have generated a new process to handle the conversation with the client. Using OS/2, the server program does not have to go through the overhead of starting a new process. OS/2 could spawn a thread to handle this conversation: instant multi-threaded application.

Listing 22.2 Lunch Socket Server Code

```
/* A simple OS/2 socket server to respond
 * to an invitation for lunch.
 */

#include <types.h>
#include <netinet\in.h>
#include <sys\socket.h>
#include <stdio.h>

#define LUNCH "Pizza at noon sounds good."

main( void )
{
    unsigned short      port_number;
    char                info_buffer[100];
    struct sockaddr_in  cli_address;
    struct sockaddr_in  srv_address;
    int                 connect_socket;
    int                 info_socket;
    int                 cli_name_length;

    /* Socket Initialization */
    sock_init();

    /* The "well-known" port number on the server machine */
    port_number = 1027;

    /* Set up the stream socket and get a socket descriptor */
    connect_socket = socket( AF_INET, SOCK_STREAM, 0 );
    if( connect_socket < 0 )
    {
        exit( 2 );
    }

    /* Set up the server's ability to receive connections */
    srv_address.sin_family      = AF_INET;
    srv_address.sin_port        = htons( port_number );
    srv_address.sin_addr.s_addr = INADDR_ANY;
```

(continues)

Listing 22.2   Continued

```
    if( bind( connect_socket, (struct sockaddr *)&srv_address,
              sizeof( srv_address ) ) < 0 )
    {
       exit( 3 );
    }

    /* Listen for a connection request */
    if( 0 != listen( connect_socket, 1 ) )
    {
       exit( 4 );
    }

    /* Accept a connection */
    cli_name_length   = sizeof( cli_address );
    info_socket = accept(   connect_socket,
                            (struct sockaddr *)&cli_address,
                            &cli_name_length );
    if ( -1 == info_socket )
    {
       exit( 5 );
    }

    /* Use the client connected socket to receive a message */
    if( -1 == recv( info_socket, info_buffer, sizeof( info_buffer ),
0 ) )
    {
       exit( 6 );
    }

    /* Set up message to send */
    strcpy( info_buffer, LUNCH );


    /* Use the client-connected socket to send a message*/
    if( send( info_socket, info_buffer, sizeof( info_buffer ), 0 ) <
0 )
    {
       exit( 7 );
    }

    /* Close the connection socket and the client socket */
    soclose( info_socket );
    soclose( connect_socket );

    exit( 0 );
}
```

The socket server program starts out by calling sock_init to setup socket use for the program. The server uses the socket call to get a socket descriptor that it can bind to. Binding is not the same as connecting. Binding allows the server program to listen to the socket for activity. The `listen` call blocks the server program until a client attempts to connect to the socket. The server program then accepts the connection using the `accept` call that returns a new socket that it can use to communicate with the client program using the `recv` and `send` calls to get and send information. When the server program is finished talking with the client, it should close the socket used for communication using the `soclose` call. The server should not close the socket used to listen for requests for connection. This listening socket should only be closed when the server is done accepting requests for communications; normally this is when the system is shut down or the system requires no connections from clients.

CPI-C and APPC

Advanced Peer-to-Peer Communications (APPC) is the protocol of choice for SNA networks. On IBM systems and many other non-IBM systems, APPC provides data and session protocol transparency and many other advanced services. The format of an APPC call is a verb and control block format. The verb-based command action provides a natural cross-platform interoperability, but variations evolved on different platforms. To correct this problem, IBM developed the Common Programming Interface - Communications (CPI-C).

CPI-C uses the familiar call-based API and layers it above APPC. CPI-C has been licensed by other vendors, including the X/Open consortium, Novell, and Apple. IBM is working on a multiprotocol format that will allow CPI-C to be layered above SNA, TCP/IP, OSI, NetBios IPX/SPX. Figure 22.2 provides an abstract view of the multiprotocol approch that CPI-C will use.

SNA Terms

To understand CPI-C programming, you should understand many of the terms used by System Network Architecture (SNA). Many of these terms will have logical equivalents in other peer-to-peer communications methods.

APPN Network Nodes (NN)

An APPN network node performs the functions of a gateway machine on an SNA network. A network node is automatically updated to the changes in the network and its conditions. It knows how to handle congested routes, and it keeps its own list of related network nodes via automatic discovery and the automatic management of additions and removals of network partners.

Fig. 22.2
The CPI-C
network layer.

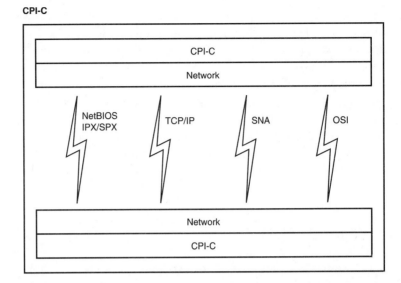

Transaction Program (TP)

A transaction program consists of an 8-byte identifier and a 64-byte name. In an APPN network, this is the program's logical network name. A TP has an advantage over many other peer-to-peer network communications in that it can define itself to handle multiple transactions per logical network name. This allows a TP to take advantage of multi-threaded platforms such as OS/2.

Logical Unit (LU)

A logical unit is SNA's connection point to gain access to other LUs' physical units (PU). The APPC verb commands are performed on a logical unit. After connection to the local logical unit, communication can be established with a remote logical unit called partner logical units.

Physical Unit (PU)

A physical unit manages the required resources on a machine for that machine's logical units. A physical unit also manages communication between logical adjacent physical units. This program handles the physical data links.

APPC Conversation

An APPC conversation is the transfer of data between two transaction programs. The two transaction programs are known as partners. In APPC programs, it is considered advantageous to keep a single conversation to a minimum, because even though multiple conversations can occur using a logical unit, only one conversation can be used at a given moment. The normal conversation strategy is to have a series of small conversations that allow other conversations to take place in the interim.

SNA Session

An SNA session is the logical connection between two logical units. Two transaction programs cannot communicate through logical units until a session is established between the logical units. Sessions provide reliable protocol services. The number of sessions that two partner logical units can have is configurable. Sessions normally remain active even when a conversation is not taking place. This allows rapid establishment of new conversations.

Attach Manager

The attach manager is the service that handles the starting of local transaction programs requested by remote conversation requests. If the attach manager is not running, remote conversations cannot be established.

CPI-C Calls

APPC calls use a verb-based format that uses a large block of information as the parameter to the verb command. Due to various platforms implementation inconsistencies, the control blocks vary from platform to platform. CPI-C uses the function call format that takes multiple parameters in a given order. This allows a CPI-C call to be used unchanged across platforms.

Common CPI-C

The common CPI-C calls are available on all platforms supporting APPC and CPI-C. The CPI-C layer above APPC orders the information passed to the CPI-C function call. The OS/2 implementation of CPI-C provides both simple and complex formats for APPC functional operations:

- cmaccp—This call accepts a conversation from the cmallc call. It also returns the conversation identifier needed by other calls.

- cmallc—This call initiates a conversation with a partner transaction process. In CPI-C terms, this is allocation.

- cmcfm—This call initiates a confirmation from a partner transaction process.

- cmcfmd—This call responds to a confirmation request call.

- cmdeal—This call initiates the termination of a conversation with a partner transaction process. This can be a confirmed or non-confirmed call.

- cmecs—This call gets the current state of the conversation.

- cmect—This call gets a flag that indicates if the conversation is basic or mapped.

- cmemn—This call gets the transmission service mode name.

- cmepln—This call gets the name of the logical unit that the transmission process is using.

- cmesl—This call gets a value indicating the synchronization level used.

- cmflus—This call causes the logical unit to flush its send buffer.

- cminit—This call sets up the conversation characteristics before the conversation is called. This call returns a conversation identifier for initiator use.

- cmptr—This call gives the transaction partner permission to send data.

- cmrcv—This call receives data, a confirmation request, and a conversion status from the transaction partner.

- cmrts—This call asks the transaction partner to accept a conversation send.

- cmsct—This call sets the conversation type to be basic or mapped. The default is mapped.

- cmsdt—This call sets the action taken if a deallocation causes an abnormal end of a conversation. You can confirm a deallocation or do nothing. The default is to confirm.

- cmsed—This call sets if an error value is to be generated if an error is detected on a send or receive. The default is to generate an error.

- cmsend—This call sends data to the transaction partner.

- cmserr—This call tells the transaction partner that an error has occurred.

- cmsf—This call sets the send buffer to be filled with more than one record.

- cmsld—This call sets a message to be generated in an error log if an error occurs. The default is nothing.

- cmsmn—This call sets the mode name to be used when the conversation is initiated.

- `cmspln`—This call sets the logical unit name of the transaction partner to use when the conversation is initiated.

- `cmsptr`—This call sets the form of synchronization used for the "preparation to receive" call. You can confirm, or force the logical unit to flush. The default is to confirm.

- `cmsrc`—This call sets the response to immediate allocation. The default is to wait for connection, but you can also have the call return immediately.

- `cmsrt`—This call sets the response to immediate receiving. The default is to wait for the send, but you can also have the call return immediately.

- `cmssl`—This call sets the synchronization level for a conversation. Only the calling transaction partner can set this, and it cannot be set after allocation. The default is to confirm, but you can also have no confirmation.

- `cmsst`—This call sets options for sending data. Options include send control information, immediate buffer flushing. The default is to send the data when the buffer is full.

- `cmstpn`—This call sets the name of the transaction partner to be used for allocation.

- `cmtrts`—This call gets the flag giving the transaction partner permission to send data.

OS/2 CPI-C

The OS/2 CPI-C calls are available only on the OS/2 platform. These calls manage "side information." Side information is knowledge necessary to initialize conversations on the OS/2 platform. Side information is normally configured by the receiving or server side of conversations, but can be done using these calls:

- `xcmssi`—This call sets side information for the destination name. A new side information entry is created if one does not already exit.

- `xcmdsi`—This call removes the side information entry for the destination name, if it exists.

- `xcmesi`—This call gets the side information entry for the destination name, if it exists.

V

OS/2 Development

- `xcecst`—This call gets information about conversation security and whether it is being used in the conversation.

- `xcecsu`—This call gets the user identifier for the conversation.

- `xcint`—This call is similar to `cminit`, but also allows the conversation to be associated with a specific transaction process.

- `xcscsp`—This call sets the security password for a conversation to be allocated.

- `xcscst`—This call sets security options for a conversation to be allocated.

- `xcscsu`—This call sets the user identifier to be used for a conversation to be allocated.

- `xcendt`—This call releases all CPI-C resources for an active transaction partner instance.

- `xceti`—This call gets the transaction partner identifier for a given conversation.

- `xcstp`—This call starts a new transaction partner instance.

Examples

A brief overview of OS/2 CPI-C has prepared us to look into development examples. The relative ease of implementing our client and server programs stems from the fact that many of the repetitive tasks that must be coded in other client/server methods are handled by the APPC and CPI-C setup of networking software. A few CPI-C calls handle alot of networking ability.

Client

The client program, Listing 22.3, will establish a connection to a waiting server program using the connections identifier. This example does not wait for a response, but it does check for completion of the communications. It is not hard to see the similarities between CPI-C and socket programming. The CPI-C source code is smaller than the socket source. This is a direct result of many network management abilities being handled by the network, not the developer. If you are the network administrator, this may come as a mixed blessing. You have much tighter control of the network, but you become a larger part of the development system.

Listing 22.3   Lunch CPI-C Client Code

```
/* A simple client program to extend
 * a lunch invitation to Edward Q.
 */

#include <cpic.h>
#include <stdio.h>
#include <stdlib.h>
#include <string.h>

#define  ADDRESS_LUNCH  "EDWARDQ "
#define  ADDRESS_LUNCH_SIZE   (strlen( ADDRESS_LUNCH ) + 1 )

#define  LUNCH     "Time for lunch, pizza at noon. Be there."

void  main( void )
{
    char           connection_id[8];
    char           diner_name[ADDRESS_LUNCH_SIZE];
    char           info_buffer[100];
    CM_INT32       info_buffer_length;
    CM_INT32       problem;
    CM_INT32       answer;


    strcpy( info_buffer, LUNCH );

    info_buffer_length   = (CM_INT32) strlen( info_buffer ) + 1;

    strcpy( diner_name, ADDRESS_LUNCH );

    /* init conversation and get communication id */
    cminit( connection_id, (char *)diner_name, &problem );

    if (problem != CM_OK)
    {
        exit( 2 );
    }

    /* Establish a conversation, allocate */
    cmallc( connection_id, &problem );

    if( problem != CM_OK) {
        exit( 3 );
    }

    /* Send information */
    cmsend( connection_id, info_buffer,
            &info_buffer_length, &answer, &problem );
```

(continues)

V

OS/2 Development

Listing 22.3 Continued

```
    if( problem != CM_OK)
    {
       exit( 4 );
    }

    /* Close the conversation, deallocate */
    cmdeal( connection_id, &problem );

    if ( problem != CM_OK) {
       exit( 5 );
    }

    printf( "Offer for lunch sent to Ed.\n" );
}
```

The client program uses simple calls to connect to the server program. The call cminit initializes the connection to the network and verifies the server that the client program wants to converse with. The cmallc establishes the connection to the server using the connection ID set by cminit. The call cmsend uses the connection ID to send information to the server and closes the connection using the cmdeal call. All through the client program, the CPI-C calls set a flag to tell the calling program if there were any errors so the program can respond to the problem.

Server

The server program in Listing 22.4 will wait for a connection, receive the message, print the message, and shut down the server program. This program is not a traditional server program in that it does not transfer information back to the client. The client does receive confirmation that the message was received, but that is all. It does present the simplicity of using CPI-C calls and the power provided by a cross-platform design.

Listing 22.4 Lunch CPI-C Server Code

```
/* A simple server program to wait
 * for a lunch invitation.
 */

#include <cpic.h>
#include <stdio.h>
#include <stdlib.h>

#define  INFO_BUFFER_SIZE 100
```

```
void main( void )
{
   char         connection_id[8];
   char         info_buffer[INFO_BUFFER_SIZE + 1];
   CM_INT32     problem;
   CM_INT32     max_amount;
   CM_INT32     info_gotten;
   CM_INT32     gotten_amout
   CM_INT32     answer;
   CM_INT32     answer_gotten;
   int          finished

   finished = 0;


   /* Set variable to maximum storage to receive */
   max_amount  = (CM_INT32) BUFFER_SIZE;

   /* Wait for a connection, Accept the connection */
   cmaccp( connection_id, &problem );

   if( problem != CM_OK )
   {
      exit( 2 );
   }

   /* Repeat receive until we get the message or   */
   /* an error occurs                              */
   while( !finished )
   {
      /* Receive information from client */
      cmrcv(  connection_id, info_buffer, &max_amount,
              &info_gotten, &gotten_amount, &answer,
              &answer_gotten, &problem );

      /* We received information or               */
      /* the client quit on us via deallocation */
      if(   (problem == CM_OK)                     ||
            (problem == CM_DEALLOCATED_NORMAL) )
      {
         /* If we received information, show it. */
         if( info_gotten != CM_NO_DATA_RECEIVED )
         {
            /* Just in case there is no terminator */
            info_buffer[gotten_amount] = (char)NULL;
            printf( "You have a message : \"%s\"\n", info_buffer );
         }
         else
         {
            /* Message received, no information */
            printf( "Problem -> No Info?\n" );
         }
      }
      else
      { /* an unexpected return_code */
```

(continues)

Listing 22.4   Continued

```
            printf( "Problem -> %lu\n", problem );
        }

        if( problem == CM_DEALLOCATED_NORMAL)
        {
            /* Normal termination of communications */
            finished = 1;
        }
    }
}
```

The server program is a little longer than our simple client program, but is just as straightforward and easy to develop using CPI-C. The server program uses the cmaccp call to wait for a client request and to get the connection ID. The call cmrcv is used to wait for the message from the client that corresponds to the connection ID. The problem flag is tested after the cmrcv call returns control to the server program. The problem flag tells the server program if information was received from the cmrcv call, if the client is no longer connected, or if no information was transferred and the connection with the client is still in place. There is no shutdown of the connection; this is handled by the network software in place when the server program quits.

More OS/2 Options

This chapter has focused on the dominant standard for client/server development in TCP/IP sockets and has looked at the major contender for this position in CPI-C, but we have not even begun to show the depth of OS/2's ability to handle communications and client/server development. OS/2 offers NetBios, Netware, DB/2, and SQL; Groupware offerings such as Lotus Notes, RPCs, Object Request Brokers, CORBA ORB, SOM and DSOM, OSI, and DCE. This is by no means an exhaustive list, but it does cover the major names. Development of new options for OS/2 continues, and the improvement of the old options goes on as the demand for them grows. OS/2 provides one of the best options for all the client/server elements. If marketing hype is set aside and the true abilities of a platform are searched for, OS/2 can stand on its own merits and abilities.

From Here...

This chapter discussed the basics of socket development for OS/2 and CPI-C for OS/2. These tools and more like them provide OS/2 with the means to operate in most of the client/server areas required of an advanced operating system. This chapter should give you a good starting point for your development efforts using sockets and CPI-C.

The following chapters will provide broader information on selected topics that relate to this chapter:

- Chapter 1, "What is Client/Server?," gives an extended introduction to client/server systems.

- Chapter 3, "Communications Protocols," provides a deeper view of TCP/IP protocol stacks that is the model for TCP/IP for OS/2.

- Chapter 4, "Client/Server Development Overview," shows the steps necessary for planning and implementing a client/server project.

- Chapter 13, "What is DCE?," describes the Distributed Computing Environment elements that make up the OSF services for a DCE environment.

- Chapter 23, "Multiplatform Applications," shows development styles for handling a multiplatform environment.

V

OS/2 Development

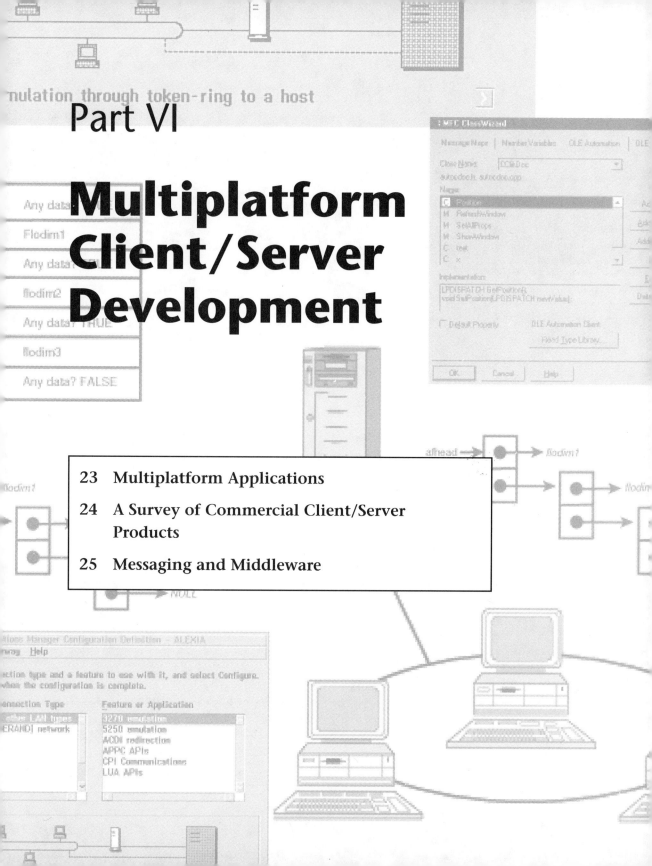

Part VI

Multiplatform Client/Server Development

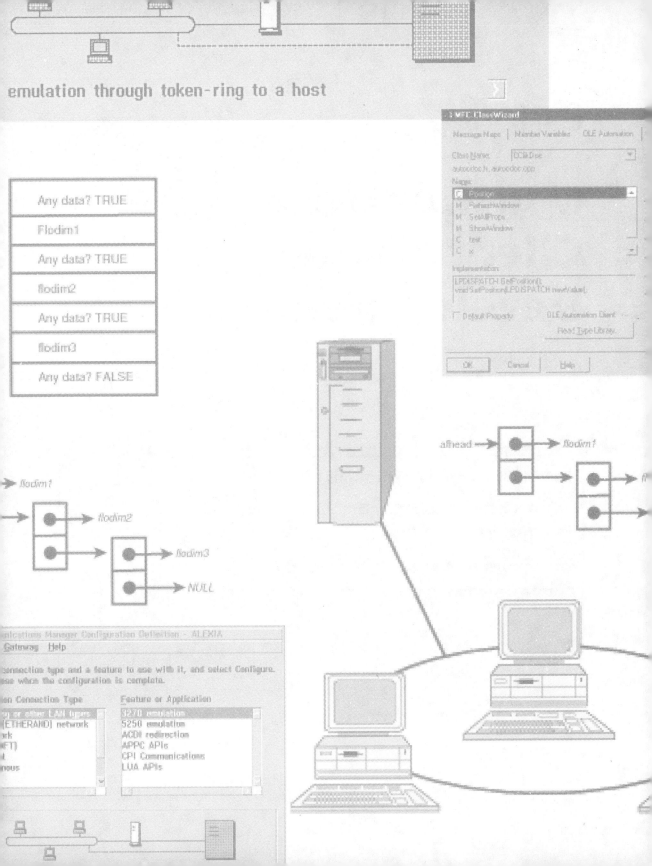

Chapter 23

Multiplatform Applications

When developing client/server applications for multiplatform environments, there are a number of issues that need to be considered. How should one go about developing a client/server application? How does developing a client/server application differ from developing traditional applications? Are there any migration strategies for migrating current applications? What methodology should be followed?

This chapter presents an overview of the key considerations for developing client/server applications in a multiplatform environment. It provides the following background information for an understanding of the following issues involved:

- Considerations for designing and building client/server applications

- Application development strategies

- Considerations in cross-platform development

- Things to think about in multiplatform application development

- Migration strategies for legacy systems

- Client/server application development tools

Designing and Building Client/Server Systems

In the past, most applications were built on a single system. Users accessed applications by way of terminals. All functions associated with an application ran on the same machine. When designing traditional applications, the application usually began with the data. Screens were merely input mechanisms for the database.

The client/server model has added a change to the structure of applications. Developers now need to worry about dividing applications into components. The network adds complexity to the problem, but middleware helps to minimize this problem. Client/server applications are modular applications, with portions running on different platforms. It allows for specialization in application environments. In other words, each part of an application runs on the platform best suited for it. This modular approach is also beneficial for maintaining systems.

Application Partitioning

Modularization is often referred to as *application partitioning*. Application partitioning determines which portion of an application should be processed where. It involves breaking client/server applications into reasonable layers. Developers must decide where to distribute the three primary components of a client/server application (data, business logic, and presentation) across multiple platforms. The goal is to minimize network traffic or movement of data between client and server, while taking advantage of all the systems in the enterprise. In addition, applications can process in parallel on multiple servers, both increasing performance and allowing for better resource utilization.

Application partitioning is one of the most complex aspects of client/server development. It is not a simple problem of knowing where data can be processed most efficiently or where business rules should be stored. There is an added problem of locking data, which sometimes occurs with two-phase commits or with data that is kept on the server and accessed by multiple applications. A two-phase commit involves a client updating data to multiple servers and multiple processes. Many client/server tools on the market help developers manage this problem.

Client/server development projects go through the same software life cycle that any software project entails. The software life cycle is often referred to as the "waterfall" model, because information about an application cascades down from one level to another (see fig. 23.1). The life cycle consists of analysis, code construction, testing, maintenance, and documentation. The key difference is that developers must now consider more than one platform. This difference has tremendous implications for the analysis and design stages, as well as for the choice of development tools.

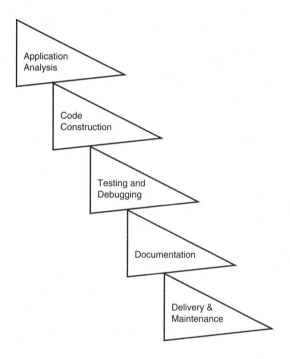

Fig. 23.1
Software engineering is a discipline that follows specific software development steps to minimize system errors and failures.

A Conceptual Framework

The client/server model consists of four primary parts—presentation logic (user interface logic), business logic (routines for the applications), middleware (software that hides the network and operating system details from developers), and data (information that the application uses). These parts interact through well-defined interfaces. Figure 23.2 shows the four main parts of client/server computing.

Note

Middleware is an essential component of the client/server architecture. Its purposes are to isolate developers from the heterogeneous networking and operating system environments common to most organizations and to facilitate development of networked applications.

Middleware consists of five fundamental technologies: Remote Data Access (RDA), Remote Procedure Calls (RPCs), Messaging and message queuing (MOM), Object Request Brokers (ORBs), and Distributed Online Transaction Processing (DOLTP).

VI

Multiplatforms

Fig. 23.2

The advantage of the client/server model of computing is that the graphical user interface, data, and business logic can reside on the system where it can maximize response time and performance.

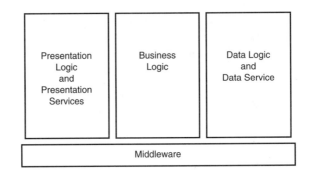

Presentation Logic

Presentation logic is the application code that resides on an end user's terminal or workstation. This code interacts with end users to perform such tasks as screen management, reading and writing information from the screen, and keyboard and mouse interaction. Examples of graphical user interfaces are X/Windows, OSF's Motif, OS/2 Presentation Manager, and Microsoft Windows.

Client/server applications need a flexible interface that gives end users more latitude in actions at their desks. GUIs and Object Oriented User Interfaces (OOUI) change the way end users interact with client/server applications.

> **Note**
>
> Object Oriented User Interfaces integrate multiple on-screen objects that run concurrently. This allows the exchange of information by dragging and dropping live links. For example, OLE 2.0 allows objects of information to be dragged between an Excel spreadsheet and a Word document. When information is updated in the Excel spreadsheet, a live link is associated to the Word document that is then updated. Technologies such as OpenDoc and OLE 2 will continue to evolve the OOUI paradigm to allow users to assemble, link, script, store, and transport objects.

Today, developers are designing application interfaces to look and feel like real-world objects, not simply following rigid logic to task-oriented applications. User interfaces today are becoming more complex and more interactive. When designing client/server applications, developers must keep in mind how they want to interact with the system.

In the presentation logic, developers must develop the graphical user interface to support an event-driven paradigm. It is important to design code so that it can respond to a wide range of actions or events from end users. This is a major paradigm shift from early applications, where the developer determined all sequences and events for end users.

The primary graphical user interface issue facing developers of multiplatform client/server applications is portability. From an end user point of view, the GUI might look the same, but from a developer point of view, each GUI has a different application programming interface (API). The lack of standardization in this area requires developers to work with a different API for each client platform in the enterprise. Many client/server development tools facilitate porting of GUIs. Some examples of tools that help users build portable GUIs are:

- CA-CommonView from Computer Associates—CA-CommonView is a C++ application framework for building portable GUI applications.

- Essential Graphics GUI from South Mountain Software—Essential Graphics GUI is a C programming toolkit for creating portable GUIs.

- Extensible Virtual Toolkit (XVT) from XVT Software, Inc.—XVT toolkit is a software library that provides a common programming interface for multiple platform development.

- Easel Workbench from Easel Corporation—Easel Workbench is a GUI builder for enhancing existing applications or for creating new GUI applications.

- Wind/U from Bristol Technology, Inc.—Wind/U allows developers to compile and execute Microsoft Windows applications on OSF's Motif.

Business Logic

This portion of the application code takes input from the screen and/or databases to perform the business function. The business logic is the component that manages the transformation, such as calculations on the data. For example, say you are updating a customer database and you enter new information into the graphical user interface. Business logic defines the processing that takes place to update the customer record.

Data

This portion of the application code manipulates data and stores it in the database management system (DBMS). The location of data plays a key role in developing client/server applications. Data can be distributed in many ways. For example, partitioning divides data among various locations, and replication allows data to be located in multiple locations.

VI

Multiplatforms

Middleware

In the middleware portion, developers must design distributed applications to take advantage of the network and prevent the latency inherent in application communications. In other words, middleware developers minimize network traffic for better application performance.

Before client/server computing, all these components resided on the same machine and were combined into the same execution code. Now developers can take advantage of the computer resources available on the network. Developers use an application programming interface (API) to take advantage of communication services. Most middleware products offer a single interface across multiple platforms.

Application Development Strategies

Client/server applications have become popular in the past few years as more companies begin to re-engineer business processes. Business process re-engineering is concerned with technology adapting to the business rather than the business adapting to the technology. The goals have been to downsize, upsize, and rightsize applications.

Different Models for Processing Distributed Applications

Client/server applications run the gamut from client-centric systems to distributed applications (see fig. 23.3). Client-centric applications are called *fat* clients, in which the goal is to transparently access data on systems across the enterprise to distributed applications, splitting processing logic between many systems. Developers are pressured to develop client/server applications in the most effective distributed model. Client-centric models are used when the client hardware (such as personal computers or workstations) has a high price/performance gain or when end users want more application autonomy. The other extreme of the distributed model is pushing all the logic to a centralized server (see fig. 23.4).

> **Note**
>
> When developing distributed applications, it is important to evaluate your business goals and determine how computing resources should be distributed to achieve them. Another consideration is how to implement intercommunication facilities among the different computing resources. The resources must include all components, such as data, business logic, and graphical user interface. In the end, the distributed application will appear to be a single application to the end user.

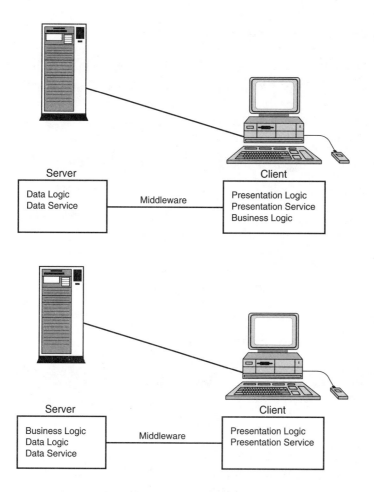

Fig. 23.3
One approach for application distribution is to place the presentation layer and business logic on the client. The client then uses SQL as a standard protocol to access data located on the server.

Fig. 23.4
Another approach places both the business logic and the data logic on the server, with only the presentation logic on the client. With this approach, the client performs simple presentation functions and the server remains the heart of the system.

The important point is that a client/server application must take advantage of the processing power that is available. It is important to understand the business process and know what the application is all about from a business perspective.

> **Note**
>
> A rule of thumb is to place data as close to the primary end user as possible, while still protecting data integrity and security. The requirements of the business rather than the needs of individual users should take precedence.

VI

Multiplatforms

Business Process Re-engineering

When moving to a client/server architecture, it is important to consider the business objectives and processes that your applications must support. This aspect of client/server computing will ultimately drive your application architecture and the computing model that should be used. A good place to start is to determine how the business processes will be re-engineered. The following questions should guide your thinking:

- Are you going to combine several processes into one?

- Are the steps in the process performed in a natural order?

- Is the process being executed in the place that makes the most sense? (Observe how work patterns are changing.)

- What is the rationale for the current business process?

- What is the logic behind the information flow?

- What is the logic behind who is performing the work?

- Is there a way to improve this business process?

> **Note**
>
> In business process re-engineering (BPR), an organization evaluates the way it works and redesigns each process to promote greater efficiency and align better with the organization's core business. To achieve the goals for BPR, an organization must look at the entire end-to-end processes that are important to its success. When attempting a BPR project, organizations cannot be limited by the current organizational structure or thinking.

When redesigning business processes, developers need to first map out the current process. Once developers understand how the old process works, they can begin to refine the old process. Developers need to identify business objects, business events, and business rules. As they identify these business processes, the application integration requirements begin to surface.

Next, determine the current information flow in the organization and the changes that need to be made. One way of determining the information flow is to look at organizational charts. They provide developers with a pattern of communication. Remember to look outside the boundaries of the corporation to customers and suppliers. They, too, provide information that is part of most business processes. In addition, developers need to work with a business domain expert to capture a mental model of the business. The objective is to understand the process by which the corporation operates to achieve its business goals or intended results. A thorough understanding of the business process generates detailed descriptions of the system requirements that support the key business activities.

After mapping the information flow, determine the types of applications users need by conducting an analysis of the users' requirements. Developers need to identify all primary and secondary users. A sales representative might be the primary user of a system, but the vice president of sales could be a secondary user. Requirements are the raw materials for client/server software development. The requirement stage also helps determine the technology, staffing, and training needs for the client/server project. The only way to build software that end users want is to thoroughly understand the end user's world and determine what the customer wants.

Selecting a Pilot Project

When selecting a client/server pilot project, remember to think big but begin small. Determine the long-term needs of the entire corporation, but begin with a strategic project to gather client/server development and middleware tool requirements. The goal is to determine a systems foundation that all client/server applications will be based on. A solid foundation eliminates the need to reinvent the wheel for each individual client/server project.

Developers need to take a close look at the types of problems that the pilot is trying to solve. Each type of application has its own requirements. For example, the characteristics of a decision support system and an online transaction processing system are very different. An online transaction processing system requires high performance and high availability. The data in a decision support system tends to be more static, but must be more flexible. In addition, the performance requirements of these two systems vary greatly.

The pilot project needs to be characteristic of future client/server applications and should be beneficial to the corporation. After all, the pilot project can become the basis for considerable future development.

Another major criterion for pilot selection is platform availability. The key decision when selecting platforms is whether to adopt a portable strategy or to take advantage of the inherent differences between platforms. The strategy selected will have an impact on the client/server tools available. Platform selection can ultimately determine your client/server tool selection, based on the availability of a tool on a particular platform.

A final consideration when selecting a pilot application is enabling services. Does the pilot project require use of a database, storage management, transaction monitors, mobile communications, multimedia support, and so on? All these services need to be identified up front to simplify application development. Also, developers need to determine whether they need enabling services on all platforms or only on specific ones. Although the pilot's fundamental requirements will largely determine the need for enabling services, these services should still be considered when deploying client/server applications.

Choosing a Middleware Strategy

Once requirements are gathered, the next task is to distribute resources among the different systems. Middleware links the front and back ends of an application into a cohesive system. Most corporations are defining a single client/server architecture to serve the entire enterprise, which means that middleware becomes a strategic component of that decision. The larger the scale of the client/server application, the greater the need for a robust middleware architecture.

Middleware is a strategic decision that should be considered carefully. Today, middleware encompasses many components including application programming interfaces (API), global and naming services, security, system and network management, network transport, application-to-application programming interfaces, and application development tools. Client/server development tools frequently include their own middleware or require a particular third-party middleware product. Many users fail to capitalize on middleware because they fail to see that selecting a client/server development tool also constitutes a middleware decision. Therefore, middleware needs to be considered during the initial requirements assessment.

In application-to-application programming interfaces, there is a wide-range of options, depending on the pilot project. The project could require synchronous communications (remote procedure calls, or RPCs), asynchronous communications (messaging or message queuing), or a mixture of both. In addition, requirements might call for remote data access, distributed online transaction processing, or object request brokers. The goal is to find the communication paradigm that best fits the pilot application, and that will also best meet the long-term strategic goals for the corporation. Will the middleware product selected be able to meet the long-term needs for the corporation? Does it provide all the paradigms needed to integrate diverse applications in a complex environment? Does the middleware product provide scalability, robustness, platform support, and other middleware features to meet users' needs?

> **Note**
>
> When building large-scale client/server applications (multiserver applications), a variety of sophisticated middleware paradigms such as RPCs, messaging, message queuing, distributed transactions, and Object Request Brokers (ORBs) are needed to solve the problems you may encounter. It is important to understand the advantages and disadvantages of each of these paradigms for solving business problems.

Different Client/Server Development Methodologies

Development methodologies are principles and procedures for the requirements gathering, analysis, and design phases of the software development process. Methodologies keep the software development process focused on the corporation's processes, structures, and requirements. In addition, methodologies are important because they help developers share the corporation's vision for software development and allow developers to share the same mental model of the business problem. This is very important in large, complex projects in which coordination between developers is key.

The analysis and design tools that automate methodologies in client/server computing include rapid application development (RAD), joint application development (JAD), and prototyping, to name a few. The up-and-coming methodology tool for client/server computing is object-oriented analysis. Some of the techniques and tools used in structured analysis, such as entity-relationship diagrams (ERDs), dataflow diagrams, and data modeling are experiencing a resurgence when combined with object-oriented techniques.

The point of these different methodology tools is to define the logical structure of the client/server application before worrying about its physical structure. The output from these various methodology tools is either high-level code or source code used to develop client/server applications.

Rapid Application Development (RAD)

RAD was developed by James Martin as a technique for systems development that emphasizes developing systems incrementally. RAD breaks the application down into smaller components so that each can be developed and deployed faster. RAD includes automated design and development tools, as well as analysis, design, prototyping, and coding tasks that receive constant feedback from the end user.

VI

Multiplatforms

> **Note**
>
> RAD is a prototyping methodology that places end users at the center of the application development process. RAD allows developers to create detailed markups of an application (for example, the user interfaces) without any of the complex database access and distributed functionality required for the application. RAD significantly alters the system design phase of the traditional waterfall model of developing software. RAD is used as a methodology for brainstorming and fast development, but there is no proof that the RAD methodology results in superior or more efficient code than other methodologies.

In the client/server era, RAD has evolved to mean a graphical user interface tool that allows developers to depict end user environments by using a set of diagrams. These tools employ visual techniques to speed application development. The process is very interactive, with significant user involvement in every stage of development. RAD and Joint Application Design (JAD) are intended to develop a specification for the information system. Some examples of RAD products are the following:

- PowerBuilder from Powersoft Corporation (a subsidiary of Sybase, Inc.)—PowerBuilder provides the ability to design and build graphical front-ends to client/server databases.

- Delphi Client/Server from Borland International, Inc.—Delphi Client/Server provides a native-code compiler and a visual development environment.

- Magic Rapid Application Development System from Magic Software Enterprises, Inc.—Magic Rapid Application Development System provides an integrated set of design tools, including screen and report designers, a report writer, and a program generator.

- Sapiens Ideo from Sapiens USA, Inc. (a subsidiary of Sapiens International Corporation)—Sapiens Ideo provides a client/server, object-oriented RAD tool that builds GUI-based and database access applications.

RAD and JAD grew out of the limited time developers had with business users. A strong advantage of RAD and JAD is that they allow developers to work with end users to obtain business requirements quickly. Dataflow diagrams allow end users to visualize the process and provide instant feedback. RAD and JAD encourage communication with end users.

Joint Application Development (JAD)

IBM introduced JAD in 1977 as a methodology that emphasized teamwork between end users, system analysts, and developers. The system objectives and business transactions are determined up front between the end users and developers. JAD is usually a one-way communication effort from the end user to system analysts and developers for gathering requirements. This methodology varies from prototyping, which is more of a two-way communication effort, although both share the same goal—a working prototype. The stages of JAD are project scoping, project definition, and detailed requirements. The steps for a successful JAD project are similar to the traditional "waterfall" stages where phase one is the analysis or project definition and scoping stage. In this stage, the developer answers the questions of purpose, who, what, and how. This results in a preliminary specification in the initial working document to prepare for the JAD session.

The next stage is preparation, in which a completed working document is produced along with a JAD session script (a map of what to do and when to do it).

The JAD session stage is where a workflow diagram is produced, along with a functional specification and prototype. The final stage is a JAD design document and signoff from each team member. Each stage builds on the previous stage in a sequential and iterative process.

The purpose of JAD is to facilitate the flow of information from an identified group of people called a team. The JAD techniques allow for consensus building for developing a project. The drawback to JAD is that there needs to be a knowledgeable facilitator to implement that process.

Prototyping

Rapid prototyping allows developers to build a client/server application incrementally. Developers take small steps, refining the design as they add pieces to the client/server application. Prototyping is a building block approach.

> **Note**
>
> It is important to involve the end user in every stage of the interface design. Developers cannot lose sight of their target customer for the GUI.

In this methodology, developers continue to refine their prototype until they have a working prototype to move into production. Because this methodology does less up front analysis and design than the more traditional

VI

Multiplatforms

approach, developers can get into a "perpetual prototyping syndrome." Frequently, developers demand perfection, and the working prototype is enhanced but never completed. The opposite can also occur. Rapid prototyping can give end users and management a set of false expectations. When end users and developers see the first iteration of a prototype, they often feel that it is complete and want to put it into production immediately. Remember, the advantage of rapid prototyping is the many iterations of the prototype that develop into a production system.

Rapid prototyping allows end users and managers to see results quickly. It is easier to encourage communication among end users if they have a live demonstration and can see themselves as an integral part of the development of the client/server application. A rapid prototyping methodology lends itself well to client/server application development because it allows developers to see major obstacles (such as performance, network overhead, and system management issues) before the application goes into production.

Developers usually encounter the following steps when they use a prototyping methodology. All software engineering projects begin with a request from a customer. If that request is determined to be a good candidate for prototyping based on the application area, complexity of the problem, and customer and project characteristics, the next step is to develop an abbreviated representation of the project requirements.

Develop an abbreviated design specification that focuses on the top level architectural and data design issues rather than the detailed procedural design. The following step is to create, test, and refine the prototype software. There are many tools used for prototyping on the market today. The following is a list of some of those tools:

- PowerBuilder from Powersoft Corporation (a subsidiary of Sybase, Inc.)—PowerBuilder provides the ability to design and build graphical front-ends to client/server databases.

- ART*Enterprise from Inference Corporation—ART*Enterprise provides a rapid prototyping, deployment, and object-oriented programming tool.

- ObjeX Programming Environment Toolkit from Auto-trol Technology Corporation—ObjeX Programming Environment Toolkit is a suite of tools for editing, compiling, running, and debugging applications.

- Vivid Clarity from Intek Technologies, Inc.—Vivid Clarity is an integrated set of visual modeling tools for client/sever development.

After completing the prototype, it is presented to the customer. The customer then tests the software to make sure it meets all requirements. The customer suggests changes, and the developer repeats the process iteratively until all requirements are formalized or a prototype has evolved into a production system.

Object-Oriented Analysis and Design

Object-oriented technology promises to improve developers' productivity and increase their ability to maintain applications. Object-oriented design is concerned with identifying discrete entities of a business process called *objects*. Objects store both the data and the behavior of an object. For the value of an object-oriented approach to be realized, developers need to consider reuse and extensions to objects.

The difference between traditional software development and object-oriented software development is that traditional development begins with a problem that is then decomposed into a number of smaller problems. This decomposition continues until it reaches the point at which code can be written. This is traditionally known as a "top-down" approach. The object-oriented software development methodology, on the other hand, uses a "bottom-up" approach. The problem to be solved is an object that is then built up to address particular tasks by creating logical objects that correspond to the elements of the different problem.

Many analysts believe that object-oriented technology is the wave of the future in client/server computing because objects are a better methodology for modular programming. Each object communicates by way of message passing. These objects do not need to know about one another's implementation details. In turn, object-oriented analysis and design techniques are easier to maintain in an environment that is constantly changing. Objects also map better to real-world business structures and concepts.

Object-oriented analysis models the business problem as objects that interact with one another. An object is defined by its class, data, and method. During the analysis stage, the application is broken down into entities. The nature of communications between these entities is determined. The next step is to take these models and determine the specification needed to create the client/server application. Once the problem is analyzed, the translation into an object-oriented design becomes simple.

Object-oriented languages have been around for many years. These tools are more stable than object-oriented analysis and design methods. Because the object-oriented analysis and design methods today were developed from a developer's point of view, it is harder to model business logic. In addition, the current object-oriented methodology and tools do not support the full life cycle of client/server application development. The object-oriented methodology should be as good as RAD and JAD in the future, but is still in its infancy.

A sign of the object-oriented methodology's immaturity is the number of object-oriented methodology models for describing business processes. These major models are event-oriented, process, data-oriented, transaction-driven (similar to information engineering), and object interaction. Some models are better suited for describing some business processes than others. A mixture of many of these models is needed for developing enterprise-wide client/server applications.

There are many object-oriented methodologies for designing software. For example, Grady Booch's Object Oriented Design methodologies consists of identifying the classes and objects, identifying the semantics of classes and objects, identifying the relationships among classes and objects, and implementing classes and objects. Other methodologies include the Buhr, Chen, Constantine-DeMarco, Hatley-Pirbhai, Ward-Mellor, and Yourdan development methodologies. Most software development tools on the market today allow developers to use many different methodologies from within the tool.

Tip

The key to object-oriented analysis and design is to view software applications as a series of interconnected objects that represent the many aspects of the problem. The goal for the software is to represent the problem described by the user.

Cross-Platform Application Development

Traditionally, developers created applications for a specific platform. Despite multiple platforms being the norm today, corporations frequently do not have the resources to develop an application more than once. The goal is to develop a client or server application that runs on all clients or servers in the enterprise. In turn, developers are now required to develop an application that can run on multiple platforms—creating a single source code for multiple platforms. Ideally, developers want to maintain a single code library that contains both client and server code.

The following are the three approaches for developing cross-platform applications:

■ Develop the application to run natively on all target platforms—This means that the developer must develop the software to the lowest common denominator of all target platforms. The application still needs to be recompiled with different libraries for each platform, but the source code is the same.

- Use a shell or front-end software tool that runs on all the platforms—In turn, the application is designed for that shell or tool. The majority of these tools address development on clients and do nothing for the server.

- Use one of the many multiplatform development tools on the market— These tools usually provide a common graphical user interface, and isolate the application from specific differences in operating environments.

Which approach is best depends on the number of platforms and the complexity of the application being developed. Although it is often easier and faster to use the many development tools on the market, this can lock you into rigid solutions.

> **Note**
>
> It is important to determine all the platforms on which the application will execute. If the client application is to run on OS/2, Macintosh, and Windows, then developers must be aware of the differences among these three operating environments. This is why cross-platform development tools often provide greater flexibility.

Multiplatform Application Development Issues

The C programming language is the most portable multiplatform language, with C compilers available for a wide variety of client and server platforms. Unfortunately, even if developers only used the C constructs, there would still be issues that they would need to be aware of when developing for a multiplatform environment.

Internationalization

As client/server computing begins to stretch enterprise-wide, many corporations are faced with the issues of internationalization. Traditional applications designed in the United States use the American Standard Code for Information Interchange (ASCII). ASCII was developed by the American National Standards Institute (ANSI) as a standard for seven-bit code for transferring information. Most of the client systems, including IBM's personal computers, use the ASCII encoding scheme. Another popular eight-bit code for transferring information is Extended Binary Coded Decimal Interchange

Code (EBCDIC), developed by IBM for its mainframe environment. When these standards moved overseas, there was a need to extend them to accommodate accent marks and extended alphabets for other countries.

The standard that evolved was the seven-bit International Standards Organization (ISO) codepage. This works well in European countries, but fails in the Asian Pacific market. The Asian market requires the use of double-byte characters (also called wide characters). This character code allows for the use of Han characters that are used in Chinese, Japanese, and Korean to represent whole words and concepts. This wide character became known as the Unicode standard. Unicode is a superset of ASCII that uses 16-bit codepage for each character instead of seven bits.

Unicode was developed by a not-for-profit consortium called Unicode, Inc., founded in 1991 to develop a common character set. Unicode is also investigating technologies, such as uniform compression techniques, that will help its member companies such as Apple, Digital, IBM, and Microsoft interoperate.

ISO and its four-byte character set is also working on internationalization issues, such as a world-wide alphabet. ISO standard is a superset of the Unicode character set.

Developers must consider these internationalization issues when dealing with international enterprise-wide client/server applications. Even a simple function, such as a two-phase commit across database servers located in Japan, Russia, France, and the United States, can be difficult (see fig. 23.5).

If global client/server applications are a requirement, developers must plan for these internationalization issues. There are middleware solutions in the market today that can help developers with codepage conversions.

Graphical User Interface

When designing a graphical user interface, developers need to consider the hardware platforms where the client application will be deployed. Graphical user interfaces between platforms are not created equal. Developers need to ask some fundamental questions when designing the graphical user interface. These questions are:

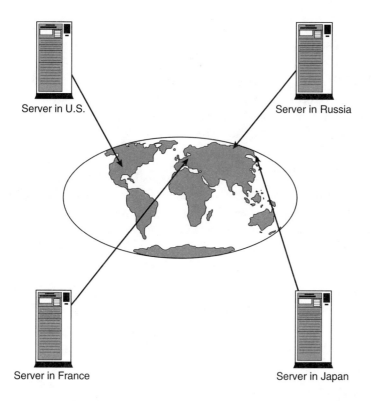

Server in U.S.

Server in Russia

Server in France

Server in Japan

Fig. 23.5
Corporations today
view their scope of
operations
worldwide.
Developers need to
consider interna-
tionalization issues
when analyzing
user requirements
when designing
their applications.

- Will the application only use a graphical user interface or does the legacy system still require a terminal-based screen?

- What is the structure of the graphical user interface?

- Does the GUI have to "look and feel" the same across platforms?

By answering these questions up front, developers can ease the burden of porting GUIs across multiple platforms. After all, the compatibility between platforms depends on the design of the interface. A rule of thumb is the less platform specific functionality, the more portable the GUI. There are tools available to help developers in GUI portability. These tools need to generate code for multiple GUI toolkits, as well as for hardware platforms and operating systems. There are also tools that generate a single source code for multiple GUIs and character-based terminals.

VI

Multiplatforms

When developing a GUI for multiplatform portability, developers need to consider two major components of application design. One is the software, which allows the application to receive input and display output. This software must be developed to the lowest common denominator for all relevant platforms. The second component to consider is hardware, or the device used to communicate with the client/server application. These input devices range from a keyboard to a mouse to a voice. Obviously, the input device must be common across all deployment platforms. The lowest common denominator, unfortunately, is the keyboard.

IBM has defined a Common User Access (CUA) interface standard. This standard's goal is to define a consistent view of applications across multiple platforms. The standard defines such functionality as how a window's layout appears, how push buttons and pull-down menus operate, and how fields should be formatted. This standard has not gained widespread support.

When developing a pilot application, make sure to consider all platforms that the system needs to support and the method for communicating. The easiest method to develop multiplatform GUI applications is to take advantage of graphical user interface tools on the market. These tools are robust and provide high ease-of-use.

File and Data Access

File and data access can differ between platforms. The primary difference in the file access area is the naming scheme used for files. Filename lengths differ among platforms. Developers need to use a standard naming convention between platforms that takes platform differences into account. For example, Windows 3.1 files can have a name length of 11 characters (8-character name with a 3-character extension) while a Macintosh file can have 31 characters. In Windows 95 and Windows NT, filenames can have 255 characters.

In the area of data access, developers have three approaches for multiplatform developing. One is to use a database system to develop the application. This locks you into a specific database vendor and does not allow you to go across different databases. Another approach is to write a C program that does the interfacing to the different databases. This approach can be a challenge because of the many differences between databases. The last approach is to use a remote data access middleware product that provides a cross-platform data access facility. This approach locks you into the middleware company.

Graphics

Graphics are the most complicated type of software to port across platforms. Most vendors support bit-mapped images (.BMP), but there are many other formats available on the market such as Macintosh (.PCT), Paintbrush (.PCX), and Windows Metafile Format (.WMF). The problem is that many of these other formats are not supported and require special drivers to display the file. The easiest approach when doing multiplatform development is to convert all these graphics to .BMP files.

> **Note**
>
> Whenever possible, avoid using any platform-specific service or extension. The best approach is to use a portable API for all services. Many client/server development tools provide an API for integrating other applications into client/server environments.

Migration Strategy

Because of the enormous effort required to maintain code, some developers would love to dump all legacy systems and develop client/server applications from scratch. The chance of this happening in most organizations, however, is next to none. Consequently, a migration strategy for legacy applications needs to be evaluated. Many times, legacy systems can be adapted to run in client/server environments.

Remember that migration does not mean conversion. Conversion means to take application programs written in one source language and change them to another. Migration means to adapt an application to a new environment.

The steps developers should consider before migrating an application from a stand-alone environment to a client/server model are shown in figure 23.6. These steps are only a guideline for analyzing the migration effort. The ultimate decision for whether applications should be migrated or rewritten is a long-term business decision. The entire organization should make this decision based on the costs to maintain a legacy system versus the cost to migrate or rewrite applications.

VI

Multiplatforms

Fig. 23.6
This diagram shows a flow-chart of the steps that should be considered when evaluating a migration strategy. Be sure to consider all costs (including intangibles such as job security) in the cost/benefit analysis.

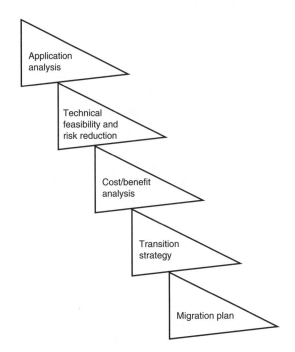

The first step in analyzing a migration strategy is to technically evaluate the current application. The ease of migration correlates to the modularity of the code and whether the original code follows good structured programming design and techniques. The more the original code is like spaghetti code, the harder the migration, and the higher the likelihood that redesigning the original application is the best approach.

If the original code is designed well, the modification to the code is easier. The current system calls will have to change to call the middleware API. The system will not have to be reworked, but merely integrated into the present environment. This is a safer approach because it allows the present system to remain structurally intact. Another extreme is to begin taking pieces of the code and retargeting them for new platforms.

The next questions are the technical feasibility, the risk of migration, and the cost/benefit analysis to the current environment. Even if the current code can integrate into the client/server environment, what are the technical feasibility and cost of maintaining the older hardware, software, and applications as part of the client/server enterprise? (Remember that the cost of maintaining includes the entire solution—hardware and software maintenance, training, documentation, consulting, and all other costs associated with the current system and future system.) Will maintaining this original code hinder the long-term migration to a client/server architecture? Is the code worth salvaging, or could other alternatives such as commercial software packaging be just as effective for solving the problem? These questions can only be answered based on the initial requirement for developing a client/server solution. These questions should be addressed during the application analysis, technical feasibility, and cost/benefit analysis stages of the migration plan.

The next consideration is a transition strategy. Once a decision is made to migrate the current application, there is still a need to develop a transition strategy. The strategy is to find the most appropriate way to transition the current application to a client/server model. The approaches may vary, from running the original system to running a mirror of the system in a client/server environment (running in parallel). Another approach is to take a risk and switch from one system to the other without a transition. A more conservative approach is to transition with a phase-in approach. First, integrate the older system into the client/server environment. Over time, transition different pieces of the application over to a client/server model. Eventually, components of the original application can be migrated to other platforms. Whichever approach you select, a transition strategy must be in place before migrating your systems.

Finally, a migration plan needs to be written that documents all the different findings from this investigation. When implementing a migration strategy, developers need to be aware of a multitude of non-technical issues. Some of these issues include the political shifts that might take place based on more users having access to information, changes in training requirements for end users, and changes in relationships with external groups, such as customers and suppliers. Some other areas affected by implementation of a migration strategy are the current workflow, business processes, and internal organizational relationships between departments. A migration strategy from a single-system architecture to a client/server one must be carefully planned to ease the transition and provide a greater probability of success.

Availability of Development Tools

Many analysts believe that client/server development tools will enjoy major growth in the coming years. These tools provide an easy interface to many of the client/server issues described in this book. The best tools provide a simple graphical user interface for developing enterprise-wide client/server applications.

There are many categories of client/server application development tools available, each having its own strengths. These tools range from client-based offerings to distributed processing tools.

Development Tools for Different Client/Server Applications

There are many tools on the market targeted to the development of client/server applications. The tools vary in functionality and methodologies. Some are geared more for development of the client side while others emphasize the server side. Developers should always keep the business requirements and long-term goals in mind when selecting a client/server tool.

Client Tools

Tip

If you understand your business requirements, then selecting a product that meets your long-term needs is easier. Many products offer tools that solve only some of a user's requirements, but do not fulfill the entire product life cycle.

The client tools originated from a LAN environment, so applications are biased toward the client. These tools tend to be event-driven visual programming tools, and unable to distribute logic among different platforms. These tools encourage a rapid-prototyping methodology.

In this type of client/server application, processing logic and the graphical user interface reside on the client, whereas data resources are on the server. Companies often take this approach because they want to add a GUI to their legacy systems. The GUI runs on the client and accesses an existing system. Tools such as Gupta's Quest allow developers to develop a front end to a SQL database. Other GUI-centric client/server tools are Visual Basic and PowerBuilder. Some tools simply provide a simple way for developers to build cross-platform graphical user interfaces, such as Galaxy from Visix Software.

Distributed, Processing Tools

These tools vary widely in their capabilities and ease-of-use. Most of these tools grew out of mainframe environments. They emphasize the structure as well as the analysis and design approaches to client/server application development. These tools tend to use RAD, JAD, or structured techniques for application methodologies. Some of the more robust tools give developers the flexibility to use all the different methodologies as they see fit.

The distributed, processing tools market includes tools that provide data modeling, code generation, multi-user repositories, and complete life cycle management tracking. In addition, these tools provide various forms of partitioning of application logic between client and server or multiple clients and servers. Tools that fall into this category are Seer*HPS from Seer Technologies, Inc., Ellipse from Bachman Information Systems, Inc., and Composer by IEF from Texas Instruments.

Object-Oriented Tools

Object-oriented tools must provide encapsulation (the ability to bundle data and corresponding procedures together), inheritance (a way for attributes to be shared among objects in classes above them on the class hierarchy), and polymorphism (allows functions to be performed on different objects). The standards in the object-oriented tools market are not clearly defined, because this area is evolving. In turn, many tools do not offer all the functionality needed to support a true object-oriented client/server environment. Kappa from IntelliCorp, Inc. and Development Environment from Forte Software, Inc., are examples of object-oriented tools.

> **Note**
>
> Object Request Broker (ORB) standards are just beginning to evolve. Many object-oriented tools today use a proprietary ORB. It will be interesting to see the impact on these tools when standards in object-oriented technology mature.

Key Requirements for Client/Server Development Tools

The basic needs for client/server tools are connectivity and high productivity for developing business logic, process logic, and graphical user interfaces (GUIs).

In addition to the typical characteristics that users look for in a software package such as features, support, training, technical environments (does it support the operating systems, network operating systems, and DBMSes that are currently part of the environment?), and price (total price per developer and per end user), what other characteristics are important to consider when selecting a client/server development tool? It is important to have a set of criteria by which to compare different client/server development tools. The following is a brief list of some of those criteria:

- Does it allow the developer to isolate the different components of an application?

  Tools should allow developers to isolate different components of an application. Modularity allows for easy entry and exit at various points in the application. Each component should also be a self-contained unit for easy maintenance.

- Does the tool provide an application programming interface (API) to integrate legacy systems?

The tool should provide a way to integrate existing applications with applications written with the client/server tool. These APIs give developers flexibility for enterprise-wide integration.

- Does the tool generate both the client and server components of the application?

  The tool should be able to generate components of an application for all clients and servers in the enterprise.

- Is the tool capable of supporting the different areas of an enterprise-wide application, such as the graphical user interface, database access, transaction management, business logic, repository interface, and so on?

  The tool should provide a diverse set of capabilities for solving enterprise-wide application problems.

- Does it allow developers to port the application across multiple platforms?

  The tool must allow you to develop and deploy for multiple platforms, operating systems, and networking protocols.

- Does the tool provide data import/export capabilities?

  It is important to be able to include data that is developed outside the tool. There is always legacy data on the network that needs to be captured for an enterprise-wide, client/server application. In addition, it is important to evaluate the quality of the tool's SQL support.

- Does the tool allow developers to have user-defined data?

  The tool should provide developers with the flexibility and capability to import images, binary large objects (BLOBs), and other data types.

- Is the client/server tool all encompassing?

  The tool should support the entire development life cycle, from requirements definition through application deployment and maintenance.

- Does the tool provide the flexibility to choose the methodology most appropriate to the application being developed?

  The client/server development tool should give developers the ability to select the methodology most appropriate to their application, such as structured analysis, object-oriented, information engineering, rapid-application development, joint-application development, and prototyping. A methodology that is too rigid leaves little room for project-specific improvements.

■ Does the system have the flexibility to provide additional packages that enhance the client/server application?

Ideally, a client/server tool allows you to enhance the client/server application environment by providing capabilities such as system and network management, documentation revisions, configuration management, and software changes and upgrades.

■ Will the tool grow with the organization into the future?

The tool must provide scalability. Otherwise, it will need to be abandoned entirely as the organization and its applications grow.

From Here...

Software development practices are constantly evolving as the dependence on computers and the complexity of applications grow. The steps and processes involved in developing software for a single system environment versus a multiplatform environment are similar, but multiplatform development adds a dimension of complexity. As a result of these complexities, a well-understood plan for moving into a client/server environment becomes important. Don't skimp on up-front analysis of the business or requirements gathering. After all, the more questions you ask up front and plan for in the design of the application, the easier these applications will be to test and maintain in the future.

For more information on the topics covered in this chapter, refer to the following chapters:

■ Chapter 3, "Communications Protocols TCP/IP, TCP, and UDP," teaches you about TCP, UDP, and other lower-level network protocols.

■ Chapter 10, "External Data Representation," acquaints you with the XDR routines that are at the heart of data transmission under RPC.

■ Chapter 13, "RPC Under UNIX," provides much greater platform-specific detail on how all levels of RPC work in a UNIX environment.

VI

Multiplatforms

Chapter 24

A Survey of Commercial Client/Server Products

The client/server model separates your process into a client and server portion, allowing you almost unlimited freedom in choosing your best solution for the client, the server, and the connectivity between the two. This freedom of choice gives you power.

However, as Spider-Man said, "With great power comes great responsibility." The power to choose includes the freedom to make a bad choice. Client/server technology still has many problems to solve, among them compatibility between products, accessing a heterogeneous database, and distributed systems management. As an example of one problem, how do you provide online help for your distributed application when the application may run on any of several widely differing platforms?

The purpose of middleware, which can be broadly defined as an interface between the operating system and the application, is to make itself invisible to the following:

- The manager who doesn't want to learn SQL but wants to know last quarter's earnings.

- The applications programmer who doesn't have time to re-create the client application on another platform and create the network programming required to communicate between the two.

- The information systems administrator who has to oversee it all.

Middleware fills in the seams of heterogeneous and supposedly homogenous networks, helping users to ignore the differences.

The previous chapters of this book gave you advice and guidelines on programming in client/server environments. This chapter is intended to give a sampling of some of the many tools available to help you practice what the rest of this book has discussed in theory. This chapter is not intended to be an exhaustive or complete review, or even to judge the relative quality of the products. However, this chapter should serve as a starting point for your search for the right software tool.

Middleware Tools

Middleware allows a developer to spend more time on his or her application and less time on converting one set of system, protocol, or application requirements to another. If two people share only a little of a common language, their conversation will proceed slower and clumsier than if an interpreter was present who could translate the speakers' discourse with clarity, richness, and depth.

This section will first examine one of the basic middleware models: the remote procedure call, or RPC. The Open Software Foundation's Distributed Computing Environment (DCE) is a standardized form of RPC, which will be mentioned separately. Tools for implementing the Object Management Group's CORBA standard for distributed object environments, and the database standards of SQL and Microsoft's Open Database Connectivity (ODBC) will follow.

Remote Procedure Calls

RPCs were developed because the older model of interprocess communication (IPC) is limited to communicating between processes that may share a common shared memory area and file space structure. Applications now need to address communication between processes that may be located on different types of processors or operating systems. RPC may be one of the few real solutions for developing a true distributed cooperative processing application, where pieces reside on multiple systems.

An RPC is intended to look like a C function call. A local procedure call is replaced with an RPC procedure (sometimes called a "stub") that diverts the call to a procedure of the same name located on another machine. Like a standard C function call, the stub includes the name of the routine and needed parameters.

> **Note**
>
> Major variations of RPC include Sun Microsystem's ONC-RPC, NFS/RPC, the Open Software Foundation's DCE/RPC, and TI/RPC (Transport Independent RPC).

EZ-RPC

NobleNet supplies three toolkits that ease the task of network programming with RPCs: EZ-RPC, WinRPC, and RPCWare. EZ-RPC is the UNIX version, and WinRPC and RPCWare are the DOS/Windows and Novell Netware platform versions, respectively. The three toolkits offer the same user interface and functionality.

EZ-RPC makes RPC programming a little different from C language application programming, without requiring you to have an extensive background in network development. Only a single function call typically needs to be added to the client portion to open communication with the server portion. In order to reduce ambiguities inherent in C that can cause difficulties across a heterogeneous network, EZ-RPC extends the XDR specification to handle complex data typing. Although RPCs are generally considered synchronous activities that tie up the client until the server's response, EZ-RPC allows for the use of other, more complex RPC types including batch, callback (role-switching between client and server), no-wait (asynchronous), broadcast, and forking.

In order to convert a current application for use in a client/server environment, follow these steps:

1. Divide the source code into the client and server portions.

2. Create an `.RPC` specification file, which contains descriptions of the data to be passed between the two portions of the application.

3. Run the EZ-RPC compiler to create a new makefile and C language files containing the RPC stub code for the application portions.

4. Use the new makefile to recompile the source code portions with their stub code specifications.

EZ-RPC's compiler generates readable and commented C code. The programmer has many optional settings for the compile process, and then is able to modify the code on a line-by-line basis if necessary. EZ-RPC's compiler creates

VI

Multiplatforms

a set of functions to control memory management (leakage) in both the client and server portions. EZ-RPC supports the TI/RPC and NFS/RPC formats, with the addition of a direction indicator that is added to every function argument.

WinRPC

EZ-RPC itself aids client/server RPC development on several varieties of UNIX, but the company's support extends beyond only UNIX. NobleNet also has two other products: WinRPC and RPCWare. WinRPC gives you the option of creating DLLs (Dynamic Link Libraries), C code, or Pascal code. Using the DLL option can ease integration of WinRPC's output into common Windows development environments. WinRPC supports Win16 and Win32 for Windows, and Windows NT on both x86 and Alpha processors. WinRPC also adheres to the WinSock (Windows Sockets) TCP/IP Windows standard.

RPCWare

Like its close relatives EZ-RPC and WinRPC, RPCWare creates C source code stubs for Netware client and server EXEs and NLMs (Netware Loadable Module). Other supported platforms include VMS, OS/2, and the Macintosh OS.

DCE

The Open Software Foundation's DCE (Distributed Computing Environment) provides one of the many standards for RPCs. In an attempt not to spawn more sub-standards from DCE, the OSF chose to emphasize strict specification of a core group of RPC standards and limitations in the ability of applications developers to alter it. Strictness may limit the flexibility of customizing which some see as a strength of RPC; but conversely, the strictness serves to promise an improved chance that members claiming to adhere to the standard in theory may be able to function together in reality. Other major elements of the DCE specification include Kerberos from MIT for authentication and security features, a multiple threading model for UNIX, a distributed naming service, and a timing-synchronization service for the entire network. DCE was adopted by the Object Management Group (OMG) for the CORBA standard, on which more discussion will follow later in this chapter.

Microsoft is also committed to supporting the DCE standard, having included DCE in Windows NT as part of an effort to tightly weave network protocols and services with the basic operating system. NT currently includes DCE and WinSock. For further integration, Microsoft has announced plans to add an extension of DCE called Distributed OLE to allow remote calls to OLE (Object Linking and Embedding) objects.

One toolkit for DCE usage is IBM's Software Developer's Kit (SDK) for DCE. The SDK was released for use in the OS/2 and Windows environments, and IBM has extended DCE support to other operating systems that they developed such as AIX, OS/400, and MVS.

CORBA

An Object Request Broker (ORB) is an interconnection area for objects to communicate in. Like a system bus, an ORB allows everyone shared access to the object area. An ORB is designed to route client application queries to the right object. An ORB can also do load-balancing and best-path routing if multiple systems share a desired resource. The Object Management Group's *Common Object Request Broker Architecture* (*CORBA*) is a specification for a messaging mechanism for a distributed object environment, defining the common features ORBs are expected to share.

An ORB is implemented as a library for the server that allows sending and receiving the remote object operation requests, and a subset of that library replicated for the client that only allows sending. A client may request a service from an Interface Definition Language (IDL) stub or a Dynamic Invocation Interface (DII). IDL stubs are precompiled for the client and server sides of the application, and use a static approach to object access by requiring applications to have prior knowledge of the objects that will be available at runtime. The DII is an API that can build an object list at runtime. DII is therefore more flexible for use than IDL, but DII is also more complex than IDL.

The OSF's DCE standard is specified for communicating between ORBs, granting specific services such as security, timing, network-wide unique name generation, and other features described in more detail in an earlier chapter of this book.

Overall, the OMG's strategy for defining CORBA does not seem to be oriented toward the creation of newly distributed services. Instead, the plan for extending CORBA seems to be on selecting an extant distributed service, such as DCE, and defining a standardized "wrapping" of an IDL interface for it.

Orbix

NobleNet's Orbix is an OMG CORBA-compliant toolkit providing C++ language binding for ORBs. Orbix is available for the following platforms:

- Windows NT
- SunOS
- IBM AIX
- OSF/1

VI

Multiplatforms

- Solaris (Sparc and x86)
- Silicon Graphics IRIX
- HP-UX

- Ultrix
- UnixWare
- Sinix

Releases for Windows 3.1, Vx/Works, SCO UNIX, OpenVMS, Macintosh, and OS/2 are promised shortly.

ORBeline

Another CORBA development package is PostModern Computing's ORBeline. ORBeline is a full implementation of the OMG's CORBA specification, including static (IDL) compiled stubs and dynamic (DII) libraries. ORBeline's IDL compiler supports all CORBA IDL features for static libraries with C++ mapping. ORBeline's DII works with an Interface Repository to provide dynamic runtime object access from the client's side of the client/server connection. ORBeline's DII has been extended past OMG's basic CORBA standard to work with the Tcl/Tk scripting language, and is also compatible with Visual Basic. ORBeline supports multi-threading for improved performance on appropriate platforms.

ORBeline includes a SMART Agent to select the most efficient communication mechanism between a client and its called object. This Agent also monitors client-object communications, and initiates reconnection attempts if a communication failure occurs. For example, a client is linked to an object on a server when the server crashes. The SMART Agent will attempt to reestablish the link when the communication fails, then will search the network for alternatives. If a replica of the missing object is found on another server, the SMART Agent links the client process to the replica object.

ORBeline is available for use on the following platforms:

- Cray supercomputers
- SunOS and Solaris
- OSF/1
- HP-UX
- IBM AIX

- Windows 3.1
- Windows NT
- UnixWare
- VxWorks
- Lynx

Remote Database Access

Almost every relational database uses SQL as an industry-wide programming language. The term "SQL front-end" is commonly applied to any development tool used for creating a user interface for a SQL-compliant database.

A company will rarely choose the GUI tool before it chooses a database management system (DBMS). Therefore, the primary quality of a SQL front-end is the capability to access any database.

Gupta's SQLWindows

Gupta's SQLWindows was the first Windows-based GUI tool of its kind, and has not been left to stagnate since its introduction. Feature-rich as it is, SQLWindows deserves a look for database front-end development. Gupta's SQLBase database is bundled with the development environment. Given the common origin of the GUI front-end development environment and the database back-end, you should expect a very strong and reliable linkage between the two components.

SQLWindows provides extensive support for team development efforts involving multiple users, with access level and promotion level definable for each user, and protection of modules using a library check-in and check-out metaphor preventing out-of-synchonization updates for version control.

> **Note**
>
> Access levels and promotion levels are related concepts. Access level defines what part of the SQLWindows environment a user has access to—for example, is the user allowed to create a new project? Promotion level in SQLWindows defines how much authority the user has to declare a module as complete in one phase, and to promote it to the next phase of its development life cycle.

One possible drawback to SQLWindows is the unfamiliarity developers are likely to have with the SQL Application Language (SAL) used within SQLWindows for development. As SAL is not based on a common programming language such as BASIC or C, this unfamiliarity may cause delays on a first contact with SQLWindows.

PowerSoft's PowerBuilder

Another tool used to develop GUI front-ends for SQL-format databases is PowerSoft's PowerBuilder. PowerBuilder is a very graphically oriented development environment. Although the graphic nature of PowerBuilder is

VI

Multiplatforms

stressed in common use, the source code is quickly and simply reachable from the GUI. The internal programming language PowerScript is similar to BASIC, shortening expected adaptation time.

One strength of PowerBuilder is the large number of supported database back ends. PowerBuilder supports the ODBC (Open DataBase Connectivity) standard as a common layer for connecting the GUI front-end to an ODBC-compliant database back end. This reliance on ODBC extends to Power-Builder's communication with the Watcom SQL database engine bundled with PowerBuilder.

ODBC

Microsoft's ODBC (Open Database Connectivity) can be considered a sort of middleware optimized for database access. ODBC 3.0 is expected to adhere to database connectivity rules laid down by the SQL Access Group which created the original ODBC specifications in 1991, allowing for more flexibility through a less proprietary solution. The goal of using ODBC is to allow an application to have a single user interface and access multiple databases built with different applications.

> **Note**
>
> One company working to make the ODBC standard useful and efficient is Visigenic Software. Visigenic's three products are the ODBC DriverSet, the ODBC SDK, and the ODBC Test Suite.

The ODBC DriverSet is compatible with the ODBC 2.0 standard, and allows cross-platform access to SQL databases using a single API. The drivers allow direct access to Oracle, Sybase SQL Server, Ingres, and Informix. DriverSet does not directly access Microsoft SQL Server as of this writing, but is expected to do so by the time this chapter sees print. The DriverSet is available on Windows, HP/UX, SunOS and Solaris, and IBM AIX.

The ODBC SDK 2.0 permits development of C or C++ applications or database drivers for multi-platform use. The SDK is available on SunOS, Solaris, HP/UX, and IBM AIX. The Test Suite is an exhaustive set of individual C test programs for every API call in the ODBC 2.0 specification, from the Core set and including Levels 1 and 2. The Test Suite is available for Windows and UNIX.

Developer's Tools

The first half of this chapter presented some middleware solutions to transparency between applications running on multiple and sometimes widely varying platforms. Use of these products, of course, assumes that you already have an application or applications running on more than one homogeneous platform or environment. This is a level of assumption avoided by the famous recipe for roast duck which starts "First, shoot a duck." The rest of this chapter describes some tools used to "shoot the duck" and get your application onto multiple platforms.

Note

In order to port your application, you should write portable code. Writing portable code involves simple guidelines:

Keep functions short and modular.

Isolate the user interface (client) from the processor-intensive application code (server).

Debug with every tool you can find.

Document everything.

While not all applications should be destined for a multi-platform distributed environment, considering the possibility in the initial design process can mean not having to rewrite the application cleanly later.

GUI 4GLs

A typical 4GL development tool should have five major characteristics:

- An open system which supports industry-wide standards such as SQL.

- Scalability, or the ability to process requests from a user base of possibly as many as thousands.

- Team support features—including such capabilities as version control and project management.

- Object-based or object-oriented programming—inheritance of features from a parent object.

- Portability, or the ability to create applications that perform almost identically on multiple platforms.

Visual Basic

Microsoft Visual Basic includes the Access Relational Database Management System (RDBMS) database engine, allowing access to many of the common Windows database formats. Like other 4GLs, Visual Basic's GUI interface creates ties to the databases without requiring you to write code. This 4GL includes strong Windows database access, including ODBC and OLE standards support.

Visual C++

Microsoft Visual C++ is a widely used 4GL development environment. The standard view in Visual C++ is of the Integrated Development Environment (IDE) which improves the integration of the major components (resource editor, debugger, and so forth) from previous editions. The improved integration reduces the need to constantly launch additional windows. Visual C++ as of version 2.1 and later has one significant limitation: it cannot build 16-bit applications, so converting your application is a decision which may be reversed only with difficulty. Microsoft currently provides workaround support for 16-bit Windows applications by including an older version of Visual C++ for 16-bit development.

Visual C++ includes support for Microsoft Foundation Class (MFC) 3.0, which supports ODBC and OLE. An OLE Control Developer's Kit for building OLE control containers is included. An OLE control container is an MFC class which acts similar to a standard OLE client, but uses a few additional calls between the control and the container.

Microsoft Visual C++ also has a Cross-Development Edition for Macintosh. The Cross-Development Edition runs under Microsoft Windows NT 3.x and generates Motorola 680x0 code which runs on any Macintosh that has a 68020 or higher CPU and is also running a version of Macintosh System 7. While the Power Macintosh line does run 680x0 code using an emulator, software written for the PowerPC processor ("native" code) runs significantly faster. A future version of Visual C++ is expected to produce native Power Macintosh code. The APIs supported are a subset of the Win32 library and MFC 3.0. The Cross-Development Edition is not a stand-alone package, it is an extension to Microsoft Visual C++ 2.0 or later.

Caution

If you are considering porting an older Windows application to the Macintosh, you need to convert the application to Win32 library usage.

Progress

Progress Software's Progress is another 4GL and RDBMS which is intended primarily for a transaction-oriented environment. Progress consists of three components: the RDBMS, the Applications Development Environment (ADE), and DataServer Architecture. The ADE is a GUI-based environment that is strongly integrated with the RDBMS for rapid development. The RDBMS conforms to the ANSI SQL standard. Access to other relational databases is provided for Oracle and Sybase in UNIX.

Progress runs in several environments including OS/2, multiple varieties of UNIX, Digital's VAX, and IBM's AS/400. Using a multi-threaded, multi-server process model, Progress is designed to make full advantage of the power of a multi-processor system, allowing better scalability. While still hardly universal, Symmetric Multi-Processor (SMP) systems can only become more common with time.

VisualAge

IBM's VisualAge is a development environment for Windows and OS/2 using the object-oriented programming language IBM Smalltalk. IBM's version of a Smalltalk development environment complies with the proposed ANSI standard for the Smalltalk language. Like many of the object-oriented 4GL programming tools, many applications may be created without you having to directly write a line of code. New objects for your VisualAge library may be written in IBM Smalltalk, or written in COBOL or C and then imported into VisualAge.

VisualAge supports team programming and version control, two important considerations for large applications programming. Version control can be used for both source and object code. Database access is provided for DB2/2 and DB2/6000, with drivers for Microsoft SQL Server, Sybase SQL Server, and Oracle also included. VisualAge contains an interactive SQL query builder.

Delphi

Borland's Delphi is another GUI-based development environment which uses Object Pascal rather than BASIC or C/C++. Not just a client/server tool, Delphi is a full object-oriented programming language.

The four major portions of Delphi are the Component Palette, the Object Inspector, the Form Designer, and a Code Window. To start development with Delphi, you create a form with elements chosen from the Palette and define the elements' characteristics using the Object Inspector. Components may be created and added to the Palette, or purchased from a third party.

VI

Multiplatforms

In addition to the library of Delphi component elements, Delphi supports Visual Basic format VBXs. One highly praised feature of Delphi is the ability of users' components to display data during the development phase. The Database Engine contains native drivers for use with Borland's InterBase, dBASE, Paradox, Sybase, and ASCII tables, as well as the general ODBC standard. Delphi has only partial support for OLE, however. You cannot create OLE servers or controls, only containers. Delphi does include a single-user license for InterBase to allow prototyping of front-ends.

Delphi client/server adds several important features for distributed development, such as the following:

- SQL Links, which allow access to remote SQL databases including Oracle, Sybase, and Microsoft SQL Server.

- Complete source code of the Delphi component library.

- An unlimited distribution license for InterBase.

- A visual SQL query builder.

- Versioning control.

As it stands, the basic Delphi compares with other 4GLs such as Visual Basic. Delphi client/server compares more closely with PowerSoft's PowerBuilder Enterprise than it does with Visual Basic, adding several important features for distributed development.

One of the few criticisms leveled at Delphi is its lack of cross-platform capability; it can only run under Windows 3.1. Borland has announced plans to deliver a 32-bit version of Delphi for use with Windows 95. The ability to create OCXs, or OLE custom objects, is also expected to be added in the Windows 95 release.

Oracle Power Objects

Oracle Power Objects is a drag-and-drop object-oriented environment for client/server applications development. The scripting language (OracleBasic) is compatible with Microsoft's Visual Basic, minimizing the learning curve associated with a new programming language. Full inheritance of object characteristics allows you to modify a parent object of the appropriate generation once, and not repeat the effort elsewhere.

For database connectivity, Power Objects provides several native drivers supporting the full range of ability in several databases, including Oracle7, DB2,

Microsoft SQL Server, and Sybase, as well as full ODBC support. Other standards adhered to are OLE, OCX, OpenDoc, and Windows DLL usage.

Oracle emphasizes cross-platform development for Power Objects, having released the environment for Windows, OS/2, and Macintosh. Applications built with Power Objects are intended to run unmodified on all supported platforms. Finally, Power Objects is designed to be used for development on machines with only 8 MB of RAM.

> **Note**
>
> It is attractive to consider that the older desktop on a back shelf in your office is capable of developing for *anything* without a hardware upgrade.

Object Engineering Workbench

Terasoft's Object Engineering Workbench (OEW) is an object-oriented C++ development tool with a single integrated user interface incorporating a modeler, a C++ code generator, and a parser. Terasoft claims one of OEW's strengths is the parser's strength, which makes OEW a powerful reverse engineering tool. OEW is described as more of a programmer's tool than a designer's tool, as its use requires more knowledge of the C++ language than CASE tools usually do.

The recommended use for OEW is to parse the output of a CASE tool into OEW. OEW can parse the header files off of your preferred C++ class library and present the object classes graphically. OEW's support of class libraries is extensive, including Microsoft's MFC, Borland's OWL, and many others. You use OEW to build the application, and then compile and produce source code for multi-platform use.

OEW's multi-platform support extends to Windows, Windows NT, and OS/2. OEW has drivers supporting all features of the POET and ObjectStore object-oriented database management systems, including the schema designers.

CASE Tools

Popkin Software's System Architect (SA) is a CASE tool for client/server and database application development. System Architect is available for Windows and OS/2. One strength of SA is its flexible approach to design methodology. Where some CASE tools easily allow only one methodology for a designer's use, and may allow another design approach only with difficulty, SA supports multiple methodologies in the base product, with two object-oriented (Booch and Coad/Yourdon) methodologies supported in a separate drop-in module.

The SA Reverse Data Engineer creates Entity Relation, IDEF1X, or physical table diagrams from an existing database or schema. Specific databases supported are DB2, Informix, Oracle, Microsoft SQL Server, and Sybase SQL Server. SA is also ODBC-compliant. One scenario for use of the SA Reverse Data Engineer module would be one in which you are the new MIS director, and the department's DBMS is only partially documented. Add to this scenario the possibility that the original designers of the system are no longer available, and you have a potential disaster. The SA Schema Generator translates ER, IDEF1X, or physical table diagrams into schema definitions, and is described by Popkin Software as a perfect complement to the SA RDE.

Windows to UNIX Transfer Tools

Windows platforms make up a majority of the desktop market; therefore, developers who create applications for Windows are virtually guaranteed a large potential market. However, the number of installed seats of the many flavors of UNIX is estimated to be over one million. Porting to a UNIX environment can be profitable if the re-engineering cost stays low enough. Many of the software design considerations for Windows NT are similar to that of a UNIX environment, thus reducing the effort needed to port from NT to UNIX. The next two products described in this section attempt to further reduce the cost of converting a Windows application to UNIX.

Wind/U

Wind/U from Bristol Technology is a cross-platform development tool which speeds conversion of Windows applications to the UNIX environment. Wind/U is intended to aid the cross-platform developer to create and maintain only a single source code base, rather than two, by being essentially a licensed port of the Windows API to UNIX, X, and Motif. Wind/U is used to convert the 16-bit Windows API calls to X and Motif calls. Wind/U supports Win16, Win32, and MFC. Other Windows features supported by Wind/U include Dynamic Data Exchange (DDE) and DLLs. DLLs may be loaded at runtime, as is normal for Windows. Bristol's Xprinter is part of the Wind/U package, and controls PCL5 and Postscript printers from an X display.

Wind/U is not a complete development environment, however. You will need both a development system on your UNIX system and a Windows SDK; but porting is simpler and faster than attempting to re-create the entire application from the beginning in UNIX. HyperHelp, a separate application bundled with Wind/U, ports Windows help files directly to UNIX by converting Windows RTF files created for use with the Windows Help compiler.

Wind/U supports the following UNIX flavors:

- SunOS
- Solaris (Sun and x86)
- IBM AIX
- HP-UX

- Silicon Graphics IRIX
- DEC OSF/1
- Santa Cruz Organization ODT
- UnixWare x86

MainWin

Mainsoft's MainWin is another Windows-to-UNIX conversion tool that takes a slightly different approach from Bristol's Wind/U. Where Bristol inserts the Wind/U layer of library code on top of Motif as a filter, MainWin replaces the X-Windows layer entirely with a port of the Windows API to UNIX platforms. While some may criticize that this loses the benefits of the Motif X toolkit, MainSoft takes the position that bypassing any X toolkit gives independence from version changes of that X toolkit. MainSoft estimates the initial port of a Windows application requires about .1% of the source code to be modified for portability to a 32-bit RISC architecture, comparing the amount of work required to the amount of work you would need to port your application to Windows NT. To aid the cross-platform porting, MainSoft includes a source processor tool that prepares PC source files for UNIX.

Two specific portions of the ported Windows API that deserve mention are the Windows Help Engine and the MFC class library. The Help Engine is a complete port that runs any standard Windows .HLP help file. MainWin was used to port the MainWin help engine from the original Microsoft source code to UNIX. The MFC 3.0 class library conversion to UNIX does not include support for ODBC, WinSock, and OLE.

MainSoft supports Windows 3.1 and NT in 16-bit and 32-bit versions for development, and supports the following platforms as destinations: SunOS and Solaris on SPARC processors, and HP-UX, IBM AIX, Silicon Graphics IRIX, and OSF/1 on the DEC Alpha processor.

Multiplatform Applications

To port your application to another platform, rewriting or recompiling your application may not always be the best answer. Two different companies have taken roughly the same approach to helping the developer support

VI

Multiplatforms

multiple platforms by providing one environment which supports many platforms' user interfaces for the client side of the application. Choosing either Neuron Data's Client/Server Elements or Visix's Galaxy Application Environment can eliminate some of the "fear of the abyss" in client/server programming. You have only one company to call which has already solved the multi-platform connection problem, and you are left free to concentrate on solid application design. The down side is that you are then tied to a single company's survival. In order to improve overall flexibility, both of these products have multiple open industry standards such as ODBC included.

Client/Server Elements

Neuron Data's C/S Elements is a development environment intended for developing one application with a wide variety of available GUI front-ends to run simultaneously on several platforms. Originally known as an expert systems software supplier, Neuron Data presently focuses on providing Elements Environment, an object-oriented environment for client/server cross-platform application development.

C/S Elements is one of the four major portions of Elements Environment, and has three main components—Open Interface Elements, Data Access Elements, and Script. Open Interface Elements is a GUI-based C/C++ code generator with a broad cross-platform support. Neuron Data addresses the problem of online help in a cross-platform environment by including a hypertext help engine. Data Access Elements provides support for using Informix, Oracle, Sybase, Ingres, ANSI SQL, Neuron Data's own NXPDB, and ODBC-compliant DBMSes.

C/S Elements may be used for development on the following platforms: Macintosh OS, DOS/Windows/Windows NT, OS/2's Presentation Manager, Open Look, and OSF/Motif. Once an application is developed, it may be run on any one, or several, of approximately 35 platforms.

Galaxy Application Environment

Visix Galaxy is another object-oriented multi-platform development environment. Like Neuron Data, the Galaxy Application Environment is a C or C++ API with a rich variety of target platforms. Many multi-platform development environments choose to implement a "lowest common denominator" approach. Galaxy's design philosophy seems to be "if it's not there, add it." If Galaxy has a fault, it could be that its richness of detail creates a fairly steep learning curve for its users.

The Visual Resource Builder, abbreviated as *Vre* after its original name of Visual Resource Editor, is the center of Galaxy. One interesting characteristic of Vre's GUI development is Galaxy's concept of "springs" and "struts" for controlling the resizing behavior of objects in the display. (Struts are created by selecting two points.) For example, a text display may have a strut drawn between its left and right edges to ensure that the display will always be drawn no narrower than the length of the strut. You may define the strut as a fixed dimension, where the text field will always be the specified size, or as a minimum dimension, where it may be stretched wider than the strut's length, but never less.

A spring is another relationship between two points of an object that defines the maximum value that object is permitted to grow along that value. Maximum and minimum values of object display size may not sound thrilling to read about, but it is impressive to define such characteristics without having to enter numeric values for the distance in pixels, inches, or centimeters between two points.

Although the Visual Resource Builder is not as simple to customize as Borland Delphi's Palette, Vre was built with the same tools (the Galaxy APIs) it provides for your use. Therefore, Vre may be used to customize itself as extensively as your development style would wish. An add-on Visual Builder Integration Kit makes it possible to edit the Visual Resource Builder and incorporate the new panels directly into Vre. Both custom-built items and third-party extensions may be added to the Vre Palette. One example of an available extension is Widget Workshop's port of the KL Group's business graphics package XRT/Graph. Widget Workshop has converted XRT/Graph from the Motif X-Windows toolkit to the Galaxy Applications Environment as a native visual gadget for business-oriented graphical display.

Galaxy's Distributed Application Services addition extends the Galaxy Application Environment to client/server usage. The DAS managers use an asynchronous peer-to-peer protocol for communication between applications. For database access, Galaxy is SQL-standard compliant. For further connection options, PostModern Computing's ORBeline has been integrated with the Galaxy Application environment, giving full CORBA connectivity to any application built with Galaxy.

VI

Multiplatforms

Like Neuron Data's Elements Environment, Galaxy solves the issue of efficient development on online help for a multi-platform application by including its own hypertext engine. The Help Server has the use of all Galaxy presentation features—including multiple fonts, text sizes, text styles, and the addition of embedded images—and supports a single help document for use on different platforms by linking to the current display platform. Instead of having to create four help documents for four separate platforms, you can construct one help server and link four screenshots to one image location in the document. When the help is opened on a given document, the illustration specific to that platform will appear. Galaxy applications may be compiled to run on several versions of UNIX (SunOS, Solaris, HP/UX), DEC Ultrix, Silicon Graphics (IRIX), Windows, Windows NT, VAX/VMS, OS/2, and Macintosh System 7.

From Here...

All of these toolkits, 4GLs, development environments, and compilers are designed to ease various programming tasks. While one of these tools—or one of the many other tools not mentioned here—may make the task of applications development for a client/server paradigm easier, caution is in order. None of these products are likely to be a "magic bullet" that is the one solution to your problems. However, you just might be at exactly the point in your work where one of these products will leap your work forward.

For more information on the topics discussed in this chapter, refer to the following:

- Chapter 3, "Communication Protocols," teaches you about TCP, UDP, and other lower-level network protocols.

- Chapter 12, "RPC Under UNIX," provides much greater platform-specific detail on how all levels of RPC work in a UNIX environment.

- Chapter 19, "Using Open Database Connectivity (ODBC)," focuses on ODBC and how it relates to Visual C++ and Visual Basic.

- Chapter 23, "Multiplatform Applications," gives an expanded view of using different platforms to create a client/server system.

Chapter 25

Messaging and Middleware

Middleware is the hottest industry buzzword, and the most misunderstood. The word encompasses many technologies that are fundamental for distributed client/server computing. It is important to understand the different technologies because they provide a transparent, high-level method for implementing client/server computing. Each technology also has a specific role to play in completing the client/server picture.

> **Note**
>
> Middleware is commonly defined as the "network-aware" system software that resides between an application, the operating system, and network transport layers. The purpose of this software is to facilitate distributed cooperative processing. Examples of middleware include message passing mechanisms, distributed TP monitors, directory services, object request brokers, remote procedure call (RPC) services, and database gateways.

Middleware, by definition, sits in the "middle" between client and server. It hides the complexity of the network and allows developers to concentrate on the application logic. This architecture frees programmers from having to worry about coding to the network protocol, allowing them to concentrate on the application logic. This architecture also ensures that if the underlying network changes, the application continues to operate normally.

Message-oriented middleware (MOM) is one area of middleware that is gaining industry attention. MOM has some unique characteristics that distinguish it from other types of middleware. It provides a peer-to-peer distributed computing model that is important in some application environments.

This chapter presents a brief overview of the evolving middleware market and subset of that market called message-oriented middleware. This chapter provides the following background information for an understanding of middleware and message-oriented middleware:

- Discussion of the role of middleware in client/server computing

- Description of different types of middleware

- Discussion of the role of standards in the middleware market

- Overview of message-oriented middleware

- Explanation of key differences between message-oriented middleware and remote procedure calls (RPCs)

The Role of Middleware

Middleware technology integrates the "islands of automation" that were common in the 1980s. At that time, different departments solved their own business problems by purchasing their own computers, operating systems, and software from different vendors. Even companies that mandated staying with one vendor began to see a need to connect their computers to their vendors, suppliers, and even their customers. Alliances, joint-ventures, and mergers and acquisitions have made it crucial to bridge information gaps.

Now, because instant access to information is key for helping corporations respond to changes in market conditions, the need for middleware has risen. Middleware is addressing the need to provide connectivity and interoperability between diverse, multi-platform systems that include everything from the desktop to workgroup and departmental servers and even mainframes.

What is Middleware?

In the days before open systems and client/server computing, life was simple. The mainframe was the heart of computing. From a terminal, you could access all the information that was stored on that system. There was no distributed computing.

Today, however, we own more personal computers and workstations than cars or VCRs. Have you ever wondered how all these different computers are going to be able to communicate? The majority of these personal computers and workstations do not live in isolation anymore. Communication is the central theme of today's information technology (IT) industry. Today, the network is the heart of the computing environment and distributed computing is a de facto standard.

To end users, the system is what they see through the graphical user interfaces on their monitors. Having access to the enterprise needs to be transparent, as depicted in figure 25.1. Users want to be able to get to any information located on any system through a simple user interface. This graphical user interface should also allow users to share data on the network. This ideal—to allow clients to communicate, share data, and interoperate with clients, servers, and mainframes—is the basis for middleware.

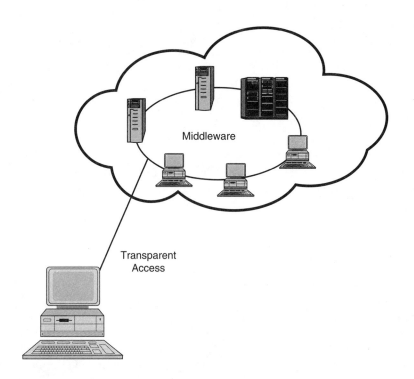

Fig. 25.1
This is how a typical end user views the world. The system on the desktop is a window into the corporate environment.

To programmers, middleware is an insulator that isolates them from the complexities of diverse, heterogeneous network protocols. Programmers need software in the "middle" between different clients and servers to raise the level of abstraction for all the different operating systems, network protocols, and hardware platforms found in multi-platform client/server development. Now application programmers don't have to worry about programming to a specific network protocol. Middleware takes care of the details associated with making the physical and logical connection to the server that contains the data source. Middleware takes much of the technical complexity and system dependencies out of the application program. It is the basis for peer-to-peer and client/server computing. In short, middleware can be thought of as the glue that ties it all together.

Types of Middleware

Middleware has been around for a long time and covers a wide variety of areas. In fact, many of the subjects discussed in this book so far, such as remote procedure calls (RPCs) and messaging, are classified as middleware. Even UNIX socket commands can legitimately be called middleware. Middleware is a catch-all phrase that refers to any high-level service that helps the client access remote resources on a server.

When you examine middleware solutions, you need to look at the total solution. It is helpful to begin with a pilot project that is in line with your long-term business requirements. A pilot project is a small initial application that is strategic to your company, but not so complex that it discourages future development. The pilot will generate requirements for a middleware product. Based on the requirements of your pilot project, you can determine whether your company simply needs data access or more elaborate server processing capabilities such as RPCs and message-oriented middleware. In addition, if your company plans to move into an object-oriented paradigm, then object interactions through object request brokers will be important; and, you need to consider whether your initial middleware selection will work in an object-oriented model.

Middleware is more than just a connection—it is a complete distributed environment. Although this chapter concentrates on application-to-application communication methods, remember that middleware solutions have various other components, such as the following:

- *Directory and Naming Service*—In a distributed client/server environment, the state of systems is often in flux. Systems come in and out of the environment all the time. There must be a way to let other clients know who you are (*name services*) and where you are located (*directory services*). The naming service is analogous to your area code, telling you what area you belong to; and, the directory service is like your phone book, telling you everybody's name, address, and phone number in that area.

- Ideally, these services should be a *single-system image*. A single-system image means that you can have a common view of your enterprise and all its services from the desktop as if it were local. There are several standards evolving in this area. For naming services, federated namespace is gaining support quickly. In the area of global directory services, the standard is International Telephone Union-Telecommunications Standardization's X.500 (ITU-TS, formerly known as CCITT), which is also an ISO/IEC 9594 standard and Domain Naming Service (DNS).

> **Note**
>
> A single-system image is defined as an operational view of multiple physical central processing units, multiple networks, or distributed databases that appear as one system.

- *Security*—In the mainframe days, security was straightforward. You only had one machine that you needed to secure. In a distributed client/server environment, the issue becomes complex. Security in middleware needs to control access to resources and protect those resources from inappropriate use. Once again, to maintain a single-system image (single-system logon), the middleware must transparently provide access to all resources, no matter what machine or operating system on which that information resides. Currently, no vendor provides a complete solution for single-system logon. Some of the most popular commercial security solutions are Netware's NDS, OSF's Kerberos, and Sun's NIS+. For more information on security, refer to Chapter 14, "DCE Security."

- *Distributed Management Tools*—In a large, distributed client/server environment, you need to worry about how to manage, monitor, and control that environment. Some important features of distributed system and network management are dynamic load and resource balancing, monitoring of the network, backup/restore of files and directories, printing services, remote software installation, software distribution, and user management. Distributed management tools are still evolving in the middleware market. Today, nobody provides a complete solution to this problem. Some examples of distributed management tools are Microsoft's System Management Server and Open Software Foundation's Distributed Management Environment.

- Two standard management protocols are being defined for distributed management tools: the Internet's Simple Network Management Protocol (SNMP) and OSI's Common Management Information Protocols (CMIP). In addition, many standards are evolving to isolate applications

VI

Multiplatforms

from the underlying management protocols (i.e., SNMP or CMIP) and raise the level of abstraction to a higher level. X/Open has defined two application programming interfaces (API) sets: Management Protocol (XMP) and Object Management (XOM).

> **Note**
>
> Simple Network Management Protocol (SNMP) is a TCP/IP derived protocol governing network management and monitoring devices. The standard is evolving to SNMP2, which provides enhancements including security and a remote monitoring functionality.
>
> Common Management Information Protocol (CMIP) is a protocol formally adopted by the International Standards Organization (ISO). CMIP is used for exchanging network management information. Typically, information is exchanged between two management stations, but it can also be used to exchange information between an application and a management station.
>
> X/Open's Management Protocol (XMP) is an API used for process-to-process communication between a managing system and a managed system. The XMP interface shields developers from the details of the underlying SNMP or CMIP protocols.
>
> X/Open's Object Management (XOM) is used to manage the data structure associated with managing an object. XOM is an abstract data manipulation API. XOM is generic enough to be used outside the network and system management arena.

In application-to-application communication, there are different methods of integrating clients and servers, from *remote data access* (*RDA*) to *distributed on-line transaction processing* (*DOLTP*). These methods even include remote procedure calls (RPCs), message-oriented middleware (MOM), and *object request brokers* (*ORBs*).

Middleware begins with the *application programming interface* (*API*) on the client that invokes a service. The location of the service on a server is transparent to the client. The client views the network from a common view or a single-system image. The request goes out on the network and possibly returns a result to the client.

> **Note**
>
> An application programming interface (API) is a set of calling conventions used by an application program to communicate with another program that provides services for it. These services are usually low-level.

Imagine ordering a hamburger in a fast-food restaurant. You order a hamburger (request for some service to be done) and the attendant hands you a hamburger (service is provided and the request is accomplished). You did not have to know that the attendant needed to first grill the hamburger on a grill located in the back of the restaurant, then toast the bun in a toaster in a completely different area, nor do you care. To you, it is a single-system image of requesting a hamburger and having it handed to you.

Trends in Middleware

The middleware market is expanding, with predictions for a high rate of growth and increased competition. Middleware is also evolving to solve more complex, enterprise-wide applications. There are different middleware technologies designed to meet various business requirements. As you move into a heterogeneous environment with mixed protocols, operating systems, and hardware, the importance of standards grows.

The Role of Standards and Consortia in Evolving Middleware

Standards have played a large role in evolving technology, as well as in users' awareness of the technology. When you look at standards, you need to look at all standards, including the de facto standards, de jure standards, standards bodies, and consortia. Remember, standards are really a point of reference and not necessarily a complete solution. You must still look at the problem you are trying to solve and decide how standards play a role in helping you solve them.

De Facto Standards

The deliberations of standards groups are so lengthy, and the progress is often so slow, that standards sometimes are born out of technology providers. We call these *de facto standards*. De facto standards are in wide use, and other technology providers implicitly recognize them as the standards to design, develop, and copy. In the PC world, Microsoft, which supplies the MS-DOS operating system, controls the de facto standard for operating systems.

De Jure Standards

De jure standards come out of a recognized standards development organization such as the International Organization for Standardization (ISO) or American National Standards Institute (ANSI). These standards are developed by an open committee and approved through the consensus of its members.

VI

Multiplatforms

Oftentimes, because they are created through an open process, these standards take a long time to evolve. For example, it took the FORTRAN computer language 10 years to evolve into an ANSI standard.

Standards Organizations and Consortia
Standards organizations are accredited organizations that develop formal, or de jure, standards through an open process. These standards are published standards and interfaces, encouraging other hardware and software vendors to develop similar technology.

A *consortium* is an association of companies, vendors, or users who are working together toward a common vision. Consortia do not develop standards, but they develop specifications that frequently become part of the standards process. Some examples of consortia are the Open Software Foundation (OSF), Message Oriented Middleware Association (MOMA), Object Management Group (OMG), and X/Open.

Client/server computing and open systems have created a large market for middleware. The market currently has many players who frequently do not provide complete solutions. Standards are necessary because they allow for modular solutions that can play together. Middleware has many standards that are still evolving. The following section analyzes several important standards.

Middleware Directions in the 1990s
The architecture of middleware is evolving rapidly from remote data access to more sophisticated application-to-application communication models such as message queuing. Remote procedure calls (RPCs) have been popular for client/server computing for the past several years, and have also had a long history of success in large-scale client/server development projects. They do, however, have some limitations that messaging can solve.

Messaging has been gaining popularity because it brings inherent decoupling and asynchronous capabilities to play in enterprise-wide client/server applications. Messaging, too, has some limitations, especially when it comes to transaction processing. Although some messaging products provide a limited form of transaction processing, they often cannot take the place of distributed online transaction processing products. Client/server applications that require high-transaction volumes necessitate distributed online transaction processing middleware. The main point to consider when deciding what application-to-application communication model to use is what business problem you are trying to solve.

Selecting a real-world application can be a useful method for evaluating middleware technologies. Select an application that is as close as possible to the problems your corporation is trying to solve daily. The next step is to determine where you would like to evolve your application in the next couple years. This largely determines what requirements you have for middleware technology. It may be that you require a mixture of many of the application-to-application communication models described in the following sections, as each has its place in multi-platform client/server development.

Remote Data Access (RDA)

Users originally wanted only to access data located on a server. These were highly data-intensive client/server applications. A client would make a single request of an SQL command to a remote relational database management system, and the server would return the data. These applications were often called *fat clients*, because the application and processing logic resided on the client, and the server was merely a database server (see fig. 25.2). Early adopters of client/server computing used this methodology for distributed database and remote data access.

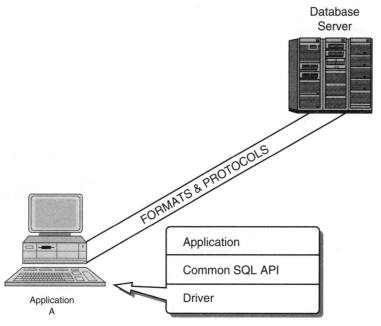

Database Server

FORMATS & PROTOCOLS

Application

| Application |
| Common SQL API |
| Driver |

Application A

Fig. 25.2
The middleware architecture for distributing data across multiple heterogeneous platforms usually provides Structured Query Language (SQL) access to different databases.

This approach sounds great until you realize that not all SQLs are created equal. Because no recognized standard exists, a market for database middleware products has appeared. The goal of these products is to smooth out the differences between different SQL dialects and extensions. The problems that these database middleware products are trying to solve include developing a common SQL interface, developing common formats and protocols (FAPs), and creating a single database administration interface.

Standards in this area are lagging behind technology. The de jure standards in this area are Microsoft's Open DataBase Connectivity (ODBC), IBM's Distributed Relational Database Architecture (DRDA), and the two variants of RDA developed by the International Organization for Standardization (ISO) and the X/Open consortium.

Users of client/server computing have not been satisfied by simply asking database systems to send them information. Rather, they have been looking for a more distributed logical model of computing. This created an opportunity for remote procedure calls.

Remote Procedure Calls (RPCs)

Remote procedure calls have been discussed in other parts of this book. Basically, an RPC is a synchronous form of middleware. A client makes a request, just like an ordinary procedure call, and the system is blocked until an action is received from the server (see fig. 25.3). RPCs were used often in the UNIX environment to link C programs on different UNIX platforms. It has evolved since then through the Open Software Foundation (OSF) and its Distributed Computing Environment (DCE).

Fig. 25.3
Remote procedure calls extend the notion of local (contained in a single address space) procedure calls to a distributed computing environment.

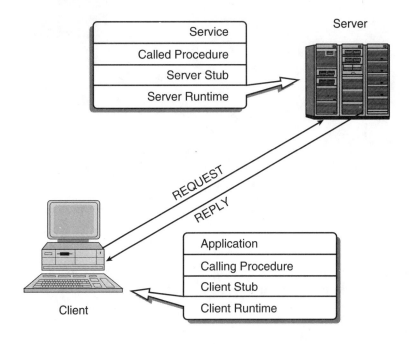

In this model, logic is slowly becoming more distributed between the client and the server. The only drawback is that the client is blocked from processing the program until the server returns a response. For certain applications, users wanted a more asynchronous approach to distributed computing. This drawback set the stage for message-oriented middleware (MOM).

Message-Oriented Middleware (MOM)

Messaging's popularity in the middleware market has surged only recently. This has a lot to do with its asynchronous capabilities. There are two distinct types of messaging paradigms—*message queuing* and *message transport*. While message queuing principles have been around for many years as part of operating system technology (for example, in IBM's Information Management System (IMS)), distributed queuing emerged as a form of middleware much more recently. (IMS applications run in what are called message-processing regions, each in its own address space. IMS also has a queuing mechanism to store messages.) Messaging technology meets a wide variety of application functionality, from e-mail to high-performance online transaction processing.

A message is a collection of data sent by a client program intended for a server program. Messages are stored in queues so the client doesn't need to wait for the server to process the information (see fig. 25.4). This is often referred to as *non-blocking*.

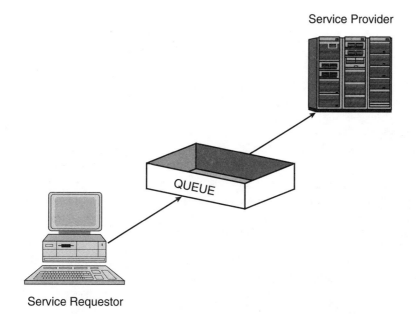

Service Provider

Service Requestor

Fig. 25.4
The message queueing architecture allows asynchronous message exchange between applications. An application can send a message to another application and have it received by a software queue if the receiving application is not able to accept it.

VI

Multiplatforms

Many industry analysts believe that this method of application-to-application communication will receive a boost when the X/Open XTP group releases their specification for transactional queuing and messaging interfaces. In addition, the MOMA group is trying to develop a standard API that will make messaging products portable across different implementations. In other words, the API would enable users to exchange one messaging middleware product for another without changing application software. If the MOMA group acts quickly, this could have significant ramifications in the middleware market. At this time, however, no messaging standard exists.

In the message handling category, standards abound, such as Vendor Independent Messaging (VIM) from Lotus Development Corporation, Messaging API (MAPI) from Microsoft, and Common Messaging Call (CMC) from the X.400 API Association (XAPIA). In the mail API category, standards include the Open Collaborative Environment (OCE) from Apple Computer, Inc. and Federated Naming from Common Software Environment (COSE).

Object Request Brokers (ORBs)

Object request brokers (*ORBs*) are the new kid on the middleware block. ORBs are based on either RPCs, messaging, or a combination of both. ORBs enable objects to communicate across the network. ORBs are not a transport mechanism, but rather an object service. This means that object request brokers support standard communication transports, such as RPCs, TCP/IP, sockets, or message technology, as the network transport mechanism. ORBs provide the means by which clients make and receive requests and responses. In other words, ORBs allow clients to invoke methods that reside on remote servers, as shown in figure 25.5. The objects are depicted in the diagram as circles that encompass a real-world entity. That entity encapsulates states and operations and responds to requester services.

Object Management Group in Framingham, Massachusetts has defined the de jure standard for ORBs, called the *Common Object Request Broker Architecture* (*CORBA*). The CORBA specification includes Interface Definition Language (IDL) and Distributed Services. The client object issues its service request through an IDL to the object request broker. The ORB can translate the request to another object, which can then provide the service. The service provider can then send a message back through an IDL to the object and request broker and to the original client (see fig. 25.5).

The popularity of ORBs will be directly related to how fast object technology takes off. Microsoft is doing an excellent job of pushing Object Linking and Embedding (OLE) and Component Object Model (COM). OLE/COM is quickly becoming the de facto standard for ORBs.

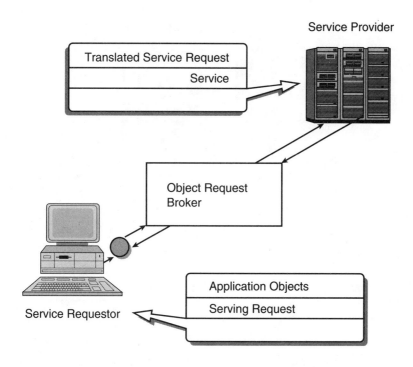

Service Provider

Translated Service Request

Service

Object Request Broker

Application Objects

Serving Request

Service Requestor

Fig. 25.5
The Object Request Broker middleware architecture allows objects to transparently make requests to and receive responses from other objects located through-out the enterprise. The objects can be local or remote.

Distributed Online Transaction Processing (DOLTP)

Distributed online transactional processing middleware allows clients to invoke services across multiple transactional services, as shown in figure 25.6. The distributed transaction processing model consists of transactional RPCs. DOLTP includes TP monitors that ensure transactions remain in a consistent state across multiple transactional services. DOLTP is typically used to employ two-phase commits. In a two-phase commit, the system first prepares to commit by seeking confirmation from the target databases that it can complete the transaction. In the second stage, if the system is able to make this transaction, it completes the commit. That is, it actually does the updating.

As in all middleware, DOLTP needs standards to ensure compatibility between different platforms, databases, and resource managers. The standards for TP monitors are as follows:

- International Standard Organization (ISO) with its OSI-CCR, which defines message protocols.

- OSI-TP, which defines two-phase commit protocols.

- X/Open with its Distributed Transaction Processing specification, which defines APIs for transaction processing.

Tip
According to many industry analysts, interest in DOLTP in the middleware market will surge in the late 1990s, as users realize that they still need transactions to run their businesses.

VI

Multiplatforms

Fig. 25.6
A two-phase
commit is used
to ensure that
a transaction
successfully
updates all
appropriate files
in a distributed
database environ-
ment.

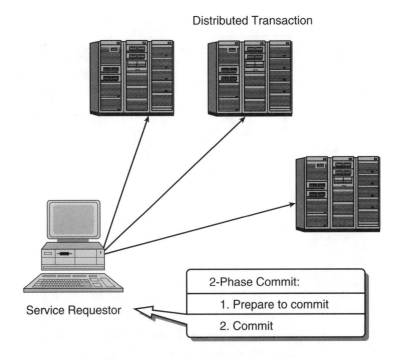

Distributed Transaction

Service Requestor

2-Phase Commit:

1. Prepare to commit

2. Commit

The Role of Messaging and Message Queuing Services

Message-oriented middleware (MOM) is a subset of overall middleware technology that is important for a specific class of client/server applications. Interest in message-oriented middleware is rapidly accelerating. MOM is often
characterized as *message queuing services*, which use an intermediate collection
point called queues. The queue model has advantages in that the client and
server do not need to be active at the same time. Message queuing services are
gaining acceptance in the middleware market because of an increased demand for mobile communications.

What are MOM and Message Queuing Services?

Messaging is a basic communication paradigm designed to ease communications in a distributed environment. It deals specifically with the many ways
in which a message can be passed between applications, such as process-to-

process communications. There are two types of messaging middleware. One type is *process-to-process communication*, such as PeerLogic's Pipes. This type of messaging middleware requires that both the client and server process be active at the same time to pass information. The other type of middleware is *message queuing*, such as IBM's MQseries or Digital's MessageQ. Queuing does not require the client process and the server process to be active at the same time. Although it has been used for a long time with file servers to collect data access requests, queuing technology is now moving into the distributed client/server domain. Message-oriented middleware has proven to be reliable for high-volume processing of large applications in a distributed environment.

Message queuing middleware is good for client/server applications where responses can be time-independent, and for applications where outgoing transactions can be queued and later uploaded to a server when a connection is established, as is the case in mobile communications. In other words, the application can communicate across the network without having a dedicated, logical connection to the other application.

Architectural Overview of MOM and Message Queuing Services

Message queuing provides a time-independent means of communicating in a distributed environment. Program A requests can be dropped off in a mailbox or in a queue. Program A can continue working or processing the program that does not rely on Program B's response. Program A does not wait for completion of the request, but intends to accept results later. These are independent events rather than concurrent ones. When Program B is available, it can take the information out of the mailbox or queue and process it. When Program B finishes, the thread is completed.

Programs communicate by putting messages on message queues, and by taking messages from message queues. A program becomes aware of a message in its queue by continuously polling its queue to see if there are any messages, or by callback mechanisms that notify the sending program that the message has been received or processed (see fig. 25.7).

The communication channels between Program A and Program B can be two-way, as shown in figure 25.8. Program A can send a message to Program B and Program B can send a message back to Program A.

VI

Multiplatforms

Fig. 25.7
The message queuing architecture is versatile. The architecture can be tailored to your environment. In this example, the message queuing middleware architecture allows the client to send requests to one server queue.

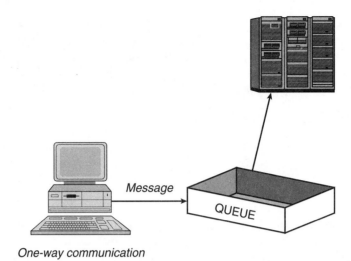

One-way communication

Fig. 25.8
The message queuing architecture can have two-way message queuing. Program A can make a request, and that request is placed in Program B's queue. When Program B completes its request, it places the response in Program A's queue.

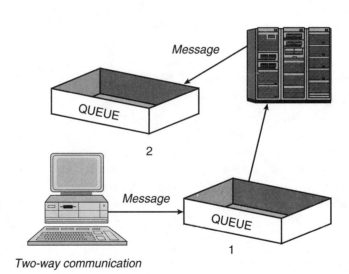

Two-way communication

Another approach would be for Program A to send a message to Program B, which triggers a response or a reply back to Program A (see fig. 25.9). A trigger is a mechanism that initiates an action when an event occurs (for example, receiving a message on a queue). Triggers are usually message-based communications that bypass the queue. Triggers can also cause a program routine to be executed in response to an occurrence of an error or some other event.

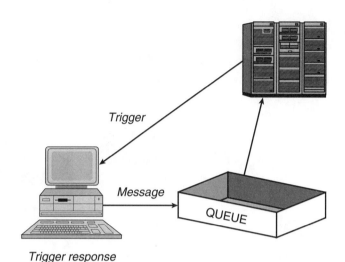

Fig. 25.9
The message
queueing architec-
ture can be set up
to receive a
response using an
automatic reply
back when
requests are made
to a queue.

The interesting thing about queues is that message queues are independent of the programs that use them. These programs and queues can be on the same processor in a single environment, on different processors in different environments, or any combination in between.

Message queues can either be persistent, non-persistent, or transactional. Persistent simply means that the queues are stored on disk, so messages are saved if the system goes down, the program aborts, or communication fails. This provides guaranteed message delivery. Non-persistent means that the queues are stored in memory, and can thus be lost if the system goes down. Non-persistent queues are created from the local operating system's virtual memory, and achieve better performance than the persistent queues. Transactional message queues function like transactional processing databases, in which the message queue can have commits and rollbacks.

Queues are managed by queue managers, which are system programs that provide queuing services to application programs. The system administrator can customize the message queuing middleware environment by determining whether a queue is local or remote, how many messages the queue can contain, and the maximum size of messages.

Some message queuing products go beyond the simple, one-to-one communications paradigms described previously. Other products have a one-to-many or many-to-one communications paradigm.

The one-to-many paradigm is often used for load balancing. Program A places a message in a queue and the three servers can run one program

VI

Multiplatforms

concurrently. This paradigm splits up the work among the three servers, as shown in figure 25.10. The program can fork multiple processes for execution on different platforms that are more likely to accommodate the request. Once the request is completed, the queue assembles the program to return it to the client.

Fig. 25.10

The message queuing architecture can have a one-to-many relationship between a client and multiple servers.

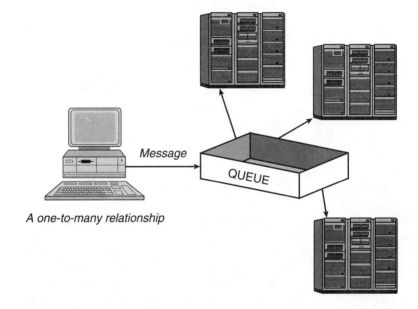

A one-to-many relationship

Some message queuing products provide a store-and-forward capability that allows Program A to send a request to Program B. If Program B determines that it cannot fulfill the request, then it forwards it to Program C. If Program C determines that it can fulfill the request, it processes the request. When Program C completes processing, it forwards the request directly back to Program A. This functionality can be very helpful in wide-area networks, where servers are not always available.

Returning to the restaurant analogy, say that it is finally your turn to order. You decide that you want a hamburger, fries, and a shake. The order is entered into a cash register (like a queue) and the three attendants behind the counter each go off to get your part of your order. One gets you a shake, another your fries, and the last attendant brings you a hamburger. They all bring your order back to the register and place it in a bag, completing your order. The three attendants each relied on taking the order (the message) from the cash register (the queue).

The many-to-one paradigm is often used in workgroup situations where multiple clients communicate with a single server (see fig. 25.11). The clients all place their messages in a queue. The server then takes messages off the queue on a first-in/first-out (FIFO) priority basis, or a load balancing scheme.

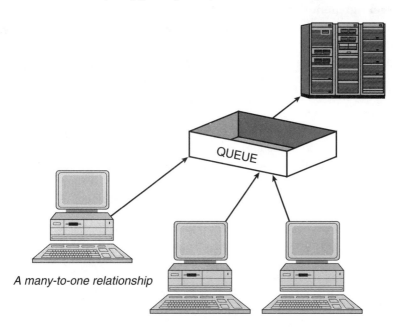

A many-to-one relationship

Fig. 25.11
The message
queuing architec-
ture allows a
many-to-one
relationship
between clients
and a server.

Say that when you come into the fast food restaurant, you must take a number. You wait in this queue until your number is called. Similarly, under workgroup situations the message sits in a queue while it waits for its turn, usually in a first-in/first-out basis. If the owners of the restaurant came in, they might jump to the front of the queue based on their high priority. Message queuing systems allow you to place a higher priority on certain messages that come from specific clients.

Remember that any one of these paradigms (one-to-one, one-to-many, many-to-one, or even many-to-many) could be on a single processor or distributed on several machines located in geographically different locations, or even in different time zones.

The Benefits of Message Queuing Systems

Message-oriented middleware provides a simple paradigm for platform-independent application-to-application communication. Messaging primitives—such as open, close, send, and receive—are simple to understand

VI

Multiplatforms

and can be used to develop distributed applications across heterogeneous protocols. There are many advantages to using a message-based middleware for developing distributed applications.

System Independence

When a client program executes and wants to communicate to a server program, whether it is within the same system or remote, the client program places a message in a message queue. The server program picks up the message immediately or hours later, and processes the information. Because messaging queuing systems use an intermediate stop at the queue before the server processes information from the client, it is classified as *indirect program-to-program communications*, meaning that the two systems are independent of one another and do not require each other for transmitting information. There is no physical connection between programs that communicate between queues. Therefore, one application can send a message to another application even when the intended receiver is not available.

Messages are transported throughout the network, as with e-mail, on a store-and-forward basis. In other words, if there are two systems (System A and System B) on the network and the link to System B is down, System A continues to collect messages in a message queue until the link to System B is restored. When it is restored, System A forwards to System B all the messages that System B should have received.

Time Independence

Message queuing uses the asynchronous communications model. Client programs can send a message to server programs and continue processing. When the server process is done, it can send a reply to the client program. The client program can either deal with it then or later. Client programs are not burdened with waiting for a response from the server program.

> **Note**
>
> Some message-oriented middleware also allows for synchronous communications. For example, PeerLogic's Pipes allows a message to wait for a server to respond so that tasks are completed synchronously.

When making a request using typical RPCs, the client makes a request of the server. The client program then must wait until the request is completed by the server before it can continue to process. The client cannot do further processing from the time it makes a request until the server sends a response. This is called *blocking*. Message queuing avoids tying up the system, because the client can simply continue processing until the server returns a reply.

Program Modularity

Message queuing allows program developers to design small, modular, self-contained programs that can be processed independently. Instead of a large program that must be processed sequentially, they can design several independent modules. The requesting program can send a message to each independent program, requesting that it perform its function. When each program finishes, the results can be sent back as one message. This modularity scheme allows for program reuse.

Guaranteed Message Delivery

Guaranteed message delivery ensures that a message arrives at its destination. With the use of store-and-forward and message queues that are stored on disk, messages remain in the queue until they are processed, even if the system or links go down. In other words, message queues provide a form of recoverability. This is similar to using an answering machine when calling someone. If there is a power failure, the message remains on tape and can be retrieved.

Guaranteed message delivery is not fault-tolerant. Fault-tolerant applications identify the failure and correct the action without interrupting the application. It is transparent to the user that a failure has occurred. Fault-tolerant applications are often expensive because they require complete redundancy of system resources. In guaranteed message delivery, there are still many possible scenarios for failure. For example, the middleware could fail before passing the message to the queue. In addition, guaranteed message delivery extracts a performance penalty, because it takes time to realize that a queue has failed.

> **Note**
>
> Some message-oriented middleware products bundle other capabilities, such as transaction control, deferred delivery, acknowledgment, safe storage of message, and ACID (Atomicity, Consistency, Isolation, and Durability) transaction properties. At a minimum, most MOM products provide platform-independent transports for heterogeneous communications.

VI

Multiplatforms

Evolving Standards in Messaging

Message queuing standards are still in their infancy. The goals behind these standards are to enhance interoperability and functionality for multi-platform client/server development. There are many organizations looking at message queuing issues.

International Organization for Standardization (ISO)

The International Organization for Standardization (ISO) is a worldwide federation of standards bodies. The ISO standard committee for Open Systems Interconnection (OSI), transaction processing (TP), and message queuing (MQ) is working on specifications for message queuing. This functional specification is looking at the MQ model, service definition, and protocol specification. ISO is currently not addressing application programming interfaces (API). ISO's specification is currently in draft.

X/Open

X/Open is an international consortium with a mission to develop specifications based on user requirements and industry de facto standards. X/Open has been active in developing a specification for transactional queuing and messaging interfaces. In the message queuing area, many vendors have submitted their technology alone or as joint submissions with other vendors to X/Open for consideration in the Common Application Environment (CAE).

MOMA

MOMA is a consortium formed in 1993 to establish specifications to enhance the interoperability and functionality of messaging and message queuing technologies. MOMA's other objective is to educate the market on the benefits of message-oriented middleware. The MOMA organization was established by product providers such as IBM, Covia, Digital Equipment Corporation, Horizon Strategies, and PeerLogic.

MOMA could have a significant impact on the message queuing middleware market if they act quickly. Message-oriented middleware is just beginning to gain momentum. Users will soon realize the need to establish standards for enhancing the interoperability and functionality of message-oriented middleware for distributed environments. MOMA could play a key role in driving these specifications. They could also have a major impact on middleware technology if they continue to have discussions with other middleware consortia such as Open Software Foundation and Object Management Group, and if these groups came to a mutual consensus on the interoperability of middleware. Unfortunately, MOMA is so new that only time will tell if they have the momentum to make the changes needed in the middleware market.

Differences Between Messaging and Remote Procedure Calls (RPCs)

RPCs and messaging are two approaches to developing distributed applications, but they are uniquely different. You can visualize the difference between messaging and RPCs by thinking about a fax machine and a phone. With the fax machine, you can receive faxes without interruptions. The fax is placed on a queue. When you have the time, you can retrieve faxes from the machine and prioritize your work. You control your work flow. Once you complete your work, you can fax it back to the sender. This is similar to a message queuing architecture, with faxes queued up on the fax machine.

Using the phone (without an answering machine attached), you can immediately conduct your business and receive an instant response from the other party. When the phone rings, you pick it up and begin to talk (a request is made). When the phone conversation ends, you have completed a unit of work. This is similar to a remote procedure call, in which the client requests information from the server. When the server completes the request, a unit of work is completed.

On the other hand, the phone can be obnoxious when it continually interrupts you. With a fax machine, you have the option of staging your work. Also, it is nice to be able to receive a fax without having to be there. While both of these technologies have a major role to play in business, it is important to know which tool is called for in a specific situation.

Messaging uses a peer-to-peer distributed computing model in which both systems can take on the role of a client or a server. Remote procedure calls use a client/server, distributed computing model where Process A acts as a client and initiates the request. Process B listens for the request and responds to the client. In this model, there is a sequence to how these two processes interoperate. The server must always be up first before the clients can initiate a conversation. With the advent of OSF's DCE 1.1, DCE servers may or may not be active when a client request is initiated, because DCE 1.1 supports dynamic allocation of servers through OSF's Cell Directory Services. In the peer-to-peer model, there is no fixed sequence.

Note

DCE's RPCs can be both a client and a server on the same machine. Servers can call other servers through delegation chains.

VI

Multiplatforms

RPCs use a blocking mode of operation. In other words, when an RPC client makes a request from the server, the requesting application must wait until the request is completed before it can continue to process. Messaging uses a non-blocking mode of operation. When a request is made to another system, the requesting application continues processing and is notified when the request is completed. The appropriate mode of operation depends on the business problem. The blocking mode of communication is appropriate in situations where an immediate response is necessary. The non-blocking mode is appropriate in large-scale, transaction-oriented applications with diverse platforms, or when the method of communicating is slower, as in wide area networks or mobile communications.

> **Note**
>
> Many analysts believe RPCs will be important for Online Transaction Processing (OLTP) and legacy connectivity. They also believe that RPCs will dominate the local area network (LAN) because they are confined to a smaller geographical area.
>
> In addition, analysts believe that message queuing will dominate high-availability, wide area networks and mobile communications by the end of this decade. Messaging will be an important component of evolving object request broker architectures (ORBs).

RPCs have a more synchronized method, in which components are more tightly linked and dependent on one another. The client/server relationship is tightly integrated, and servers must keep up with clients. In the synchronized method, components are loosely integrated. One component sends a message to another component, not knowing when there will be a response, or even if there will be a response. There are many applications in the banking industry for example, where an immediate response is needed, such as verifying funds before withdrawal.

RPCs can perform asynchronous communications through the use of threads, but this requires a lot of programming. The programmer needs to create a separate thread that invokes an RPC and returns a result when completed. Another method of providing asynchronous capabilities with ONC's RPC is by setting the time-out value to zero. This returns control to the client immediately after the RPC is sent. This method does not guarantee delivery of the RPC request. The client must poll the server to ensure it receives the RPC request. The client polls the server through the RPC APIs provided with ONC's RPC package. Message queuing has this capability inherent to its underlying architecture making asynchronous communication simpler.

> **Note**
>
> Open Network Computing (ONC) is a family of networking products provided by SunSoft that includes an RPC mechanism. ONC was developed to implement distributed computing in a multi-vendor environment. SunSoft has evolved ONC (called ONC+) to include Federated Services, an interface for allowing third parties to connect into the ONC distributed environment.

Message queuing can provide store-and-forward, where Program A can forward a request to Program B. Program B determines whether it can process it. If not, it forwards the message request to Program C. Program C can then process the request and return it directly to Program A. Because RPCs are a client/server model, they require Program C to return the completed request to Program B, which would then return it to Program A. In this scenario, message queuing is faster at processing store-and-forward requests.

RPCs, because of their stub architecture, automatically provide data marshaling (encode data) for network transmission on the client side and unmarshaling (decode data) on the server side. Most message-oriented middleware simply transmits buffers so that all data marshaling and unmarshaling is handled by programmers or tools. Many message-oriented middleware products and value-added resellers are addressing this issue, so there are products on the market that can help you data marshal with message-oriented middleware.

With RPCs, clients request a service from a server. This request will be met with either success or failure. RPCs are oriented to online processing. When failure occurs, it may be difficult with RPCs to detect where that failure occurred. OSF's DCE 1.1 does have some new features that help detect failure and allow users to add their own messages. These messages are in a common message format across the code base. In addition, Encina from Transarc provides an add-on product to DCE's RPC called RQS. It provides a queuing mechanism that allows off-line processing. In addition, TOPEND from AT&T GIS, Tuxedo from Novell, and Encina offer transactional message queuing.

Message-oriented middleware is oriented to both online and off-line processing. With a pure messaging system (without queuing), message transmission fails if the server is not available. Messaging can have message recovery through queues, audit files that can reconstruct the message, or automatic resend functionality. Messaging provides you with more than just success or failure.

VI

Multiplatforms

Many messaging companies are implementing a hybrid system of both on-line and off-line processing. Developers can implement applications that attempt online processing. If online processing isn't available, it will queue the message (off-line processing). In this hybrid system, developers can develop applications that process critical operations online, deferring less critical operations to off-line processing. This hybrid system gives you the best of both worlds.

Message-oriented middleware is more flexible than RPCs for program development. Programmers must develop applications with RPCs in a very synchronous method, following sequential logic. With message-oriented middleware, developers can take advantage of asynchronous capabilities by modularizing their code and having different processors process different modules of the application. This, in turn, takes advantage of the parallel processing aspects of messaging. Through threading and the thread library, OSF's DCE can provide parallel processing at either the kernel space or at the user space. This requires more programming than what is inherent in message-oriented middleware. DCE also provides multi-threaded capabilities at runtime, so you receive the benefits of threads without having to program them in your applications.

RPCs have a simpler method for program development. RPCs work the same way as subroutine calls, except that they are over the network. Developers are accustomed to this method of developing, so oftentimes it is easier, simpler, and more efficient to program with RPCs. Messaging allows you to send and receive messages between applications. Messaging, however, requires training for developers to be productive.

> **Note**
>
> While RPC technologies from different vendors provide similar features, message-oriented middleware products vary widely in their scope and functionality.

Table 25.1 summarizes the differences between these two paradigms.

Table 25.1 Comparison of Message-Oriented Middleware and RPCs

Feature	RPCs	Message and Message Queuing
Program logic	Follows a standard procedure call format	Follows a new programming logic

Feature	RPCs	Message and Message Queuing
Program synchronization	Synchronous	Asynchronous (with queues)
Distributed computing model	Client/server model	Peer-to-peer model
Processing mode	Blocking	Non-blocking
Provides automatic data marshaling	Yes	No
System independence	No (RPCs require that both the server and client be available)	Yes (Messages can be queued until a server is available)
Time independence	No (RPCs require that both processes run concurrently)	Yes (Message-oriented middleware allows both processes to operate at different times)
Error detection	Success or failure	Message recovery with queuing
Load balancing	Requires a TP monitor like Encina or Tuxedo	Can be done as part of the message queuing paradigm with different message queuing schemes
Similarity of technology from different vendors	Consistent	Varies widely

From Here...

Middleware is an important consideration when entering the world of distributed client/server computing. It is important to choose the right middleware to solve your long-term business needs. Each type of middleware provides unique features that could be important in your environment. It is nice to have the flexibility and scalability provided by multiple types of middleware, such as RPCs, RDAs, MOM, ORBs, and DOLTP. However, you must choose the right tool for the job. It is a lot easier to drive a nail into a wall with a hammer than with your shoe.

The same is true when selecting a type of middleware to solve a problem. There are many middleware products in the market, all claiming to have a mixture of these different application-to-application communication capabilities. You must look at their total solution, including security, directory services, development tools, and error recovery.

VI

Multiplatforms

For more information on the topics discussed in this chapter, refer to the following:

- Chapter 4, "Client/Server Development Overview," acquaints you with the client/server model.

- Chapter 11, "Techniques for Developing RPC Clients and Servers," shows you actual XDR routines in action in clients and servers.

- Chapter 12, "RPC Under UNIX," gives you the UNIX-specific information you will need to create and manage remote procedure call code.

Index

Symbols

% directive (rpcgen), 275-276

56-Kbps WAN service, 82

A

a (ACL access permission), 380

A-ABORT (OSI ASCE primitive), 68

A-ASSOCIATE (OSI ASCE primitive), 68

A-P-ABORT (OSI ASCE primitive), 68

A-RELEASE (OSI ASCE primitive), 68

accept (socket core calls), 619

Access Control List, *see* ACLs

Access Control Services (LAN Server), 556

access levels, defined, 683

Accounting Services (NWCalls), 551

accounts, DCE, 377

ACCT command (FTP), 112-113

ACF (Attributes Control File), customizing interface, 394-398

ACID test (Atomicity, Consistency, Isolation, and Durabiltity), 189

ACLs (Access Control List)
  ACL Manager, 437
  DCE (Distributed Computing Environment), 378-380
    management function calls, 383-384

actual remote procedure, 413

add-ons, OS/2 servers, 542

address fields (A), HDLC, 95

addresses, 78-79
  data link, 78
  network, 78
    converting to host name, 321
  OSI reference model, 64-65
  physical, 78
  protocols, 21
  sockets, 611-612

Administrative Server, DFS (Distributed File Service), 371-372

Administrator (ODBC), 503

ADSP (AppleTalk Data Stream Protocol), 104

Advanced Peer-to-Peer Communications, *see* APPC

AEP (AppleTalk Echo Protocol), 104

AFI (Authority Format Identifier), 65

AFP (Apple File Services), 551

aggregates (OLE), 452-453

Alert Services (LAN Server), 556

algorithms, LSA (Link State Algorithms), 64

allflodim list (XDR routine), 246

allflodim List Pointer (XDR routines), 245

analysis phase (SDLC), 133
  multiple platform applications, 146
  one platform applications, 135-136

anonymous pipes (OS/2), 535

any_other (ACL access permission entity), 379

API conformance level (ODBC drivers), 504-505

APIs (Application Programming Interface)
  defined, 561-562, 700
  event semaphores
    DosCloseEventSem, 580
    DosCreateEventSem, 577
    DosOpenEventSem, 579
    DosPostEventSem, 580
    DosQueryEventSem, 580
    DosResetEventSem, 579
    DosWaitEventSem, 579

DosWrite (API), 564
parameters, 565
downsizing, 523-524
downward multiplexing (splitting), 62
DRDA (Distributed Relational Database Architecture), 190
drivers
defined, 490
ODBC, 503
API conformance level, 504-505
defined, 503-504
Desktop Database Driver Set, 492-493
driver manager, 490
multiple-tier, 500-502, 505-506
selection criteria, 506
single-tier, 500, 505-506
SQL statements, 505
DROP statement (SQL), 494
DSP (Domain-Specific Part), 65
DTS (Distributed Time Service)
components, 438
DCE, 366-367, 437-439
DXI (ATM), 93
Dynamic Link Libraries (DLLs), 538

E

e-mail, OSI (MOTIS), 70-71
Easel Workbench, 653
Echo Protocol, 99
editing
in-place editing (OLE), 460
visual editing (OLE), 449
Electronic Private Automatic Branch Exchange, *see* EPABX
EMS (Endpoint Mapper Service), 443

encapsulation
bridges, 38-39
defined, 673
OSI protocol, 62
encryption, 211
End Systems, *see* ES
endpoint mappe, defined, 401
Endpoint Mapper Service (EMS), 443
endpoints, binding methods, 203
enhanced data sharing, 26
entry Type (rpcgen databases), 279
enum keyword (rpcgen), 266-268
EPABX (Electronic Private Automatic Branch Exchange), 30
error control (OSI protocol), 61
error correction, 80-81
error detection, 80-81
bridges, 40
MOM (Message-Oriented Middleware), 721
protocols, 21
routers, 40
RPCs, 721
error detection and recovery class (OSI transport layer), 66
error handling
clients, 296-298
DCE clients, 406-407
exception handling, 409-412
selecting approach, 412
synchronous, 407-409
Error Protocol, 99
error recovery and multiplexing class (OSI transport layer), 65
ES (End Systems), 63-64
Essential Graphics GUI, 653
Ethernet, 84-86
transmission specifications, 86

event semaphores (OS/2 API), 533
DosCloseEventSem, 580
DosCreateEventSem, 577
DosOpenEventSem, 579
DosPostEventSem, 580
DosQueryEventSem, 580
DosResetEventSem, 579
DosWaitEventSem, 579
named pipes, 599-604
multiple event semaphores, 604-607
exception handling
DCE
clients, 409-412
threads, 362-363
OS/2, 538
execution, ODBC statements, 510-511
execution agency, 72
explicit binding method, 202
DCE clients, 404-405
Extended Attributes Services (NSCalls), 552
Extended Networking Package, 550
extended services, 181
Extensible Virtual Toolkit (XVT), 653
Extension Level 1 API conformance (ODBC drivers), 504
Extension Level 2 API conformance (ODBC drivers), 504
External Data Represenation, *see* XDR
EZ-RPC, 679-680

F

facilities, DCE, 422-423
RPC, 423-425
Failure transparency, 544
families (socket famlies), 611
FAT (File Allocation Tables), OS/2, 538-539
fat clients, 654

I

SMDS, 97
SMTP (Simple Mail Transfer Protocol), 115-116
SNA (Systems Network Architecture), 102-103
SNMP (Simple Network Management Protocol), 116-118
SNMP (Single Network Management Protocol), 700
SONET (Synchronous Optical Network), 98-99
SPP (Sequence Packet Protocol), 99
STA (Spanning Tree Algorithm), defined, 35
synchronizing, 21
TCP/IP (Transmission Control Packet/Internet Protocol), 107-110
TFTP (Trivial File Transfer Program), 113
Token Ring, 87-88
UDP (User Datagram Protocol), 119-120
WANs (Wide Area Networks), 82-83
XMP (X/Open's Management Protocol), 700
XNS (Xerox Network System), 99-100
XOM (X/Open's Object Management), 700
ZIP (Zone Information Protocol), 104
prototyping, 661-663
pthread_join( ) routine, 361
PU (Physical Unit), 636
NAUs, 103
public key cryptography (RSA), 213-214
public protocols, defined, 75
PWD command (FTP), 112-113

Q

queries
ODBC (Object Database Connectivity), 512-513
sending, 164-169
queues
defined, 561
message queuing, 705
OS/2, 535
QUIT command (FTP), 112-113

R

r access permission
ACL, 380
UNIX, 379
RAD (Rapid Application Development), 659-660
RAISE verb, 363
raw sockets, 611 RD (Routing Domain), 63
RDA (Remote Data Access), 190, 703-704
RDBMS (Relational Database Management System), security service, 223
readrequest Structure, 324
readv (socket core calls), 616
ReceiveAll( ) function, 286
record streams (XDR), 249-251
recv (socket core calls), 615
recvfrom (socket core calls), 617
re-engineering business processes, 656-657
reference counting (OLE), 452
reference functions, 237
DCE, 389
XDR, 242-243
multiple references, 252-254
registry, DCE (Distributed Computing Environment), 377-378

regular priority, 531
Relational Database Management System, *see* RDBMS
relational databases, 185
see also ODBC
relational model (ODBC), 493-494
relaying frames, 33
Reliable Transfer Service, *see* RTS
Remote Data Access, *see* RDA
remote data management architectures, 10
remote database access, 683
ODBC (Open Database Connectivity), 684
PowerBuilder, 683-684
SQLWindows (Gupta), 683
remote procedure, 413
Remote Procedure Calls, *see* RPCs
remote procedure interface compiler, *see* rpcgen
remote requests, 189
Remote Resource Access, LAN Server, 555
remote transactions, 189
rendezvous, UNIX RPC, 316
client broadcast function, 319-323
client identification, 323-326
client selection, 323-326
clnt_call( ) function, 316-318
NULLPROC, 318
pormapper, 327-331
replication, filesets, 441
Replication Server (DFS), 372
requests
ACID test, 189
distributed, 189
remote, 189
Resource Management Services, LAN Server, 556

Y-Z

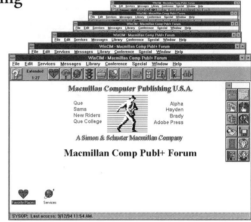

Complete and Return this Card
for a *FREE* Computer Book Catalog

Thank you for purchasing this book! You have purchased a superior computer book written expressly for your needs. To continue to provide the kind of up-to-date, pertinent coverage you've come to expect from us, we need to hear from you. Please take a minute to complete and return this self-addressed, postage-paid form. In return, we'll send you a free catalog of all our computer books on topics ranging from word processing to programming and the internet.

Mr. ☐   Mrs. ☐   Ms. ☐   Dr. ☐

Name (first) ☐☐☐☐☐☐☐☐☐☐☐☐☐ (M.I.) ☐ (last) ☐☐☐☐☐☐☐☐☐☐☐☐☐☐☐☐☐☐

Address ☐☐☐☐☐☐☐☐☐☐☐☐☐☐☐☐☐☐☐☐☐☐☐☐☐☐☐☐☐☐☐☐☐

City ☐☐☐☐☐☐☐☐☐☐☐☐☐☐☐☐ State ☐☐ Zip ☐☐☐☐☐ ☐☐☐☐

Phone ☐☐☐ ☐☐☐ ☐☐☐☐ Fax ☐☐☐ ☐☐☐ ☐☐☐☐

Company Name ☐☐☐☐☐☐☐☐☐☐☐☐☐☐☐☐☐☐☐☐☐☐☐☐☐☐☐☐

E-mail address ☐☐☐☐☐☐☐☐☐☐☐☐☐☐☐☐☐☐☐☐☐☐☐☐☐☐☐☐

1. Please check at least (3) influencing factors for purchasing this book.

Front or back cover information on book .... ☐
Special approach to the content .... ☐
Completeness of content .... ☐
Author's reputation .... ☐
Publisher's reputation .... ☐
Book cover design or layout .... ☐
Index or table of contents of book .... ☐
Price of book .... ☐
Special effects, graphics, illustrations .... ☐
Other (Please specify): _____ ☐

2. How did you first learn about this book?

Saw in Macmillan Computer Publishing catalog .... ☐
Recommended by store personnel .... ☐
Saw the book on bookshelf at store .... ☐
Recommended by a friend .... ☐
Received advertisement in the mail .... ☐
Saw an advertisement in: _____ ☐
Read book review in: _____ ☐
Other (Please specify): _____ ☐

3. How many computer books have you purchased in the last six months?

This book only .... ☐   3 to 5 books .... ☐
2 books .... ☐   More than 5 .... ☐

4. Where did you purchase this book?

Bookstore .... ☐
Computer Store .... ☐
Consumer Electronics Store .... ☐
Department Store .... ☐
Office Club .... ☐
Warehouse Club .... ☐
Mail Order .... ☐
Direct from Publisher .... ☐
Internet site .... ☐
Other (Please specify): _____ ☐

5. How long have you been using a computer?

☐ Less than 6 months   ☐ 6 months to a year
☐ 1 to 3 years   ☐ More than 3 years

6. What is your level of experience with personal computers and with the subject of this book?

	With PCs	With subject of book
New	☐	☐
Casual	☐	☐
Accomplished	☐	☐
Expert	☐	☐

Source Code ISBN: 0-0000-0000-0

7. Which of the following best describes your job title?

Administrative Assistant ☐
Coordinator ☐
Manager/Supervisor ☐
Director ☐
Vice President ☐
President/CEO/COO ☐
Lawyer/Doctor/Medical Professional ☐
Teacher/Educator/Trainer ☐
Engineer/Technician ☐
Consultant ☐
Not employed/Student/Retired ☐
Other (Please specify): _____ ☐

8. Which of the following best describes the area of the company your job title falls under?

Accounting ☐
Engineering ☐
Manufacturing ☐
Operations ☐
Marketing ☐
Sales ☐
Other (Please specify): _____ ☐

9. What is your age?

Under 20 ☐
21-29 ☐
30-39 ☐
40-49 ☐
50-59 ☐
60-over ☐

10. Are you:

Male ☐
Female ☐

11. Which computer publications do you read regularly? (Please list)

_____
_____
_____
_____
_____
_____
_____
_____
_____
_____

Comments: _____
_____
_____

Fold here and scotch-tape to mail.